The Blackwell Companion
to Christian Ethics

Blackwell Companions to Religion

The Blackwell Companions to Religion series presents a collection of the most recent scholarship and knowledge about world religions. Each volume draws together newly commissioned essays by distinguished authors in the field, and is presented in a style which is accessible to undergraduate students, as well as scholars and the interested general reader. These volumes approach the subject in a creative and forward-thinking style, providing a forum in which leading scholars in the field can make their views and research available to a wider audience.

Published

The Blackwell Companion to Judaism
Edited by Jacob Neusner and Alan J. Avery-Peck

The Blackwell Companion to Sociology of Religion
Edited by Richard K. Fenn

The Blackwell Companion to the Hebrew Bible
Edited by Leo G. Perdue

The Blackwell Companion to Postmodern Theology
Edited by Graham Ward

The Blackwell Companion to Hinduism
Edited by Gavin Flood

The Blackwell Companion to Political Theology
Edited by Peter Scott and William T. Cavanaugh

The Blackwell Companion to Protestantism
Edited by Alister E. McGrath and Darren C. Marks

The Blackwell Companion to Modern Theology
Edited by Gareth Jones

The Blackwell Companion to Christian Ethics
Edited by Stanley Hauerwas and Samuel Wells

Forthcoming

The Blackwell Companion to Religious Ethics
Edited by William Schweiker

The Blackwell Companion to the Study of Religion
Edited by Robert A. Segal

The Blackwell Companion to Eastern Christianity
Edited by Ken Parry

The Blackwell Companion to Christian Spirituality
Edited by Arthur Holder

The Blackwell Companion to the Bible and Culture
Edited by John Sawyer

The Blackwell Companion to the New Testament
Edited by David Aune

The Blackwell Companion to Christian Ethics

Edited by

Stanley Hauerwas and Samuel Wells

Blackwell Publishing

© 2004 by Blackwell Publishing Ltd
except for editorial material and organization © 2004 by Stanley Hauerwas and Samuel Wells

BLACKWELL PUBLISHING
350 Main Street, Malden, MA 02148-5020, USA
9600 Garsington Road, Oxford OX4 2DQ, UK
550 Swanston Street, Carlton, Victoria 3053, Australia

The right of Stanley Hauerwas and Samuel Wells to be identified as the Authors of the Editorial
Material in this Work has been asserted in accordance with the UK Copyright, Designs, and
Patents Act 1988.

First published 2004 by Blackwell Publishing Ltd

3   2005

Library of Congress Cataloging-in-Publication Data

The Blackwell companion to Christian ethics / edited by Stanley Hauerwas
and Samuel Wells.
       p. cm. – (Blackwell companions to religion)
Includes bibliographical references and index.
    ISBN 0-631-23506-X (alk. paper)
1. Christian ethics.   2. Public worship – Moral and ethical aspects.
I. Hauerwas, Stanley, 1940–   II. Wells, Samuel.   III. Series.
  BJ1251.B54 2004
  241–dc22

                                                        2003015469

ISBN-13: 978-0-631-23506-4 (alk. paper)

A catalogue record for this title is available from the British Library.

Set in 10 on 12.5 pt Photina
by SNP Best-set Typesetter Ltd, Hong Kong
Printed and bound in the United Kingdom
by TJ International, Padstow, Cornwall

The publisher's policy is to use permanent paper from mills that operate a sustainable forestry policy,
and which has been manufactured from pulp processed using acid-free and elementary chlorine-free
practices. Furthermore, the publisher ensures that the text paper and cover board used have met
acceptable environmental accreditation standards.

For further information on
Blackwell Publishing, visit our website:
www.blackwellpublishing.com

To the people and parish of
St Elizabeth's, North Earlham, Norwich, UK

Contents

List of Contributors

Nicholas Adams is Lecturer in Theology, University of Edinburgh, Edinburgh, Scotland.

Scott Bader-Saye is Associate Professor of Theology, University of Scranton, Scranton, Pennsylvania.

Frederick Christian Bauerschmidt is Associate Professor of Theology, Loyola College of Baltimore, Baltimore, Maryland.

Daniel M. Bell, **Jr** is Assistant Professor of Theological Ethics, Lutheran Theological Southern Seminary, Columbia, South Carolina.

John Berkman is Assistant Professor of Moral Theology, Catholic University of America, Washington, DC.

Michael L. Budde is Professor of Political Science, De Paul University, Chicago, Illinois.

Michael G. Cartwright is Professor of Theology, University of Indianapolis, Indianapolis, Indiana.

William T. Cavanaugh is Associate Professor of Theology, University of Saint Thomas, St Paul, Minnesota.

Jim Fodor is Associate Professor of Theology, Saint Bonaventure College, Saint Bonaventure, New York.

Stephen Fowl is Professor of New Testament, Loyola College of Baltimore, Baltimore, Maryland.

Timothy Jarvis Gorringe is Professor of Theology, University of Exeter, Exeter, UK.

Amy Laura Hall is Assistant Professor of Theology, the Divinity School, Duke University, Durham, North Carolina.

Michael Hanby is Assistant Professor of Theology, Villanova University, Philadelphia, Pennsylvania.

Stanley Hauerwas is Gilbert T. Rowe Professor of Theological Ethics, the Divinity School, Duke University, Durham, North Carolina.

Kelly S. Johnson is Assistant Professor of Theology, University of Dayton, Dayton, Ohio.

Emmanuel Katongole is Professor of Theology and Ethics, University of the Martyrs, Uganda, and the Divinity School, Duke University, Durham, North Carolina.

Philip Kenneson is Professor of Theology, Milligan College, Johnston City, Tennessee.

D. Stephen Long is Professor of Theology, Garrett-Evangelical Theological Seminary, Evanston, Illinois.

M. Therese Lysaught is Associate Professor of Theology, University of Dayton, Dayton, Ohio.

David Matzko McCarthy is Professor of Theology, St Mary's College, Emmitsburg, Maryland.

Joseph L. Mangina is Professor of Theology, Wycliffe Seminary, Toronto, Canada.

Mark Thiessen Nation is Professor of Theology, Eastern Mennonite Seminary, Harrisonburg, Virginia.

Michael S. Northcott is Reader in Christian Ethics, University of Edinburgh, Edinburgh, Scotland.

Charles Pinches is Professor of Theology, University of Scranton, Scranton, Pennsylvania.

Ben Quash is Dean of Peterhouse, University of Cambridge, Cambridge, UK.

Hans S. Reinders is Willem van der Bergh Chair of Theology, Vrije Universiteit, Amsterdam, The Netherlands.

R. R. Reno is Associate Professor of Theology, Creighton University, Omaha, Nebraska.

Gerald W. Schlabach is Associate Professor of Theology, University of Saint Thomas, St Paul, Minnesota.

Joel James Shuman is Assistant Professor of Theology, King's College, Wilkes-Barre, Pennsylvania.

Robert Song is Lecturer in Christian Ethics, University of Durham, Durham, UK.

Carole Bailey Stoneking is Professor of Theology, High Point University, High Point, North Carolina.

Kevin J. Vanhoozer is Professor of Theology, Trinity Evangelical School of Theology, Chicago, Illinois.

Paul J. Wadell is Professor of Theology, St Norbert's College, De Pere, Wisconsin.

Samuel Wells is Priest-in-Charge of St Mark's, Newnham, Cambridge, UK.

Rowan Williams is Archbishop of Canterbury.

Tripp York is a PhD student at Garrett-Evangelical Theological Seminary, Evanston, Illinois.

Preface

We hope that, years from now, this book will be seen as a milestone for Christians. That is a high ambition, but one we risk. We do so because we are convinced that this book represents a new turn not only for Christian ethics, but also for the way Christians learn to live in that time often identified as "late modernity." Of course, this book would not have been possible if the decisive turn we believe this Blackwell Companion represents had not already happened.

The evidence that such an event has and is taking place is that authors existed to write the essays that form the chapters of this book. We are in their debt because, without their courage to think against the grain of their times, and with the grain of the Eucharist, this volume could not exist. For a long time, people have been goading Hauerwas to write the definitive "big book," but he has resisted because he has always seen such a book as stifling rather than provoking the kinds of conversation his work has sought to make possible. Finally here, after all, is Hauerwas's "big book," but his friends have written it for him. It is not a monologue; it is a book begun, continued, and ended in conversation. This is the way it should be.

We are in debt to all those who have written the essays for this Companion. We suspect that seldom have authors taken their responsibilities (and their deadlines) so seriously. We owe a great debt to our editor, Rebecca Harkin, who invited us to imagine this book, and gave us permission and encouragement to be different. Perhaps our largest debt is owed to Jana Bennett, a doctoral student in theology and ethics at Duke University. Jana not only overcame Hauerwas's technological limits, but also added invaluable insights to the conversation that this book represents. Without her organizational skills, good humor, and passion for the faith, this book would not exist.

This book was made possible by God's joining strangers – an Englishman and a Texan – in an unlikely friendship. We hope that those reading *The Blackwell Companion to Christian Ethics* will sense some of the joy that our working together gave us.

PART I
Studying Ethics through Worship

CHAPTER 1
Christian Ethics as Informed Prayer

Stanley Hauerwas and Samuel Wells

The aim of this volume is to stretch, inspire, and develop the reader's conception of Christian worship in order to challenge, enrich, and transform the reader's notions of the form and content of Christian ethics. To suggest that assumptions about Christian worship could benefit from an overhaul might be regarded as uncontroversial. To suggest, however, that assumptions about Christian ethics might be altered, and, furthermore, that that alteration might take place through the exploration of the liturgy, might come as rather more of a surprise. The purpose of this chapter is to explain why the authors of this volume have chosen to perceive the discipline of Christian ethics through the lens of Christian worship, most particularly the Eucharist.

The book is written for those who sense that the problem with Christian ethics is not just the complexity and elusiveness of the questions it faces, but also the methods and environments in which it is understood to be studied. Hence the book is written in a style that is designed to be accessible to an introductory student, but it is hoped that even the most experienced practitioner in the field will have much to discover and ponder in its pages. The issues raised concern not just Christian ethics but Christian theology as well. Christians approach worship with an expectation that God will make himself known through the liturgy, and Christians who approach ethics in ways informed by worship come with a similar expectation that God will make himself known in their deliberations, investigations, and discernment. The study of how God makes himself known is, of course, generally regarded as the field of theology, and it is hoped that students who find the living God in the pages of this study will pursue their enquiry through more conventional theological literature.

Why Study Ethics through Worship?

But first we must confront the understandable reaction that may come from some quarters that to study the practice of worship is no way to explore the field of Christian ethics. What has the altar to do with the lecture theater? The connection of the two may seem incongruous to many, absurd to some. The simplest reason for this reaction is that the connection has not often been made. Its apparent novelty might seem to be its weakness. For those involved in pastoral ministry the disconnection of the two is frequently experienced as a cause of great bewilderment. So often it appears that lay Christians have a thriving life of personal devotion, an active life within a worshiping community, and an engaged life fulfilling a range of professional and public roles in the workplace, neighborhood, and family, but comparatively seldom do lay Christians have an equally developed way of bringing these three parts of their life together. Similarly, a great many theologians, at every level of seniority, have a corresponding range of involvements and commitments. But how often do the convictions and assumptions that shape one aspect of life genuinely interact with the key dynamics of another?

For a certain view of ethics – perhaps a dominant one within the academy over recent generations – this is just as it should be. The assumption has been made (or the aspiration has been held) that ethics is something *more* than worship – that it is broader, or deeper, or more objective, or more significant. Hence worship has been relegated to the lower divisions of the academy, regarded as the realm of the "merely pious," open to sociological and psychological investigation certainly, but remote from the frontiers of truth. Of the reasons why worship has tended to be separated from ethics, four appear to stand out.

(1) Ethics is about the real, worship is about the unreal. This kind of assumption can be expressed in a number of different ways. Ethics is about the tangible, worship about the spiritual. Ethics is about the real world, in which it is taken for granted that the flesh is weak, people break their promises, and every motive is mixed. Worship aspires to the ideal world, in which hearts find their rest in God, resolutions are kept, and heavenly justice and peace rain down. In short, ethics knows that people are bad, worship tries to make them good. More subtly, worship is a kind of play, a temporary escape from real life to an environment where normal rules are suspended; by contrast, ethics is serious, by no means play, and an uncompromising squaring up to the sometimes unpleasant responsibilities and requirements of adult life.

Such an understanding stands very much in the tradition of Immanuel Kant. His distinction, between the immanent world of experience available to us through our senses, and the unreachable (though interesting) transcendent world of which religious language speaks, has been immensely influential and represents the foundation of conventional distinctions between doctrine and ethics. It undergirds all perspectives that regard talk of God as speculation, while describing talk of ourselves, human beings, as observation.

This book challenges these assumptions because its authors believe that, contrary to the popular slogan, life *is* a rehearsal. Worship is indeed a kind of play with a different set of rules – for, without such games, who would recognize that "real" life is also a set of games with their own rules? Worship has a set of rules that time, tradition, and providence have honed and honored, and Christians believe that the set of rules they practice and embody in worship is a *good* set of rules, a set by which they may identify and judge other sets. In the process they may critique the kinds of binary distinctions that appear to make terms like "unreal," "spiritual," and "ideal" meaningful and at the same time secondary, exposing the social locations and power relations of those who unself-consciously describe their own perspective as "real." More ambitiously, many of the authors of this volume would go further in terms of outnarrating Kant, and suggest that life is in fact a rehearsal for worship – that, within an eschatological perspective, it is worship for which humanity and the creation were made, and it is worship that will make up the greater part of eternity, within which what is called "life" and "the real" will appear to be a tiny blip.

(2)   Worship is about beauty, ethics is about the good. (The logic would generally follow that theology – or philosophy – is about truth.) A set of corresponding assumptions follow, which see worship as subjective, ethics as objective. Worship is about the heart, ethics about the head. It may, for example, be supposed that ethics is about judgments of right and wrong, whereas worship is more about discerning what is "fitting." It may be assumed that ethics is about establishing unarguable reasons for decision, while worship is about exploring aesthetic grounds for choice. More significantly, worship is an activity in which only a limited number of people, perhaps a minority in North Atlantic cultures, would see themselves as engaging. It is therefore a practice for only some, whereas ethics is generally taken to be a discipline that has a bearing on everybody. Worship is something of an occasional voluntary pastime, whereas ethics touches on an obligation for which one may be accountable at any time.

This set of understandings rests on an assumption that goodness, truth, and beauty are detachable from one another, so that they may even come into conflict with one another. It is one of the foundations of modern liberal-democratic culture that this detachment is not only possible, but is also necessary, if peoples with diverging and even contradictory perceptions of goodness, truth, and beauty are to live among one another without violent conflict. What tends to happen, however, is that a different set of "forms," notably the functional, the instrumental, and the transferable, become the central language of liberal-democratic culture. These are regarded as "objective," and those who insist on talking of, still less practicing, goodness, truth, and beauty are tolerated under the label "subjective." Ethics therefore deals with the functional, the instrumental, and the transferable, leaving worship muddling along in the backwaters of goodness, truth, and beauty.

This book challenges the distinction between "subjective" and "objective" that characterizes these assumptions. This challenge shares the already-mentioned suspicion about binary distinctions that presuppose the speaker has the global view. It distrusts the notion of "objectivity," if objectivity assumes there was ever such a thing as a disinterested observer. It similarly questions the idea that goodness, truth, and beauty are detachable from one another. For, in worship, Christians seek the God who combines all three while maintaining their overflowing abundance. To exemplify or amplify one in no way reduces or downplays either of the others. Worship proclaims a universality that invites people to unite about where they are going to, not to dissent about where they are coming from. There is no shortage of goodness, truth, and beauty: there is no need for competition for scarce resources, or deliberation over their just distribution.

Meanwhile, worship challenges assumptions about what goodness, truth, and beauty mean in the light of the gospel. That which might appear to exemplify beauty may look very different in the context of worship. For example, as preachers we have both found that in almost every congregation in which we have preached regularly, across every social class, there has been at least one adult who would leave no rhetorical question unanswered. Such a feature of worship, such an embodiment of the way in which a community can welcome, nurture, and empower people who might be seen as having a disadvantage or a disability, might at first, perhaps jarring, experience be regarded as undermining the goodness, truth, and beauty of the liturgy; but, on reflection, might be relished as embodying all three.

(3)   Worship is about the internal, ethics is about the external. This perception is similar to the subjective–objective assumption discussed previously, but it rests rather more on a distinction familiar in contemporary culture. Ethics is public, worship is private. To put it a different way, ethics is political, worship is (or should be) apolitical. Ethics is concerned with the good ordering of issues that affect the public sphere: crises over the beginning and ending of life, questions over the conduct of business, medicine and technological research, the rights and wrongs of war, justice, the distribution of wealth and human rights. Worship has no specific contributions to these questions: it merely concentrates on reconciling people with their God. (An exception is often made for issues that are considered to belong in the "private" sphere, notably questions of sexual relationships and the family.)

This portrayal of ethics and worship clearly rests on a very particular notion of politics. Here is a remarkably tidy world, where every question that arises can be filed neatly under either "public" or "private." Politics is about the reasoned distribution of scarce resources, about the efficient management of publicly accountable and fiscally funded services, about the maintenance of order and the integrity of borders, about the upholding of legitimate rights and the respect for diverse expression. In this notion of politics, ethics is likely to be drawn into the constraints of the legislative process, the reduction of what is right to what can become legal, the exaltation of tolerance and the tendency to address the virtues, justice, truth-telling, peacemaking, as if they could be isolated from one another and fulfilled alone.

By contrast, this book portrays a rival perception of politics. It aspires to a politics that discerns the best use of the unlimited gifts of God, rather than the just distribution of the limited resources of the world. It regards the contrast between public and private as yet another binary distinction that misrepresents the call of the gospel and the nature of the Christian life. For example, in baptism, Christians (or those speaking on their behalf) are called to give up any sense that they "own" their bodies. So the notion of "private" makes no sense. Yet this creates a profound conception of politics, seen now as the best working of an organism – the Body of Christ – that sees itself as being genuinely a body, rather than a mass of discrete individuals. Worship is, or aspires to be, the manifestation of the best ordering of that body, and is thus the most significantly political – the most "ethical" – thing that Christians do.

(4)   Finally, worship is about words, ethics is about action. This may seem a strange way of talking about ethics, which, for a discipline that is taken in this sense to be about action, has nonetheless generated a remarkable number of words. So it may help to give another corresponding portrayal. Worship commemorates the past, ethics empowers the present – and prepares for the future. Or again, worship is about stories from the past, ethics is about life in the present.

This perception rests on a fundamental misunderstanding of the nature of worship. Worship is about words and actions. Worship is an ordered series of activities that Christians carry out regularly together in obedience to Jesus's command, as a way of becoming more like him, and as a witness to God's world. Words constitute these actions as well as enrich and amplify what is done. This is an easy point to miss in an age of constant liturgical renewal, driven largely by the production of huge numbers of words, available in every kind of paper and electronic format. This mass of words should not obscure the fact that Christian worship is shaped primarily by instructions and habits of action: "Baptise them . . . ," "Do this . . . ," "Whenever you eat this bread and drink this cup," "When two or three are gathered."

Worship does indeed commemorate the past because it sees the past as the theater of God's definitive and self-revelatory actions in his world. But worship also anticipates the future, particularly through the Eucharist, in which Christians share a meal that anticipates the heavenly banquet. Ethics that has no conception of good patterns of action, treasured from the past, that has no place to go to find communities that inhabit such corporate action in the present, and has no embodied configuration of the communal eschatological future to anticipate, is a discipline that is almost bound to experience its context as one of daunting scarcity. The liturgy offers ethics a series of ordered practices that shape the character and assumptions of Christians, and suggest habits and models that inform every aspect of corporate life – meeting people, acknowledging fault and failure, celebrating, thanking, reading, speaking with authority, reflecting on wisdom, naming truth, registering need, bringing about reconciliation, sharing food, renewing purpose. This is the basic staple of corporate Christian life – not simply for clergy, or for those in religious orders, but for lay Christians, week in, week out. It is the most regular way in which most Christians remind themselves and others and are reminded that they are Christians. It is the most significant way in which Christianity takes flesh, evolving from a set of ideas and convictions to a set of practices and a way of life.

How Does the Liturgy Inform and Shape the Christian Life?

The American Roman Catholic priest Vincent Donovan was sent in the late 1960s to evangelize the Masai people of Tanzania. In his remarkable book *Christianity Rediscovered* (1982) he portrays the successes and failures of the mission. In vivid terms he describes how a series of communities came to grasp the significance of the Eucharist, and how the regular practice of the liturgy informed and shaped their common life.

Reluctant to pass on to new converts the more rigid and formalistic aspect of Roman Catholic liturgy, Donovan began with the essentials.

> The first Masses in the new Masai communities were simplicity itself. I would take bread and wine, without any preceding or following ritual, and say to the people: ". . . On the night before he died, Jesus took bread and wine into his hands, blessed them and said, 'This is my body. This is the cup of my blood of the New Covenant, poured out for the forgiveness of sins. Do this in my memory.'" That served as Offertory, Preface and Canon. The people took it from there. (Donovan, 1982: 121–2)

But already the ethical dimensions of this practice were profound, and were lost on no one:

> Masai men had never eaten in the presence of Masai women. In their minds, the status and condition of women were such that the very presence of women at the time of eating was enough to pollute any food that was present . . . How then was the Eucharist possible? If ever there was a need for the Eucharist as a salvific sign of unity, it was here . . . Here, in the Eucharist, we were at the heart of the unchanging gospel that I was passing on to them. They were free to accept that gospel or reject it, but if they accepted it, they were accepting the truth that in the Eucharist . . . "there is neither slave nor free, neither Jew nor Greek, neither male nor female." (Donovan. 1982: 121)

They did accept it, after a traumatic period of discernment; and a group of teenage girls told Donovan later that the "good news" was really good news for them.

Donovan began to develop some misgivings, however, that the Eucharist had almost too significant a role in the people's notion of Church:

> At one point I thought the people were badly confusing the meaning of the Eucharist, or that of the church, or both. They already referred to the church as the *orporor*, the brotherhood. Now, from time to time, I heard them calling the Eucharist the *orporor sinyati*, the holy *orporor*, or the holy brotherhood. They would ask questions like "Next time you come, are we holding or making the holy *orporor*?" It did not seem to make sense until I remembered St Paul's saying, "This bread that we break, is it not the *koinonia* of the body and blood of Christ?" . . . These Masai communities did, in fact, build up and make the church in each Eucharist they celebrated. (Donovan, 1982: 123)

The Masai's way of resolving arguments was for one person to offer a tuft of grass (the vital food of cattle) and a second to accept it, as a guarantee and embodiment of peace. And this helped the elders to decide whether today there was Eucharist.

> We had tried to teach these people that it was not easy to achieve the Eucharist. It was not an act of magic achieved by the saying of a few words in the right order . . . If the life of the village had been less than human or holy, there was no Mass. If there had been selfishness or hatefulness and lack of forgiveness . . . let them not make a sacrilege out of it by calling it the Body of Christ. And the leaders did decide occasionally that, despite the prayers and readings and discussions, if the grass had stopped, if someone, or some group, in the village had refused to accept the grass as the sign of the peace of Christ, there would be no Eucharist at this time. (Donovan, 1982: 127)

With this understanding of the Eucharist, it became the principal way in which the priest and people discerned the good for their common life. A highly significant example of this came in relation to another tribe, the Sonjo, who were expert dancers. In the hands of the Sonjo, the Eucharist took on a new dimension. It became the practice through which the community discerned the good. The following words epitomize the understanding that this volume seeks to present of the role of worship in ethics:

They brought their music directly to the place where the bread and wine were later to be blessed, and performed it there deliberately and carefully. Some of their music was decidedly secular. The elders in that community pointed out to me that the purpose of such a procedure was to make an actual judgement on a very important area of their lives. The time of the Eucharist was the time for that judgement. They were not ashamed of that dance in their own lives, so they wanted that part of their lives to be offered with the Eucharist. There were some dances they were ashamed to bring into the Eucharist. By that very fact, a judgement had been made on them. Such dances should no longer be a part of their lives at all. Eucharist served as judgement for them. (Donovan, 1982: 125)

It will be clear by now that the ethos of this volume is entirely constructive. While the "judgment" of the Eucharist found some aspects of the Sonjo's culture wanting, so likewise the judgment of the Eucharist as explored in this volume finds some aspects of contemporary culture and some of the methods often used in Christian ethics wanting. In particular, a number of chapters find that the consumer culture prevailing in contemporary North Atlantic countries and elsewhere creates a hazy mist through which it is difficult to see the gospel, indeed any aspect of life, straight. By suggesting that worship, especially the Eucharist, offers a lens through which to see life, this volume seeks to offer to its readers what Vincent Donovan offered to the Masai: a corporate practice for discerning the good. And it is not a new practice: it is one that has been at the heart of many of the world's cultures for hundreds of years.

Worship as a Series of Practices

Because the Eucharist incorporates so many practices, one could easily fall into the habit of using the term in a sweeping manner to suggest that the Eucharist is the answer to every question that arises in contemporary Christian ethics. This is a danger because not only does it risk overlooking the detail of what those specific practices are and how they are best carried out, but also it can slip into making the Eucharist an abstraction, a theoretical panacea detached from embodied practice – the very opposite of the intention. Thus, even though the Eucharist must always be understood as a whole, this volume largely treats it as an ordered series of specific practices. By so doing, detailed attention may be given to these particular practices, and concentrated emphasis may rest on how the performance of these practices shapes the character of Christians and the mind of the Church as a whole.

The volume is shaped in an ecumenical spirit, and includes contributors from the Roman Catholic, Anglican, Methodist, Presbyterian, Mennonite, and Pentecostal traditions. The outline of the Eucharist is intended not to mimic that performed in any one of these traditions alone, but nonetheless to take a form that any Christian would recognize. Indeed, no effort has been made to elide differing perceptions of the nature and significance of aspects of the liturgy. The variety of ecclesial identification is part of the reality of the Church, and conflict is part of that heritage. To establish an internal consistency in the volume that ignored the unhealed divisions in the Church would be hopeful but less than truthful.

The practices of the Eucharist have been treated under five broad sequential headings. All the headings are participles, emphasizing the kinetic, or action-based, emphasis of this volume's understanding of worship. No effort has been made to make each chapter's treatment of a particular moment in the liturgy an exclusive one. It is inevitable and right that most of the chapters treat not only their specific practice but make reference to other practices in the liturgy and in some cases to the Eucharist as a whole. There is bound to be a small dimension of arbitrariness in the way the practices and the ethical "issues" have been assigned, but the reader is encouraged to treat the volume as a whole, rather than to judge the argument on any one particular chapter. The overall objective is to take worship from being a curiosity in ethical discussion to being considered so significant that it is taken for granted in every debate and permitted to generate questions that shape the whole discipline.

The first heading, describing the first group of practices, is "Meeting God and One Another." This refers to the four principal introductory activities that most congregations carry out early in their time together. They gather; they greet God and one another; they confess sin; and they celebrate forgiveness and other blessings, often musically. The chapters on the themes of gathering and greeting consider the social and political significance of the very fact that Christians gather at all, and the questions of identity and purpose that arise from such basic elements of being Church. The chapters on praise and celebration consider how hymn singing and similar practices inform the Church's understanding of the arts in general and modern communication in particular. The chapter on confessing sin focuses on how the practice of reconciliation might shape general understandings of juridical punishment.

The second group of practices is called "Re-encountering the Story." This is perhaps the most conventional part of the volume because it considers how the Scripture shapes the character of Christians and the mind of the Church. But this section is interested in the Scripture not just as a written text, but as a performed and enacted Word. Thus reading and preaching are only two of the practices discussed: there is also consideration of the discipline of listening, the recital of the Creed, and, most easily missed, the pause between sermon and Creed in which the Body discerns the ways in which the truth of the gospel reveals both God and the world for what they are and empowers the Church to anticipate, experience, and participate in liberation. The chapters in this section consider such significant issues as authority, justice, truth, and description, issues that underlie any approach to Christian ethics.

The third group of practices is treated under the name "Being Embodied." This is the point in the service, after the proclamation of the Word, in which other elements may be included before the sharing of food begins. Hence the volume includes two specific practices that are not a part of most celebrations of the Eucharist, but are a part of some – namely baptism and marriage. All the chapters in this section consider aspects of what it means for the Church to regard itself as living as one Body. The practice of intercession is considered in relation both to human need (poverty) and one highly influential model of response to scarcity (management). Baptism offers a series of practices that shape Christians' understanding of the body, and thus is the right way in which to consider abortion and cloning. Likewise, marriage is about a shared embodiment. And, lastly, the sharing of the peace provides a corresponding chapter to that on confessing sin, underlining the practices necessary to maintain trust and thus sustain the Body.

The fourth and largest group of practices considers the preparation and consumption of the eucharistic food itself, and this section is called "Re-enacting the Story." The first three chapters address the material of the Eucharist and the way it is handled, and reflect on how this informs Christians' relationship with the material world, an issue that causes deep concerns to many of the authors in this volume. The next two chapters reflect on the powerful forces at work at the altar, and notions such as sacrifice that emphasize the dimension in which blessing and breaking bread is the heart of the Christian response to what seem to be the most powerful forces in the world – such as war and capitalism. After that come three chapters that meditate on the practice of eating together as the definitive form of Christian witness, and the way in which this simple but profound activity might shape a wide range of issues from euthanasia to homosexuality. The last three chapters in this section all consider the "conclusion" of the meal, and include differing notions of how the meal ends and the way those different endings offer significant statements about the Church's understanding of its membership, purpose, and witness.

The final group of practices concerns the two principal ways in which the service as a whole is completed. There are two reflections on being blessed, one that addresses the notion of blessing as material abundance, another that treats blessing in terms of having and rearing children. Lastly comes the dismissal, and the comprehensive understanding of how what has taken place in the service has informed, shaped, changed, or transformed the Body and whether it will now better carry out its vocation in the world.

A Story

Some years ago one of us became the vicar of a small church in a notoriously marginalized and antagonistic neighborhood. One distressing aspect of life there was that services would frequently be interrupted by children and young people who were not interested in participating, but nonetheless took to bursting in, looking for attention, and hoping to get some kind of a reaction. On one particular occasion, at the Sunday Eucharist, things became more sinister. A gang of seven surly twelve- and thirteen-year-old boys entered the church purposefully just as the prayer of consecration had been completed and the bread was being broken. They strode up and stood tall across the altar. The leader, pointing at the consecrated bread, said "Are you going to give us some of that?" The congregation winced – not just from horror (sadly, this was no more than an extreme example of confrontational behavior), but because the question of how best to respond in such circumstances had for some time caused a good deal of conflict amongst the regular church members. It was time to put the consecrated bread down for a few moments, and try persuasion. The words flowed. "If you look behind you, you will see a small group of people who are here to do the most important thing in their lives. I don't think this is the most important thing in your life. I hope it may become so one day. But for now, I suggest you wait outside until we've finished, and then we'll have a chat about what things are really important and how we learn how to do them." Contrary to expectation, the boys did exactly as they were asked. A conversation followed the service, about what things matter, how to treat oneself, people and things, and whom to trust.

This book is written to inform such a conversation. It is written to show how the Eucharist really is the most important thing we do in our lives. And it is dedicated to the congregation in that challenging neighborhood, and others like them, who have allowed their characters to be shaped by the worship of the living God, who accompanies his disciples, and makes himself known to them in the breaking of the bread.

Reference

Donovan, Vincent (1982) *Christianity Rediscovered* (London: SCM).

CHAPTER 2

The Gift of the Church and the Gifts God Gives It

Stanley Hauerwas and Samuel Wells

God gives his people everything they need to follow him. In the context of contemporary Christian ethics, this claim may seem incomprehensible, bewildering, and absurd. Incomprehensible, because it suggests that ethics is about being disciples and witnesses (following him); bewildering, because it speaks of the abundance of resources rather than their scarcity (everything they need); absurd, because it suggests that the subject of ethics is not those who self-define and self-express, but about the one who gives (God). This chapter sets out to witness to this extraordinary claim.

It suggests that what God wants is for his people to worship him, to be his friends, and to eat with him: in short, to be his companions. The Eucharist offers a model of this companionship. Disciples gather and greet; are reconciled with God and one another; hear and share their common story; offer their needs and resources; remember Jesus and invoke his Spirit; and then share communion, before being sent out. Through worship – preparation, performance, repetition – God gives his people the resources they need to live in his presence.

If God offers his people this gift, why would anyone overlook, ignore, or neglect it? Yet that is what conventional Christian ethics does. This is a great mystery. God has shown his people how to commune with him, but much contemporary Christian ethics strives to act Christianly without using the resources designed for the purpose. It tries to make "Christian" an adjective, an epithet, a style – when what God offers his people is particular actions – verbs – through which they can become and be distinctive nouns – people, disciples, witnesses. Thus conventional ethics so often finds its task impossible. It is trying to make a better world without us needing to become better people. Not only is the task impossible, but it is neglecting its chief resource – the way God chooses to form his people. This chapter is about that resource and how the Church is to use it.

What follows has been inspired by a range of theologians, some indicative, some interrogative, some imperative. In its emphasis on worship, it owes much to the Reformed tradition, though the importance of corporate worship is a more Catholic theme; on friendship, it follows Thomas Aquinas (1981), and before him Aristotle

(1980). In its concentration on God as subject, it follows Karl Barth (1936–69); in its perception of God's abundance in the face of quasi-Stoic scarcity, it follows John Milbank (1997); in its emphasis on tradition and practice, it follows Alasdair MacIntyre (1984). When it comes to seeing the heart of Christianity in corporate discipleship, it is aided by George Lindbeck's (1984) cultural-linguistic proposal; perhaps, most of all, its careful delineation of practices is inspired by John Howard Yoder (1984). In its portrayal of exile, it follows Tom Wright (1996); in its perception of God's commitment to the poor, it follows Gustavo Gutiérrez (1988). Its attempt to see the practices of the local church put under proper theological scrutiny follows the invitation of Nicholas Healy (2000), and its confidence that they will meet the challenge is encouraged by William Cavanaugh (1998).

If this chapter lies within some traditions, it clearly lies outside others. It is not an attempt to ground an ethic on a reading of human nature and society in the style of Immanuel Kant (1960); it does not seek a calculus of happiness like Jeremy Bentham (1996), or a litmus test of love like Joseph Fletcher (1966). It does not seek to secure a valued place for Christianity in a liberal-democratic consensus bounded by sin and compromise after the manner of Reinhold Niebuhr (1941), nor seek a middle path between gospel values and contemporary realities with William Temple (1976). It makes no claim for a God that all can subscribe to as James Gustafson (1984) does, or a global concern that all can share as pursued by Hans Küng (1997). It seeks not to deride or pity these approaches, but simply to demonstrate the resources they have neglected, and inspire the reader to explore the gifts and demands of worship, discipleship, and witness. Then may the Church set aside what it knows of human scarcity, and open its life to divine abundance. For ethics begins and ends with God.

God

> Then Jesus came from Galilee to John at the Jordan to be baptized by him. John would have prevented him, saying, "I need to be baptized by you, and do you come to me?" But Jesus answered him, "Let it be so now; for it is proper for us in this way to fulfill all righteousness." Then he consented. And when Jesus had been baptized, just as he came up from the water, suddenly the heavens were opened to him and he saw the Spirit of God descending like a dove and alighting on him. And a voice from heaven said, "This is my Son, the Beloved, with whom I am well pleased." (Matthew 3: 13–17)

The baptism of Jesus is the foundation of Christian ethics. Here Jesus speaks his first words in the Gospel, explaining to John the Baptist the purpose of Christian ethics: "to fulfill all righteousness." Here is revealed the source of Christian ethics, which lies in the interrelationship between the members of the Trinity: the Father who opens heaven and speaks, the incarnate Son who goes down, rises, and fulfills all righteousness, the Holy Spirit who descends and rests upon.

The context of Christian ethics emerges in understanding the setting of the baptism story. The story is set at the River Jordan, the very river that Joshua had crossed to take possession of the Promised Land. The crossing of water echoes the crossing of the Red

Sea, the definitive act by which God shows his power and his love for Israel and his will to give them freedom from slavery. Yet at the time of Jesus's baptism, Israel does not possess the Promised Land, and has not done so for centuries; the land belongs to an occupying power. And Israel does not experience the freedom enjoyed in the Exodus from Egypt – indeed, she experiences that the Exile has in many ways not yet come to an end. In these circumstances, Israel's plea is a constant hope for God's intervention: "O that you would tear open the heavens and come down" (Isaiah 64: 1), and her prophecy similar: "Shower, O heavens, from above, and let the skies rain down righteousness" (Isaiah 45: 8). The setting of the story is thus one of bewilderment, longing, desperation – in short, need – and fervent expectation. This is the context of Christian ethics. Need and expectation are also the context of Christian intercession. Intercession brings human need to God in an expectation that he will transform that need. Thus, as for the blind man, the hope is always that "God's works might be revealed" through the concerns raised (John 9: 3). Ethics and intercession are two halves of the same Christian practice.

Christian ethics is therefore a discipline that seeks to help Christians fulfill all righteousness from and with the Trinitarian God of Jesus Christ. And it is a practice that takes place in the context of need and in the spirit of expectation that God will make himself known through the faithful pursuit of his will.

Within this context takes place the event – the content – of Christian ethics. The gospel proclamation is that God has decisively acted to change the context of life. This is what is enacted in the baptism of Jesus. Three dimensions of the baptism of Jesus constitute the event of Christian ethics, and make possible the whole discipline. First, heaven, which has been closed for a long time, is opened. This epitomizes the fruit of Christ's work. The gospel begins with the tearing of the heavens and ends with the tearing of the temple curtain. The veil between God and his people has been torn. Heaven is open to those who stand where Christ stands. There is no limit to God's purpose for his people: it is an eternal purpose. The open heaven also confirms that earth is the theater of God's action. The author has joined the drama. The key events of the world are key also to the life of God. He has shaped his life – and that of the world – so as to be for and with his people. God hears his people's prayers.

Second, God's Spirit descends like a dove. At the end of the Flood, the dove brought the twig of new life back to Noah. Now the dove descends on Jesus, bringing the gift of the Holy Spirit. He is the Temple of God's Holy Spirit. He is the place where others will encounter God. He bears the promise that through him his people may become the Temple of the Holy Spirit, the place where God's glory dwells, the place of encounter. God gives his people power.

Third, God speaks, and he tells his people how precious is the gift they have in Jesus. The voice tells God's people that Jesus means everything to God, and that God makes himself fully known in Jesus. It also holds out the promise that, just as God gives everything to Jesus, everything he gives to Jesus he gives through Jesus to his people. And, ultimately, the promise of this is that God's people mean everything to God. "Jesus has everything the Father has to give, and he gives us this everything in the unlikely place called baptism in the church" (Bruner, 1987: 94). God gives his people everything they need.

Thus Christian ethics is the study of how God meets the needs of those who call upon him in need and expectation, thus enabling them to fulfill all righteousness. The attitude of Christian ethics should be one of intercession, from an experience of need. But heaven is open, and prayers can be heard. God is intimately concerned with the destiny of his people. God makes his people new through the power of the Holy Spirit. Christian ethics is about how God makes people who are capable of fulfilling all righteousness; it is about how people are shaped to live good lives before him. God gives his people Jesus – who is everything they need. Christian ethics names the ways in which the Church inherits and embodies what God gives his people in Jesus.

We have witnessed the foundation, the source, the context, and the content of Christian ethics – all of which lie in God's gracious action, crystallized in the baptism of Christ. It remains to witness the goal of Christian ethics. The goal of Christian ethics names the things that the baptism of Christ enables Christians to do. These are also the purposes for which God created his people. They are the same things that exile and slavery inhibit them from doing. The baptism of Christ announces the end of slavery and exile, and inaugurates the new crossing-over into dwelling with God. God wants his people to worship him. He made his people to glorify and enjoy him forever. He also wants his people to be his friends. Friendship is at the center of the moral life because the virtues God's people learn in being friends of one another are vital in learning what it means to be God's friends forever.

The word that best expresses this friendship is companion – one who shares bread. The principal eschatological image of the Gospels is the banquet. The image of the great feast declares that God longs for his people to worship him in a friendship that is embodied in eating together. Christians practice this longing when they habitually and faithfully share the Eucharist. In the Eucharist they recognize that God wants them to worship him, to be his friends, and to eat with him. It is through baptism, the baptism of Christ embodied in their own baptism, that Christians are enabled to realize these goals; and it is in the Eucharist that the goals of God's creation and redemption come to fruition. The goals of Christian ethics are none other than these very same longings and realizations. This book is a study of how Christians, in great things and small, may practice Christian ethics by fulfilling God's longing for them to worship him, be his friends, and eat with him.

The Gifts of God

God has given his people everything they need. What he wants is for them to worship him, be his friends, and eat with him. Through employing what he has given them to these ends, they will become the people he wants them to be. So to understand Christian ethics, it is necessary to explore the gifts God gives to his people. We shall explore how God gives his people one gift, Jesus, in three forms. These three meanings of the gift of Christ are a way of understanding how Jesus epitomizes all of God's gifts. Each of these three meanings is conveyed by the term "the body of Christ."

In the first place, the body of Christ means Jesus, born of Mary, who suffered under Pontius Pilate, was crucified, dead, and buried, and who rose again. In understanding the gift of Jesus, God's people recognize the gift of Scripture. Scripture is the story that identifies God's people. It is the memory and heritage that they share. It is a story that reminds them that they are not the first to be loved by God; that he has unfolded his call and purpose over countless generations; that in each era many have tried to follow, and a great number – perhaps most – have failed significantly: but that as much can be learned from the failures as from those whose faith was strong. The story teaches that the service of God is perfect freedom. It tells how this freedom can be sustained despite human fragility, iniquity, and hostility. It delights in the embodiments of God's faithful purpose – the Commandments, the ark, the Temple, the Land. It recalls how precarious was the thread by which the exiled people held on to their vision. It acknowledges how far from God's freedom his people many times strayed, and the perils of those who called them back. It shows how Jesus embodied all the promises of God and the yearnings of Israel, how he recapitulated Israel's life as prophet, priest, and king, how his death and resurrection broke open the purposes of God and the possibilities of his people, how his Church began, grew, and faced early setbacks, how finally dispersion became no longer a sign of defeat and despair but always a sign of growth and joy.

This is the gift of Scripture: a story that shows the definitive workings of God, but invariably shows how those workings are laced around the strivings of his people. Jesus embodies the way God's action takes shape in human form. He is the direction and the purpose of the story. But Jesus also steps out of the pages of Scripture, in a way no other character does. He is part of a story about the past, but he is not limited to that story. He points always beyond the story, to the kingdom. The kingdom is the fulfillment of the purposes of God, all creation in perfect service and harmonious relationship and joyful communion. The kingdom expresses the hope of God's people, just as Scripture incorporates their memory. And just as Scripture points to and illustrates the gift of Jesus, so likewise the kingdom is defined and identified by Jesus. God's people long for a time of perfect service because they have seen perfect service in Jesus ("not what I will, but what you will"). They long for harmonious relationship because they have seen harmonious relationship in Jesus ("I am in my Father and you in me, and I in you"). They long for joyful communion because they have seen joyful communion in Jesus ("Father, may they be one, as we are one"). If Scripture is about heritage, kingdom is about destiny. For God's people, if Jesus is the person they remember, Jesus is also the person they look forward to. They look back to the one crowned on the cross, and forward to the one enthroned in judgment. They thus perceive that those in distress and agony are by no means outside God's purposes now, and that those who have been trodden down and abused may look forward to vindication on the great day.

If Scripture points back to the pattern of God's action expressed fully in Jesus, and kingdom points forward to the fulfillment of God's purpose expressed in Jesus, then God's people look to him to bring these gifts into their present life. This he does through the work of the Holy Spirit. The Holy Spirit brings the remembered word of Scripture to life and transforms the anticipated hope of the kingdom into action. Through the gift of the Holy Spirit the gift of Jesus is made ever present and ever new. Through the ministry of the Holy Spirit what would otherwise be words, stories, ideas become practices, habits, patterns of action. The Holy Spirit teaches God's people and thus makes followers into disciples. People learn how to read Scripture, and to read their own story as narrated by the scriptural story. People learn how to look to and pray for the coming of the kingdom, and how to let the form and content of their practice be transformed by the anticipated character of life with God. Thus the Holy Spirit trains God's people to recognize God's hand at work, shapes the ways in which they reflect God's character, and empowers them to express that character in the world.

An understanding of Scripture, the hope of the kingdom, and the work of the Holy Spirit are all therefore needed in order to explore what it means to see God's gift of the body of Christ as Jesus. A second understanding of the body of Christ is as God's gift of the Church. Up to this point we have used the designation "God's people" to refer to that aspect of creation that has responded to its creator and redeemer in faith. That we now begin to use the word "Church" is an affirmation that the Church is itself an aspect of God's gift in Jesus. The Church is not (and was not) an assembly of people whom Jesus happens (or happened) to visit; it is a people assembled only in the strength of Christ's coming and being among them. To call the Church the Body of Christ does not appeal to a static, hegemonic identification with a timeless ideal; it simply confirms that the Church's existence is always a gift and that that gift is always delivered and shaped by the incarnate, crucified, and risen Jesus.

God gives many gifts to the Church to form, shape, and maintain its life. Some of these gifts are practices, regular patterns of action that embody the goods that God conveys. Others are powers or charisms, faculties that enable the Church to carry out the sometimes demanding practices God has given it. We shall briefly explore the dimensions of the gifts God gives his people in his gift of the Church.

The gifts God gives to the Church for its formation are those that bring people into the company of the faith. Preaching alerts the listener to the awe and wonder of the scriptural testimony. The preacher's role is to unfold the breadth of God's purpose, the depth of his love, the length of his forbearance; to acknowledge the mystery of human indifference, the tragedy of alienation, the waste of glory; and to focus on the urgency of the moment, the intensity of God's longing, and the faithfulness of his promises. While preaching should certainly aspire to renew the Church through conviction, its primary goal is to constitute the Church through conversion. Preaching is by no means the only way that people come to faith, but it symbolizes the other routes because it emphasizes that the gospel is good news in the form of a liberating story. This liberating story is accompanied by transforming practices, such as catechesis. Catechesis names the process by which the new believer is conformed to Christ in body, mind, and spirit and made ready to become a disciple. In catechesis the new believer discovers how the story and practices of the Church enable disciples to worship God, be his friends, and eat with him. The process of catechesis prepares new believers for the event of baptism. Baptism embraces the whole of God's story, from the water of creation to the fire of judgment. It enacts the crossing-over from slavery to freedom, darkness to light, death to life, despair to hope. It is the principal way in which those who turn to God are incorporated into Christ's body. It defines the Church.

Another set of gifts and practices shape the regular life of the Church, the continuing deliberation of common goods and purposes that is called politics. These practices begin with praise, in which God's people accord to him all that they long to offer, responding to his love with listening ears, singing hearts, and serving hands. Praise is a continual blend of the joyful telling of God's wondrous deeds and the humble joining of the angels' constant celebration. It is the stretching of words to their limit, and the embracing of action when words fail. Closely associated with praise is thanksgiving, in which the Church records not just God's deeds, but their grace and mercy, and the miracle that they extend to the most unlikely and unworthy and unexpected. In silence, God's people recognize that God's activity in the world always precedes their own, listen for signs or indications of that activity, and are drawn into the intimacy of God's presence. Meanwhile, in intercession, the Church comes before God with the anticipation of the kingdom and the burden of all in creation that falls short of the kingdom's fulfillment. Much of the rest of the regular practice of the Church may be taken together under the single designation "witness." For witness names the Christian hope that every action − whether for peace, for justice, for stability, for alleviating distress, for empowering the young or weak, for comforting the lonely, for showing mercy to the outcast, for offering hospitality, for making friends, or for earning a living − points to God, and invites an inquiry into the joy that inspires such actions.

While the foregoing gifts and practices form and norm the Church, a third set is needed for the many times the Church's supposed witness and discipleship fail to imitate God and jeopardize his friendship. God gives the Church practices through which he maintains and restores its character as the Body of Christ. These include admonition, the speaking of truth for the sake of God and the sinner; and involve penitence, the sinner's naming of his or her own sin and request for forgiveness. They center on reconciliation, the restoration of perpetrator and victim to relationship and communion, with self, one another, community, and God. They can require discipline, the use of persuasion, warning, constraint, and even punishment in an effort to bring the offender to truthfulness, penitence, and reconciliation.

This then is the second understanding: the gift of the Church and the accompanying gifts that enable God's people to be formed, to witness, and to be restored to relationship. The first two portrayals of the body of Christ have explored what it means for God's people to worship God (through Jesus) and to be his friends (through the Church). The third understanding therefore concerns what it means to eat with him. This is the body of Christ as the Eucharist − or, more particularly, the living bread, broken for the life of the world. This third understanding is the one most commonly considered and received as a gift. Indeed, the president says in some traditions, when inviting the congregation to the table, "the gifts of God for the people of God." What gifts accompany the gift of the body of Christ in the food of the Eucharist?

The regular practice of a shared meal on the day of the Lord's resurrection is the principal way in which Christians bind time. If it were not a meal, which requires preparation, it could take place anytime, anywhere Christians spontaneously came together. If it were not a corporate activity, it could take place privately, whenever was convenient for an individual. But because it must be corporate and requires preparation, it makes the Church find a regular rhythm of celebration. And this regular rhythm of celebration comes to order the shapelessness of time. Life is no longer a linear flow of one thing after another, but an ebb and flow, a constant sending out to love and serve and share, a constant return and gathering to praise and repent and ask. What is not done by the beginning of the next celebration can wait; and all that has been done is transformed. Each celebration looks back to the last, and forward to the next; and meanwhile looks back to the Passover and Exodus, the Lord's Supper, Crucifixion and Resurrection, and forward to the final banquet. Thus worship gives the Church time.

Likewise, gathering gives the Church space. Because Christians need each other if they are to be able to experience the gift of the body of Christ in the food of the Eucharist, they cannot be just anywhere when they worship. Because the Eucharist is an embodied, corporate practice, God's people need to come together in one place. They become for that period, if for no other, a visible community. The Church is not, for that period, a vague idea, a marvelous principle, an invisible influence. It becomes *some*-thing, and thus can no longer be *any*thing, gives up being *every*thing, and is much more than *no*thing. This is a sacrifice because being able to be "anything" offers flexibility, to be "everything" offers power, and to be "nothing" offers anonymity and therefore safety. By becoming something, somewhere, the Church locates itself in space, and is made visible. Only thus can it begin to relate to all in God's creation who have taken the freedom of God's patience not yet to believe.

Gathering to eat together gives the Church its identity because it gives God's people a definitive practice. Learning to perform this action well informs and educates Christians in their performance of all other actions. In performing the action well the Church realizes its need to incorporate into its worship most of its other characteristic practices, at least in elemental form. To be ready to receive the body of Christ, people of God need to remind themselves of the identity of Christ, and of the nature of their existence as a body. By so doing, they prepare themselves to become what they eat – the body of Christ. This activity, eating, is particularly related to sustaining the body. It therefore locates the Church in relation to the whole of creation, as a body that, like other bodies, needs food, but, being a special body with a special purpose on behalf of all other bodies, is given special food.

Thus the gift of the Eucharist comes alongside the gift of the Church and the gift of Jesus as the third understanding of the body of Christ. The gift of the Eucharist demonstrates and, in many ways, embodies God's gift to his people of time, space, and action and their relation to the rest of creation. It completes the argument of this chapter that, in the body of Christ, God has given his people everything they need: everything they need to know about the past and the future; everything they need to do to form, shape, and maintain their shared life and witness; everything they need in time, space, and action. Just as this comprehensiveness is prefigured in Jesus's first words in Matthew's Gospel ("to fulfill all righteousness"), so it is announced in Jesus's last words ("All authority in heaven and earth has been given to me: go therefore . . ."). It is time to consider the character of this body, which has been given so much, and from which so much is expected.

The Gift of the Church

We shall attempt to characterize the Church in response to five familiar questions. What, where, and who is the Church? Which Church? And how does the Church embody Christ? Three of these questions are helpful, one, though frequently asked, is unhelpful, and the fifth opens the way to the final section of this chapter.

What is the Church? The foregoing treatment of the body of Christ has addressed this question so far as to outline some of the practices that constitute and maintain the Church. To the extent that the Church is what it does, then, we have identified it as that part of God's creation that seeks to respond to his love by taking up his invitation to worship him, be his friend, and eat with him. Beyond this, the Church believes it exists not for its own sake but for the world. It hopes to inherit God's words to Abraham: "in you all the families of the earth shall be blessed" (Genesis 12: 3). It thus sees itself as a gift of God to the world. What form should this gift take?

Jesus embodied the memory and hope of Israel by enacting the roles of prophet, priest, and king. The Church, the Body of Christ, is called to imitate Jesus in some respects – but not all. It follows much of the prophetic and priestly aspects of Jesus's ministry, and should share some of their cost. But it goes seriously awry when it takes on a kingly role. Assuming a kingly role invariably directs attention away from Christ and toward itself. The Church thus has a twofold ministry, pointing to both the sovereignty of Christ's person and the pattern of his work. In short, the Church is a prophet and priest that points to a king.

The Church is a prophet in two respects. The first is that it points people to God. One much-loved cathedral has a famous sequence of roof bosses along the length of the nave, depicting salvation history from the tree of knowledge in Genesis 2 to the tree of the Lamb in Revelation 22. It would be too easy for the worshiper or visitor to miss it, so in the aisle are several mirrors, facing heavenwards. Lest viewers peer into the mirror and become distracted or fascinated by their own image, the mirrors are tilted slightly. Those mirrors are an apt analogy for the prophetic ministry of the Church. Without them, few would look up at all, and fewer still would realize what beauty and order lay above. With them, all will have an opportunity to see, some will use them to look in detail, and others will be inspired to look heavenwards for themselves. The work of the mirrors is not even ruined when their glass is badly damaged or broken: for even a small piece of glass can help to highlight a part of the roof, and the existence of the mirror will eventually provoke the viewer to look up. This is the role of the witness.

The second role of the prophet goes beyond the analogy of the tilted mirror. If all prophets were as subtle as that, few would have died horrible deaths. Prophets have died horrible deaths because they have pointed out to the world that it is not the Church. The world is all that in God's creation have taken the opportunity of God's patience not yet to believe in him. But that unbelief in the God of Jesus Christ does not inhibit misplaced confidence in the abiding power or truth of other theories, practices, or stories. And it is against these idolatries that the prophetic ministry of the Church speaks. The choice is not always a stark one: the Church may work with a great variety of movements in the world, valuing their wisdom, courage, and insight, but a point invariably comes when a faith that hinges on cross and resurrection must challenge other models of formation and transformation. A culture pervaded by the management of limited resources must eventually contradict the limitless goods of God; a society sustained by the benevolent models of therapy must eventually be challenged by the foolishness and wisdom of the cross; an economy that depends on the competition of the market must eventually confront the perpetual communion of the Trinity.

If the prophetic ministry of the Church is directed chiefly to those outside it, in the form of witness, the priestly ministry of the Church is principally concerned with ordering the life of those inside the body. The prophet exposes what is impossible without God; the priest demonstrates what is possible with him. The priestly role of the Church is to model sustainable life before God – to show what God makes possible for those who love him. This life in the presence of God has the three features noted in the previous section. The priestly role is concerned with the formation of disciple and community, with the way in which the believer and the body negotiate the boundary between Church and world. It is concerned with the politics of the body, with the practices through which it embodies its vocation of worship, witness and service, and the continuing conversation over the best ways to follow Christ. And it is concerned with the character of the disciple and the body, the way it perceives and experiences setback, quarrel, and sin not as the end of harmony but as an opening for the wonder of transformation and the weaving of grace.

The Church does not have a kingly ministry. Its task is, through prophetic and priestly witness, to point to the kingship of Christ. The kingship of Christ is, indeed, exercised in a prophetic and priestly way, but the Church worships Christ because of his sovereignty not because of his style. He is king not because he is good, but because he is God; not because he is just, but because he is true. Christ achieved things the Church could never have achieved, and because Christ achieved them the Church does not need to. To take upon itself a kingly ministry thus either assumes Christ was not victorious, or that he no longer reigns. Either way, it points away from and inhibits the prophetic and priestly ministry. The Church's role is like the role of the disciples at the feeding of the five thousand: to plead for the people, to bring their resources to Christ, to wonder at his work, to distribute his gifts, and to ensure nothing is wasted by gathering up what is left over. But Christ alone presides and multiplies.

The second and third questions may be taken together. Where and who is the Church? The question of where the Church is appears in a clearer light when one refers to the discussion in the previous section. If God's gifts crystallize around the paradigm of the body of Christ, and if the Church is itself one aspect of that paradigm, then it is easier to see how no one part of that paradigm is found without the others. Thus the answer to the question of where the Church is – is that it is where Jesus is, and where the Eucharist is.

As the earlier discussion showed, to speak of Jesus means to speak of people reading Scripture, people encountering the kingdom, people meeting the Holy Spirit. Jesus is God bringing his people out of slavery and exile: Jesus showed this by the people with whom he spent most of his time. The Church is therefore found in people reading Scripture and entering its narrative; it is found in people anticipating the coming reign of God; it is found in people being open to the work of the Holy Spirit in making Christ present to them. The Church is found where Jesus spent most of his time: with those whose knowledge of their neediness led them to expect most from God; with people who knew they were in slavery and exile, and who longed for the liberation that only God could bring. Thus the questions "where?" and "who?' belong together. The Church is made up of the hungry. The hungry are those who have no abiding city and whose hope is in God alone. The Church is made up of the lonely. The lonely are those who have given up the lone search and have accepted the disciplines and shared responsibilities of common life.

If "where Jesus is" responds to the question of where the Church is in a general way, a more specific definition comes from the second answer – "where the Eucharist is." This corresponds to Calvin's understanding of "where the Word of God [is] purely preached and heard, and the sacraments administered according to Christ's institution" (Calvin, 1960: 4.1.9). Celebrating the Eucharist means much more than eating bread. It means gathering, and thus becoming a visible people. It means being reconciled, and thus finding unity in Christ, rather than in "common humanity." It means listening and responding to the scriptural story, and thus sharing a tradition. It means remembering God's action and invoking the Spirit's presence, and thus being redirected to true power and unique sacrifice. It means being sent out to witness and serve, and thus being given a shape for living. The Church is not the limit of God's activity – the kingdom has already been detailed – but it names the specific gifts and practices that become available to people when they meet together in his name. Putting the general and the specific answers together, the Church is God bringing people out of slavery and exile through people coming together to identify with him and through him with one another. Where these things happen, there the Church is. Those who do these things, they are the Church.

So the three questions – "what, where, and who is the Church?" – are helpful in characterizing the gift that God gives the world in giving the world the Church. This brings us to the less helpful, but equally common, question: "which Church?" The Church finds itself divided into countless communions, most of which claim for themselves a unique understanding of the faithful following of Christ. A theological principle that "you did not choose me, no, I chose you" now offers disciples a bewildering set of choices to be made on doctrinal, historical, cultural, racial, social, liturgical, aesthetic, catechetical, and geographic grounds. Just as the central reality of Jesus is his broken body on the cross, and the central reality of the Eucharist is the broken body enacted on the altar, so it seems the central reality of the Church is the broken body of the many communions. Which church is the Church? Which church fulfills the criteria outlined in this chapter?

It is an understandable question, but not a helpful one. It is unhelpful because it encourages a sense of finality that diminishes, rather than builds, the Church. This is a finality that suggests it is possible to "arrive" at a "right" Church. Such a Church would be almost bound to foster pride rather than honesty, complacency rather than confidence. It would resemble a too-tidy dogmatics, in that it would provide such a conclusive guarantee of God that witness would seem unnecessary and service would be neglected. It would misunderstand every aspect of worship. It would misrepresent gathering, if it assumed it was the only community to which people could gather. Reconciliation would become even more problematic because failure and guilt would seem absurdities in the Right Church. Scripture reading would be impoverished if it suggested the story could be told no other way. Communion would be impaired if it were assumed that divisions were simply the fault of others. Mission would be confused if other

Christians were taken to be part of the "world." The response of Christians to the brokenness of the Church can only be to be even more committed to worship, witness, and service, hoping that in so doing they may form partnerships and friendships that concentrate less on the discordant contexts from which each is coming than on the harmonious glory to which each is heading.

The fifth question – "How does the Church embody Christ?' – leads us to our last section, the question of ethics.

Ethics

At the end of his Gospel, John describes how Peter looks at the beloved disciple and seeks from Jesus some promise or prediction of what the future may hold. Jesus's answer is brusque. "What is that to you? Follow me!" (John 21: 22). So begins the journey of Christian ethics. Jesus's statement recognizes that there are mysteries, wonders, problems, and troubles that the disciples – even Peter – will not be able to resolve, at least not with a simple, verbal explanation. The statement asserts that there is, nonetheless, a valid way forward, despite the lack of a comprehensive solution. And it claims that the way lies in faithfulness to the God revealed in Jesus Christ. What does following Jesus mean? The following characteristics of discipleship may be offered as illustrative, rather than exhaustive.

The disciple is conformed to Christ. This is the activity of the Holy Spirit and the Church, as well as of Christ himself. Through catechesis, study, fasting, reflection, direction, imitation of the saints, and baptism, the disciple becomes part of Christ's body.

The disciple participates in the politics of the Church. The members of the body deliberate over the goods of their life and the gifts God has given them; through casuistry they establish the practicalities of witness in the particularities of service; through mission they seek to extend the goods of their fellowship into partnerships in all corners of the world, especially the most benighted ones, longing for the kingdom, looking for the work of the Spirit, and expecting to meet Christ in friend and stranger; through prayer they adore the God they have seen and heard, and implore him to reveal and rescue where witness and service fall short.

The disciple engages in the reconciling practice of God and the Church. Through admonition, discipline, repentance, confession, reconciliation, and restoration the disciple and the community experience and practice God in Christ, reconciling the world to himself. Through peacemaking, the disciple and the Church extend this encounter beyond the Church to the world, seeking to show the glory of God in human beings restored to life and relationship.

And in all these ways the disciple enters into the rhythm of God's life, the pattern of the dance of the Trinity. The disciple who accepts the humility of repeating the same practices over and over again receives the wonder of discovering through them the God who is ever new. Following Jesus is not just about making commitments, facing temptations, forging patterns, extending gestures, and restoring relationships. It is also about the ordinary, the routine, the common, the everyday, the trivial. Following the incarnate Christ means handing over to God the salient features of existence, and being surprised to receive back the humdrum as a wonderful gift.

Each dimension of following Jesus – conformation, participation, restoration, and rhythm – is incorporated in worship. In worship Christians meet God in time-honored ways. Worship is where people are conformed to Christ, join in his work, are accepted back into his fellowship, and dance to the beat of his drum. Worship anticipates heaven, where all these things are gloriously fulfilled. But worship is also a training for discipleship on earth. It is the time when Christians learn how to be God's friends by eating with him.

While all disciples face crises in life, the great preponderance of things they do they take for granted. Meanwhile, what they regard as a crisis will probably be an interruption in the flow of events and practices and relationships that they take for granted. So what they take for granted shapes and determines what they regard as a crisis, an issue, or a dilemma. And the way to resolve such a quandary can only be by reference to other things they take for granted. That is why worship is the key to Christian ethics. Through worship God trains his people to take the right things for granted. When Christians gather they learn to value every person God has made, big, small, bright, slow, not because they are each individuals with rights (which inevitably conflict) but because each one has been given gifts by God that the Church needs to receive if it is to be faithful. When Christians confess their sins they recall the passion and recklessness of God and realize that every saint has a past and every sinner has a future. When Christians listen to Scripture they remember that God's purposes can never be limited by the meanness of the human imagination. When Christians share bread together they rediscover that every person brings different things to the table but each receives back the same. When Christians are sent out they are reminded that each one has a vocation to witness and service and that ordinary discipleship can find an elixir in the words "for thy sake."

Worship is the time when God trains his people to imitate him in habit, instinct, and reflex. The people who listen to children talking about God learn to listen to children talking about growth and sadness. The people who expect God to communicate with them in worship learn to discern his voice in the shopping queue or the news bulletin. The people who hear the story of the homeless young mother who became a refugee learn to welcome such people whom they meet elsewhere. Together, God's people reform the descriptions they use to name the outcast, the sinner, and the unclean, and reshape the ways people are received, nurtured, respected, and empowered. Together they reflect on the patterns of life that build up the body. In discussing whether, how, and when it is appropriate to speak in tongues or dance or prophesy or use contemporary music or pray extempore, the body discovers when it is appropriate to campaign, denounce, protest, or be silent. In discussing who should lead, preach, preside, pray, and how much people should attend, pray, give money, be patient, the body discovers the gifts God gives the Church and the instincts of community.

Above all, worship trains God's people to be examples of what his love can do. Worshiping God invites him to make the life of the disciple the theater of his glory. Worshiping God together invites him to make the body of believers the stage of his splendor. Over and over, God's people see the way God's Son took, blessed, broke, and gave, so that this pattern might give life to the world. The next day he himself was taken, blessed, broken, and given, for the life of the world. Over and over, they ask God to take, bless, break, and give them, for the life of the world. The saints are those whose lives have been transformed in this way – those through whom God has given life to the world. Worship trains Christians to be saints.

We have seen how God opens the heavens in response to the cry of the oppressed. He gives his people the body of Christ, thereby shaping their lives through Christ, the Church, and the Eucharist. The Church exists to practice the life made possible by Christ and to offer that life to the world in witness and service. Ethics names the ways in which disciples discern and embody Christ's life in the world, and the chief way they learn how to do this is through worship.

While all prayers are important, the disciplined practice of worship is about forming good prayers, prayers appropriate to God's mercy and justice and to his people's fragility and character. Ethics that stems from worship is this kind of informed prayer. It begins with the simple "Help!" of the crisis; it becomes the plaintive "What should I do?" of the dilemma; it emerges as the retrospective "What else could I have done?" of the confessional. Each of these is a prayer. But the worship commended by this book is a more informed prayer. It is a corporate prayer, honed by the traditions of centuries into an orchestrated dance of practices that, over time, the believer learns to perform and inhabit. It is these practices, not the crisis, that define ethics, for they are about being Christians, all the time – not about acting Christianly, on occasion. When serious challenges arise, which the Church must face together, it is to these practices, to the pattern of practices called the Eucharist, that Christians turn. And what they find is an enacted prayer, a prayer that articulates the call to God to rend the heavens and pour down righteousness, and a prayer that at the same time embodies his response. His response is the presence of his Son, the empowerment of his Spirit, and the encouragement of his Word. Who could ask for anything more?

References

Aquinas, Thomas (1981) *Summa theologica*, vols 1–2, trans. the Fathers of the English Dominican Province (Westminster, MD: Christian Classics).

Aristotle (1980) *Nicomachean Ethics*, trans. David Ross, rev. by J. L. Ackrill and J. O. Urmson (Oxford: Oxford University Press).

Barth, Karl (1936–69) *Church Dogmatics*, ed. G. W. Bromiley and T. F. Torrance, 13 vols (Edinburgh: T. and T. Clark), esp. vol. 3, pt 2, sections 44–5.

Bentham, Jeremy (1996) *The Collected Works of Jeremy Bentham: An Introduction to the Principles and Morals of Legislation*, ed. H. L. A. Hart and J. H. Burns, with an introduction by F. Rosen, rev. edn (Oxford: Clarendon Press).

Bruner, Frederick Dale (1987) *The Christbook: A Historical/Theological Commentary: Matthew 1–12* (Dallas: Word).

Calvin, John (1960) *Institutes of the Christian Religion*, ed. John T. McNeill, trans. Ford Lewis Battles, 2 vols (Philadelphia: Westminster).

Cavanaugh, William (1998) *Torture and Eucharist: Theology, Politics and the Body of Christ* (Oxford: Blackwell).

Fletcher, Joseph (1966) *Situation Ethics* (Philadelphia: Westminster).

Gustafson, James (1984) *Ethics from a Theocentric Perspective*, 2 vols (Chicago: University of Chicago Press).

Gutiérrez, Gustavo (1988) *A Theology of Liberation: History, Politics, Salvation*, rev. edn (London: SCM).

Healy, Nicholas (2000) *Church, World and the Christian Life: Practical-Prophetic Ecclesiology* (Cambridge: Cambridge University Press), esp. pp. 154–85.

Kant, Immanuel (1960) *Religion within the Limits of Reason Alone* (New York: Harper and Row).

Küng, Hans (1997) *A Global Ethic for Global Politics and Economics*, trans. John Bowden (London: SCM).

Lindbeck, George A. (1984) *The Nature of Doctrine: Religion and Theology in a Postliberal Age* (Philadelphia: Westminster), esp. pp. 30–45, 112–38.

MacIntyre, Alasdair (1984) *After Virtue: A Study in Moral Theory*, 2nd edn (London: Duckworth), esp. pp. 146–64, 204–25.

Milbank, John (1997) *The Word Made Strange: Theology, Language, Culture* (Oxford: Blackwell), esp. pp. 219–32.

Niebuhr, Reinhold (1941) *The Nature and Destiny of Man*, 2 vols (Welwyn: James Nisbet).

Presbyterian Church, USA (1983) *Book of Confessions* (Louisville: Office of the General Assembly), esp. the *Westminster Shorter Catechism* 7.001.

Temple, William (1976) *Christianity and Social Order*, with a foreword by Edward Heath (London: SPCK).

Wright, N. T. (1996) *Jesus and the Victory of God* (London: SPCK), esp. pp. 244–74, 576–92.

Yoder, John Howard (1984) *The Priestly Kingdom: Social Ethics as Gospel* (Notre Dame, IN: University of Notre Dame Press), esp. pp.15–45.

CHAPTER 3

Why Christian Ethics Was Invented

Stanley Hauerwas and Samuel Wells

Once, there was no "Christian ethics." And yet the Church was able to form and sustain disciples. To ears used to hearing the confident assertions of modernity, this may seem a curious, almost unintelligible claim. It seems curious because Christians and non-Christians alike assume that insofar as Christianity is credible in modernity it is so because of the "morality" represented by the description "Christian." It seems unintelligible because Christian ethics names the compromise that theology made in modernity by which Christian convictions would still have a hearing in contemporary debates so long as they were detached from the Church's practices. This book challenges the notion of "Christian ethics" because it seeks to reunite convictions with practices, specifically the key practices of the liturgy, thereby revoking the compromise that theology has made in modernity.

We are not the first to make this challenge. "Once, there was no 'secular.'" John Milbank's remarkable book, *Theology and Social Theory: Beyond Secular Reason* (1990: 9) begins with this counterintuitive claim in the hope of preparing readers to challenge the normalizing intellectual practices and presuppositions of modernity – practices and presuppositions shared by those who count themselves Christian as well as those who have no use for any form of the practice of the Christian faith. According to Milbank, if churches are to reclaim the politics necessary to be able even to understand what it means to proclaim "Jesus Christ is Lord," Christians must be freed of the practices and forms of thought that make descriptions of "the secular" unproblematic.

For reasons similar to Milbank's stark claim about the secular, we begin this chapter on the history of Christian ethics by observing that: "Once, there was no 'Christian ethics.'" At least, there was no "Christian ethics" prior to the time that is now described as "modern." To deny that Christian ethics existed until recently may seem even more counterintuitive than Milbank's assertion that once the "secular" did not exist. Surely we do not mean to deny that from the beginning what it means to be Christian is associated with an "ethic"?

We are, of course, not denying that the Christian Scriptures seem to be full of moral judgments and advice. The Ten Commandments and the Sermon on the Mount have long been used as paradigms of Christian morality. The problem, however, is that such examples too easily confirm current presumptions about what constitutes an "ethic." As a result, the grammar – the necessary pattern of practices – that makes Christian behavior intelligible is not thought important for any account of the lives Christians should live. This is why this book is organized around the Church's primary work, the liturgy, the worship of God. For we hope to show that an admonition such as "Do not resist an evil person" (Matthew 5: 39) is unintelligible when divorced from the early Christians' presumption that they worshiped Jesus as God's Messiah through practices such as admonition, penance, reconciliation, and absolution.

The problem with attempts in modernity to write a "history of Christian ethics" is that they assume the Enlightenment's turn to the subject, with the result that the "ethics" that becomes the main character in such accounts reflects more the self-understanding of the contemporary Western individual than the practices of the Christian tradition. A key example is the enormously influential Protestant liberal theologian, Ernst Troeltsch. Troeltsch observes at the beginning of his great work, *The Social Teaching of the Christian Churches* (1992), that a history of Christian ethics is necessary to be able to answer the question: "What is the basis of the social teaching of the Christian churches?" (1992: 24). But, according to Troeltsch, no such history is in existence; so he must attempt to write such a history in the hope that his readers can better understand the "Christian ethos in its inward connection with the universal history of civilization" (1992: 25).

The Social Teaching of the Christian Churches was first published in 1912. In the "Introduction" to this massive work, Troeltsch made clear that he undertook the task of writing a history of Christian ethics in response to the "social confusion of the present day, with its clamor of conflicting voices" (1992: 23). The Protestant churches rightly seek to make a contribution to the challenge presented by such "social confusion," according to Troeltsch: but to do so, they required a better understanding of how Christians in different times and places understood the role the Church should play in terms of the "social question." According to Troeltsch, Roman Catholicism and Calvinism had hitherto been the forms of Christianity best capable of shaping society and state, but their accomplishments had come to an end with the legal and social disestablishment of the Church. Therefore, by the "social question," Troeltsch sought to explore how liberal Protestant churches harness Christianity's ability to sustain the ethos of the past social orders in the modern era.

He thus begins the first chapter of *The Social Teaching of the Christian Churches* with the observation that, in order to understand the foundational principles of Christianity in relation to social problems, one must begin with the recognition that the preaching of Jesus and the creation of the Church "were not due in any sense to the impulse of a social movement" (1992: 39). Early Christianity was apolitical, having nothing to do with a class struggle or with the "social upheavals" of the ancient world. It is true that Jesus preached primarily to the "oppressed" and that the early Church gained new adherents from the lower classes. Moreover, it is clear that in the whole range of early Christian literature, within and without the New Testament, there is no hint of any formulation of the "Social" question; the central problem is always purely religious, dealing with such questions as the salvation of the soul, monotheism, life after death, purity of worship, the right kind of congregational organization, the application of Christian ideals to daily life, and the need for severe self-discipline in the interests of personal holiness; further, we must admit that from the beginning no class distinctions were recognized; rather they were lost sight of in the supreme question of eternal salvation and the appropriation of a spiritual inheritance. It is worthy of special note that Early Christian apologetic contains no arguments dealing either with hopes of improving the existing social situation, or with any attempt to heal social ills; it is based solely upon theology, philosophy, and ethics; further, these ethical considerations always aim at fostering habits of sobriety and industry, that is, they are concerned with the usefulness of the Christian as a citizen. (Troeltsch, 1992: 39–40)

Troeltsch acknowledges that Jesus began his public ministry by proclaiming the Kingdom of God; but such a kingdom was never thought to be a perfect social order to be created by the power of God. Nor was the kingdom an attempt to console those who were suffering from social wrongs by promising some future compensation. Rather, the message of the kingdom was primarily an ethical ideal presuming a world controlled by God in which spiritual values would be recognized for their true worth. Later, when the idea of a future redemption receded into the background and was replaced by the idea that redemption had already been achieved through the life and death of Christ, "the values of redemption were still purely inward, ethical, and spiritual, leading inevitably and naturally to a sphere of painless bliss. This is the foundation fact from which we have to start" (Troeltsch, 1992: 40). Troeltsch's characterization of the "ethic" – his assumption that it involved no response to the "social question" – is one this book is meant to counter. Troeltsch has a profound presupposition about ethics, one that leads him to suggest that the marks of the early Church – the concern for purity of worship, congregational organization, the application of Christian "ideals" to daily life, the need for self-discipline for personal holiness – at best represent an ethic that has nothing to say about the "social question." His assumption is that the "ethics" that matters is the ethics that he sees as necessary to sustain modern liberal social orders.

Such an understanding of "ethics" – that is, an ethic that can be acknowledged by "anyone" – is a recent invention. By "recent" we mean such an understanding of ethics received its determinative intellectual formulations in the eighteenth century. Immanuel Kant (1724–1804) is justly singled out for his attempt to provide an account of moral obligation based on reason alone. Kant provided elegant and complex arguments to establish what he called the categorical imperative: "Act only according to that maxim by which you can at the same time will that it should become a universal law" (Kant, 1959: 39). Kant elaborates the categorical imperative in formal terms because he presumes that "ethics" has a law-like character that makes possible cooperative forms of life between people who may not share common beliefs or history.

This account, which lends great power to the attempt to justify ethics, so to speak, on its own base, presumes a particular reading of history. The story goes something like this. For many years, usually identified with the Middle Ages, the advanced society we now call Europe was dominated by Christianity and, in particular, Catholicism. That world, however, came to an end with what we now call the Reformation. The disintegration of Christendom resulted in interminable warfare between Protestants and Catholics over who would control the different parts of Europe. Exhausted by these wars in which Protestants and Catholics, when they were not fighting one another, fought fellow Catholics and Protestants, courageous thinkers sought a morality that was not based on rival perceptions of revelation and could thus bring peace to war-ravaged Europe. Kant's ethic represents the climax of this effort just to the extent that it promises to make peace a possibility.

Closer inspection of European history suggests that the modern state in fact rose prior to the wars of religion. Meanwhile, both before and after Kant, states and peoples have found plenty of reasons to fight one another without recourse to religious justifications. That Kant's story happens not to be true nonetheless does little to qualify the power of this kind of legitimation of "modernity" (Cavanaugh, 1998).

Kant's achievement is often hailed as one of the most important expressions of the historical movement called the Enlightenment. In his essay "What is Enlightenment?" Kant expressed the essential character of this rediscovery of "man," declaring:

> Enlightenment is man's release from his self-incurred tutelage. Tutelage is man's inability to make use of his understanding without direction from another. Self-incurred is this tutelage when its cause lies not in lack of reason but in lack of resolution and courage to use it without direction from another. *Sapere aude!* "Have courage to use your own reason!" – that is the motto of enlightenment. (Kant, 1989: 85)

Accordingly, autonomy (i.e. self-liberation) became the great watchword of the Enlightenment. The autonomy of the individual was but a correlate of the autonomy of ethics; that is, both the individual and the ethics that established the moral dignity of the individual were assumed to be free of any historical and religious determination.

Kant's ethics seems so commendable because the ahistorical character of his account of the categorical imperative suggests that there might be some way to get people, who otherwise have little in common, to resolve conflicts short of war. If people respect one another as rational beings, then perhaps they might discover commonalities that might be a basis for peace. Ironically, the result of the Kantian revolution was the increasing growth of bureaucratic states that did nothing to eliminate war but rather made bigger wars – such as the two world wars of the twentieth century. Kant's politics results in the wan hope that a war could be fought "to end all wars." We obviously think that the Christian refusal of war comes from a quite different source than that provided by Enlightenment presuppositions.

The key point for our narrative – the narrative of how what is known today as Christian ethics became possible and necessary – is to note that Kant all along understood himself to be a Christian. For this reason, and for its influence on so many subsequent thinkers, Kant's important book *Religion within the Limits of Reason Alone* can be regarded as *the* great book of Protestant moral theology. Kant took as his task to save Christianity after the metaphysical and historical presuppositions once thought to be essential to the truth of Christianity had been decisively called into question by the development of Newtonian science and historical scholarship. Christianity having lost its metaphysical power, Kant sought to rescue it by showing that Christian claims could be justified to the extent that they were consistent with the moral law.

Accordingly, Kant argued that Christian belief could not depend on an historical figure like Jesus as an authority to sustain the moral life. It was not possible to depend on such a figure and yet sustain the autonomy necessary to be a moral agent. Having removed the historical Jesus as the fulcrum of Christian ethics, Kant nonetheless maintains his Christian identity by arguing that the "archetype" is already present in human reason, making it possible for the autonomous person to identify Christ as the embodiment of the moral law. Kant observes

> Now if it were indeed a fact that such a godly-minded man at some particular time had descended, as it were, from heaven to earth and had given men in his own person, through his teachings, his conduct, and his sufferings, as perfect an *example* of a man well-pleasing to God as one can expect to find in external experience (for be it remembered that the *archetype* of such a person is to be sought nowhere but in our own reason), and if he had, through all this, produced immeasurably great moral good upon earth by effecting a revolution in the human race – even then we should have no cause for supposing him other than a man naturally begotten. (Kant, 1960: 57)

Kant did not think that this meant Christians needed to deny that such a man might be supernaturally begotten, but he did not see how such an affirmation would accrue any practical benefit. Indeed, the presence of such an archetype in the human soul is sufficiently incomprehensible without "our adding to its supernatural origin the assumption that it is hypothesized in a particular individual. The elevation of such a holy person above all the frailties of human nature would rather, as far as we can see, hinder the adoption of the idea of such a person for our imitation" (Kant, 1960: 57).

Protestant liberal theology thereafter became an endless set of variations on these Kantian motifs. Protestant theologians attempted to demonstrate the significance of Jesus by attributing to him a peculiar moral significance. This often meant that Jesus's "ethic" of love was contrasted with Jewish legalism. The debates of the Reformation concerning the relation between law and gospel became the way in which the relation between Jesus's ethic and that of Judaism was understood. It is against this background that Christian ethics became an identifiable discipline distinct from theology. Even though the intellectual background for this development took place primarily in Germany, it was in America that Christian ethics came into its own.

At the end of the nineteenth century the Social Gospel movement began in America in the hope that "salvation" could be brought to the social ills facing American society. Under the influence of the great Protestant liberal theologians, Albert Ritschl and Ernst Troeltsch, figures such as Walter Rauschenbusch tried to "Christianize the social order" by organizing society on the principles set forth in Jesus's teaching and life (Rauschenbusch). The "principles," which were primarily associated with Jesus's proclamation of the Kingdom of God, were a theological expression of Kant's ethic, that is, the dignity of the individual and the brotherhood of man. The Social Gospel was first a movement for social regeneration, but soon courses in ethics appeared in seminary and college curriculums in America, confidently demonstrating how Christian ethics underwrote the liberal social order. The discipline of Christian ethics was born.

If Christian ethics was to be a discipline in the modern university and seminary, however, it could be so only if requisite scholarly procedures could be put in place. Troeltsch's *Social Teaching* became the model for the development of the kind of intellectual work necessary to justify the discipline of Christian ethics. No book better represents this kind of work than H. Richard Niebuhr's *Christ and Culture* (1951). Drawing on Troeltsch's work, Niebuhr sought to offer a richer canvas to display the variety of ethical "types" than Troeltsch had provided. While Troeltsch had presented a threefold typology of church, sect, and mystical forms of addressing the social order, for Niebuhr there are five types of Christian ethics: Christ against culture (First John, Tertullian, and Tolstoy); Christ of culture (Gnosticism, John Locke, A. Ritschl, Rauschenbusch); Christ above culture (Justin Martyr, Clement, Thomas Aquinas); Christ and culture in paradox (Paul, Marcion, Luther, Kierkegaard); and Christ the transformer of culture (the Gospel of John, F. D. Maurice).

Niebuhr's five types were extremely persuasive, providing a way for the Christian ethicist not only to characterize the "ethics" of past Christian theologians but to characterize various contemporary alternatives. Martin Marty (1986: xiii) has rightly called *Christ and Culture* a classic because any future alternative readings must take Niebuhr's book into account. Marty's claim for the significance of *Christ and Culture* has certainly been true of the development of Christian ethics until very recently. Yet we hope that this book at least begins to provide an alternative to Niebuhr's account.

Niebuhr's types are thought to be self-evident by many, perhaps most, who have written in the field of Christian ethics over the past 50 years. But they are not self-evident. John Howard Yoder correctly argues that not only do Niebuhr's types fail to do justice to the rich texture of Christian practices from the early Church to our own time, but, more problematic still, the Trinitarian and Christological assumptions that shaped Niebuhr's account are less than orthodox (Yoder, 1959: 31–89). Niebuhr's depiction of the "enduring problem" of the relation between Christ and culture reproduces a Kantian Christ freed from ecclesial embodiment, who can do no more than hover as a transcendental reminder of human finitude. Moreover, Niebuhr's understanding of "culture" underwrites the normative status of cultural achievements to judge the gospel in the name of a doctrine of creation. As Yoder observes, H. R. Niebuhr fails to see that the

> intention of the post-Nicene doctrine of the Trinity was precisely not that through Father, Son, and Holy Spirit, differing revelations come to us. The entire point of the debate around the nature of the Trinity was the concern of the church to say just the opposite, namely that in the Incarnation and in the continuing life of the church under the Spirit there is but one God. (Yoder, 1959: 62)

What Yoder's criticisms of H. Richard Niebuhr's famous book show is that "Christian ethics" has become – indeed, for the 200 years of its life has, perhaps, always been – the story of how the Church has set aside its practice and adopted a Kantian epistemology in an effort to secure relevance and consensus. It has been so much taken for granted that the Church had a fundamental stake in the sustenance of liberal social orders that it has gone without question that the Christianity applicable to Christian ethics was that outlined by Kant and characterized by Ritschl and Troeltsch – a Stoic inner conviction of human dignity and individual autonomy, with a sense of finitude and a orientation toward common striving, sometimes called brotherhood. There is no significant place in such an account for the concrete practices of the Church – practices such as baptism, preaching, interceding, breaking bread, being reconciled. Such practices require the Church to explore what it means to worship Father, Son, and Holy Spirit – not just as concepts but as habits, attitudes, and forms of life. When practices such as baptism are ignored on the grounds that baptism has nothing to do with "ethics," then the history of Christian ethics cannot help but become an account of what this or that historical figure said about this or that moral problem.

And this is exactly what it did become. Four years after the publication of *Christ and Culture*, H. Richard Niebuhr and Waldo Beach put together a collection of readings documenting the historical development of Christian ethics, appropriately entitled *Christian Ethics: Sources of the Living Tradition* (Beach and Niebuhr, 1955). Assuming that most readers of their source book owned a Bible, they provided an overview essay introducing "Biblical ethics." They called attention to various "ideas and themes" in the Bible such as covenant and law, directed attention to the importance of the prophets, and discussed the Sermon on the Mount and the Pauline understanding of law and gospel. It was a perfectly reasonable selection, although it failed to discuss one of the most important decisions to determine the character of Christianity; namely, the Church's decision that the gospel was unintelligible without the Old Testament.

Beach and Niebuhr helpfully provided selections from Clement on the problem of riches, Augustine's "On the Morals of the Catholic Church" and portions of *The City of God*, examples from monasticism such as Benedict of Nursia's *Rule*, Bernard of Clairvaux's "On the Love of God" and Eckhart's "Sermons" to illustrate the "ethics of mysticism," followed by selections from Aquinas, Luther, Calvin, Baxter, Barclay, Butler, Wesley, Edwards, Kierkegaard, and Rauschenbusch. Again, these are good selections that anyone who wishes to understand the struggle of Christians to be faithful should know. But such a selection cannot help but give the impression that "ethics" is a subject that can be distinguished if not isolated from the liturgical life, daily habits, and elementary practices of the Church. Beach and Niebuhr give the impression that the study of Christian ethics is the study of ideas about ethics by theologians.

We need to be clear why we believe this criticism of Beach and Niebuhr is so important. The problem is not that Beach and Niebuhr's selection of people to represent "ethics" is arbitrary, but, rather, that they are plucked out of a context in which one could recognize they were engaged with the tradition. Following Troeltsch, Beach and Niebuhr attempted to write a story about Christian ethics that makes the development of Christian ethics appear as a series of "talking heads," that is, as if Christian theology could be divorced from the ecclesial context necessary for theology to be intelligible.

Moreover, the "ideas" that are identified as "ethics" too often, as we argued above, reflect our modern understanding of the moral life, and the selection fails to acknowledge that the authors quoted did not know they were doing "ethics." Those authors thought they were writing theology. For example, it surely makes sense to include Augustine's "On the Morals of the Catholic Church." But equally important to understand Augustine are his *Confessions* and *Enchiridion*. To read only "On the Morals of the Catholic Church" would be to miss one of the major themes in Augustine's life and works, which is the importance of friendship – so apparent in the *Confessions*. To read only "On the Morals of the Catholic Church" is not sufficient to understand Augustine's emphasis on the importance of the forgiveness of sins for the building up of the Church and why the practice of forgiveness is made possible by the resurrection of Christ. No Church Father, and in particular Augustine, would have known how to distinguish theology from ethics.

It may be objected that no source book can include every text that may touch on the formation of Christians. No doubt this is true, but we are not simply objecting to the problem of limited space. Rather, given the problem of limited space, we are suggesting that too often a limited notion of what constitutes "ethics" determines the selections. For example, Augustine's *De Trinitate* may well be considered the "heart" of Augustine's ethics. After all, Augustine believed that only through the work of the Holy Spirit can a human life be constituted by the charity that makes all that is done or not done pleasing to God. Source books such as that of Beach and Niebuhr were put together with the best of intentions, but they cannot help but give the impression that Christian ethics is determined primarily by issues about which there is conflict. Conflict produces writing and writing provides something for later generations to read and turn into history. But the most important aspects of human life are often matters that do not become explicit sources of conflict.

The practices that shape human lives are seldom points of conflict: on the contrary, they are the very things that people take for granted. When a person is taken ill while shopping, an ambulance is called, a hospital bed is made available, relatives come to visit, health professionals attend: these are unremarkable things, noted only in their absence. Each has become part of a network of practices, underlying which are a host of habits and virtues, such as hospitality, patience, charity, kindness, skill. Such habits and practices generally go unnoticed because they make people what they are. Without countless such habits, which those involved in health care take for granted, the conventional points of conflict, often surrounding limited resources and the beginning and end of life, would be meaningless. Similar practices constitute the Church, and, without them, the celebrated conflicts, such as those over sexuality, have no context. No reader of Paul's letters to the church at Corinth can miss the fact that the early Church was often filled with conflict, but what can be missed is that they understood themselves to be constituted by their worship of Jesus.

We do not doubt that scholarly divisions of labor can often be of service to the Church. But we have argued that attempts to distinguish ethics from theology in modernity have distorted the character of Christian convictions and practices. Should there be any lingering doubt that our argument runs counter to the culture of Christian ethics, consider the contrasting account of the widely influential contemporary writer James Gustafson. Writing in praise of *Christ and Culture*, Gustafson observes that *Christ and Culture* is not as such an historical study of Christian theological ethics. According to Gustafson, such a study requires two dimensions not present in *Christ and Culture*: "an account of the cultural, ecclesial, social, religious, and theological circumstances in which each author wrote; and a chronological ordered account of influences from antecedent to subsequent writings" (Gustafson, 2001: xxvii). For example, an adequate account of Augustine's ethics would have to include an account of the character of the Roman Empire in his time, the theological controversies in which he was embroiled, and his biography, "and many other matters of his context." Gustafson observes that we do have a few historical studies of this sort, but we do not have a comprehensive history of Christian ethics, if for no other reason than that of human finitude.

We think Gustafson is right to call attention to the problem of the limits of any scholar to accomplish such a history, but our concerns about that task are different from those of Gustafson. We agree that we need to give an account of the cultural, ecclesial, social, and religious circumstances surrounding any account of a theologian's ethic. He thinks that this is required if we are to understand the background that makes a theologian's view intelligible. We think that such accounts are important in order to help us see how their worship shaped all that Christians did and did not do. Indeed, we think "social history" is not simply a development in historical disciplines, but rather that it is required by the theological rediscovery of the significance of practices for sustaining the Church across the centuries. Put starkly, we believe that as important as Augustine may have been for the development of theology, far more important is the eucharistic practice that sustained the Church that made Augustine such an important theologian. That is why this book is focused on the practices that make the Church the Church rather than on the individual theologians who were formed by those practices.

The other reason Gustafson gives for why a history of Christian ethics cannot be written is that:

> the ethics of Christianity are not unique in any way comparable to the uniqueness of the doctrine of the Trinity, Incarnation, Sacraments, and others. Ethics, both theoretical and practical, in the Christian tradition are much more like Jewish ethics and the ethics of the classical Greek and Roman world than the theology of the Christian tradition is like Jewish theology or Greek metaphysics and religion. (Gustafson, 2001: xxvii)

We could not wish for a clearer contrast to the methodological presuppositions that have informed the chapters in this book. Some may well think we have, for example, made Kant more important than he is. Certainly, not all the work done in Christian ethics is shaped by Kantian habits. But Gustafson's presumption that the ethics of Christians can be made intelligible abstracted from Christian convictions about the Trinity, Incarnation, and Sacraments clearly continues to be shaped by Kantian habits of mind. We have no reason to deny that the way Christians lived, as well as how they thought about how they lived, was often quite similar to the way in which Jews, Greeks, and Romans lived and thought about how they lived. But we also believe such comparisons only demonstrate how different Christian, Jewish, Greek, and Roman "ethics" were from today when a Kantian frame is used in place of Jewish, Greek, and Roman ethics.

Gustafson's assumption that ethics can be isolated as a subject from Christian convictions about the Trinity, Incarnation, and Sacraments not only distorts the character of Christian theological convictions, but also implies a moral psychology that separates an agent from an agent's action. Gustafson is certainly right that there are deep similarities between Plato's and Aristotle's and Christian understandings of the moral life. All three traditions thought *how* people do what they do is every bit as important as *what* they do. This is not a means/end distinction (that is, any account of the institution of the end must take into account the means to accomplish the end), but rather a reminder that what people do is indistinguishable from how they do it. If ethics names the process through which people acquire habits and the virtues that habits make possible, in ways shaped by the determinative narratives shaping a community, then the "ethics of Christianity" cannot help but be different from the ethics of Plato and Aristotle.

The reader will have gathered that we are not always sympathetic to typological distinctions, but one recent treatment may prove helpful in locating this study. Robert Gascoigne distinguishes between three principal conceptions of Christian identity in contemporary theology, each with a distinct view of the relationship of Christianity to other realms of meaning and belief: "firstly, Christian identity as a praxis based in and inspired by a particular narrative; secondly, Christian identity as an interpretation of universal meaning, based in a theology of mediation; thirdly, Christian identity as a self-contained tradition" (Gascoigne, 2001: 97). The second conception, represented by theologians such as Karl Rahner, Wolfhart Pannenberg, and David Tracy, trusts the power of rational dialogue to elicit convergence between the gospel and other projects of meaning. It is a conception that sits comfortably with the notion of "Christian ethics" that this chapter has critiqued. The third conception, represented by George Lindbeck, John Milbank, and Joseph Ratzinger, ridicules the suggestion that there is common language that can convey meaning, and demands that the Christian narrative be regarded as the world in relation to which other narratives gauge their truth and meaning.

This book belongs in the first category. The first conception insists that Christian identity is not primarily to be found in statements or debates or arguments, but in particular practices, commitments, and habits. Christianity is not principally something people think or feel or say – it is something people *do*. The narrative of the Gospels is the story of what Christ *did*, and what God did in Christ, and the scriptural narrative shapes and inspires disciples to go and do likewise. This emphasis on praxis as the center of theology affirms the common cause between this book and the movement known as liberation theology. We note how some of the poorest communities of South America have pointed the attention of the Church in the West to the way in which theology and ethics arise out of reflection on the key practices of God's people. Liberation theology begins with the recognition that God's people are oppressed by slavery and injustice. This book seeks to aid that struggle by recovering the key practices of the Church, and showing how those practices constitute the most significant Christian witness in the face of oppression *and* indifference, blind injustice *and* bland tolerance.

Theology will always be about theologians, as well as about God. But we hope this study affirms that theology is primarily about the Church. This means that theological ethics is a discipline that reflects on the practices of the Church, seeking to understand how those practices shape the character of Christians. We hope it is clear that we need the kind of studies of Clement, Augustine, and Thomas Aquinas that Gustafson describes. But if such studies are well done, they will not be about "ethics." If done well, we believe such studies will make it difficult to distinguish between theology and ethics, ecclesiology and ethics, sacraments and ethics. This chapter has described how ethics became a separate discipline from theology, and how both became separate from the practices of the Church. But it comes within a book that is intended to make those separations things of the past.

References

Augustine (1955) "On the Morals of the Catholic Church," in *Christian Ethics: Sources of the Living Tradition*, ed. Waldo Beach and H. Richard Niebuhr (New York: Ronald), esp. pp. 110–17.
—(1961) *Confessions*, trans. R. S. Pine (Harmondsworth: Penguin).
—(1965a) *De Trinitate*, trans. John Barnaby (Philadelphia: Westminster).
—(1965b) *Enchridion*, trans. Albert C. Outler (Philadelphia: Westminster).
—(1972) *City of God*, trans. Henry Bettenson (Harmondsworth: Penguin).
Beach, Waldo and Niebuhr, H. Richard (1955) *Christian Ethics: Sources of the Living Tradition*, 2nd edn 1973 (New York: Ronald).
Cavanaugh, William (1998) *Torture and Eucharist: Theology, Politics and the Body of Christ* (Oxford: Blackwell).
Gascoigne, Robert (2001) *The Public Forum and Christian Ethics* (Cambridge: Cambridge University Press).
Gustafson, James (2001) "Preface: An Appreciative Introduction to H. Richard Niebuhr's *Christ and Culture*," in H. Richard Niebuhr, *Christ and Culture* (San Francisco: Harper).
Kant, Immanuel (1959) *Groundwork to the Metaphysics of Morals*, trans. with an intro. by Lewis White Beck (New York: Liberal Arts Press).
—(1960) *Religion within the Limits of Reason Alone* (New York: Harper and Row).
—(1989) "What is Enlightenment?," in *Foundations of the Metaphysics of Morals* (Englewood Cliffs, NJ: Prentice-Hall), esp. pp. 85–92.
Marty, Martin (1986) "Foreword," in H. Richard Niebuhr, *Christ and Culture* (New York: Harper Collins), esp. pp. xiii–xx.
Milbank, John (1990) *Theology and Social Theory: Beyond Secular Reason* (Oxford: Blackwell).
Niebuhr, H. Richard (1951) *Christ and Culture* (New York: Harper).
Troeltsch, Ernst (1992) *The Social Teaching of the Christian Churches*, trans. Olive Wyon, with a foreword by James Luther Adams (Louisville, KY: Westminster/John Knox).
Yoder, John Howard (1996) "How H. Richard Niebuhr Reasoned: A Critique of *Christ and Culture*," in *Authentic Transformation: A New Vision of Christ and Culture*, ed. Glen H. Stassen, D. M. Yeager, and John Howard Yoder (Nashville, TN: Abingdon).

CHAPTER 4

How the Church Managed Before There Was Ethics

Stanley Hauerwas and Samuel Wells

The argument we have made in the previous chapters does not mean that we think students of Christian ethics do not need to read and know well the great theologians of the Christian tradition. But it is those same theologians who have directed our attention to the importance of worship so that we may learn how to live and think in ways that are faithful to what God has done in Jesus Christ. Indeed, the change of perspective about "ethics" can be indicated by calling attention to "reading," and in particular the reading of Scripture, as moral formation. For the early Christians, to learn to read Scripture well, one had to learn to read in a community of readers. Often this meant that one needed to be apprenticed to a master reader.

In this respect James Gustafson (2001) is quite right to argue that there are strong continuities between Christian formation and other forms of ancient ethics. Plato and Aristotle assumed that the only reason to study philosophy was to become good, that is, to acquire the virtues. Philosophy was not "ideas" a person might consider, but immersion into a way of life. To become a philosopher meant that one must be trained by being formed into a hierarchy of skills (which often began with learning basic skills necessary to perform physical tasks) through which one became what was sought. For example, Aristotle observes that the virtues are acquired by putting them into action: "For the things which we have to learn before we can do them we learn by doing: men become builders by building houses, and harpists by playing the harp. Similarly, we become just by the practice of just actions, self-controlled by exercising self-control, and courageous by performing acts of courage" (Aristotle, 1962: 34).

Yet Aristotle also understood that simply doing this or that act that is generally considered "courageous" or "just" is not sufficient to make a person courageous or just. Nor, for an act to be courageous and just, is it sufficient for it to be done by a courageous or just person; rather, for Aristotle, "acts" and "agents" cannot be isolated from one another. Accordingly, what matters is not only that the acts are of a certain kind, but that the agents have certain characteristics as they perform them: "first of all, he must know what he is doing; secondly, he must choose to act the way he does, and he must choose it for its own sake; and in the third place, the act must spring from a firm and unchangeable character" (Aristotle, 1962: 39). Thus, Aristotle did not think moral excellence open to everyone, but only to those willing to undergo the appropriate training.

In the ancient world, philosophy was not so much a body of knowledge one could take or leave, but rather a way of life. That is why there were schools of philosophy. To become a Platonist or an Epicurean meant one was quite literally taking on a way of life. The head of the school acted as a spiritual director, working with each student to discern what that student might need to progress on the path of virtue. All the work of such schools, even if it was apparently theoretical or systematic, was "written not so much to inform the reader of a doctrinal content but to form him, to make him traverse a certain itinerary in the course of which he will make spiritual progress. One must always approach a philosophical work of antiquity with this idea of spiritual progress in mind" (Hadot, 1995: 64).

Often the reason Christianity appeared so foreign to pagans was not because of the discipline and virtues necessary to become a Christian, but because Christians staked their lives on such a strange "philosopher," Jesus of Nazareth. Moreover, they did not just follow Jesus, they worshiped Jesus – a Jesus, moreover, who had died a convict's death. No text in the New Testament is more telling for understanding what it meant to be a Christian than Philippians 2: 1–11:

> If you have any encouragement from being united with Christ, if any comfort from his love, if any fellowship with the Spirit, if any tenderness and compassion, then make my joy complete by being like-minded, having the same love, being one in spirit and purpose. Do nothing out of selfish ambition or vain conceit, but in humility consider others better than yourselves. Each of you should not look to your own interests, but also to the interest of others. Your attitude should be the same as that of Christ Jesus:
> Who, being in very nature God, did not consider equality with God something to be grasped, but made himself nothing, taking the form of a servant, being made in human likeness. And being found in appearance as a man, he humbled himself and became obedient to death – even death on a cross! Therefore God exalted him to the highest place and gave him the name that is above every name, that at the name of Jesus every knee should bow, in heaven and on earth and under the earth, and every tongue confess that Jesus Christ is Lord, to the glory of God the Father.

This remarkable passage illuminates how Christians once reasoned about the moral life. Issues of how Christians were to conduct themselves in relation to one another forced Paul to make cosmic claims. To do so, Paul resorted (at least according to many) to music, reminding the Philippians of a well-known hymn that they had no doubt sung. That hymn makes clear that the humility necessary for the kind of community they must be to be Christians is the humility of Christ. Moreover, that same humility is possible only because the humble Jesus has been exalted, becoming Lord so that all worldly lords are put in their place. This passage is at once theological, ethical, and political – if it still seems important to distinguish the theological, ethical, and political. But a people willing to sing this hymn would surely not need to be told that by becoming Christian they were taking on a new way of life that might entail being seen by some as politically subversive. Here was a subversion that forced the Church to discover why the doctrine of the Trinity is a necessary reading rule if we are rightly to read not only this text, but the whole of Christian Scripture. For, in discovering the identity of Christ in worship, Christians found that political subversion was both necessary and possible.

This text is also an important reminder that Christians worshiped Jesus before they had the Scripture we now call the New Testament. The text that was Scripture for the people that gave us the New Testament was what Christians now call the Old Testament. This is but a reminder that Christians' perception of their identity and activity arose not only from absorbing and critiquing Greek influences, but equally, if not more importantly, from inheriting the assumptions of the culture now known as Judaism. For centuries, theologians have emphasized contrasts between Jewish and Christian modes of moral reflection. They have insisted that Jews believe righteousness comes from observing the law, whereas Christians assume grace comes before the law, which means Christians think love more important than law. But recent scholarship makes increasingly clear that contrasts of this kind, in the context of the early Church, simply cannot be sustained (Bockmuehl, 2000).

The difference between Jews and Christians was not therefore how they reasoned, but quite simply Jesus. This is why the Gospels remain the texts that Christians must learn to read if we are to be followers of Jesus. But the very existence of the New Testament can mislead Christians because it makes it easy to think that a Christian ethic can be identified with Jesus's teachings. To be sure, no Christian can think that what Jesus taught is unimportant. But what he taught cannot be separated from what he was. Accordingly, we believe the Gospels are best read as training manuals for discipleship. This means that no matter how similar the way of life of Christians may seem to other ways of life, such similarity will be qualified by the Church's conviction that Christians are to be disciples of Jesus. There may be, for example, family resemblances between Christian humility and Immanuel Kant's awe at the "starry heavens above and the moral law within." But even Kantian awe, if it is faithfully to witness to the God who created all things anew from the cross of Christ, must be made subject to Jesus.

Christianity names the continuing history of a people gathered across time and space to worship this Jesus. One of the constant temptations that has beset Christians is to believe that they are saved by Christianity rather than by the work God has accomplished in Christ. One of the tasks of Christian theology is to explore how Christians may get their worship of God wrong and as a result fail to witness to the God whose love moves the sun and the other stars. Christians do not believe they ever "get it right." This is why one of the first lessons Christians learn is to confess their sins. They confess with sadness but also with thankfulness, knowing that they would not even be able to know their sin without God's grace. Accordingly, Christians can never have their lives focused on "how to avoid sin": instead they recognize that because of God's good work they have been given good work to do.

The "good work" to which Christians are called has often resulted in martyrdom. "Martyr" is but a word for witness. All Christians are called to be witnesses, but for some this means nothing less than the sacrifice of their lives. Martyrdom is unavoidable if the Philippian hymn is to be sung truthfully. The Church, as the New Testament makes clear, will be persecuted and some will become martyrs. This martyrdom is clearly anticipated in baptism. For some, who rightly see the Christian dying in Christ as a threat to worldly presumption, it is made all too actual. Those who die for the faith are those who either cannot, or will not, use force to persuade or coerce in order to convince. They are witnesses whose witness does not allow them to kill.

A Church that faces persecution, a Church that is clearly out of step with the world that surrounds it, seldom feels the need to make explicit the relation between how it worships and how it lives. Such a Church has no time to contemplate or produce an "and" between theology and ethics. This is why the writings of the Fathers, the Patristics, have remained a touchstone for Christians. By reading Clement, Gregory of Nyssa, Basil, and Augustine, we hope to learn again how to live as Christians, that is, in a world where to be a Christian is a mark not of safety, but of danger.

The Church does not seek to be persecuted in order to "prove" her faithfulness. There have been many times when the Church has been seen as a benefit both by those that rule and by those that are ruled – whether because of the Church's network of organization, its significant practices, or its reputation for instilling good character in its adherents. This positive climate is one for which Christians should rightly be thankful. The eucharistic feast Christians share is believed to anticipate the heavenly peace. Christians, therefore, seek the peace of the city in which they find themselves (Jeremiah 27). Christian peace is one that makes them friends of God, one another, and the stranger. Christians, therefore, were and are obligated to offer hospitality to the stranger, a stranger they hope may become a friend, having learned from their Lord that he will continue to make himself known in the face of the hungry and despised. Christian witness will continue to be identified not by those to whom Christians give money, but by those with whom Christians take time to eat. That the Church can live as a people who believe they are sustained by the gifts of strangers is part of what it means for the Church to live eschatologically. Eschatology names the journey that Christians believe God has called them to undertake with his people Israel.

The Church, therefore, is not surprised that in some circumstances those who do not share its Eucharist may nonetheless find Christian practices beneficial. Any organization that has survived lengthy periods of oppression must have developed networks, whether overground or underground, that would be very useful to those seeking to govern. They may therefore even seek to harness the Church as useful for maintaining a more nearly just world. However, when the Church is so established – an establishment that most identify with Constantine's recognition of the Church in the fourth century – the Church is forced to face new challenges (Yoder, 2002). No longer were Christians killed for worshiping Christ rather than the gods of Rome. Prior to Constantine, it took courage to be a Christian. After Constantine, it took courage to be a pagan. Before Constantine, no one doubted that Christians were different. After Constantine, it became increasingly unclear what difference being a Christian made. At least one of the signs of God's continuing faithfulness to the Church after the Constantinian settlement is that an accommodated Church refused to forget the martyrs. Such remembering remained a judgment on a Church that too often exchanged its obligation to receive the stranger for the safety this or that Caesar promised.

One of the challenges faced by a Church no longer persecuted was how to form Christians in a world in which it was no longer dangerous to be Christian. The journey of Antony into the desert in the fourth century symbolizes the way in which the frontier between good and evil had changed from an external threshold into an internal one. Temptation had succeeded persecution as the testing arena for faith, and thus holiness had replaced martyrdom as the paradigm of discipleship (Hook and Reno, 2000). Confession of sins, penance, and reconciliation became the ways in which Christians learned to live lives commensurate with their worship of the Father, Son, and Holy Spirit. It is not accidental that the practice of penance was discovered through monasticism. Nor do we believe it accidental that monasticism became a movement at just the time that the Church was beginning to be recognized by the powerful. Indeed, Troeltsch's (1992) great insight was that Christians' understanding of Jesus and reading of the Bible were determined by the sociology of the Church's relation with the world. The Church that was recognized by Caesar was also the Church that could not forget it was first and foremost called to be holy – that is, to be a people sanctified by their worship of God. Monastics were those called to lives of poverty, chastity, and obedience, offering a witness that made it impossible for the more "worldly" Christians to forget the radical demands of the gospel.

Augustine's work is often taken to be the beginning of the Church's compromise with the world. By the late fourth century, Christians increasingly found themselves in positions that made it impossible for them to "forgive their enemy." Some attribute Augustine's account, in his magnificent work, *The City of God*, of the two cities – the one ruled by love of God and the other by love of this world – to be the theological justification for Christians to engage in ways of life that made it impossible for them to be holy. To be sure, Augustine had no illusion that either the Church or Christians could pretend in this life to be free of sin, but he never suggests that their sinfulness could or should become an explanation for Christian unfaithfulness.

The City of God was written to counter the charge that the fall of Rome to the barbarians was the result of tolerance toward Christians. Augustine set out to show that Rome fell by her own vices, not the least being the worship of false gods. Augustine applies two parallel arguments: worship is what makes all that Christians are and do intelligible; meanwhile, no politics can be true that is not based in the worship of the true God. Thus in book XIX of *The City of God*, Augustine observes:

> Justice is found where God, the one supreme God, rules an obedient City according to his grace, forbidding sacrifice to any being save himself alone; and where in consequence the soul rules the body in all men who belong to this City and obey God, and the reason faithfully rules the vices in a lawful system of subordination; so that just as the individual righteous man lives on the basis of faith which is active in love, so the association, or people, of righteous men lives on the same basis of faith, active in love, the love with which a man loves God as God ought to be loved, and loves his neighbor as himself. But where this justice does not exist, there is certainly no "association of men united by a common sense of right and by a community of interest." Therefore there is no commonwealth; for where there is no "people", there is no "weal of the people." (Augustine, 1972: 890)

We believe we are right to stress the importance of practices for any account of how Christians have had or should have had their lives formed to be followers of Christ. This emphasis, however, does not mean that the significant contributions of Augustine (or

Aquinas and innumerable others) should be forgotten. Indeed, accounts of the Christian life after the fourth century (in quite diverse ways to be sure) can be read as footnotes to the above quotation from Augustine. There we see the essential topics articulated for subsequent attempts to understand the Christian life: (1) the Christian life is shaped by the virtues; (2) all the virtues must be shaped by love; (3) love is nothing less than God's will to make us his friends (Burt, 1999); (4) the appropriate ordering of loves has direct implications for how Christians should understand their relations to the social orders in which they find themselves; (5) the Church as God's people can never be made subordinate to the interests of those who rule; (6) for all its faults the Church remains the only true political reality.

Augustine's works were widely read and were extremely influential. Many, particularly in recent times, blame Augustine for burdening the Church with an exaggerated understanding of human sinfulness in general and of the disordered character of sexual behavior in particular. Augustine certainly saw the effects of sin in human lives and especially in his own life, as he made clear in his *Confessions*. But sin, for Augustine, is literally powerless when faced with God's grace. Just as the lie is only possible because of the primacy of truth, so sin is parasitical on the good. Accordingly, Augustine never tired of reminding the Church that God's forgiveness is deeper than our sinfulness. Through confession, penance, and reconciliation, Christians are formed by grace into a commonwealth that cannot help but be a challenge to the human cities. It should never be forgotten that when Augustine became a Christian he also became a monk, a form of life that has often found itself in tension with those who rule.

There is no way of knowing how penance began to be practiced, or the forms that it took in early monasteries. That monks found it necessary to confess to a fellow monk was but a way of following Jesus's command in Matthew 18: 15–20 as well as the admonition from the Book of James (5: 16) that Christians should confess their sins to one another. Jesus tells his followers that if they believe a brother or sister has sinned against them, they must seek the brother or sister out in the hope of reconciliation. They are to do so because a sin against them is not just against them but against God. If the Church is to be God's community of peace in a violent world, Christians cannot afford to let sin determine their lives. The monks sought to confess their sins not only for themselves, but for the Church and, therefore, for the world.

The practice of confession, penance, and reconciliation in monasteries began to be practiced in the wider church in Ireland perhaps as early as the fifth century. Monks would be asked by lay Christians to hear their sins. The practice became so common that some record of how such confessions should be conducted was needed. This led to books called "penitentials" being written in which sinful acts were enumerated and appropriate penance was suggested. These sins were correlated with the eight deadly sins (gluttony, avarice, anger, dejection, lust, languor, vainglory, pride) and the virtues that were their cure (temperance, generosity, meekness, spiritual joy, continence, zeal, docility, compassion) (see Connolly, 1995 for more on Irish penitentials). These penitential books were carried across Europe by Irish monastic missionaries, making the practice of confession – even if only once a year for the laity – universal in the Church. Catechismal instruction also became increasingly formalized in the late Middle Ages.

Catechism had long been practiced in the Church. For example, Augustine's *Enchiridion* was written for the training of new Christians so that they could learn the essentials of the faith. But the first book called a "catechism" was written in 1357 and, significantly, was translated into the vernacular so it could be used to ensure that the laity knew the fourteen articles of the Creed, the Ten Commandments, the seven sacraments, the seven works of mercy, the seven virtues, and the seven sins (Marthaler, 1995: 9–14). Penitential manuals and catechetical instruction did not ensure that medieval Christians, most of whom could not read, had a thorough cognitive understanding of what being a disciple of Jesus entailed. Such practices were, of course, subject to misuse. But in a world in which everyone was now a Christian, catechism and confession were reminders that the Church was called to be holy.

Penitential practice required the development of casuistry, which simply means the identification of the good through the careful comparison of cases. Casuistry became increasingly formalized. Casuistical manuals began to be written to enable confessors to discern the moral seriousness of this or that act. A large part of Thomas Aquinas's *Summa theologiae* is dedicated to the work of casuistry. For example, as part of his analysis of the virtue of temperance, Aquinas asks if the "adornment of women" is devoid of moral sin. Aquinas is well aware that Cyprian had forbidden the use of "yellow pigments, black powders, or rouge" as an "assault on the Divine handiwork, a distortion of the truth." However, observes Aquinas, if such adornment were always a sin, then makers of such adornments would sin mortally, which seems absurd. To be sure, suggests Aquinas, Christians must avoid excess, and women (particularly women who are not married) must not use adornment to create lust in men. But he concludes that since it is written in 1 Corinthians 7: 34 that the woman that is married thinks on the things of this world so that she might please her husband, a married woman may "adorn herself in order to please her husband and she can do this without sin" (Aquinas, 1981: II-II, 169, 2).

This kind of casuistry could become "legalistic" to just the extent that it tempted Christians to think avoiding sins more important than being good, but Aquinas certainly never let his readers forget that casuistical reflection was always in the service of living lives of virtue. Indeed, for Aquinas, humans are creatures destined to be made friends with God. Therefore, any good they do is done only through the gift of the Holy Spirit. So he is led to say, echoing Augustine's "The Spirit and the Letter", that "the letter denotes any writing that is external to man, even that of the moral precepts such as are contained in the Gospel. Wherefore the letter, even of the Gospel would kill, unless there were the inward presence of the healing grace of faith" (Aquinas, 1981: I-II, 106, 2).

The *Summa theologiae* is a vast and complex work that many take to be the most comprehensive account ever given of the Christian faith. Aquinas was writing at a time when the works of Aristotle, which many Christians took to be antithetical to the Christian faith, had recently been recovered. One of Aquinas's tasks was to show how Aristotle could, on the contrary, be an aid for the presentation of the Christian faith. Because of his extraordinary philosophical skills, Aquinas has often been understood to be more the philosopher than the theologian. This way of reading Aquinas often stresses his understanding of "natural theology" as well as his account of natural law.

Those that read Aquinas in this fashion give the impression that Aquinas thought one should try to proceed as far as possible with unaided "natural reason," which can then be supplemented by truths known through revelation. But Aquinas did not think of himself as a philosopher, whose task was to reflect on the workings of nature. He thought of himself as a theologian, whose primary task was rightly to interpret the Scripture (Rogers, 1995).

Aristotle was certainly important for Aquinas, but Augustine was equally, if not more, his primary conversation partner. Indeed, at least one aspect of Aquinas's extraordinary achievement is to have represented essential themes in Augustine. Thus the virtues, rather than the law, are the principal subject of Aquinas's understanding of the Christian life. However, he departs from Augustine in his account of the virtues. Following Aristotle, Aquinas stresses the importance of habitual formation – whereas Augustine, following Plato, sees all the virtues as forms of love. For Aquinas, it is not so much that the virtues are forms of love, but rather that charity – which is nothing less than the work of the Holy Spirit to make us friends with God – is the form of courage, temperance, justice, and prudence (Aquinas, 1981: I-II, 65). Indeed, the "natural virtues," which to be sure are of some use, are but sin unless they are vivified by the Holy Spirit (1981: II-II, 23, 7).

In the *Summa theologiae* Aquinas was not attempting to provide an account that avoided the continuing struggle Christians must undertake in this life. Indeed, his favorite way of describing the Christian life was that of being "wayfarers" (1981: II-II, 24, 4). The *Summa* was his attempt to help the Church continue to develop the skills to discern the work of the Spirit. That is why the very structure of the *Summa* is determined by the story of creation, fall, and redemption. Thus, theologians like Augustine and Aquinas never forgot that their task was to help Christians remember that their lives are shaped by story-determined practices that make all that they do and do not do intelligible.

It would be a mistake, however, to exaggerate the extent to which the moral formation of Christians in what we now call the "Middle Ages" was determined by work such as Aquinas's *Summa theologiae*. It may be that the distance in the Middle Ages between the university, which was just beginning, and the Church was not as large as we experience today. So what went on in the universities in the Middle Ages may well have reflected as well as changed how Christians lived. Indeed, controversies in the universities, for example between Franciscans and Dominicans over whether Jesus's disciples owned possessions, often had an immediate effect on the life of the Church. But, as important as theology may have been, the everyday life of the laity was more determinatively shaped by the regularity of time rung by the monastic bells, by the rhythm and shape of the Christian year, by the form of the cathedrals, by the stone and glass shaped by the stories of the Bible. Consider the roof bosses of Norwich Cathedral. So far off the ground that the naked eye cannot discern them in detail, and thus pitched between earth and sky, they nonetheless carefully trace the path of salvation history from Adam to Revelation as a constant conversation between humanity and God. Only the embodiment of the Christian narrative in the ordinary practices of the people could have produced craftsmen able to tell that story, and content to let their handiwork be distinctly visible to God alone.

The most important book for medieval Christians was Jacobus de Voragine's *The Golden Legend: Readings on the Saints* in which the lives of the saints informed the learned and unlearned alike about how Christians should live as well as understand the character of God's world. Not only did saintly lives provide examples of what it meant to live as a Christian, but such lives, and particularly the saint's ability to perform miracles, determined how Christians negotiated their world. William Ryan, in his "Introduction" to *The Golden Legend*, observes that for modern readers the miracle stories require a special effort if we are to make sense of them. In contrast to us, medieval Christians did not consider God to be a philosophical abstraction, but an ever-present actor. The question they asked about an unusual occurrence was not so much "Did it happen?" or "Was it a trick?" but "Who did it?"

> Their life was a pilgrimage through a world that was passing, to which they were not to become attached, since the reason for their being was to be united with God in heaven; meanwhile they grubbed a hard living from the reluctant earth. The world was a scene of warfare between good and evil, a world peopled with demons and angels. The demons, in order to deceive and mislead God's children, resorted to a marvellous bag of tricks but always wound up looking foolish. The angels protected God's people. The Church, the sacraments, the mysteries of Christ celebrated in the liturgy, formed a milieu for the Christian's progress from birth to death, from earthly life to eternal life. "If you be risen with Christ, seek the things that are above, not the things that are upon the earth" (Colossians 3: 1–2). (Ryan, 1993: xvi)

In modernity, in which most people cannot imagine what it means to be a Christian, it is tempting to romanticize the Middle Ages. The power the Church possessed in that age often resulted in unfaithful forms of life. Yet at the same time the gospel was proclaimed, even making possible what John Bossy calls "the social miracle." For the definitive miracle in the Middle Ages was the Eucharist through which Christians were made one with their Lord and one another. Accordingly, the Eucharist quite literally functioned for "the reconciliation of the parts and the whole, the union of social limbs in the body of Christ" (Bossy, 1985: 71–2). In such a world it is not surprising that heresy was seen as a threat not only to the Church, but to the very existence of society.

It is important to remember that the Crusades and Inquisition, so habitually derided in modernity, both gained general support from their ability to transform elitist spirituality into popular practices. The Crusades captured the imagination of the medieval Church, not so much because Islam presented a mortal threat, but more because here was a chance for ordinary people to find salvation. Those who were not spiritual or material aristocrats, and especially those whose sins strained their confessors' ears, found in the Crusades a pilgrimage that could reincorporate them into the body of the faithful. Likewise the Spanish Inquisition, while it promoted disturbing degrees of hostility to Jews and Muslims, gained its strength from the revival of Catholic piety in Spain and Italy in the late fifteenth century through oratories devoted to works of charity – a revival that led also to the establishment of the Capuchins and the Jesuits. It is not far from the discovery that everyone *could* be holy to the insistence that everyone *should* be.

Of course, all was changed by the movement we now call the Reformation. The "unity" of Christendom – a unity that often hides from us the extraordinary divisions and diversity that continued throughout the Middle Ages – was destroyed. Other factors, such as the printing press, transformed the world in which Christians would have to discover how they must live to be faithful disciples to Jesus Christ. The rupture that the Reformation names, however, can mislead people to overemphasize the discontinuities between Luther, Calvin, and the practices and the theologians now identified as Roman Catholic. For example, neither Luther nor Calvin thought "ethics" was a subject separable from the way of life necessary for the building up of the Church.

Though Luther emphasized "justification by faith through grace," he could also say: "Anyone who knows the Ten Commandments perfectly knows the entire Scriptures" (Luther, 1959: 5). No one who reads Luther's *Large Catechism* can doubt that Luther believed by the grace of God Christians are called to be disciples of Christ. In his *Institutes* Calvin treats sanctification before justification, even suggesting that "to wake us more effectively, scripture shows that God the Father, as he has reconciled us to himself in his Christ (2 Corinthians 5: 18), has in him stamped for us the likeness (Hebrews 1: 3) to which he would have us conform." Calvin then challenges anyone to find in "moral philosophy" a more "excellent dispensation." Moral philosophy can at best only ask people to live in accordance with nature, "but Scripture draws its exhortation from the true fountain. It not only enjoins us to refer our life to God, its author, to whom it is bound; but after it has taught that we have degenerated from the true origin and condition of our creation, it also adds that Christ, through whom we return into favor with God, has been set before us as an example, whose pattern we ought to express in our life" (Calvin, 1960: III, 6, 686).

The Protestants of the Reformation, including the Anabaptists, assumed that their "ethics" was inherent in their attempt to renew the Church. They differed to be sure. For example, the luminaries of the first and second generation of the English Reformation, Thomas Cranmer and Richard Hooker, could not imagine a world in which Christian practices were not at the very heart of all that they – and we – would call political. We are inspired by their assumption that the practices of the Church shape how Christians understand the nature of politics. But they also assumed that Church and state were coterminus. By contrast, the Anabaptists refused to use the sword not only in ensuring ecclesial discipline but in all matters. We take this to be a particular gift that they have given the Church. And that they saw the disciplines and practices of their common life as their politics we have taken as an inspiration for this book.

But Protestantism, whether established or radical, "worked" because it could continue to rely on habits – habits as basic as the assumption that marriage means lifelong monogamous fidelity – developed over the centuries. Once those habits are lost – and modernity names the time of the loss of Christian habits – Protestantism has often found it lacks even the resources to know how to form those that wish to be Christian.

So we are brought back to the beginning, to the development of Christian ethics. Desperate to find a substitute for the habits that make us Christians, Protestants as well as many Catholics have assumed that they can think their way out of the challenges that face being Christian in modernity. Thus there has been the creation of the discipline of Christian ethics. Yet no ethics, philosophical or theological, can ever be a substitute for what only communal habits can provide. To be sure, some people trained in ethics may help communities see the connections between the habits that constitute their lives (though more likely help will come from people we now call artists). But such connections cannot be made if the habits are no longer in place. What can be done, however, is what we have tried to do above; namely, to use the past to help us see what has been lost, in the hope that our imaginations will be renewed and begin to see what we must now do.

That we hope to use our past to see our present in the hope of the future is why this book, a book about ethics, makes the liturgy the central organizing focus. We do so because we believe the churches in their various forms share the intention to worship God truly. We wish we could say that the churches share a common worship, but that is clearly not the case. Indeed, many will find the liturgical form used to shape the chapters in this book far too Catholic. We have no apology to make for having made it so. It is our conviction that any attempt to help Christians recover what it means to be disciples of Jesus requires the shaping of our lives through word and sacrament. One unfortunate legacy of the Reformation is the transformation in the way Christians came to understand the context in which the Bible should be read. The laudable desire that lay people should have regular access to the Scripture led to the normative manner of reading becoming the privacy of personal devotion, rather than the liturgy of public worship. It is easy to see how this encourages the sense that "ethics" is about the agony of individual decision, rather than the public formation of character through the rhythm of corporate practice. We see the normative place in which Scripture should be read as in the context of the practices and traditions of the community of faith – just as we see the normative context for understanding Christian ethics as surrounded by the narrative and habits of the Church.

Charles Taylor (1989: 30) has observed that "to say we live in a secular civilization is to say that God is no longer inescapable." We think that is not only a correct description of our world, but a good thing. That Christians can no longer depend on the habits of the surrounding world to reinforce what they think makes them Christian should force us to the kind of rethinking we hope this book represents. That does not mean that Christians can try to retreat to a past in which we "got it right." Christians, of all people, should know that we have never been able to say that we have "got it right." But we do think the challenges before us provide the opportunity for us to get back to the basics and nothing is more basic than the worship of God.

Whatever the virtues and vices of the establishment of the Church, in either legal or cultural forms of establishment, that day has passed. That recognition is one of the determinative judgments that has informed the shaping of this book and explains why we cannot be content to write about the history of Christian ethics as if we knew what we were talking about. Christians seldom will to be faithful, but we believe God is using this time to force them to be faithful.

Christianity names the lives, events, and ideas that the Church traces across hundreds of years and perceives as a purposeful story. The Church names the community that abides across time and space, making it possible for people to know and to become part of that story, the story of God's way with creation, the story of a friendship begun, frustrated, restored, sustained, and destined to be fulfilled. The Eucharist names the ordered series of practices that Christians carry out regularly together in obedience to Jesus's command, as a way of becoming more like him, and as a witness to God's world. In the Eucharist Christians recall the glorious story of salvation, recognize how inadequately their lives have reflected it, and then retell that story as they gather all that they are and hope to be into the one great prayer of thankfulness to the One who has given life. All that Christians do and do not do thus finds its intelligibility in the worship of God. The chapters in this volume attempt to do no more than help Christians recover the story and practices that are the form and substance of their lives.

References

Aquinas, Thomas (1981) *Summa theologica*, trans. the Fathers of the English Dominican Province (Westminster, MD: Christian Classics).

Aristotle (1962) *Nicomachean Ethics*, trans. Martin Ostwald (Indianapolis, IN: Bobbs-Merrill).

Augustine (1956) "The Spirit and the Letter," in *Nicene and Post-Nicene Fathers*, ed. Phillip Schaff (Grand Rapids, MI: Eerdmans).

—(1972) *City of God*, trans. Henry Bettenson (Harmondsworth: Penguin).

Bockmuehl, Marcus (2000) *Jewish Law in Gentile Churches: Halakhah and the Beginning of Christian Public Ethics* (Edinburgh: T. and T. Clark).

Bossy, John (1985) *Christianity in the West, 1400–1700* (Oxford: Oxford University Press).

Burt, Donald, OSA (1999) *Friendship and Society: An Introduction to Augustine's Political Philosophy* (Grand Rapids, MI: Eerdmans).

Calvin, John (1960) *Institutes of the Christian Religion*, ed. John T. McNeill, trans. Ford Lewis Battles, 2 vols (Philadelphia: Westminster).

Connolly, Hugh (1995) *The Irish Penitentials and their Significance for the Sacrament of Penance Today* (Dublin: Four Courts).

Gustafson, James (2001) "Preface: An Appreciative Introduction to H. Richard Niebuhr's *Christ and Culture*," in H. Richard Niebuhr, *Christ and Culture* (San Francisco: Harper).

Hadot, Pierre (1995) *Philosophy as a Way of Life: Spiritual Exercises from Socrates to Foucault*, ed. Arnold Davidson, trans. Michael Chase (Oxford: Blackwell).

Hook, Brian and Reno, Rusty (2000) *Heroism and the Christian Life: Reclaiming Excellence* (Louisville, KY: Westminster/John Knox).

Luther, Martin (1959) *The Large Catechism*, trans. Robert Fishes (Philadelphia: Fortress).

Marthaler, Berard (1995) *The Catechism of Yesterday and Today: The Evolution of a Genre* (Collegeville, MN: The Liturgical Press).

Rogers, Eugene (1995) *Thomas Aquinas and Karl Barth: Sacred Doctrine and the Natural Doctrine of God* (Notre Dame, IN: University of Notre Dame Press).

Ryan, William (1993) "Introduction" to Jacobus de Voraigne, *The Golden Legend: Readings on the Saints*, 2 vols (Princeton, NJ: Princeton University Press).

Taylor, Charles (1989) *Sources of the Self: The Making of Modern Identity* (Cambridge, MA: Harvard University Press).

Troeltsch, Ernst (1992) *The Social Teaching of the Christian Churches*, trans. Olive Wyon, with a foreword by James Luther Adams (Louisville, KY: Westminster/John Knox).

Yoder, John Howard (2002) *Preface to Theology: Christology and Theological Method*, ed. Stanley Hauerwas and Alex Sider (Grand Rapids, MI: Brazos).

PART II
Meeting God and One Another

CHAPTER 5

Gathering: Worship, Imagination, and Formation

Philip Kenneson

No issue is more central to Christian ethics than worship. Moreover, human gatherings always involve worship, and worship always implicates human gatherings.

That many people would regard such assertions as controversial, if not patently false, reveals more about the assumptions and convictions that underwrite Western cultures and societies than it does about the assertions themselves. Two assumptions, in particular, make it difficult to acknowledge both the centrality of worship to human life and the inextricable connection between human gatherings and worship. First, worship is widely assumed to be a "religious" activity that belongs to a specific and circumscribed sphere of human life called "religion." Because there are many kinds of human gatherings that lie outside this religious sphere, it is assumed that many kinds of human gatherings have nothing to do with worship. Second, human beings are most often regarded fundamentally as individuals and only derivatively as social creatures. As a result, human gatherings are widely considered as primarily *expressive* of common self-understandings rather than being *formative* of them.

This chapter rejects these two assumptions, arguing instead both for a broader, less-circumscribed understanding of worship, and for the fundamentally formative power of human gatherings. Human gatherings powerfully shape the human social imagination, inevitably forming the horizon within which all human action – including worship – takes place. In underscoring the formative power of human gatherings, this chapter identifies some of the considerable resources that Christian worship and its requisite gatherings offer Christian moral reflection and practice. Just as the chapters in this volume take up the specific practices of the Christian liturgy in order to show their potential relevance for Christian ethics, this chapter explores the close connection between, as well as the ethical significance of, the gathering and worship of Christians.

The Pervasiveness of Worship

One of the primary impediments to recognizing the ethical significance of worship is that people in Western societies have been formed to think of worship as a strictly "religious" affair. As such, worship is widely understood to involve participating in certain cultic or ritual practices. Moreover, these practices are routinely circumscribed not only *physically* by taking place in certain "holy spaces," but also *intellectually* and *morally* by finding their rightful place in the so-called "religious sphere." Thus, it is usually assumed that if the activity of worship is to have any bearing on life outside that place or sphere, it will need to be translated into the established discourses of those other spheres (such as the economic, political, or educational spheres). Within the assumptions of this view of religion and worship, therefore, the regular activities associated with economics, politics, and education have nothing inherently to do with worship.

But there is no compelling reason to begin with the assumption that worship is a peculiarly "religious" activity confined to a particular physical location or cultural sphere. Indeed, if we begin with the notion that worship involves, as the etymology of the English word itself suggests, the activity of "ascribing worth," we are quickly led to see that every human endeavor both presupposes and reinforces certain judgments regarding worth. Moreover, the words routinely translated as "worship" in Christian Scripture point in a similar direction, though in an even more vivid way, for they derive from roots that mean "to kiss," "to bow, bend or prostrate oneself," and "to serve." Kissing, bowing, and serving – all are embodied ways of ascribing worth to something or someone. Not surprisingly, therefore, Christian worship has often included these activities as part of its liturgy.

Yet such explicit and ritually intensified examples of ascribing honor and worth in Christian worship should not blind us to the fact that human lives are always formed and shaped in specific ways that either explicitly or implicitly ascribe worth. Every human life is an embodied argument about what things are worth doing, who or what is worthy of attention, who or what is worthy of allegiance and sacrifice, and what projects or endeavors are worthy of human energies. In short, every human life is "bent" toward something. Every human life is an act of worship.

Understood in this way, the inextricable connection between worship and ethics comes more clearly into view. Regardless of how one understands ethics, the human judgments involved will be inseparable from judgments regarding the relative worth and worthiness of certain actions, projects, dispositions, values, principles, persons, or ideas. In many respects, this is what the ancient Greeks were articulating with their notion of "the Good": all human life is bent toward something or someone that defines ultimate worth. All human life, therefore, is doxological, for its shape and direction always ascribe honor and worth to something or someone.

Such an acknowledgment of the pervasiveness of worship suggests that every answer to such typically "ethical" questions as "What should I do?" presumes certain (often unacknowledged or unexamined) judgments about worth. This in turn leads to a further question: "How do human beings learn to what or to whom they should ascribe ultimate and relative worth?" How, in other words, do they come to render the world as this particular kind of world inhabited by these particular kinds of beings who ought to be engaged in these particular kinds of actions rather than others? Sociologists call this process "socialization"; Christian theologians have often called it "formation." In both instances there is the clear acknowledgment that human beings are shaped or formed by forces and influences beyond the individual.

Learning to Worship

Human beings are social creatures. As such, they are always being formed and shaped by structures and powers outside themselves, as well as participating in those structures and powers that form and shape others. Aristotle affirmed this long ago, and contemporary social sciences have only deepened our awareness of this central dynamic of human life. An intimate connection exists between how people come to understand themselves and their various gatherings and assemblies. Indeed, the answers that people offer to the "big questions" – Who am I? Who are we? What is the purpose of human life? What is the basic shape and character of the world in which we dwell? – are inseparable from the ways that they have come to understand themselves as the result of social interaction, which by its very nature involves human gatherings.

Because human beings are social creatures, when they gather together they inevitably presuppose and reinforce much about the shape, meaning, and purpose of the world that they understand themselves to inhabit. Indeed, all human gatherings are a kind of worship to the extent that they presuppose and reinforce certain ascriptions of worth. For this reason, human gatherings are inevitably formative, not least because such gatherings construct an imaginative landscape (a "world") within which all future action and reflection upon it will take place. People come to have a world as they gather together and share stories about the shape and meaning of that world, as well as their place and role within it. People come to have a world as they gather together and engage in common practices that only "make sense" within a world so understood. People come to have a world as the above activities presuppose, instill, and intensify certain desires and dispositions, and as certain virtues are commended and instilled as being requisite for flourishing in this kind of world. People come to have a world as they construct and maintain institutions that order and support ways of life that are congruent with the ways they understand the world and their place within it.

Taken as a whole, these multiple features of life together might be called a way of life. As such, a way of life is not simply a particular style of human living, but an entire way of rendering the world as a certain kind of inhabitable space in which people seek to dwell and flourish. For this reason, every way of life is inevitably a form of ascribing worth, a form of worship.

Gatherings, the social imagination, and human action

Another way of underscoring the formative power – and therefore the ethical significance – of human gatherings is to draw attention to the critical role that these gatherings play in forming the human imagination and, thus, the moral space or horizon within which human beings think and act. Yet such a strategy is impeded by the fact that ethics has so rarely considered the social imagination as central to its concerns.

There are, of course, various competing ways of understanding the human imagination. Prior to Kant and the German idealists, imagination was largely discussed in terms of its *mimetic* and *reproductive* capacities, and as such was largely associated with unreality, fantasy, illusion, and unreason. In contrast, most contemporary discussions of imagination take their bearings from Kant's focus on the *productive* aspects of imagination. This understanding was picked up by the Romantic movement, which went on to associate the imagination with creativity, genius, autonomy, and freedom (Engell, 1981; Kearney, 1994).

However, my arguments in the balance of this chapter concerning the human social imagination take an approach significantly different from either of these two familiar trajectories. In speaking of the human social imagination in what follows, reference will be made to that complex human social capacity to receive and construct an intelligible "whole" of which particular parts are considered to *be* constituent parts. In many respects, this usage parallels what one scholar has helpfully called the "paradigmatic imagination" (Green, 1989). Within such an understanding, imagination is not set in opposition to a separate human faculty called "reason," but is instead regarded as inseparable from human understanding and human action. In short, the human activity of imagining a "whole" in which any particular action "makes sense" suggests that imagination cannot in any simple way be pitted against practical reason or judgment, since such judgments always assume and make use of prior imaginings.

Understood in this way, it is not difficult to see in what sense the paradigmatic imagination is always social; that is, it is not something that individuals create for themselves, but is something that they largely receive. Human persons are always the recipients of an imaginative world within which they are called to live and through which they are encouraged to understand themselves and their place within that world. This imaginative whole is produced and reproduced by means of various human social structures, institutions, and practices, all of which shape and animate human lives in ways that presuppose and reinforce a particular understanding of how things hang together. Thus, every time that people engage in particular practices, interact with and have their lives shaped by certain institutions, come to believe certain things and hold certain convictions, and in all of this have certain desires instilled or fulfilled, these people are having their imaginations profoundly shaped with regard to what the "whole" of human life is about.

Finally, all this implies that there is no neutral way of narrating or rendering human behavior or the imaginative horizon within which it is engaged. Both social theory and theology, for example, offer a comprehensive rendering of the world and human behavior within it (Milbank, 1990). Both discourses are rooted in fundamental commitments about the shape of the "real" world, what it means to be human, and how those kinds of beings should act in that kind of world. Both discourses are in service to those specific renderings of the world and those who understand themselves to live in those worlds. What neither offers is a value-free or commitment-free rendering of the world. Thus, even the human activity of rendering the world as a particular kind of inhabitable space within which meaningful human action may take place is itself an act of worship, that is, an act of "ascribing worth."

To see an example of this complex social dynamic of human gatherings, social imagination, and action at work, one need only briefly reflect on a kind of gathering familiar to most readers: an assembly of students, teachers, and staff who gather as a school. Here, regardless of the level of schooling, one sees the complex interaction among – as well as the formative power of – the stories humans tell, the practices in which they engage, the desires, dispositions, and virtues they seek to instill, and the institutions they create and sustain in order to support all of this over time.

Schools function within a matrix of broadly shared cultural stories about why people should attend, stories that structure the curriculum as well as the expectations of what should happen in and out of the classroom. Inseparable from these stories are certain common practices in which people engage that presume and reinforce these stories. A school requires students to read and discuss common texts, master certain information regarded as critically important, and demonstrate certain skills considered to be essential. Moreover, faculty members assess and evaluate this student work, making it possible to rank those students, who, in turn, may use those rankings to impress prospective employers. In this way, the practice of grading in higher education commonly underwrites the widespread cultural story that society is largely a meritocracy, with the best jobs (and best pay) going to those who have earned it by means of their hard work and demonstrated achievement.

The moral and imaginative framework presupposed by such stories and practices also presumes that certain desires, dispositions, and virtues are requisite for flourishing in this world. The desires to excel, compete, "get ahead in life," as well as the virtues of diligence and open-mindedness, are all presupposed and reinforced by the "world of the school." Not surprisingly, ordering these projects toward a common end requires institutions capable of supporting them as "worthy" enterprises over time.

This complex web of stories, practices, institutions, and instilled passions and dispositions reveals schooling as a kind of formation system, for it participates – and requires those who are part of it likewise to participate – in a particular rendering of the world. And to the extent that a school sees itself as offering at least a partial answer to what it means to be a human being and what it means to live a good life, the school commends this understanding and way of life to all people, not just to those immediately engaged in the enterprise.

The relative power of gatherings

Schools are not, of course, the only kind of gathering; human beings gather in lots of different places for lots of different purposes. These manifold gatherings also differ enormously with respect to their formative impact. The gathering of a group of strangers at a subway station likely has less transformative potential than does a group of fellow employees gathered at a workplace. Similarly, a gathering of fellow devoted fans at a sporting event is likely to have less influence on one's view of the world than the regular gathering of one's family around the dinner table. The difference in relative impact among gatherings is the result of many factors, including such things as their frequency (how often these gatherings take place), their stability over time (whether a relatively stable group of persons gathers), their intended scope (how much of human life this gathering seeks to influence and order), the type and intensity of interaction fostered (the kind of social relations those gathering engage in and the potentially formative influence of that intimacy), and the willingness on the part of those gathered to be caught up in vision of the world being presupposed and reinforced by that gathering.

For example, consider the relative differences in formative power between a military boot camp and an amusement park. A boot camp is a gathering of human beings for a purpose so specific and focused that this shared purpose becomes capable of guiding everything that happens during and after that gathering. By contrast, a gathering of human beings at an amusement park is a much more diffuse and therefore much less potentially transformative gathering than the boot camp. That is, although the gathering at the amusement park still has woven into it some shared judgments regarding purpose and relative worth, the intended outcomes of the gathering are not nearly so tightly controlled or circumscribed.

Of course, the relative differences between the transformative power of the amusement park and of the boot camp are also due to a number of other factors. These include such things as the relative differences in the intensity of social interaction constitutive of each, as well as the vastly different degree to which each demands a total commitment or "conversion" in order to be initiated into a peculiar, distinctive, and comprehensive way of life.

This raises an obvious question. Should Christian formation, in terms of scope and focus, look more like an amusement park or more like a boot camp? That is, should gatherings of disciples understand themselves primarily as loosely knit aggregates of individuals who come together for assorted reasons and purposes, and whose fundamental orientation is dictated primarily by concerns other than the right worship of the triune God? Or is the way of Jesus Christ a peculiar and distinctive way, requiring an intentional and disciplined formation, the central component of which is the Christian liturgy? The chapters in this volume affirm the latter view. A person does not simply wake up one day and find she is a disciple of Jesus Christ any more than a person wakes up one day and finds she is a Marine. Although this formation takes place in various ways and in different venues, a certain priority is given to the community gathered for worship, for here, more clearly than in any other context, disciples of Jesus Christ are initiated into the comprehensive vision, the social imagination, that animates Christian life. Because this priority underwrites the approach of this entire volume, a couple of clarifying comments are in order.

First, priority is given to the community at worship not because the actions practiced there are in themselves *inherently more important* than the actions engaged in outside of the liturgy, but because the actions of the community at worship are taken to be *paradigmatic* for all other actions. That is, the community of disciples gathered for worship seeks to have its imagination so shaped by these formative liturgical actions that its entire life outside the liturgy will itself be a powerful expression of the worship of this God. In short, the reason the liturgy is given priority is not because offering praise and adoration to a deity is inherently more important than feeding the hungry or sheltering the homeless, but because learning to praise and adore this God who was revealed most fully in the flesh and blood of a first-century carpenter from Nazareth has everything to do with the care we offer our neighbors.

Second, granting the liturgy priority in the formation of those gathered is not itself sufficient, for engaging in the liturgy does not automatically shape those gathered in the desired ways. Those gathered rightly confess that the liturgy may be a powerful means of grace in God's economy of salvation, but the *ekklesia* also rightly confesses that the God it worships is not coercive. Just as Mary's consent was necessary for the Spirit to come upon her, so the *ekklesia* must consent to its own *re*-formation. One of the *ekklesia*'s central and continuing concerns, therefore, will always be not simply *if* it gathers and engages in the liturgy, but also *how* it gathers and engages in the liturgy. This central concern will always demand discernments regarding the spirits that animate this gathering.

This final concern is not unique to our age; indeed, it informs one of Paul's sternest admonitions to the disciples in Corinth (1 Corinthians 11: 17–22). Paul insists that it is not enough that they simply gather to celebrate the Lord's Supper; they must also attend to *how* they gather, that is, to the spirit that animates and therefore shapes their gathering. The Lord's table, which is intended to draw together and reconcile those whom society divides, has been dishonored because this occasion has been used to reinforce the social divisions between rich and poor. Because Paul is convinced that they gather in a spirit that violates the very purpose of the table, he can maintain that they are not in fact eating of the Lord's table. Paul's warning stands as a sober reminder to the gathered community, for it underscores the need not only to engage in certain practices, but also to attend to the spirit that animates and directs them.

The *Ekklesia* as Formative Gathering

In order to illustrate the potentially formative power of Christian worship, as well as its pivotal role in matters of Christian ethics, the remainder of this chapter identifies some of the crucial skills, convictions, and dispositions that are nurtured in and through the community of disciples gathered for worship. As would be expected, the specific liturgical practices and contexts within which many of these are nurtured will be discussed and illustrated more directly and explicitly in the chapters that follow. The remainder of this chapter will of necessity, therefore, paint with rather broad strokes, with the understanding that the following chapters will use finer and more detailed ones.

In what follows, I refer to the community of disciples of Jesus Christ as "the *ekklesia*." The reason for doing so is straightforward. When most people hear the word "church" (the word most commonly used to translate the New Testament Greek term *ekklesia*), they quite naturally think of a special building set aside for "religious" gatherings and activities. Because such usage presupposes and reinforces an understanding I am arguing against, I have chosen simply to transliterate the Greek word in the hope of offering a modest linguistic restraint against too quickly foreclosing on the scope and purposes of this assembly. In its New Testament context, the word "*ekklesia*" did not refer to a "religious" gathering, but rather to any assembly gathered to engage in important business. Thus, in what follows, this assembly is understood to be the primary context in which disciples of Jesus Christ learn the skills, convictions, and dispositions that animate its life in the world. It is within this communal form of life that it learns how to make the prudential judgments necessary for living out the *ekklesia*'s mission in the world: to be an embodied sign and foretaste of God's continuing work of reconciliation and healing in the world.

Learning to glorify and enjoy God

Christians affirm that all human life – including gatherings for engaging in intentional and ritually focused practices of worship – has as its ultimate horizon the glory of the triune God and the enjoying of communion with that God. Or, as stated succinctly in the Westminster Shorter Catechism of 1647: "Man's chief end is to glorify God, and to enjoy him forever."

From the time of the call of Abraham, God has moved to create a gathering of people from all the nations that would do precisely that. Just as ancient Israel was called to be a light to the nations, so the *ekklesia* is called to embody before the world God's deepest desires for all of creation. That desire is for communion, for participation in the very life of the triune God. Such communion, such participation is rooted in the very relationship within the triune God, where the Son serves the will of the Father and the Spirit bears witness to the Son in such a way that both bring glory to the Father. To the extent that the *ekklesia* likewise serves the will of the Father, bears witness to the Son, and opens its life continually to the animation of the Spirit, it too participates in the life of God, anticipating in embodied form the eschatological gathering of the people of God.

Thus, the first petition of the Lord's Prayer – "Hallowed be thy name" – when read against the background of ancient Israel's Scripture, is a call for God to sanctify God's own name by gathering and renewing the people of God. As one New Testament scholar has noted, it means "Gather to yourself a renewed people that is truly holy, so that the reign of God can shine forth and your holy name may stand in its full glory before the eyes of all peoples" (Lohfink, 1984: 124). Therefore, when the *ekklesia* in any concrete time and place gathers to worship, it does so not at its own initiative, but in response to the triune God's continuing work of gathering a sanctified people who will participate in the very life of God, thus bringing glory and honor to God. Seen from this perspective, the gathering of the *ekklesia* does not begin at the processional, or with the call to worship, but with God's determination to call out a sanctified people. God's work of sanctification – God's work of bringing wholeness, healing, and reconciliation to the entire cosmos – does not happen by means of magic, but rather by means of a people who have been formed and animated by the Spirit of God in Christian worship to serve as agents of God's reconciling work in the world.

Consequently, the regular gathering of the *ekklesia* for worship is always already an embodied response to God's prior action: it is an act of trust that God will, through these people and practices, form the *ekklesia* in ways that will edify it for further service and embodied witness in the world. Rightly understood, therefore, the gathering of the *ekklesia* is not simply a prerequisite to worship, but is already itself an act of worship. The *ekklesia* gathers the gifts of the people of God – both the gifts and stories they bring and the gifts and stories they are – as a witness to God's continued work in and care for the world. The triune God's action in the world has a certain shape, direction, taste, aroma, and tenor, and the *ekklesia* gathers to learn to recognize, acknowledge, and participate in that action.

Learning to pay attention

More than one cultural commentator has noted that we live in an age of distraction. More and more, people in contemporary Western societies find that their attention is increasingly fragmented, diverted, and unfocused. Although every society demands that certain things be given proper attention, contemporary Western societies are incredibly proficient at bombarding their citizens with vast arrays of objects that compete for their attention. It is within this context that the *ekklesia* gathers to learn to attend to the right things rightly.

Although this critical process of formation takes place throughout the liturgy, most ecclesial traditions seek to focus the attention of gathered worshipers from the moment they enter that space set aside for the practice of the liturgy. As a result, liturgical space itself is typically arranged to focus the attention of those gathered on certain vital matters. For example, Christian liturgical space is usually arranged so that focal attention is drawn to the altar or communion table, the pulpit and lectern, and to the central symbol of the Christian faith, the cross of Jesus Christ.

The centrality of the cross to ecclesial attention is underscored in many concrete ways. Crosses not only frequently adorn the steeples and domes of church buildings and cathedrals, but also provide the architectural pattern for those buildings whose cruciform shape itself bears material witness to this central focus. Moreover, the liturgy in many ecclesial traditions begins with a procession in which the cross, followed by the Gospel, leads the procession. By following the cross and the Gospel into (and, later, out of) the sanctuary, the *ekklesia* dramatizes not only the focus of this gathering, but also the deliberate direction of its life. Hence, in many concrete ways the *ekklesia* is reminded that the way of Jesus Christ is the way of the cross.

Yet, for Christians, the way of the cross is never one traveled alone. The *ekklesia* gathers as part of the communion of saints across time and space, a communion whose reality is powerfully evoked by means of the stained glass windows or icons that often appear prominently within the liturgical space of the *ekklesia*. In each case, the *ekklesia* is encouraged to have its understanding of the world transformed by viewing it *through* these renderings of the saints, who offer the *ekklesia* much needed perspective by reminding it that the grace of God is sufficient for those who embark on the way of the cross. Moreover, the liturgy as a whole is an enterprise engaged in together. In entering this space, those who gather as the *ekklesia* are drawn out of their private and narcissistic worlds in order to enter the cosmic arena of God's reconciling purposes. That God's purposes and initiative, rather than their own, are the focal point of this gathering is underscored by the call to worship, which appropriately uses words from Scripture to remind those gathered that they do so in response to God's call on their lives.

The *ekklesia* likewise learns to pay attention rightly through its practice of prayer. Correctly understood, prayer is not simply a speaking to God, but a deep and abiding communion with God. Such communion requires that we both listen to God and open ourselves up to the transforming power of God's Spirit. In short, prayer invites us to attend to the desires of God and to make those desires our desires. This is one reason why the *ekklesia* gathered for worship often prays using words from other times and places: such words have the power both to focus our attention and to serve as models for our own prayers. In this way, those gathered learn how to attend more faithfully to the things of God.

Learning to speak truthfully

Contemporary life is filled not only with distraction, but also with deception and falsehood. Few citizens expect to hear the truth from their elected leaders; most people are daily subjected to a steady stream of inflated and deceptive claims from advertisers; and nearly every one of us, in our quiet moments, is painfully aware of our own capacity for falsehood and self-deception. In contrast, Christian worship offers those gathered important resources for learning to speak truthfully about God, the world, and themselves.

First, and most importantly, in worship the *ekklesia* learns to speak truthfully about God. The *ekklesia*'s truest speech *about* God is its speech directed *to* God. That is, in offering its ultimate praise, adoration, and thanksgiving to the triune God, the *ekklesia* truthfully embodies the cornerstone of Christian worship: this God alone is worthy of all honor and glory and praise; this God alone is worthy of complete devotion and allegiance; this God alone is worthy of being the axis around which all life revolves. Such speech, as well as human embodiment consonant with that speech, has far-reaching formative potential. To proclaim in the gathered assembly that God is the source of all life, as well as the source of every good and perfect gift, is to affirm a fundamental orientation deeply at odds with contemporary society. In this way, the liturgy potentially reconfigures the imaginative landscape within which those gathered think and act.

For this reason, the *ekklesia*'s truthful speech does not stop with its praise and adoration of the triune God. The *ekklesia* also seeks to speak truthfully about the world as the arena of God's redemptive purposes, as the realm of God's work of transforming the kingdoms of this world into the kingdoms of our Lord. Gathering to worship reminds those gathered of this larger horizon within which they live and serve. The *ekklesia* gathers to participate in something it did not initiate and which it will not bring to completion, but which nonetheless has the power to shape it profoundly. In the liturgy, the *ekklesia* learns to see the world as the realm of God's work and God's glory, as well as learning to see a world that is passing away in its current form, being transformed by God's grace into the reign of God. This recognition, which is itself an act of worship, an activity of ascribing worth, relativizes in an important sense all other loyalties and commitments, demanding that they become subordinate to God's ultimate purposes rather than become themselves ultimate, absolute, and controlling.

Thus, in gathering, the *ekklesia* confesses that it can only know its true identity and purpose as it finds its story within the more comprehensive story of God's work in the world. In gathering, the *ekklesia* embodies its continued willingness to see itself first of all as a participant in God's cosmic drama rather than as a participant in the puny, if not petty, dramas that humans script for themselves in which they play the leading role. In gathering, the *ekklesia* confesses that God plays the leading role in this cosmic drama, while the *ekklesia* is cast in a supporting role. To participate in the life of God is to participate in the life that God offers to the world, a life that the *ekklesia* is called not only to enjoy but also to serve. In short, in gathering, the *ekklesia* learns to receive its true identity as the Body of Christ. In so doing, the *ekklesia* confesses that there is no "I" apart from that body: that every person receives his or her truest identity as a part of the Body of Christ. This is why gathering is neither secondary nor incidental, for in so doing, vital and life-giving connections are nurtured and sustained.

Finally, it is precisely in the light of such truthful speech that the *ekklesia* is able to speak truthfully about its own waywardness, its own sinfulness and resistance to the purposes of God. It is only in the light of the *ekklesia*'s rightful praise of God and the revelation of God's reconciling purposes for the world that the *ekklesia* becomes fully enabled to confess its sin as sin. In other words, it is by means of the formation that takes place most fundamentally in worship that the *ekklesia* learns to recognize and name its idolatry as idolatry. Whereas much contemporary life is devoted to exalting and extending the reign of the gods of fashion, convenience, efficiency, novelty, violence, excess, fear, and insecurity, the *ekklesia* is called to devote itself to worshiping the only true and living God. The gospel announces the good news that these false gods need no longer hold us in bondage. Like the idols that Isaiah satirically mocked (Isaiah 44: 9–20), these gods are the work of our own hands. In a world in bondage to gods of its own making, the *ekklesia* dares to gather, both to give praise and honor to the only one worthy of such worship and to denounce and confess its own idolatrous life. In so doing, the *ekklesia* learns the rudiments of truthful speech.

As far back as Aristotle, ethics was understood to be centrally about praise and blame. Ethics is about learning to recognize, praise, and commend the right actions done in the right way, as well as learning to praise those who engage in such action, while also learning the proper use of the language of blame. When praise and blame are rightly spoken, those who hear and are guided by such truthful speech are rightly formed to make the judgments necessary to live well. Seen in this light, the adoration and praise of God in worship, as well as the confession of human sin, are profoundly moral activities.

Learning good posture

As already noted, the gathering of the *ekklesia* for worship is itself a response to God's prior action. The Christian liturgy assumes that God, by virtue of who God is and what God has done, is worthy of praise, adoration, and thanksgiving. Such an assumption has important ethical implications to the extent that the liturgy forms those gathered with a particular orientation or posture toward God, the world, and other people that flows from and is consonant with the *ekklesia*'s practice of worship.

First, worship cultivates a posture of dependence. It matters enormously for Christian ethics whether human beings see themselves as autonomous and independent of

God and each other, or whether they see their lives as gifts from God that in turn might be offered for the life of the world to the glory of God. The *ekklesia* confesses that human flourishing is best understood as and sustained through participation in the circulation of God's good gifts; in contrast, much contemporary life assumes that human flourishing is best understood and sustained through participation in human self-making. People who dwell in these very different imaginative moral spaces will inevitably find themselves making very different kinds of practical moral judgments.

For example, the imaginative moral space within which much contemporary ethical reflection takes place assumes that the highest human good is something called "freedom," understood as the capacity to create, choose, and pursue one's own purposes and goals. However, within the imaginative moral space fostered by Christian worship, the notion of being required to create and live out one's own self-chosen purpose is regarded as a form of bondage. In this sense, the Christian worship of God may itself be liberating, for it forms those gathered to acknowledge that human life has a transcendent purpose and goal that is not simply self-created and self-chosen.

Furthermore, the regular gathering of the *ekklesia* fosters a posture of dependence in that it affirms our need not only for God but also for each other. In contrast to those many voices that encourage us to construct our identities primarily by purchasing various products ("I am what I buy"), the gathering of the *ekklesia* for worship encourages us to have our identities forged both through the reception of word and sacrament, and through the reception of guidance and admonition offered by the communion of saints. Thus, whereas for many kinds of human gatherings the interaction among persons is relatively minimal and incidental, the gathering of the *ekklesia* in a particular time and place calls for a relatively consistent group of people who are open to both the gifts and demands brought by those gathered.

A second and corollary posture nurtured in worship is that of humility. If human beings truly and profoundly are dependent upon God and other people, as Christian worship affirms, then such an affirmation should foster a deep sense of humility. As an assembly of creatures gathered to worship their Creator, the *ekklesia* rightly bends its will to the One whom it confesses as Lord of all. As an assembly of sinners gathered to worship a righteous, holy, yet merciful God, the *ekklesia* falls on its face to honor the judge and justifier of all that is. Such willful submission presupposes and reinforces a posture of humility, one that is physically embodied, for example, in those traditions where genuflecting and kneeling remain critically important gestures.

Although worship nurtures a number of other postures, two more may be briefly mentioned: trust and hope. Both are closely tied to what has already been noted. If the triune God is who the *ekklesia* confesses God to be – the one who unrelentingly pursues our well-being – then the *ekklesia* is right to place its trust in that God and wait patiently and hopefully upon that God and the future that God is bringing. In the liturgy the *ekklesia* rehearses the story of this triune God, a story that testifies that this God is worthy of our trust and deepest hopes.

As a result, the *ekklesia* gathers to wait. In a world that urges people to be always doing something productive with their time and energies – something that makes a noticeable difference in the world – the *ekklesia* dares to gather and wait upon God. At the heart of the liturgy stands a kind of waiting, a kind of disciplined inactivity. In the liturgy Christians learn to hold together two important, yet seemingly contradictory, affirmations: the *ekklesia waits* for God's reign; the *ekklesia* offers itself to be used by God to *extend* that reign. The coming of God's reign is not driven by human initiative; however, God is capable of sanctifying human action in ways that extend God's purposes. The *ekklesia* has not been given the task of engineering a future of its own devising, but instead one of recognizing, announcing, welcoming, and "midwifing" a future that God is bringing. The *ekklesia* gathers both to honor and praise the One who promises that future, and to be shaped and formed for its part within that future.

Conclusion

There are, of course, many other ways in which formation takes place when the Body of Christ gathers to worship; many of these will be taken up in considerable detail in the chapters that follow. Yet perhaps an adequate enough sketch has been offered in this brief chapter to suggest why the gathering of the *ekklesia* is vital to its very identity and purpose, an identity and purpose that are themselves irreducibly ethical. The *ekklesia* gathers to worship the triune God, and, in so doing, bears embodied witness that this God alone is worthy of undivided allegiance and devotion. For this reason, the *ekklesia* gathers to have its potentially idolatrous imagination renewed by the narratives of Scripture and the practices of the Christian tradition. Such renewal makes possible the confession of idolatry, as well as the opportunity to assume a more appropriate posture toward God and the world. When the *ekklesia* gathers to worship, it does not gather to grumble, compete, or secure for itself what is needed; rather, the *ekklesia* gathers to rest and be renewed by giving thanks and praise to the One who so graciously supplies all its needs. In gathering to worship, the *ekklesia* opens itself up to receive the proper orientation to all that is, in order that it might live in *that* world in ways consonant with the reign of the triune God. In gathering to pay attention to the right things, to speak the truth, and to adopt the proper posture toward God and the world, the *ekklesia* opens itself up to being formed into the kind of people who can glorify and enjoy God forever.

Over the centuries, the people of God have gathered to worship the God revealed in Jesus Christ. By the grace and power of God, such worship has often transformed the lives of those who have prayed "your kingdom come, your will be done," nurturing within them an alternative social imagination and thereby enabling them to bear embodied witness to the desires and purposes of God. In this way, such worship across the centuries has created and sustained new identities. For example, countless Christians across time and space have learned what their African American sisters and brothers learned through their experience of worship: that they were "no longer named by the world but named by the Spirit of Jesus" (Cone, 1978: 140). Such worship has also encouraged those gathered to see their lives not as something to be grasped, but as gifts to be given for the service of God. As a result, such worship has led countless gatherings, animated by the Spirit of Christ, to feed the hungry, give drink to the thirsty, cloth the naked, take in the stranger, bind up the wounded, and share their possessions with those in need. Such worship, by making focal God's reconciling work in Jesus Christ, has also led countless Christians to seek reconciliation with their enemies and to offer forgiveness to those who have sinned against them. Likewise, such worship has nurtured the imaginations of those who have non-violently resisted oppressive regimes and powers in the name of the coming reign of God, often at the price of their own lives. No less importantly, such worship has, across the centuries, also enabled those gathered to name and confess their own sin. At times, such worship has even empowered those gathered to denounce the unfaithfulness of their own brothers and sisters, as was the case with the Confessing Church in Germany.

Has the gathering of the *ekklesia* and the worship of God always in all places led to the transformation of those gathered into the image of Christ and to the further manifestation of God's reign? Certainly not. Nor can such failures be simply ignored. Disciples of Jesus Christ who rightly understand their purpose in the world can neither glibly excuse themselves nor hide behind the privatization of modern "religion," protected by the anonymity that such privacy affords. Indeed, the act of gathering itself sets in motion a complex social dynamic that may lead to transformation not only by means of the liturgy, but also by means of heightened expectations and critique. By gathering to worship the triune God, the *ekklesia* offers an embodied witness to its primary allegiance and so raises its own and the world's expectations. For if disciples of Jesus Christ really gather to be transformed and to make themselves available to be used by God to transform the kingdoms of this world into the kingdoms of our Lord, then the *ekklesia* and the world should rightly expect to be able to see some of this transformation taking place. So, in gathering, the *ekklesia* becomes visible and addressable, opening itself up to being probed and criticized, not only by God, but also by the world.

Yet this is as it should be. The *ekklesia*, as an imperfect anticipation of what God desires for all of creation, seeks to conceal neither its faithfulness nor its unfaithfulness. For if the *ekklesia* exists for God's glory and not its own, then its willingness to name its own sinfulness – as well as have its sinfulness named by others – is itself a form of faithful witness to this God and this God's work. Thus, the *ekklesia* has its own reasons, internal to its own story and vocation, for carefully examining and critiquing the shape of its own embodied life. In other words, it is precisely *because* the *ekklesia* believes that its embodied life is part of the gospel that it must ask about the *shape* of that life, asking hard questions about how it might more faithfully devote its entire life to the right worship of the triune God.

References

Cone, James H. (1978) "Sanctification, Liberation, and Black Worship," *Theology Today*, 35: 139–52.

Engell, James (1981) *The Creative Imagination: Enlightenment to Romanticism* (Cambridge, MA: Harvard University Press).

Green, Garrett (1989) *Imagining God: Theology and the Religious Imagination* (Grand Rapids, MI: Eerdmans).

Kearney, Richard (1994) *The Wake of Imagination* (New York: Routledge).

Lohfink, Gerhard (1984) *Jesus and Community: The Social Dimension of the Christian Faith*, trans. John P. Galvin (Philadelphia: Fortress).

Milbank, John (1990) *Theology and Social Theory: Beyond Secular Reason* (Oxford: Blackwell).

CHAPTER 6

Greeting: Beyond Racial Reconciliation

Emmanuel Katongole

Christian worship provides one of the best resources and contexts for Christians to unlearn race and resist racism. For instance, the greeting, which Christians receive and offer to one another during worship, is a witness to the fact that Christians are drawn beyond themselves into the story of God's own life and self-sacrificing action in the world. It is by standing within this story that Christians learn to see themselves and others as gifts which, in their bodily differences, are called to be the visible Body of Christ. In the act of being greeted and of greeting one another in the name of the Trinity they bear witness to this story. Accordingly, when Christians take worship not as an occasional act but as a way of life, they acquire resources that enable them to see and relate to one another in ways far more interesting and truthful than any recommendations for racial reconciliation would ever be.

My appreciation of worship as the best context for a discussion of race has been shaped by many factors, among which are my own resistance to a newly acquired racial identity, and a determined effort to recover a vision and way of life beyond such an identity. And so, for the reader fully to appreciate "where I am coming from," I thought it would be helpful to begin with this personal story.

On Discovering Race: A Personal Story

I did not know that I was black until the summer of 1991, when I first came to the United States. That it took me so long to discover my "race" was, however, never due to any confusion about my parentage or doubts about my skin pigmentation. It is just that in Uganda "black" is simply an adjective, and a black person is simply one with an unusually dark complexion. And since, as far as complexion goes, I am "brown" or "dark brown" I was never black. I was therefore surprised, on coming to the United States, to discover that these distinctions were not significant in the same sort of way, and that I was simply "black." Moreover, what I soon discovered was that, here, "black" was not an adjective that operated among other adjectives to describe a person, but an ethically and ideologically coded designation of what a person is, in this case, my very identity.

To be sure, I do not remember if there was any particular incident or decisive moment at which I became "black." In fact, during this first visit in the summer of 1991, I must have gotten away with a number of things that were outside the usual or "normal" range of expectations of black and white interactions. This was particularly the case since I happened to be assigned as summer resident priest at a rural, predominantly white parish in Indiana. And since I was not aware that I was "black," I just went about discovering America and American culture in the most innocent manner. And if people were extra nice to me, this did not strike me as odd. It simply confirmed my impression of Americans as generally very friendly people. In this way, Americans reminded me of the people back at home in Uganda.

I do, however, remember being amazed by the fact that, even after a very short time at the church I served, everybody in the town seemed to know me. Whether at a supermarket, or at an ice cream parlor, or on an evening walk, I met people who greeted me with a friendly "Hi Father." I remember at first thinking to myself: everybody here must be Catholic, and so they must have seen me at mass. It was only when I asked one woman whether she came to St Mary's and she said "no" that I was curious to know how she knew me. Her swift reply: "This is a small town, and word goes around very quickly." It had never struck me that I was the only "black" person in town.

This fact was, however, brought home to me one afternoon when, as I prepared to take my driver's license, I needed some practice in parallel parking. I chose a relatively quiet street in the neighborhood for this exercise, and when I was satisfied with my skills, headed back home. Just a couple of blocks away from the church, a police car pulled me over. The police officer was very polite, and when he had examined my documents and found nothing wrong explained that he had received a call from a concerned neighbor who had seen a "black" person doing a couple of parking maneuvers in the neighborhood.

The discovery of myself as "black" continued and even became heightened when I went to study in Belgium in the Fall of the same year. And though I was never able to understand Flemish fully, I was aware of how frequently the word *zwart* came up in reference to or in conversations about me. Not that all these references were "racial" in the negative sort of way. They just confirmed the extent to which race had become the dominant grid through which my life was read, and through which I was supposed to see my life. This discovery made me angry. For, as far as I was concerned, "black" or "*zwart*" did not name anything about me – not even my skin color. It was just an identity that I was assumed to have; something I was supposed to be.

What I found particularly difficult to understand is the fact that all my characteristics, roles, and functions did not seem to be as significant as the fact that I was "black" or "*zwart*." I was particularly shocked that my being a Christian among fellow Christians, or my being a priest in a predominantly Catholic country like Belgium, did not make any difference. I was "black" and that greatly determined my social interactions, the church I went to, the type of housing that was open to me for rent, and even how well I did in some courses. To be sure, most of this was very subtle, though there were other incidents where racism was just in your face.

I remember, for instance, when Sam, a priest from Ghana who was in the same program as me, asked me to go with him to check out his new apartment. He had been shopping around for a while for an apartment, and had called a number of landlords whose ads he had seen in the paper. At detecting his African voice, the majority of them had told him that the apartment in question had just been rented out, even though the ad for the same apartment would appear in the paper the following day or week. Sam got a brilliant idea. He asked Rob, a Belgian student in our program, who agreed to call on Sam's behalf. Sure enough, the apartment was available. So, Sam invited me to go over with Rob to check out the apartment. On seeing the three of us, the landlord realized the trick. And even though Rob immediately explained that he had called for the apartment, the landlord apologized for the mistake, but the apartment was not available.

I am sure there is nothing unique about my story, except perhaps in the sense that for me this was a novel experience, a recent discovery of what it means to be "black." But this is perhaps what made me all the more determined not to accept this new identity of myself as a racialized person. For I soon realized that I was beginning to hate not only myself, but others as well, for no other reason than their being "black" or "white." It was then that I realized that I would either have to accept and learn to live with my new identity, or find ways to resist it. But, even as I faced the challenge, the choice seemed to be clear. For how could I allow such a recent discovery to become the overriding characteristic for my self-understanding?

It is this personal biography that perhaps best explains why I have come to see the need to move theological discussions beyond the search for guidelines and principles that foster racial reconciliation. For, helpful as many of these recommendations might be, they are based on a realism that accepts "race" and racial identity as a fact. Accordingly, their greatest relief seems to be one of providing insights and skills (theological, ethical, political) to help us "manage" or deal with the reality of race. However, given my story above, even as I hoped for and expected justice and racial equality, I constantly found myself longing for spaces and practices in which I could recover a sort of pre-1991 racial innocence. Accordingly, it became increasingly clear to me that, more than racial reconciliation, the far more urgent ethical and theological challenge was the recovery of a vision and way of life "beyond race."

But, if I understood this to be the challenge, I also soon discovered that the standard philosophical and theological discussions did not offer much in terms of concrete resources with which to meet the challenge. For, whereas philosophical and theological discussions could shed light on the issue of race, their recommendations nevertheless still fell short of providing *concrete* alternatives to, or resources for a way of life beyond, race. A simple theoretical digression will help to make this clear.

The Consolation of Philosophy

One can learn a great deal from the philosophical discourse on race. In my case, for instance, it was my philosophy background that helped me to see the connections between the notions of "race," "civilization," "reason," "progress" – in a word, the connection between race and the Enlightenment project. It is this connection that led me to see the extent to which assumptions of "race" still underpin the social, political, and economic institutions of Western civilization. More specifically, philosophy helped me to see how the modern problem of race is connected to the modern accounts of the self and human flourishing. If philosophy helped me to begin to make these connections, it also helped to expose the arbitrariness of the notion of race. For instance, I found Hannah Arendt's attempt to connect race and imperialism highly instructive, especially her observation that both are grounded in practical economic interests (Arendt, 1951). Similarly, by connecting the notion of race to the "invention" of Africa as the dark, uncivilized other of European Enlightenment, Mudimbe (1988) was able to show how race classification is just one factor reflecting the anxiety at the heart of Western claims to "civilization." Thus, both Arendt's and Mudimbe's argument helped me to see the deep connection between colonialism and race.

But, for all these insights, philosophy was still far from providing skills and resources for a vision of life "beyond race." In fact, the best that philosophy seemed to offer in terms of relief were *theoretical* skills. No doubt, one could *do* a lot with these and similar intellectual insights. I remember, for instance, how, armed with such insights, my African colleagues and I often found ourselves in a spirited conversation in which we discussed, debated, and eventually deconstructed "blackness" as simply an invention, a political and ethical construct, meant to advance particular political and economic interests. But even with the consolation of such deconstruction we were still without any concrete skills or practices with which to live out our lives beyond "the political and ethical construct" that we had discovered race to be. At the end of the day, we were all still "black" and my friend Sam could still not find an apartment.

Theology and Racial Reconciliation

The challenge of providing concrete alternatives to racism and race categories is also one that theological discussions have tended to shy away from. For, in turning to theology, one is first confronted with the astonishing realization that the observation that James Cone noted in 1975 is still largely true today. That is, that in spite of the fact that race and racism are a major social problem, white theologians have, on the whole, had very little to say against racism (Cone, 1975: 45–53). The silence may, of course, be an indication of the realism with which the mainstream of Western theology has come to accept race and racism as a fact, about which nothing much can be done. It may also be, as Cone suggests, that the fact that white theologians have remained virtually mute on issues of race is because they have been unwilling to question their own cultural history, particularly the political and economic structures of Western societies. What the silence does however, is to turn the theological discourse on race into just another area of special interest, one that black theologians are expected to pursue. My being asked to contribute a chapter on racism to this volume may itself not be unrelated to this observation.

Secondly, one notes that theological discussions of race have been greatly dominated by recommendations for "racial reconciliation." Whereas this might sound like a very concrete recommendation, one soon discovers that a great many of these theological discussions are not only abstract, they leave us at the level of principles and insights. For, even when the discussions begin by making reference to Scripture or Christian tradition, the goal is quite often to draw from these traditions *ethical* implications or insights which could be applied generally.

This is also perhaps the reason why, within many of these discussions, the problem of race is easily reduced to a general problem of difference, one that is common to all societies. Craig Keener's "The Gospel and Racial Reconciliation"(Keener, 1997) provides a good example. In this essay, Keener first notes that, whereas differences in skin color and other physical features were noticed but rarely understood in a prejudicial manner in the New Testament, "racism in the sense of various cultures viewing themselves as superior was widespread" (Keener, 1997: 118). He then examines Paul's theology of reconciliation in order to show that the gospel provides insights and guidelines for how Christians can overcome this problem of "prejudice" and transcend "all other human barriers we have erected among ourselves" (1997: 118). I draw attention to Keener's essay because it offers a clear example of how once the problem of racism has been reduced to a universal human problem, the Christian response cannot but itself be limited to one of discovering what *insights* the gospel can shed on this general problem. To the extent that a great many theological recommendations for racial reconciliation move in this manner, they leave us at the level of insights and principles, and do not draw attention to specific Christian practices, which might offer concrete skills of resistance and an alternative to racism.

Even more problematic, however, is the fact that the attempt to reduce racism to a general problem of difference and prejudice tends to obscure the particular history and assumptions that sustain racism as a distinctively modern problem. In the absence of any attention to that narrative, it is simply assumed that race is a natural category, and, therefore, all that one can hope for is tolerance or some form of racial reconciliation or harmony.

What my excursus into philosophy had allowed me to appreciate, however, is the fact that race is not a natural category, but one that is somehow connected to modern accounts of the self and human flourishing. And so, by not questioning the category of race, theologies for racial reconciliation may unwittingly reproduce the same accounts of the self as those responsible for giving rise to the problem of racism in the first place.

This observation is connected to a wider problem facing theology in modern times; namely, that in an attempt to remain a respectable discipline, we theologians often feel that we have to appeal to the modern accounts of culture, race, and history to provide us with an account of reality. But since it is these accounts that are responsible for giving rise to the problem of race in the first place, appealing to the same accounts leaves us with little or no resources with which to move beyond the limits that the vision of these accounts imposes. This is one reason why I personally find the theologies of racial reconciliation not to be radical enough. For while these discussions offer insights and ethical guidelines on how to deal with or manage the problems of racism, they leave us within the same politics and social history where race is still a dominant story.

But if, as I have noted, the challenge is one of recovering a vision and way of life beyond race, then what is required is a different story and a different set of practices that would not have to assume "race" or "racial" identity. If this sounds like a utopian or idealistic expectation, it is because Christian theology and ethics are, by their nature, idealistic in the sense that they reflect God who constantly calls the Church to new imaginations of the real, of what is possible. Moreover, my own idealism was also made possible by my personal biography. For, while I knew race and racism to be a fact in the West, I also knew as a matter of fact that it is possible not be "black" or "white." In fact, what my personal story had led me to see is the fact that being "black" or "white," or for that matter any other racial identity, was an acquired identity, which is to say, a *learnt* vision of life and set of corresponding habits. This, I think, is what Cornel West has in mind when he notes that blackness has no meaning outside a system of race-conscious people and practices (West, 1993: 39).

This is what makes a Christian response to race not so much a matter of principles and insights but one of *practices*. In other words, if racial identity is a matter of community, an alternative identity is not only possible, it is a matter of an alternative community, embodying different practices and a different vision of the self. If racism is at home within modern Western societies, then the Christian challenge to racism is really one of being able to step outside the vision of modern Western society, and find oneself part of a community and practices in which race and racial identity simply make no sense. Christian worship provides precisely such an opportunity in the sense that, within the practice of Christian worship, a new unique community is being constituted in a manner that both challenges, and offers a concrete alternative to, the story of race and racism.

Christian Worship as a "Wild Space"

Such a claim needs to be qualified in at least two ways. First, we all are sadly aware that worship can be, and has so often been, one of the most segregated spaces. And so, far from offering an alternative to the cultural patterns of racism, Christian worship has often simply confirmed and even re-enforced the racialized boundaries and interactions within modern society. That is why an appreciation of worship along the lines we are calling for involves a re-assessment of the relation of worship to modern culture. While worship has tended to provide an opportunity for a spiritual confirmation and affirmation of the dominant cultural patterns and values, I suggest that we see worship as a site for imagining and embodying concrete alternatives to the dominant cultural patterns and values. In this way, Christian worship is able to provide Christians with the resources and possibilities for living out of, and living out concrete alternatives to, the vision of modern society.

Secondly, the notion of "stepping outside" might strike many as encouraging a form of Christian sectarianism. Without getting into the so-often misleading assumptions connected to this impression (Katongole, 2002: 189–203), there is nothing about Christian worship that forces Christians to withdraw from engagement in their societies. What is meant instead is that through a practice such as worship, Christians are able to develop the skills and practices required to engage critically with their societies, or, which is the same thing, to live as "Resident Aliens" (Hauerwas and Willimon, 1989) within the societies they find themselves in.

More recently, I have found McFague's (2001) notion of "wild spaces" a helpful way to characterize the practice of Christian worship. In an attempt to recover ethical existence in the face of a consumer-oriented economy and culture, McFague suggests the cultivation of "wild spaces" as a normative requirement if the individual is to resist, survive, or creatively reshape the draft of an all too powerful consumerist worldview. A "wild space," according to McFague, is whatever does not fit the stereotypical human being, or the definition of the good life as defined by conventional culture. What is particularly significant, however, is that, for McFague, a wild space is not the province of a self-sufficient way of life "outside" Western capitalist and consumer society. Rather, wild spaces are created or discovered in the rifts of that very culture.

> Imagine conventional Western culture as a circle with your world overimposed over it. If you are [a] poor Hispanic lesbian, your world will not fit into the conventional Western one. It will overlap somewhat (you may be educated and able-bodied), but there will be a large crescent that will be outside. That is your wild space; it is the space that will allow – and encourage – you to think differently, to imagine alternative ways of living. It will not only give you problems, but possibilities. (McFague, 2001: 48)

Christian worship is precisely such a wild space, which allows – and encourages – Christians to think differently, to imagine and embody alternative ways of living. Worship enables Christians to break out of the status quo of conventional culture, but also offers resistance to it in ways that a new change in rules does not. For, it is by standing within the wild space that is worship that Christians can now *see* themselves in a different perspective. Such seeing, of course, is not theoretical, but is, in fact, made possible to the extent that the Christian is located within concrete practices, which reflect a different story of the self than that named by race.

And so, in the remaining part of this chapter, I would like to draw attention to just one such practice of Christian worship, namely the act of greeting, in order to highlight the conclusion that the greeting which Christians receive and offer to one another during worship provides resources for Christians to *unlearn* race, and come to embody a new pattern of life.

On Being Greeted in the Name of the Trinity

When Christians gather for worship, they are greeted and in turn take time to greet one another. The Catholic liturgy of the mass, for instance, begins with the priest greeting the congregation in these or similar words: "May the Grace of Our Lord Jesus Christ, the Love of God the Father, and the Fellowship of the Holy Spirit be with you . . ."

Although I have been quite familiar with this formula, I first began to appreciate its full theological significance on a visit to Malaysia in 1997, when, on one afternoon, I was invited to participate in the celebration of mass at a Kampung (village) community outside Kuching. Mass began outside the church, with the priest greeting the congregation, and everyone in the congregation greeting everyone else. What I found particularly striking was not just the orderliness of the whole exercise, but the fact that we had to extend greeting not only to those next to us but to each person in the congregation. For what happened was that the greeting was part of the procession into the church whereby the congregation formed two lines, with the person at the end of each line passing through the formed lines and greeting everybody in the line. Although it was quite a while before the last person got into the church, by that time we had all had a chance to touch, kiss, shake the hands, and look into the eyes of everyone else in the congregation.

I draw attention to this example not only because I do not know any other congregation that takes the practice of liturgical greeting as seriously, but also because this Kampung community is one of the most racially and ethnically diverse communities I have experienced. A simple survey confirmed that the congregation comprised Christians of Chinese, Malay, Indian as well as a host of *Orang Asli* (indigenous or tribal) backgrounds. Thus, the more I have had a chance to reflect on this experience, the more I have realized its profound theological relevance, and the rich resource that greeting provides for Christian ethics in the context of race.

Beyond Modern Anthropology

Ordinarily, greeting can be a good way to help people drop their guard and feel at home. Within the context of Christian worship, greeting accomplishes a similar goal. This was certainly the case at the mass at the Kampung. On a deeper level, however, what greeting does is to help Christians drop the guard of their modern self. This is so important if we are to begin to imagine ourselves and others beyond racial categories. For I suspect that one of the reasons why racism is such an intractable problem for us is that it reflects the story of the modern self, particularly the constant anxiety at the heart of the modern project. The anxiety has somehow to do with our desire to become both autonomous and our own self-makers. For, having repudiated any story beyond its own choosing, the modern self must now seek to justify not only its own existence, but also the certainty of its knowledge, as well as the worthiness of its undertakings and values. However, with self-interest as the one and perhaps only story to live for, self-justification becomes both tenacious and ever suspect.

This anxiety cannot but give rise to a distinctive politics of power as control, and an economics of exploitation of those different from us in the name of "self-interest" and "self-preservation." In fact, as McGrane (1989) puts it, it is this constant anxiety that gives rise to practices in which the meeting with the other is policed by theories of race, history, or culture – all of which are meant to assure the modern self's place at the center of history, as the climax of civilization, or as the "most advanced." It is perhaps not surprising that the result of this self-arming has been a history of colonialism, imperialism, and slavery. What this history reflects, however, is nothing but the endless thrust of the desire for control and conquest of the modern self, a self haunted by the need to justify its own existence and place in history. Racism is just one aspect of this story.

That is also why, unless this story of the modern self is questioned, ethical recommendations for racial reconciliation may unwittingly reproduce the same politics of anxiety. That is what makes an ethics of "tolerance" problematic. For it reproduces a problematic form of inclusion by which power and privilege are extended but not questioned. In this way, white privilege may be extended to black folks without, however, questioning the underlying politics and accounts of the self and of human flourishing that are responsible for giving rise to the problem of racism in the first place. What is required if such a politics is to be resisted is an altogether different story of the self, a different politics in which the self is "relieved," so to speak, of the need to provide the grounds for its own existence or to prove its importance. The relief can only come to the extent that the self is not at the center of life. Christian worship is precisely the performance of this different story, which draws the self into the wider story of God's creation and redemption.

In other words, if modern anthropology, in which the theories and practices of racism are at home, is an "arming" strategy, Christian worship is a "disarming" practice. That is what being greeted "In the name of the Father, and of the Son, and of the Holy Spirit . . ." does. For the greeting is an invitation to the Christian to "relax," as it were, in the knowledge that his or her life needs no other grounds for its justification since it has already been justified and the Christian is already part of that new creation that is made possible by "the love of God, the grace of the Son and the fellowship of the Holy Spirit." Becoming thus aware of, and learning to relax in, this good news, Christians can now be aware of other Christians – not as strangers competing for limited resources, but as fellow pilgrims, fellow citizens of this new creation.

The Performance of a Christian Anthropology

The greeting at the start of worship places the Christian at the very heart of a Christian anthropology, or, which is the same thing, the very heart of ecclesiology. For what the greeting announces is the fact that the Christian is part of a peculiar gathering, one that is based not in the self-interested accumulation of economic or political gains, but a gathering or assembly (ecclesia) of reconciled sinners, performed by the self-sacrificing love and forgiveness of God.

To put it differently, the story is not one of Christians gathering, but of *being* gathered, *being* assembled, of *being* greeted. The greeting at the start of worship announces the wonderful news that the Christian is the recipient and not the provider of this new dispensation. That Christians are greeted just goes to confirm that they are not the ones who initiate this story of grace, love, and forgiveness. In fact, the story is not about them. Rather, it is the story of what God has done and continues to do on their behalf. Not just them, but God's whole creation. In other words, this is a story whose existence and truth precedes us. That is why the greeting is at the same time a reminder of the story of "in the beginning" – a beginning that reflects God's superabundance and goodness. For this is what the very name of Trinity names – the superabundance of love, fellowship, and communication as it exists within the three persons of the Trinity. It is into this superabundance of creation and fellowship that the Christian is invited and drawn by the act of being greeted "in the name of the Father . . ."

Thus the greeting pronounces us as the gifts that we are. And, having received the good news of our being gifts, we can learn to see others similarly as gifts. Thus, having been greeted in the name of God the Father, God the Son and God the Holy Spirit, Christians can now greet one another in the same name. In this way, the greeting becomes a benediction, which is offered to the congregation, and which they, in turn, offer to one another. But it also becomes an invitation to mimic or model the same story of differences as embodied by God the Trinity. This does not mean that we can now dismiss as irrelevant all differences, but rather it is an invitation to learn to name our differences and particularities in the name of the Trinity. The act of greeting, whether it is by kissing or shaking the hands of the one next to us, is the way in which Christians make this conviction concrete.

Once the issue has been put in this way, then one realizes that, within the act of greeting, the range of Christian theology from creation to eschatology is being played out. In other words, being greeted and taking the time to greet one another in the name of God, the Christian is standing in between creation and eschatology; witnessing to the peaceful abundance and differences within God's creation, while at the same time anticipating the final display of the fullness of God's love, fellowship, and grace in the whole of creation at the end of time, when Christ will be all in all. In the meantime, Christians become part of this new creation, this new gathering or assembly; a new community of worship, not just one that performs this act of worship, but one for whom worship has become a way, *the* way of life.

A Christian Ethics

Greeting thus becomes a mode of being in the world in between times; it does not have ethical "implications," it *is* Christian ethics. And as ethics it announces and opens up a revolutionary future in which, as McCabe says (1969: 75), "we do not merely see something new, but we have a new way of seeing" God, the world, ourselves in it, and others. Similarly, as Christian ethics, worship does not simply encourage or facilitate racial reconciliation. Rather, it institutes a whole new social reality in which being "black" or "white" just makes no sense. That is why worship itself is the revolutionary future, a "wild space" in which a different story, a different performance is being played out and rendered visible in the world.

That is why it is significant that the greeting comes at the start of worship. In fact, one reason why I found the practice at the Malaysian Kampung so remarkable was that the greeting was the way, the only way, that anyone could get into the church, and thus to listen to the word of God and share the Eucharist. This in itself is highly significant since it confirms that greeting is the concrete embodiment of a key Christian claim; namely, that we cannot know God, we cannot even hear his word rightly let alone share his table, unless we have learnt to greet each other, including the stranger, with the sign of peace. In fact, within the context of greeting each other "in the name of the

Father . . . ," the very concept of "stranger" is being challenged and redefined from a radically Christian perspective.

Significant as it is, the rite of Christian greeting cannot be isolated from the full context of Christian worship and presented as an "ethic" for racial reconciliation. The fact that greeting is located at the beginning of worship simply goes to show how it is this concrete practice that initiates us, draws us into the full politics and economics of what it means to be a worshiping community. Anyone able to stand the greeting should be willing and ready to go all the way. In the particular case of the Malaysian Kampung, this was perhaps the reason why the worship did not end with the usual "dismissal," but with an invitation to "fellowship." What I found particularly remarkable about the fellowship, apart from the fact that everybody stayed, was the fact that all the cans of Coca-Cola that different people had brought with them were broken open and poured into one jug. It was from this one jug that the Coca-Cola was served using only one cup, which was passed on from one person to the next. As I thought about this practice, I found myself thinking that it would have been much easier, more time-efficient, and even more "hygienic" to hand each person a can of Coke (or invite people to take one) since there were more than enough to go around. Only gradually was I able to see in this "awkward" practice, a form of resistance to the individualism inherent in a market economy that, for instance, neatly packages Coca-Cola in cans and bottles that are so convenient for "individual" consumption.

This is what is meant by the claim that greeting is both an invitation and a concrete embodiment of what it means to go all the way. For through the act of greeting, the otherwise racially and ethnically diverse Kampung community found ways of moving beyond the dominant cultural identifications of being Malay, Indian, Chinese, Dayan, or Kadazan. At the same time, worship constituted a visible wild space, which allowed and encouraged resistance to other dominant stories, including resistance to the individualism of capitalistic consumption, even as they were already standing within the story of modern economics – thus drinking Coca-Cola.

But that the entire gamut of Christian theology and ethics should be embodied within such a gesture as greeting just confirms how God is not abstract, but as concrete as the handshakes, voices, hugs, and kisses of a people who greet each other "in the name of the Father . . ." And so, abstracted from such concrete practices, "God" remains just an idea, a hypothesis, to be believed or contested.

Beyond Docetism: On "Touching Color"

We can highlight the point above by noting how Christian worship, the act of greeting in particular, provides Christians with an opportunity to be present to one another in ways that challenge the docetism that may very easily be masked by theologies of "racial reconciliation." Early Christian docetism was an attempt to downplay the significance of Jesus's bodily incarnation. Because the docetists felt that attributing full bodily incarnation to Christ would limit the claims to Jesus's divinity and attributes, they taught that Jesus's bodily incarnation was just an appearance, which Christ had to assume in order to effect for us his saving operations.

Jennings (1997) is right to note that there is an unrelenting docetism that haunts the way in which Christians in the West deal with race, culture, and the problem of racism. For though racism is, in great part, an imagination involving bodies, the danger now is to claim an easy and quick "racial harmony" – one, however, that avoids the need to confront, touch, feel, and relate to bodies that are different from us. Thus, the temptation, as Jennings reminds us, is to claim: "I do not see anyone as black or white, just my sister or brother in Christ. There is no such thing as race. We are all one in Christ." Or we say, "we just need to learn how to forgive, respect and live together and go on to the future." Or we say, "where I was raised there were no black people. Therefore, race was and is not an issue for me" (Jennings, 1997: 47)

Such claims, however, are so often a reflection of our desire to see racial harmony without facing the need for the transformation of our usual forms of social existence and community. Moreover, the claim to color blindness may be, as Mary McClintock Fulkerson (2001: 140) suggests, just another strategy of condescension associated with liberal claims to tolerance whereby the one who is "tolerant" can still position the other in his or her sphere of influence. In this way, claims to color blindness are just a way of avoiding face-to-face bodied relation in situations of reciprocity. Without such bodied interaction, however, Christians cannot fully appreciate what it means to be the Body of Christ. That is why the practice of greeting within Christian worship is a good place to begin if we are to recover the significance of the body for Christian salvation.

This is another reason why I found the practice at the Kampung very significant, in that the greeting was so much about the body. It involved movement, touch, hugs, kisses, and handshakes. There was therefore just no way one could avoid touching and relating to other bodies. In so doing, however, a key conviction of Christian life was being played out – namely that the body matters for Christian salvation since as Christians we believe that we are saved in and through the body, our own bodies, but ultimately the Body of Christ. Such concrete bodily interaction is therefore a good way to learn what it means to be that very Body of Christ – the one Body of Christ which is made up of different members (bodies). And so, in the very act of Christian greeting, in kissing or touching other bodies, including those that look very different from one's own, one is being introduced to the very mystery of the Body of Christ.

Which means that, in our modern time-conscious world, in which greeting is often nothing more than a disinterested "hi," the challenge is, at the same time, one of recovering an embodied account and practice of greeting like the one at the Malaysian Kampung. What is, however, even more important is the need to recover Christian discipleship as a practical way of life at the margins of the dominant cultures of our day. For I suspect that the fact that the Christian community in Malaysia had learnt to take worship so seriously has to do with the unique situation of their being a minority in a predominantly Muslim country. Finding themselves in a marginal (8 percent of the population) and often marginalized position, Christians in Malaysia may have no choice but to turn to their tradition and practices for resources with which to lead meaningful lives at the margins of the dominant culture.

That is why the specific challenge facing Christians in the West, as well as in other cultures where Christianity is the dominant religion, has to do with the recovery of worship as a "wild space" that can foster an alternative imagination to the one of the dominant culture. This challenge is particularly urgent in the West given the fact that, as already noted, worship here tends to reflect and reinforce the same neat, racialized interaction as the dominant culture. In this respect, Martin Luther King Jr's comment that 11 o'clock is the most segregated hour in America is not only a true sociological observation, but it is also a deeply disturbing theological assessment of a Church that has long given up on the challenge to embody an alternative imagination. What makes King Jr's observation more disturbing is the realization that it is true not just of the Church in the West. For, whereas the case of racism that we have been examining makes this obvious in relation to America, Martin Luther King Jr's observation reflects a more global phenomenon of a Christianity that has become comfortable – too much at home – within the dominant cultures of our time.

In Africa, for instance, similar versions of a cultural Christianity are so easily reproduced through an uncritical quest for inculturation. The effect is that here, too, instead of providing an opportunity for re-imagining African identities and societies from a Christian perspective, Christian worship tends to reflect and reproduce the same ethnic or tribal divisions within African society. This is also what leads us to suspect any attempts to encourage racially or ethnically homogeneous congregations even when their existence is justified in terms of a need or appreciation of cultural diversity or authenticity. For if what we have said about worship and greeting is true, there seems to be no greater challenge relating to our invitation to be the Body of Christ than to resist these new forms of segregation, which might easily ride on a postmodern celebration of culture. Such fascination with "difference" and "culture" might just be another way to assume a kind of superficial "racial diversity," one, however, that avoids the need to resist the dominant forms of our social and cultural existence.

Conclusion

Here, by way of conclusion, I can only recount my own experience of the transformation that worship makes possible, which brings me to where I began my story. For, during the years I lived in Europe, I was lucky to belong to the St Mary and St Martha English-speaking parish of the university. It was through worship with and in this multicultural, multiracial congregation that I not only got a chance to meet people from all parts of the world, but also to recover somewhat the sort of pre-1991 racial innocence which I had longed for so much. Through our weekly worship and the concrete greeting and interaction this provided, I was able to become part of a community for whom being black or white had ceased to be an interesting identity. Not only did this allow a certain relaxation and lack of pretentiousness in our worship, it opened up possibilities for friendship based on what we discovered to be more interesting stories of our lives.

This was the very same "relief" that had helped me to survive the summer of 1991, when I first discovered that I was black. For, even as I discovered my race, I was lucky to be part of the community of St Mary's parish. The opportunity to worship in and together with the "white" congregation of St Mary's again proved to be one of the transforming spaces for both me and my "white" congregation. I remember, for instance, an elderly man who tearfully later confessed to me that I was the first black person whose hand he had shaken. Another man whispered to me at the end of mass how he had at first been reluctant to receive communion from the hands of a black person. The most telling case, however, was that of Dorothy, a woman in her late eighties whom I had seen regularly and greeted at Saturday five o'clock mass. When I learnt that she had been taken to a nursing home, I went to visit her. She was very happy to see me, and excitedly called on her roommate: "Come and say hello to Fr Emmanuel," she said. "Fr Emmanuel is not a Negro. He is a priest!"

If, through the greeting we receive and offer within Christian worship, we can, like Dorothy, begin to see each other not as strangers in competition for limited resources, but as gifts of a gracious God, then we will already have discovered ourselves within a new imagination, on the road to a new and revolutionary future, which worship both signals and embodies. Part of this new future consists in discovering that there are more determinative, and far more interesting, stories that we can tell about ourselves and about others than just being "white" or "black."

References

Arendt, Hannah (1951) *The Origins of Totalitarianism* (New York: Harcourt, Brace).

Cone, James H. (1975) *The God of the Oppressed* (New York: Seabury).

Fulkerson, Mary McClintock (2001) " 'We Do Not See Color Here': A Case Study in Ecclesial Cultural Invention," in *Converging on Culture: Theologians in Dialogue with Cultural Analysis and Criticism*, ed. Delwin Brown, Sheila Greeve Daveney, and Kathryn Tanner, pp. 140–58 (Oxford: University Press).

Hauerwas, Stanley and Willimon, Will (1989) *Resident Aliens: Life in the Christian Colony* (Nashville, TN: Abingdon).

Jennings, Willie (1997) "Wandering in the Wilderness: Christian Identity and Theology," in *The Gospel in Black and White*, ed. Dennis L. Okholm, pp. 37–48 (Downers Grove, IL: Intervarsity).

Katongole, Emmanuel (2002) *Beyond Universal Reason: The Relation between Religion and Ethics in the Work of Stanley Hauerwas* (Notre Dame, IN: University of Notre Dame Press).

Keener, S. Craig (1997) "The Gospel and Racial Reconciliation," in *The Gospel in Black and White*, ed. Dennis L. Okholm, pp. 117–30 (Downers Grove, IL: Intervarsity).

McCabe, Herbert (1969) *What is Ethics All About?* (Washington: Corpus).

McFague, Sallie (2001) *Life Abundant: Rethinking Theology and Economy for a Planet in Peril* (Minneapolis, MN: Fortress).

McGrane, Bernard (1989) *Beyond Anthropology* (New York: Columbia University Press).

Mudimbe, Valery (1988) *The Invention of Africa* (Bloomington, IN: Indiana University Press).

West, Cornel (1993) *Race Matters* (New York: Vintage).

CHAPTER 7

Naming the Risen Lord: Embodied Discipleship and Masculinity

Amy Laura Hall

Greeting

Our Sunday mornings begin with a series of Sabbath practices that are worn like ruts in the hallways. We all usually wake late, having disrupted our daughters' bedtime routine the night before. Hearing Emily shriek on the monitor, we nudge one another, playing a parental game of chicken. Someone loses and stumbles wearily to pick up Emily, who is, blessedly, almost always happy in the morning. The slow one out of bed responds as Rachel calls out her all-purpose "Mommy, Mommeeeeeey!" It is then back to the big bed, where I nurse Emily, while Rachel builds a cave with pillows and blankets. John walks the dogs while listening to the People's Pharmacy (the dregs of public radio, but the path to NPR is extremely well worn). We all somehow make it to the table for breakfast, and we spend too long there, thinking every week "Hey, this is the Sabbath, we should not rush." But then one of us reminds the other that we will have miffed parents checking their watches in the foyer if we do not make it to our classrooms by Sunday School hour. So comes the mad dash, hurrying both girls into half-ironed clothes that will (hopefully) not make the older members gasp in horror, slipping on shoes and tie and hair bow, checking the bag for diapers and Cheerios and sippy cups, and running (literally, and often clumsily) to the car. The routine culminates in the dreaded Drive to Church. We spend the next eight minutes in a tetchy argument to determine who is to blame for the fact that we are *always* late for church.

The grace of the Lord Jesus Christ be with you.

The cruciform grace of God is with us, in the form of the risen Christ. He is there, in our midst, through the power of the Holy Spirit, infusing us with faith, hope, and love, in spite of ourselves.

We enter this place from households that still smell of the morning's burned waffle, from dormitory rooms that reek of last night's pizza and yesterday's quarrel, from apartments where the scent of a missing father's aftershave still lingers like a phantom limb. Entering the door, taking our seats or kneeling heavily, we smell the candles, the incense, the heated wood of pew and cross, and we know the Lord is risen, the Lord is risen indeed. The gathered people of God sing an opening song of praise, interspersed with the coughing of a kindergartener in the third row who is getting over the flu. Heads turn as the acolyte bears the cross forward, the same acolyte who, just fifteen minutes ago, disrupted class with her baseball cards. The scents and sights mingle, and God's grace is intertwined with our particular sickness and sin. Doubting Thomas would be convinced: this Body of Christ bears the marks.

The risen Christ is with us. Praise the Lord!

The household of God and the households from which we enter it are sites marked with embodied vice, error, and mere annoyance, with suffering, illness, and simple eccentricity, and with complicated grace. When we greet one another in the name of the risen, incarnate Lord, we become privy to the otherwise avoided intricacies of friends, families, and church. The untidy and tedious tasks of discipleship in these settings of holiness involve receptivity, patience, and a vulnerability to grace. While during the week we may scurry to cubicle or office, turn on the tube to avoid conversation with our kids or spouse, and sit always on the *back* porch to eschew our neighbors, when we enter the doors of our church we become part of one messy, holy, body. The form of our worship thus takes on the form of Christ's work. The Lord and Savior who greets us at the door of his house took the form of a servant, washing dirty feet, touching the ulcerated sores of a blind man, and weeping with a grieving sister. He did not travel from town to town dispensing disembodied wisdom but brought wisdom into the otherwise hidden crevices of people's lives. If Christians greet one another in his name, we are both exposed to such grace and called to encounter the exposure of others.

Perhaps one may interpret the words with which Christians meet in worship through Christ's first greeting to his disciples: "Follow me, and I will make you fish for people." Seeing Peter, Andrew, James, and John depicted in long robes with eyes heavenward may obscure this point, but Jesus invites them to move from one fairly predictable and respectable line of work to another erratic and odd one. Once one has caught a fish in the net, brought it on board, and taken it to shore, that fish is quite definitely caught. How does one know when a person is truly caught? One can fashion a net sufficient for the task of catching fish, but, as Jesus shows, catching people requires nimble adaptation, attention to the particular story of the person to be caught, and the capacity to read just which hook will do the trick. Even then, one can hardly haul her to shore, add her to the pile, and count her later. If sufficiently caught, she will instead follow you around, ask probing questions, beg you to come and lay hands upon her dying daughter, and pull you toward others who need catching. Finally, a fisherman who intentionally searches for half-rotten or runty fish is not much of a fisherman.

Jesus does just this, calling his disciples, and us, to become very strange fishermen. Christians greet one another in the name of such service.

Gender

This discipleship calls for a peculiar kind of courage, one not akin to wielding swords and fighting grand battles that result in death or definitive triumph. In most settings applicable to the readers of this volume, the courage toward which the greeting calls is less about heroics and more about patient hope. If one honestly describes the bare bones of daily discipleship, they most often involve abiding another parishioner's strange interpretation of a favorite passage, mowing the parsonage's overgrown lawn, stumbling in at 2 a.m. to hear the obscure details of a child's diagnosis, folding bulletins and sharpening pew pencils, changing the diaper of an aging or newly baptized member, stirring stew for the homeless, painting the third grade Sunday School room, or writing tomorrow's gospel message for a parish from whom you are estranged.

As Lillian Daniel, a pastor and cherished colleague, puts it, the greeting is a sort of wake-up call, abruptly summoning us to become alert to the practices of worship and discipleship. It should come as little surprise that many of my generation and social class have chosen instead to check out, sleep in, read the *Times*, and breath the scents at Starbucks, or that, if we do cross the threshold of God's house, we expect to be greeted with something less intrusive than the risen Christ. If the Church is a site where each one of us becomes – quite disconcertingly – part of an interdependent mass that reveals the risen Christ, fewer and fewer men and women are ready for the intimacy and intrusion involved. To be frank, many of my generation and social class in the US hardly have the time or the inclination to endure the work that sustained earlier generations of holy communities. There is little time or energy left in the day to change the oil (hence Jiffy Lube), throw the football (hence the sports channel), or grill a steak (hence your local Gristle-Sizzle). Tending to the chronically ill, visiting the incarcerated, and stitching garments for those shivering on street corners is quite simply out of the question. Who has time to see Jesus?

While this evasion of discipleship may be particular to class and locale, it is, within that class and locale, less and less particular to gender. While the generic mainline men's group has been anemic for some time, with many chapters typically hosting a pathetically symbolic pancake breakfast once a year, up until fairly recently one could rely at least on the good old United Methodist Women, or a similar group of dedicated mainline ladies, to maintain the practices of incarnate discipleship. But no more. The stalwart ranks of such faithful are thinning (as are the ranks of sisterly orders in the Roman Catholic Church), because women have better things to do. Although upper-class women have long avoided the "women's work" relegated to their gender, middle-class women are now increasingly expected to forgo, or they jettison by their own choosing, the work of feeding, clothing, nursing, and otherwise tending real bodies. As women have entered the workforce in earnest, the middle and upper-middle classes in the one-third world have hardly redistributed these tasks. Rather than men joining women in the servant ministry of mopping floors, washing dusty feet and touching broken bodies, women who are economically capable of doing so are joining men in the avoidance of this work. Men and women are all alike, disembodied and self-deceptively self-sufficient, in the new economy. There is, increasingly, neither male nor female, or at least many in the "developed" West are seeking in this vein. Christians thus face in the US and Western Europe a push towards a novel type of gender symmetry or equality, led in part by a middle-class job market that demands more hours behind a desk and fewer in the actual care of real homes, churches, and dependent bodies.

Such self-sufficiency is a lie against which Christians must testify. The middle and upper classes are hardly self-sufficient; rather, they are dependent upon an underclass that cares for other people's children, runs the cash registers, and serves the burgers. To broaden the circle of inquiry, the goods served to the disembodied classes by these underpaid employees are packaged, glued, and stitched together by even lower paid workers in the two-thirds world (see Ehrenreich, 2001). Economically vulnerable workers here and abroad are now the "women" of late-capitalist culture, doing the undervalued work to which no one wants to stoop. While many homes are cleaned by the "Merry Maids," and too many offices are serviced by meagerly paid workers employed by the (purportedly Christian, union-busting, and outrageously named) "Service Master," the liturgical greeting calls, and calls for mainline Christians to wake up. Inasmuch as Christians accept these patterns as given, we are not testifying to an incarnate Word, a Word that calls us to resist patterns of economically coerced servitude and to encourage embodied Christian service. In my own experience, many mainline churches are sorely tempted not only to accept these patterns and eschew discipleship, but to mimic our culture's expectations – to hire inexpensive caterers to replace the covered-dish supper, foreign nannies to soothe the babies in our crèche, and low-wage orderlies to spoon food into the mouths of the Church's patriarchs and matriarchs. Mumbling something about "gifts," about who is best suited to such service, some Christians attempt to robe this parasitic economy in theological garments.

In sum, the present manifestation of capitalism in the West strongly encourages those with sufficient funds to avoid precisely the patterns of embodied care on which our discipleship depends. If Christians are to live in the greeting with which we remember one another – "The risen Christ is with us!" – we must resist the gnosticism inherent in such cultural patterns. Churches and Christian households are not and should not be sites of seamless beauty and efficiency, wherein we hire out the messy work to hidden, menial workers. Witnessing to the truly risen Christ involves the complicated marks of frailty and sin. It involves building and baking and teaching and healing and feeding, and all the other untidy, loving works by which Christians are to be known.

I should here make explicit a contested, but working, assumption: such practices of incarnate discipleship are not essentially feminine, even though they have often been culturally constructed as such (cf. Butler, 1999; Ward, 1999; Coakley, 2002). Those who assume that gender is largely constructed (and often constructed in the service of men) can take that assumption toward various ends. Some constructivist feminists aim toward the liberation of women from the bonds of interdependence and service. I wish to suggest otherwise: the assumption that gender is largely constructed can, alternatively, serve anew to call Christian men to the embodiment of service out of which much of Western culture pulls them. I wish thereby to challenge a well-meaning, but subtly evasive hagiography of "the feminine" as "essential" to Christian community. Recent retrievals of previously neglected female saints in the communion have been a blessing, but such retrievals have, at times, aided and abetted a convenient romanticization of the inherently self-giving female body. This need not be the case. To put the point rather bluntly, I find it no more defensible for Christian men to follow Julian of Norwich, Simone Weil, or Dorothy Day from a safely gendered distance than it is for them to follow Jesus at such (see Bauerschmidt, 1999, on an unmistakable call to the messy proximity of embodied discipleship). The deconstruction of gender can serve to renew a longstanding Christian tradition of communities – whether all male, all female, or mixed – who worshiped, studied, and wrote while also feeding children left at the doorstep and tending the sick who had nowhere to go.

A focus-on-the-family retrieval of the feminine mystique is thus a problematic way to address this neglect of embodiment. One can almost hear the call: Where are the United Methodist Women when you need them? What happened to the good old days when women stayed home and also stayed late at church to clean up after the covered-dish supper? But the suggestion that those with breasts are best suited to perform the small and crucial tasks of Christian discipleship is too convenient to be trustworthy. For too long, men who write and preach have stood back and assessed: "Yes, indeed, women are simply better suited than men to the task of [insert practice of embodied discipleship]." This call is as impractical as it is dubious. The few women who presently have sufficient power (whether worldly or ecclesial) to encourage a retrieval of embodied care have often procured their status by becoming adroitly habituated into the patterns that necessitate the changes. I thus submit that the impetus for the complicated tasks of incarnate grace should come from men. This will require a redefinition of masculinity according to popular (and even churchly) standards, and a different kind of moral courage.

Masculinity

The diagnosis that follows is thus not about original sin, grace, and gender in general but about one particular manifestation of the Fall that besets my own North American culture: destructive norms of masculinity. This is a risky endeavor for at least two reasons. First, I am not male. I am not fully privy to the constructed assumptions of manhood in the twentieth century. Yet I attempt this analysis of gender and grace drawing on ten years of pastoral and pedagogical experience with boys and men, and with the girls and women who attempt to love and/or emulate them. In talking about "the facts of life" to twelve-year-old boys and listening to the stories a retired army officer, now in the nursing home, tells of his son, I hope to have gathered some wisdom about the struggles of Christian manhood within at least one slice of the Church in North America. And, after counseling a college freshman who has decided never to have children so that she can succeed as a computer programmer, I have learned that mainline feminism has not yet altered the norm of unencumbered, individual success. The second risk is the necessarily limited scope of my analysis; I will draw on culturally particular constructions of masculinity. Consider this my attempt to make visible the otherwise assumed center of North American manhood (see hooks, 2000). While I very much hope that these observations will be useful to the readers of this volume, I do not expect them to be universally applicable. There are nuances even to dominant Western culture that I will miss, and I cannot even begin to speak of "masculinity" as some sort of Platonic form that floats from land to land. So be it.

Untangling the threads that lead to dominant images of power and manhood in English-speaking culture is complicated. But at least one strand leading into the knot emerges from post-World War II popular mythology. From Superman (on US television from 1952 to 1957) to Tolkien's Aragorn (1954–7) to Gary Cooper's Will Kane (1952), there ran during this period an account of masculine maturity that was not conducive to the complicated flourishing of Christian community. These narratives, forged after a seemingly clear battle of good versus evil, may be aesthetically satisfying, but they do not easily fit the daily work to which Christians were called then, or now. Whether fighting alongside elf and dwarf or flying above the fray, the heroes of North American culture continue to face grand conflicts – saving the world, saving Middle Earth, or saving Hadleyville – rather than the relatively boring details of daily discipleship. While I will admit to loving *High Noon* (*the* greatest Western ever made), it ill prepares one for enduring and cherishing the tedium of life in God's household or my own. There may be men out there who, after imbibing such normative accounts of manhood, have found themselves newly called to live in community with Latino immigrants at a Catholic Worker house, to protest against nuclear weaponry every week at the Savannah River Plant, to teach autistic children (or even their own "normal" but normally difficult children), or to pastor a small rural parish, but sustained engagement in such work requires gifts quite different from the ones writ large and exciting on the big screen.

In her book *Stiffed: The Betrayal of the American Man* (1999), Susan Faludi suggests that, as the United States in particular shifted, in the second half of the twentieth century, from an industrial economy to one of information and service, conceptions of masculinity became increasingly a matter of Hollywood fantasy. Upon their return from fighting for freedom against evil incarnate, World War II veterans found themselves stuck with the task of forging a new life in the suburbs. Their sons and grandsons, Faludi argues, have tried repeatedly to retread their struggle – to achieve the perceived victory in film and then to re-narrate masculinity in North America to fit the image on screen. Interviewing men from the Citadel, West Coast shipyards, and the Cleveland Browns Municipal Stadium, to name only a few locations, Faludi reads one major problem facing men in the US at present to be the entertainment industry, which emerges to perpetuate the myth of victorious masculinity.

Faludi begins her book at the closing of a shipyard, and the myth of effective, physically courageous masculinity begins to deteriorate precisely with such closings. While industrial capitalism allowed some men to continue working toward big projects with large results, the post-industrial economy leaves men bereft of even an illusory glory approximating that of the "Great Generation." Seeing themselves interpreted through the see-and-be-seen culture of entertainment and service capitalism, men now have little to do besides watch and pose. Passing through the tragic bloodshed of Vietnam,

the image of the moral warrior became increasingly problematic, and a new generation of men sought instead to negotiate the shallowly "rebellious" images of glamor
culture. Following Faludi's trajectory, I suggest that late twentieth-century masculinity split in two on or about 1982, when gorgeous, snarling, British boy band Duran
Duran released an early music video wearing make-up and shaking their posteriors in
leather pants ("Girls on Film," no less) while Sylvester Stallone, in *Rambo: First Blood*,
played a wandering Vietnam vet who wages war after being jailed and humiliated for
vagrancy.

Today, both ostentatious beauty and forceful valor exist in an uneasy mix that is
apparent in both film and print media. *Men's Journal* offers go-to-the-office dads the
chance to imagine themselves climbing large mountains with thick, wavy hair and
pouting lips. They are tempted to purchase vehicles designed originally for combat
alongside sexy leather jackets originally worn by their fighter-pilot grandfathers. More
upscale magazines are merely more subtle, as readers of *The Atlantic Monthly* are
encouraged to join the History Book Club so that they may escape their currently inconsequential lives with the narratives of men who truly made what most count as
"history."

All of these images glitter with blood and make-up in the blockbuster Tolkien trilogy,
as absolutely fabulous men battle evil hordes quite literally forged in the fires of hell,
while wearing costumes to die for. Although any reader worth his salt knows that the
heartbeat of Tolkien's *Lord of the Rings* is the rhythm of hope, friendship, and emerging greed among the Hobbits and the fallen Hobbit Gollum, the young male viewers
with whom I saw the movie version were hardly interested in this part of the tale. Every
time a new sword emerged, there was a collective sigh and cheer, "YES!" (Freud would
have had a field day). Longing for a battle more clearly cut and well won than that
which Frodo and Sam must fight, it is easy to miss their patch of grass for the (rather
large) trees (and I don't mean the Ents). As Ralph Wood (2003) so perceptively
observes, the film writes large and long the battle at Helm's Deep, while diminishing or
ignoring all together Tolkien's narration of mercy. The tale thus becomes a newly effective march for a nation eager to fight a virile battle against evil itself. As North American viewers move with another son intent on recapturing his father's past glory, the
pacific undercurrent of the story is hardly noticeable. But there, in Frodo's struggle to
trust or suspect ambiguously fragile and treacherous Gollum, is something more akin
to the real tasks to which men in North America are most often called.

About a Man

> The thing was, Will had spent his whole life avoiding real stuff. He was, after all, the son
> and heir of the man who wrote *Santa's Super Sleigh*. Santa Claus, whose existence most
> adults had real cause to doubt, bought him everything he wore and ate and drank and sat
> on and lived in; it could reasonably be argued that reality was not in his genes. He liked
> watching real stuff on *EastEnders* and *The Bill*, and he liked listening to Joe Strummer and
> Curtis Mayfield and Kurt Cobain singing about real stuff, but he'd never had real stuff
> sitting on his sofa before. No wonder, then, that once he'd made it a cup of tea and offered
> it a biscuit he didn't really know what to do with it. (Hornby, 1999: 117)

Written by Nick Hornby, a novelist with an uncanny eye for the predicament of post-industrial manhood, *About a Boy* came out in film the same year as *The Fellowship of the Ring*. This modern-day confession of a self-avowed sinner writes large the predicament of vicarious masculinity – of manhood defined by images that are wholly without the routines of truly interdependent life – and it subtly describes the vulnerable fragility of life with a real person on your sofa. I suggest that this merely human hero is an apt one for the next generation of Christian men, who are encouraged either to live vicariously off the heroics of big men with big swords or to survive on the songs of angst-ridden rebels like Cobain, who simply can't endure the burden of mere existence. Wandering around in the service/entertainment economy, seeking aimlessly for a True Quest to die for, many men may miss the challenging work under their very noses. Nick Hornby's novel is a trenchant pointer toward the holy and humble households with which we began, suggesting what it might take for more men to take up the call to holy tedium.

We are first introduced briefly to Marcus, a twelve-year-old boy, eating boxed pizza and watching the nature channel with his mum, Fiona, in the uneasy but familiar aftermath of her break-up with a recent boyfriend. Then, in chapter 2, we shift sharply to Will Freeman: "How cool was Will Freeman?" Terribly cool, "dry ice," according to the men's magazine quiz. Owing to his very cool outerwear, record collection, and deftly casual drug use, our hero is "with the cool and powerful." This is a good thing, for "that was the point of fashion [to be] against the alienated and the weak, just where Will wanted to be" (Hornby, 1999: 141). Hornby's character is not-so-subtly the epitome of Faludi's entertainment era man, living off the royalties of his father's one-hit silly song, which plays incessantly two months a year in the malls and grocery stores of London. Will has posters of real men on his wall – "That's Charlie Parker, and that's Chet Baker. And they're on my wall because I like their music and they're cool" – kitchen gadgets that could do real tasks, but don't, and an infinite capacity for avoiding the work that stains said gadgets and said life. Drifting from mall to mall, watching the telly, spending his hours and days consuming and dreaming and avoiding, Will is the quintessence of cool – decidedly *not* aligned with the pathetic losers who open the book.

But Will has two nagging questions that will not allow him complete respite within the chic-leather cocoon he has created for himself, and these questions propel his story: how to secure sex that is safe from real engagement, and how to tell women with whom he would like to have frequent sex that he really doesn't, well, do anything. In an early conversation with an attractive single mum, Will suggests obliquely that he might be a good "at it." "Good at what?" she asks, "Right. Good at what? What was he good at? This was the million-dollar question, the one he had never been able to answer about anything" (1999: 21). Having too much time on his hands, having *every single moment* quite literally on his hands, Will has not done much. He has tried out various things, in theory: "after a fit of remorse following a weekend of extreme self-indulgence, [Will had] volunteered to work in a soup kitchen, and even though he never actually reported for duty, the phone call had allowed him to pretend, for a couple of days, that he was the kind of guy who might" (1999: 36).

A fortuitous exchange with a single mum gives him a new *raison d'être*. He can kill two birds with one stone, have his cake and eat it too, by pretending to be good at kids. This might give him a leg up, so to speak. After all, most men "didn't like the kind of mess that frequently coiled around these kids like a whirlwind" (1999: 24), and to tolerate them seems a small price to pay for frequent sex.

After a reasonably satisfying tryst with this first mum, he decides to try his hand again by attending a meeting of SPAT (Single Parents Alone Together), incognito as a single father. Intending to breeze in and hope for the best, Will quickly finds himself in over his head. Hornby intersperses chapters told from Will's perspective with chapters on Marcus's life with Fiona, who is teetering on the verge of suicide, and, through no choice of his own, Will finds himself stuck in the wrong chapter. At the hospital with Fiona and Marcus after she attempts suicide, Will adroitly dodges the grit of the ensuing scene by imagining himself to be both watching and interacting with the characters on some reality-TV show. Taking on his now well-honed persona of someone who *might* care, internally he is clear: "Will didn't know if he was part of the 'we' or not, but it didn't matter one way or the other. However absorbing he was finding the evening's entertainment, he certainly didn't intend repeating it: this lot were just too weird" (1999: 69). In this rich section, Hornby makes strong use of the contrast between Marcus's agonized disorientation and Will's detached resolution. When Marcus wonders whether the hospital workers will confuse Fiona with one of the usual suspects who appear with regularity in an emergency room, Will scoffs.

> For once, Will thought, Marcus was asking the wrong question. The right question was: What the hell difference did it make? Because if the only things that separated Fiona from the rest of them were Suzie's reassuring car keys and Will's expensive casual clothes, then she was in trouble anyway. You had to live in your own bubble. You couldn't force your way into someone else's, because then it wouldn't be a bubble any more . . . if Fiona couldn't afford these things, and didn't have an equivalent bubble of her own, then that was her lookout. (1999: 70)

However, to continue this metaphor, his bubble bumps repeatedly into theirs. Overestimating his capacity to retreat, underestimating the glimmer of decency somewhere deep under the surface of ironic distance, Will becomes increasingly enmeshed in Marcus's life.

Hornby delicately reveals the odd combination of insouciance and expectancy that draws Will into the mess of this story. These are traces not so much of virtue, but of unexpected grace in the narrative, and one begins to cheer for Will in spite of himself. As Will casually tries on various identities, Hornby seems almost to be suggesting in Will an opportunity, an opportunity for a kind of heroism that travels well below the radar of "effective" masculinity. The reader cannot help but think of Edmund, that redeemed scoundrel of C. S. Lewis's Narnia series, when Will remembers a story from his childhood to explain his penchant for hopeful mendacity:

> He always felt something would turn up, even though nothing ever did, or even could, most of the time. Once, years ago, when he was a kid, he told a school friend (having first ascertained that this friend was not a C. S. Lewis fan) that it was possible to walk through the back of his wardrobe into a different world, and invited him round to explore. He could have cancelled, he could have told him anything, but he was not prepared to suffer a moment's mild embarrassment if there was no immediate need to do so, and the two of

them scrabbled around among the coathangers for several minutes until Will mumbled something about the world being closed on Saturday afternoons . . . [B]ut he hadn't learnt a thing from the experience: if anything, it seemed to have left him with the feeling that he was bound to be lucky next time. (1999: 51)

Against all sense, Will expects that a small son will suddenly materialize and make real his charade as a legitimate member of SPAT. He cannot make it so, he cannot even perceive that such an appearance would overwhelm his defenses, and the gift he receives, from beyond the wardrobe, is hardly what he would have chosen.

Or is it? For a while, Will tries on the idea of making this twelve-year-old and his mum his own little project. Given his inheritance, he has no need to build anything or dig anything or paint anything, so perhaps he can make them his work. He begins to "entertain strange and probably unhealthy notions of entering their lives in some way" (1999: 82) and maintains "this sense that Fiona and Marcus could replace soup kitchens . . . possibly forever . . . [T]he occasional swordfish steak, the odd visit to a crappy film that he might have gone to anyway. How hard could that be?" (1999: 99). For a brief time, Will coasts on a "natural high!" – "He couldn't recall having felt like this before, so at peace with himself, so convinced of his own self-worth"(1999: 126) – but the intrusion of reality continues. Will and Marcus's daily ritual of watching contrived gameshows on the telly is contaminated with Marcus's real fears over his mother's real illness and the actual terror he faces daily at school. Hornby narrates the clash between artifice and incarnation as our hero becomes increasingly uneasy about the meshing of his life with this boy's. Hardly fitted for much beyond a heartfelt "that sucks," Will repeatedly tries to pull out of the whole thing:

When [he] had conceived this fantasy and joined SPAT, he had imagined sweet little children, not children who would be able to track him down and come to his house. He had imagined entering their world, but he hadn't foreseen that they might be able to penetrate his. He was one of life's visitors; he didn't want to be visited. (1999: 105)

What started as a healthy desire for sex quickly throws Will flat on his back, and he scrambles to get back on top. He learns that there are no truly random acts of kindness, that real interaction involves penetration, and he wants out: "He'd made a big mistake thinking that good works were a way forward for him. They weren't. They drove you mad. Fiona did good works and they had driven her mad: she was vulnerable, messed-up, inadequate" (1999: 102). Yet even while struggling to maintain his "depression free life," Will is unexpectedly redeemed. Although his "first instinct was to turn the volume on the TV up and ignore it all . . . in the end some sense of self-respect drove the cowardice away," and he answers the door, day after day, to allow Marcus into his life. He is stuck, now part of a larger mess that he cannot avoid, even while turning up his stereo and watching the Three Stooges.

Through Will's clumsy attempts truly to fall in love and Marcus's struggle to find a friend, any friend, while attending his hostile secondary school, Hornby makes clear that this book is a description of growing up, and of the *risk* necessary for a boy to become a man. Will must be a real man, a father for a boy who will eventually also become such, and the requisite virtue is courage defined differently from what one usually finds in print. Realizing that, ironically, "his own experience of growing up with a batty parent" gives him precisely the capacity "to guide the boy through to a place of safety," Will becomes a third person to Marcus and Fiona's fragile two (1999: 141). The masculine maturity forged in the story is thus not about becoming fully functional, but instead is about recognizing that even a dysfunctional slacker can be an adequate member of a pyramid that holds up kids like Marcus. This, we have learned, is Marcus's (perceptive) goal, to ensure that "if someone dropped off the edge, you weren't left on your own" (1999: 75). "It's like those acrobatic displays," Marcus explains at the close of the book, "those ones when you stand on top of loads of people in a pyramid. It doesn't really matter who they are . . . as long as they're there and you don't let them go away without finding someone else" (1999: 299).

Having learned that "sometimes good news came in unpromising shapes and sizes," Will receives this very strange new world of reality, "caught up in this sort of messy, sprawling, chaotic web . . . it was almost as if he had been given a glimpse of what it was like to be human" (1999: 292). In the last pages, Hornby makes this point beautifully, that Will's transformation is decidedly not about becoming a "real man" as usually defined:

> He felt as if he were a chick whose egg had been cracked open, and he was outside in the world shivering and unsteady on his feet (if chicks were unsteady on their feet – maybe that was foals, or calves, or some other animal), without so much as a Paul Smith suit or a pair of RayBans to protect him. (1999: 301)

Will's shaky redemption and Marcus's acrobatic salvation are not about grand tasks taken on by sturdy, determined men. Our hero falls into this work somewhat by accident, somewhat through a wacky hope that there should be something worthwhile for him to do. And the doing, oddly enough, is less about solidity and more about allowing his life to become permeable. Will becomes a man inasmuch as he becomes vulnerably receptive to the lives of others: "people who could not control themselves, or protect themselves, people who, if only temporarily, were no longer content to occupy their own space" (1999: 191). And, by the way, he gets the girl, an artistic woman named Rachel, who also has a difficult son. But, like Jacob, Will does not win Rachel until he first proves his love – in this case for Marcus and Fiona.

Hornby offers a different prescription from a hearty reclamation of the glory days when men were men and women were women. His is a vision of hope that emerges precisely out of the rubble of the "good old days" when men built ships of war and fought battles to secure freedom and safety. Located in London, where much is up for grabs, Hornby's story explores the possibility for idiosyncratic interdependence even in the quirky chaos of the unreliable city. Where many Christian commentators might see very little promise in the midst of consumer-driven, reality-deprived postmodernity, Hornby suggests a differently real reality. I would even suggest that his story bears the faint traces of a baptismal transformation that muddles up gender in untidy, but graced, ways. Gender "equality," whatever precisely that means, is not something for women to "win," but for men to *receive* as a gift – not through efficient participation in a busy economy, not through excellent works, but through the unlikely grace of a crucified king. We are no longer male and female; for all of us are one in Christ Jesus.

The grace of the Lord Jesus Christ be with you. The risen Christ is with us. Praise the Lord!

In the chapters that follow in this volume, we are invited to perceive the world differently from many of the popular narratives that define success. We are summoned to enter into worship and know anew the liturgical patterns of embodied life together. This summons requires of us at least one move that is deeply counter-intuitive in a culture bent on self-sufficiency and masterful beauty. We are required to be exposed sufficient to receive the grace of the risen Christ. Such reception involves not just the relinquishing of our time, but the relinquishing of our willed determination to *win* at the games of worldly success.

But, as Hornby subtly attests, such relinquishing, if it is true, will involve the work of attending to dependent lives. Discipleship, adequately formed, will lead us to be aligned with precisely the losers that our life is set up to avoid. And this alignment must go much deeper than such random acts of kindness as those by which Will seeks to assuage his nagging sense of responsibility. If Christians greet one another in the name of the risen Christ, and are inconveniently penetrated by that greeting, then we should become newly able to engage in the lives of those who are most obviously in need, not because they are somehow better or more worthy than us, but because, losers that *we* are, we share in their plight.

What would this look like? To script the changes generally is beyond my limited scope. But, from where I stand in the upper-middle class, there seem to be some basic necessities. At present, the average father in my social class spends twice as much time each evening watching television as listening to his children. The average professional mother is steadily catching up with him. While businessmen, lawyers, professors, and doctors may like *looking* at BabyGap babies, few of us want their messy needs to interrupt our *real* work. North American mainline Christians increasingly pay immigrant women from the two-thirds world to do that (and then find ourselves shocked when they lose patience with the child we can hardly take the time to tend). For the *Atlantic Monthly*-reading, Starbucks-sipping, J. Crew-wearing classes, an alignment with dependent life must involve a change in the pace of life, to clear real time (not "quality" time) to do the work that has become increasingly hired out.

Allow me one very concrete example. It is my prayer that a significant number of the boys I teach in Sunday School will decide eventually to use their gifts as teachers in the chaotic corridors of public schools. They may not be able there to share their faith verbally, but I can think of few places better suited for tending the biggest losers of the flock.

This prescription for real time and real discipleship applies also, of course, to the work performed under the auspices of the Church proper. If Christians become more fully shaped by the liturgy, we should find ourselves pulled toward those who society deems to be hardly worth the time and effort. More Christian men should thus be teaching children's Sunday School, visiting nursing homes, and serving up meals to the homeless. If we move from the alignment of the eucharistic table, into the halls of the church building, we should see as many male as female faces digging into the tasks that dirty us. While an occasional stint building a Habitat House is a great step toward embodied, masculine discipleship, we must admit that the most avoided tasks in the Church require tools much more complex than hammer and nail. In other words, do not wait for a miraculous resurrection of the United Methodist Women.

In the name of the Father, and the Son, and the Holy Spirit, we have reason to hope.

References

Bauerschmidt, Frederick (1999) *Julian of Norwich and the Mystical Body Politic of Christ* (Notre Dame, IN: University of Notre Dame Press).

Butler, Judith (1999) *Gender Trouble* (New York, Routledge).

Coakley, Sarah (2002) *Powers and Submissions: Spirituality, Philosophy and Gender* (Oxford: Blackwell).

Ehrenreich, Barbara (2001) *Nickel and Dimed: On (Not) Getting By in America* (New York: Metropolitan).

Faludi, Susan (1999) *Stiffed: The Betrayal of the American Man* (New York: W. Morrow).

hooks, bell (2000) *Feminist Theory: From Margin to Center* (Boston, MA: South End).

Hornby, Nick (1999) *About a Boy* (New York: Riverhead).

Ward, Graham (1999) "Bodies: The Displaced Body of Jesus Christ," in *Radical Orthodoxy*, ed. John Milbank, Catherine Pickstock, and Graham Ward (London: Routledge).

Wood, Ralph (2003) "Hungry Eye: The Two Towers and the Seductiveness of Spectacle," in *Books and Culture*, March/April.

CHAPTER 8

Being Reconciled: Penitence, Punishment, and Worship

John Berkman

A Reconciled and Reconciling People

When the Christian community gathers for eucharistic worship, there is an expectation of formative preparation. The preparation expected is not a change of clothes, a quieting of one's heart, or a pious countenance. Rather, for the eucharistic worship of God, members of the community are to have repented and are to be reconciled to God and each other. The earliest Christians knew St Paul's admonition about "eating and drinking the body and blood of Christ unworthily" (1 Corinthians 11: 27–32) and were also well acquainted with the Lord's words "if you are offering your gift at the altar and there remember that your brother has something against you, leave your gift there in front of the altar. First go and be reconciled to your brother; then come and offer your gift" (Matthew 5: 23–4). The *Didache* and Hippolytus' *Apostolic Tradition* both assert that admission to the Eucharist is predicated on being reconciled (Cavanaugh, 1998: 238).

The centrality of the practice of reconciliation for eucharistic celebration is not limited to the practice of the early Church. Nor is reconciliation apart from the eucharistic celebration. "At the Eucharistic meal . . . by joining him or herself with the blood shed in forgiveness of sins, each believer . . . finds in communion through the power of the Lord's *agapé* the necessity and possibility of a life of reconciliation with his or her brothers and sisters" (Tillard, 1971: 41). Eucharistic worship is the primary context for reconciliation and conversion in the Christian life.

This chapter focuses on the reconciliatory facet of the Eucharist, highlighting its transformative and restorative character. In so doing, it seeks to show how the Eucharist can shape our perception and practices with regard to penitence and retributive justice, two controversial aspects of reconciliation. The chapter proceeds in three sections. The first section focuses on how acknowledgment of our need for reconciliation shapes our identity, showing us not only who we are as sinners, but also who we are called to be as a reconciled people. The second section examines practices of penitence in the

Church's history to show how these practices of penitence contribute to the practice of what I shall call *eucharistic reconciliation*. The third and final section will examine both ecclesial and secular practices of punishment in the light of the practice of eucharistic reconciliation, and in doing so seek to show how punishment – properly understood and applied – can be understood to be a part of the practice of eucharistic reconciliation.

Who Needs to Repent and be Reconciled? Discovering Who We Are

As a eucharistic people, we are a reconciled people. To know ourselves as reconciled presupposes three other self-understandings. First, since to be held responsible for sin requires that we be free to act, we know ourselves as agents who judge and are judged. Second, since only a sinful people need reconciliation, we know that we are a sinful people. Third, we know that reconciliation of sinners requires repentance.

Accounts of our freely acting and being judged for our actions are as old as the story of our first parents. But we do not need to ponder the serpent and the apple to know that, willy-nilly, our free actions and those of others are judged. Judging is ubiquitous in our lives, whether in the workplace (e.g. performance evaluations), in education (e.g. grades), in child-rearing, in athletic competition (e.g. prizes and penalties), on the stage (e.g. reviews), or by the law (e.g. fines and/or incarceration). It is impossible to imagine our lives without such judgments, without appropriate praise and blame. In acting, we can hope (and experience should teach us to expect) that our acts will be met similarly, that our acts will be requited. Although we now associate "retribution" (from the Latin *retribuere* "to pay back") with punishment, its meaning is more general; i.e., giving to someone what they deserve. Discerning "what we owe to whom" is more popularly known as the exercise of the virtue of justice. Giving someone what he or she is "owed" when he or she has offended has traditionally been referred to as retributive justice.

As a people of God, we know that we stand under the judgment of a holy and just God, who justly judges us according to our deeds. We also know that we worship a merciful and forgiving God who seeks our reconciliation. These latter characteristics necessarily complement rather than negate God's holiness and justice, for we cannot have one without the other. As disciples of a savior who comes to save us from our sins and is crucified for our sins, Christians cannot but be clear about our status as sinners deserving God's retributive justice *and* reconciled by God's merciful initiative in Christ (O'Donovan, 2000: 19).

Our understanding of ourselves as sinners in turn shapes our understanding of the character of our reconciliation. As sin is both social and individual, so too is reconciliation both social and individual. While our discussion will focus on the reconciliation between individuals and God, the Church, and our society, it must also be recognized that the unreconciled character of the world is a cosmic reality, a theological view of the world seen most clearly in the early Christian account of Genesis 3 as the Fall, and the Augustinian doctrine of original sin, later developed and modified by Anselm and Aquinas. Our work of reconciliation as Christians is not exclusively a matter of repairing individual relationships or even of overcoming or mitigating the effects of social sin, but also involves our participation in God's efforts to reconcile the entire cosmos.

Scripture provides us with two particularly prominent images of sin. First and foremost, Scripture pictures sin as a rupture of our communion with God. This understanding of sin as a break in communion is sometimes articulated as idolatry (for which moderns sometimes substitute "alienation" or "addiction") and at other times described as a breaking of God's law. What these descriptions share is the conviction that sin affects our *status*. Second, Scripture also envisions sin as a kind of stain or sickness. This outlook focuses not so much on our spiritual status, as on our spiritual *health* (Kennedy, 1996: 237–55; McFadyen, 2000: 221–6). These two pictures of sin point us toward two (complementary) forms of reconciliation. Since sin compromises our status, reconciliation restores us to community; since sin defiles and wounds us, reconciliation heals and transforms us. God's reconciliation of us is twofold: it transforms us as individuals and restores us to and as a community. This practice of reconciliation is what I am calling eucharistic reconciliation.

Mere recognition or acknowledgment of one's sinfulness is not sufficient to be reconciled. In order for reconciliation to occur, the offender must repent. Also referred to as contrition, repentance is sorrow for one's sin and resolve to turn away from it. Although one's sincere repentance absolves one's sin, it does not address the disorders caused by one's sin. Justice requires that, where possible, we make some form of reparation for our sin (e.g. restoring someone's goods, or his or her reputation, or seeking to compensate someone who has been wronged). In reconciliation, efforts toward restoring justice (either commutative or retributive) in the situation are known as "satisfaction" or "penance." A penance serves both the transformation of the penitent (seeking his or her spiritual good by involving him or her in some offering or sacrifice) and the restoration of the good of the community (re-establishing a just state insofar as possible through commutative or retributive justice). This restoration of the offender as a communal restoration is also a restoration of those offended, both the particular victims and the integrity of the good of the community as a whole.

Eucharistic Reconciliation: Restoration and Transformation

Reconciliation is an essential and central element of the gospel message. The theme of reconciliation is ever present in Jesus's ministry. This theme pervades Jesus's parables and is an integral element of Jesus's ministry of healing. An adequate understanding of Jesus's life, death, and resurrection must incorporate the theme of God's continuing work of reconciling the world to God. The life of the Church and of Christian disciples is none other than a life of reconciliation.

At different times in Christian history, the restorative and transformative aspects of the practice of eucharistic reconciliation have been variously emphasized. When the restorative aspect is more prominent, penitential practices tend to focus on the Christian's identity; that is, the Christian's status in relation to God and the Church. When the transformative aspect is emphasized, practices of repentance have stressed its significance for moral and spiritual formation, for the healing and/or growth in maturity of the penitent. At its best, these two dimensions of eucharistic reconciliation are seamlessly interwoven (McCabe, 1994).

For the early Church, the primary context for the practice of reconciliation is the Eucharist. Although all Christians continue to sin, penitential practices of prayer, fasting, almsgiving, and acts of charity serve to prepare believers to be reconciled in eucharistic worship. The eucharistic celebration both disciplines and reconciles, and thereby maintains the unity of the Church. However, the Church also discerns that some grave sins require another remedy, and disqualifies those who commit them from the Eucharist for a time. The status (i.e., identity as believers) of such sinners is in question. To be reconciled, these Christians enter the "order of penitents," undergoing a penance commensurate with the seriousness of their sin. The *paenitentia* is carried out in the context of the Church community, administered by the local bishop. The penitent does not receive Eucharist while undergoing penance; ecclesial forgiveness coincides with readmission to the Eucharist (Poschmann, 1964: 19–25; Vogel, 1968: 181–208).

Key aspects of the practice of penitence are formulated in the second and third centuries. *The Shepherd of Hermas* (c.100–150), the earliest post-Apostolic document focused on the subject of repentance, affirms both the necessity and possibility of post-baptismal reconciliation with the Church for grave sins, but insists that this second repentance is possible only once. Tertullian (c.160–225), the most important early source for understanding the development of penitence, describes the penitents' unique garb when among the community, their penitential practices, and their reconciliation with the community. Origen (185–254) emphasizes that all penitence has a remedial aspect, aimed toward the healing and conversion of the penitent. In dealing with widespread apostasy during the Decian persecution (250–251), Cyprian, the Bishop of Carthage, and Pope Cornelius argue against the reconciliation of apostates *too quickly*. Cyprian insists that, for some penitents, the process is lengthy, even extending to their deathbeds.

Although a uniform set of penitential practices does not emerge in the churches in the second and third centuries, the authors discussed above agree on key characteristics. First, penance for grave sin is a form of fraternal correction, an aspect of charity. Second, as a discipline, penance is not a substitute for forgiveness, but its embodiment (Cavanaugh, 1998: 239). Third, penance goes on in the context of the Church community. Fourth, penance is administered by a bishop (or other leader) on behalf of and in the name of the Church. Thus, from the earliest days, the Church has its own distinctive notion of penitence for the grave sinner. Eucharistic reconciliation is practiced in (a) reforming both the individual and the community and (b) restoring the individual to communion with God and the Church. Penitence in this period is generally referred to as ecclesiastical penance (Rahner, 1982: 79ff; Woods, 1998: 98–123).

As the Church is transformed in the period of Constantine from a relatively small sect of believers into the official religion of the Roman Empire, new problems and inadequacies concerning ecclesiastical penance emerge. Whatever its successes with a relatively motivated group of believers, ecclesiastical penance becomes increasingly unworkable and undesirable as churches are confronted with increasing numbers of relatively "nominal" Christians. Confronted with the Church's rule of one penance after baptism, many Christians choose not to receive penance until their deathbed (*paenitentia in extremis*). Unfortunately, this form of reconciliation undermines its formative aspect and indefinitely postpones its restorative aspect. By the sixth century, ecclesiastical penance is almost exclusively *paenitentia in extremis*. Reconciliation is concerned exclusively with the penitent's eternal status.

Understandably, many fifth- and sixth-century church leaders are exercised by this situation, and respond in divergent ways. For example, St Leo the Great, Pope in the middle of the fifth century, has little sympathy for those whose lives show no signs of repentance, but who seek reconciliation on their deathbed. If they receive the *paenitentia* in their final moments, but die before *reconciliatio*, Leo does not consider them to belong to the communion of the faithful. On the other hand, St Caesarius of Arles, Archbishop of Arles in the early sixth century, knowing that entering the *ordo paenitentia* is extremely rigorous and demanding, and has grave implications for those who abandon the penitential state or return to grave sin afterwards, forbids the granting of ecclesiastical penance to young persons or to married persons who are not of advanced age. Owing to its severity, and the general indifference of most Christians to its practice, the *ordo paenitentium* gradually ceases to function as a means of reconciling grave sinners with the community. Instead, it comes to function as a "third order" practice for Christians (known as *conversi*) seeking perfection (Vogel, 1968: 247–62). In Leo and Caesarius, we have divergent practices of eucharistic reconciliation, based on different understandings of what it means to be restored to the Christian community.

Meanwhile, in the British Isles, another form of penance functions. Among Celtic Christians, there are no explicit records of the practice of ecclesiatical penance. However, as early as the fifth century, Celtic monks and nuns practice private auricular confession in their monasteries. For these monks, confession is a form of spiritual direction and formation, by which one is guided to a holier life. A key development with this form of repentance occurs when the monks expand the practice, offering it to those living in proximity to the monasteries. Those living outside the monastery are provided opportunities to confess their sins privately to a monk and are absolved in conjunction with their performing appropriate penances. By the seventh century, the monks take their "tariff penance" to Europe. While tariff penance initially faces some opposition, it gradually gains acceptance throughout Europe over the next two centuries. While the Carolingian reform of the ninth century attempts to limit tariff penance and recover ecclesiastical penance, it only succeeds in further establishing this new penitential practice (Vogel, 1968: 260–76; Dooley, 1982). With tariff penance, both the transformative and restorative aspects of the practice of eucharistic reconciliation are evident. However, the restorative aspect is subtly altered. In ecclesiastical penance, one's restoration to the community is a practice visible before and involving the whole community. While tariff penance, assigned in private auricular confession, is undoubtedly often visible to the community, the process of reconciliation is no longer an act of the community as it is with ecclesiastical penance in the early Church.

As the practice of tariff penance spreads across Europe in succeeding centuries, it has a significant impact on the conversion and transformation of the continent (McNeill, 1922; Driscoll, 1997). The Fourth Lateran Council of 1215 is the culmination of this development. By mandating both an annual confession of sins and an annual reception of the Eucharist as a requirement for a member of the Church in good standing, it definitively links these two practices of reconciliation. In so doing, the Fourth Lateran Council focuses on penance (and Eucharist) as the means of determining the believer's status.

In the centuries before and after the Fourth Lateran Council, the practical concerns of theologians that penitents be efficaciously reconciled spurs many of the period's most important theological developments. For example, St Anselm composes his work on the atonement as a means of understanding why it is that, despite Christ having forgiven the sins of all persons through his cross, it is necessary for Christians to undergo penance to be reconciled to God and the Church. Beginning with Abelard, medieval scholastics seek to articulate more precisely the nature of action and intention, to the end of more appropriately determining moral freedom and culpability and thus assisting the administration of confession. A significant purpose of the new mendicant orders (i.e., the Franciscans and Dominicans) is to improve the administration of the practice of penitence. Leonard Boyle argues that his fellow Dominican Thomas Aquinas composes his *Summa theologiae* primarily as a resource to aid his fellow Dominicans in their role as confessors (Torrell, 1996: 144, citing Boyle, 1982: 15ff). While the concerns of the scholastics to better understand the nature of penitence are all in themselves legitimate, taken together they seem to have served to place an inordinate emphasis on the *status* – rather than on the *transformation* – of the penitent.

The late-medieval preoccupation with the status of the penitent is undoubtedly an impetus for the Reformers attack on the practice. The Reformers' criticisms of penitence (for example, its being overly detailed, its requiring works of penitence, its challenging the absolute gratuity of God's grace, and its requiring a priest) are all focused on claims about the significance of penance for one's status. What is largely missed amongst discussions of the disagreements is that Luther and Calvin both acknowledge the importance of penitence as a practice of formation for both the individual and the Church. Luther and Calvin wish to retain a form of ecclesiastical penitence similar to that of the early Church (Luther also wishes to retain penance as a sacrament), and both recognize that confession to a minister can contribute to a person's formation (von Allmen, 1971: 112–15).

In the midst of this controversy, moral theology is born. When the Council of Trent institutes the seminary system for priestly education in the sixteenth century, the main subject of study is the newly created discipline of moral theology. Its primary task is to train clergy in the proper administration of the sacrament of penance. From Trent until the middle of the twentieth century, the primary purpose of the Anglican and Catholic manuals of moral theology is to assist clergy in helping people confess their sins appropriately and be reconciled to God and the Church. While the formative aspect of the practice is not entirely absent, the restorative aspect, understood individualistically and juridically, continues to dominate (Vereecke, 1986; Mahoney, 1987: 22–36; Pinckaers, 1995: 259–68).

In the wake of Vatican II's *Constitution on the Sacred Liturgy*, as a result of a renewed appreciation of the ecclesiastical penitence of the Patristic period, and in the light of an increased recognition of the structural aspect of sin, there have been two developments with regard to the practice of reconciliation. First, there is a renewed appreciation of the Eucharist as the primary sacrament of reconciliation. Second, in the light of that and a more general appreciation of the communal dimensions of both sin and reconciliation, there has been a movement to ritualize the restorative aspect of penitence in more communal settings (Congregation for Divine Worship, 1973). Offenses against God are also offenses against the people of God and vice versa. While these developments by no means presage a return to the tradition of ecclesiastical penance, it is perhaps indicative of a renewed appreciation that both the reformative and restorative aspects of reconciliation are better served if we can find contexts in which they can be more visibly linked together.

The Practice of Eucharistic Reconciliation: Punishment in Theological Perspective

The previous section portrayed the historical contours of the practice of eucharistic reconciliation by displaying its evolving practices of transforming and restoring penitents. In this section, we examine the historical influence of Christian practices of reconciliation (and specifically monastic penitential practices) on practices of punishment in modern societies. Parallels between these two practices are rarely if ever drawn. In examining the analogies, the suggestion is not that ecclesial practices can simply be translated into the practices of civil society. Nor am I proposing a method or blueprint for "Christianizing" the penal system. Rather, the goal is to (a) understand the extent to which the assumptions of eucharistic reconciliation inform modern penological practices, and (b) show how the practice of eucharistic reconciliation instructs Christians about transformative and restorative punishment as they witness to a civil society that wrestles with the appropriate means and ends of criminal punishment.

While the purpose of this section is to show similarities and continuities between penitence and punishment, two important distinctions must be noted. First, whereas the penitent is actively involved in the process, accepting some form of punishment (i.e., traditionally called "satisfaction" or reparation), the person being punished may not be active in the process, may not be repentant. Although punishment without repentance cannot bring about true eucharistic reconciliation, it does not follow that the unrepentant should not be punished. A person may be in some important sense reconciled to the community without his or her acknowledgment or acceptance of this reconciliation. In such situations, punishment may bring the offender to recognize and acknowledge his or her offense, but there is no guarantee that the one punished will repent and grow in the good rather than, for example, becoming embittered and resentful (Milbank, cited in Jones, 1995: 273). Part of what may sustain hope for reconciliation with unrepentant wrongdoers is the acknowledgment that God's reconciliation of us is a drama rather than an event, a drama reflected liturgically in the celebration of Easter, which is preceded by the season of Lent, a season involving weeks of prayer and penitence necessary to adequately celebrate Easter (Dallen, 1986: 85–8). Herbert McCabe highlights both the dramatic character of reconciliation and its relation to the Eucharist in speaking of the sacrament of reconciliation as a sacrament of return

(McCabe, 1964: 86–108). Thus, efforts at punishment and reconciliation always need be infused with the virtue of hope.

Second, whereas penitence is associated with sin, punishment is associated with crime. Although, for the first Christian millennium, "sin" and "crime" are virtually interchangeable (Berman, 1983: 185–6), in contemporary parlance sin is a violation of God's laws, whereas crime is a violation of society's laws. Although an action can be a sin without being a crime (and vice versa), many serious sins are crimes and serious crimes are also typically sins (see Gorringe, 1996: 17–22, for a more nuanced account).

The earliest Christians wrestle with the dilemma of how it can be that baptized Christians – freed from sin – can lapse into wrongdoing and how the community should respond to such persons. The Church's response to this is to set into motion penitential practices. Thus, in the Gospels and Epistles we read directions to and by the disciples to chasten and, if need be, shun members who are obstinate in wrongdoing (Matthew 18: 15–17; 1 Corinthians 5: 9–13; 2 Thessalonians 3: 14–15). Some are excluded (for a time or until repentance occurs) as a recognition that the community's unity has been broken and the necessity of the wrongdoer admitting fault and seeking reconciliation with the community that desires their restoration.

While the New Testament texts on confronting wrongdoers and excluding or shunning them seem unexceptional, they inaugurate practices in the early centuries of the Church that prefigure the Western judicial and penal system. As was discussed in the previous section, those in the early Church who sin grievously but who wish to be restored to the community of the Church enter an order of penitents. The *ordo paenitentium* is not simply a means of burdening and shaming the penitent, but is a practice designed to transform the penitent *and* the entire Church community. For example, the ritual for entering the order of penitents involves the imposition of hands, an action analogous to that involved in ordination. While the order of penitents involves a ritualized period of separation and repentance for the penitent, it also calls forth the active participation of the Church community in the process, including their prayerful support. Community members are expected to keep watch over the penitents, assuring that the penitents maintain their exculpatory behavior (Poschmann, 1964: 87–9).

Those in the *ordo paenitentium* are excluded from the Eucharist, are supervised by the Church as a whole, are assigned a specific place in the assembly (probably in the rear of the church), and typically wear distinctive and symbolic clothing; for example, the goatskin (as opposed to lambskin) *cilicium* worn by penitents symbolizes their exclusion. Taken together, these features show a symbolic group of excluded penitents, made to wear distinct clothing, placed under supervision for a period of time in an assigned place. While the early Church does not have prisons, ecclesiastical penance of that time does provides "sentences" of determinate length, based on a judgment as to the seriousness of the sin. Taken as a whole, these ecclesial practices reveal a "sense of both penal geography and the image of the convicted offender that would have a powerful impact on monastic culture in regard to the practice of incarceration" (Skotnicki, 2002).

From the beginnings of monasticism, incarceration (i.e., placing a monk in his cell for a period of time) is seen to be the appropriate response for certain wrongs. The rule of St Pachomius, the earliest monastic rule, states that one who slanders "shall be separated from the assembly of the brothers seven days and shall receive only bread and water until he firmly promises to convert from that vice. Then he shall be forgiven" (Pachomius, 1981: 178–9; cited in Skotnicki, 2002). This is an example of a penance of a specific duration. For some wrongs, Pachomius' rule specifies a specific dwelling, and for others the penitent is to be excluded from the Eucharist.

The same key elements regarding monastic incarceration can be found in the rules of St Basil and St Benedict. While the different rules vary on the specifics of different punishments, practices of ritual exclusion, isolation, prayer, and silence for a set period of time are typical monastic forms of punishment. Such practices are judged to be the appropriate means by which the penitent is to be reconciled.

Over time, the monastic model of punishment by incarceration gains popularity. Other ecclesiastical and royal officials begin to employ penal seclusion as an alternative to other more brutal forms of punishment that are typical of the time. Papal blessing for monastic incarceration can be found as early as the fourth century when Pope Siricius, in advising Bishop Himerus on a number of disciplinary questions, ordered lascivious and sacrilegious monks to be confined in "continual lamentation" so that they might be purified through "penitential fire." By the time of Gregory the Great, confinement for both monks and disobedient clergy is a common theme. Gregory writes to the Bishop of Milan that an ex-presbyter should be forcibly sent to Sicily and be deprived of any hope of departure so that he will focus on penitential bewailing. The Council of Orleans, the first Council of Seville, and the first Council of Matison all make reference to confinement for clergy for a variety of offenses (Skotnicki, 2002).

The degree of similarity between monastic incarceration and contemporary penology is striking. For example, both the physical structure of the monastery and the spiritual discipline of monastic life are prototypical for later developments. Mimicking the physical structure of monastic incarceration, the modern penitentiary is made up of numerous "cells." Mimicking the ascetic and interior goals of monastic life, the modern penitentiary emphasizes silence, isolation, self-denial, with liberal opportunity for prayer and self-reflection.

This influence is not accidental. John Howard, the eighteenth-century ascetic and pious non-conformist who first formulates the ideal of penitentiary discipline, is significantly influenced by the promise of monastic discipline. Howard, whom Ignatieff calls the "father of solitary confinement," models much of his plan for the English penitentiary on the work of J. P. Vilain, whose conception of a prison with individual cells is in turn based on Pope Clement XII's prison of San Michel. Clement's prison, named the *Silentium*, is built in 1703 to reform juvenile delinquents by applying the monastic discipline to the purposes of punishment (Ignatieff, 1978: 47–67).

In order to fully grasp the influence of these Christian ideals of punishment and reconciliation in the first Christian millennium, it is necessary to contrast Christian penitential practices with the practices of punishment in the societies of which the Church is a part. These societies typically practice a rather different form of criminal justice, largely consisting of retributive blood feuds. In such societies, prisons as we know them do not exist, relatively few wrongdoings are punished, but existing punishments are typically severe. For example, eighth-century Frankish law attempts to mitigate blood feuds by a law of "composition," in which the kinsmen of the offender turn the wrongdoer over to the plaintiff, and then can negotiate economic reparation with the plain-tiff for his injury. Under this system, various injuries and wrongs are assigned an economic value, either in terms of property, cattle, or human servitude. However, the aggrieved party is free to forgo such (typically economic) reparation in favor of the death of the offender. Goebel speculates that, as a result of "ecclesiastical pressure," a new kind of law is instituted in this time, the law of redemption, where a wrongdoer is not automatically turned over to the aggrieved party, but can instead be "ransomed" (Goebel, 1937: 83–92). The influence of the penitentials in this sudden shift in the prac-tice of penal law is likely, especially considering that this shift occurs at the time when penitential manuals are rapidly increasing in number and influence on the European continent.

In medieval England, the earliest records of secular jails are in the tenth and eleventh centuries, and typically refer to tiny buildings operated by the local sheriff. They are typically places for short-term custody until other means of punishment have been executed. This is in sharp contrast to European monasteries, which all have prisons suitable for incarceration for extended periods. For example, a twelfth-century Cister-cian ordinance states that a monk of sound body who kills another member is to be kept in confinement and fed on bread and water for the rest of his days (Pugh, 1968: 1–25, 347–90). Although the sixteenth and seventeenth centuries witness periodic efforts to establish workhouses and/or "corrective" prisons, the sharp contrast between the style, scope, and purpose of secular and monastic punishment largely remains up until the advent of the modern penitentiary in the eighteenth century (Ignatieff, 1978: 11–14).

Thus, we see that, prior to the past two centuries, monastic prisons are not merely a predecessor for modern imprisonment, they are apparently the only model for such prisons. The goals of monastic punishment – like ecclesiastical penance – are twofold: the reformation of the penitent and his or her restoration to the community. The formative aspect is directed primarily at the prisoner, typically viewed as a kind of spiritual medicine. The restorative aspect is directed not only at the restoration of the individual to the community, but the restoration of the community itself. As such, this restoration is a species of commutative and retributive justice. In this sense, it is clear how the restorative aspect involves retributive punishment.

We see both the reformative and retributive aspects of punishment articulated by Augustine and Aquinas. Augustine emphasizes the retributive aspect of punishment, arguing that punishment is necessary as a means of restraining evildoers and bring-ing about a relative peace. Regarding such peace, Augustine says "nothing is desired with greater longing, in fact, nothing better can be found." However, Augustine also recognizes the reformative or medicinal aspect of punishment, that it is "for the benefit of the offender, intended to readjust him to the domestic peace from which he has broken away" (Augustine, 1972: XIX, 16). On the other hand, while Aquinas also acknowledges the retributive justification for punishment as important for the preser-vation of societal order (i.e., the virtue of *vindicatio*: Aquinas, 1947: II-II, 108), he places greater emphasis on the reformative aspect of punishment. Aquinas typically speaks of punishment as medicinal, believing that punishment can be a means by which the penitent grows in virtue (Aquinas, 1947: II-II, 64, 3).

While Augustine and Aquinas describe well the specifics of these two aspects of punishment, a fuller, and more adequately contextualized, description of monastic punishment is to be found in the most famous of monastic rules – that of St Benedict. In his discussion of the purpose of punishment in the monastery, Benedict includes a more general discussion of the lens through which the roles of both abbot and offending monk should be seen. Benedict employs Christological images (e.g., Christ the good shepherd) and parental images of attentive care in describing the role of the abbot, and he also uses Christological images to describe the offender (e.g., Christ as prisoner). For example, Benedict instructs the abbot that he is to be solicitous of the erring monk even while he places upon him the necessary cross of sentencing, isolation, and reduced rations. The abbot is seen as taking on the role of Christ with regard to the erring monk, and is instructed to "imitate the good shepherd's devoted example: He left the ninety-nine sheep . . . looking for the one who had strayed . . . placed it on his sacred shoulders and carried it back to the flock." This Christological theme is reiterated when Benedict reminds the Abbot that, with regard to the erring monk, "it is not the healthy but the sick who need a physician" (Benedict, 1996: ch. 27, cited in Skotnicki, 2002). Similarly, the erring monk is seen as taking on the role of Christ the prisoner, and the goal for the erring monk is to be liberated from his bondage and restored to the flock.

In this very brief historical synopsis of the goals of monastic punishment, we see that it is aimed at both the good of the prisoner as well as the reconciliation of the whole community. Of course, this is an ideal in the tradition, an ideal that is often far from the reality. Much brutality and cruelty have at times passed for "the good" of the prisoner. However, the ideal of monastic punishment has at times been realized in history, and we can and should ask how this approach might continue to inform Christian visions of a reconciling punishment. In other words, how might these images of Christ the good shepherd as sentencing judge and Christ the prisoner continue to inform and challenge practices of punishment in the United States, for example, with the return to capital punishment and explosive rise in prison populations in recent decades?

The vision of punishment as a potential means of individual reform and growth and communal reconciliation, a vision shared by Benedict, Augustine, and Aquinas, is in stark contrast to much of what is currently thought to justify punishment. For example, contemporary accounts of punishment, which emphasize "deterrence" or "a desire to protect society," depart from the classical Christian approach in that their focus does not remain on the integral good (i.e., the reformation) of offenders with the specific victims of their offenses and/or the community which has been harmed. Even many undoubtedly well-meaning Church statements abandon the tradition's reformative and retributive justifications of punishment, focusing instead on "deterring crime" and "guarding the public's safety" without locating such notions in the broader purpose of reconciliation.

If the ultimate goal of punishment (either for sin or crime) is to move us toward our practice of eucharistic reconciliation (or something approximating that as nearly as possible), then the integral relation between its pursuit of (a) the good of the offender and (b) the good of the community to which the offender is to be restored must be maintained. With the dominant images of Christ as the prisoner, and the exhortation that when Christians perform the work of mercy of ransoming prisoners, they are ransoming Christ, no Christian justification for punishment can set aside the good of the prisoner.

One difficulty with defending – as this chapter does – retributive justice as inherent in both the reformative and restorative aspects of the practice of eucharistic reconciliation is that "retribution" is often employed to represent accounts of punishment that are not ordered to the goal of reconciliation. For example, some advocates of "retributivism" link it to the *lex talionis* (i.e., "an eye for an eye, a tooth for a tooth"). On this view – more accurately referred to as "retaliationism" – any failure to retaliate (i.e. to defraud the defrauder, rape the rapist, or execute the murderer) is a commutation of the ideal. But defenders of the death penalty who are true retaliationists are rare, as practically no one advocates that *all* persons who kill be killed. However, the retaliationist impulse can be seen in contemporary trends such as the "penal harm" movement. A response to the call to have more concern for the victims of crime, it sees the offender and victim in a zero-sum relationship, in which the victim can only be benefited by equivalent losses to the offender. Since it does not hold together the restorative and reformative aspects of reconciliation, the retaliationist understanding of retribution is not theologically defensible (Berkman and Hauerwas, 1996: 102–4).

Perhaps the most controversial practice associated with punishment is capital punishment. In light of the practice of eucharistic reconciliation, the death penalty is simply not reconcilable with fundamental theological convictions regarding punishment. The primary theological objection to the practice of the death penalty will not be that it is "cruel" or "unusual" or "barbaric" or even "incommensurate" punishment. The primary objection will be that in light of the Christian imperative of reconciliation, it is not punishment at all. For while punishment is rightly seen as part of God's justice, it is a justice ordered to reconciliation, whose ultimate earthly manifestation is the practice of eucharistic reconciliation. But "capital punishment" undermines the realization of the reformative or restorative aspects of the practice of reconciliation, to which any theologically defensible form of retributive justice must be ordered. At times, in the Church's history, its understanding of reconciliation was such that, as long as the criminal's soul was reconciled to God, the civil magistrate was free to punish the body with death. At best, on this approach, "reform" was restricted to the offender's soul, and "restoration" was restricted to an offender-less community, at least on this side of the eschaton. But recent appreciation of the created dignity of even a murderer has led to Pope John Paul II to challenge the traditional view that some crimes are commensurate with the death penalty. Although the Pope acknowledges the possibility of emergency situations or settings in which it might be necessary to kill unjust aggressors as the only means of defending innocent persons, such judicial killings would not be retributive. Whereas retributive justice is always backward-looking, a response to what was done, these "emergency" judicial killings are essentially forward-looking, justified to prevent further harm to innocents. As such they are extrinsic rather than intrinsic to the logic of punishment (John Paul II, 1995; O'Donovan, 1998). This move to disentangle the death penalty from the logic of punishment is reflected in changes in

The Catechism of the Catholic Church, which can be seen by comparing sections 2266–7 of the 1993 and 1997 versions.

Of course, the Christian practice of eucharistic reconciliation has implications not only for the question of capital "punishment." A whole range of contemporary judicial practices can be evaluated in relation to it: the present mass incarceration practices in the United States (with a prison population exceeding 2,000,000 for the first time in 2003); the "three-strikes-you're-out" laws which mandate what are often grossly disproportionate sentences; the statistical disparities of punishments along racial and socioeconomic lines; what O'Donovan calls "execution-on-arrest by a gun-happy police," reports of which are all too common in our local newspapers.

In the midst of a culture whose practices of punishment seem remote from practices of eucharistic reconciliation, there are movements of hope. The past twenty years has seen the rise of a movement known as the "restorative justice" movement. It seeks to embody the two key elements of eucharistic reconciliation: first, in seeking to have offenders accept responsibility for their wrongdoings and find concrete and creative ways to acknowledge and, to the extent possible, make restoration for their offenses, the restorative justice movement attends specifically to the reform of the offender; second, in having the offender respond to interaction with their community (including the victim(s) and/or the victim(s) representatives) and to establish a punishment deemed appropriate by all parties, the restorative justice movement actively seeks to restore the offender to his or her community.

A people shaped by eucharistic reconciliation have much to learn from the restorative justice movement. There is also much to be recovered from the history of the practice of eucharistic reconciliation. In the *ordo paenitentium*, a penitent was ritually separated from the Church, but was being prepared to be received again into the Body of Christ, and the entire Church was involved in the process of reconciliation. One body of people who are palpably separated from the practice of eucharistic reconciliation, who are also part of the "least of these," are the countless imprisoned in the US. As Timothy Gorringe shows, efforts to "ransom" and reconcile such people to the eucharistic body are rare (Gorringe, 1996: 268–71). However, Matthew's Gospel warns us that we are to be judged according to how we receive, not only the hungry, the sick, and the stranger, but also the prisoner.

Anyone who is familiar with recidivism statistics for criminal offenders in our society knows that the practice of eucharistic reconciliation with this group of the "least of these" will not do well to measure its success in earthly terms. In ministry to those imprisoned and in thinking about punishment in our society more generally, the Body of Christ will greatly need the theological virtue of hope. In the *Summa theologiae*, Aquinas notes that the twin vices corresponding to hope are despair and presumption. Many of our current practices of punishment, especially the return of capital punishment and the move toward mandatory sentencing, are exemplifications of the vice of despair, despair over the possibility that a prisoner can be reformed and restored to the community. In their worship, in their eucharistic reconciliation, believers are given gifts of charity and hope, a gift that can and should be shared with those – whether on the "inside" or on the "outside" – who are captive to fear and despair.

Acknowledgments

Thanks to R. Alspaugh, K. Dooley, G. Hallonsten, F. Maloney, C. Pinches, S. Wells, and J. Wiseman for critical and constructive comments on earlier drafts of this chapter, which previously appeared as "Eucharistic Reconciliation: Penitence, Punishment and Worship" in the *Journal of Peace Studies*, 14 (2) (Fall 2003).

References

von Allmen, Jean-Jacques (1971) "The Forgiveness of Sins as a Sacrament in the Reformed Tradition," in *Sacramental Reconciliation*, ed. E. Schillebeeckx, pp. 112–19 (New York: Herder and Herder).

Aquinas, St Thomas (1947) *Summa theologiae* (New York: Benziger).

Augustine, St (1972) *The City of God*, trans. H. Bettenson (Harmondsworth: Penguin).

Benedict, St (1996) *Benedict's Rule*, trans. T. G. Kardong (Collegeville, MN: The Liturgical Press).

Berkman, John and Hauerwas, Stanley (1996) "Capital Punishment," in *Dictionary of Ethics, Theology, and Society*, ed. P. B. Clarke and A. Linzey, pp. 100–5 (New York: Routledge).

Berman, Harold (1983) *Law and Revolution* (Cambridge, MA: Harvard University Press).

Boyle, Leonard, OP (1982) *The Setting of the Summa theologiae of Saint Thomas* (Toronto: PIMS).

Cavanaugh, William (1998) *Torture and Eucharist: Theology, Politics and the Body of Christ* (Oxford: Blackwell).

Congregation for Divine Worship (1973) *Ordo paenitentia: editio typica* (Rome: Typis Polyglottis Vaticanis).

Dallen, James (1986) *The Reconciling Community: The Rite of Penance* (New York: Pueblo).

Dooley, Kate (1982) "From Penance to Confession: The Celtic Contribution," *Bijdragen*, 43: 390–410.

Driscoll, Michael (1997) "Penance in Transition: Popular Piety and Practice," in *Medieval Liturgy*, ed. Lizette Larson-Miller (New York: Garland).

Goebel, Julius (1937) *Felony and Misdemeanor* (Philadelphia: University of Pennsylvania Press).

Gorringe, Timothy (1996) *God's Just Vengeance: Crime, Violence and the Rhetoric of Salvation* (Cambridge: Cambridge University Press).

Ignatieff, Michael (1978) *A Just Measure of Pain: The Penitentiary in the Industrial Revolution 1750–1850* (New York: Columbia University Press).

John Paul II (1995) "*Evangelium vitae* [The Gospel of Life]," *Acta Apostolicae Sedis*, 87: 401–522.

Jones, L. Gregory (1995) *Embodying Forgiveness* (Grand Rapids, MI: Eerdmans).

Kennedy, Terence, CSsR (1996) *Doers of the Word* (Slough: St Paul's).

McCabe, Herbert (1964) *The New Creation* (London: Sheed and Ward).

—(1994) "Manuals and Rule Books," in *Considering Veritatis Splendor*, ed. John Wilkins, pp. 61–8 (Cleveland: Pilgrim).

McFadyen, Alasdair (2000) *Bound to Sin: Abuse, Holocaust and the Christian Doctrine of Sin* (Cambridge: Cambridge University Press).

McNeill, J. (1922) "The Celtic Penitentials and their Influence on Continental Christianity," *Revue Celtique*, 39: 257–300; 40: 51–103, 320–41.

Mahoney, John, SJ (1987) *The Making of Moral Theology* (Oxford: Oxford University Press).

O'Donovan, Oliver (1998) "The Death Penalty in *Evangelium vitae*," in *Ecumenical Ventures in Ethics*, ed. Reinhard Hütter and Theodor Dieter, pp. 216–36 (Grand Rapids, MI: Eerdmans).

—(2000) "Payback: Thinking about Retribution," *Books and Culture*, 6 (4): 16–21.

Osborne, Kenan, OFM (1990) *Reconciliation and Justification* (New York: Paulist).

Pachomius, St (1981) *Pachomian Koinonia*, vol. 2, trans. A. Veilleux (Kalamazoo: Cistercian).

Pinckaers, Servais, OP (1995) *Sources of Christian Ethics* (Washington: Catholic University of America Press).

Poschmann, Bernhard (1964) *Penance and the Anointing of the Sick* (New York: Herder and Herder).

Pugh, Ralph (1968) *Imprisonment in Medieval England* (Cambridge: Cambridge University Press).

Rahner, Karl, SJ (1982) *Theological Investigations XV: Penance and the Early Church* (New York: Crossroad).

Skotnicki, Andrew (2002) "Foundations Once Destroyed: The Catholic Church and Criminal Justice," unpublished paper.

Tillard, Jean-Marie, OP (1971) "The Bread and the Cup of Reconciliation," *Sacramental Reconciliation*, ed. E. Schillebeeckx, pp. 38–54 (New York: Herder and Herder).

Torrell, Jean-Pierre, OP (1996) *Saint Thomas Aquinas, Volume 1: The Person and his Work*, trans. Robert Royal (Washington, DC: CUA).

Vereecke, Louis, CssR (1986) "Le concile de Trente et l'enseignement de la théologie morale," in *De Guillaume d'Ockham à Saint Alphone de Liguori: études d'histoire de la théologie morale moderne, 1300–1787*, pp. 495–508 (Rome: Collegium S. Alfonsi de Urbe).

Vogel, Cyril (1968) "Sin and Penance: A Survey of the Historical Evolution of the Penitential Discipline in the Latin Church," in *Pastoral Treatment of Sin*, ed. P. Delhaye, pp. 177–282 (New York: Desclée).

Woods, Walter J. (1998) *Walking with Faith* (Collegeville, MN: The Liturgical Press).

CHAPTER 9

Praising in Song: Beauty and the Arts

Kevin J. Vanhoozer

The work of art is the object seen *sub specie aeternitatis*; and the good life is the world seen *sub specie aeternitatis*. This is the connection between art and ethics. *Wittgenstein*

Doxology: In Praise of Beauty?

Our local Presbyterian church sings the doxology as the deacons bring forward the collection, acknowledging that God has given far more to us – "all blessings" – than we can ever give back. We sing the *Gloria Patri* after confessing our sins and hearing the absolution, acknowledging the greatest divine gift of all: forgiveness, together with the new share in the triune life that ensues. These and other musical offerings enhance the quality of our worship. But how? Wittgenstein's insight into what connects aesthetics and ethics also forges a tie to worship: praising God in song enables the Church not simply to see things *sub specie aeternitatis* but to enter the antechamber of heaven, to stand on eternity's very brink.

We praise what we prize, just as we worship what we consider worthy. Praises may be said or sung, but singing accomplishes something that saying cannot. First, singing is social, uniting the whole assembly in a harmony that both manifests and constitutes a community. Second, singing is personal, engaging all one's faculties: "singing clearly demonstrates worship – and therefore the divine kingdom and human salvation – to be an affair of the whole person, mind, heart, voice, body" (Wainwright, 1980: 200). Third, singing is sensational: one perceives both visual art and music through the senses (the original Greek sense of aesthetics was "perception").

The present chapter is not about styles of music in the Church; it seeks rather to investigate the role of beauty and aesthetics in the Christian life. Specifically, how does praising God in song form Christian character? We listen to Scripture readings to hear the Word of God, but what should we be trying to perceive when we listen to Church music? Aaron Copland's question to would-be music lovers provides a helpful starting-point: are you hearing everything that is going on; are you really being sensitive to it? (Copland, 1957: vii). Just what is going on in hymns? What should Christians listen for in Church music? What does praise have to do with aesthetics? And why has the contemporary Church so often neglected aesthetics, and what are the consequences of so doing?

Let us make a preliminary distinction between "aesthetic" and "aesthetics." "Aesthetic" refers to a dimension of human being in which an experience of what is beautiful leads to a self-transcending delight. "Aesthetics," by contrast, is a branch of philosophy that deals with judgments about works of art. "Beauty" is central to the former, but not necessarily to the latter. While a theological aesthetics treats the role of art in the Church, a theological aesthetic examines the role of beauty in the life of faith (Farley, 2001: 117). The present chapter is primarily a consideration of theological aesthetic.

There is something about praising God in song that goes beyond both doctrine and piety. The argument of the present chapter is that *praising God in song – a staple practice of the Church – forms our imaginations and hence our sensibilities as to what is fitting in the created (and redeemed) order*. The imagination, particularly at work in the arts, is a vital means for perceiving and commending the good and the true hidden and revealed in Christ.

The True, the Good, and the Beautiful: The Ancient/Modern Quarrel

The fate of beauty is tied to that of truth and goodness. What the ancients united, the moderns have differentiated and the postmoderns have deconstructed. Society is still learning to live amidst the ruins.

Auld alliance, ancient quarrel

Ancient philosophers parsed "being" in terms of the true, the good, and the beautiful, transcendental properties that may be predicated of everything that is: flowers, bird song, sunsets, geometrical proofs and, as we shall see, human virtues and actions. According to Plato, all instances of worldly truth, goodness, and beauty participate in ideal or eternal forms. For Christian thinkers, the application was obvious: God, as perfect being, is himself the source of the true, the good, and the beautiful. The glory of God consists in the sublime conjunction of the true, good, and beautiful.

Plato also spoke of an "ancient quarrel between philosophy and poetry" (and, by extension, the other arts as well). For Plato, the arts, whether visual, literary, or musical, are actually crafts (*techne*) that make images. These images may imitate their originals but, precisely because they are imitations of objects that are themselves imitations of eternal forms, they are two steps removed from the realm of reality. Plato nonetheless allowed that poetry and music, at their best, may be means of character formation, capable of inculcating moral virtue. Beauty has subsequently been the Cinderella of philosophy, the poor stepsister of truth and goodness.

The modern quarrel

Beauty became dispensable in modernity for both metaphysics and morals. Indeed, beauty has become the "beast": alternately seductive, elitist, trivial, subjective – "an ornament of the bourgeois past" (Farley, 2001: 1). Discourse on beauty disappeared in the academy, and beauty itself largely disappeared from society and the Church.

"Modernity" names a process of rationalization and differentiation, in which social forces and institutional forms – secularization, industrialization, bureaucratization – came to embody the Enlightenment ideals of rationality, individual autonomy, and progress. Modernity is the triumphalistic exercise of instrumental rationality in the domain of the social. The result is an ever-increasing differentiation or fragmentation of life, where every aspect of human experience becomes a new field for the specialist. From another perspective, modernity is the turn to the subject: a turn away from a consideration of the world in itself to a consideration of the world as it appears in human experience. The arts thus come to be associated not with being, but with feeling; beauty gives way to the study of aesthetic sensibility.

Kant's philosophy illustrates both trends. Kant fragments the auld alliance between the true, the good, and the beautiful by showing each to be a corollary of a separate realm of human experience, each with its own a priori principles and rationality. For Kant, aesthetic judgments are neither cognitive nor moral; they concern neither truth nor moral goodness. Of what value, then, is aesthetic sensibility? Kant's own answer was that art mediates the realms of nature (fact) and freedom (value) by enabling us to view the world *as if* it had purpose, *as if* nature were a meaningful context for moral action.

Modern thinkers responded to the fragmentation of the true, good, and beautiful in two diametrically opposed ways. Some saw art and beauty as a dispensable luxury or "extra" to the essentials of life; others saw art and beauty as essential, the very things that make life worth living. Matthew Arnold and Leo Tolstoy argued that art has social value only when it is morally useful, an incentive toward virtue. On the other hand, others like Oscar Wilde advocated aestheticism, the notion that art needs no justification by reference to anything outside the work itself. The artist's calling is to strive for formal perfection as a value in its own right: art for *art's* sake. A poem, painting, or prelude need not "mean" but simply "be." Everyone agreed that aesthetics named a discrete aspect of human experience and that art had become a specialization in its own right; the disagreement was over how central to the rest of society artists actually are. Is beauty necessary to the good life or not?

The postmodern quarrel

Where moderns differentiate, postmoderns deconstruct, exposing claims to absolute truth, goodness, or beauty as expressions of the merely individual or cultural will to power. Yet the same two tendencies that characterize the modern quarrel are also apparent in postmodernity.

Postmodern aestheticism has become a veritable "first philosophy." Yet the post-modern celebration of creative interpretation sits uneasily with a certain despair of the imagination. Postmoderns revel in stories and images, while simultaneously draining them of ultimate significance by insisting that one cannot really *believe* in them. That ideology-criticism ultimately devalues the imagination is the great irony of post-modernity. Meta-narratives shrink to mere narratives; deep symbols give way to super-ficial spin.

Dorothy Sayers correctly foresaw the malaise of our time: *sloth*, the inability to believe in, or *do*, anything. Romantic passion has shriveled into anemic irony. A lack of beauty in one's diet leads to spiritual malnutrition, a deficiency of vital symbols and stories in the bloodstream of the soul that results in world-weariness. Postmoderns suffer not, as is commonly thought, from over-sensation but from de-sensitization, an anesthesia of the spirit. One is hard pressed to identify that for which postmodern men and women are willing to live or die.

In contrast, Lévinas makes ethics his "first philosophy." On this view, recognizing one's infinite obligations to the other clearly takes priority over aesthetic delight. Indeed, for many today, a preoccupation with beauty is politically incorrect because art, like religion, can act as the people's opiate, distracting them from situations that cry out for social justice. Scarry (1999) believes that such arguments for the irrelevance of beauty are misguided because the same sensibilities that enable the perception of beauty also oppose injustice. As she notes, the word "fair" means both beautiful and just. Moreover, to perceive beauty is to undergo a transformation of sorts from self-centeredness to other-centeredness. Experiencing beauty prompts us to give up our imaginary position at the center and forces us to recognize that we are in the presence of something larger than ourselves.

Beauty and Imagination in the Christian Life: Beholding and Beholden To

Christian ethics concerns our responsible response to the gift of Christian freedom. It is about using or creating forms of freedom that participate fittingly in the form of Jesus Christ. Appropriate action, however, requires understanding and, for this, we need the evangelical imagination: the ability to see what God is doing for the world in Jesus Christ. The beauty of what God is doing is not merely in the eye of the beholder. On the contrary, "beholding" is the ability to see everything that is going on in Christ. The imagination is the power of synoptic vision, the ability to understand complex wholes. As such, it is related to wisdom: the discernment of how things fit together, and hence of what one should do in a given situation. *To behold is thus to be beholden.*

The ethos of the mythos

There is an important, though often overlooked, tie between a culture's imagination and its ethics. The foundation stories of a given culture, its stock of narratives and meta-narratives, create a sense of the stage on which human freedom lives and moves. *Culture cultivates an ethos via the work of the imagination (mythos).*

The imagination cultivates an awareness of a dimension of things inaccessible to empirical science and shapes our sense of the meaning of the whole. The arts, "that human activity that goes beyond the useful to embody in allusive color, shape, or sound the joy or pain of being human" (Dyrness, 2001: 99), is one of the principal means of cultivation. Art, music, and literature (not to mention dance, architecture, and film) indirectly communicate views about human life and love, about the meaning of life in its cosmic setting. Cultures thus cultivate the human spirit, encouraging certain forms of life rather than others. The irony of our time is that, though we have more powerful image-making technologies than ever, we continue to be caught in what Paul Claudel called "the tragedy of a starved imagination."

But we began with music – "sonorous forms in motion." What we encounter in all works of art are meaningful forms – visual, verbal, or audible – that communicate some kind of promise, project, or proposition ("real presence," to use Steiner's [1989] term) that calls for our response and has the potential to affect us. Readers, viewers, and listeners have an ethical responsibility to be hospitable toward the work of art instead of using it for one's own purposes. Genuine encounters with a work of art are non-violent. I receive in order to understand.

Music conveys one's sense, conditioned but not determined by time and culture, of what it is "to be in the world." Being-in-the-world involves both a grasp of one's environment and of oneself: of one's place in the world and of one's possibilities. What music conveys, then, is not so much a message as it is a *mood*. Martin Heidegger prefers to speak of "mood" rather than ethos, but both terms refer to a person's sense of being-in-the-world. The German term for "mood" (*Stimmung*) originally referred to the tuning of a musical instrument, which may be why Heidegger also speaks of "being attuned." Mood thus involves one's sense of self, one's sense of the world, and the relation between them (the "tuning"). Because music always conveys some sense of being-in-the world, all music is "mood" music.

What is the ethos of contemporary music? Much popular music is more conducive to protesting than to praising. After all, how does one compose music after Auschwitz? How can one make sense of anything after the demise of the Enlightenment project, after the violent and absurd twentieth century? This is a problem for theologians, ethicists, artists, novelists, and composers alike. The waltzes of Johann Strauss may be charming, but we cannot take them too seriously. They are apt evocations of the lightness of being that characterized nineteenth-century Viennese bourgeois society: carefree, yet shallow. Strauss wrote music for dancing one's cares away, not for helping us bear one another's burdens. His waltzes are neither true nor beautiful. Brahms's music is more true to life, more in touch with human joys and sorrows, more *authentic*, to use Heidegger's language. Brahms wrote music for mortals, music that conveys the inevitability of death yet a certain refusal of that very finality.

Insofar as culture acknowledges the negativities of existence, it may be true to a certain penultimate point, but it is not beautiful. For much in contemporary culture is based on the premise of God's absence, and this premise creates an ethos that is distinctly hostile to attempts to make experiences of joy, hope, and love intelligible. One persuasive present-day story is that only the fittest survive. This Darwinian *mythos* generates an ethos of conflict and competition. It is a violent, ugly story that views the world *sub specie evolutionatis*.

What evolution is to nature, the market is to society. Many churches have been possessed by the spirit of the financial times, where "success" means numerical growth. The Church growth movement, with its "seeker-sensitive" appeal to the lowest common denominator, is as ugly as the popular culture it mimics, and so is its result: a "McDonaldization" (Ritzer, 2000) of worship. It is a sad case of the bland leading the bland. Ironically, Marva Dawn (1995) argues that such dumbing-down leads many to stop participating in worship because of boredom. Even more tragic than a starved imagination is an imagination that starves in church!

Against such a background of cultural bleakness and despair, Church hymns act as powerful catalysts for counter-cultural world-making. The stories and songs of the Church are indispensable moments in ethical and spiritual pedagogy, arrows to a glorious other (i.e., eschatological) order. William Brown (1999) has convincingly shown how the biblical pictures of creation helped shape Israel's moral character. Yet it is the *logos* made flesh that compels us to reimagine God's glory in terms of "the face of Christ" (2 Corinthians 4: 6). The biblical imagination depicts the entry of the eternal into human time and thus generates an evangelical ethos: "God with us." There is nothing depressing or boring about that.

Wisdom as moral imagination: right attention, right action

Wisdom – the virtue that orders all other virtues – is intrinsically linked to the imagination, and to beauty, via the theme of fittingness. The wise person perceives and participates fittingly in the ordered beauty of creation. Wisdom thus integrates the true, the good, and the beautiful. Works of art and music provide the lighting on the stage of human existence. They also cultivate the ability imaginatively to discern certain features of our situations that cannot be perceived with the physical senses. Right perception, the capacity to discern, is therefore the connecting link between aesthetics and ethics. "The capacity to see what is there . . . is integrally related to the capacity to love" (Harries, 1993: 106).

Modern philosophers often spoke dismissively of the imagination as a faculty of fancy that produces images of the unreal. Scripture is aware of this pathology, acknowledging the possibility of "vain imaginings" or of Satan appearing as an angel of counterfeit light. The present problem is not so much a demonic as a downsized imagination: an imagination that can neither grasp the whole nor project the sublime. "Kitsch" is art without seriousness, art that takes pretty, fashionable, and cute forms. But the cute is rarely curative: "The failure of kitsch is a moral and spiritual failure as much as an aesthetic one" (Harries, 1993: 60). The problem is not too much imagination but too little.

The imagination is an essential ingredient in wisdom. Gerard Manley Hopkins once wrote that the touchstone of great art was seriousness: "not gravity but the being in earnest with your subject – reality" (cited in Harries, 1993: 50). Imagination is the ability to grasp how things fit together, the capacity for beholding wholes. "Imagination is the tool by which we perceive reality concretely" (Brown, 1999: 20). John McIntyre (1987: 64), in a telling phrase, refers to the Holy Spirit as "God's imagination let loose . . . in the world." This is the same Spirit of truth, the Spirit who ministers the Word, and the Spirit who ministers the real by opening our minds and hearts to God.

Art demands what Simone Weil calls "attention": the ability to transcend oneself in order to see things as they are. According to Martha Nussbaum, perception – "the ability to discern, acutely and responsively, the salient features of one's particular situation" (1990: 37) – lies at the core of practical wisdom. For wisdom is the ability to see what is right and fitting in a particular situation given one's understanding of the larger whole of which it is a part. To act only according to general rules easily degenerates into a kind of ethical Philistinism where one fails to appreciate the shape and nuances of one's situation. It is to act without seeing what one is doing. The wise person, by contrast, is imaginatively attentive: "finely aware and richly responsible."

Great art can bring about what Edith Sitwell calls "heightened consciousness": a kind of inner clarification and cleansing that refines our capacity for discernment and inclines us to respond more sensitively to the world and those around us. Similarly, growing up into Christ and speaking the truth in love (Ephesians 4: 15) involves learning to see what is fitting, appropriate – beautiful – in concrete situations. To see the glory of God in the form of Christ is to be able actively to participate in – not simply intellectually apprehend – the drama of redemption. To be wise is to discern and to participate in evangelical truth, goodness, and beauty – the way of Jesus Christ. The best ethics is therefore a good – which is to say gospel-centered – aesthetics.

The ends of beauty: the ethos of the eschaton

Christian worship fosters an eschatologically charged ethos: a sense of being-in-the-world but not of it. Hymns make explicit what experiences of beauty in general implicitly suggest, namely, that there is a new world emerging out of the shed skin of the old. The *kalos* of Christian beauty includes the pathos of the cross. The cross is beautiful, not because of some numeric ratio that obtains between beam and crossbar, but because it irradiates the splendid form of God's self-giving love. "He hung therefore on the cross deformed, but his deformity is our beauty" (Augustine, cited in Sherry, 2002: 74).

Experiences of beauty have eschatological significance inasmuch as they anticipate the transfiguration of the people of God and the cosmological shalom, when all will be well. Presently, however, humans inhabit a fallen world where "passing away" inexorably attends experiences of beauty. Beauty in its truth and fullness is seen only in the resurrection, the breaking in of the eschatological into human history (Jüngel, 1995). In the meantime, the Spirit communicates the first fruits of the beautiful end in Christ: "true beauty is the radiance of the Holy Spirit, the holiness and the participation in the life of the world to come" (Leonid Ouspensky, cited in Sherry, 2002: 142).

"Praise without Ceasing": A Diet of Doxology

Worship, like art, partakes of the pedagogy of eternity. As with great art, worship awakens our senses and imaginations to the contours of the created order. Yet, unlike art, it engrafts us into the drama of redemption, into that Trinitarian design for living in which beauty is loving consent toward the other.

Doxological aesthetics

There is a precarious relation between the arts and worship. Art is not an end in itself; we must not worship art. On the other hand, the aesthetic quality of our worship may well be an index of our appreciation of God's beauty, and our wisdom. Those who lack aesthetic sensibilities risk being tone-deaf to God's Word and color-blind to God's glory. The fool says in his heart, "There is no beauty," and thus refuses to see the fittingness of the gospel. Things fall apart; wisdom is no more. Where the capacity to see and appreciate beauty is absent, the true and the good lack compellingness.

Beauty is not simply a value-added extra to worship, or to life; on the contrary, human beings are made for beauty, as they are for truth and goodness. Stated differently: human beings are created for fellowship with God, the one in whom the true, the good, and the beautiful are ultimately grounded and find their unity. To discern the fittingness of the new order of things "in Christ" requires a robust imagination, nurtured on compelling and intelligible forms. Hymns help to discern and to project the intelligible form of the new order in Christ. Because wisdom, too, is a matter of perceiving what is fitting, imaginative worship – the use of song and story and ritual to cultivate one's sense of evangelical and eschatological fittingness – also makes one wise.

It is precisely through learning to worship that our aesthetic sensibilities themselves can be galvanized and restored. Still, the church is not a concert hall, nor are worshipers concert-goers whose primary focus is disinterested aesthetic experience. No, those who worship in spirit and in truth must do more than appreciate the music on a purely aesthetic level. One must praise God, in singing and in listening. Listening, in the words of the composer Roger Sessions, implies "a real participation, a real response, a real sharing in the work" (cited in Wolterstorff, 1980: 25). To experience beauty is to be drawn beyond oneself into an experience of something greater than oneself. Encountering a beautiful form provokes a moral response, a desire to lead a changed life. Apart from such experiences, our worship and praise risk being about us – "instances of natural egocentrism and even idolatrous self-securing" (Farley, 2001: 106) – rather than God.

Worship, like experiences of beauty, solicits our attention and seeks to shape our character into the image of the one to whom we are attending in our prayers and praise: the triune benevolence. The shape of primary beauty is love; it follows that praise edifies the Church insofar as it enables us to become like what we adore; the shape of Christian freedom is the shape of love. *The present proposal is thus less about using the arts to enhance worship than it is about indwelling worship practices in order to enhance the arts. Specifically, participating in worship practices prepares the people of God to proclaim the good news of redemption in Christ in myriad forms of articulate action, including the creative activity of the arts.*

Being-toward-resurrection: living hymns

Praising God in song shapes our sense of space and time, the conditions for all experience. Praising God in song helps us attend to the wonder and the wideness of the love of God, enabling us to perceive it, to celebrate it, to rehearse it, to take comfort in it. Praising God in song creates a specific "mood," a sense of being-in-the-world-before-God. Specifically, praising the God of Jesus Christ forms a sense of "being-toward-resurrection." Doxology thus turns out to be much more than a moment in a service of worship; it is, or should be, the Christian's everyday mode of being-in-time. Christians glorify God in all that they do not simply as living letters, but as living hymns.

Hymns that celebrate   A doxological aesthetics forms Christian character by helping us to attend to the depths of the riches of the love of God. Hymns celebrate the resurrection and so make those who sing them celebrants. Hymns celebrate not the joy of Strauss's Vienna, but of Jesus's Jerusalem – a joy that has been tested, and refined, by fire. So-called "praise choruses" whose words and harmonies are too trite risk trivializing their subject matter and minimizing the cost of discipleship.

Genuine experiences of beauty do not simply entertain but transform. Even secular psychologists distinguish joy from pleasure: "Joy arises only when there is a transcending of egocentric pleasure into the life of the other" (Farley, 2001: 106). Joy is the perception of, and the participation in, a larger "fittingness" that satisfies our longing for ultimate meaning. Joy is not a passing feeling so much as a perduring mood or orientation to the whole of life. Christian joy is *being-toward-resurrection*.

Hymns that rehearse   One does not have to be a Christian to enjoy great music. But it is one thing to be a spectator, quite another to be a participant. The saints, living hymns, become part of the music, fitting into the created and redeemed order as witnesses to the new life made manifest in Jesus Christ. To worship well is to live well, and vice versa. Aesthetics and ethics alike cultivate sensibilities that enable one to make judgments concerning fittingness.

To praise God in all that we do is to join in the company of the redeemed who have been performing parables of the kingdom of God for centuries. To worship in spirit and in truth is to witness to the evangelical and eschatological nature of reality, giving holy substance to what would otherwise be hollow shades. As living hymns, Christians create forms of life that participate in the drama of redemption. Worship must be part of the disciple's daily diet, for worship is nothing less than the appropriate response to reality, to the reality of what God has done, is doing, and will do in Jesus Christ.

Hymns that console   Music consoles. Yet the unanswered question posed by Brahms's music (and not only his) is whether music's power to console is rooted in reality rather than in wishful singing. Consolation that is not grounded in the way things are is only an effect of rhetoric. Indeed, whether the power of music to console is grounded in rhetoric or in reality is perhaps the unanswered question of all art. The gospel provides the answer: Immanuel, "God with us." The birth of Christ is the eucatastrophe of human history. Music has become fact. Yet, like all truth, it needs to be embodied in beautiful lives in order to be compelling. True religion – and this probably includes worship and ethics too – is "to visit orphans and widows in their affliction" (James 1: 27). Christians must be living hymns of consolation.

Beauty consoles, not because it promises material blessings but because it enables us to see the larger whole of which our histories are a part. Being-toward-resurrection means living toward the joy of Christ, while not forgetting the sufferings of Christ, or his followers. Christians have a responsibility to live lives of solemn joy, acknowledging both present pain and future hope. In sum, to be a living hymn means to live and love in ways that show forth joy, faith, and hope: being-toward-resurrection.

Conclusion: Living Beautifully

Wittgenstein was almost right. The connection between art and ethics is a function of the way in which primary and secondary beauty anticipate the eschatological order inaugurated in Christ. The beautiful conveys an ethos of eternity that cultivates the wisdom for living well in time. Praising God in song informs and energizes the whole of Christian life, ministering to the whole person, heart, mind, and imagination. Hymns are harbingers of the new creation, the beauty of holiness its dawn. Christian existence is not merely pretty; the beauty of holiness is not without pathos. Yet the wisdom implied in beauty sees that even suffering has a place, or rather a time, within the broader drama of redemption. *The eschatological ethos conveyed in hymns and Christian worship, precisely by helping us to see the radiance of God's eternal glory, equips us for life in our time.*

To think aesthetics and ethics together along the lines suggested above leads one to consider art as an instance of responsible action, but also *action as a work of beautiful art*. Indeed, one might say that ethics is all about "designs for living," though such a notion can be understood in two very different ways which we can abbreviate by asking: Nietzsche or Kierkegaard?

Nietzsche preached, and to some extent personified, the gospel of art. He believed that art reveals values beyond the reach of reason and morality. Art is holy because it is the product of human creativity. Nietzsche's highest calling was to become the creator of his own life. He sought to "aestheticize" life, striving to become like God, not in the sense of imitating divine creativity but rather by challenging it. To make one's own life a work of art is a Promethean task that would only have appeared possible to one, like Nietzsche, who held to a Romantic view of the imagination as the capacity for the infinite. But why believe in human creativity? Nietzsche was ultimately unable to avoid the conclusion that art is merely a beautiful lie humans tell themselves in order to make life bearable. Ironically, the products of the creative imagination, like truth claims and moral values, are only masks for the will-to-power.

Kierkegaard seems an exceedingly odd "or" to counterpoise to Nietzsche's "either." Does not Kierkegaard himself distinguish the "aesthetic" from the "ethical" stage of existence, and then distance them both from the stages of religion and Christian faith? Indeed, both Balthasar (see Mongrain, 2002) and Farley (2001) fault Kierkegaard for disjoining beauty and faith. While it is true that Kierkegaard held the aesthetic stage to be inimical to Christian faith, it is important to note that by aesthetics he meant a way of living given over to the senses and to sensual pleasure (see Walsh, 1994). Kierkegaard's focus on inwardness makes room for the notion of inner beauty, the beauty of holiness – not the self-made beauty of the creative genius, but the Spirit-made beauty of the faithful disciple.

Kierkegaard believes that one's life must conform to one's message; one's politics follows one's passion. The Christian's passion must be the Passion of Jesus. The Christian life acquires a beautiful shape when it takes on the shape of the cross. Inner beauty expresses itself outwardly through works of love, through works of self-emptying humility and self-giving action.

According to Johann Sebastian Bach, the highest activity open to human beings is praise, and the only object worthy of praise is the triune God. Bach wrote all of his music, sacred and secular, for the glory of God alone. He therefore exemplifies Kierkegaard's passion for the beauty of holiness, not Nietzsche's passion for the holiness of beauty: "The motif of Enlightenment theology was the generally religious, the motif of Bach's theology was the specifically Christian" (Pelikan, 1955: 151). The glory of the cross of Christ was for Bach the criterion of true beauty.

William Morris, the founder of the Arts and Crafts Movement, engaged in the secular equivalent of a "holy war" against the ugliness of nineteenth-century industrial culture and against the dehumanizing utilitarianism of factory labor. Along with other knights of beauty, Morris formed his own company of designers and decorators that sought to recapture the dignity and quality, and especially the sense of vocation, that characterized the work of medieval craftsmen. Over the years, Morris and his partners designed furniture, wallpaper, tapestry, stained glass, books, tiles, homes, and gardens, transforming the stuff of everyday life into myriad beautiful forms. If Morris, an agnostic, could transform the humdrum world about him, how much more should the Christian seek to transfigure the ordinary by being an icon of Christ – not by designing beautiful tapestries, but by creating a beautiful tapestry of life.

In a sermon on 1 John: 4, Augustine remarks that it is by loving that we are made beautiful. We have been given the dignity of glorification, a fitting dignity for creatures who have received the gift of freedom. A somewhat obscure passage from the Gospels brilliantly illustrates the beautifying nature of right action. An anonymous woman approached Jesus in a house in Bethany and poured an expensive ointment over his head as he sat at table. Jesus's rebuke to his disciples' criticism of her act is swift and unequivocal: "She has done a beautiful thing to me" (Matthew 26: 10; Mark 14: 6). Beauty is something to be done, a generous self-giving love for the other that anticipates the eschatological "and all things shall be well." Perhaps it is for this reason that "wherever this gospel is preached in the whole world, what she has done will be told in memory of her" (Matthew 26:13).

The chief end of life is to glorify God and enjoy him forever, and the chief means for doing so is to achieve a beautiful body. This is the task of the Holy Spirit, who creates and perfects the Church, the Body of Christ. Primary beauty is best seen in persons who love as God loves. Praising God in song is a vital part of the curriculum of worship, part of the pedagogy of the Church as that beauty school that seeks to produce forms of individual and communal holiness. As the etymology of the term reminds us, persons are sounding boards (*per + sonare* = to sound through). The Christian life is itself a sonorous form in motion, a distinctive shape of being-in-time. Art and ethics thus converge in persons through whom the praise of God is shown and sounded in lives that display forms of holiness and wisdom. The Church's highest calling is thus to be a beautiful body, a community of persons in and through whom the love of God – the way, the truth, and the life of Christ – sounds through, a sonorous form in active, loving motion.

References

Begbie, Jeremy (2000) *Theology, Music and Time* (Cambridge: Cambridge University Press).

Brown, William P. (1999) *The Ethos of the Cosmos: The Genesis of Moral Imagination in the Bible* (Grand Rapids, MI: Eerdmans).

Copland, Aaron (1957) *What to Listen for in Music* (New York: McGraw-Hill).

Dawn, Marva (1995) *Reaching Out without Dumbing Down* (Grand Rapids, MI: Eerdmans).

Delattre, Roland A. (1968) *Beauty and Sensibility in the Thought of Jonathan Edwards: An Essay in Aesthetics and Theological Ethics* (Hartford: Yale University Press)

Dyrness, William A. (2001) *Visual Faith: Art, Theology, and Worship in Dialogue* (Grand Rapids, MI: Baker).

Eco, Umberto (1986) *Art and Beauty in the Middle Ages* (New Haven, CT: Yale University Press).

Farley, Edward (2001) *Faith and Beauty: A Theological Aesthetic* (Aldershot, Hants: Ashgate).

Harries, Richard (1993) *Art and the Beauty of God: A Christian Understanding* (London: Mowbray).

Jüngel, E. (1995) "Even the Beautiful Must Die," *Theological Essays II* (Edinburgh: T. and T. Clark).

Lewis, C. S. (1949) "The Weight of Glory," in *Transposition and Other Addresses* (London: Bles).

McIntyre, John (1987) *Faith, Theology and the Imagination* (Edinburgh: Handsel).

Mongrain, Kevin (2002) *The Systematic Thought of Hans Urs von Balthasar* (New York: Crossroad).

Nussbaum, Martha (1990) *Love's Knowledge: Essays on Philosophy and Literature* (Oxford: Oxford University Press).

Pelikan, Jaroslav (1955) *Fools for Christ: Essays on the True, the Good and the Beautiful* (Philadelphia: Muhlenberg).

Ritzer, George (2000) *The McDonaldization of Society* (Thousand Oaks, CA: Pine Forge).

Scarry, Elaine (1999) *On Beauty and Being Just* (Princeton, NJ: Princeton University Press).

Sherry, Patrick (2002) *Spirit and Beauty: An Introduction to Theological Aesthetics*, 2nd edn (London: SCM).

Steiner, George (1989) *Real Presences* (Chicago: University of Chicago Press).

Wainwright, Geoffrey (1980) *Doxology: The Praise of God in Worship, Doctrine, and Life* (New York: Oxford University Press).

Walsh, Sylvia (1994) *Living Poetically: Kierkegaard's Existential Aesthetics* (Philadelphia: Pennsylvania State University Press).

Wolterstorff, Nicholas (1980) *Art in Action: Toward a Christian Aesthetic* (Grand Rapids, MI: Eerdmans).

CHAPTER 10

Collecting Praise: Global Culture Industries

Michael L. Budde

Before the practice was discontinued by a committee convinced that "punctuality" was among the theological virtues, our parish had a distinctive way of "Meeting God and One Another" (as this Part of the volume is called). After being gathered to worship "in the name of the Father, and the Son, and the Holy Spirit," our pastor told us to greet one another. So we did. Everybody greeted everyone: not a perfunctory shake-hands-and-run exercise in obligation and awkwardness, but a get-out-of-your-pew-and-roam-around-the-church sort of thing. An embrace for someone you know, a real handshake for someone you don't, sometimes a hug for someone you've seen a few times but whose name you haven't yet mastered, and plenty of time to say hello, inquire about someone's health and family, and report on yours.

The process usually took 20–30 minutes. When it was done, you felt more ready to worship God because you'd already felt something of God's love in the arms and hands, smiles and touch, of the people God gathered that day for worship. You could bring your offering to the altar with more of a clean conscience since this way of welcoming made it difficult to postpone the process of reconciling with those with whom you were at odds. It is easy to avoid the person who has offended or annoyed you when interaction is limited to those in your immediate vicinity, but much harder when the whole church erupts in a free-for-all of motion, roaming, and unregulated interactions.

My congregation is a medium-to-small Catholic parish, predominantly but not exclusively African American in make-up, with a degree of class, racial and lifestyle diversity unusual in contemporary American churches. The time of greeting didn't have the feel of papering over real differences, never proffered a fake, feel-good sort of community so dear to liberals (white and black) everywhere. In fact, in my early visits to the congregation I couldn't help but feel deeply suspicious of the whole enterprise – all these people, black and white, rich and poor, actually seemed *glad* to see each other. It had to be false, a product of wishful thinking and white self-deception. But, over time, I became convinced that it wasn't any of those things – it was authentic, at least as authentic as the loose ecclesiology of contemporary Catholicism could produce.

As I said, this form of greeting God and one another was time-intensive. It made for liturgies that often broke the two-hour mark. Surprisingly, even the kids seemed better able to focus and attend to the business at hand, thanks to the whirl of attention and friends that swept them up along with the adults at the outset. And I believe it enabled the congregation to give itself more fully to the stories and songs – the embodied performances of Christianity – that help to form Christian disciples.

My church no longer does such a greeting at the beginning of the mass. We start on time more often these days, and jump directly into the business of the liturgy without delay. It's still a good community of persons trying to find their place in the great Christian story, but it seems more difficult than it used to be.

"Learning our place in the Christian story" might be a serviceable definition of Christian discipleship. It reminds us of a few important things: that we don't invent what it means to be a Christian, that being Christian is a learned (not innate or "natural") condition, and that we require others to help us understand and embody the role of disciple. Mostly it draws attention to the inescapable reality that serious followers of Jesus are made, not born. They are formed by the stories, symbols, songs, and exemplars of the Christian experiment. In particular it involves the internalization of the priorities, affections, and dispositions of Jesus of Nazareth, he through whom God reveals most fully who God is and what God desires of us.

Stories, symbols, songs, and exemplars – in our day, of course, it is not the Church that carries these to most people, even to most Christians. For people in advanced capitalist countries (and in ever-larger parts of the euphemistically labeled "developing world"), most of their stories, narratives, images, and sounds come from centralized, for-profit transnational corporations – the so-called global culture industries. From Disney to AOL TimeWarner, Newscorp to Microsoft, and many more – from cradle to grave, people are immersed in a "cultural ecology" constructed by these firms and their myriad subsidiaries. While once the term "culture industries" seemed limited to direct producers of cultural products – movies, books, music – the digitization of media products requires the expansion of the category to include distributional players (e.g., cable television and telecommunications firms) and information-processing firms (e.g., market research, software creators). If the world is now a global village (a distinctly unhelpful metaphor I reject), it is one in which the sages and teachers, town criers and shamans, all work for the company store.

One would think that the Church, more than any other group, would look with alarm on the increased power and influence of global culture industries. For, however else they differ, both the Church and the culture industries seek to "form" people in highly specific ways. What stories will become embedded in human desires and affections: those of the gospel, or those of the Gap clothiers? Will Christians "sing the Lord's song" (Psalm 137) in this foreign land of ours, or will they sing the latest MTV saturation-play hits *du jour*? Will they become a people trained in the ways of seeing that find God in "the least of these" – surely a countercultural skill not naturally given to humanity – or will they create their sense of the good, the true, and the beautiful from the pages of glossy fashion magazines and digitally (and medically) augmented celebrities?

To the extent that culture industry formation succeeds, Christian formation fails. The irony, of course, is that the commercial "orchestrators of attention," as Michael Warren calls them, are winning a contest that church leaders scarcely recognize as underway. For the Church to understand better its present and future in the cultural ecology created by contemporary capitalism, it must think more clearly than it has in the past about the power of global culture industries.

Culture Industries as Industries

The market structure in culture industries, while showing some variation across sectors, is one in which a handful of firms enjoy oligopoly advantages. Be it television, film, music, radio, publishing, advertising, market research or software, small players exist on the margins of a field dominated by transnational, for-profit conglomerates. Most of these firms are based in the United States (e.g., AOL TimeWarner, Disney, Microsoft), Japan (Sony), or the European Union (Bertelsmann), with smaller regional conglomerates simultaneously competing and cooperating with global firms (e.g. Globo in Brazil).

In advanced industrial countries like the United States, culture industries play an economic role disproportionate to their size. While the sector as a whole is relatively small compared, for example, with the automotive or petrochemical industries, its role in the overall economy is significant. Along with agriculture and military products, cultural products generate consistent trade surpluses for the United States. In countries like Canada and the United States, entertainment spending has become a major part of the overall consumer budget.

Aggregate sales figures do not capture the full importance and power of media and culture industries. Not only do such firms sell directly to consumers (books, DVDs, movies), they also provide critical intermediate goods for other firms (e.g., advertising, market research, product design, promotional tie-ins), as well as important distribution mechanisms (cable and satellite television, broadband Internet services). In other words, firms not generally considered to be media or culture industries in themselves nevertheless depend on such industries to succeed. Appliance makers, insurance companies, food processors, and the like depend on culture industry inputs in ever-increasing measure.

Ways to Think about Media and Communications

It is the media and communications part of the culture industries that has attracted the greatest degree of attention and debate from secular and Christian commentators. Sex and violence, stereotyping and commercialism, cultural imperialism, and prospects for cross-cultural dialogue and understanding – these are just a few of the topics typically explored in many contemporary settings. In assessing the state of the discussion among Christian ethicists, it may be helpful to identify several general approaches to the issues at hand. These are orientations concerned primarily with content, control, and context.

Content

Much Christian commentary on media focuses on problems of content. For some, too much sex or violence or crudity is the problem. Others criticize gender and ethnic stereotyping, and the exclusion or under-representation of various groups and perspectives. Still others draw attention to the Western orientation and bias of news and entertainment worldwide as evidence of "cultural imperialism."

Content is a major concern of the Vatican in its institutional statements on mass media, and Christian critiques across the ideological spectrum often focus on the "what" of media messages and programming. Content-specific approaches seek variously to protect vulnerable audiences (for example, children) and include hitherto marginalized groups (ethnic, religious, and cultural minorities) by two sorts of strategies. The first appeals directly to media professionals and associations to reduce or eliminate undesirable content while increasing more desirable fare. These appeals may include positive inducements (prizes and acclaim, appeals to professional ethics and social responsibility) as well as negative sanctions (threats of protest, condemnation, boycotts). The second approach focuses on media audiences. Consumers are encouraged to support – with their patronage and resources – desirable sorts of media content (uplifting, family oriented, multicultural, and so on). They are also asked to avoid or withdraw from providers of socially or religiously undesirable products, sometimes also avoiding corporate advertisers or sponsors tied to parent firms offering materials with objectionable content.

In the United States and Canada, most Church-related commentary on media focuses on questions of content. Much of this literature – pastoral and scholarly – assumes that media firms have a high degree of discretion in matters of program content, such that an infusion of good will and reinforcement can make for substantive changes.

Control

Christian and secular ethicists concerned with media control criticize the exclusion of women, ethnic minorities, poor people, and other marginal groups from positions of decision-making within media enterprises. They also draw attention to the lack of access to media outlets for cultural products from these same groups.

Questions of media control are tied in part to the changing patterns of media ownership: fewer independent outlets, with concentrated power in fewer hands. Public interest programming, either via quasi-governmental organization (for example, the BBC, CBC, PBS) or regulatory mandates (via the Federal Communications Commission in the United States), have been weakened by the twin moves toward deregulation of for-profit media companies and the privatization of the airwaves and broadcast spectrum (and the de-funding of public broadcasting corporations). The net result has been the strengthening of socially entrenched groups and an expansion of commercially driven media usage worldwide.

Ethicists and commentators concerned with questions of control call for renewed government regulation of media in some cases, guaranteeing access for currently under-represented groups and voices. Some call for state action designed to weaken or abolish media monopolies, and the creation of well-funded public (or non-commercial) broadcasting and publishing.

During the 1970s, questions of media control and ownership at the international level led to calls for a New International Information Order (NIIO) by Third World countries via UNESCO and the United Nations. This movement to curb the power of global media conglomerates was described as an argument in favor of state censorship of information by the United States government and media conglomerates, and was crushed by their lobbying efforts (severely weakening UNESCO for the next several decades in the process).

Finally, Christian ethicists and activists focusing on the control of the media also champion media literacy in churches, religious schools, and secular settings. By teaching people how media products are made and how to interpret them more critically, such programs intend both to inoculate consumers against some types of media effects and to invite them to become media producers themselves if they wish. Doing so, allows individuals to 'take control" of media products and tools, so that they may more effectively pursue their own ends rather than accept passively those of media firms.

Context

The sort of contextual approach I describe here incorporates many of the concerns of the content and control approaches, but situates them in a broader and more adequate framework. It also points to a broader set of implications for the Church that go to the heart of Christian life and practice; rather than being one issue among many others on the Church's public policy agenda, the power of the media and culture industries threatens to undermine many of the preconditions necessary to have any Christian community or agenda worthy of the name.

Unlike content and control approaches, which focus more on state action and on secular institutions, the contextual approach defended here is radically ecclesiocentric. The purpose of the Church is nothing less than forming communities of disciples whose priorities, practices, dispositions, and affections are modeled on those of Jesus of Nazareth and the exemplars of the Christian way at its best. Not an "idea," nor a menu of postures and notions, Christianity is a way of being in the world charged with being a foretaste of the promised Kingdom of God – "God's demonstration plot," according to New Testament scholar Richard Hays (1996). Media and culture industries matter to the Church not simply because the media affect public morals, social cohesion or tolerance, or awareness of social problems and pro-social options. More fundamentally, the Church must assess media and culture industries as systems (rather than as discrete parts), judged by how they affect the Church's ability to be a community that exemplifies justice, compassion, and forgiveness in the manner of Jesus.

A contextual Christian approach to media analysis is more impressed by the impact of the *flow* of mediated and commercially driven images than by the effects of individual messages, programs, or images. Like a control-focused approach, a contextual analysis takes seriously the corporate domination of media and culture industries, but in a contextual analysis these industries are so central to the structural workings of contemporary capitalism that changes in media ownership (or greater access to media outlets by outsiders) will leave untouched the most important and deleterious aspects of the culture industries as they affect the Church and its mission in the world.

The statistics on time spent interacting with commercial media would be staggering to persons not already numbed by the cultural ecology of contemporary capitalism. Television viewing in the United States and Japan (West European figures are closing in on them) consume more waking hours than all activities except paid employment. Young people watch 20–25 hours per week of television, and add several hours per day of radio, computer games, Internet entertainment, and the like (multiple media exposures experienced simultaneously are often missed in earlier media involvement studies; see the important Kaiser Family Foundation study as reported in Roberts et al., 1999).

A child born in the United States will spend the equivalent of 2.1–2.7 years of his or her life in school by age 18 (assuming he or she doesn't drop out); by contrast, over a 75-year life span, that child will spend nearly 13 years watching television (3 years of which will be commercials) (see Ekstrom, 1992: 135; Jacobson and Mazur, 1995: 41). The volume of media flow into most people's lives is far more than most people realize, as is the amount of time they spend interacting with for-profit culture products. The bulk of these interactions and engagements are with culture products with commercial intent: they are selling things, in other words. One expert estimates that Americans are exposed to ads, logos, brand identifiers, and jingles at the rate of 16,000 per day (Savan, 1994: 1).

Thanks to the imposition of neoliberal policies worldwide via the International Monetary Fund, the World Bank, and the American and British governments, the US model of for-profit cultural finance is ascendant worldwide. Journalism, cinema, television, radio, publishing – to name only a few sectors – are designed to attract various audiences of interest to persons selling things, or are themselves end products sold to consumers via advertising and marketing. Media content is driven increasingly by market imperatives; in the current context, were control of for-profit culture industries turned over to more pro-social owners tomorrow, the sales imperative would continue to determine the prerogatives of the new owners and operators, lest they see their properties deteriorate in value and usefulness.

From this sort of contextual perspective, the proper response to corporate culture industries is neither chaplaincy (pleading with the powerful to make more wholesome decisions) nor *coup d'état* (making one's own group a media mogul, however large or small, or by imitating the tactics and tools of the corporate moguls). The way forward in a cultural ecology inundated by culture industries and commercially centered products lies in forming Christian communities capable of discernment and selectivity. It requires greater attention to the processes by which Christians are "formed," and how these processes are affected by the formative power of capitalist culture industries.

Media and Ecclesial Formation

One of the biggest problems with a Christian ethics focused on content or control is that it assumes the continuing integrity of a Christian community capable of discerning and acting Christianly in the cultural ecology of contemporary capitalism. It is precisely this assumption that seems dubious if one takes seriously the contextual power of global culture industries. So many of us come from churches deeply accommodated to secular power (the so-called Constantinian compromise) that we seem to have lost a sense of how substantial Christian identities and convictions could be formed *without* the support of the dominant culture. Some clues may be derived by examining practices from the first centuries of the Church – not to imitate their ways unreflectively, but to learn from a time when no one labored under the illusion that being a Christian was automatically identical or compatible with being a good citizen, ruler, or secular subject.

It was during this period that the Church developed its early catechetical practices, in which would-be Christians underwent a lengthy formation period. Becoming a Christian meant making discipleship and the Body of Christ one's prime identity and allegiance, circumscribing and sometimes abrogating the rival claims of family, profession, and sovereign. The changes required in one's life – how one earned a living, with whom one associated, what one considered desirable or valued – required a long period of apprenticeship (often three years) under more mature adult Christians whose advanced formation was itself continuing. The profound mysteries of faith – that one could love enemies, that Jesus could be fully present in the eucharistic meal, that neither Caesar nor the sword had the final word in God's redemptive plan – were things novices could not appreciate unless and until they had passed through prerequisite changes in attitude, lifestyle, and commitment (newcomers were typically allowed to hear the liturgy of the word in early worship services, but were required to leave before the Eucharist). Even after several years of learning the language of faith, some candidates for full membership in the *ecclesia* were turned away; unless formation was sufficiently deep and rooted, one could not think, feel, pray, or desire as God intended for members of his new form of human association on earth – namely, the Church (Budde and Brimlow, 2002: 77–8).

Whatever local variations existed among local churches in the pre-Constantinian era (after which the practice was abandoned in the rush to absorb as many new members as possible), the formation of Christians was taken to be a matter of great importance central to the existence of the Church. However it was conducted, "making a Christian" seemed to require:

- A substantial investment of time on the part of the initiate and the community.
- A process of sequential learning, with knowledge building upon knowledge and practice upon practice. People gradually developed the religious competencies and

appetites necessary to appreciate and benefit from later practices and lessons. There remained reserved knowledge and practices, things for which the initiated had to demonstrate themselves adequately prepared and formed.

- An apprenticeship with a Church member, with the latter acting as an exemplar or role model for the neophyte. Processes of mimetic, or imitative, learning were of central importance.
- Materials of instruction, most of which were steeped in the narratives of Jesus, stories of Israel and the Church, and parables of the Kingdom.
- Formal examination of candidates, with rejection a live possibility.
- Obligations on the part of the receiving community to live up to the standards expected of the catechumen, and to walk with the newly baptized along the path of discipleship.
- A developed capacity for an interior spiritual life; in other words, the ability to pray as a Christian (see Budde, 1997: 67, 69–70).

Suffice to say that we are a long way from the formative practices of early Christianity. Indeed, in most precincts of mainstream Christianity, it seems almost inconceivable that "being a Christian" might be incompatible with the "natural" demands of state, market, or family. The loose ecclesiology of most churches in North American and Europe presumes a smooth fit between Christianity and almost anything else; there is no need to change one's life, or submit to disciplines of formation, if Christianity is redefined as a purely interior disposition (the modern turn) or relegated to an ancillary role in individual and communal life similar to membership in a club or hobbyist group.

Contemporary practices of Christian formation and post-baptismal faith development in many parts of mainline Catholicism and Protestantism are marginal to ecclesial life and practice. Consider the priorities of Catholics in the United States as one illustration of the negligible involvement of adherents in formative disciplines, practices, or time commitments (as derived from what is still one of the most comprehensive studies of parish life). Keeping in mind that behavioral measures of religious involvement tend to be higher in the United States than in other advanced industrial countries (and that the self-reporting typical of most US studies tends to exaggerate involvement), only 3 percent of parish-registered Catholics spend six hours or more per week on parish activities outside of mass attendance. To put that in context, only 3 percent of American Catholics spend as much time *per month* in Church-centered activities as the average American Catholic spends *watching television* per week. In the course of a year, most American Catholics will read no books on classical or contemporary Catholicism or Christianity, will subscribe to no religious periodicals (diocesan or independent, regional or national) – will do nothing, in short, to familiarize themselves with contemporary expressions of the faith, or even to add to their information base regarding the tradition to which they are nominal adherents. Nearly all their news on contemporary Catholicism comes from secular media sources (see Castelli and Gremillion, 1987: 30–52, 67; Budde, 1997: 83).

If American Catholics invest virtually no time in Christian learning, spiritual disciplines, or ecclesial involvement (the mainline Protestant denominations do not fare much better), what are they doing with their time? They're immersed in the products of global culture industries, of course – recall the time-and-use statistics mentioned earlier, in which Christians do not differ from their contemporaries in any significant degree. Internalizing the priorities, practices, and dispositions of the gospel is virtually impossible with as little time as most mainline American Christians invest in ecclesially centered practices – what they can and do internalize, of course, are the priorities, affections, and dispositions of for-profit storytellers and amusements. If they do nothing else, global media and culture industries extract so much time from contemporary Christians in rich countries that there is no time left for anything else more central to the mission and purpose of the Church. Were Christians to invest in other activities the time they spend engaged with commercial cultural products, a new world of possibilities could take shape; with as little time as they devote to practices that enable them to internalize the Way of Jesus, the wonder is not that churches are what they are, but, rather, that they are not even worse.

Media and culture industries inhibit processes of ecclesial formation in other ways as well. The deluge of messages, logos, ads, and jingles present problems for media firms seeking public attention: they must find ways to break through the media "clutter," to provoke recognition and attention to their product before it gets buried under the next wave of appeals, stories, and songs. Especially in advertising and marketing, firms are constantly seeking out cultural resources that have not yet been despoiled by commercial exploitation and over-exposure: these repositories of songs, symbols, and stories can then be affixed to ads and sales pitches likely to resonate with people from whose tradition those cultural resources have been drawn. Such a process is now well underway as advertising and marketing firms have begun to mine the symbols and images of religion, especially Christianity, for commercial gain. In this, advertising firms act as "symbolic predators," cultural parasites aiming to profit from legacies of meaning and socialization they did not create and which they weaken by their use. The broad-but-not-deep religious socialization of Christians in North America and Europe over the past several decades ironically contributes to the attractiveness of this strategy: with most people possessing nothing more than a surface familiarity with biblical and religious symbols, advertisers can utilize cultural resources that are both vaguely familiar to millions of people and yet not especially vital to most of them.

Consider a few examples: Volvo claims its cars will now "save your soul," Spirit soap boasts a classic Trinitarian formula for cleanliness in its three-soaps-in-one formulation, and clergy are used to sell everything from a long-distance telephone service to computer operating systems. *The Times* of London advertised itself via a photo of a crucified Raquel Welch, Volkswagen in France used Jesus at the Last Supper to celebrate the launch of the new Golf model car, and one particular detergent claims to be powerful enough to wash clean the Shroud of Turin. Some of the utilizations are clever, others are crude, but all ultimately degrade the formative power of the Christian heritage through a sort of Gresham's Law of symbolism: bad uses drive out good ones (see Budde, 1997: 91–2; Budde and Brimlow, 2002: 59).

Given this, the unvarnished confidence expressed by many Christian ethicists and activists that the Church can "use" the institutions, tools, and techniques of the global culture industry without being used by them seems naïve in the extreme. Churches whose members know the theme songs to old television shows more deeply and easily than they do the Psalms or Christian hymns are poorly placed to wield tools of such transformative power. Consider the degree to which many churches have internalized the ideology and worldview of advertising and marketing: the complete package of focus groups, psychographic research on pre-cognitive "resonances," and associative strategies that tie the Church to fun, increased self-esteem, uncritical acceptance, and entertainment. This capitulation to market formation expresses itself in the so-called "Church growth" movement, and the new embrace of advertising and marketing by church agencies.

The Church growth movement has been adequately criticized elsewhere (for example, Kenneson and Street, 1997). The degree to which the Church has been co-opted by its use of advertising, marketing, and corporate sponsorship can be seen in these examples of recent Catholic initiatives (Budde and Brimlow, 2002: 55–8):

- To finance the Pope's 1998 visit to Mexico City, the Archdiocese of Mexico City received corporate sponsorship from more than two dozen firms. The single largest sponsor was the Pepsi-owned Sabritas chip company, which paid $1.8 million for the right to use the Pope's image on its packaging. The Spanish-language play on words – "Las Papas del Papa" ("the potatoes of the Pope") – was lost on absolutely no one.
- In 1999, the Vatican approved a licensing deal with Miami-based Siesta Telecom to issue a Pope John Paul II pre-paid telephone card. The card comes with a signed certificate and the Pope's likeness on the card; the company already sells telephone cards with the Virgin Mary's picture on them.
- The physical structures of the Church are now within reach of corporate advertising and promotion. In October 1999, live television across Europe carried the formal presentation of the refurbished St Peter's Basilica. The $5 million bill for the two-and-a-half-year restoration was paid by a host of corporate sponsors, most notably ENI, the Italian state oil company. This most recent restoration-by-sponsorship continues a precedent set in the 1980s, when a Japanese broadcasting network paid for the restoration of Michelangelo's ceiling frescos in the Sistine Chapel (in exchange for high-profile visibility for the firm). Similarly, in 1998 a German appliance manufacturer underwrote the cleaning of Bernini's Colonnade at the edge of St Peter's Square in exchange for promotional rights.

Comparable exercises in the marketing of the Church have appeared in Anglican and Reformed churches, and is rampant among evangelical and non-denominational congregations in many countries. While not all have followed the Full Gospel Chapel of Denver in using market research to rename itself officially as "The Happy Church," the trends are not encouraging for people who believe that the Church can adopt the tools and tactics of the culture industries without cost to the identity and mission of the Church.

Worship as a Site for Christian Resistance and Formation?

Given the present ecclesiology of mainstream Christianity, I do not hold high expectations for worship as a site for resistance to the effects of the culture industries, nor as an occasion for formation into Christian discipleship. For most Christians, worship is a once-a-week activity. To expect one occasion per week to counteract the effects of hundreds of thousands of images, symbols, and logos – to provide an effective counter-formation to the dozens of hours the faithful spend immersed in the fictive worlds of television, the Internet, movies and the like – is to demand the miraculous on a regular basis. Doing so will make for bad worship, disappointed congregants, and perhaps the same sort of insistence on performance that typifies the technique-driven operations of advertising/marketing and other culture industries.

Part of the problem, of course, rests in the conventionally constricted view of worship as a once-a-week activity. A more expansive understanding of worship – that which focuses our attention and desires, which opens us up for transformations of many sorts – would highlight the degree to which Christian worship and culture industry formation represent rival liturgies. Seen in this way, worship can rightly claim an important role in conjunction with stronger ecclesiologies that put formation of human affections, dispositions, bodies, and practices near the center of their common life. Worship properly understood can contest and make visible some of the more pernicious effects of global culture industries, and it can model other ways of life with the potential to intrigue, inspire, and invite Christians in our day.

Sooner or later church leaders must come to terms theologically with the emotional satisfaction that people derive from viewing, listening, playing, and engaging with media and culture products. In fact, the production of emotion and emotional states is central to media and culture productions of nearly all sorts. In assessing "the ubiquitous rise of emotion-saturated narrative" in mass-media culture, critic Hal Niedzviecki notes a corresponding diminution of the role of serious literature. As he notes: "Our movies of the month, television spectacles and pop-song moments are all about how we feel. In such an environment, what is left to literature to evoke except, perhaps, the deadening sense of being so saturated with feeling that we can't really feel much at all?" (Niedzviecki, 2002: D-8). Media sociologist Todd Gitlin (2001: 5–6) makes comparable observations:

> We have come to care tremendously about how we feel and how readily we can change our feelings. Media are means. We aim, through media, to indulge and serve our hungers by inviting images and sounds into our lives, making them come and go with ease in a never-ending quest for stimulus and sensation. Our prevailing business is the business not of information but of satisfaction, the feeling of feelings, to which we give as much time as we can manage, not only at home but in the car, at work, or walking down the street.

Gitlin and others argue that the emotional indulgence conveyed via culture industries is mostly shallow, sentimental, and non-threatening. It is the affective equivalent of kitsch, about which, in the context of art, Catherine Madsen (herself relying on the work of Tomas Kulka) observes:

> A kitsch painting's reason for being . . . is its subject matter: the bug-eyed child, the cute kitten, the sunset with palm trees. The style of the painting is not particularly important, except that it must not interfere with the subject matter, whose purpose is to trigger a strong and unreflective emotional response. The unreflectiveness is the point; kitsch does

not expand one's definition of beauty, but satisfies an established definition. It does not shake the beholder's certainties but fulfills an existing expectation. It delivers a reliable emotional charge and does not incite the mind to thought. Kitsch never says anything for the first time, only for the tenth. (Madsen, 2001)

The ability to "produce a dependable stock response" is the appeal of kitsch, and why it dominates our cultural life. This emotional provisioning has profound implications for spirituality and religion, at least of a watered-down sort.

At one level, kitsch intends nothing less than to restore the soul – to supply abundantly, and in an accessible shorthand, a reminder of what we love. This is surely why children, animals, landscapes, Jesus, the American Flag, and the smile supply so much of the subject matter in the wider culture; these images give us instant access to a world of feeling that is suppressed by our daily work. (Madsen, 2001)

Madsen notes, however, that 'the restorative effects of kitsch depend, of course, on the viewer's not probing too deeply . . ." It is significant to Madsen that, while Americans see kitsch mostly as a matter of taste, many Europeans see it as a political problem.

The willingness to be satisfied with a schema, the insensibility to anything but one's own satisfaction [is the current American situation] . . . People who are strongly attached to kitsch will fight fiercely to preserve it as their only aesthetic form; they have, they claim, the right to their simplicity, the right to be protected from anxieties and ambiguities, the right not to know. Ethics recapitulates aesthetics; if we want a comforting simplicity that badly, we will get it at the expense of anyone who unsettles us. (Madsen, 2001)

In an entertainment-driven cultural ecology produced by the deluge of commercial appeals and media products, what can we reasonably expect from worship and liturgy? Can Christian communal worship provide another place to stand, a way through the engrossing clutter toward the Way of Jesus?

For worship and liturgy to contribute to forming disciples rather than children of the culture, at a minimum they must resist the temptation to ape the techniques of the culture industries. They must resist another sort of contextual argument – very different from the one I outline here – that claims that, since the world is now defined electronically and digitally, the Church *must* adapt the same ways of seeing, experiencing, and interacting in its worship life. Some variants of this technological determinism are couched in scholarly terms about a "change in epochs," in which the move from a literary world to an electronic one is as revolutionary as were earlier shifts from an "age of orality" to the age of literacy. To resist is futile, bad ecclesial practice, and likely to alienate Christians who are already more deeply in tune with the rhythms and spectacles of the Nintendo world.

Comparable arguments flourish at the level of pastoral life, in which consultants and advocates abound calling the Church to styles of worship, music, and prayer that accommodate media-formed sensibilities. If the Church doesn't embrace electronic media in its communal worship it can expect to die out in a matter of decades, according to one advocate of the "Media Reformation," a message he delivers to crowds of 500-plus paying customers (at $90 per person) in his M3 ("Multimedia, Multisensory,

Multicultural") seminars. This self-styled Martin Luther and countless advocates like him insist, in Caroline Tiger's words, that the Church must "become as attractive as secular forms of entertainment, as gripping as the Super Bowl, MTV, or 'the X-Files,' or perish" (Tiger, 2002).

Tiger shows such an imperative in action in Milburn, New Jersey, where a two-year-old non-denominational church has no building of its own, yet already owns two truck-trailers full of multimedia equipment that requires a four-hour setup each week in a rented high school space. The intent is to construct video wallpaper to run continuously through the worship service, "montages and constant surges of images," featuring sunsets, mountains, oceans, and the sky. Superimposed on the floating images are reassuring phrases, including "Don't be afraid," "There's nothing to fear," and "Be patient."

Such worship may draw large numbers and may build edifices that, according to professional audiovisual supply companies, are more akin to professional theater complexes than traditional worship spaces (McKeon, 2002). What worship like this cannot do is put emotion in service of the gospel. While the imperative of the culture may be to "take charge of your head!" (Gitlin, 2001: 57), Christian worship aims to facilitate the handing over of our emotions, our passions, and our allegiances to the God that aims to make us a new creation for the good of the world God loves.

It remains true that there is no such thing as unmediated, precultural "experience" to which we add the particularities of our time and place. Contrary to liberal anthropology and social theory, experiences and emotions are themselves constructed – by the narratives, symbols, songs, and other constitutive elements of culture. Worship is one way (not the only one) through which Christians learn to feel, to experience emotions, in a Christian fashion. Where the world feels revulsion for lepers and the ugly, Christians are taught to see the face of the hidden Christ, hardly a "natural" or universal experience of emotion, but one in which Christians are schooled via the reading and hearing of the Scriptures on a regular basis. Worship done well constructs what Jon Mitchell calls "social memory," which he describes as "a set of cultural competencies or dispositions that enable people to live in a social setting" of a particular sort. Not only can worship provide a framework for interpreting the past that is unavailable to persons not schooled in its rhythms and practices, it can also make it possible to experience particular sorts of emotions of a determinate sort (Mitchell, 1997).

Madsen sees the proper role of liturgy in media-saturated culture as one that seeks "to educate feeling, to teach it discrimination, renunciation, refusal, as the only means of expansion and compassion and grace." Liturgy that is unafraid to break free of pious platitudes and flattering the congregation by occasionally providing unsettling images, stories, and emotions, has the potential to craft more adequate "neural pathways for emotion and action." Such will require a break with the standards cultivated by mass-culture industries, and will definitely require keeping them out of the worship experience: "In the contemporary public hysteria about moral breakdown, we hear nothing about aesthetic breakdown. People who agitate for prayer in the schools seem to have no concern for the quality of prayer in the churches . . ." (Madsen, 1996–7).

Having once called for a worship service in which "a Madonna video be played with superimposed quotations from Teresa of Avila scrolling slowly across the bottom of the screen," best-selling author Tom Beaudoin admits to a change of heart away from enthusiasm for media-drenched liturgy and worship:

> At a Midwestern university, I preached at an ecumenical campus ministry service where the "altar" was a television set surrounded by candles. I played in a rock band at a very, very low-church Protestant service that featured a homily built around "the Simpsons," and a free-form communal use of Crayola markers. I preached at a liturgy during which an introductory reflection was read comparing the basic theological commitments of "Star Wars" to that of Jesus in the Gospels. Each of these experiments left a disappointing after-taste. Instead of catalyzing the carbonation of spiritual electricity that I had anticipated – multiplying opportunities for an appropriation of the Holy Spirit – each was liturgically a flat soda. In each case the worship space felt cheapened instead of elevated, both during the service and upon later reflection. (Beaudoin, 2001)

An alternative that Beaudoin now recommends is to consider worship as a sanctuary from media culture:

> as a worshipful haven, safe from the symbolic order of popular media culture, [with] liturgy as the place of media fasting; sanctuary, then, as the place that offers a counter-cultural symbolic order to that of popular media culture. The essential element here would be a pedagogy of the awe and grandeur of God as mystery present in the glorious and suffering mystery of human life – against the temptations to modes of life that are often over-active, overstimulated, and self-absorbed in media culture. (Beaudoin, 2001)

Conclusion

The irony remains that even the most compromised of multimedia churches always have recourse to specifically ecclesial forms of "global communication" – in their inter-cessory prayers, the communion of saints, and acts of solidarity and exchange with fellow Christians from around the world. The Church has carried news – even Good News – across national borders long before CNN appeared on the scene.

I started this chapter by thinking about how my congregation used to convene for worship each week. I end by thinking about that time and space in the light of the pre-ceding reflections. When I think of the 20 or more minutes spent greeting and wel-coming one another, mixing liberally with people whom I know well and not at all, I am struck by what doesn't happen. It often represents the longest period of time in my week in which I interact with large numbers of people who are my peers, none of whom is trying to sell me anything. We are not gathered to consume the latest offering by Paramount, Disney, Universal, or Castle Rock films. I am not being hectored regarding life insurance, a telephone service, or an electronic device I can't live without. It is among the only times in our culture in which people gather for a purpose without com-mercial intent. We are gathered not as consumers of this or that style of popular music or high art, but as consumers of the body and blood of the One who was in himself the medium and the message.

It is also unmediated, direct contact with lots of people. We don't welcome one another via cell phones, e-mail, Instant Messenger services, personal digital assistants, broadcasts, web pages, or PowerPoint presentations. We encounter each other's eyes and hands and bodies – sometimes you can tell how well or poorly someone is faring by how they smell – and we absorb something of the miracle of the incarnation whether we realize it or not. When untrained volunteers change into "our choir," they strike a blow against the commodification and corporate control of song and rhythm.

We now spend less time preparing to worship God and now move straight into the business at hand (ironically, we often start late now just because things are a bit disorganized). We have gained punctuality, and a bit more of our Sunday for other purposes – watching televised sports for some of us, alas. But we have lost a precious bit of free space ordered toward the love of neighbor that properly accompanies the love of God. I fear we worship and reason together less well as a result.

References

Beaudoin, Tom (2001) "Liturgy in media culture," *America*, 158: 8 (September 24).

Budde, Michael L. (1997) *The (Magic) Kingdom of God: Christianity and Global Culture Industries* (Boulder, CO: Westview).

—and Brimlow, Robert (2002) *Christianity Incorporated: How Big Business is Buying the Church* (Grand Rapids, MI: Brazos).

Castelli, Jim and Gremillion, Joseph (1987) *The Emerging Parish: The Notre Dame Study of Catholic Life Since Vatican II.* (New York: Harper and Row).

Ekstrom, Reynolds R. (1992) "Consumerism and Youth," in *Media and Culture*, ed. R. R. Ekstrom New (Rochelle, NY: Don Bosco/Multimedia Press).

Gitlin, Todd (2001) *Media Unlimited: How the Torrent of Images and Sounds Overwhelms our Lives* (New York: Metropolitan).

Hays, Richard (1996) *The Moral Vision of the New Testament* (New York: HarperCollins).

Jacobson, Michael and Mazur, Laurie Ann (1995) *Marketing Madness: A Survival Guide for a Consumer Society* (Boulder, CO: Westview).

Kenneson, Phil and Street, James (1997) *Selling Out the Church: The Dangers of Church Marketing* (Nashville, TN: Abingdon).

McKeon, John (2002) "Pulpit Fiction: With Drama, Concerts, and More, Churches are Putting Entertainment to Work in the Service of Mission," *Entertainment Design*, 36: 4.

Madsen, Catherine (1996–7) "Liturgy for the Estranged: The Fascination of What's Difficult," *Cross Currents*, 46 (Winter).

—(2001) "Kitsch and Liturgy," *Tikkun*, 16 (2) (March/April).

Mitchell, Jon (1997) "A Moment with Christ: The Importance of Feelings in the Analysis of Belief," *Journal of the Royal Anthropological Institute*, March.

Niedzviecki, Hal (2002) "Pundits and Pedestals," *Globe and Mail*, Toronto, August 3, p. D8.

Roberts, Donald F., Foehr, Ulla, Rideout, Victoria, and Brodie, Mollyanne (1999) *Kids and Media at the New Millennium: A Kaiser Family Foundation Report*. San Francisco: Kaiser Family Foundation.

Savan, Leslie (1994) *The Sponsored Life* (Philadelphia: Temple University Press).

Tiger, Caroline (2002) "The Father, The Son, and the Holy Jumbotron," *Salon*, April 15.

PART III
Re-encountering the Story

CHAPTER 11

Reading the Scriptures: Rehearsing Identity, Practicing Character

Jim Fodor

The liturgical reading of Scripture is, for Christians, the paradigmatic instance of reading. Only in reference to this definitive practice do all other modes of reading in the Christian life acquire their intelligibility, find their bearing, and attain their practical and ethical import. The substance of Christian existence derives from the Scriptures; from the Word of God Christian life inherits its peculiar character, discovers its orientation, and continually receives its nourishment and power. Indeed, it is from the hearing of God's Word repeatedly read in public worship that a life of faith takes on something of its measured rhythms and cadences, its distinctive orchestration, but also its peculiar vision. Worship is Scripture's home, its native soil, its most congenial habitat. Liturgy marks the privileged site where God's Word is proclaimed, received, expounded, commented upon, and responded to in prayer and praise. For it is in the liturgy that the Word first begins to insinuate itself within the assembled body; in worship the people of God feed and feast upon the Word of God. Here Scripture is broken, ingested, and assimilated; here the Scriptures become kneaded into the whole bread of faith. By having Scripture read in worship, God's people discover that their imaginations are fired, their hopes enlivened, their vision expanded, their sensibilities reformed and refashioned. It is in the liturgy, too, that Christians are schooled and exercised in the scriptural logic of the faith; here desires are cleansed, realigned, and given concentrated focus. Indeed, the repetition and regularity with which the faithful gather to listen to God's Word serves to collect, arrange, position, and coordinate the entire spectrum of practices and habits that comprise Christian life.

The liturgical assembly is God's people gathered in prayer, praise, and remembrance. But it is important to bear in mind that this gathering happens only and always as a response to a prior summons, a call to assemble, from God's Word. The first truth recognized by Christian faith is one of grace – namely, that the Church has been constituted by God himself, called together principally to hear God's Word. Indeed, the authors of Scripture characteristically assumed reading aloud would be the normal form of engaging the Word. Like the "Qahal Yahweh" of the Old Testament, the Church is summoned into one body so that first of all it might hear God speak to it. "O that today you would hearken to his voice! Harden not your hearts . . ." (Psalm 95: 7–8, RSV).

The mode and purpose of liturgical gathering is neither artificial nor contrived, but deeply accords with the way in which the biblical texts themselves were produced, deployed, preserved, and transmitted. An intimate bond is established, then, between the *what* of the address, the Scripture's contents, and the *way* in which they are always to be received: openly read, proclaimed, and responded to worshipfully and obediently. Answering God's "Qahal," in other words, means precisely to hear the Word of God that brings the faithful together, and, having heard the Word, to accept it in faith, collectively pledging obedience to it. At Mount Sinai especially, but at all subsequent renewals of the covenant too, the announcement of God's Word constitutes the central and decisive means of forming a people of God's own choosing, a people whose very identity and form of life are inextricably bound up with the practice of reading Scripture. Reading the Scriptures before the assembled faithful reminds those gathered that they are a people of the covenant, a people to whom God has vowed his fealty and love.

The portrait of the liturgical reading of Scripture that follows is deliberately a "composite" construction. It is designed not so much to offer a description of how Scripture reading occurs at one particular, "special" place or time in the Church's history. For no such privileged time or place exists. Details of ceremony and liturgical practice have varied greatly throughout the Church's history, yet distinctive patterns are present across confessional frontiers and historical epochs. By calling attention to these family resemblances, the hope is that something of the integrally theological/ethical character of reading, its peculiar logic, but also its formative powers and transformative operations, will become evident. The self-consciously "composite" character of this portrait underscores the modest but important objective of this chapter; namely, to show how any accurate understanding of Christian ethics presupposes an appreciation of the ethos of Scripture reading and the form of life within which that reading unfolds.

Reading Scripture Liturgically: A "Composite" Portrait

Early Christian worship closely followed the synagogue model in placing at its center the public reading of Scripture. However, to the reading from the Old Testament, the Church added "the teaching of the apostles" (Acts 2: 42) and, above all, the words of Jesus as found in the Gospels. By the time of Justin Martyr (100–165 CE), these readings – but also the ministry of reader or "lector" – were already established as a traditional and essential part of the Sunday assembly: "The memoirs of the apostles or the writings of the prophets are read for as long as time permits. Then when the reader ceases, the president in a discourse admonishes and urges the imitation of these good things" (*Apology* I. 67. 3–5). Besides Scripture, other ecclesiastical writings, including letters from the neighboring churches, sermons of famous bishops, and accounts of martyrs' lives, were also read aloud in liturgical gatherings. From the early Middle Ages onward, however, it became customary that the liturgical readings be restricted to the Scriptures alone.

Liturgical "reading," then, consists primarily and focally of the public proclamation of Scripture; but reading entails much more than the mere oral conveyance of Scripture's linguistic content. Indeed, what initially appears as a relatively straightforward and transparent activity turns out to be, upon closer investigation, a complex and multifaceted phenomenon; namely, a bodily engaged and socially embedded set of practices into which the faithful are inducted and according to which they are regularly exercised. In order to appreciate its multifaceted character, attention must be given not only to the *content* of liturgical reading but to the *modes* of reading as well as the *setting* in which they take place. The entire "liturgical scene" is significant: its aural peculiarities and unique architectural spaces, its rich auditory, olfactory, and visual elements, its ambiance, the gestures and movements of the worshipers, the prayers and acclamations, the sermon and the hymns. How Scripture arranges and orchestrates this entire panoply of interrelated movements and activities is exactly what reading entails.

Even before the human voice is sounded, the public "reading" of Scripture begins. It commences with the very appearance of the sacred books themselves as they enter the sanctuary. The Bible or lectionary is processed in a solemn entry, elevated above the lector's head. A cross-bearer leads the way, followed by acolytes, a censer, deacons, the celebrant, and others who will preside and assist in worship. The gathered faithful musically escort the procession – instrumentally or vocally (chants or songs sung by cantor, choir and/or congregation) – as it makes its way toward the altar. Light, in the form of candles or tapers, also accompanies the procession, dramatizing the psalmist's words: "Your word is a lamp to my feet and a light to my path" (Psalm 119: 105, RSV). The altar is circled, after which the Scriptures are placed, sometimes upon a special cushion, in a designated place, symbolically marking Christ's triumphal entry and enthronement in the midst of the assembly.

Signs of respect and veneration of the Word of God are also exhibited in the custom of kissing the book – first by the president upon entering the church, then by the lector or deacon before ascending the ambo (the elevated platform from which the Scriptures are read), and, finally, by the celebrant after reading from the Gospel and just prior to beginning the homily. Often, in the procession of the book to the ambo, the Scriptures are incensed. After the reading, "the fragrant smoke emanating from the censer and swirling around the Gospel book" is carried through the congregation. "[E]veryone wants to be touched by it, to be blessed by the blessing of this consecrated incense" (Jungmann, 1951: 451). The Scriptures, too, are handled in a special way, not with bare hands but with covered hands. For this purpose, the lector wears a *planetum* (a bell-shaped chasuble), which he rolls up and with which he covers his hands before handling the book. The desire to grasp the Word of God, to secure its blessing, also finds expression in the sign of the cross. As the congregation signs forehead, lips and breast, the celebrant extends this gesture to the pages of Holy Writ, thereby pledging on behalf of the entire assembly allegiance to the Word of God. "For the word which Christ brought and which is set down in this book we are willing to stand up with a mind that is open; we are ready to confess it with our mouth; and above all we are determined to safeguard it faithfully in our hearts" (Jungmann, 1951: 454).

The numerous and diverse ways in which the Word of God is "elevated" in worship testify to its inestimable importance, its supreme authority. In this regard, the reading *site*, but also *changes in liturgical location* at which the Scriptures are read, proves highly significant. The ambo (from the Greek *anabainein*: to mount, to climb up), typically in the form of a reading desk or lectern set upon a raised platform, marks the special place set aside for the presentation of the Word. The placement of the reader on a raised podium allows the reader's voice to be more articulate and audible. But even more importantly, reading the Scriptures from a lofty position concretely displays the Church's conviction that the Word of God comes to it first and foremost as an address "from on high" – distinguishable (though not separable) from the congregation's own words of response to God, which, in its prayers and songs of praise, freely borrows from and is deeply guided by the Scriptures themselves. Like Ezra reading the Law before the assembled people of Israel (Nehemiah 8: 4), reciting the Scriptures from the ambo re-enacts and visibly manifests the authoritative status of God's Word in the community of the faithful. The *placement* or *location* of the readings is unquestionably important, but likewise so are the *shifts*, the *changes in locale*, from where the Scriptures are read. Because these shifts involve both a transference of the Bible from one reader to another and a movement from one place to another, the cumulative effect is to *re-orient* the congregation, physically and theologically, *vis-à-vis* the Word.

The practice of lectors conceding the Gospel readings to a higher minister (bishop, priest, or celebrant) is one example of the physical transference of the Scriptures. Indeed, the Gospel becomes demarcated from the rest of the readings not only by the *office* of the person who reads but also according to the *mode* of reading. The lector, in other words, reads the non-evangelical Scriptures in a *tonus rectus* – avoiding every change of pitch and refraining from injecting the readings with the reader's own sentiments so as, presumably, better to preserve the "objectivity" of God's Word. Despite the lector's prosaic presentation and the conscious effort to keep the readings free of "melodic overgrowth," each of the divisions of readings (Old Testament, "Epistle," and Gospel) nonetheless acquires its own distinctive style. Customarily, "the Epistle" refers to the first of the two readings of the Roman mass, even though in all cases they may not actually come from the apostolic letters (Jungmann, 1951: 418). Specific cadences and melodic figures serve especially to signal that the Gospel is above the other readings, with the result that even for those incapable of comprehending the sense of the words read (say, in Latin, as opposed to the vernacular), they would nonetheless be able to identity that the Gospel is being read by the distinctive melody alone.

The differentiation of readings according to the readers' office tracks the gradation among scriptural readings. The undisputed centrality of the Gospel over other readings exhibits itself, moreover, in variations in liturgical design and fixtures – the ramifications of which are that, because readings take place at different locations in the sanctuary, fundamental alterations in spatial arrangement and orientation are thereby produced. Typically, in Christian worship, there is but one ambo or podium, which serves for all the lessons as well as the homily. Nevertheless, at the same time specially built desks – often in "the form of an eagle with wings outspread" (Jungmann, 1951: 418) – are constructed specifically for the reading of the Gospel. Despite variations in liturgical layout, the underlying logic remains the same. Where there is only one ambo, the lector who reads the lesson (but also the cantor who sings the responsorial) mounts but does not stand at the top of the ambo, as this platform is reserved for the Gospel. Instead, the lector and/or cantor (sometimes the same person performs both functions) is satisfied with one of the steps (*gradus* – hence the chant takes the name *graduale*) of the stairway from which to read the Old Testament and the "Epistle" or to chant the responsorial.

In liturgical settings where two ambos are present, the Old Testament and "Epistle" are read on the south side of the sanctuary, while the north side becomes the site where the Gospel is intoned. This transversal shift from south to north, combined with a vertical movement (the once-sitting congregation now stands to hear the Gospel) creates a fundamental re-alignment inseparable from the actual reading performance. The custom of standing, either erect or slightly bowed, and orienting oneself to the ambo as the Gospel is read underscores the inescapably bodily discipline that constitutes liturgical reading. This practice points up, furthermore, the way in which reading is simultaneously a communal and corporeal reorientation inasmuch as it engages, redirects, and disciplines the body.

That reading is a fully engaged, arduous bodily activity is often under-appreciated. There is, however, no mistaking this fact in the reading practices of antiquity, where no clear distinction obtained between speech and singing. For whenever *legere* and *lectio* are used without qualification or further explanation in classical Christian sources, "they mean an activity which, like chant and writing, requires the participation of the whole body and the whole mind." In fact "doctors of ancient times used to recommend reading to their patients as a physical exercise on an equal level with walking, running, or ball-playing" (Leclercq, 1982: 15). Reading, in short, presupposed that one be in good physical form. While the ways in which the body becomes engaged are perhaps not as obvious in contemporary modes of reading, the body is nonetheless actively and unavoidably involved. Reading necessarily implements and trains the body to the extent that it demands the vocalization of the page, which means that the differences between ancient and contemporary modes of reading are more one of degree than of kind.

Processing, lighting, incensing, kissing, and signing the Scriptures are key liturgical gestures by which Christ's presence in the Word is honored, as are the various customs regarding the handling and placement of Scripture. In Christian communities that follow a less "liturgical" form of worship, the Scriptures are also given prominent place. Witness the custom of displaying an open Bible on the altar or podium, of individual congregants carrying their own Bibles to worship and following along in the readings. Justice cannot be done in this short space to the full range of the Church's liturgical practice, which is but another way of saying that the composite portrait sketched above is more representative than exhaustive. Two exemplifications or illustrations of the spiritually transforming and ethically constituting nature of reading deserve closer attention: (1) how Scripture reading is tantamount to an inculcation, training, and exercise in scriptural reasoning which better enables a life of faithfulness; and (2) how Scripture reading is at once an identity-constituting and character-building activity to the extent that it both produces a fundamental re-orientation and effects a bodily "incorporation" into the communal life of faith.

Scripture Reading as Scriptural Reasoning: Exercises in the Grammar of Faith

The early Church adopted and adapted the synagogue custom of reading Scriptures consecutively, in their entirety (*lectio continua*: "continuous reading"). At each gathering for worship, the reading of a book of the Bible begins at the point where it was left off at the previous assembly and continues until the president gives the signal to stop – witnessing not only to the connection with synagogue custom but also to the conviction that it is from Christ that the whole history of salvation derives its unity. Although fundamental to the Church's self-understanding, continuous reading of Scripture within an annual cycle is not always possible in practice. Hence, the tradition of discontinuous reading (*lectio selecta*: "selected reading") emerges where representative *pericopes* (relatively short, self-contained passages of Scripture) are read in order of their appearance within a biblical book rather than the entire book. But even here the convention of observing a consistent and orderly reading of *pericopes* is never rigorously followed. In order to "avoid an excessively long reading or to highlight parallels or to emphasize one or other particular point" exceptions to this rule are always admitted (Dalmais et al., 1987: 138). In fact, the practice of "centonization" is not all that uncommon; that is, extracts from different biblical books are combined to form a single, albeit patchwork, reading ("cento").

Further interruptions to and variations on *lectio continua* developed with the evolution of the Christian calendar. As the Christian year became differentiated according to feast days and liturgical seasons, the set readings, whether continuous or discontinuous, began to be organized in such a way that particular books of the Bible became reserved to certain periods of the year. Despite the number, selection, and arrangement of readings, a more or less invariant and universally recognized rule came to be observed: "that there should be at least two readings (lessons) of which the last in all cases is to be taken from the Gospels" (Jungmann, 1951: 393).

Juxtaposing Old Testament readings (Law, Prophets and Writings) with the New ("Epistle," Acts and Gospel) helps foster within the faith community a profound typological or figural imagination. Allowing the biblical readings room to resonate deeply and fully with one another in the marvelous echo-chamber that is God's revelatory voice, proclaimed in worship from the pages of Scripture, serves to accentuate the central motifs of faith, reinforce its principal themes, and rehearse its characteristic movements. At the same time, crucial dissonances and disharmonies are awakened, identified and, in certain instances, even accentuated. Whether these countervailing forces are taken up directly and explicitly addressed in the homily – thereby intensifying the tensions among the scriptural readings, exacerbating the discordances and widening the fissures, sometimes even to the point of rupture – or whether they are glossed over and muted, the dissonances nonetheless do their work. The effect of such a reading practice is to set the various biblical passages in motion, encouraging them to reverberate and play off one another to generate specific melodies and harmonies, and sometimes harsh discords. The faithful quickly learn through *lectio selecta* (reading by fragments) that harmonies and dissonances together form an integral part of scriptural reading/reasoning. Indeed, one might say that *lectio selecta* serves as a centrifugal force, shattering the deceptive tendency to appropriate Scripture on one level, uniformly, homogeneously, mechanically.

Rightly emphasizing the distinctive "voice," the "irreplaceable tonality," of each biblical book is vital to sound reading practice. Nevertheless, no matter how important, indeed indispensable, are the individual traits and personality of a particular instrument, *lectio selecta* never entirely loses sight of the fact that it is finally the orchestration of their unique qualities and sounds that matters. Hence, *lectio selecta* yields to *lectio continua*, which in turn gives way once more to *lectio selecta*, in an endless oscillation, a continuous alternation of part to whole and whole to part. What begins to occur in these subtle and complex movements is that slowly, steadily, indelibly the reading community becomes marked by, attuned to, and conversant with the distinctive rhythms, accents, and cadences of the faith.

Transposing this musical imagery into narrative terms, the goal of Christian life might be said to approximate:

> an alignment with the inner harmony of the Bible, which, like the universe as a whole, is the expression of a unified and rational wisdom under the guise of an apparently diverse and even conflict-ridden surface. The spiritual reader of the Bible discerns what is beneath the surface, the spiritual sense of the biblical narratives and injunctions, and learns to sit a bit light to the apparent (but potentially deceptive) surface difficulties. (Williams, 1999: 5)

By repeated exposure to and immersion in liturgical readings of the Bible, the gathered faithful begin to acquire a peculiar kind of scriptural competence, which is but another way of describing "faithful living." Scriptural aptitude and fluency presuppose both an acquaintance with and an actual working knowledge of the rudiments of the faith, a basic grasp of key motifs and specific vocabulary, the "surface elements." However, more importantly, theological literacy implies an acquired sensibility for and attunement to the "deep structure" of language: its grammar and syntax, its inflection, its idiomatic expressions and local colorings, dialects and accents, an attunement to its virtually endless modulations.

The liturgical reading of Scripture performs a central didactic function. For much of the Church's history the public reading of the canonical books was really the only practical way most Christians had of acquainting themselves with the contents of Scripture. That the public readings are usually arranged on the basis of *lectio continua* testifies to the Church's continuing commitment (if not always its actual practice) to lay the subject matter of Scripture before the gathered assembly in a thorough and systematic fashion. This commitment is further evidenced by the custom of following the reading with "a homily or explanation, or alternatively by a period of silent meditation in which the meaning of the words is internalized" (Bradshaw, 1992: 38). But it would be a mistake to conclude, because one of the principal purposes for reading Scripture in worship is educational or catechetical, that therefore this aim is principally (or even most effectively) achieved by means of imparting discrete teachings or "lessons." For faith is less about learning beliefs in the abstract and more about being apprenticed, trained, exercised, disciplined, and formed into a life of faith whose fount and source is the Word of God. Equating reading with the acquisition of information, the distillation of didactic truths from the Bible, simply fails to do justice to the rich, all-encompassing pedagogy that is Scripture reading. "Christian worship," in brief, "requires that our bodies submit to a training otherwise unavailable" (Hauerwas, 1998: 101).

Scripture Reading as Conversion: Ethical Formation and Identity Constitution

"Vision" and "orientation" mark the all-embracing character of religious reading. The two are integrally linked precisely insofar as "seeing" aright means properly comporting or aligning oneself toward God, the world, self, and others. Indeed, to hear the Word aright requires that one must be realigned and re-oriented. The entire congregation physically stands and turns to face first the south, for the reading of the "Epistle," and then the north of the sanctuary for the Gospel. Reading Scripture liturgically signifies the continual striving on the part of the congregation to occupy a certain sort of place that allows one to grasp *where* and *who* one is. Thus construed, reading is less "a solitary function of the mind and memory" and more "a collegial action that is simultaneously cognitive and kinetic, spiritual and sensate" (Mitchell, 1999: 170).

Over time, through continual repetition, reading Scripture works to convert, transform the reader, by providing "a broad imaginative territory" in which readers allow themselves to be "defined afresh." Reading competency thus amounts to an ability to follow "the entire rhythm of [Scripture's] argument and the detail of its imagery" and to ask the question: "What does this writer want me to see? What of my own story am I being invited to retell or recast in the light of the way the text presents the story of God's action in Jesus Christ?" (Williams, 1999: 12). Through the liturgical reading of Scripture, Christians become educated, schooled, and trained into a new way of seeing and being. Reading is the pivotal rite of dislocation – of re-orientation by disorientation, if you will – whereby one's identity becomes radically transposed.

Scripture reading elicits but also exercises its own distinctive gestures and actions, which are aspects of its sacramental character. As the deeper movements and rhythms within the pages of Scripture are regularly intoned and proclaimed in worship, they begin to set in motion within the assembled body characteristic movements of faith. This is crucial, given the ways in which the body marks the inescapable site of identity. But Scripture reading also simultaneously disrupts certain cadences and patterns by repeatedly intercepting, interrogating, and re-describing received social arrangements and judgments. As Rowan Williams notes:

> the sacramental action itself traces a transition from one sort of reality to another: first it describes a pre-sacramental state, a secular or profane condition now imagined, for ritual purposes, in the light of and in the terms of the transformation that is to be enacted; it tells us that where we habitually are is not, after all, a neutral place but a place of loss or need. It then requires us to set aside this damaged or needy condition, this flawed identity, so that in dispossessing ourselves of it we are able to become possessed of a different identity, given in the rite, not constructed by negotiation and co-operation like other kinds of social identity. (Williams, 1996: 89–90)

Faithfully reading the Scripture thus means permitting oneself to be cross-examined, challenged, and remade by the Scripture. Reading the Bible *for* oneself and for one's community also means reading it *over against* oneself and one's community. In this way, ethical formation both precedes and follows the reading of Scripture.

The transformative function of Scripture reading complements its didactic function, which is another way of saying that *the manner* in which reading "actualizes" itself is considerably more somatic, strenuous, and challenging than is often appreciated (especially if the normative construal of "reading" is, as is customary within modernity, equated with a capacity mentally to lift information off the page). It would be more accurate to say that faithful reading of Scripture entails developing moral sensibilities, hermeneutical skills, and powers of discernment that enable the reader to negotiate God's world. To be sure, navigating, getting around a scripturally constituted world, entails (at least in part) an ability to move between part and whole *within* the pages of Scripture (a form of intertextuality or "inner-biblical exegesis"). But it also involves a capacity to move *from* the life-world of the page *to* the life-world of the reader, and back again. A common mistake is to think that reading mainly concerns extracting meaning-content "out of" Scripture by means of a process that bypasses the body altogether (with the possible exception of the eyes). The truth of the matter is that reading is "not mere mental activity aroused by the eye moving across a page." Rather, it involves a full, complete, bodily engagement and as such it is "an unavoidably social and communal enterprise" (Mitchell, 1999: 172). To be sure, this may appear less the case now than in times past when, for example, monastic modes of reading (*lectio divina*: prayerful, meditative reading) dominated Christian existence.

For much of the Church's life prior to the advent of printing technology, the widespread availability of relatively inexpensive and portable books, and the educational push towards universal literacy, reading Scripture was very demonstrably a "carnal" – i.e., fleshly – and communal activity. This is not to say that liturgical reading has subsequently ceased to be an embodied practice; only that its corporeal and communal dimensions have largely been overlooked or ignored. The liturgical reading of Scripture, then as now, is very much "a bodily motor activity" to the extent that the Bible still becomes, via the reader's lips and tongue, a reverberating, resonating, "sounding page." The reader activates the words in such a way that "the sequence of letters translates directly into body movements." Reading "patterns nerve impulses. The lines are a sound track picked up by the mouth and voiced by the reader for his own ear. By reading, the page is literally embodied, incorporated" (Illich, 1993: 54). Recall that reading is also often cantillation, suggesting that, in a significant sense, reading is rhapsodic. The Scriptures become a "score" to be performed and, as such, the act of reading is necessarily kinesthetic, bodily: it "flows from words as they move through the body, feel on the tongue, mean in the mouth." Performing the Scriptures as liturgical enactment means making them part of the performer's biography, memory, and physiology (Mitchell, 1999: 172).

Indeed, the links between movement and memory are extraordinarily intimate. Witness the way in which utterances are tied to "a well-established sequence of muscular patterns," when, for example, "the child is rocked during a cradle song, when the reapers bow to the rhythm of a harvest song, when the rabbi shakes his head while he prays" or "when the proverb comes to mind only upon tapping for a while" (Illich, 1993: 61). Careful attention to the way in which "the psychomotor nerve impulses ... accompany sentences being learned" in Yeshiva study further illustrate how reading and memory are actually remembered movement. Students sit on the floor with the book open upon their knees. Each one chants his lines in a singsong, and while they read, "their bodies sway from the hips up or their trunks gently rock back and forth." These students use their whole bodies to embody the lines. Indeed, "the body movements re-evoke those of the speech organs that have been associated with them" (Illich, 1993: 60). Reading, "thinking, cognition and comprehension are not merely 'mental processes,' they are embodied performance. Thinking emanates not solely from the brain's neocortical layer; it also flows from the skin. We quite literally [read and] remember with our *bodies*" (Mitchell, 1999: 173). In short, the ethical/theological specificity of Christian life is written/inscribed on our bodies before it is expressed in our words.

By being read, Scriptures work themselves into the lives of the faithful just as yeast is kneaded into dough. However, the "working" of Scripture proceeds not primarily by way of the apprehension of meaning or sense "inherent" in or otherwise "contained" by texts. Texts, especially the pages of Scripture, do not "hold" meaning in the way that bottles hold water. Nor do readers come to "possess" the sense of Scripture in the way a landlord owns his property. Readers, rather, relate to the Scriptures more like a musician relates to a score, or an actor to a script, or a cartographer to a map. In learning how to follow a complex set of rule-keeping activities, the reader becomes, in effect, "a living text before God" (Saliers, 1998: 25). By means of weekly, liturgical Scripture readings – Old and New Testament (Law, Prophets and Writings, but also "Epistle," Acts and Gospel) – readers acquire a finely honed Scriptural sensibility and imagination. They become, over time, figured and re-figured by Scripture, much in the same way that an actor, by rehearsing his or her part, learns to "take on" a character in the play or a musician, through hours of diligent practice and rehearsal, becomes a virtuoso.

That reading "attunes" the reader to the world and to the page also highlights the vital affective and aesthetic dimensions of reading. The appropriate affections, emotions, desires, dispositions, and attitudes of Christian faith are not only shaped by, but are actually constituted through, the liturgical reading of Scripture. For as faithful readers continually re-enter and gain their bearings from the biblical narrative that depicts God's identity in Jesus Christ, they come to learn not only *what* affections and desires are appropriate, but *how* and *when* and *with whom* to exercise and express them. Reading schools the faithful so to discipline and direct their desires that the life of God's people might become transparent to the divine character – revealing and bearing witness to God's faithfulness, steadfast love, mercy, compassion for the powerless, and so on. Thus, while there clearly is an intellectual dimension to reading Scripture liturgically, cognitively apprehending God's Word never occurs apart from affective refinement, aesthetic enhancement, or moral amplification.

Reading works variously on, in and through the reader. Reading Scriptures liturgically allows for a greater appreciation of the character of the reading body – which is simultaneously both the subject and the object of reading. Complex and subtle indeed are the ways in which the reader's fleshly body (*corpus*) interacts and interrelates with the literary *corpus* of Scripture. The idea that the Scriptures are to be inscribed directly in the thought and heart of God's people is a very ancient one. See Jeremiah 31: 31ff and Ezekiel 36: 25ff and Hebrews 8: 8–12: "I will place my laws in their thought, I will engrave them in their heart." Hence, the Word of God is not written simply outwardly (on tablets of stone or in a book which remains exterior to humans), but by liturgical proclamation, by the interior adherence of the believer, it becomes inscribed on the reader's body, enfleshed in the community of faith. As Paul says to the Corinthians, "Clearly you are a letter of Christ's, inscribed by our efforts, written not with ink but with the Spirit of the living God, not on tablets of stone, but on tablets of flesh, on your hearts" (2 Corinthians 3: 3).

There is perhaps no better way of summing up that complexity and subtlety than by underscoring the ways in which reading exhibits an inescapable "performative" character. The pages of Scripture are "living" – in the sense of "being alive", in motion, "life-giving" – which implies that they are meant to be "rendered", performed, lived out, displayed, embodied. Demonstrating Scripture's "liveliness," then, is not limited to an exposition of the intelligibility of God's creating and saving actions as depicted by Scripture, but is also a matter of following, extending, "filling out" God's actions in history. The task of readers of Scripture, in other words, is to render comprehensible God's historical performances. They do so by turning

> to the text of the Bible for clues and models useful for unraveling as much as they can of what they think they discern as the mysterious working of God in the lives of people over time. What is always ultimately at stake is the reality and the proper characterization of a divine performance in the material world of space and time, a performance that defines the personal, social, ethical, and political obligations of Christians. (Dawson, 2002: 216)

Invoking reading's inescapable performative qualities thus points up the ways in which reading is also a necessarily communal and collaborative enterprise. As Nicholas Lash aptly puts it, "It is no more possible for an isolated individual to perform [the texts of Scripture] than it is for him to perform a Beethoven quartet or a Shakespeare tragedy" (1986: 43). The *dis*analogies with performance models of reading, however, are perhaps as important as the analogies. There are clearly significant differences between dramatic "enactment" or musical "performance" and "living a life".

> For even the most dedicated musician or actor, the interpretation of Beethoven or Shakespeare is a part-time activity. Off-stage, the performers relax, go shopping, dig the garden. But there are some texts the fundamental form of the interpretation of which is a full-time affair because it consists in their enactment as the social existence of an entire human community. The scriptures, I suggest, are such texts. (Lash, 1986: 43)

Reading, then, is a practice enmeshed in social relations, which is but another way of signaling the fact that reading is more about exhibiting together as a faith community "the intelligibility of an embodied performance" than it is a matter of individually detecting the presence or absence of meaning in texts.

If reading has more the quality of a divine performance than that of a purely mental decoding of signs, then considerably more attention ought to be paid to the practices and regimes of reading (which include their material conditions and social contexts) if reading's ethical efficacy is to be better appreciated. On one level, of course, reading clearly does include making sense out of black marks on the page. But this is, even on the most generous analysis, a mere epiphenomenon. Whenever a single dimension of reading is considered in isolation, or, worse, made the defining feature, what is advanced amounts to a severely truncated view. In its fuller and broadest sense, reading encompasses a much wider semiological enterprise whereby the Scriptures themselves become a structural pattern for understanding and negotiating the entire created universe.

Augustine, who is perhaps the one most responsible for inaugurating and promulgating this semiological approach, considers the cosmos as legible as Scripture itself: "The very countenance of creation is a great book. Behold, examine, and read this book from top to bottom" (Augustine, 1966: 224). Applying his textual model broadly beyond the physical world, Augustine compares "the progression of time to the successive syllables of a psalm, the course of history to a divinely composed poem, and even God himself to a heavenly book studied by the angels" (Jager, 2000: 27). However, it is in the *Confessions* – replete with its metaphors and images of carving or cutting, inscription and circumcision – where Augustine ascribes to reading its most "carnal" (fleshly) and vivid expressions and functions. Here Augustine powerfully expounds "the radically transforming power of God's word upon the inner self and even the violence of that word as it operates on the human heart" (Jager, 2000: 32). Not only does he see the many ways in which humans resemble a text – for example, the animal skins that originally clothed their bodies (Genesis 3: 21) are of a piece with Scripture, likewise written on cured animal hides – but Augustine correlates God's creational/redemptive actions with the reparative, regenerative, and transformational movements of reading and writing. That is to say, human moral history is explicitly based on a readerly model. For Augustine "reading signifies the capacity of God's word, as externally embodied in Scripture, to convert or transform the reader's innermost self. Augustine highlights the readerly conversion of the heart by contrasting the external, bodily aspects of reading (eye movement, voicing) with its internal, spiritual effects (recollection, understanding, spiritual arousal)" (Jager, 2000: 33).

Important as it is that the reader should enter into the meaning of Scripture, it is just as vital that the Scriptures should enter into the reader. Eucharistic overtones are unmistakable here, as are the intimations of mutual indwelling and mystical union. Reading the Word is always also to ingest the Word; indeed, the intelligibility of Word and the intelligibility of the Eucharist are reciprocally dependent. For without the liturgy of the Word, the Eucharist remains incomplete or, worse, it runs the risk of turning into a kind of magic. Likewise, without the celebration of the Eucharist the proclamation of the Word risks promoting a view of Scripture as a mere archive of information, a set of doctrines, ideas, and beliefs quite independent of its need for appropriation. Interfusing liturgical reading of Scripture and celebration of the Eucharist is the practice of *lectio divina*, a practice that in its varied self-descriptions draws heavily on tropes of eating (ingestion, mastication, rumination, digestion).

This repeated mastication of the divine words is sometimes described by use of the theme of spiritual nutrition. In this case the vocabulary is borrowed from eating, from digestion, and from the particular form of digestion belonging to ruminants . . . To meditate is to attach oneself closely to the sentence being recited and weigh all its words in order to sound the depths of their full meaning. It means assimilating the content of a text by means of a kind of mastication which releases its full flavor. (Leclercq, 1982: 73)

Reading as a form of prayer or meditation thus means "to read a text and to learn it 'by heart' in the fullest sense of this expression, that is, with one's whole being: with the body, since the mouth pronounced it, with the memory which fixes it, with the intelligence which understands its meaning, and with the will which desires to put it into practice" (Leclercq, 1982: 17). On this view, reading becomes a mode of "incorporation" – by which is meant the process through which one is taken up into the life of God and transformed daily, bit by bit, more fully into God's image.

The beauty of *lectio divina* – inasmuch as it flows out of the liturgical reading of Scripture and is but its prolongation – is that its goods are internal to its very activity. In other words, with *lectio divina* "one does not read in order to have read. One reads for the act of reading." Its inestimable worth, in brief, derives not from "what we learn from it but through what it makes us become" (Bouyer, 1955: 169). Hence reading that is "true" and "faithful," in a properly theological/ethical sense, is *disinterested* reading. It is non-instrumental, impervious to being converted into a means to some other end. Reading's *telos* is not "to launch into a swift voyage of discovery, but to trace and retrace our path, to explore thoroughly, to make truly our own some part of the country hitherto known but superficially and assimilated imperfectly" (Bouyer, 1961: 52). Reading here becomes an absorption of the reader into what is being read, which is nothing short of a conformation to and union with the Word. Religious reading is training in the art of attention, a listening that anticipates creative obedience, an abandoning of oneself to the Word. As Gregory the Great so aptly observes: "We ought to transform what we read into our very selves, so that when our mind is stirred by what it hears, our life may concur by practicing what has been heard" (cited in Hugh of St Victor, 1961: 220). Reading, then, forms the reading community into a virtuous body, a corpus of character and charity.

Conclusion

Part of the Church's challenge of retrieving and restoring these vital but largely forgotten dimensions of reading for Christian life is to overcome the hegemony of modern, post-Enlightenment conceptions of reading. Regnant notions of reading are largely disembodied and disembedded. They construe the reader as a solitary, silent individual before the printed page whose objective is mentally to harvest the text's meaning or sense. The extent to which reading nonetheless remains a practice is thus rendered largely invisible. Indeed, on these accounts, the reader appears not to be *doing* anything – or at least whatever the reader is "doing" involves the body and/or a community in only a tangential or secondary sense. When reading is viewed as silent mental, "inward" process, a private and thus hidden cognitive operation, it is not recognized as a practice that is at once identity-constituting and ethically formative.

Clearly, reading has not always been thought of as a private, solitary act. In fact, such conceptualizations of reading arise from and are intimately linked with Romantic notions of the self. The prejudice in favor of the silent, solitary reader is often reinforced by the further assumption, equally mistaken, that because texts "contain" meaning (therefore "meaning*ful*"), the process of extracting sense from texts is the reader's primary objective. Added to that is the further misleading assumption that this objective can be achieved through mental operations of the sort that any person with the requisite literacy skills can deploy without any further apprenticeship or training. What this chapter has striven to show, however, is that reading is unavoidably bodily and communal in character; it is at once ethically formative and identity-constituting, which means that reading is a practice made intelligible only with regard to a larger form of life. Reading is never simply a cognitive decoding of written signs, a logical assessment of linguistic content, or following an argument; it is also – and perhaps even primarily – a means of forming and disciplining the emotions and affections, offering an orientation, schooling dispositions, re-ordering desires.

In the Christian tradition, reading is a communal speech act *par excellence*, a collective "performance" of the Book, the Word of God. To the extent that Scripture reading embodies itself in specific gestures, spaces, and habits, it is incarnational; reading "enfleshes" the Word; reading gives human form to the Word in space and time. Part of what it means for Christians to read, then, involves a life-long apprenticeship, the peculiar habits, gestures, and practices of which constitute Christian existence. Learning to read "Christianly" – i.e., spiritually and ethically – means conforming oneself to and being united with the ceaseless, gracious act of God's utterance, which is God's very own self-offering of his Word in Jesus Christ.

References

Augustine, Saint (1966) *Selected Sermons of St Augustine*, trans. Quincy Howe, Jr (New York: Holt, Rinehart and Winston).

Bouyer, Louis, CO (1955) *The Meaning of the Monastic Life* (New York: P. J. Kenedy).

—(1961) *Introduction to Spirituality*, trans. Mary Perkins Ryan (New York: Desclee).

Bradshaw, Paul (1992) "The Use of the Bible in Liturgy: Some Historical Perspectives," *Studia Liturgica*, 22: 35–52.

Burton-Christie, Douglas (1993) *The Word in the Desert: Scripture and the Quest for Holiness in Early Christian Monasticism* (Oxford: Oxford University Press).

Casey, Michael (1995) *Sacred Reading: The Ancient Art of Lectio Divina* (Liguori, MI: Triumph).

Dalmais, Irénée Henri, et al. (1987) *The Church at Prayer: An Introduction to the Liturgy*, new edition, *Volume I: Principles of the Liturgy*, by Pierre Marie Gy, Pierre Jounel, and Aimé Georges Martimort, trans. Matthew J. O'Connell (Collegeville, MN: The Liturgical Press).

Dawson, John David (2002) *Christian Figural Reading and the Fashioning of Identity* (Berkeley, CA: University of California Press).

Fowl, Stephen E. and Jones, L. Gregory (1991) *Reading in Communion: Scripture and Ethics in Christian Life* (Grand Rapids, MI: Eerdmans).

Gamble, Harry Y. (1995) *Books and Readers in the Early Church: A History of Early Christian Texts* (New Haven, CT: Yale University Press).

Griffiths, Paul J. (1999) *Religious Reading: The Place of Reading in the Practice of Religion* (Oxford: Oxford University Press).

Hauerwas, Stanley (1998) "Worship, Evangelism, Ethics: On Eliminating the 'And'," in *Liturgy and the Moral Self: Humanity at Full Stretch Before God*, ed. E. Byron Anderson and Bruce T. Morrill, pp. 95–106 (Collegeville, MN: The Liturgical Press).

Hugh of St Victor (1961) *The Didascalicon: A Medieval Guide to the Arts*, trans. Jerome Taylor (New York: Columbia University Press).

Illich, Ivan (1993) *In The Vineyard of the Text: A Commentary to Hugh's Didascalicon* (Chicago: University of Chicago Press).

Jager, Eric (2000) *The Book of the Heart* (Chicago: University of Chicago Press).

Jungmann, Joseph A., SJ (1951) *The Mass of the Roman Rite: Its Origin and Development*, vols 1 and 2, trans. Francis A. Brunner (New York: Benziger).

Lash, Nicholas (1986) "Performing the Scriptures," in *Theology on the Way to Emmaus* (London: SCM).

Leclercq, Jean, OSB (1982) *The Love of Learning and the Desire for God: A Study in Monastic Culture*, trans. Catherine Misrahi (New York: Fordham University Press).

Mitchell, Nathan D. (1999) "Ritual as Reading," in *Source and Summit Commemorating Josef A. Jungmann, SJ*, ed. Joanne M. Pierce and Michael Downey, pp. 161–81 (Collegeville, MN: The Liturgical Press).

Saliers, Don E. (1998) "Liturgy and Ethics: Some New Beginnings," in *Liturgy and the Moral Self: Humanity at Full Stretch Before God*, ed. E. Byron Anderson and Bruce T. Morrill, pp. 15–35 (Collegeville, MN: The Liturgical Press).

Stock, Brian (1996) *Augustine the Reader: Meditation, Self-knowledge, and the Ethics of Interpretation* (Cambridge, MA: Harvard University Press).

Williams, Rowan (1996) "Sacraments of the New Society," in *Christ: The Sacramental Word*, ed. David Brown and Ann Loades, pp. 89–102 (London: SPCK).

— (1999) "To Stand Where Christ Stands," in *An Introduction to Christian Spirituality*, ed. David Brown and Ann Loades, pp. 1–13 (London: SPCK).

CHAPTER 12

Listening: Authority and Obedience

Scott Bader-Saye

As the Scripture reading begins, the congregation listens with expectation and eagerness. The desire to hear God's Word silences all other voices and focuses the concentration. Well, sometimes. Other times, the congregation fidgets, glances down at the bulletin, quiets a noisy child, looks out of the window, notices the time, all the while wondering whether to go out to lunch or fix something at home. Listening is not always easy. Even when the preacher begins to preach – making eye contact and using expressive gestures – listening requires effort. Twice a day observant Jews recite a prayer called the *Shema*, beginning with the words "Hear (*shema*), O Israel" (Deuteronomy 6: 4). By reciting these words so often, they are reminded that their first task as God's people is to listen. The prayer continues by reminding them that listening calls forth obedience, "You shall love the Lord," and that listening for God's Word is a continuing process, "keep these words that I am commanding you today in your heart. Recite them to your children . . . Bind them as a sign on your hand . . . and write them on the doorposts of your house" (Deuteronomy 6: 6–9). God's command that Israel "hear" is not so different from a parent asking a child, "Are you listening?," by which the parent really means, "If you are listening you will do what I ask you." To hear God is to obey God. (The word "obedience" derives from the Latin root *ob* + *audire* "to hear.")

Modernity: The Crisis of Authority

In a "do what feels good" and "be yourself" culture, talking about obedience is hardly popular. Because modern people have learned to value autonomy as one of their highest goods, authority often appears to be a threat. Of course, one must admit that authority *can* be threatening, especially when it serves as a mask for domination. In modern times, however, it is not just the abuse of authority that has come under question, it is the idea of authority itself. Given the reservations many have about the legitimacy of authority and the presumption that authority is incompatible with freedom, the challenge of this chapter is to reclaim the possibility of wise authority and joyful obedience though an examination of the Christian practices of speaking and listening.

Why has authority become a bad word for those shaped by the Enlightenment ideal of individual autonomy? At the beginning of the modern period, authority (especially that of the Church) came under fire from the forces of Renaissance humanism and Enlightenment rationalism. René Descartes, the seventeenth-century philosopher and scientist, began his search for truth by first doubting everything that could be doubted: all that he had been taught, all that tradition had declared, even what his own senses told him, for here too he could be mistaken or deceived. What he could not doubt, he determined, was that he existed, because just when he tried "to think everything false," he realized that he must exist in order to be thinking – concluding famously, "I think, therefore I am" (Descartes, 1956: 21). Descartes tried, in a sense, to recreate the wheel of knowledge, to start at the very beginning and determine for himself, apart from the authorities of the past or present, what was most certainly true. The philosophical success of his project is less interesting now than the spirit of his project. Descartes stands as a particularly vivid illustration of the modern turn to the self, the ascendance of the individual as arbiter of truth and the decline of traditional authorities as trusted sources of knowledge and guidance.

Almost 150 years later, Immanuel Kant made clear that this aspect of the Enlightenment project was still going strong. In a 1784 essay entitled "What is Enlightenment?," Kant wrote:

> Enlightenment is man's release from his self-incurred tutelage. Tutelage is man's inability to make use of his understanding without direction from another. Self-incurred is this tutelage when its cause lies not in lack of reason but in lack of resolution and courage to use it without direction from another. *Sapere aude!* "Have courage to use your own reason!" – that is the motto of enlightenment. (Kant, 1959: 85)

Though Kant's work is seen by some to mark the conclusion of the Enlightenment as an historical period, he clearly embraces the spirit of Enlightenment that would throw off the shackles of authority (what Kant calls "tutelage") in favor of the free pursuit of knowledge by the individual.

This spirit of Enlightenment, this challenge to "think for yourself," has outlasted Kant and the modern period and continues today as a driving force of postmodernism. Michel Foucault, the twentieth-century French philosopher, wrote his own response to the question "What is Enlightenment?" Like Kant, Foucault affirmed an ethos or attitude of Enlightenment that goes beyond any particular historical period or body of knowledge. He described this ethos as "a philosophical life in which the critique of what we are is at one and the same time the historical analysis of the limits that are imposed on us and an experiment with the possibility of going beyond them " (Foucault, 1984: 50). Foucault's postmodern desire to transgress imposed limits corresponds closely to the modern quest for liberation. Indeed, on this point, postmodernity is but an extension of modernity.

Lest I give the impression that the rejection or suspicion of traditional authority exists only in philosophical circles, consider the ways in which popular culture reinforces this attitude. "Must see" TV shows, such as *Seinfeld*, *Friends*, and *Will and Grace*, normalize a world in which the characters are guided by no authority beyond their personal fulfillment. Indeed, part of the humor in these shows comes from the levity with which the characters treat such serious matters as sex and death: think of the death of George's fiancé in *Seinfeld* or Joey's inability to remember the names of women he sleeps with in *Friends*. Popular culture urges us to "Just do it" and "Obey your thirst." Such messages both exploit and encourage a conception of freedom that is little more than lack of restraint.

Another way of putting all this is to say that authority has not vanished but has been relocated within the individual. The word "autonomy" derives from the Greek *auto* "self" + *nomos* "law, rule," meaning literally "the rule of the self" or "a law unto oneself." In a culture infatuated with autonomy, personal experience and individual preference become the arbiter of what is true and right. In such a context all outside voices are treated with suspicion, and rightly so if we assume that those in authority are also answerable to nothing outside themselves. Once we imagine the world as an arena of conflicting autonomous wills, authority can hardly avoid being construed as dominance and coercion.

The perceived conflict between authority and freedom turns out also to be a conflict between community and individual. Communal life requires some kind of authority structure that makes life together possible. Lacking a common vision and common guidance, a community of self-interested individuals could hardly avoid being fractured by competition and conflict, as in William Golding's novel *Lord of the Flies* or an episode of *Survivor*. Proper authority turns out to be the necessary condition of community, though of course authority can be exercised to produce good or bad communities. Neither authority nor community can be considered good in the abstract; each becomes good as it is used rightly and directed toward the right ends. What the Christian story provides is a way of naming the ends that authority and community should serve. Specifically, Christians use language like "the reign of God" and "the Body of Christ" to describe the goal of authority and the nature of community. Apart from the service of God's reign, authority, even ecclesial authority, loses its credibility and quickly descends into domination that serves the interests of the powerful. Apart from the service of God's reign, freedom becomes little more than license to pursue one's own desires without question or constraint. Such "freedom" can quickly devolve into slavery to greed, lust, ambition, pleasure, and power.

Scripture: Authority as Transparent and Cruciform

The crisis of authority in modernity was not the first or only such crisis. Already in biblical times, Israel and the early Church struggled over the proper exercise of authority in their communities. Israel's transition from a confederacy of tribes ruled by judges to a unified nation ruled by a king presents a particularly instructive case. The book of Judges displays the moral decay of Israel under the rule of judges, and, as if to punctuate the decline, the book ends with the horrific story of the rape, murder, and dismemberment of the Levite's concubine. The editor of Judges concludes this story, and the book, saying, "In those days there was no king in Israel; all the people did what was right in their own eyes" (Judges 21: 25). Governance by judges fails precisely in that it cannot control moral anarchy. Without a central authority figure, individuals fall prey to arbitrary judgments and end up serving nothing more than their own preferences, that is, doing "what was right in their own eyes." The book of Judges ends, then, with the hope that a king could deliver Israel from its moral corruption.

1 Samuel 8–12 narrates the rise of kingship in Israel. Following the book of Judges, one might assume that the naming of a king would be greeted with great joy and expectation, but, in fact, the text reveals a deep conflict about the monarchy. In these chapters, the editor has apparently woven together two literary sources, one pro-monarchy and one anti-monarchy, giving the reader a vertiginous sense of spinning between the poles of an unresolved argument. The pro-monarchy source sees kingship as God's answer to Israel's problems. In this source, God calls on Samuel to anoint Saul who, God promises, "shall save my people from the hand of the Philistines" (9: 16). Samuel anoints Saul and the spirit of God is poured out upon him. Saul immediately shows his courage by delivering Israel from the Ammonites and shows his mercy by refusing to punish those Israelites who have opposed him (11: 1–15).

However, woven into these pro-monarchy passages are sections that present the monarchy as a grave mistake on Israel's part. In the anti-monarchy account, the idea of kingship comes not from God but from the people. They ask Samuel to appoint "a king to govern us, like other nations" (8: 5). Samuel takes the request as a personal rejection of his judgeship, yet God tells him "they have not rejected you, but they have rejected me from being king over them" (8: 7). Samuel recounts for the people what a king will do, conscripting their sons and daughters into his service, taking the best of their fields and produce, essentially turning them into his slaves. The people reply: "we are determined to have a king over us, so that we may also be like other nations" (8: 19–20). This passage presents a double indictment of Israel: that they wish to replace God as king and that they wish to be like the nations. As the chosen ones, their election had been predicated on the rule of God and their distinctiveness from the other peoples of the world. Now both were in jeopardy. After Saul has been chosen and anointed as king, the people recognize their mistake and beseech Samuel: "Pray to the Lord your God for your servants, so that we may not die; for we have added to all our sins the evil of demanding a king for ourselves" (12: 19).

The central question that arises in this story is whether the one who exercises earthly authority among God's people, in this case the king, will displace God as the true ruler of the people or will be a transparent vehicle for God's authority. The rules for kingship in Deuteronomy 17: 14–20 (written long after the establishment of the monarchy, though canonically preceding it) suggest that there may be a way to balance the need for visible earthly authority with the recognition that this authority is but a vessel to mediate God's reign. This passage begins by placing restrictions on the king: he must not acquire many horses, many wives, or much silver and gold (17: 16–17). Power, sex, and money were seen as potential threats to the proper rule of the king. Kingly power was not to be an excuse for excess, and the king was not to exalt himself over others in the community. Next comes the positive command: the king was to have a copy of the Torah written for him and he was to make its study a daily habit. The good king would rule by making his kingship transparent to the authority of God revealed in the Torah.

In the New Testament a crisis of authority arises among the disciples as Jesus moves toward his final days. In Luke's Gospel it is just after the Last Supper that the disciples begin to argue "as to which one of them was to be regarded as the greatest" (Luke 22: 24). Jesus says to them:

> The kings of the Gentiles lord it over them; and those in authority over them are called benefactors. But not so with you; rather the greatest among you must become like the youngest, and the leader like one who serves. For who is greater, the one who is at the table or the one who serves? Is it not the one at the table? But I am among you as one who serves. (Luke 22: 25–7)

Having just risen from the table where Jesus has offered himself to them in weakness, as broken body and spilled blood, the disciples immediately show their lack of perception by arguing over worldly power: who will be greatest in Jesus's administration? Jesus quickly challenges them to recognize that they are acting like the Gentiles (the nations). God's people are not to embrace power as a means of "lording it over" others. In fact, they are to witness to a radically new kind of authority, the authority that comes through service and through a dispossession of power. Jesus turns their attention to the table from which they just arose: he is greater than they, yet he served them. This is the pattern of vulnerable authority that Jesus leaves for his Church. It is not an abdication of authority, but neither is it a grasping after control. It is the rule of God mediated through service and weakness. It is an authority that would die for the truth but would not kill for it.

What may we conclude from these biblical struggles with authority? First, any human ruler who would stand over God's people must exercise authority in a way that is transparent to the authority of God. The real danger of the monarchy in ancient Israel was that it would function as a replacement for divine authority, occluding God's rule rather than mediating it. Second, leadership within the Church must bear the imprint of the cross. Cruciform leadership refuses to lead from power, but rather leads from weakness. The authority of the cross comes from Jesus's willingness to be a servant unto death.

Liturgy: Speaking and Hearing the Authoritative Word

By attending to its liturgical practice, the Church may recover resources for embodying a transparent and cruciform authority. In the liturgy, the people of God re-encounter the story of Israel and Jesus as the Word of God is spoken and heard in three different ways: in the Scripture lessons, in the sermon, and in the recitation of the Creed. In this threefold movement of the liturgy, the preaching of the Word is bracketed by the words of Scripture and tradition, while Scripture and tradition rely on the spoken sermon to bring their authority to life for this particular community.

In my Episcopal tradition, the Old Testament, the Psalm, and the Epistle are read by lay readers from the lectern. After each selection, the reader proclaims "The Word of the Lord." The congregation responds, "Thanks be to God." I must confess that on some days this feels like an odd response. For instance, we recently heard this reading from the book of Joel: "Let all the inhabitants of the land tremble, for the day of the Lord is coming, it is near – a day of darkness and gloom, a day of clouds and thick darkness! Like blackness spread upon the mountains a great and powerful army comes; their like has never been from of old, nor will be again after them in ages to come" (Joel 2: 1–2). And for this we give thanks? Importantly, the response of gratitude is not particular to the Scripture lesson for the day. Christians give thanks for every Scripture, knowing that however dark or challenging or puzzling the passage may be, this too can, by the work of the Holy Spirit, become for us God's Word. So, we respond not with the "Yes, sir!" of forced compliance but with the "Thank you" of one who has received a gift, the gift of truth telling. The Bible does not mince words; it does not lie to us to make us feel better. In a world that is all too often full of darkness, it is sometimes a relief to hear that hard truth spoken aloud, and so we give thanks.

The response of gratitude also reminds us that the authority of the Word does not seek to bind us but to free us. As one collect from the *Book of Common Prayer* puts it, "to serve you [God] is perfect freedom." How can service be freedom? It cannot be, if freedom means what many commonly take it to mean: "doing what I want." Yet a "freedom" that is but lack of external restraint is nothing more than license to become enslaved to one's passions. In a Christian understanding, freedom is not "doing what I want" but "being who I am." Of course, *being* who I am requires that I *know* who I am. Only as I move more deeply into my identity as a child of God, created, redeemed, and loved, will I begin to understand how the service of God is the truest expression of who I am. Thus, while the service of God will not always mean that I get to do what I want, I am perfectly free because in God's service I am enabled to be who I am. For this, Christians give thanks and welcome the authoritative Word of God as a word of freedom.

At the point of the Gospel reading, the priest and the congregation make the sign of the cross over their forehead, mouth, and heart. (The first time I tried this, having come from another tradition, I found myself accidentally crossing my *nose* in a rather uncoordinated gesture. I realized then why repetition and habit are so important!) This preparation to hear the Word recalls the congregation to its commitment to cruciform discipleship in thinking, speaking, and acting. Only as we are willing to make our lives like Christ's own will we be able to hear and understand the Word he speaks to us. In other words, the listening we are about to do is deeply tied up with obedience. Are we willing to take up our cross and follow? Are we ready to do what we hear? Unlike the Old Testament, Psalm, and Epistle readings, which come from the lectern, the Gospel is read from the center aisle in the midst of the congregation. Here, in the story of Jesus, the Word has come close to us, and so, liturgically, we bring the Word close. This says something important about its authority. One might imagine that the Gospel reading, pointing most directly to the life of the one we proclaim as Lord, would be read from the highest place, reminding us that Christ stands over us in lordship. But Jesus understood his own authority as a challenge to all domination; thus, his rule takes the form of service. So, as the Gospel of Christ is brought low into the congregation, the gathered people hear it as an authority that humbly stands alongside us rather than above us.

After the Gospel reading, the preacher stands in the pulpit (or, in my local church, sometimes continues to stand in the midst of the congregation) to proclaim God's Word for the community. Before beginning, she invokes the name of God, "In the name of the Father, the Son, and the Holy Spirit," and again both priest and congregation mark themselves with the sign of the cross. With our words and our gestures we situate Christian speaking and hearing in a Trinitarian context where the goal is the formation of a community marked by the cross of Christ. Placing authority and obedience in a Trinitarian context is crucial for a proper Christian understanding. Herbert McCabe, writing about obedience in his own Dominican order, observes: "Christ lived his whole life and died in total *obedience* to his Father and yet was *equal* to his Father ... Now, our obedience, our relationship to the community, is not just *like* the relationship of God the Son to God the Father; it *is* a sharing into that relationship" (McCabe, 1992: 233).

The Christian story does not equate obedience with subordination. As Jesus modeled authority through service, so he also modeled obedience among equals. In the garden, Jesus, the Son, prays to his Father in heaven that the cup of suffering might pass from him, yet he concludes "not what I want, but what you want" (Mark 14: 36). The Son is obedient to the Father through the power of the Spirit, yet Father, Son, and Spirit are equal, united as one God. This unity in difference is the mystery of the Trinity. As the body of the Church seeks to be drawn more deeply into this mystery, it will learn to enact authority and obedience in ways that mirror both the unity and the difference in the Godhead. As the laity participates more fully in Christ, submission to pastoral authority will not be seen as weakness or loss but as a Spirit-led participation in the submission of the Son to the Father. Likewise, the exercise of pastoral authority will be seen not as domination but as a humble participation in Christ's cruciform lordship. In this way, both those who lead and those who follow become transparent to the model of Christ and thereby bear witness to his life.

After the invocation of Father, Son, and Holy Spirit, the preacher delivers the sermon. Central among the preacher's concerns in the sermon must be transparency to the Word that authorizes her speech. Martin Luther thought so highly of preaching that he once said we should listen to the preacher as if we were listening to the very words of God. Certainly no preacher could live up to such pressure if this were understood to be some kind of human achievement. Luther's injunction, however, was meant to remind us that the preacher's words ought, by God's grace, to become utterly open to God's own. Unlike the kings in ancient Israel whose authority all too often became a rival to God's authority, the preacher must point away from herself toward the one before whom the whole congregation bows. Her obedience to the Word that has been read serves to ground her authority as God's spokesperson to the congregation. It is given to her to bear and interpret the communal memory that allows us to test our present obedience against Scripture and tradition. Her judgments are neither arbitrary nor optional.

The sermon, then, should be both transparent to God's authority and cruciform in its message. Paul reminded the Corinthians that, when he first came to preach among them, "I did not come proclaiming the mystery of God to you in lofty words or wisdom. For I decided to know nothing among you except Christ Jesus, and him crucified" (1 Corinthians 2: 1–2). The goal of Paul's preaching was to witness to Christ crucified and, in so doing, produce in his hearers a conformity to the mind of Christ. "Let the same mind be in you that was in Christ Jesus," he tells the church in Philippi (Philippians 2: 5). Proclamation ought to guide the congregation into a unity of mind that reflects the *kenosis*, the self-emptying of Christ. As the priest proclaims the Word, the congregation enters into a time of learning, of allowing our minds to be conformed to Christ so that as a community we share one mind. The authority of the pastor arises from shaping this shared mind rather than commanding the isolated will.

After the sermon, there is a time of silence. This is not a time for the congregation to assess the preached word to decide if we agree or disagree. Such acts of judgment are not the proper work of worship. Rather, we are to listen, again, to hear what God would call forth from the sermon as a word to us, here and now, as a call to obedience. It is time to let the Word sink in like rain on dry soil. Karl Barth (1961) has famously said that silence in worship is as useful to the devil as it is to God, but in this moment between sermon and Creed, the silence allows our human words to recede and again become transparent to the God who bears all true authority.

After the silence, the congregation stands to speak the words of the Creed. Here the listening turns to speaking. The power and authority to bear the tradition forward is handed over to the congregation as a whole. In a recent ordination sermon Episcopal Bishop Paul Marshall noted that "the newly ordained are immediately put to work delivering the sacrament and pronouncing God's blessing so that they and we know that *they are not ordained to accumulate power, but to disperse it*" (Marshall, 2002: A3). The speaking of the Creed in common is a sign of that dispersal of power and authority. Those who have listened and heard the Word in obedience now become those who speak the Word with authority.

Community: Authority in Strength and Weakness

Within any healthy community authority is necessary. This claim may strike some as odd, for many assume that authority is a necessary evil that exists to respond to problems and failures. Surely, they say, when a community is healthy and functioning well it needs authoritative voices less and less. This view assumes that authority has no positive, directive role, only a negative, constraining role; thus it fails to see that the need for authority can arise not only from deficiency but from abundance. Yves Simon, a French Catholic philosopher, lived during the first half of the twentieth century and witnessed two world wars. He responded to the perversions of authority that accompanied those conflicts not by rejecting authority altogether but by probing more deeply into the basis and purpose of true authority. He concluded: "The truth may well be that authority has several functions, some of which would be relative to deficient states of affairs and others to features of perfection" (Simon, 1962: 21). What he meant was that authority properly functions to educate, form, and reform in situations where there is a deficiency of knowledge or character (think of the authority of the teacher or the parent), as well as to direct and organize in situations where there is such a plenitude of gifts that they need coordination (think of the authority of the orchestra conductor or the lead dance partner). Simon writes:

> Given a community on its way to its common good, and given, on the part of this community, the degree of excellence which entails the possibility of attaining the good in a diversity of ways, authority has an indispensable role to play, and this role originates entirely in plenitude and accomplishment . . . An ideally enlightened and virtuous community needs authority to unify its action. (Simon, 1962: 49–50)

To some extent, both types of authority will always be necessary in the Church, for it is a community that is both sinful and redeemed, full of gifts and battered by wounds. Authority in the Church serves to form the character of the community as well as to coordinate the many gifts poured out by the Holy Spirit. The more faithful and mature a church community becomes, the more those in authority can serve as conductors of a skilled performance rather than as teachers of those still learning to play the music.

To try another metaphor, authority in a healthy Christian community should resemble a dance in which one partner leads but both partners make the dance possible. Such cooperative partnership was vividly enacted in the recent enthronement of Rowan Williams as Archbishop of Canterbury. After the congregation had gathered and the participants had processed, the Archbishop arrived at the closed cathedral door. Breaking the silence, he struck the door three times with his staff. The choir began to sing *Jubilate Deo* and the door to the cathedral was opened. The Dean then spoke: "Most Reverend Father in God, we have looked forward to your coming with great joy. In the name of the Lord we greet you and welcome you into your Cathedral church." All the congregation then spoke in unison: "In the name of the Lord we greet you." The Archbishop responded: "With all my heart, I thank you for your welcome. I hope to serve you and to serve with you in Christ's name and in the joy of his Spirit. May the peace of God our Father be upon this house and upon this company."

What was remarkable about the moment, aside from the sheer power of the spectacle, was the sense of partnership between the Archbishop and the people. Williams did not appear in the chancel from a side door to claim his authority from a position above and in front of the people. Rather, he came knocking, asking entrance, mirroring Christ's humble invitation, "behold I stand at the door and knock" (Revelation 3: 21). He waited for the door to be opened and for the people to welcome him. His first words were reminders of the servant nature of his authority, "I hope to serve you and to serve with you," giving himself to the people in service as they, in turn, gave themselves to his authority. In the enthronement liturgy, the relationship of power and obedience, leadership and submission, was played out in such a way as to echo the mutual self-giving of the persons of the Trinity. As I reflected on the many symbolic gestures in the service, Williams's own words came to mind:

> those who are charged with speaking authoritatively for or in the community stand in a very peculiar and paradoxical place. The distance from the community that is built into

their role has to be something other than a claim to share the kind of distance that exists between the risen Jesus and the community. They remain under the judgment of the Risen One, along with the rest of the community, and their task is to direct attention away from themselves to Jesus, to reinforce the community's awareness of living under Jesus' judgment. (Williams, 2000: 192–3)

What happens, though, when the dance is disrupted, when some in the community refuse to welcome the authority of the bishop or pastor? What is to be done when members of the body refuse the pastor's teaching and resist being of one mind? Just as there can be abuses of authority there can be failures of obedience. Often resistance to pastoral leadership comes not from the prayerful and humble conviction that such leadership has strayed from its own ground and source, but from the misguided sense that one's personal preferences should be catered to. Such views assume a bureaucratic model of leadership in which the balancing of rights and interests becomes primary. On this model, members vie with one another to have their needs and desires met or at least balanced alongside the interests of others. Such a model makes ecclesial unity impossible. In the life of cruciform discipleship, personal preferences may have to be set aside for the good of the community. The priest or pastor has the responsibility to name those instances where dispossession of interests is necessary and to help the members of the body see that such self-giving is part of their imitation of Christ for the good of others.

In the church at Philippi, two of Paul's co-workers, Euodia and Syntyche, were quarreling. We do not know the nature of the conflict, but, in his letter to their church, Paul calls them to agreement. The language he uses is instructive: "I urge Euodia and Syntyche to be of the same mind in the Lord" (Philippians 4: 1). Further, he asks another member of the community to assist the women in reconciling. The unity of the body is the concern of everyone, and it comes not through coercion but by the patient movement of every member toward conformity with the mind of Christ. Again, some members may actively resist this unity, and in such cases the pastor may need to exercise authority for the good of the whole.

It is easy enough to see the importance of Church discipline in extreme cases, such as adultery or abuse, but what about the more common causes of division: personality conflicts, resistance to change, and hurt feelings? Imagine a church that has just hired a new rector. He comes in with great enthusiasm and many ideas. Unlike the previous rector, he has an informal style of worship leadership and he begins to include more contemporary music in the service. Some members of the congregation find these changes troubling and begin to gossip and spread rumors, dividing the body. What is the rector to do in such a situation? Discipline in the Church, like all ecclesial authority, is primarily about making community possible. So, steps taken to discipline a member or members can only make sense as part of a continuing attempt to reconcile and restore unity. Discipline such as "fencing the table," that is, excluding certain people from communion who are actively dividing the body, stands at the far edge of attempts to reconcile. Such action, however, should not be understood as the priest or bishop dividing the body but rather as the truthful acknowledgment that someone has already divided the body and will continue to rupture the community until there can be truthful speech and honest repentance.

This is why Jesus gives guidelines for seeking reconciliation before invoking the pastoral power to "bind and loose" in the community (Matthew 18: 15–19). He urges community members to confront the offender alone, with another, and finally with the whole church before treating that one "as a Gentile and a tax collector." Such exercises of authority, while rare, may be important to save the unity of the body, and ultimately to serve the good of the offending members. What needs to happen is for the offenders to come to understand that proper Christian obedience requires them to set aside certain preferences or interests, actions or desires in the service of *their own* greatest good. Again, McCabe's thoughts are helpful: "Obedience for us is not a denial of self but a discovery of self. For – to say it again – obedience is not the suppression of our will in favor of someone else's, it is learning to live in community, in solidarity, which is simply learning to live" (McCabe, 1992: 231). Discipline involves helping others embrace obedience as a way of embracing communal life. Rightly practiced, the dance of authority and obedience involves for both parties the loss of self in order to gain the self again in communion with Christ's Body.

World: Mission and Parable

So far, we have focused our attention on speaking and listening, authority and obedience within the Church. The question remains whether there is something in this understanding of a cruciform and transparent authority that can serve as a model for those outside the Church, from community leaders to heads of state. In other words, does the Church have a mission, a calling, to speak to the world about the ways in which it exercises authority?

In recent years, we have seen no more powerful example of cruciform authority in the face of political conflict than that of Archbishop Desmond Tutu of South Africa. Tutu, who now works for peace and restorative justice around the world, bears an authority that is recognized both inside and outside the Church. His authority comes not simply (or even primarily) from the title of Archbishop, but from his willingness to live and lead in the way of the cross. His leadership of the Truth and Reconciliation Commission guided South Africa through a peaceful transition out of apartheid and into democracy (see Tutu's account of his leadership of the Commission in *No Future without Forgiveness*, 1999). Tutu refused to support a violent or vengeful response to those who had routinely committed torture and murder under apartheid. Instead, he offered South Africa a third way between a retaliation that enshrined vengeance and a forgetfulness that would move on without facing the past.

This third way, the path of restorative justice, was rooted in Tutu's conviction that all people are children of God and that justice should be focused on bringing the truth to light and reconciling enemies. In the proceedings of the Commission, the victims of violence and their family members were called on to tell their stories, freely and without interruption. Then, those charged with crimes were invited to come and tell the full truth about what they had done. In exchange for a truthful confession the offender was granted amnesty. Though it was not required, in many cases the offender asked forgiveness of the victims or their families. In a remarkable number of instances, forgiveness was granted. By leading South Africa through a process designed not to punish but to reconcile, Tutu embodied servant authority before a watching world and brought the Church's resources to bear on what seemed an intractable political situation. In this way he bore witness to the kind of rule made possible in Christ and he continues to challenge the world to embrace such a model.

Alongside speaking *to the world* of a new kind of authority, can the Church recognize *in the world* authoritative words to which it must attend? In other words, does the Church have a monopoly on the speaking and hearing of the authoritative Word of God? Is it not also called to *listen* for God's Word in the voices of strangers?

As the Israelites were making their way from Egypt to the Promised Land, they had to pass through the land of Moab. The Moabites had heard of their strength and how they had recently defeated the Amorites. Fearing this wandering people, the king of Moab, Balak, called upon Balaam, a priest-diviner for hire, to come and curse Israel so that they could be defeated (Numbers 22–4). Balaam, however, heard from the Lord that Israel was to be blessed and not cursed, so he refused Balak's offer. Again Balak sent an envoy with money in hand, and again he was refused. Finally, God allowed Balaam to go, but when Balak took him to see the Israelite troops Balaam blessed them rather than cursing them. Three times Balak tried to convince Balaam to curse them and three times he blessed them instead. What is most interesting about this story is that here a foreign prophet who had never encountered Israel was able to hear the voice of Israel's God and speak a word of true blessing. God spoke to Balaam and Balaam spoke for God without the mediation of God's people. Balaam is paralleled in the New Testament by the Roman centurion at the foot of Jesus's cross. While the disciples in Mark's Gospel were unable to see Jesus's identity clearly, this outsider, an occupying soldier no less, saw and spoke the truth, "Truly this man was God's Son!" (Mark 15: 39). Both Balaam and the centurion stood outside the people of God and the normal avenues of revelation, yet each spoke a true word through the guidance of the Spirit.

These episodes suggest something about the power of the "unauthorized word" and they raise questions about God's means of speaking authoritatively to the community today. Just as there were voices among the Jews authorized to speak for God, so there are authorized voices today – deacons, pastors, bishops. And, as in biblical times, God does in fact speak through those chosen and authorized voices. This does not mean, however, that God cannot speak an authoritative word from an unauthorized source. Indeed, God may choose to speak truth from quite unexpected places. When U2's lead singer, Bono, convinces North Carolina Senator Jesse Helms to fight the spread of AIDS in Africa by reading the Bible with him, it appears the Spirit of God is at work in unlikely ways. When a movie like *The Matrix* challenges us to open our eyes to the dark truth about the world through its allegorizing of the Christian story, it appears God is speaking even in the unlikely voice of popular culture.

Karl Barth (not known for his affirmations of secularism!) reminds us of God's ability to speak from unexpected places. We should not, he tells us:

> have too little confidence in the One who extends His dominion also over the kingdoms of this earth, nor expect too little in the way of signs of this lordship. How many signs he may well have set up in both the outer and inner darkness which Christianity has overlooked

in an unjustifiable excess of scepticism, to the detriment of itself and its own cause! We are summoned to believe in Him, and in His victorious power, not in the invincibility of any non-Christian, anti-Christian or pseudo-Christian worldliness which confronts Him. The more seriously and joyfully we believe in Him, the more we shall see such signs in the worldly sphere, and the more we shall be able to receive true words from it. (Barth, 1961: 122)

Faithful ecclesial authority will not waste time guarding its turf, but will have its ears ever tuned to God's voice as it issues from whatever source. True Christian leadership may well lead best when it points away from its own authoritative word and teaches the people of God to listen for the unexpected word in the weak ones among them and the worldly ones around them. When the congregation is sent forth at the end of the service, it is sent into the world, not only to minister to the world but to listen to the world, for here too God's lordship is real and God's authoritative Word may be heard.

References

Barth, Karl (1961) *Church Dogmatics*, ed. G. W. Bromiley and T. F. Torrance, vol. 4, part 3. (Edinburgh: T. and T. Clark).

Descartes, René (1956) *Discourse on Method*, trans. Laurence J. Lafleur (Indianapolis, IN: Bobbs-Merrill) (originally published 1637).

Foucault, Michel (1984) "What is Enlightenment?," in *The Foucault Reader*, ed. Paul Rabinow (New York: Pantheon).

Kant, Immanuel (1959) "What is Enlightenment?," in *Foundations of the Metaphysics of Morals and What is Enlightenment?* (Indianapolis, IN: Bobbs-Merrill) (originally published 1784).

McCabe, Herbert (1992) "Obedience," in *God Matters*, pp. 226–34 (Springfield, IL: Templegate).

Marshall, Paul (2002) "You Are Ordained to Disperse Power," *Diocesan Life*, 13 (10): A3.

Simon, Yves (1962) *A General Theory of Authority* (Notre Dame, IN: University of Notre Dame Press).

Tutu, Desmond (1999) *No Future without Forgiveness* (New York: Doubleday).

Williams, Rowan (2000) *On Christian Theology* (Oxford: Blackwell).

CHAPTER 13

Proclaiming: Naming and Describing

Charles Pinches

An Introduction to Preaching

For some Christians, the sermon is the highlight of the service of worship, the main course of the meal. Setting aside such motives as, for instance, wanting to be entertained, the interest these Christians show in the sermon has something to do with the truth. People want to get hold of some truth, which they can ruminate over or take to their lives in the coming week. Liturgically, however, if someone sits down in the pew with truth and the sermon on his mind, he is told to wait.

Of the many reasons why this is the right thing to do liturgically, I should like to highlight one: simply, Christians believe that truth always needs an introduction. Or, in connection to Christian preaching, the truths we are told in the sermon do not start off anew, but rather always build upon what we have heard before. Specifically, preaching extends the reading of Scripture; it is bound to it. Since Scripture comes in words, the binding is linguistic. A preacher may weave a compelling pattern with words masterfully chosen, but if none of these words echoes and re-echoes Scripture, the sermon has failed, the Word of God has not been proclaimed.

This may seem like a limitation for preachers. But it is actually their salvation. For it allows them to speak on someone else's behalf. As Karl Barth suggests, they are heralds; they speak for someone else. As such, they do not need to establish their own authority as they speak; rather they borrow it, from the text and from the God who speaks in it. Mercifully for them, the Christians in the pews listen not directly to them but to God who speaks through them. These listeners listen to the preacher not based on who he is but because of the authority of the Word to which the preacher is bound – "the Word of the Lord" read just before.

Preaching, we might say, leans back upon Scripture for support, and then springs forward from it to the congregation. Preachers are not to utter their own words but rather deliver God's Word to the gathered faithful. Likewise, those Christians who receive it are to regard it as spoken directly to them. This is not because they should listen to and obey their pastor; indeed, they need not think he or she is a particularly good preacher. Rather, locked as they are right now in the action of worship, they must listen as the ones to whom the Word is moving. They are the receivers, and without reception the Word returns void.

So the preparation and waiting before the sermon binds both the preacher and the gathered Christians. It binds to the appointed lessons just read, yes, but it goes beyond. It requires that preaching should never separate itself from the words and descriptions that have been handed down among the people called "Church." Christian preachers are not at liberty to start afresh, as if with a clean slate. They must always look back before going on. Likewise, the hearers gathered in the pew cannot skip right to the "truths" of a meaty sermon. That they must wait reminds them that the delivery of truth and wisdom in the sermon requires preparation, an introduction in which they are taught and re-taught the *vocabulary* of the Church.

This is not to say that Christians must be scholars before they can listen to the sermon. Yet the requirement that those in the pews wait and listen before the sermon does teach Christians something about history, especially their own: while they have the distinction of being the ones at whom the Word of God is this day aimed, they are by no means the first ones. Indeed, the aiming of the Word, and its reception, began long before the preacher opens his mouth, and will continue long afterward. As "Word of God" implies, it is not the preacher behind the sights aiming the Word, but God. As recipients of the Word of God, Christians must find their place in an historical company of "hearers," a fact that constrains how they can receive the Word well. They may, as some of Jesus's hearers, receive it with astonishment; or, as with Peter's hearers in Acts 2, they may be "cut to the heart." They may be disturbed by it, or even dispute it, as Jeremiah disputes with God about why the wicked prosper. What they cannot do, however, is dismiss it or pass it off. Nor, for that matter, can they find it deliciously entertaining or interesting or even tremendously emotionally uplifting. Underneath these false ways of receiving the Word is the idea that the lives of the Christians in the pews are independent of the Word, as if their history had nothing whatsoever to do with its history. Such history-less people do not exist, despite modern claims to the contrary. If Christians are tempted by this false imagination, the time spent in worship, waiting and preparing for the proclamation of the words, is training to the contrary.

Doing Things with Words

As just suggested, proclamation in the sermon and the appropriate reception of it have something to do with learning a vocabulary. This may seem difficult, and it is, but not in the way it sounds. Some may worry that they are not good with foreign languages: they have no ear for them or always mix up expressions. But, as I have said, a key part to learning to speak as a Christian is recognizing an inheritance. Much of what must be learned is already present, although it goes unnoticed. In addition, even what is new is not rightly called "foreign," for the Word has been with us all along, since creation. Finally, we learn the Word not so much by thinking but by doing. It is practical, not theoretical.

Interestingly, words, not just the Word but all words, are far more closely tied to practice than we typically think. We associate words more with theory than practice, more with thinking than doing, a well-ingrained association that actually informed much thinking about ethics for centuries. Working against this pattern, the philosopher J. L. Austin wrote an important mid-twentieth-century philosophy book with an unphilosophical title: *How to Do Things with Words* (1962). Austin pointed out that we actually act when we speak. This is easiest to see with dramatic speech acts, like a nation's leader declaring war or a groom saying the words "I do" in a wedding ceremony. Austin noted such utterances could be "happy" or "unhappy," by which he meant that they could fail or succeed as acts. For example, if a person said "I do" in a wedding ceremony, but turned out later already to have been married (thereby rendering the new "marriage" void) then the speech act would be "unhappy."

Not all words or utterances are so clearly performative as the "I do" in a wedding ceremony. However, Austin's analysis helps to overcome a tempting but misleading view about words. This is that words are sounds or collections of written characters whose function is to point to objects in the world. As a paleontologist mixes up plaster and pours it on a recently discovered fossil imprint, so we might think of words as little replicas, in sound and symbol, of a world that exists independently of these words. Yet, plainly, we come to the world equipped with our words. Indeed, not only when we act with our words (i.e., by saying "I do" in the right context), but also in using them to describe the world we bring a linguistic history to bear on what is. There is no separating the shape of our world from the shape of our words. As words come to us through time and by tradition, so does the world.

This point was initially unsettling to Ludwig Wittgenstein, Austin's teacher. For it meant that truth about the world is mediated by words, language that has a history and is tied inextricably to the way in which a particular people has come to live. In his earliest work, the *Tractatus*, Wittgenstein attempted to deal with this problem by using precise prepositional formulations of those truths about the world he thought he could speak, passing over the rest in silence. Wittgenstein later came to regard the effort of the *Tractatus* as mistaken. The meanings of words, he came to hold, were invariably tied to their use – and we use words together, in communities and shared traditions. Attempts to reify words, lifting them by some theory from their homes in ordinary life and talk, are therefore necessarily mistaken. Returned to these homes, words retain a power and richness they cannot have abstracted from them. This power is not that of directly and simply referring to "truth" as an arrow points to an object. Indeed, such imagined power for words is a temptation when it matches up with the hubris that we humans are like gods, surveying the world from a distance. In fact, we are not the lords, or even the detached observers, of the world; as speakers and actors we participate in it. As participants, we actively describe and affect the world with our words. Put another way, as we speak so shall we live.

This is why vocabulary is so important. Words, descriptions, do not occupy a sort of neutral space that hovers over our lives and actions, as if we might be able to describe the world in a disinterested fashion, later adding in judgments about how we will act in it. A clear place to see the falsity of this neutral picture is with "moral terms." Suppose that John and Jane, each married to someone else, are having sexual relations. We say that they are engaged in "adultery." This description is not morally neutral.

It describes what Jane and John are doing, yes, but as it does so, it draws what they are doing into a long tradition of moral reflection and description surrounding the goods of marriage. The moral judgment in the description is the judgment of this tradition. When one uses the term "adultery" to describe Jane and John's action, one joins the tradition in its judgment.

Pursuing the point about the practicality of words leads us back to the idea that learning vocabulary is not so innovative or foreign as we might think. In fact, in the sermon, it is perhaps less important that we be taught new words than that we be shown how the ones we already know are at work in our lives, for good or ill.

Ethics, Morality, and the Wisdom of the World

It is not an accident that moral descriptions such as "adultery" clearly illustrate how words are intimately related to acts and practical judgment. For morality is about "*mores*" (Latin), ethics about "*ethos*" (Greek): the practices and customs that we live by. Surprisingly, this has often proved rather difficult to see. For instance, philosophers sometimes draw a distinction between ethics and morality. The idea is that morality is the set of rules and judgments about right and wrong actions that a people actually lives from day to day, while ethics rises above to a higher level of reflection about this morality and its judgments. In the twentieth century, another level of reflection was added atop this stack: something called "meta-ethics." Meta-ethics concerned itself with how the language used in ethics or in morality could make sense. What, the meta-ethicists asked, is the cognitive content in a judgment such as that you should not steal from your neighbor? How does such a moral judgment have genuine meaning?

The comments above about Wittgenstein already help to identify a difficulty that plagued the meta-ethicists in their work. They typically came to "morality" and moral language with skewed standards of meaning and sense rooted in an understanding of language as reference, words pointing to objects. Meta-ethics has a smaller following than it once had; we can leave its specific preoccupations aside. Yet this ascending pattern of justification – morality to ethics, ethics to meta-ethics – offers important clues about how scholarship about "ethics," even widely popular views of "ethics," even widely shared Christian views of "ethics," took a long and costly detour around moral and theological words and descriptions. Each step up revealed the concern that particular moral judgments must be secured in some higher and more universally applicable principle or theory. The idea was that moral judgments needed some rooting or justification in something ever more basic. The most basic thing was a broad theory that encompassed the whole of morality (or ethics). So, we should not steal because each person possesses a basic right to property, and this right is anchored in the fact that persons (who have rights) are fundamentally worthy of "respect," and this respect implies that persons should be treated as ends, never merely as means, and such treatment follows from the very form of the supreme moral law, the only thing worthy of being genuinely called law since it rests, finally, in rationality itself.

The pattern of justification just mimicked is commonly known as Kantian, for it was Immanuel Kant who first worked it out. The point in following him along is not to show that he was wrong in talking about "respect" – we will need this word. Rather, the point is that Kant, a brilliant and original thinker, nonetheless presumed the aforementioned ascending pattern of justification. In this he was like his contemporary across the English Channel, Jeremy Bentham, the founder of Utilitarianism, although Utilitarianism skips many of Kant's complicated steps. According to the Utilitarian, we need to check to see if a particular instance of stealing is morally right or wrong by testing it on the one foundational principle of morality: the maximization of happiness for the greatest number. So, if I catch my Utilitarian neighbor stealing my stuff and he asks me what is so bad about stealing, I'll need to make an argument that connects his stealing with the more basic concern about maximizing happiness.

Kantianism and Utilitarianism are philosophical theories of ethics. However, their presumptions about how ethics should be done, the pattern of their justifications, spilled liberally into Christian thinking. For a time, many became concerned that "Christian ethics" needed firmer theoretical grounding. To find it, they frequently turned to the philosophical theories. Joseph Fletcher, who wrote the immensely popular book called *Situation Ethics* (1966), equated Christian love, *agape*, with the Utilitarian principle. For Fletcher, Christian love meant that one should always act to maximize happiness for the greatest number.

Fletcher's thinking, while popular in some circles, was widely repudiated by other Christian thinkers, including Paul Ramsey (1968). Now Ramsey was not quite a Kantian. However, the 1960s' debate between Ramsey and Fletcher was very much like a debate between a Utilitarian and a Kantian: Fletcher held that the end of an action, its outcome, could justify any means used in bringing it about, while Ramsey maintained that there were some actions Christians were duty bound by the "*agapic* principle" not to do, irrespective of the consequences. Both thinkers followed the theoretical pattern above. They presumed that ethics involved the discovery and articulation of a basic principle by which actions could be judged moral or immoral, faithful to the Christian God, or unfaithful. With them, and other thinkers of their time, Christian ethics took the familiar shape: ethical thinking needed to drive back behind or underneath particular descriptions like "adultery" to find a root principle (Kant's categorical imperative, Utilitarian happiness, Christian *agape*, and so on) that could support the judgment "adultery" implied. Actually, sometimes descriptions like "adultery" were called into question by the root principle, since (as Fletcher, 1966, noted) one can easily think of times when refraining from adultery does not maximize happiness.

Once pointed out, the common pattern in these approaches to ethics is easy to see. It is more difficult to come up with an alternative. Indeed, as some might say, is not the alternative, in effect, to give up doing ethics altogether and return to a conventional morality wherein we live by and pass on to our children whatever descriptions we received from our parents? So, if we were brought up to avoid adultery or taught not to steal, then we should simply keep this up, giving little thought to why, or ever questioning whether, in some cases, the prohibitions each of these descriptions implies might require reinvestigation?

A frank response to this worry must include the observation that many people throughout human history have lived in just this way, and thinking of them as Lawrence Kohlberg (1981) might – that is, as locked in the first obedience/punishment stage of moral development – is not necessarily to be preferred over thinking of them as "faithful" or "steadfast." Indeed, the idea that each individual must question the wisdom about life that is passed from one generation to the next is a distinctively modern idea, one of only a few ideas our current culture is successfully passing on. Put differently, the worry about conventionalism – that we really ought not to accept what is passed down to us without checking it on some securer and more theoretically sophisticated moral theory – is itself a conventional worry, i.e., according to the conventions (the ethos, the mores) of our time.

Here we see that, despite our best efforts to climb above our words and descriptions, we end up returning to them. The oddity of modernity is that this is understood to be a problem to be overcome. In a way peculiar to them, the moderns have tried to navigate around the plain and simple fact that human beings are born into human communities, they are raised up into ways of life that have histories and traditions that are not of their own making. Within these communities there are certain accepted ways that things get done, certain practices that are commonly engaged in, certain descriptions that are used to describe the human world in which the common life is lived out, and, as part of the descriptions, certain words that give the descriptions meaning and certain stories that seat them in the history of the common life of the community. These sets of practices, descriptions, and stories include a great number of judgments, about what is true (or false), good (or bad), right (or wrong). These are not added in on top of the common life and language of the community, as if we might begin living in one of these communities and then later develop the felt need to make some judgments about whether what we are in the midst of is "moral" or not. No, what we call "morality" is already shot through the practices, descriptions, and stories by which we are already living.

Beyond this "simple fact," morality is anything but simple. Since virtually all of what we say and do is shot through with judgments about what is true or good or most worthy or most fittingly human, then thinking about these matters will require that we discover and consider judgment after judgment, pick carefully through one practice or description and then another, considering its nuances and relating it to other descriptions or words that carry connected but perhaps also subtly different sorts of judgments. To enter this complex world of judgment, however, requires something the moderns hope to avoid. We must acknowledge that we are members of a "we." Like others with whom I live, I am the inheritor of a great range of descriptions, words, and practices that have brought me to this day, and will take me beyond it. As such, my way is not really my way, but ours. And the next step along it, if it is to head in the right direction, must be well guided by what is best called "shared wisdom," drawn from the best of what we have come to know about our human lives together, especially as this is expressed in our daily speech and practices.

For Christians, the sermon is a place were the "we" is particularly evident. As argued earlier, rightly hearing the Word of God requires the recognition that our lives are already bound up with it. Moreover, we hearers and speakers are neither the first nor the last to which it is directed. The Church extends through time, which we are always in the midst of. This time-laden pattern, as we noted earlier, helps explain why the sermon should be neither the first nor the last thing Christians do in their liturgical worship. It also makes clear that the "we" is not any and everybody. As Christians have prepared for the proclamation of the Word of God by reading and listening to Scripture, they have placed themselves firmly in a particular community whose vocabulary is tied inextricably to the biblical story. Indeed, the reading has already placed them in that story, and it is now their business to think and act wisely in relation to it.

It should therefore come as no surprise if the wisdom in the sermon seems rather unwise according to some *other* "we." As Paul tells the Corinthians, he has been sent "to proclaim the gospel, and not with eloquent wisdom." For, after all, the

> message of the cross is foolishness to those who are perishing, but to us who are being saved it is the power of God . . . Has not God made foolish the wisdom of the world? For since in the wisdom of God, the world did not know God through wisdom, God decided, through the foolishness of our proclamation, to save those who believe. For Jews demand signs and Greeks desire wisdom, but we proclaim Christ crucified . . . Christ the power of God and the wisdom of God. (1 Corinthians 1: 17–24)

Paul does not repudiate wisdom *per se*. Indeed, it is precisely the wisdom of God, Christ, which he thinks he is called to proclaim. Rather, if what Christians say about life, from the pulpit or elsewhere, turns out to be what everyone else is saying, something has gone wrong. Christian wisdom is kind of wacky, for it rests on the crazy idea that God has come to live and die as one of us. Insofar as it is to be God's Word and not the herald's, all Christian proclamation begins and ends with this. This is what we call the gospel.

The Miracle of the Multiplication of the Words

These last comments may seem to imply something we had hoped to avoid: a reduction of the great variety of moral life and wisdom to one judgment according to one thing. In one sense the reduction is genuine: Christians have long held that all our various moral judgments, including surely our various moral terms, must be brought under subjection to Christ. In fact, in answer to the earlier worry expressed that Christianity simply perpetuated vocabulary and descriptions from one generation to the next without thought, we can say that all inherited moral descriptions should in one way or another be examined critically in the light of Christ. Yet this process of judgment and critique does not follow the ascending pattern of justification of the modern moral theorizers. This is because the Word of God is not a theory. Indeed, the Word has been with us from the beginning when it moved over the waters. Moreover, as we Christians say, the Word has become flesh and lived among us.

Here again, an apparently simple point turns out to be complicated. It leads as well to a much more complicated pattern of moral thinking, one the Christian sermon might demonstrate. The gospel is in one sense simple, yet preaching it well is a complicated task. Christians have sometimes missed this. The revivalist D. L. Moody reportedly told others that all his many sermons were really the same sermon. For, there is really only one thing to say: John 3: 16. Following Moody, some Christian preachers in revivalist America yet feel obliged to make the theme of personal salvation the refrain of every sermon. Besides demonstrating a theological individualism, this approach fails to see that God's Word becomes many words as it meets human life.

Words, as we have noted, are tied inextricably to actions and to life. Speaking genuine wisdom in the sermon, and discerning it in the pews, will therefore involve the vital but complex task of connecting the gospel to human life in all of its facets. This is not a theoretical task, but a practical one. As Christians hold, the gospel as living Word goes out from the book to the gathered Church, later (at the dismissal) to be dispersed into the world. In the sermon, then, the Word must meet the world in which Christians live. Perhaps more than anything, the task of the sermon will be that of naming this world in the light of the gospel.

"Naming" involves the right use of words to describe the world truthfully. This includes our previous example: sexual relations between a man and a woman married to other partners is "adultery." This may need to be named in a particular sermon, although it cannot be turned into a name-that-sin game. Good sermons will also display, likely by story and example, what it means for one human being to offer hospitality to another; who are the poor, and what they mean to God; what sadness in the face of death involves and how it can be borne; and so on. As this list illustrates, the full resources of Scripture and of the common life of the people called Church stands available for use in the pulpit where the Word is enfleshed. Indeed, it is precisely as the Word has become flesh that so many other words have come to life, and the world once created by the Word can now rightly be named.

Jean Bethke Elshtain has noted that our time is one in which many have lost confidence in our capacity to name our world.

> One extraordinary sign of our times is a process of radical alteration in language, understanding and meaning . . . [W]e are painfully aware of what happened when totalitarian regimes had the power to control language and to cover mass murder with the rhetoric of "improvement of the race" and even "mercy and compassion." We are much less attuned to the ways in which our language, hence our understanding of the world, may be contorted by drawing us away from, rather than closer to, that which we are depicting. (Elshtain, 2000: 128)

Elshtain is concerned that we will kill people, as Hitler did, and call it by another name. (Indeed, this may be well along the way.) Another concern is that we will kill ourselves and go on living, becoming people so lost in lies that we give up any vision of saying and living the truth. By contrast, Christians, according to Elshtain, must be a people "claimed by hope." Joined with others, "the first project for citizens who live in hope is to insist that we name things accurately and appropriately."

It is likely that hope is not the first thing that comes to mind when naming is considered. Yet Elshtain's connection is important to preachers as they begin the daunting task of speaking words of truth about life to congregants who, despite their thirst for wisdom and truth, may nonetheless cling stubbornly to comfortable lies. The hope rests not in the fact that the preacher has prepared well for this moment, or that he or she is good with crowds. It is rather rooted in the fact that God has actually spoken, in human tongue, and will do so again. Scripture is not the only such actual, historical speaking, but it is the one on which Christians can always depend. Whatever her precise articulation of the doctrine of scriptural authority, a confident and hopeful preacher must hold that in Scripture God has given us the resources we need rightly to describe God's world.

Christian preaching directs the inherited descriptions of Scripture out into the world of the day. But, of course, they are directed to the hearers in the pews who live in this world. Here, Elshtain's confident insistence that Christians can yet truthfully name is put to the test. We like truthful descriptions much better when they are about someone else. But, like David's words of outrage at the rich man in the prophet Nathan's story who appropriates his poor neighbor's one sheep, Scripture's words have a way of turning round to point back at us. Good sermons often follow this pattern.

In the Episcopal Church we make a great deal of the "institution" of our rectors, which generally occurs some months after a new priest has taken the helm. In my parish, which includes many faithful souls whose long ties to Episcopal traditions make change difficult, we recently called a new rector, our first woman in that position. She is learned, focused, and challenging as well as gracious and godly. Almost instantly after her arrival she became the subject of a great chorus of whispers passing between this person and that. "Can you believe she speaks from the aisle not the pulpit? How could she have the nerve to move the baptismal font?" And so on. The chorus of whispers swelled to a deafening roar just at the time of her institution, which was, fittingly, especially joyful but also quite elaborate and adventurous. The Sunday immediately after the institution, our associate pastor, who had been with us for some time and had gained the confidence and love of many in the parish, took her turn to preach.

The Gospel lesson that day was Matthew 25: 14–30, Jesus's parable of the talents. Our associate pastor began her sermon with a story of Mrs Griggs, her ninth-grade English teacher, whom she had at first sorely disliked for her uncompromising demands, but whose rigor ultimately uncovered a gift for writing she (our associate) never knew she had. With Mrs Griggs, the two faithful servants in the parable, who multiplied their talents by actively trading them, understood that growing a gift takes work, determination, and risk, something the third servant knew but failed to act on. He knew his master was one who "reaped what he did not sow," but "being afraid . . . he hid the talents in the ground" (verse 25). With careful, sincere words, our associate told us that the unfaithful servant's "fatal flaw was *timidity*. Out of fear of failure, he refused even to try." She went on to suggest that perhaps it was our turn to do "some hard thinking about how trustworthy we are with tending God's church . . . Do we do more than maintain it? Do we better it? What kind of risks do we take in order to help it flourish and thrive?"

"These are particularly important questions," she continued, "to ask on the day after our rector's institution – our dynamic, gutsy, visionary new rector, a priest with a heart for those on the margins." At the institution we had entered into a covenant, we had begun something new together, rector and congregation. "So what now? Can we find the trust, can we communicate with one another honestly and kindly, can we stretch in new directions and try things we have never tried before, or will we cling to the status quo? Really, the choice is ours!"

Who would have thought to describe the whispering among us in terms of timidity? But that was its root: a clinging tightly to a precious thing out of fear of losing it.

Scripture gave our associate pastor the means to name this truthfully. (It remains to be seen if we had ears to hear.) Importantly, the truth she spoke was particular, about the particular life of a little parish in the hills of north-east Pennsylvania. This is the hardest kind of truth to take, but it is the form the Word takes among us.

Another story in Matthew displays how Scripture is the first resource not only in naming things truthfully but also in identifying when things have been falsely named, especially as temptations to mis-name arise in the specific needs of our daily lives. In the fourth chapter a hungry Jesus responds to the tempter's suggestion that he turn stones into bread as follows: "It is written: you shall not live by bread alone but by every word that proceeds from the mouth of God." Bread – its multiplication to feed the hungry, eating it in communion with his disciples, its being broken for many – will come to play a central role in the story of Christ's life, as well as in the liturgy following the sermon, when the gathered company turns its attention toward the Eucharist wherein bread becomes body. Yet here, early in Christ's ministry, he resists the temptation to turn one thing, stones, into something else. Reading liberally, we might take the tempter's strategy to be to confuse about what nourishes by renaming: "this stone is really bread." In response, Christ refuses a certain power of re-naming by which he might re-form the world to fit his desires. The resistance is rooted in Christ's awareness that human life is nurtured by word as much as by food. The nurturing word is from God, and has, for Jesus, issued in the many words of Hebrew Scripture: every word from God's mouth.

Jesus's dependence on Scripture as the source of our names for the world will raise suspicion among some. Why suppose that the naming that has gone on in this one tradition, Israel's, is truthful naming? Yet within Israel's tradition, or Christianity's, or the two traditions in relation, precise names are always open to dispute. That is particularly clear for Christians since they depend so much on borrowed namings (i.e., from Judaism) which are necessarily reinterpreted as Christians use them. That this goes on explicitly is especially plain in the sermon if, as is generally required by the liturgy, it is preceded by a lesson from the Old Testament, as well from the New. Rather than always harmonizing these, it is sometimes the preacher's task to remind his or her hearers that they live on borrowed descriptions whose meanings are yet open to continuing dispute.

Sabbath, for instance, is one of these. Jesus, plainly, was locked in a dispute with his fellow Jews about just what "Sabbath" was. The dispute should not mask underlying agreements that the Sabbath is the Lord's Day, and therefore one of rest for us all. Yet it is also not inconsequential quarreling. For dispute about how the Sabbath should be kept is dispute about what it is, even about who is its Lord. Appropriately, this dispute can be engaged in practically rather than theoretically. To show what "Sabbath" means, one needs to keep it, in one way or another. And, importantly, if the Sabbath is not kept at all, in Jesus's way or the Pharisees' or even the Seventh Day Adventists', the claim "this is the Sabbath day" means nothing.

This last point is of the greatest importance for understanding what follows from the various namings that are offered in the sermon. They are meaningless if not carried out into the world by those who have heard and will shortly be dismissed to "do the work God has given them to do." Will my parish communicate honestly and kindly? Will "the Sabbath day" be faithfully kept? The descriptions of the sermon must now be tested in the world by the lives of the hearers, who become what the New Testament calls "doers" of the Word. Perhaps more than any other piece of the liturgy, the sermon points beyond its own time in worship to the life the assembled Christians have lived last week or last month or will be living in the weeks ahead, the life of the Church in the world. As doers of the Word, these many Christians multiply it, offering it as bread to the world.

Living Tradition

That a key purpose of the sermon is to equip its hearers to do God's work in the world explains the relatively obvious fact that an elegant and learned sermon that skates gracefully over the heads of most of its listeners is a failed one. The threat of such an elegant failure is greatly increased if the sermon is directed only one way, from Scripture read or Creed recited to the practical lives of the believers in the world. Rather, successful sermons go both ways: back and forth from life to Word to life. This follows from what we have said about the Word. If it is a living Word, it is not really a matter of the word (in text) read, spoken, and then applied as, for example, a theory might be, but rather that the lives of the congregants become the Word, particularly following the dismissal into the world at the worship's end.

This suggests that there is to be a certain porous quality to the descriptions that are deployed in the sermon. While preachers need to be confident in their naming, they also must name in anticipation, recognizing that they can only fully learn what the names mean as they are carried into the world in the lives of the faithful. Meaning is tied to use, and the Word's use is in the Church's life in the world.

The porous quality of Christian descriptions – that they will be opened to further meanings as they are used in life – can actually re-enter the sermon in the form of what we might call worldly stories. Jesus's own proclamation was full of such stories: the parables. As Rowan Williams observes, "the parables of Jesus are not religious stories or expositions of a tradition." They begin in life: "a sower went out to sow," or (as we have seen) "a man summoned his servants and entrusted them with talents." Jesus's parables, in fact, seem often to carry us outside "religious language" so that we can rejoin it, often with a quite different understanding of its rightful meaning. This is not necessarily a new meaning; more frequently it is a recovered or renewed one.

For instance, consider the well-loved parable of the good Samaritan. A man traveling the road to Jericho is attacked and severely injured by thieves, is ignored by two religious leaders who later pass by, but is finally rescued and gently cared for by a good Samaritan. The context for the parable is a question put to Jesus about the meaning of a description: "who is my neighbor?" (Luke 10: 29). The term "neighbor" carried considerable weight in the Jewish tradition to which Jesus spoke; so many laws rotated around it. Jesus does not deny this tradition as he speaks in response; but he also does not simply rehearse it. Rather, he takes the term into worldly life for closer investigation. The investigation results in a bold challenge to certain traditional religious understandings of the description "neighbor."

The challenge is pressed by the introduction of another term; one that surely had a popular life as well as a biblical one for Jesus's audience: "Samaritan." The surprise that animates the story is that neither the priest nor the Levite but rather the Samaritan, viewed by most Jews as unclean, turns out to be the neighbor. So the story brings a challenge to that inherited meaning. In essence, Jesus is asking: do we really know what we mean when we use the term "Samaritan" as we typically do? Is that meaning not challenged by real Samaritans in the world?

When he does this, Jesus trusts his listeners to be able to see things as they are. Moreover, he refuses to perpetuate pious descriptions that do not fit the world his hearers know precisely because they live in it. No doubt, his hearers need the story's help to re-understand "Samaritan" or "neighbor," but the help does not come in a religious pronouncement but in a story from their everyday life. The story does not trump or brush aside Scripture or received tradition. "Samaritan" and "neighbor" are not obliterated as descriptions but redirected and rethought so as, finally, to be better used. Of course, the redirection of the descriptions redirects the community that uses them. In fact, combined with certain other redescriptions, such as Paul's regarding who is a child of Abraham, Jesus's "neighbor" or "Samaritan" eventually opens the way for a new community to emerge that speaks a related but also different language from the Jewish community that first heard the story.

So the naming that takes place in the sermon is not simply the "application" of the tradition. As Alasdair MacIntyre (1984) notes, a tradition must actively engage with itself and the world or else die. This engagement is perhaps the fullest description of what goes on in a good sermon, most especially in the pews and subsequently in the lives of the hearers who also become doers of the Word. The names carried forward to this day in Scripture and tradition are read, exposited, and probed for meaning in the context of the biblical world. But these names must also be brought to bear, even tested, in the life of the assembled Church. They will come to be used in new (although not discontinuous) ways as they are tried and tested in this life.

In a word, it is in the sermon as much as in any other place in the common life of the Christian community that "ethics" is done – that is, ethics understood neither as theory nor application but rather as the continual testing and rethinking of inherited moral terms and descriptions within the realities of a life shared by a community that is committed both to the terms and the testing. It should not surprise us that other moral communities may wish to borrow the sermon's form. Indeed, the best place to see a community's morality at work is when it assembles for encouragement, for practical advice about successful living – the topic so many seminars in our own time so earnestly address, usually (like the Christians) with a distinctive vocabulary of terms like "stress management" or "self-actualization." Unlike other integral pieces of the liturgy, the form of the sermon is relatively transferable, and, since the Word has been active among us since creation, Christians need not decide beforehand that sermons outside the Church will necessarily mis-describe. Yet, as Augustine (1993) noted about his teachers the Platonists, while those outside the Church may discover the Word spoken in creation, it will be more difficult for them to hear it as having become flesh. The naming, describing, and acting Christians do in and of the world, their "ethics," will be perpetually wrapped around this truth, which comes by faith. It is world transforming.

References

Augustine (1993) *Confessions*, book 7, trans. F. J. Sheed (Indianapolis, IN: Hackett).

Austin, J. L. (1962) *How to Do Things with Words*, ed. J. O. Urmson and Marina Sbisa (Cambridge, MA: Harvard University Press).

Bader-Saye, Demery (2002) "Enter into the Joy," unpublished sermon.

Barth, Karl (1936–69) *Church Dogmatics*, ed. G. W. Bromiley and T. F. Torrance, 13 vols (Edinburgh: T. and T. Clark), esp. vol. 1, part 1, section 3.

Bentham, Jeremy (1996) *The Collected Works of Jeremy Bentham: An Introduction to the Principles and Morals of Legislation*, ed. H. L. A. Hart and J. H. Burns (Oxford: Clarendon Press).

Elshtain, Jean Bethke (2000) *Who Are We?* (Grand Rapids, MI: Eerdmans).

Fletcher, Joseph (1966) *Situation Ethics* (Philadelphia: Westminster).

Kant, Immanuel (1981) *Foundations of the Metaphysics of Morals*, trans. Lewis White Beck (Indianapolis, IN: Bobbs-Merrill).

Kohlberg, Lawrence (1981) *The Philosophy of Moral Development: Moral Stages and the Idea of Justice* (San Francisco: Harper and Row).

MacIntyre, Alasdair (1984) *After Virtue: A Study in Moral Theory*, 2nd edn (Notre Dame, IN: University of Notre Dame Press).

Pinches, Charles R. (2002) *Theology and Action: After Theory in Christian Ethics* (Grand Rapids, MI: Eerdmans).

Ramsey, Paul (1968) *Norm and Context in Christian Ethics*, ed. Gene Outka (New York: Scribner).

Williams, Rowan (2000) *On Christian Theology* (Oxford: Blackwell).

Wittgenstein, Ludwig (1953) *Philosophical Investigations*, trans. G. E. M. Anscombe, ed. G. E. M. Anscombe and Rush Rhees (New York: Macmillan).

—(1961) *Tractatus Logico-philosophicus*, trans. D. F. Pears and B. F. McGuinness (New York: Routledge).

CHAPTER 14

Deliberating: Justice and Liberation

Daniel M. Bell, Jr

In recent decades, the claim that the Christian faith is about justice and liberation has achieved the status of a veritable truism. And this is as it should be, for the Word rightly proclaimed is a word of justice and liberation. Yet how Christians are to respond to that Word, what doing justice and liberating the oppressed entails, is not self-evident. Rather, it is a matter of discernment.

In what follows, the history of such discernment is sketched, beginning with an overview of the dominant philosophical accounts of justice and their contemporary theological appropriation. A brief consideration of the difficulties that attend the dominant theological accounts clears the way for appreciating how the Christian pursuit of justice, rightly conceived, is distinctively shaped by its arising as a liturgical response to the Word. Put more provocatively, this chapter aspires to make sense of Augustine's startling claim that true justice is found only in the City of God, the Church, whose ruler and founder is Christ (Augustine, 1950).

What is Justice?

In the West, reflection on justice has traditionally taken as its starting-point the ancient definition, *suum cuique*: "to each what is due." Yet, as Alasdair MacIntyre (1988) has reminded us, how this is understood is far from monolithic. "What is due" can be calculated according to a host of discordant logics.

The classical background: good prior to right

The classical understanding of *suum cuique* finds its definitive statement in Aristotle. He distinguishes between what is called "general" and "particular" justice. General justice is a virtue concerned principally with the good or end (*telos*) of the community as a whole. As such, general justice functions to guide and coordinate the virtues, actions, and relations of individuals so that they harmonize with or enhance the good of the community as a whole. Particular justice, on the other hand, addresses principally the good of individuals, ensuring that they share in the common good by receiving what is due to them in the context of particular relations and exchanges. Particular justice is itself further divided into distributive and corrective ("commutative") forms. Distributive justice deals with the division of communal goods among individuals, whereas corrective justice deals with exchanges between individuals and, in particular, the rectification of harms incurred in the course of individual relations.

This classical understanding embodies several characteristics that, in the light of future developments, are particularly noteworthy. Perhaps chief among them is that this account is founded on what in contemporary parlance is known as the "priority of the good over the right." According to the classical vision, determinations of what is just are dependent upon a prior conception of the good of humanity, of a thick or substantive conception of the good that embraces both the community and individuals. In other words, agreement on what justice is is only possible subsequent to agreement on what constitutes the proper end or good of humanity. Furthermore, this account entails an hierarchical ordering of goods and merit. What is due persons is "not same" but correlates instead with one's role and function, and corresponding excellences, in the community. Fairness, one could say, is not a matter of strict equality in the modern egalitarian sense but of proportion. Like are treated alike, but unlike are treated differently and this is just.

Modernity: right prior to good

This classical vision of justice carried the day (albeit with important theological modifications during the era of Christendom discussed below) for over a millennium, when developments associated with the birth of modernity and the ascendancy of liberal political philosophy (the Enlightenment) gave rise to a host of competing theories of justice erected upon a very different vision of society. With the advent of modernity, the classical sense of community as a matter of solidarity in a shared *telos*, of agreement around a thick conception of what constitutes the good of humanity, gave way to a more fragmented understanding of community, to a thinner conception of the good that brings people together in society.

Liberalism re-imagined society as a teeming mass of individuals, each with their own interests, ends, and conceptions of what constitutes the good life. Consequently, justice was reconfigured; in contemporary parlance, now the right is given priority over the good. What constitutes justice is arrived at apart from any substantive agreement about what constitutes the good or *telos* of humanity. Justice in modern liberal social orders becomes essentially procedural. Under the sign of modernity, justice is a matter of arriving at a procedure for securing effective cooperation between and security among discrete individuals pursuing an irrepressibly diverse plethora of self-determined interests and private goods. In this situation, justice is no longer conceived as a unitive force. Indeed, with the arrival of modernity, the general virtue of justice is invariably reduced to "legal justice" and equated simply with following the positive laws of the state, or it is discarded altogether. Henceforth, the particular virtue of justice moves to center stage and increasingly takes on the fundamentally distributive hue that is common-place today. Correlatively, "right" becomes a matter of discrete "rights" and these rights, instead of being anchored in a (common) good that is external and prior to the individual, adhere to sovereign individuals who possess them prior to (and frequently over against) any communal bonds. The result is a justice that functions essentially as a police force, as a procedural power that attempts to supervise the competition of rival interests struggling for access to society's resources for the sake of the pursuit of private ends.

This modern vision of justice is manifest in three dominant philosophical accounts. Deontological theories, associated pre-eminently with Immanuel Kant, stress adher-ence to universally applicable rules coupled with respect for the individual. The em-phasis on adherence to rules without regard for ends, coupled with the stress placed on respect for individuals, leads deontological accounts toward an ethic of rights. Utili-tarian theories, associated with John Stuart Mill and Jeremy Bentham, construe justice in terms of what produces "the greatest good for the greatest number." Given the absence of agreement concerning what constitutes the greatest good, however, Utili-tarian theories inevitably become defenses of procedural protections for rights. Justice is equated with maximizing individual rights (to the extent compatible with the rights of others) so that individuals may pursue their own goods, with the sum of all these individuals pursuing private goods amounting to the greatest good for the greatest number. Finally, contractarian theories, associated with John Locke and, more recently, John Rawls, cast justice as the product of a pact ("social contract") between individu-als who surrender rights to the state for the sake of mutual advantage and protection. Here again, the predominant idiom of justice is that of rights. Self-interested individu-als pursuing private goods cooperate in reaching agreement on certain rules or pro-cedures of justice for the sake of a more efficient pursuit of those private ends.

Contemporary theological appropriations

The dominant contemporary theological efforts to discern what justice is start from the classical formula *suum cuique*. However, they quickly jettison the substance of the clas-sical vision in favor of the presuppositions of modernity. First, pluralism – the modern fragmenting of the common good into irreconcilable, private goods and interests – is either embraced as a positive good or simply acknowledged as an unavoidable fact. This is not to say that contemporary theological accounts lack any understanding of the common good. Rather, the point is that the content of such good is much thinner. It becomes instrumental, in the sense that where it is retained it is equated with access to that pool of societal resources from which individuals draw for the sake of the pursuit of private interests and goods. If theologies attempt to say more than this, they quickly move beyond the sphere of what they recognize as justice and into the realm designated by love, charity, or the spiritual. Second, the dissolution of a strong sense of the common good leads inexorably to an elevation of the status of the individual as well as a reconfiguration of what constitutes equality. Justice is no longer a matter of merit and proportion, of a person's fit or function within the larger whole; now justice becomes egalitarian and seeks to bestow upon all individuals the same, regardless of their role or function within society.

Unsurprisingly, the loss of a robust sense of the common good and concomitant elevation of the individual results in modern theological accounts of justice reproducing the procedural bent of their secular counterparts. Inevitably, justice is defined as a procedure for regulating the distribution and exchange of goods in a society now understood as an aggregate of autonomous individuals. Noteworthy is the absence of justice as a general virtue concerned with nurturing a community's solidarity in a shared love. Occasionally, the general virtue appears just long enough to be equated with adherence to the laws of the state, but, for the most part, theological discussions of justice revolve around the problems of clarifying and enacting it in its distributive and commutative forms. Indeed, in contemporary theological circles what is meant by justice is essentially distributive justice. Moreover, the parameters of this distributive justice are cast in terms of rights. Hence, when it is said that God is one who does justice, what is typically meant is that God promotes and protects human rights. Likewise, the Christian struggle for justice is the struggle to liberate those whose rights are violated.

The tendency toward theories of rights highlights another important characteristic of contemporary theological trends; namely, the extrinsic character of justice. Justice is presented as if it were an external standard to which Christianity is properly accountable. This is to say, justice is presented as something that can be understood apart from Christian theological convictions and practices. For example, justice as the promotion of human rights hardly depends upon the doctrine of the Trinity or the practice of baptism for its intelligibility. Moreover, it is frequently asserted that Christianity is credible only insofar as it underwrites the pursuit and promotion of (secular) justice. Thus, theological accounts often amount to efforts to prove that Christianity is up to the challenge, that it is a faith that does (secular) justice.

To the extent that they embrace many of the presuppositions of modernity, contemporary theological accounts of justice resemble secular philosophical accounts. Indeed, many theological accounts explicitly state such affinities. Such affinities, however, should not obscure important differences that remain. For the theological *adoption* of secular theories entails a process of *adaptation* as well. Typically, secular theories are adapted by way of origin and/or addition. This is to say, theological appropriations generally anchor a given account of justice in the theological; for example, recognizing God as the source of rights and/or Christianity as the historical stimulus for a particular vision of justice. Likewise, theological accounts frequently suggest that secular theories of justice require theological completion, whether in the form of tempering justice with love/mercy or the reminder that human flourishing exceeds social justice to embrace religion as well.

There is no easy typology of contemporary theological accounts of justice. While shared commitments place them within the contours of modern political liberalism, the particulars of their accounts diverge significantly. Take, for example, the defense of human rights. Although there is agreement that justice concerns the protection of rights, there is significant disagreement regarding how this conclusion is reached. Some theologians trace the development of the biblical notion of covenant through the Puritans and Locke to arrive at a defense of modern liberalism and rights that has strong affinities with secular contractarian theories (e.g., Harlan Beckley, Clinton Gardner, Max Stackhouse). Others, like Latin American liberationists and Roman Catholic proponents of natural law, found modern rights in a transcendental appeal to the dignity of the human person created in the image of God, while Christian Realists reach similar conclusions beginning from a doctrine of sin. Still others arrive at a vision of justice as the guarantor of modern liberal rights on grounds that come closer to Utilitarianism by means of an explication of biblical principles, such as freedom or the value and equality of persons, under the conditions of finitude and sin (e.g., Michael Novak, Phillip Wogaman, Charles Curran, Richard McCormick).

A second example of diversity among contemporary theological conceptions involves the relation between rights. There is little agreement, for example, concerning the proper balance between freedom and equality. Some theologians lean in a libertarian direction, while others have more egalitarian inclinations. Likewise, there are those who emphasize political rights (e.g., Novak, Richard John Neuhaus), while others privilege economic rights (e.g., Latin American liberationists, political theology), and yet still others attempt to stake out a mediating position (e.g., Stackhouse, Robert Benne, Dennis McCann).

The agony of modern justice

For all their theological caveats, addenda, and praiseworthy intentions, the dominant theological accounts of justice finally owe more to modern liberal politics than they do to the Word. This is to say, they are accounts of justice that fall short of true justice, which, Augustine observed, finds its political correlate not in the city of man but in the City of God. That such accounts are inadequate is not necessarily a suggestion that their proponents would find objectionable. Indeed, many of them profess an uneasiness with their accounts. Christian Realists, for example, acknowledge that the gospel finally exceeds what they describe as justice in the direction of love and mercy. Likewise, the Latin American liberationists insist that, although justice is necessary, forgiveness and mercy ultimately have the last word. And, in recent years, theological feminists have begun to question the liberal presuppositions that diminish relations between and communion among persons.

These reservations gesture toward the fundamental problem with theological accounts that find their political correlate in modern liberalism. That these accounts recognize that justice conceived in terms of rights does not finally mesh with Christian charity, forgiveness, mercy, and communion is tacit acknowledgment that such justice cannot redeem. Which means that liberalism fails. After all, liberalism and its justice are frequently defended as a sort of secular soteriology meant to deliver humanity from conflict. Moreover, contemporary theology has embraced this soteriology insofar as it lauds the collapse of the strong sense of the common good and embraces the pluralism that prompted the reconfiguration of justice in terms of the primacy of the right over the good. Yet, liberalism's justice does not live up to its promise; it does not deliver us from conflict. The peace modern justice delivers is not true peace, but only a simulacra. It is the fortified peace (for the peace and justice of liberalism are always backed by the threat of force) that is better labeled a "truce." Insofar as justice as the guarantor of rights entails a shift from functioning primarily as a *unitive* force that coordinates the pursuit of a common love to a *distributive* force overseeing the pursuit of private goods, it relinquishes its connection with a genuine peace that comes from the harmonious interaction of people who share a common good. Even when successful, it does not pave the way for new relations among peoples, relations that might transcend the truce of mutual advantage. Instead it keeps humanity trapped in an agonistic logic, where the mutual recognition of rights is constantly threatened by the pull of competing visions of the good.

Jesus, the Justice of God

The failure of modern justice clears a space for hearing the good news of God's justice and liberation again and for appreciating the claim that true justice and liberation can only be a response to the Word. Augustine's assertion that true justice is found in Christ and that its political correlate is the City of God provides our entryway. More specifically, we turn to the medieval Christian vision of justice as articulated by Augustine, Anselm, and Aquinas. Here we discover an account of Jesus as the justice of God that transforms – indeed, we might say redeems – the classical conception of justice as *suum cuique* by repositioning it within the divine order of charity. And it is this redeemed justice that promises to liberate us from the agony of modern justice.

The Word (I): atonement

At the center of the Christian faith stands a supreme act of justice and liberation. Jesus Christ is the justice of God who liberates humanity from sin. More specifically, the heart of the Christian gospel is the good news of the justice of God as that justice is displayed in Christ's work of atonement. Accordingly, an attempt to discern what justice is that is self-consciously a response to the Word must begin with the atonement.

Traditionally, the center of the atonement has been identified with Christ's death on the cross. Furthermore, at least in the West, it is Anselm of Canterbury who provides what is perhaps the most influential account of the atonement, what is called the satisfaction or substitutionary theory. According to the standard reading, Anselm explicates the logic of the atonement as follows. In the face of human sin, which is an offense against God's honor, God, as one who must uphold justice, cannot simply forgive sin but must enforce a strict rendering of what is due. Because sinful humanity cannot fulfill its debt, the God-man, Christ, steps forward and fulfills justice, renders what is due, through his substitutionary death on the cross. In this way, redemption is a result of the payment of a debt incurred through sin by means of a compensatory death that satisfies divine justice.

While many contemporary theologies endorse this theory, many more reject it, often in favor of some version of the "moral influence view" of atonement associated with Peter Abelard. What is noteworthy about either response is, first, the way they leave intact justice as a strict rendering of what is due. On the one hand, this theory is used to support the claim that God sanctions a strict rendering of what is due (with a host of implications for social ethics). On the other hand, the objection is either that Anselm misconstrues what is due (e.g., the killing of an innocent is hardly "what is due"), that Jesus's relation to what is due is misunderstood (e.g., he effects what is due not with a compensatory death but by his moral example) or that Jesus is about mercy and not justice. A second noteworthy characteristic of these responses is that both reflect the culmination of a development that traces its roots back to nominalist currents of medieval theology, namely, the sundering of justice from love/mercy. Both proponents and opponents of the standard reading of Anselm accept the division between justice and mercy that the reading propounds. Indeed, that mercy and justice are distinct if not opposing logics is a commonplace of modern theology.

The standard reading of Anselm, however, is a misreading. It errs by reading Anselm, and thus Christ's atonement, through the juridical lens of late medieval and early modern theology. As a result, Christ's atoning work is displaced from its proper setting, which is the ecclesial penitential order understood as a means of grace, an order that transformed or redeemed justice as *suum cuique* by subsuming it in the divine order of charity. Instead, the atonement is interpreted in an alien legal context governed by a logic of debt, equity, and retribution that leaves the classical conception unredeemed, instead separating justice and mercy, thereby preventing justice from being formed by charity. Hence, making proper sense of Jesus as the justice of God entails recovering the atonement in its correct setting, the divine order of charity. Only then can we make sense of Augustine's extraordinary claim that true justice is found in Christ alone, or Thomas Aquinas's equally striking assertion that justice has as its end, charity, which is nothing less than friendship with God. Only such a repositioning promises not to pit justice against mercy but instead confirms that the beauty of justice is in complete accord with grace (Augustine), that mercy implements perfect justice (Aquinas), and the rule of God's justice is mercy (Anselm).

When read in its proper context, Anselm's account of the atonement reveals that Jesus's death on the cross was not a matter of juridical reckoning and the strict exacting of what was due sin, but rather was first and foremost a matter of ontological union, of the taking up of humanity into the communion of love that is the life of the blessed Trinity (*theosis*, deification). In other words, according to Anselm, God became human not in order to meet the demands of an implacable justice before which even God must bow, nor to overcome a conflict within God between justice and mercy, but so that humanity might be restored to the place of honor that God from the beginning intended for humanity, namely, participation in the divine life. In this regard, the injury to God's honor that is effected by sin is a matter of the absence of humanity from full communion with its creator. Thus, rightly understood, God's honor is not a barrier to humanity's reconciliation with God but rather it is the origin of God's free act to provide humanity with a path to renewed communion. Accordingly, the atonement displays the plenitude of divine charity, of God's giving and giving again. God has always given to humanity in the form of love, and when humanity rejected that gift, God gave again in the form of love incarnate, which is the Son. Christ's work is that of giving again, of communicating God's love and grace (which has never ceased to flow) to humanity again (and again). The work of atonement is God in Christ bearing human rejection and extending the offer of grace again, thereby opening a path for humanity to recover beatitude. In this sense, Christ's faithfulness even to the point of death on the cross marks not a divine demand for retribution, but a divine refusal to hold our rebellion against us. Jesus is the justice of God, not because he receives what is due sin but precisely because in Christ God *refuses* to render unto humanity what is due sin, bearing offense *without* exacting compensation, instead continuing to extend the offer of communion.

Jesus as the justice of God plays havoc with justice understood simply as *suum cuique*. Here, Thomas Aquinas is helpful. He begins his treatment of justice with the classic notion of *suum cuique* and, on the surface, there appears little difference between his treatment and the classical conception. Thus, according to Aquinas, justice is a virtue with both general and particular species. The general virtue is a unitive force that nurtures solidarity in the shared love that is the common good, while the particular virtue is divided into distributive and commutative dimensions. The affinities of this account with the classical conception are clear; what transforms it and renders it unrecognizable to the classical world is the way that "rendering what is due" is located within the divine order of charity. Justice has as its end charity. According to Aquinas, charity is the form of the virtues. Charity is the form of justice. What this does to justice understood as *suum cuique* can be seen from two interrelated angles.

First, that justice has as its end or form charity means that justice is about the communion of humanity in God; it is about humanity's becoming friends with God. Justice is about building up the communion of all in the circle of love that is the Trinity. So informed by charity, the distributive and commutative operations of justice are radically altered. No longer are they enacted with the ruthless efficiency that characterizes the juridical economy of debt, equity, and retribution. Thomistic justice is not merely a matter of protecting the rights of strangers in the absence of a shared love, but is about nurturing the communion of saints in a shared love. It is not principally a matter of calculating and distributing what is due among strangers; rather, it is concerned with maintaining the unity that God establishes with and among humanity as humanity is liberated from sin. In other words, justice is an instantiation of God's redemptive activity in the world. Justice redeems; it does not enforce an economy of debt, dominion, and strict restitution. Justice is predicated on peace; it is not merely the regulator of conflict. (Thus a common canard is transposed: "Without peace there is no justice.")

Accordingly, the distributive and commutative operations of justice are determined in accord with what, under the impact of the Spirit, is discerned to best promote the communion of humanity in the divine love. Thus, at times justice may entail mercy and forgiveness, forgoing a strict accounting of what is due. For this reason, Augustine, Anselm, and Aquinas insist that there is no conflict or opposition between divine justice and mercy; they are but two names of the single love of God that draws humanity into communion. Justice and mercy are not opposing logics; rather, they share a single end: the return of all love, the sociality of all desire, in God. Justice attains its end by enacting mercy to overcome sin. Mercy overcomes sin to attain its true end, which is justice. In this way, mercy implements perfect justice (Aquinas) and the rule of God's justice is mercy (Anselm). Hence, Christ's sacrifice was perfectly just, not because it satisfied a debt but because it renewed the communion of humanity in God. At this point the classical conception ruptures, for the classical world had little or no place for mercy or forgiveness, seeing it as an alien intrusion or immoral interruption. Yet it is precisely at this moment, when justice and mercy join hands, that humanity is liberated, is provided with a path beyond the agony and conflict of sin.

The second aspect of the transformation or redemption of justice that is effected by its being repositioned within the divine order of charity is that justice is no longer a human achievement but is a divine gift, the logic of which is distinctly liturgical. It is not insignificant that Aquinas's treatment of justice in the *Summa* appears after his treatment of the supernatural virtue of charity. This is the case because justice finally is a supernatural gift. It is, as Anselm recognized, Christ's accomplishment, not ours. Christ is the Just One of God; we are just only insofar as we have been graciously made just (justified) through his gift. In other words, our being just is made possible only as we are united to Christ through participation in Christ's body – the Church – via the liturgy and sacraments. In this sense, the classical understanding of justice as *suum cuique* is transformed from a logic of debt and retribution into a logic of liturgy. In *The City of God* Augustine argued that Christianity embodied a true politics because, unlike pagan Rome, it alone worshiped the triune God. It alone was a truly just community because only it offered God the sacrifice of worship, praise, and obedience that was due God. And, of course, this is *not* because Christians are somehow able to fulfill the classic canons of *suum cuique* where pagans failed, but because Christians are incorporated into Christ, who through the donation of love to the Father transforms the operation of *suum cuique* by an act of substitution or recapitulation that miraculously (which is to say, graciously) renders the impossible possible, namely our praise and worship of God. As God in Christ bears the burden of human rebellion, the classic logic of *suum cuique* implodes as the divine refusal to render unto sinners what is due sin ironically creates the possibility that they may now return to the fold of perfect justice, where God is duly worshiped.

The Word (II): Scripture on justice and justification

This Augustinian account of Jesus as the justice of God that effects the communion of all in the divine order of charity corresponds to the vision of justice and liberation revealed in the written Word. From beginning to end, the biblical drama of liberation is the record of God's intention to gather humanity again into the communion of divine love. God calls Abraham, liberates Israel, establishes David, raises up the prophets, sends the Spirit, and gathers the Church for the sake of the participation of humanity in the divine order of charity that is the Trinity. The written Word reveals that God is just precisely as God renews and restores relations. This is to say, biblical justice is a matter of effecting communion, not the impartial administration of an abstract forensic ideal.

In the Old Testament, this is expressed in the word pair, *mispat* and *sedaqah*, usually translated as "justice and righteousness." The linking of justice, or true judgment, with righteousness is not incidental. For, in the Old Testament, what is just is intrinsically bound up with what is good. No mere proceduralism, justice is ordered toward righteousness; in particular, it is directed toward the establishment of right relations between people in God (Weinfeld, 1995). For this reason, *mispat* and *sedaqah* have little in common with modern concerns for the impartial administration of laws. Instead, they are first and foremost about the deliverance, vindication, or liberation of humanity from a situation of oppression and destitution. This is to say, justice in the Old Testament is soteriological; it redeems or saves. This is most clearly demonstrated in the way *mispat* and *sedaqah* reflect a divine partisanship on behalf of the widow, the orphan, and the poor (Donahue, 1977; Weinfeld, 1995). But it should not be overlooked that God's penchant for the poor and oppressed is but an extension of the divine intention to liberate humanity from the oppression of sin. *Mispat* and *sedaqah* are pre-eminently manifestations of God's faithful activity to renew and uphold the covenantal relation with humanity even in the face of human rebellion.

This understanding of justice is further displayed in the New Testament, where justice and righteousness are translated with a single term, *dikiaosyne*. The gospels present Jesus as the justice of God, as the one who embodies the justice that delivers people from sin (again, prominently displayed in a preferential concern for the downtrodden and oppressed) and whose presence inaugurates the kingdom where human relations are redeemed and restored. Central to this justice is the mercy or forgiveness that in the name of reconciliation forgoes retribution and retaliation. It is Paul, however, who most directly addresses the issue of the justice of God when he explicates the meaning of justification. The *locus classicus* of the doctrine of justification is his Epistle to the Romans. Although it has been subject to the same sorts of misreadings and distortions that have plagued Anselm, Paul's understanding of Jesus as the justice of God involves not a logic of penal substitution in accord with a strict accounting of what is due but rather, in harmony with its Jewish roots, displays the divine redemptive solidarity that has as its end the restoration and renewal of communion of all in God (Marshall, 2001). Jesus is the justice of God, according to Paul, precisely as the incarnation of God's fidelity to the promise of redemption made long ago to Abraham (Hays, 2002). In contrast with the classical canons of justice, the justice of God in Christ entails the endurance of offense and offer of forgiveness for the sake of justifying the unjust, so that the unjust may be gathered back into communion through participation in the death and resurrection of Christ.

Works of Mercy

At the outset it was posited that the Christian enactment of justice and liberation arises as a response to the Word and that this response is distinctively shaped by the liturgical context of the Christian life. As Augustine said, true justice is found only in the community ruled by Christ. The exposition of Jesus as the justice of God illuminated Augustine's claim as it suggested that true justice is formed by charity, which means true justice accords with mercy and forgiveness, and that this charity is finally not a human accomplishment but a divine gift that is given in Christ. That justice is not a human accomplishment, that it accords with mercy, and that its end is the communion of love prompt us in this final section to reconsider the nature of the Christian response to the Word. If justice and liberation are neither human accomplishments nor reducible to a strict calculus of *suum cuique* and the enforcement of modern "rights," then what do we do when we respond to the Word that summons us to do justice and liberate the oppressed? The Christian response is twofold.

Response (I): font and table

First, we move toward font and table. Because justice is not our accomplishment but Christ's, the first response to the Word's calling forth justice is to receive the gift of that justice. Confronted with the Word, we respond by allowing God's justice mercifully to enfold us and draw us back into the order of charity whence we have departed in sinful insurrection. Traditionally, this has been called justification, and occurs as we are joined to Christ and made members of his body through the liturgy and the sacraments. Specifically, through the waters of baptism we are joined to Christ and so justified and at the table, where we receive the body and blood offered for us and to us, that communion is nurtured as our participation in Christ is ever deepened. Thus, Augustine's claim becomes clearer: the Church is a correlate of true justice because it is there that we are engrafted into the body of the one who is the justice of God.

Response (II): works of mercy

This first response necessarily entails a second. The corollary of the reception of justice is our going forth to embody this justice and liberation in the world. The justified set forth to do justice (Tamez, 1993), as the words of the eucharistic liturgy remind us: "Eternal God, we give you thanks for this holy mystery in which you have given yourself to us. Grant that we may go into the world in the strength of your Spirit, to give ourselves for others, in the name of Jesus Christ our Lord, Amen" (United Methodist Church, 1989: 10). This response is perhaps nowhere better displayed than in poor Latin American parishes where, Latin American liberationists tell us, in response to the Word, Christians intentionally devote themselves to discerning – sometimes as part of the liturgy itself, sometimes after the formal liturgy – how they are to respond to a particular situation of injustice in light of the Word.

This going forth, however, is not merely a matter of motivation, as if the liturgy simply encouraged Christians to go out and do secular justice. On the contrary, if Jesus is the justice of God, then going forth to do justice can only be about inviting others to be joined to Christ. Doing justice does not entail leaving the liturgy behind and taking up a secular theory, but is a matter of extending the liturgy so that all might be gathered in the communion of charity that is possible in Christ.

That justice is a liturgical act, an act whose end is the communion of all in Christ, shapes how we go about discerning the form of our enactment of justice and liberation in the world. Here again Augustine is helpful. In a discussion of the Eucharist and how Christ's sacrifice unites us to God in holy fellowship, Augustine writes that true sacrifices are works of mercy that have as their end the relief of distress and the conferring of happiness. Here, the threads of this chapter converge in the recognition of the liturgy as the fount of true justice – in the Eucharist we meet the justice of God as Christ mercifully draws us into the circle of charity that is the Trinity – and in the identification of this justice as a work of mercy. Augustine then continues, asserting that, as we are eucharistically united to Christ, we take on Christ's form, the form of a servant people who give themselves to and for others as a work of mercy (Augustine, 1950: X, 6). With regard to the discipline of discernment, Augustine's insight prods us to set aside the futile ideologies of modernity and, instead, let our deliberations be guided by the ancient tradition of the works of mercy, for they are the liturgical extension of the justice of God in the world.

The works of mercy encompass seven corporal and seven spiritual works. The corporal works include feeding the hungry, giving drink to the thirsty, clothing the naked, harboring the stranger, visiting the sick, ministering to prisoners, and burying the dead. The spiritual works include admonishing the sinner, instructing the ignorant, counseling the doubtful, comforting the afflicted, bearing wrongs patiently, forgiving injuries, and praying for the living and the dead. They find their richest elaboration in the lives of the saints, and so our deliberations of what justice entails should be guided by the witness of the lives of such figures as Francis and Clare, Day and Romero as well as countless others who, while garnering less recognition and approbation, nevertheless clearly display God's justice.

As works of charity that spring from devotion to Christ (cf. Matthew 25: 31–45, one of their scriptural warrants) and as the embodiment of a substantive notion of the good that desires all to be reconciled in God, the works of mercy are not easily assimilated to either the classical or modern variants of *suum cuique*. Nor are they, when understood rightly, susceptible to the charge of being an instance of *mere* charity, that is, of being an example of the modern hobby of philanthropy that contributes a few percentage points of one's disposable income to "worthy" causes, all the while ignoring broader systemic issues (what liberationists label "structural sin or injustice"). On the contrary, the Church's practice of the works of mercy coinheres with the best insights of the liberationists regarding the struggle for justice and liberation. For example, it takes little imagination to see the correlation between various elements of the works of mercy and what liberationists call "integral liberation." With this term liberationists signal that God's justice and liberation is holistic, embracing the redemption of humanity at the personal, sociopolitical, and spiritual levels (Gutiérrez, 1988: 24–5). The works of mercy, likewise, are holistic in breadth, addressing sin and the rupture of communion in its personal, social, and spiritual dimensions. Moreover, they entail not simply tending to the wounds of the oppressed and afflicted, but also confronting the oppressor.

How the works of mercy might strike contemporary readers as most inadequate and ineffectual is in their apparent personal approach to social change and in their emphasis on forgiveness. That the works of mercy are interpreted as personal, seeking change by means of individual, one-to-one acts of kindness to the exclusion of systemic concerns, however, is an error that is symptomatic of the way in which tradition has been eroded by the acids of modernity. Modernity has little place for a public, political Church and, as a result, the works of mercy are consigned to individuals; yet, as they have been practiced across the ages (and continue to be practiced in some quarters), the works of mercy are a corporate activity. They describe the struggle for justice and liberation of a people, of a public and therefore political body named the Church. In this regard it is worth noting that Adam Smith, in his classic treatise, *The Wealth of Nations*, acknowledged that the Church's practice of the works of mercy constituted a social and economic system or structure that warded off capitalism (Smith, 1976: II, 323–6).

There is one aspect of the charge of personalism that holds, however. The works of mercy clearly imply that justice and liberation are effected through the nurturing of relationships. Far from being a deficiency, however, this is in accord with the liberationists' insight that justice entails solidarity and becoming "friends of the poor." The works of mercy are personal in the particular sense that they shift the center of the struggle for justice away from where it typically resides today, namely, in struggles for the attention of impersonal governmental agencies and in the public policy pronouncements of bureaucratic arms of ecclesial bodies that do not themselves abide by those pronouncements. Instead, the works of mercy remind us that the struggle for justice is of a piece with the expansion of community, with the ever-widening proliferation of the bonds of friendship, which is the wisdom behind the liberationists' insistence that the Church that struggles for justice cannot be a Church *for* the poor, but must be a Church *of* the poor (Sobrino, 1984).

The charge that forgiveness is out of place in a discussion of justice likewise reflects an estrangement of justice and mercy that is at odds with both the Word and traditional Christian practice. As previously noted, whereas forgiveness and mercy have little place in either classical or modern accounts of justice, the justice of God, precisely because its end is the charity that desires communion, is a work of mercy. This, however, does not mean that the justice of God sanctions impunity. After all, alongside the exhortation to forgive stand those of admonishing the sinner and instructing the ignorant. Moreover, forgiveness as a work of mercy has little in common with contemporary notions of forgiveness that do little more than traffic in pious sentimentalities and coping strategies while leaving an unjust and oppressive situation intact. Instead, it is more akin to the ancient practice of penance, which at its best was understood as a means of grace precisely because its aim was to liberate the offender from sin and effect reconciliation and the renewal of communion by means of confession, repentance, and satisfaction/reparation (cf. Jones, 1995). A good example of what this sort of justice might look like today is the contemporary movement for what is termed "restorative justice" (Zehr, 1990; Marshall, 2001).

Conclusion

Justice and liberation name first and foremost what Christ has accomplished. Christ's work reveals that true justice is formed by charity and that its rule is mercy. Before Christians enact this justice, they receive it as a gift through the liturgical constitution of the Church as the Body of Christ. The liturgical reception of justice in turn forms the Church into a servant body that serves the world justly by extending Christ's gift of renewed communion in God. This the Church does through the works of mercy. As a people whose life together is marked by the corporal and spiritual works, it embodies the justice of God that promises to liberate both oppressor and oppressed from the agony of sin and gather all around the table of the Lord to share in the eternal bounty of divine charity.

References

Augustine (1950) *The City of God* (New York: Random House).

Donahue, J. R. (1977) "Biblical Perspectives on Justice," in *The Faith that Does Justice*, ed. J. C. Haughey, pp. 68–112 (New York: Paulist).

Gutiérrez, G. (1988) *A Theology of Liberation* (Maryknoll, NY: Orbis).

Hays, R. (2002) *The Faith of Jesus Christ* (Grand Rapids, MI: Eerdmans).

Jones, L. G. (1995) *Embodying Forgiveness* (Grand Rapids, MI: Eerdmans).

MacIntyre, A. (1988) *Whose Justice? Which Rationality?* (Notre Dame, IN: University of Notre Dame Press).

Marshall, C. (2001) *Beyond Retribution: A New Testament Vision for Justice, Crime, and Punishment* (Grand Rapids, MI: Eerdmans).

Smith, A. (1976) *An Inquiry into the Nature and Causes of the Wealth of Nations* (Chicago: University of Chicago), esp. Book V, chapter 1, part 3, art. 3.

Sobrino, J. (1984) *The True Church and the Poor* (Maryknoll, NY: Orbis).

Tamez, E. (1993) *The Amnesty of Grace* (Nashville, TN: Abingdon).

United Methodist Church (1989) *The United Methodist Hymnal* (Nashville, TN: The United Methodist Publishing House).

Weinfeld, M. (1995) *Social Justice in Ancient Israel and in the Ancient Near East* (Minneapolis, MN: Fortress).

Zehr, H. (1990) *Changing Lenses: A New Focus on Crime and Justice* (Scottdale, PA: Herald).

CHAPTER 15

Discerning: Politics and Reconciliation

William T. Cavanaugh

If we are going to speak rightly about Christianity and politics, the first obstacle we must overcome is the illusion that we are talking about relating two essentially different spheres of discourse. The most common procedure for relating Christianity and politics is to begin with the assumption that one is "religious" and the other "secular." In the interests of civil peace, we have learned to separate out the particularities of religious discourse from the universal and neutral sphere of politics. Even those who maintain that Christianity has a contribution to make to politics often assume that religious language must be translated into some more neutral type of language in order to have an impact on politics.

What is partially obscured by this line of reasoning is the deeply "religious" nature of the story it tells. Modern politics – and the distinction of religious and secular – is itself based on a deeply mythological tale of human reconciliation. Once this is grasped, it becomes possible and necessary to see that Christianity and modern liberal politics do not by essence inhabit two distinct spheres or realms; they are rather two ways of describing human nature and human destiny. Both are stories of conflict and recon-ciliation. The way they are told, however, is very different. In this difference lies the Christian political task.

I will begin by telling the story as told by two of the founders of modern liberalism, Thomas Hobbes and John Locke. I will then tell the Christian story of reconciliation, and show how it is enacted in the liturgy. Finally, I will examine the Christian political practices of living the liturgy in everyday life.

Scattering

Modern politics is a story of reconciliation that is told in a tragic key. It begins with an account of the conflict that makes reconciliation necessary and urgent. For Western politics, the conflict that marks out the modern era from the medieval involves the break-up of a united Christendom into many competing worldviews. The division of Christendom into a welter of Protestant, Catholic, and Anabaptist groups – and the wars of the sixteenth and seventeenth centuries – were followed by the opening of Europe to a diverse world of belief and the development of ideologies of unbelief. The central political problem of modernity became that of trying to achieve social reconciliation in a situation of such widespread and intractable pluralism in matters of ultimate concern, a pluralism that sometimes erupted into violence.

To achieve such reconciliation, it would be necessary, so this history of salvation goes, to pry the human person free from all such lethal allegiances. Thus was born the "state of nature," a crucial analytical device for the classical period of liberal political theory. In the state of nature, the human person exists as an individual, prior to any allegiances. No claim of tradition or Church or class or location impinges on the individual in the state of nature; he or she is free, and in that freedom is equal to every other individual. Only upon this basis could a political order be constructed that is free from the violence that such claims produce.

For Thomas Hobbes, however, the state of nature does not short-circuit the tragedy of history by returning to some pristine pre-Fall condition. For Hobbes, the essential individuality and equality of human beings means that violence is inscribed in the very nature of things:

> From this equality of ability, ariseth equality of hope in the attaining of our ends. And therefore if any two men desire the same thing, which nevertheless they cannot both enjoy, they become enemies; and in the way to their end, which is principally their own conservation, and sometimes their delectation only, endeavor to destroy, or subdue one another. (Hobbes, 1962: 98–9)

In the state of nature, there is no common good. Each person has a right to everything, a *jus in omnia* (Hobbes, 1962: 103). The only ends are the relentless pursuit of one's own conservation, or simply one's own pleasure. The driving force is the *libido dominandi*, the "perpetual and restless desire of power after power, that ceaseth only in death" (Hobbes, 1962: 80). In searching for a solution to the war of all against all that results, Hobbes cannot return to the Aristotelian and medieval idea that a political order must be based on a common conception of the good. Hobbes's own experience of the English Civil War taught him that people disagree over the ends of life, and this intractable disagreement could only produce more violence. If people cannot agree about what is good, however, they can agree about what is evil. The new political order will be based on the fear of death, since the only thing people have in common is mutual enmity (Manent, 1994: 22–3).

The resolution of the war of all against all is therefore that each person give up his or her right over all things to an absolute sovereign, who will protect each individual against all other individuals. The power of the sovereign is unlimited because the *jus in omnia* transferred to the sovereign is unlimited (Hobbes, 1962: 134–41). In the state of nature the individual is weak, constantly fearful and frustrated in the pursuit of power. Fear of the sovereign imposed upon all, however, allows each person to realize his or her nature as an individual free from the interference of others, free to pursue his or her own ends. Absolutism is therefore not an oppressive but a liberating force. Nevertheless, with Hobbes, political power has now been constructed not from God's strength but from humanity's weakness (Manent, 1994: 30). To thus construct a political order from the flaws in the human character is to acknowledge that politics can only be a tragic enterprise. True reconciliation among humans is impossible. The most we can expect from politics is the displacement of violence through a sovereign will strong enough to keep individuals' pursuit of power in check.

Absolute sovereign power does not contradict freedom in Hobbes's scheme because it is based on the tacit but willing consent of the people to transfer their rights to the sovereign, and because the law is a purely external device meant to build protective fences around individuals and their freedom. When one encounters a law, it must be obeyed, but in all the spaces between fences the law is absent, and the individual is free to do whatever he or she wills. This is the essence of modern liberal political orders: the law is meant to protect the freedom of individuals from interference, not to promote any particular conception of the good. In his individualism, his emphasis on consent, and his giving priority to freedom over the good, Hobbes is the founder of liberalism. It would be up to John Locke, however, to give liberalism the characteristic form that we recognize today. Though Locke was fundamentally in sympathy with Hobbes's scheme – and himself proposed an absolutist political project in his early work *Two Tracts on Government* (1660–2) – Locke sought to make rights an intrinsic property of the individual in nature and sought to limit the power of the sovereign state.

For Hobbes, rights were not yet an intrinsic property of the human person as such because the *jus in omnia* depended on the instinct to self-preservation, which depended in turn on hostile others with whom the individual was already locked in rivalry. In order to make rights intrinsic to the person as such, Locke sought to show that rights arise not out of relationship with others but within the context of the individual's relationship with nature alone (Manent, 1994: 40–1). Locke is more thoroughly individualistic than Hobbes because in the state of nature the individual has no primary relationships with others, not even hostile ones. What motivates the individual in the state of nature is not primarily fear of others but the search for sustenance. From this search arises private property, the right to which is the most fundamental right and the foundation of the political order.

According to Locke, "God gave the world to Adam and his posterity in common" (Locke, 1924: 129), but it was appropriated for private property, not because of some Fall from grace, but because, in order to derive benefit from the creation, individuals made use of their God-given reason and abilities by mixing their labor with the creation, thus marking it as their own. God gave the world "to the use of the industrious and the rational" (Locke, 1924: 132). Therefore, whoever appropriates a thing from the abundance of nature through his or her own labor establishes an exclusive property right to it. This right is strictly individual and does not depend, as it had for Aquinas, for example, on its social utility. Locke says that no one may appropriate more from nature than he or she can use, for it would be wasted. With the invention of money, however, perishable goods may be exchanged for imperishable gold, thus allowing the legitimate stockpiling of great wealth. The gold may in turn be exchanged for other goods, thus allowing for the possibility that the legitimate owner of goods might not be the person whose labor produced them. The system is beneficial to all, however, for it allows for the increase and preservation of wealth. Locke thus derives the fundamental and intrinsic right of property from the solitary individual laboring with his or her hands in the state of nature, but then applies this right toward a utilitarian justification of the market economy as a whole (Locke, 1924: 131–41).

Because Locke wishes to make rights intrinsic to human being and avoid Hobbes's despotic sovereign, he makes a distinction between the state of nature and the state of war, and generally paints an attractive picture of labor and exchange in the state of nature. The problem with the state of nature, as Pierre Manent puts it, is this: "The more 'satisfying' it is, the 'happier' it is, then the more likely it is to provide the image of natural rights that the political institution should guarantee and protect; but simultaneously, it becomes less clear why men left this state to enter into a body politic" (Manent, 1994: 47–8). Locke is forced to say that, although the state of nature is not a state of war, it is inevitably fated to become so, for "the pravity of mankind being such that they had rather injuriously prey upon the fruits of other men's labors than take pains to provide for themselves," they are compelled out of the state of nature and into political society (Locke, 1955: 47). Without a common judge, the rights of all are imperiled. It is to protect these rights that individuals enter into a commonwealth: "The commonwealth seems to me to be a society of men constituted only for the procuring, preserving, and advancing their own civil interests. Civil interests I call life, liberty, health, and indolency of the body; and the possession of outward things, such as money, lands, houses, furniture, and the like" (Locke, 1955: 17). To protect individual rights, Locke wishes to avoid alienating them to an absolute sovereign who is above the law. Rather than follow Hobbes's solution, Locke sets the tone for the modern liberal state by making government representative, and putting the sovereign itself under the law.

Nevertheless, Locke's politics remain tragic, no less than Hobbes's. Locke's individualism is even more extreme than Hobbes's, such that the unitive project of political life consists only of making clearer what is mine and what is yours. There is no room in the political arena for the discussion of common goods, but only the management of varied civil interests. Locke is unable to stop, however, at imagining the peaceful non-interference of isolated monads. For, as we have seen, conflict and war are essential to the hypothetical state of nature if we are to explain why anyone saw fit to leave the state of nature and undertake political society in the first place. In other words, the story of the liberal political order must be told as the rescue from some primordial violence. Hostility must be natural in order to explain the social contract. But since it is natural, inscribed in creation itself, we can never fully escape it. The modern political order continues to derive its legitimacy from its continuing ability to convince us of its success in displacing the violence that constantly threatens. The stories told of the state of nature, after all, are not intended to be historical accounts of the way things actually were in the past. These stories are ontological; that is, they tell about how things really are in their nature, now and always. And, at the bottom of it, violent is the way things really are. Creation is characterized not by abundance but by scarcity. The most a political order can do is to stave off the violence, not to achieve true reconciliation but to keep individuals from interfering with each other, most especially by diverting their attention to common enemies outside the borders of the nation-state. That is, the problem of violence is solved by war. In a polity with no common ends by design, war unifies.

The lack of common ends was meant to save us from the so-called wars of religion and other conflicts over the ends of life, on which disparate individuals would never agree. Liberal politics is supposed to be more humble and peaceloving, therefore, because it leaves such ultimate questions aside to concentrate on more mundane matters. At the same time as it professes this humility, however, modern politics is simultaneously hubristic, for now that God has been bracketed out of politics, our ends are entirely self-given. The genius of modern politics is that we have abolished heteronomy; we only obey ourselves. The priority of freedom over the good, however, makes conflict inevitable; since there is no common good to adjudicate competing claims, all that remains is the force of will against will. The state must deliberately frustrate any attempt to instantiate a thick conception of the good, presumably to avoid violence. At the same time, the lack of common ends ensures that conflict is tragically inevitable, and it is upon this conflict that the legitimacy of the state depends.

Gathering

At first appearance it may seem that the biblical story is also a tragedy, marked by a fall from grace that has forever fated humanity to violence and sin. However, it is precisely the Fall that marks the biblical narrative as a story capable of true reconciliation. For the Fall indicates that there is something to fall away from. Genesis assumes that there is an original good condition from which the present state of affairs is a departure. Violence, therefore, is not the norm, but is a deviation from the norm. Genesis thus leaves open the possibility that reconciliation can be achieved, and that ultimately the drama of human evil and violence is not a tragedy.

Genesis 1–11 most likely received its final form in partial response to the Babylonian creation myth, the *Enuma Elish*. The latter narrative begins with Apsu and Tiamat, the goddess of chaos, who create gods of order but then regret it and plot to destroy them. In the ensuing battle, Apsu and Tiamat are killed. Marduk, newly acclaimed king of the gods, creates the world from the dead body of Tiamat. Marduk then makes humans from clay and the blood of the slain Kingu, chief helper of Tiamat. Humans are made for the purpose of being slaves to the gods (Heidel, 1951). In the *Enuma Elish*, as in liberal accounts of the "state of nature," there is no Fall from a pristine creation which God has declared to be good. Violence is present in the beginning. This serves as a powerful explanatory device: the world is violent because it has always been so. The state of war is inevitable. Violence is written into the very nature of being.

What can be done to minimize and displace the effects of this primordial violence is, for liberal thought, to enter into a particular kind of political community. For liberal thought, the history of salvation begins with the social contract. In the biblical narrative, the history of salvation begins with Abraham. It may seem odd to compare a "religious" narrative with a "political" one, but, as liberation theologians have reminded us, there are not two separate histories, one secular and one sacred (Gutiérrez, 1988: 86).

Salvation history is simply history itself, written from the point of view of God's action in the world. Salvation is a public, political event that unfolds on the one stage of human history. In the Scriptures, salvation is depicted as a Kingdom, a new city; in the Scriptures pharaohs, judges, kings, and caesars all play roles in the drama of salvation. There is only one stage. On it the tragedies of history are ultimately incorporated by God into the story of salvation.

In modern politics, human beings are essentially individuals in a state of alienation or separation from one another. Politics has done its job, therefore, if it can protect the autonomy of such individuals and their property from one another. In the biblical story, on the other hand, humans are not essentially individuals, but rather are essentially one. Creation in the image of God (Genesis 1: 27) indicates that all human beings participate in one another through their participation in God, for the image is the same in each person. The patristic writers speak of the creation of humanity as a whole, not of individuals. Thus Gregory of Nyssa: "the whole of human nature from the first man to the last is but one image of him who is" (de Lubac, 1988: 29–30).

For this reason Paul is able to treat Adam's fall as the Fall of the whole human race (Romans 5: 12–21). The effect of this breach of the relationship between humanity and God – the fading and distortion of the image of God in humans – also therefore has an effect on the relationships of humans to each other. That effect is the scattering of the original pre-Fall unity of the human race. From Abel's murder in chapter 4 to the scattering of the tower-builders in chapter 11, Genesis shows the effects of the Fall in the mutual enmity and violence that divide humans from each other. Hence Origen's dictum, "Where there is sin, there is multiplicity."

> True to Origen's criterion, Maximus the Confessor, for example, considers original sin as a separation, a breaking up, an individualization it might be called, in the depreciatory sense of the word. Whereas God is working continually in the world to the effect that all should come together into unity, by this sin which is the work of man, "the one nature was shattered into a thousand pieces" and humanity which ought to constitute a harmonious whole, in which "mine" and "thine" would be no contradiction, is turned into a multitude of individuals, as numerous as the sands of the seashore, all of whom show violently discordant inclinations. (de Lubac, 1988: 33–4)

This theme is common in the patristic sources. Augustine says of Adam, "Originally one, he has fallen, and, breaking up as it were, he has filled the whole earth with the pieces" (de Lubac, 1988: 34). The important point is that humans are not essentially individuals; the very existence of individuals who seek to protect their autonomy and interests is an indication that something has already gone terribly wrong. To seek judiciously to erect fences between mine and thine is not a formula for peace but an institutionalization of hostility.

In Genesis 12, salvation begins with gathering a people, Israel. Abraham is called to be a great nation, through whom all the nations on earth will be blessed. Gerhard Lohfink (1999) contends that "gathering" has been neglected as a theological term; in fact, the term captures a fundamental theme of Israel's theology (for example, Deuteronomy 30: 1–6), and is even used as a technical term in the soteriology of many of the prophetic books (Lohfink, 1999: 51–2). Thus, for example, in Isaiah 11, the vision of the peaceable kingdom is accompanied by a promise that YHWH will "raise a signal for the nations, and will assemble the outcasts of Israel, and gather the dispersed of Judah from the four corners of the earth" (Isaiah 11:12). Salvation is depicted as the re-gathering of Israel, not only for Israel's sake, but for the reconciliation of "all the nations" (e.g., Isaiah 2: 2–4).

Jesus's use of the term "gather" is consonant with the Old Testament imagination of salvation as a restoration of unity. "How often have I desired to gather your children together as a hen gathers her brood under her wings, and you were not willing" (Matthew 23: 37); "Whoever is not with me is against me, and whoever does not gather with me scatters" (Matthew 12: 30). This gathering is effected in Christ himself, the "one man" whose death and resurrection is the reconciliation of the many (Romans 5: 12–21). As the patristic writers stressed, the incarnation was the incorporation of the whole of humanity into Christ. "In making a human nature, it is *human nature* that he united to himself . . . Whole and entire he will bear it then to Calvary, whole and entire he will raise it from the dead, whole and entire he will save it" (de Lubac, 1988: 38–9). The resolution of the drama of salvation is the reconciliation that Christ realizes between humans and God and among humans themselves. Their essential unity is restored, though the drama is not yet concluded; full consummation of the Kingdom of God still awaits.

Liturgy

Liturgy is the continuing performance of the drama of reconciliation through Jesus Christ. Liturgy is the public act of remembrance, or *anamnesis*, of the history of salvation, from the creation of the world to its fall and redemption in the life, death, and resurrection of Jesus Christ. This remembrance is not just a mental act, however, but a public performance that gathers people into a particular kind of community, the Body of Christ. The original sense of the Greek word *leitourgia*, as Alexander Schmemann points out, is "an action by which a group of people become something corporately which they had not been as a mere collection of individuals" (Schmemann, 1988: 25). In the Christian liturgy, what they become is an anticipation of the Kingdom of God. The remembrance of the drama of redemption is not just a symbolic re-presentation of a past event, like the re-enactment of a Civil War battle. In the liturgy, Christians stand in the presence of the future, and come, as Hebrews says (12: 22–9), to the heavenly altar. We recall the suffering of Christ at the hands of the powers and principalities that still stalk this earth, and we recognize that we still walk as pilgrims in hope. Nevertheless, the liturgy is a real foretaste of the Kingdom, and the Eucharist calls us to be now what we will be perfectly later: the Body of Christ. The Eucharist is the true politics because it is the public performance of the City of God in the midst of another city that is passing away.

In the liturgy, we enact a politics of reconciliation that makes the Church a counter-performance to the politics of the world. This politics is evident in the very act of gathering. "The actual assembly of Christians renders visible the gathering of humankind that Christ has accomplished" (Martimort, 1987: I, 91). Since the earliest times, this assembly was seen as prefiguring heaven. This is not to say that the Church is a gathering of the perfect, for we know that the Church is full of sinners. The Church is to prefigure heaven in breaking down barriers between Jew and Gentile, woman and man, slave and free (Galatians 3: 28). The early Church was unique in Roman society for its assemblies across class, ethnic, and gender lines, people who gathered by reason of no affinity other than their common affinity to Christ.

That our churches are often segregated is a scandal about which Paul (1 Corinthians 11: 12) and James (2: 1–4) already felt obliged to complain. Nevertheless, the liturgy itself makes clear in multiple ways that reconciling these divisions is the work that Christ is about in his Church. In the Roman Catholic mass, the greeting is followed by a penitential rite in which the assembled confess together, to God and to each other, that they have sinned, and ask forgiveness and prayers. This rite is an echo of the second-century *Didache*, which instructs

> Assemble on the Lord's Day, and break bread and offer the Eucharist; but first make confession of your faults, so that your sacrifice may be a pure one. Anyone who has a difference with his fellow is not to take part with you until they have been reconciled, so as to avoid any profanation of your sacrifice. (Staniforth, 1968: 234)

The penitential rite is in fundamental continuity with the kiss or sign of peace that comes before communion. Practiced universally in the ancient Church, the kiss of peace formalizes the requirement that we be reconciled to one another so as not to make a mockery of the liturgy. According to Cyril of Jerusalem, the basis for catechetical instruction on the kiss of peace was Matthew 5: 23–4, Jesus's admonition that those who have need of reconciliation should go and be reconciled before approaching the altar (Martimort, 1987: II, 114). The third-century *Didascalia Apostolorum* reports that during the kiss of peace the deacon would cry out "Is there any man that keepeth ought against his fellow?" as a safeguard against performing the Eucharist in an unreconciled state (Dix, 1982: 106–7).

The penitential rite and the sign of peace are preliminaries that lead up to the Eucharist, which the revised Roman Catholic *Rite of Penance* refers to as "*the* sacrament of reconciliation" (*RP*, 4). It is the Eucharist that incorporates us into the very Body of Christ, for "whoever eats my flesh and drinks my blood lives in me and I live in that person" (John 6: 56). The Eucharist is human participation in the reconciliation of the world that Christ accomplishes. St John Chrysostom speaks of the Eucharist in these terms.

> The Son of God came down for this purpose, to reconcile our human nature to the Lord. But He did not come down for that purpose alone, but also for the purpose of making us, if we do likewise, sharers of His title. For He says: "Blessed are the peacemakers, for they shall be called sons of God" (Matthew 5: 9). You, according to human capacity, must do what the Onlybegotten Son of God has done, be an agent of peace, for yourself and for others. For this reason, at the very time of sacrifice He recalls us to no other commandment than that of reconciliation with one's brother, showing that it is the greatest of all. (Chrysostom, 1986: 147)

The liturgy we perform in our churches is an enactment of true reconciliation of the world in Christ. It is, therefore, a profound challenge to the politics that claims that we are essentially individuals whose reconciliation is always tragically deferred. The liturgy is more than symbolic. The communal body of people that is formed by the liturgy is meant to embody the politics of reconciliation, the politics of Jesus, in the world.

Church and Politics

Those of us who have our rears in the pews on Sunday mornings may find all of this a little overblown. It may be the case that the liturgy is a dramatic performance of what God has done for us, and participation in this ritual may have an effect on how each of us sees the world, but the performance itself seems confined to the church building. To claim it as a public act, even more a political act, seems unrealistic. Politics is what happens when people meet to deliberate about the structure of their common life together, but any gathering is not therefore a political act. In common usage, the term "politics" does not refer to the deliberations or structuring rituals of merely particular or private associations. Politics implies universality, the structure of the whole. Modern politics refers to the state and its subsidiary organs, and not to the merely particular associations that make up civil society. Such associations – unions, professional organizations, religious groups, and so on – may indeed seek to have an effect on the political process, but they do so by vying for power within the apparatus of the state. Only the state represents a gathering that transcends particular interests and deliberates for the whole.

What happens when the Church gathers? In the dominant view, the Church takes its place alongside the other gatherings of civil society. The Church may strive to be political by lobbying for influence on the deliberations of the state, but the Church is not itself the sphere where politics proper happens. This is so because the Church is one particular association among many. In a pluralistic society filled with Catholics and Protestants, with Jews, atheists, Muslims, and agnostics, with believers and non-believers of every stripe, the Church cannot claim universality. The state is the universal gathering, the place where all particular individuals and associations meet to make binding decisions for the life of the whole. Politics, therefore, is enacted on the stage of the state, the one truly public space. Other performances, such as that enacted by the Church, are relegated to the rehearsal rooms off the main stage. At most, they can prepare individual actors to enter the action on the main stage energized with new motivations and dispositions.

There is no reason why Christians should meekly accept this way of configuring politics. It has a profoundly distorting effect on the Church's proclamation of the universal message of the gospel. In trying to lobby the state for political influence, the Church often feels it must translate the supposed particularity of Jesus and the gospel into more universal and neutral terms. Despite its ostensible openness to a pluralism of ultimate ends, the liberal state will never be able to respect the integrity of the associations of civil society precisely because it is founded on the belief that pluralism is a threat. The liberal nation-state is founded, as we have seen, on a dramatic myth of salvation from pluralism. In the absence of shared ends – an absence upon which liberalism insists – devotion to the unity of the nation-state as the end in itself becomes ever more urgent. Pluralism will always be a crisis, and the solution to the crisis of pluralism is to rally around the nation-state. But the nation-state must always be in crisis in order to produce that unity. As Walter Benjamin said in a different context, the "'state of emergency' in which we live is not the exception but the rule" (Benjamin, 1968: 257).

The nation-state is inclined to solve the crisis of pluralism by directing violence outward, toward other nation-states, but it is war that most especially reveals the particularism and tribalism of the nation-state. Though the Body of Christ is truly catholic and spans the globe, Christians have become accustomed to killing Christians and others in places like Iraq out of loyalty to the narrow interests of their country. The Church, on the other hand, has always claimed to be a universal, and not merely particular, association. The synagogue, out of which the Church emerged, was exempted from military and cultic service in the Roman Empire because of its status as a *tertium quid* between *polis* and *koinon*. The synagogue was not a *polis*, or city-state, but it also rejected identification as a *koinon*, a club formed around particular interests that was a subset of the whole. The concern of the Torah was for the whole of life, from communal organization to washing before meals.

When the Church separated from the synagogue, it too refused to accept the status of merely particular organization. In adopting the term *ekklesia* – originally meaning the assembly of all those with citizen rights in a Greek city-state – the Church refused the language of *koinon* (Lohfink, 1999: 218–36). Such particular associations were based on affinity; what was distinctive about the Christian gatherings is that "they did not share a common table because they were already one for some other reason, but found their center and source of unity at the table itself" (Power, 1994: 30). Around the table gathered people from all sectors of society, including those excluded from citizenship in the *polis*, namely women, children, and slaves. The Church was not merely a part of the whole but was itself a whole. The term "catholic" came from the Greek *kath' holou*, according to the whole. The Church's interests included the redemption of the whole world. The Church saw itself as the eschatological fulfillment of the promises made to the whole world through Israel.

And yet, precisely because the Church is catholic, it is not a *polis* either. The Church is not like a territorial state, with boundaries that are policed. The Church does not occupy a fixed territory, but moves on pilgrimage through the *civitas terrena*. Furthermore, the boundaries of the Church are not always easy to delineate. "Church" is a crucial theological concept, but it often acts as more a prescriptive than a descriptive term. In practice, the Church is full of the world, full of what is not-Church. We hardly need reminding of the manifest sinfulness of those who gather in the name of Christ and his Church. In this light it is helpful to think of the Church not as a location or an organization, but more like an enacted drama; it is the liturgy that makes the Church. In this drama there is a constant dialectic between sin and salvation, scattering and gathering. "Church" names that plotline that is moving toward reconciliation. But the fact that the drama is moving ultimately toward resolution does not mean that it is immune from conflict. Indeed, conflict is necessary in order for there to be something to resolve.

Those who would face the political nature of the Christian story of salvation have seemed to run up against the following choice: either the Church can acknowledge the universality of the state and try to participate in the state as one more particular organ of civil society, or the Church can withdraw into a "sectarian" stance. To follow the language of the drama, the choice would be either to audition for a minor part in the state tragedy, or to find a separate room in which to stage a different sort of drama, without much of an audience. However, this sociological division of ecclesial stances between Church-type and sect-type (Troeltsch, 1960) is misleading and radically impoverishes the Church's imagination of its own political vocation. Troeltsch and his successors (for example, Gustafson, 1985) assume that the politics and culture of the nation-state are simply the given public reality that the Church can either accept or reject as a whole. In traditional terms, a sect was a group that put itself outside the authority of the Church; the Waldensians were considered a sect and the Franciscans were not, not on the basis of their attitudes toward "culture," which were very similar, but because of their differing attitudes toward Church authority. Since Troeltsch, however, "sectarian" has taken its meaning from a sociological and not a theological criterion, i.e., the Church's attitude toward the dominant culture and its political structures.

Rather than forcing a choice between acceptance of or withdrawal from the one public reality, Augustine's metaphor of the two cities is a far more fruitful model, for it helps us to see that there are two rival performances, the City of God and the earthly city, contending for the status of "public." Augustine helps us imagine the Church's full public participation in the drama of history without insisting that the nation-state is simply the given public reality which we must serve – albeit critically – in order to avoid withdrawal, irresponsibility, and irrelevance. For Augustine, the Church formed in liturgy constantly redirects the drama, redefining what is public and what is not. According to Augustine, the Roman Empire, despite its claims, was not fully public at all. A true *res publica*, or public "thing," is based on justice, the giving of each his or her due, which includes the worship of the true God upon which the acknowledgment of right is based (Augustine, 1950: XIX, 21–3).

The Roman Empire, by contrast, was based on the same *libido dominandi* that Hobbes identified. According to Augustine, the *libido dominandi* was the highest civic virtue, by which other lusts are controlled. Civic virtue and civil integration are based upon the conquest of rivals. When internal conflict threatens the peace of the Empire, it is necessary to direct the conquest outward. As Augustine tells it, the Punic Wars served this purpose until the destruction of Carthage in 146 BC eliminated the "wholesome fear" that, according to Scipio, was a "fit guardian for the citizens," and the Romans once again turned upon each other (Augustine, 1950: I, 30; V, 12). The Roman Empire was not truly public, but merely a temporary dam on the tragic violence that always threatened. The true public thing, says Augustine, is the Church, for it is the Church that enacts the reconciliation of creation through the sacrifice of the Eucharist (Augustine, 1950: X, 6).

If Augustine's analysis carries over – *mutatis mutandis* – to the tragic politics of the liberal state, then Christians need not imagine that our politics begins and ends with lobbying for influence over state policy. Lobbying may be useful, but mere lobbying does not significantly depart from the tragic script that liberal politics enacts. The Church may wish to ask the state to devote more of its resources to the poor, but in doing so it will be difficult to escape the overall story of competition for scarce resources that the state embodies. The Church may argue against the wisdom of a particular war, but if the model of "public theology" is followed (e.g., Himes and Himes, 1993: 15–25), the Church is required to argue in "public" terms, accessible to policy-makers, and thus must appeal to considerations of national security and the self-interest of the nation-state.

More interesting are those approaches that speak on the public stage but refuse to play bit parts in the tragedy orchestrated by the state. One such approach is exemplified by groups of Christians and others that have traveled to Iraq since 1991, bringing food, medicine, and toys, in violation of US law. Such groups refuse the tragic drama of threats to national security, and see the Iraqi people, suffering under sanctions, as the weak members of the body whom Paul admonishes us to treat as members of our own body (1 Corinthians 12: 22–6). Nation-state borders are dismissed as unreal, artificial segmentations of the universal Body of Christ, in which all people made in the image of God are members or potential members in the universal reconciliation that Christ accomplishes. War is seen, as St Cyprian said, as a "rending of the Body of Christ." War is not inevitable. In the delegations to Iraq, this is not merely said but enacted.

Another more quotidian example from the parish level may help to suggest how the reconciliation we enact in the liturgy can rearrange public space. I was invited a few years ago to speak to a church group on the injustices of economic globalization. We talked about how cheap labor is exploited for our benefit, about the Body of Christ that makes us one, and about the contradiction between the two. Some in the group suggested writing to our representatives in Congress. A more interesting approach presented itself later when we learned of a cooperative of local organic farmers that markets its products through churches. People in my parish now buy directly from the cooperative once a month, and the food is distributed at the church. We have begun to know some of the farmers' names and the specific farms from which the different products come. We know that the prices we pay ensure a sustainable living for the farmers. We have begun to short-circuit the global market in which we are accustomed to buying our food from strangers, blind to the conditions in which the food is produced. What is being created is a different kind of public space, a market that is not based on competition or the rational choice of self-interest, but on a just price and a community of producers and buyers who view each other's interests as their own. The reconciliation that we enact in the liturgy every Sunday is breaking out of the walls of the church building, as it were, and forming a different, fully public, space. This is not a withdrawal from politics, but the enactment of the politics of reconciliation that we celebrate in the liturgy.

References

Augustine (1950) *The City of God* (New York: Random House).
Benjamin, Walter (1968) *Illuminations*, trans. Harry Zohn (New York: Schocken).

Chrysostom, St John (1986) "Sermon on the Betrayal by Judas," in *The Eucharist*, ed. Daniel J. Sheerin, ch. 6, Message of the Fathers of the Church series, vol. 7 (Wilmington, DE: Michael Glazier).

Dix, Dom Gregory (1982) *The Shape of the Liturgy* (New York: Seabury).

Gustafson, James (1985) "The Sectarian Temptation: Reflections on Theology, the Church and the University," *Proceedings of the Catholic Theological Society*, 40: 83–94.

Gutiérrez, Gustavo (1988) *A Theology of Liberation*, 2nd edn, trans. and ed. Sister Caridad Inda and John Eagleson (Maryknoll, NY: Orbis).

Heidel, Alexander (1951) *The Babylonian Genesis: The Story of Creation* (Chicago: University of Chicago Press).

Himes, Kenneth and Himes, Michael (1993) *Fullness of Faith: The Public Significance of Theology* (New York: Paulist).

Hobbes, Thomas (1962) *Leviathan* (New York: Collier).

Locke, John (1924) *Two Treatises of Government* (New York: Dutton).

—(1955) *A Letter Concerning Toleration* (Indianapolis, IN: Bobbs-Merrill).

Lohfink, Gerhard (1999) *Does God Need the Church?*, trans. Linda M. Maloney (Collegeville, MN: The Liturgical Press).

de Lubac, Henri (1988) *Catholicism: Christ and the Common Destiny of Man*, trans. Lancelot C. Sheppard and Sister Elizabeth Englund (San Francisco: Ignatius).

Manent, Pierre (1994) *An Intellectual History of Liberalism*, trans. Rebecca Belinski (Princeton, NJ: Princeton University Press).

Martimort, Aime Georges (ed.) (1987) *The Church at Prayer*, new edn, trans. Matthew J. O'Connor (Collegeville, MN: The Liturgical Press).

Power, David N. (1994) *The Eucharistic Mystery: Revitalizing the Tradition* (New York: Crossroad).

Schmemann, Alexander (1988) *For the Life of the World* (Crestwood, NY: St Vladimir's Seminary).

Staniforth, Maxwell (ed.) (1968) *Early Christian Writings* (New York: Penguin).

Troeltsch, Ernst (1960) *The Social Teaching of the Christian Churches*, trans. Olive Wyon (New York: Harper and Row).

CHAPTER 16

Confessing the Faith: Reasoning in Tradition

Nicholas Adams

Saying the Creed together is an act of Christian witness. It is addressed to all, both Christians and strangers. To witness is not just to say something or show something. It is to become a sign. Christian witness means becoming a sign of Christ, who shows the God of Abraham, Isaac, and Moses by becoming man, dying, being raised, ascending to heaven, and coming again with glory.

Signs are not isolated things. A sign in a language one does not understand does not function as a sign, but as a puzzle. Signs need to be intelligible, so there need to be rules for interpreting them, and people who are skilled in using these rules. The world is full of signs of God, but they cannot function as signs unless people can read them. Likewise, Christians cannot be signs of Christ unless strangers can interpret them. To be a Christian is to be schooled in an apprenticeship of signs; it is to learn how to read the signs of God in the world. It is also to be a teacher so that others may become apprentices in turn.

Tradition and Reasoning

The common shorthand for using rules is "reasoning." Reasoning is a powerful concept, with many siblings and cousins: Reason (with a capital R), rationality, *Raison*, *Vernunft*, *Rationalität*. Many of these have a common heritage in the Latin *ratio*, a word with a wide range of meanings to do with thinking and understanding. At their heart, however, is the idea of making connections between things, and making judgments. To do this, you need rules for making connections, and people skilled in using them. Different kinds of connection-making have different rules, and they have their own names: logic, music, poetry, rhetoric, laws, ethics.

This chapter is about the rules for interpreting God's signs, including the signs that Christians are when they witness to God as they recite the Creed together. These rules are usually called theology. The Creed is important not only because it witnesses to God, but also because it is a pattern of rules; to say the Creed is to rehearse this pattern, and to learn how to interpret God's signs. We shall look at what kind of pattern it is, and what kind of reasoning is learned in using it.

Learning to reason is difficult. Everyone, from toddlers to sages, needs to learn how to reason. Reasoning well takes time, effort, patience, and wisdom. Scripture teaches that Solomon was the greatest reasoner ever, and for him it took prayer too (1 Kings 3: 7–12). However, reasoning has a dark history in modern times. Its story would take a long time to tell properly, but a short sketch can help show where things stand.

In the period after the Reformation, in which there were many wars, some Christians, not least philosophers, noticed that rules were rooted in traditions. This was especially noticeable in the rules for interpreting Scripture, and the rules for interpreting the natural world. These rules were at variance with each other and led to conflict. Stephen Toulmin (1990) has suggested that the bloodshed of the wars of religion spurred philosophers, especially Descartes, to try to find a way to coordinate all traditions, and all methods of reasoning. Christian philosophers sought a rule for all rules, a master key for all interpretative locks. Traditions seemed bound in conflict. Arguments were settled with fire; people debated with swords. Surely there was another way? Surely words could be smelted into a universal language that might bind all traditions and subject them to one method and one logic? The question is: who will forge this language? This question has never been satisfactorily answered, and the history of the rise and fall of the Enlightenment is a story about the struggles it engendered. Descartes tried to forge something that all could use and he chose to write in the language of mathematics – above all geometry – because he judged, not unreasonably at first sight, that this language was the least influenced by different religious traditions.

The problem with this did not take long to reveal itself. Every language has its heart, and at the heart of each language certain things can be said briefly and elegantly. The further one strays from that heart, the more the language has to be stretched and twisted in order to say what needs saying. The language of geometry has a heart, and that heart is calculation, clarity, and decisive distinctions between constants and variables. The surface area of a sphere can, in its language, be said briefly and elegantly: $4\pi r^2$. But if one strays to places whose character is marked by vagueness, metaphor, and more-or-less-ness, the language of geometry will need to be stretched and twisted severely in order to say what needs to be said, and perhaps will not be able to say it adequately at all. The character of Shakespeare's Lear can be sketched briefly and elegantly in the language of literary criticism, but it would take a long time to say very little of significance in the language of geometry. Geometry struggles to speak the many languages of poetry and of love.

Yet although geometry has difficulty saying some things, it showed itself well suited for saying architecture and painting, irrigation and plumbing, transport and weaponry. Geometry transformed the face of Western Europe in very few years. And, in the course of this, something extraordinary happened to the understanding of tradition. Different traditions had different styles of architecture and different approaches to weaponry; but the same geometry and logic appeared to rule them all. Having learned that geometrical reasoning governed all traditions, it became possible to imagine that reasoning *as such* transcended all tradition. As new cities grew up, and as famine and disease became gradually limited through new agricultural technology and the widespread building of sewers, it seemed that a kind of force of Reason was driving history, and leading it in a triumphant march of progress. And so, instead of informing everything, niches were found for tradition: it tended, for the moment, to govern the parts of life that Reason could not yet say briefly and elegantly: marriage and family life, cuisine and hospitality, ethical and moral life, liturgy and worship.

It would take some years for Reason to command even these, and teach ordinary people, and not just awkward philosophers, to question fundamentally why marriage is sacred, why strangers should receive hospitality, why certain things are right and wrong, and to ask whether there is any point to worship. It would take even longer for the traditions that embodied answers to these questions to wither, for the wells of institutional authority to dry up, and for the rock of Reason itself to break apart in two world wars and technologically aided genocide. Yet, by the year 2000, tradition seemed in many places to have become synonymous with "heritage" (of interest mostly to tourists), and reason, in a dark Platonic nightmare, had morphed into opinion, to which everyone was entitled, but in which few were convincing. Those fortunate to enjoy art galleries no longer understood the paintings whose strange beauty they admired, and those privileged to have their opinions heard in public discovered that they were widely distrusted. As for those too poor for Botticelli and politics, it was left to charities to sustain, but rarely to transform, their lives.

This story of reasoning's dark history needs telling because it explains why many people find themselves in modernity's poverty trap: a poverty not least of imagination. It is, however, a story that needs retelling against a different pattern which leads not to the despair of capitalism's iron cage or society's listless *anomie* but to the statement of a task, which is God's gift to modern Christians: to repair the modern imagination and bring God's healing to the body politic. That different pattern is rehearsed each time Christians recite the Creed together.

"It is not reason that is against us, but imagination." So said Cardinal Newman (1976: 159). His words, now 120 years old, concerned the relationship between science and theology in the late nineteenth century. They speak just as eloquently to current Christian questions about the relationship between reasoning and tradition in the early twenty-first century. What is the best way for Christians to characterize the interplay between what is received (tradition) and what is contributed (reasoning)? There are resources for exploring this question in the context of the Christian practice of saying the Creed together in worship, the witness by which Christians become signs.

Tradition is not a thing. It is people giving gifts to their children; they give descriptions, rules for interpreting them and making new ones, and teach the skills for using them. This has been better understood in recent times. The role of tradition in reasoning, having been suspect and eclipsed during the Enlightenment, underwent substantial changes during the nineteenth and twentieth centuries. Varied answers were offered to the question "What is the significance of tradition?" The one-sided emphasis on the cold, clear freedom of reason in Kantian philosophy in the late eighteenth century produced a reaction among Romantic philosophers, who advocated the sensuous givenness of tradition. Hans Georg Gadamer has argued that both sides err in setting up an antithesis between "free" reason and "given" tradition because every tradition is transmitted freely through the exercise of reason, and all reasoning finds that its boundaries are given by the tradition that provides it with things to think about (Gadamer, 1989: 277–85).

The nineteenth-century patchwork of ancient and modern morality, held together loosely by a Christian religious culture, produced a reaction in the philosophy of Nietzsche, who insisted that morality was another name for the bad faith of a slave mentality, that God was dead, and that liberation lay in the brute assertion of one's own will. Alasdair MacIntyre has argued that both the patchwork and its annihilation err in divorcing moral theory from traditions that, over long periods of time, teach their members what their goals are, and train them in the virtues that lead there. Nietzsche and the culture he despised over-generalize their insights and their culture respectively, and pay insufficient attention to the precariousness and historicity of traditions (MacIntyre, 1985: 109–20).

Gadamer and MacIntyre have provided many of the resources, and much of the language, for contemporary attempts to think of tradition and reasoning as two parts of one enterprise: forming theories which help make sense of the world. Their legacy is a renewed understanding that the relationship between tradition and reason is not one of a passive tradition and an active reason, but an interaction of reception and spontaneity that characterizes both – an insight that leads ultimately back to Schleiermacher. Christian theologians have learned much from these insights, especially in the areas of doctrine and its development, and in Christian ethics and its complexity as a freely transmitted tradition of schooling in the virtues.

Knowing

Reasoning is about knowing. Yet, as countless intellectual witnesses have insisted down the generations, knowledge gets strange when it comes to God. This is not primarily because there are different kinds of knowledge. It is because we have more difficulty knowing things, the less like us they are. And God is not just unlike us or even very unlike us: God is unlike anything at all! How then, can we know God? Posing this question seems natural enough, and during the modern period it led to an increasingly anxious concern with epistemology, as philosophers found ever fewer convincing rebuttals to the claim "there is no God." Such anxiety is strange, however, in the light of the pre-modern tradition, which saw many signs of God in the world, and believed that it was God who made such seeing possible. From time to time this medieval tradition had clever answers for those who do not see such signs, but for the most part it did not attribute this to intellectual failing, but tended to consider such people blind or foolish. However, in the later modern philosophy, many believing Christians became blind too. Their elaborate systems of proofs for God's existence were perhaps a kind of compensation, making up for not seeing signs of God, the striking of a human match in an imagined darkness no longer illuminated by the one they worshiped. No one ever struck a light. Epistemology never came to their aid.

If knowledge gets strange when it comes to God, and if reasoning is about knowing, then Christian reasoning is going to be a little strange. Again, this is not because its techniques are different (mostly they are not), or because it has bizarre tools that no one else uses (it does not), but because its object is not like "objects" at all. The Creed is a pattern for reasoning theologically; that is, for interpreting signs of God's life. So it is to be anticipated that the Creed will appear strange to those who are used only to reasoning about objects in the world. However, the character of this strangeness is worth sketching before too many misconceptions arise.

The Creed is not strange because it demands "blind faith" (an invention of the Age of Reason), nor even because it starts with unusual "basic assumptions." It is strange primarily for two reasons: it is Trinitarian, and it is prayerful. It is overtly Trinitarian in being divided up into three sections, concerned with God, the Father; God, the Son; and God, the Spirit. And it shows itself to be prayerful because it is recited liturgically and ends with "Amen." These two features are what make its pattern for reasoning strange to unschooled ears, including the ears of many Christians, who often wonder what the Creed means while they are saying it. Why is the Creed Trinitarian and prayerful? Because it concerns God rather than some object in the world. It is also strange for other reasons, such as some of the associations and juxtapositions it relies on and develops, some of which are ancient and unfamiliar to modern ears. We shall look at some of these.

The Creed is the principal pattern for the Christian apprenticeship of signs. To say the Creed is to rehearse and trace out the shape of Christian reasoning in the interpretation of God's signs. It is also a witness to the world in which Christians become such signs for others to interpret. The Creed sets criteria for reasoning about, and patterns for describing, the one God whom Christians worship. Such description is, again, strange and unlike other forms of description. To repeat: its strangeness resides in its Trinitarian and prayerful character. It is worth considering this double strangeness in some detail, with the help of two contemporary theologians: Nicholas Lash and Rowan Williams.

Trinitarian Reasoning

Trinitarian theology does not say three things; it says one thing, three ways. That one thing is not really a thing: it is God. Knowledge gets strange when it comes to God, or better, when God comes to it. Trinitarian reasoning is a pattern for reminding people what the shape of such knowing is, and an aid to handling the difficult relationship between knowing and not knowing. There are two errors to avoid: thinking one knows God; and thinking one does not know God. The common names for these errors are idolatry, on the one hand, and atheism, on the other.

Speaking the truth means acknowledging that, although God is unknowable, God shows himself to us. This kind of truth-telling is learned by thinking shaped by a Trinitarian pattern. It is not easy. Christianity's peculiarity lies in its identification of God's appearing with Jesus Christ, rather than some other means. It is not surprising, therefore, that for a Christian the danger of thinking that he or she knows God is most commonly manifested in a one-sided Christological emphasis. "Here is God, in Christ Jesus, and no more needs saying." This is a mistake because it wrongly implies that the divine mystery has been fully illuminated and human knowledge can describe God as satis-factorily as it can describe any human. It also implies that God's approach has been and gone, that the story is over and we grasp it perfectly: God's revelation in time is ossified into a timeless fact which can be safely shielded from making any troublesome claims upon the world. This one-sidedness can be repaired: "Here is God, in Christ Jesus, and there is no more to see." This is true, because Christology is about seeing and hearing, and there is no more to see and hear in God than what is seen and heard in Jesus Christ. There is plenty more to say, however, because the story is not over, God continues to approach us, and indeed the mystery has come close to us rather than becoming wholly intelligible. Furthermore, it is not statements, locked out of time, which best express this action, but something altogether more *dramatic*: actual human lives which bear witness to the truth by living lives of worship. Nicholas Lash shows clearly the danger of thinking that we can know God:

> We inherit rules of speech, systems of value, habits of behavior. We set great store upon particular places, people, narratives and institutions. We learn to learn, to venerate the message and the messenger: even to confess identity of both in one man worshipped as fleshed Word. This line of thought is (once again) quite sound. And yet, without correc-tive pressure from the standpoint of the other articles, it once more freezes into idolatry, this time by turning God's address, God's truth-giving speech, into our supposed posses-sion, protected by a church now shrunken to a gnostic sect. (Lash, 1992: 93–4)

Lash suggests that Trinitarian thinking is about acknowledging "corrective pres-sure" which each of the articles exerts on each other, and much of his reading of the Apostles' Creed is an attempt to show what one-sidedness looks like, and to suggest corresponding ways to center things once again. One of his most memorable tools for handling the relationship of known to unknown in speech about God is his use of the metaphor of distance:

> On the one hand, God, as creator, as the one by whom all things are made *ex nihilo*, is – as such – absolutely beyond imaginable possibility because too *far* from us, quite outside our range of vision. On the other hand, God, as given life, as intimate to all our inmost thoughts and movements, is – as such – too *near* for us to see. God only comes within our range of vision, is only visible, in Christ; is only audible in the utterance of the Word. It is the one sent whom we see, not the one who sends him, nor the one in whom we see. (Lash, 1992: 91)

The strangeness of Lash's reasoning can perhaps be emphasized by noticing that the Trinitarian pattern of the Creed does not provide much *information*. It speaks of one who is both too far and too near to be sensed. Rather, the Creed teaches that this is the case and *keeps things in play*. This way of considering things shows that the Eucharist is deeply Christological, especially in churches (like my own in Edinburgh) where wor-shipers not only taste the bread and wine, but touch each other at the sharing of the peace, hear bells ringing, smell incense, see beautiful robes and icons, and (given any opportunity at all) process solemnly round the nave.

These churches provide a rich enactment of the sensuous body of Christ. I suspect it is no accident, however, that such churches often tend to behave as if we possess our narratives, our liturgy, and even God. This emphatic Christological accessibility places a great burden on preaching to restore Trinitarian balance: in Lash's terms, to remember that God is both too distant and too near as well as perceivable and present. This burden is, however, shared by the Creed which follows the sermon; its logic is intrinsically Trinitarian and this means that it is *by definition* not resolvable into a single image, or metaphor, or rule. Instead, the three ways of saying one thing forbid the generation of speech to be arrested. It may pause, as in the contemplation of an icon, but such pausing is best thought of as the occasion for endless meditation, rather than as the conclusion of a train of thought.

Prayerful Reasoning

The Creed is a pattern of rules for interpreting God's signs. It is, however, not merely written down in a manual or recorded in some set of instructions. It is recited by a body of people, facing the altar, frequently sung, and often accompanied by gestures. It is worth noticing where it is liturgically located: in the Eucharist, the Creed is said after the sermon, as a hinge between proclamation of the Word and the intercessions, itself displaying a double character of affirmation ("I believe") and prayer ("Amen").

> The fundamental form of all our speech concerning God is as address to God, in prayer. The creeds are acts of worship. And all prayer, all worship, all human life lived in the discipline of discipleship, is, at its heart and center, dispossessive. We need continual and exacting schooling because, at every level of behavior, language, and imagination – from politics to private life, from business to religion – we seek some safety, some security, through ownership and power. And yet, however much we kick against the pricks, we do not *own* the words we say, the things we do, ourselves, our friends, our circumstances (and, when we try to do so, there are always forces, outside our control, which mock all such Promethean ambition). In liturgy and attentive contemplation, praise and prayer, we may learn to *give back* our language, and our understanding, and ourselves; learn patience, the surrender of security, sometimes in darkness not unlike Gethsemane. (Lash, 1992: 81)

Lash raises once again the question of the relationship between divine and human agency. To understand this relationship well is to give up ownership, safety, and control and to embrace dispossession and surrender through discipleship and schooling. Clearly, Lash thinks this has something to do with worship and especially prayer. Yet those who have learned about ideology critique from Karl Marx (not least Nicholas Lash) cannot help suspecting that it is going to suit some parties very nicely if large segments of the population are "disciplined" into giving up "control" and accepting their "dispossession." Is there any way of articulating this that can protect the weak?

"The Creed is a pattern of rules." Who decided these rules? How? Who supervises their use? To ask these questions is to ask about the locus and operation of power. This matters in the context of the Creed because of two important characters it possesses.

First, the Creed is a summary. It is a summary of Scripture, more particularly of the Gospels. It summarizes who God is, what the Church is, and what the Church hopes for. Summaries are products of reasoning. Whose? Secondly, the Creed contains criteria by which certain Christian communities measure their reasoning. The Creed sets limits on how members of such communities think and speak about God, humanity, and the future. Setting limits is risky and open to abuse because its job is sometimes to tell people when what they say is out of order. Who has the authority to set limits? These are hard questions, but they must not be avoided. Without a summary, Scripture has no heart or plot; instead of the interpretative discovery of wisdom there would only be recitation. Without limits to argument, without rules for debate, there cannot be ordered disagreement, only the clash of competing views. Christians argue. And for that reason, limits need to be set. One of the tasks of the Creed is to set limits in order for debate to be possible. How can it do this without being a means for the strong to silence the weak?

Lash says of the creeds that "their very form is such as to furnish a pattern of self-correction or restraint upon the range of their misuse" (Lash, 1992: 7). One very serious way to misuse the Creed is to think that, after finishing the concluding "Amen," I have successfully described the one God in whom "I believe." The reverse is true: the congregation has, in fact, just rehearsed the pattern for continuing reasoning, including resources for self-correction. Rowan Williams, putting the matter in classical terms, describes Trinitarian theology as "negative" theology. "It is 'negative' because [it is] obliged to be not only critical of the Church's language and practice, but also self-critical, suspicious of its recurring temptation to theoretical resolution and conceptual neatness" (Williams, 2000: 146). The "limitation" of the Creed is not the erection of boundaries which might suit this or that faction, but an invitation beyond the shriveled, self-absorbed human imagination toward God. To follow the patterns elaborated in the Creed is to be drawn beyond ourselves and opened to God. It is to discover and rehearse a task. Lash calls this task "endless learning" (Lash, 1992: 4–16). The Creed does not operate primarily by silencing certain types of speech but, because it is Trinitarian, by discouraging certain types of silence: the neat, the closed, the finished.

How, then, are limits set well? Williams suggests that setting and receiving limits to debate is "a skill that may be learned rather than a system to be accepted." Its goal is not to predetermine true statements, but to foster continuing conversation. "It sets out a possible framework for talk and perception, a field for debate, and so a field for its own future transmutations" (Williams, 2000: 5). This is not automatically good. What matters is not merely *that* limits are set or received: this provides only the barest formal possibilities for discussion. It is *how* this happens that counts. People readily manipulate limit-setting to conceal the true operations of power between persons or within groups, perhaps in order to evade accountability or to secure positions of rank. Nonetheless, it is possible to set limits in a way that encourages discussion without trying to retain power over the process.

This kind of discussion refers to talking about talking. It means asking: "How shall we talk? Who decides this? What are our conversation's limits?" This kind of speech is sometimes called "discourse." Discourse is talk about talk, a special kind of conversation; and its character matters. It is not yet a conversation about what needs discussing: that is not yet possible. First, you and your partner need to agree about how to have that conversation. Once that is settled, you can go on to discuss the matter in hand. For example, suppose a recently deceased member of your congregation has left a sum of money "to make the church more beautiful." You need to decide how best to spend it. There will need to be a conversation about it. First, however, you need collectively to decide who will be part of this conversation, how the decisions will be made, and who will bear responsibility. This preliminary discussion is what Williams is describing. It is the necessary talk about talk that precedes good conversation. Anyone who has tried to chair a meeting where these preliminaries have not been properly conducted knows the tangles even the lowliest committee can get into. The problems are not merely procedural: there are significant power issues at stake. Decisions need to be made about whom to invite (and to exclude), who is authorized to make decisions (and who is not). Decisions about power need to be made. They cannot be avoided: only made more or less plainly or in secret.

Williams notices that preliminary conversation, especially, *already* has to do with power. Once the later committee meets, the rules are laid out, and can be followed. The prior conversation is of a different kind. How are its own limits set? Very differently, and it is obvious why. If every conversation has to have a prior conversation which sets its limits, there would never be any conversations at all. There would be an infinite regression of committees for committees, which surely resembles a kind of hell. Discourse, talk about talk, is riskier and more dangerous than the conversation it makes possible.

Now all this discussion about committees seems banal. What has it to do with saying the Creed together? Answered simply, the Creed is bound up with issues of power that relate to setting boundaries to conversation. Setting boundaries is part of the Creed's job. It is worth noting that there are different forms of "the Creed," the two most common being the Apostles' Creed and the Nicene Creed. For the purposes of the preceding discussion, the differences between them do not much matter, as what applies to the one applies equally to the other. Nonetheless, creeds have a history. And in the case of the Nicene Creed, a statement formulated by a very ancient and very powerful committee, that history is troubled, above all because of the way a famous heretic, Arius, was treated.

Williams has investigated very thoroughly the case of Arius, one of the delegates at the Council of Nicaea (325 CE), and the kinds of "discourse" that surrounded judgments upon his theology (Williams, 2001). Arius was caught up in Trinitarian debates about Christology, especially the question of the relationship of Christ's divinity to his humanity. He insisted, for example, that the Son must have been created by the Father, and had a number of arguments to support this view, which Williams rehearses in detail (Williams, 2001: 95–116). There are problems with his arguments, and Williams patiently guides the reader through a series of evaluations. What is striking, however, is that Arius received nothing like this patient consideration at the hands of his opponent Athanasius. His arguments were misrepresented, oversimplified, and distorted. And on the basis of this, he was (to cut a long and painful story short) pronounced a heretic. Williams suggests that Arius should have been *argued against*, but instead he was brutally expelled.

This is a problem. At the time of the Council of Nicaea, something new was happening in theology. "The doctrinal debate of the fourth century is thus in considerable measure about how the Church is to become intellectually self-aware and to move from a 'theology of repetition' to something more exploratory and constructive" (Williams, 2001: 235). Williams's *Arius* is a case-study of the limiting of argument and conversation: it shows the tragic costs that being constructive and exploratory exact if such limitation is done by fearful, premature excommunication and expulsion rather than with the tough work of charitably argumentative talk. Nicaea is an example of damaged discourse, and its history affects all churches that recite the Creed. Worse, this dark history is recapitulated every time Christians seek to discredit and dislodge their opponents rather than argue skillfully and charitably against them. Saying the Creed is dangerous. Can it be said well?

Williams's arguments suggest that it can, and that this is a matter of "theological integrity." Theological integrity means treating attempts at description of the world as "strategies for responding consistently and intelligibly to the world's complexity rather than as exhaustive interpretations" (Williams, 2000: 6). Only God can adequately describe the world; humans must make their way, in the thick of things, as best they can. Theological integrity *"declines the attempt to take God's point of view"* (Williams, 2000: 6; emphasis in original). The amplitude of theology's integrity is "the degree to which it escapes its own pressures to power and closure" (2000: 7). Power and closure are prerequisites for uniformity and clarity, and the latter often hamper and ruin good theology because the world is not clear but complex, and it calls for constructive exploration and not merely repetition.

The prayerful desire to keep things in play has much in common with the rabbinic tradition in Judaism. In some ways, it might tentatively be suggested that the Trinitarian logic of the Creed performs a kind of rabbinic office in the Christian tradition, and perhaps that is why one sometimes hears Jewish scholars insisting that the condition for good conversation between Christians and Jews is that Christians be fully Trinitarian, and Jews wholeheartedly rabbinic. If this is so then the Creed, so often seen as overemphatic and divisive (and thus often omitted in ecumenical worship), might be better understood as the guardian of open-endedness and the host of good conversation. Clearly this is not an internal property of the Creed, but of the way it is uttered and used. We shall return to this.

The comments about power, closure, uniformity, and clarity bring us back to Lash's comments about dispossession and discipline. The distinctively Christian character of reasoning is not that it gives up control: this also characterizes forms of reasoning imposed on the already dispossessed. It is *what* it gives up control of: the God's eye view. If theological integrity means giving up the God's eye view and learning that human speech is directed, in prayer, *to* God at the same time as being *about* God, then startling consequences follow for saying the Creed together. If it is said with integrity, then it is not an achievement or possession that simply needs repeating; rather, it is a means of responding to the world's complexity and learning to describe it. It is the paradigmatic instance of what Williams calls "Christian reflection": "a frame of reference, a grammar of human possibilities, believed to be of unrestricted significance, an accessible resource for conversion or transformation in any human circumstance" (Williams, 2000: 7). It is not primarily the contents of this "frame" but the manner of its articulation that matters. To utter a frame of reference as a prayer is strange and unusual, but it is the characteristically Christian way of avoiding the idolatry that misidentifies God and seeks, as a result, to capture the world and control the descriptions of all who live in it. What Nicaea needed was better discourse, and that means it needed to argue and reason prayerfully. For that reason, all who do recite the Creed as a prayer contribute in a small but significant way to the healing of Nicene wounds, and simultaneously learn the pattern for good conversation.

The prayerful reasoning of the Creed is politically explosive and spiritually troubling. Lash helps reciters of the Creed to discover the political dimension to their liturgical practice. "Words take their meaning from the company they keep," he says, often (Lash, 1992: 12 and passim). This slogan is introduced to teach modern readers that the meanings of utterances arise from networks of association, juxtapositions of metaphors and contexts of speech rather than from simply pouring out the meaning that words contain (and for this reason he refers to this mistake as a "container theory" of language). This discussion of how words mean things to people is most helpful. It also has a sting. If contexts of speech affect not only how things are heard but the very meaning of those things themselves, then *where* and *how* the Creed is said matters deeply. For an affluent community to recite the Creed peacefully and even knowledgeably with respect to its theological subtleties, yet gently oblivious to the injustices that are the origin of the community's affluence is not merely unfortunate. Here, the Creed *means* something quite different from its setting in a contrasting community marked by poverty and a hope for which current economic conditions furnish no reasonable grounds. The beauty of the Creed can be not only the anticipation of a heavenly beauty, but a sharp judgment against quietism in the face of ugliness that is the product not of human nature but sin. If words take their meaning from the company they keep, the meaning of the Creed will taste bitter if the company of those who say it colludes with forces that set their faces against God's friendship in the interests of forms of "security" whose cost is other people's livelihoods and lives. Meditating on the meaning of the word "holy" in the phrase "the holy, Catholic Church," Lash insists that the holiness of the Church brings it under constant judgment:

> If it could be shown that, on the whole, Christianity had made and makes no significant contribution, by announcement and example, to the peacefulness and healing and completion of the world, then there would be no reason to give it any further serious consideration. Even allowing for the tendency of those who disapprove of Christianity to exaggerate the damage it has done, there seems no room left for complacency or for triumphalism if the facts of Christian life and history are to be tested by this stern criterion. (Lash, 1992: 88–9)

Once again, we are reminded that God's gifts do not automatically improve lives or make them whole. They set tasks, intensify judgment, and ruin all traces of human self-satisfaction which is tempted to look upon its own work and say "Behold! It is very good." To say the Creed is to face up to gifts and responsibilities. This does not mean that Christians need to overcome all obstacles and injustices before they may utter it:

absolutism of this kind encourages procrastination and ultimately leads to despair. Rather, it means that saying the Creed means making a promise: a promise to "believe in," to commit to, God's description of the world, and no other. What remains after this is hard work, and a readiness to receive the gifts that make it possible. To make baptismal vows is to announce oneself ready for labor. To say the Creed is for a community to proclaim itself engaged in it. And, because it is uttered publicly, it is to invite the rest of the world to hold us to that promise, and join us in our work.

Living Signs

Christians do not need philosophical systems in order to think well. Systems are a problem: the neater they are, the more they tend to close open questions off, shut endless debate down, and make things, if they do not suit the system, unimaginable. They are established, they perform their intellectual labor, and they cease. Credal reasoning provides something else: patterns which continue, rules which apply to endless new things, reminders for how to say what needs saying without saying too much or too little.

The Creed is a prayer that ends with "Amen." This is good news because it frees Christians from the prison of thinking it a mere bold declaration. In the Gospels, such things do not have a happy history. A rich ruler, asking about eternal life, boldly declares that he has kept all the commandments; he is told, much to his disquiet, to sell everything that he has (Luke 18: 18–27). Peter boldly declares his willingness to follow Jesus and to lay down his life; he is told bleakly that before the cock crows he will deny Jesus three times (John 13: 38). Christians might be encouraged to learn from this that making statements of faith is hazardous and far worse than merely pointless. Who knows if he or she is ready to accept the consequences of making such a statement, to have someone else put a belt around us and lead us where we do not wish to go? The more clearly such statements are uttered, the harsher the judgment they invite. Descartes's gift of clear and distinct ideas seems decidedly dangerous when it comes to statements of faith.

One of Williams's insights is that "good liturgy does what good poetry does," that is, it gives up its control over language and allows something other than itself, and supremely God, to be heard in it. Revelation, like poetry, "manifests an initiative that is not ours in inviting us to a world we did not make" (Williams, 2000: 134). Prayer, in response to this revelation, offers its statements, its patterned frameworks, not as a closure of speech but as evidence of a poetic willingness to carry on and keep things in play in pursuit of saying what needs to be said. It is not statements that keep things in play, but actual, messy, complex lives, lived as witnesses and signs of God's healing in the world.

In conclusion, a number of things can be learned from considering the Creed. Christians relate tradition and reasoning according to a Trinitarian pattern; knowledge is best sought and articulated in the form of prayer; discourse invites divine judgment; and conversations are best limited not merely by restricting their scope but by opening them out dispossessively to God.

It is the poetry of lives, rather than the clarity of statements, that shows how tradition and reasoning are woven together in the Trinitarian, prayerful recitation of the Creed. Such lives, invited to a world we did not make, are made into signs. No philosophical system, and no brilliant theory of the relationship between tradition and reasoning, can replace the embodied poetry that living signs, saints, are called to be in the world. The Creed, as an uttered part of this embodiment, simultaneously proclamation and prayer, is part of the Eucharist, and that means it is not only about speech and talk: it is an occasion in which we are shown how to share food, and, in the breaking of bread, are given a foretaste of things to come, and taught how to transform the world.

References

Gadamer, Hans Georg (1989) *Truth and Method*, ed. J. Weinsheimer and D. Marshall (New York: Continuum).

Lash, Nicholas (1992) *Believing Three Ways in One God* (London: SCM).

MacIntyre, Alasdair (1985) *After Virtue: A Study in Moral Theory* (London: Duckworth).

Newman, John Henry (1976) *The Letters and Diaries of John Henry Newman*, vol. 30, ed. C. Dessain and T. Gormall (Oxford: Clarenden Press).

Toulmin, Stephen (1990) *Cosmopolis* (Chicago: University of Chicago Press).

Williams, Rowan (2000) *On Christian Theology* (Oxford: Blackwell).

—(2001) *Arius: Heresy and Tradition* (London: SCM).

Being Embodied

CHAPTER 17

Praying: Poverty

Kelly S. Johnson

At the hinge of Christian worship, closing the liturgy of the Word and pointing us toward the sacred exchange of the Eucharist, stands the Prayer of the Faithful, intercession for the Church and the world, for leaders, for the poor and the sick. Annie Dillard tells of a minister she liked because one Sunday during these prayers, "he stopped and burst out, 'Lord, we bring you these same petitions every week.' After a shocked pause, he continued reading the prayer" (Dillard, 1988: 57–8).

So it goes. Week after week, we plead God to grant us faithfulness for the Church; wise leaders; peace throughout the world; an end to cruelty and injustice; healing for those who are sick and relief for the poor. Then the service moves on, and no one is tempted to look out of the window to see if the world has changed. No one complains, but then perhaps no one – except Dillard's minister – still expects these prayers to matter.

Yet the stories of the faith tell us that when God's people intercede in prayer, God listens. Abraham interceded for Sodom (which was not a great success story, but that was not because God did not listen). Moses interceded for Israel to much happier effect after their worship of the golden calf. The Gospel of John includes Jesus's prayer that God be glorified in him the night before his execution, and his prayer met with an answer no one could have dared to imagine. Throughout the New Testament Paul requests and offers thanks for prayers, and Acts shows the early Christian community frequently at prayer. In football stadiums, house churches, by hospital bedsides and on cable TV, Christians still pray for God's intervention. But what exactly are they doing?

Prayer and our Habits of Exchange

Prayers of petition are both so common as to seem instinctive and, on closer inspection, so strange as to seem absolutely nonsensical. It takes no particular Christian faith to cry out, "Oh, God, help us!" in a moment of panic, and yet even the most devout believer can find it hard to explain why a person *should* make such a prayer. I once heard two homeless men arguing in a way that cut right to the chase. One had urged another to pray about his needs, but the second was skeptical: "Why should I pray about it? Doesn't God already know my troubles? Do you think God needs my advice on what to do? No – if God's good and knows everything, then what's the point in my praying?" The first, who called himself "Billy the Polo-Rican" because his mother was Polish and his father Puerto Rican, answered decisively, "Because that's the system."

Billy drew his answer from a model of distribution he knew well: the welfare bureaucracy. Questioning why the system works as it does never helped anyone trying to get public assistance. Fill out the form; be polite in the interview; wait for the response; follow directions and trust that eventually some help will turn up. The inefficiency or unreasonableness of the process simply is not the point. The great Provider in the sky, rather than using omniscience to keep up a steady stream of necessities, seems fixated on an inefficient procedure. In a related if more optimistic approach, the popular devotional book *The Prayer of Jabez* (Wilkinson, 2000) claims that God holds a store of blessings for which people have only to ask. Like grant money for which no one applies, divine treasures collect dust as people fail to seek them. Once Christians learn how to use this system, their supply line is open and their prosperity, to the glory of God, will be unlimited. But if prayer is simply a requisition form, then why are deliveries from the divine warehouse so unpredictable? Does the check sometimes get lost in the mail?

Faced with the unpredictability of divine answers, many people prefer to invoke a model for prayer that holds out hope for better control over results: purchase. God has a supply of miracles; people in need can offer in exchange a certain amount of renewed obedience, penance, or some sacrifice of things held dear, even up to life itself. If the bid is high enough, the petitioner hopes, the goods will be delivered. Hospital waiting rooms see a continual, agonized flow of such attempted deals. In grief and longing, people will promise any price to gain possession of health for their loved ones. But this is a tragic market. Regardless of human readiness to pay, prayer is not, as we know, purchase. The right to control life and death is not for sale. One cannot control God.

This theological principle is the ground on which intercessory prayer faces its strongest critics. Adam Smith, the philosopher-economist, disapproved of prayer of petition as a useless and immoral attempt to bribe God. God, the impartial judge, does not care for "sacrifices, and ceremonies, and vain supplications", but for "acts of justice and beneficence" (Smith, 1971: 296). It is as though God is an honest employer who asks that we do certain work and will reward us fairly according to that work. If we plead for special consideration, we are wasting our time, condemning ourselves, and dishonoring God.

Immanuel Kant, an admirer of Smith's, is more explicit on the danger of prayers of petition, even those asking for spiritual gifts.

> *Praying*, thought of as an *inner formal* service of God and hence as a means of grace, is a superstitious illusion (a fetish-making); for it is no more than a *stated wish* directed to a Being who needs no such information regarding the inner disposition of the wisher; therefore nothing is accomplished by it, and it discharges none of the duties to which, as commands of God, we are obligated; hence God is not really served . . . (Kant, 1960: 182)

On the contrary, such prayers can only be useful as reminders to people of their own devotion. Prayer can have "only the value of a means whereby that disposition within us may be repeatedly quickened, and can have no direct bearing upon the divine approval." It is, therefore, a bad idea all the way round, and not only because it is ineffective; it is also likely to confuse people into thinking they are actually requesting something and that such a request could be appropriate. Prayer, "like everything which is aimed at a given end indirectly, rather weakens the effect of the moral idea (which, taken subjectively, is called *devotion*)" (Kant, 1960: 184–5). Prayer is not about getting something from God, but about encouraging oneself to obey God, about changing the self, not changing God.

This idea that prayer is therapeutic, affecting the petitioner rather than God, offers Christians an alluring alternative to prayer as purchase or bureaucratic hoop-jumping. In fact, a leading liturgical theologian recently argued that "Intercessions are the practice and exercise of being turned to discern and act in the direction in which God's love looks and moves" (Saliers, 1998: 29). Prayer for the poor is a reminder that we should work for economic justice; prayer for government leaders is a reminder that we must vote responsibly, and so on. In this case, the economics of prayer is not a struggle to win benefits from God, but a struggle to win support from Christians. Prayer becomes a way for Christians to lobby each other. The pro-lifers pray for an end to abortion while pro-choicers pray for greater respect for women. Peace activists pray for an end to a bombing campaign and just-warriors pray for the men and women in the military, far from home risking their lives on behalf of others. It is as though we hope that perhaps if God does not answer the prayer, at least someone else in the congregation will consider the issue more carefully. If this is the true meaning of prayer, though, Kant was right. We would do better to engage the issues directly, arguing for these commitments, rather than pretending to ourselves and others that we are talking to God. If this is the meaning of prayer, then Christians should stop praying.

Scripture and tradition will not permit Christians to accept such a conclusion, but how else can prayer be understood? A more theologically satisfying position sees prayer as analogous to begging. The person making the prayer asks for a gift from One who is not in any way obligated to respond. All of the power and right belongs to the potential Donor, before whom humanity must wait humbly. The image carries theological weight because it, better than the others, accords with the Christian conviction that God's care is unmerited and free, not to be purchased or presumed, but generous toward those who look for help. It is said that Martin Luther's last words were, "We are all beggars, that is certain."

Nevertheless, thinking of intercessory prayer as begging only sharpens the problem. Though it honors the gratuity of grace, the analogy to begging draws our attention to the assumption – common to all these models – that prayer is some sort of power-struggle with God, an attempt to get the rich Someone to hand over what poor humanity needs. If humanity is begging, this struggle becomes even more distressing. No common rule of justice or reason settles how much, if anything, should be transferred to a beggar. The outcome of the encounter seems to be a function of the donor's arbitrary will and the beggar's success at causing guilt or discomfort or pity. Power alone determines the outcome. For this reason, almsgivers sometimes associate beggars with violence, assuming – reasonably though not necessarily accurately – that beggars hate the people from whom they beg. How can one love a God who, without being in any way accountable, can give or withhold that for which people plead? In each of these explanations, deeply ingrained habits of exchange attempt to interpret the liturgical practice of intercessory prayer and fail to make sense of it.

Intercession in the Liturgy

As it turns out, then, this apparently unsophisticated practice of calling on God's help requires a substantial theological account, and the liturgical context of the Prayer of the Faithful provides it. The Church has already gathered, confessed sin, and listened to the Word, all before this prayer. The congregation does not simply launch into a wish list with God. First, the Church remembers that it is under the guidance of Scripture. *We* have been saved from slavery, have passed through the Red Sea, and been sustained through the desert, says the liturgy. We have seen God's hand on the unlikely who become great leaders. We have been faithless, suffered the consequences, and repented in hopes of returning to our own homeland of milk and honey. We have been moved by Jesus's preaching and seen his power to heal, and we lament by the cross, run away from the empty tomb astonished, and are charged with the Spirit. The Church has done these things, or else the Scripture lessons were mere exercises in nostalgia.

In prayer, the Church carries on that story as its own. The Church prays for God to do again what God has been doing: to heal the sick, to free prisoners, to proclaim good news, to bring salvation to the world. The Prayer of the Faithful, seen in this light, is less like listing off needs to a supplier or flattering a boss than it is like an encore to a wonderful performance. At the end of a concert, people clap and stomp and yell for more, expecting that the best songs have been saved for the end. They do not do this because the band is unwilling to do more. On the contrary, the audience knows that the band hopes for this outcry. They even plan for it. Nevertheless, they wait for the audience to ask. These appeals for more are themselves part of the pleasure of the show, part of the game between performer and audience that makes a live performance *live*. The cheers of the audience, which the band has worked to create, now become the cause of the band's doing just what it wants to do, with renewed vigor – playing the best-loved piece of their repertoire.

The Prayer of the Faithful is a kind of encore. In the liturgy of the Word the congregation hears testimony about God's work in the past and they can't get enough of it. They call out for more, not because they think God is unwilling, but because it is their role to play in the divine performance, a role God has given them. This prayer is neither requisition – for the band may not want to do an encore and are not compelled to do it – nor purchase, nor begging. It is a kind of gift.

Gift is a form of exchange, just as purchase and bribery are. When a person gives a gift, the receiver is in some way indebted to the giver and will have to make a return gift. But the debt is not precisely measurable. The return may come at any future time and may take a quite different form. In fact, if the return is too precise it may appear to be a mere purchase price for the earlier gift. By evening the score, such a return would actually close off the need for future gifts, for an ever-renewed exchange that is a continuing bond between the two parties. Successful gift exchange, uneven, unpredictable, and therefore on-going, is the material stuff of friendship.

Prayer, like the noise of an audience caught up in the music's energy, is simultaneously a gift to the Performer and a gift from the Performer, an invitation for the audience to be part of the event that is unfolding. Having heard God's deeds, the congregation responds in hope, hungry for more; but it is God who has created that hunger and hope, in something like the way the band moves the crowd to want more. God gives the Church the role of calling for what God intends to give.

A friend of mine heard a congregation in Haiti sing, "Sometimes it seems all we have to offer is our needs." This is an offering, and one God will certainly receive. Surrounded by confusion, danger, and discord, Christians pray for health and well-being, for peace and increasing faith and for safety for teenagers driving home from the prom. The Church calls for God's people to be whole and well and trusts that this tune is in God's repertoire. And, with Dillard's minister, the faithful wonder when these prayers will be finally, fully answered, in God's eternal encore. But in the meantime, this dynamic of gift and counter-gift continues through the rest of the liturgy, as the "sacred exchange" in the Eucharist takes the gifts of bread and wine, and returns them as the body and blood of Christ, the health of Christians and the pledge that these cries for peace and safety are being heard, because of what Christ has already done and continues to do.

The liturgy also teaches that this gift-exchange of prayer is not a role that people were born with. In the early Church, the Prayer of the Faithful marked the exit of the catechumens, those who had not yet been baptized. The faithful prayed over them, dismissed them, and only then went on with the intercessions. After their baptism, the neophytes shared in this prayer for the first time, taking up the privilege and responsibility of God's people.

The neophytes need to be prepared, for it is no small thing to come before God with requests. Abraham feared for his life as he interceded, on tenterhooks, for the people of Sodom and Gomorrah, at each step prefacing his requests with, "Let my Lord not grow angry. . . ." Moses spent forty days listening for God's word. Israel feared to come before the God who made the earth shake, the jealous God who killed the Egyptian first-born. Kant and Smith were right to be worried that no human should presume to tell the Creator what to do, or even to ask for God's consideration. Yet Christians do it regularly within the liturgy, as an ordinary element of worship. They dare to do it because they are the Body of Christ, filled with his Spirit. Their prayer joins that of the great high priest who can enter the Holy of Holies and intercede for humanity (Hebrews 4: 14ff). The "our" in "Hear our prayer" means that this is first Jesus's prayer to his Father, and now the Church's as well. "I am ascending to my Father, and your Father, to my God and your God" (John 20: 17).

What a strange and deep mystery is at work in this most common of Christian acts! The economic analogies for prayer picture a transfer of a dribble of wealth from the infinitely rich God, seated on a throne of glory, to miserable humans. This, unhappily, is a habit of thought and speech all too familiar to those who strive for security and comfort in a competitive world. But the Christian God is no monolithic moneybags, nor are Christians needy consumers. God is Trinity, the continual gift of love overflowing such that God must be both giving and receiving, both Father and Son, and the Gift of the Spirit given plentifully and joyously between the two. Prayer is not an attempt to persuade God to share the wealth. The very nature of God is outpouring Gift. Prayer is not asking for an allotment or a grant from a foundation. Being able to pray is itself a gift, the first gift that brings Christians into the continuing friendship and outpouring of gifts that is God's life.

Christian Unity and Intercession

This may seem a bit much, given the usual practice of the Prayer of the Faithful. A lector reads off a list of petitions: for church leaders, for government leaders, for peace, for the poor and sick, for the victims of whatever tragedy is most recent in the network news. The congregation responds with the laconic "Lord, hear our prayer" or a variant. Where members offer spontaneous prayer, healing for a child's cancer and requests for sunny weather stand alongside thinly veiled partisan wrangling over controversial issues. In order to avoid such disagreement, prayers are often couched in the most abstract terms possible. *This* is participation in Trinitarian gift-giving?

Again, the liturgy instructs us: these are not "the prayers of the faithful," but "the Prayer of the Faithful," one prayer offered together by God's people. And this one prayer is not merely petition, but *intercession*, which means petition offered on behalf of others. This Prayer of the Faithful concerns common needs and personal needs now made common by the prayer. Justin, Tertullian, and Hippolytus testify that the kiss of peace was offered as a "seal" on the prayer of the faithful, the one Church sharing in the one Spirit (breath) of the one Lord.

Likewise, the unity of the Church is taken to be an intrinsic element of prayer in the book of Acts. Just after an account of ardent prayer for God's reassurance is answered with an outpouring of the Holy Spirit, the author continues by noting: "The community of believers were of one heart and one mind. None of them ever claimed anything as his own; rather, everything was held in common" (Acts 4: 32). Their prayer life and their practice of sharing goods are correlative. "All who believed were together and had all things in common; they would sell their possessions and goods and distribute the proceeds to all, as any had need. Day by day, as they spent much time together in the temple, they broke bread at home and ate their food with glad and generous hearts, praising God and having the goodwill of all the people" (Acts 2: 44–7).

Why is the unity of Christians so closely connected to their prayer? Among Christians, to pray for each other's needs is to take the other's need on as one's own because it is taking part in Christ's intercession and this is what he does. Having once and for all taken on humanity, he claims no exemption from its need. "Have this mind among yourselves, which is yours in Christ Jesus, who, though he was in the form of God, did not count equality with God something to be grasped, but emptied himself, taking the form of a servant, being born in the likeness of men" (Philippians 2: 5–7). Christ intercedes for human needs as his own, and the Father who continually pours out into the Son hears these needs. For the Church to join in Christ's high priesthood is to be, as the

Body of Christ, a people for one another, whose needs belong to one another, because of Christ.

These examples from Scripture do not show humans wresting some good out of God, nor do they preach that our lives must become consistent with our prayers, as though the prayers were reminders to do some good deed later. Rather, they suggest that prayer for each other's needs, intercessory prayer, is part of the practice of communal sharing. Intercessory prayer does not *point us toward* so much as it already *is* a sharing of goods. Just as those of us whose lives are shaped by purchase or bureaucratic paperwork tend to approach prayer out of those habits, so the Scriptures indicate that Christian prayer belongs within a set of material practices. The placement of the offertory collection just after the Prayer of the Faithful is more suitable than most commentators imagine.

In this sense, when Paul urges the Corinthians to generosity toward the church in Jerusalem (2 Corinthians 8–9) he is engaging in intercession and inviting the Corinthians to join him in it. The church in Jerusalem was in need and Paul's answer was for other Christians to share resources with them. When he considers the impoverished church in Macedonia, which begged for the privilege of contributing to the needs of the church in Jerusalem, he claims that their desire to give is counted as an overflowing richness in them, in spite of their poverty. It is richness because it is their sharing in Christ, who "though he was rich, yet for your sake he became poor, so that by his poverty you might become rich" (2 Corinthians 8: 9). As Christ's becoming poor produced such a rich outpouring of blessing, so their willingness to share each other's troubles will lead to plenty: "he who sows sparingly will also reap sparingly, and he who sows bountifully will also reap bountifully" (2 Corinthians 9: 6). The more ardent that desire, the more generous the commitment, the more we know the faithfulness of the God who poured himself out for us. Paul's own commitment to getting the contributions made by distant churches to the aid of the Jerusalem Christians seems to have been crucial to his determination to return to Jerusalem, in spite of the prophecies that imprisonment awaited him (Acts 20: 22–3; 21: 11).

Unlike Paul, most Christians do intercession from a safe distance, and in this way fail to make it truly the prayer of Jesus. The alarming reality is that God's plentiful blessings poured out on the saints are first apparent in their willingness to suffer for each other. It is that solidarity, that mutual love, which distinguishes the Body of Christ. To ask for God's blessing is to be willing to accept that kind of trouble. Intercession is not a spectator sport.

On the other hand, such troublesome prayer meets with an abundant response, for it is then the prayer of Jesus who knew, at the tomb of Lazarus, that his Father heard him. In the first place, such prayer is fruitful because even making the prayer is already the gift of grace. The further return God makes cannot be foreseen or calculated or controlled. Yet saintly Christians have counted on it in a way that scandalizes those of lesser faith. Thérèse of Lisieux prayed for a convicted murderer's conversion, and she asked as well for a sign that the conversion had happened, as a way to strengthen her own faith. Nevertheless, she had no doubt that his conversion would occur, as indeed it did. As she shared in the mind of Christ, giving her life in penitential solidarity with the life of the world, she was confident in God's grace. Conversely, prayer loses this fruitfulness when it is severed from the prayer of Christ. The story is told that while displaying the beauty of the Vatican to St Dominic, the pope quipped in reference to the miraculous cure of Acts 3: 6: "Peter can no longer say, 'Gold and silver I have none.'" "And neither," answered Dominic, "can he now say, 'Get up and walk'" (Chesterton, 1956: 43).

Intercessory prayer is, then, the act of the Church united with Christ and therefore committed to bearing each other's burdens. So crucial is this unity that Cyprian claimed that failure in it displeases God and makes prayer fruitless (Cyprian, 1994: 286).

These comments show the way to understanding just what is going wrong in the intercessory prayer of many congregations. Under cover of vague phrasing and an efficient pace, Christians pray without, in many cases, anything like the presence of one heart and one mind, much less the one heart and mind of Christ. In many cases, this is simply a matter of the congregation not having endured the difficult discernment of particular goods, not having worked out among themselves what the mind of Christ has to say about present-day concerns. Unhappily, many congregations may fear that consensus on such questions is impossible. At issue here is the need for discernment and discipline in Christian language during the work of prayer. If Christian prayer is God making us the cause of the good that God intends, then Christian prayer requires people to know what that good is and to ally themselves with it. Skipping over the details may be only a way to paper over the lack of common mind, the mind of Christ. If that commonality cannot be achieved, common prayer will be impossible.

Consider what is happening when the New Testament urges Christians to pray for rulers, "kings and all who are in high positions" (1 Timothy 2: 1). Such prayer does not imply simply a general advocacy of good governance. It may be an act of obedience to Christ's command: love your enemies, pray for those who persecute you. Such a prayer, to be made in common by people who might have good reason to prefer to pray that God would smite the ruler with a good strong plague, indicates that the community disciplines its prayer in accordance with Christ's teaching. Pre-existing "felt" needs may well need to be challenged and reconsidered. As Christian lives are re-formed into Christ's life, even the needs they name are re-formed.

The problem of unity is particularly conspicuous, however, in prayers "for the poor." Members are not likely to dispute that, insofar as poverty is harmful, its relief is a good for which the Church should pray. The dissension first emerges around what role the people in the Church will play in the provision of that relief. Some leaders of congregations, in an attempt to remind people that they do have some such role, change the prayer to something like, "For the poor, and that we may answer the call to serve them generously." But even if, within the congregation, such a prayer is made sincerely and in common, it betrays a deeper failure of unity, a failure of unity in the universal Church. The prayer assumes that those who pray are the "we who should serve" rather than "the poor." "The poor" are apparently somewhere else, perhaps in another congregation on the other side of town or on the other side of an ocean, waiting on our aid. They are not, at any rate, us.

"Not so," runs a common reply, "for all of us are poor, in one way or another. As the suburban Church prays for those suffering from famine, it too may be starved, for meaning, integrity, love." Thus the Church convinces itself that all people are equally poor before God and matters of economic disparity create no significant distinction. This is mere self-deception. While all people are mortal and all depend on grace, still some have a reliable supply of food and clean water, adequate medical care, and the expectation of those same goods into old age. Others do not. Lazarus and Dives, in Jesus's parable, both died, but the point of the story is not that they were as mortals equally poor in the sight of God. Dives does not even try to make such a claim in his defense. The vast differences in property, security, and power among Christians and their congregations is itself testimony that the Church does not live in the unity of Christ, that unity of heart and mind which in Acts includes no one claiming anything as his or her own.

Nor is it sufficient that those who hold more power commit themselves to "steward-ship" or "service." Praying "that we will be good stewards of our resources, in service to the poor" seems to draw the wealthy into a unity of concern and practical problem-solving. But it also conceals a deep lack of solidarity. The "responsibility" prayer fosters a new kind of disunity, by handing managerial authority and rights over the morality of wealth to those who hold more of it, rather than calling on them to call nothing their own, sharing the burdens and gifts of their brothers and sisters. Praying "that we will be good stewards" also conveniently removes the issue of poverty from the scriptural narrative, in which God, through the prophets and in Jesus, warns and denounces the wealthy: "Woe to you rich . . ."

When Cyprian claims that the prayers of Christians are not heard when they are not made in unity, he was concerned with schism. But disunity has many forms. Insofar as the Body of Christ is not one, it fails to be the Body of Christ. "That they may be one; even as you, Father, are in me and I am in you, that they may also be in us . . ." (John 17: 21).

Here we must face a hard truth. It follows that if Christians pray for "the poor," meaning by that some distant set of people to be pitied, whose suffering has no direct connection to those who pray; if at that point the people prayed for are praying in a church in a neighborhood where "we" don't go; if the prayer is part of an order of life in which the well-being of some exists at the expense of others; then to that extent the prayer is deficient. If the "we" who pray excludes the poor, then the intercession has missed its mark from the beginning, for it lacks the very sharing that it claims. It is no longer the Body of Christ, interceding in charity for all, obedient to God, sharing in the suffering of others. Such prayer is still caught in the habits of requisition or purchase, as though the problem is how to get whoever has power – God or the state or the wealthy or our fellow Christians – to hand over the goods. It misses the liturgical point: this is the body that shares in the great outpouring of gifts already given, whether that be food, wisdom, or persecution.

This means that, to pray rightly, Christians must engage in the awkward, conflict-filled process of facing class boundaries, of overcoming fear and pride and self-decep-tion to begin to know each other as members of one body. It is not enough to send donations, nor even to work for policy and legal changes, nor is it of any use to be ashamed. The unity of the Church in liturgy, which is friendship enacted through gift-giving, requires mutuality, facing each other as peers, as family, as members of each other and therefore as constitutive of each other's well-being.

Again and again, where Christians do share needs and goods for the love of God, they attest that their prayers are answered. I was once a member of a parish where large numbers of undocumented people were turning up at the door looking for emergency shelter. Many members of the parish had themselves been immigrants at one time or had seen their parents struggle to find their own place in a new country. The parish had been their refuge. The pastor was happy to allow homeless men occasionally to stay a night in the church basement, but the community decided they needed a house of hospitality.

When a committee met to discuss starting a pledge drive that would establish a regular income for the budding ministry, one of the older parishioners reminded them of the practice of "picketing St Joseph," taking turns in prayer at the local church until the resources they needed arrived. The committee chuckled but, before the meeting broke up for the evening, they prayed. The next day a generous donation arrived, unsolicited, from St Joseph parish. When we needed beds to furnish the house, we prayed and a congregation who had heard a garbled version of our needs called to say that their youth group would build us a hundred bunk beds. God has a wry sense of humor: we had only a four-bedroom house. Remember the children of Israel who cried out to God that they wanted meat and ended up with quail "coming out their noses" (Numbers 11: 20)? Day by day, what we needed appeared. Finding sufficient supplies is not a problem for God. Prayers are answered.

Or not. Children are malnourished, people die of exposure in the winter and heat in the summer, wars and injustice and famine and disease continue. In sum, everything we pray for does not come to pass. To say that prayer is answered is also to face the evidence that a person or a congregation may call out to God in distress and receive no answer that we can hear or see.

But Christian intercessory prayer, we have established, is not a standing on the sidelines of this game between God-holder-of-all-goods and poor-suffering-humanity. This was the mistake of Ivan Karamazov, Dostoevsky's tormented believer: a child, abused by her parents, cries out to "Dear God" in the night, and no help comes to her. To this God, Ivan can only offer his refusal to be consoled later for the atrocities committed now. In fact, this temptation to despair of God's goodness in the face of human misery meets its antidote in the right practice of intercession, which is Christian solidarity. Burdens, even terrible ones, can be shared as people trust that the Father of Jesus does not abandon his children. Prayer made in this way is not the same as other prayer, just as Jesus's prayer was not the same as other prayer.

The "Civil Society of the Bees" (*Las Abejas*) of Chiapas know how Christians pray. Since 1992, they have organized themselves to work non-violently for change. In 1997, they were attacked while praying for peace in the town of Acteal, where peasants forced from their homes by violence had taken refuge. Forty-five unarmed men, women, and children were killed. After the massacre, the group's charism carried on. They buried their loved ones in one common grave, where they await redemption together. Then they announced their intention to work for justice, not vengeance, and to call their enemies to repentance and reconciliation. They made a pilgrimage to Mexico City to pray with thousands of supporters. The *Abejas* urged others to join them in what they call "strong prayer." After they hear the word of God, they kneel on the floor, and cry out with confidence for God to carry on the work of the kingdom: to bring perpetrators to justice, to create peace in Mexico and beyond, to give the poor ways to live in dignity.

This prayer goes on for a long time, each and all calling out together for the coming of God's kingdom.

These prayers do bear fruit, first in the continued testimony of this beleaguered community to the gospel. The Bees have also seen those wrongly jailed set free, unjust politicians brought to resign, perpetrators of crime named and punished. Much injustice remains, and peace seems far off in Chiapas. But hope is the backbone of prayer. The liturgy, again, instructs us: intercession is not all Christians do, nor is it the climax. Hope is fed by the Scriptures, but it stands then suspended, as the Church shares in the foretaste of the coming banquet, assured that hope is not in vain.

Of course, sometimes the lack of an answer to prayer proves to be the necessary answer. Dorothy Day, founder of the *Catholic Worker*, said once that when they were in need they would pray and would receive what they needed. And, she added, when they did not receive it, they discovered that they had not needed it. Day's reasoning, that they learned the difference between want and need retroactively, is manifestly circular. But it is a virtuous circle, rather than a vicious one. It is the claim of someone who recognizes that Christians *need* a certain kind of poverty. The temptation in prayer is to look for comfort and safety. "But," writes Augustine, "if we acknowledge ourselves as thirsting, we shall acknowledge ourselves as drinking also. For he that thirsteth in this world, in the world to come shall be satisfied, according to the Lord's saying, *Blessed are they that hunger and thirst for righteousness, for the same shall be satisfied.* Therefore in this world we ought not to love fullness" (Augustine, 1849: LXIII).

The prayerful virtue of hope can be extinguished on one side by despair, but it can also wither because of pride, since the proud are already satisfied and have no need to be on the way to anywhere else. This is the danger of "loving fullness": that, finding security, Christians will forget that their hearts are restless. Strange as it may seem, it is not untoward for a Christian to believe that a kind of poverty, the kind that makes one have to hope for better, is a gift of God. In fact, the long tradition of Christianity which associates wealth with pride sees the matter just this way: the wealthy may avoid arrogance, but their very comfort, the satiation of needs, tempts them to rest in their accomplishments rather than to hope for more.

All Christian prayer, therefore, must be for that which God wants to give, for God's will to be done. Mary, the chief intercessor of Christians, prayed this way when her moment of truth came. Mary's "Thy will be done" is not resignation (since it will be done anyway, whether I want it or not) but a welcome, an encouragement, a conscious alliance with God's purposes. This is the spirit of Christian prayer, and without it, the prayer backfires, becoming evidence only of how little people know God. "You ask and do not receive because you ask wrongly, to spend it on your passions" (James 4: 3).

Prayer may be made wrongly, it may be for the wrong thing, it may need to be tried in patience. But sometimes Christians discern a good, commit themselves at personal risk and in the love of Christ, and still what they pray for does not come to pass in any way that they can see. Intercession, at this point, becomes a proclamation to the world that God is not absent. Those making the prayer complain and lament as they pray, but they do not cease praying. When the temptation is to run for the high ground, they stay in the place of trouble, in solidarity and hope. They share in the patience of the psalmist and of Jesus, crying,

My God, my God, why hast thou forsaken me?
O my God, I cry by day, but thou dost not answer; and by night but find no rest.
Yet thou art holy, enthroned on the praises of Israel.
In thee our fathers trusted; they trusted, and thou didst deliver them.
For he has not despised or abhorred the affliction of the afflicted,
and he has not hid his face from him, but has heard, when he cried to him. (Psalms 22:
1–5, 25)

Knowing the story is answer enough, for now.

References

Augustine (1849) *Expositions on the Book of Psalms, volume 3*, from *A Library of Fathers of the Holy Catholic Church*, translated by members of the English Church (Oxford: John Henry Parker).

Catholic Church (1994) *Catechism of the Catholic Church* (Liguori, MO: Liguori).

Chesterton, G. K. (1956) *Saint Thomas Aquinas: "The Dumb Ox"* (Garden City, NY: Image).

Cyprian (1994) Epistle VII, *Ante-Nicene Fathers, volume 5: Hippolytus, Cyprian, Caius, Novatian*, ed. Alexander Roberts, DD and James Donaldson, LLD (Peabody, MA: Hendrickson; reprint of American edition of the same title by Christian Literature Publishing, 1886).

Dillard, Annie (1988) *Holy the Firm* (New York: Harper and Row).

Jungmann, Joseph A. (1986) *The Mass of the Roman Rite: Its Origins and Development*, trans. Rev. Francis A. Brunner, CSSR (Westminster, MD: Christian Classics).

Kant, Immanuel (1960) *Religion within the Limits of Reason Alone* (New York: Harper and Row).

Saliers, Don (1998) "Liturgy and Ethics: Some New Beginnings," in *Liturgy and the Moral Self: Humanity at Full Stretch Before God*, ed. E. Byron Anderson and Bruce T. Morrill (Collegeville, MN: The Liturgical Press).

Smith, Adam (1971) *The Theory of Moral Sentiments* (New York: Garland) (originally published 1759).

Wilkinson, Bruce (2000) *The Prayer of Jabez: Breaking Through to the Blessed Life* (Sisters, OR: Multnomah).

CHAPTER 18

Interceding: Giving Grief to Management

Michael Hanby

Our culture is confused about goodness and what is good. And since statements about what is good are statements about what is true, this means there is a lot of confusion about everything. To a large extent, the phrase "This is good" has come to mean "I love this," which is not a statement about the "objective" quality of a good thing, but about our subjective pleasures and emotions. "I love this," therefore, often expresses not my love for the thing, but my desire to use the thing to love myself.

Occasionally, we contradict this notion in practice. Whenever we love someone or something for its own sake, whenever we commit ourselves to it, sacrifice or suffer loss for it, and prize its well-being as our own, we affirm through our actions that the thing we love is good in itself, independent of its affect on our pleasure. (Though whether the beloved thing is genuinely good or not is another question.) At its best, a parent's love for a child can be like this.

Genesis portrays God as bringing the world to being, giving life to it, through an act of sheer generosity. When "God looked at everything he had made, and he saw that it was good" it is because his generous gift affirms that something other than God, something not God is good in itself (Genesis 1: 31). If God's creation is good by nature, then Adam's fall does not merely break a rule and incur punishment because the violation angers God. Rather Adam's disobedience, his desire to "be like God" must somehow injure him and detract from the goodness of his nature. The injury is its own punishment. Still, God's commitment to creation continues to affirm its goodness, as he blesses all the nations of the world through Abraham and Israel and finally, lovingly, assumes human flesh in Jesus Christ and gives himself over to death, "even death on a cross" (Philippians 2: 8). As an expression of the love and commitment of God, Christ's incarnation and passion affirms the objective, intrinsic goodness of creation despite its manifest violence and cruelty. Yet Jesus is both God *and* human. So while God affirms creation's goodness by giving himself to humanity in Jesus, this is only half the story. As Jesus obediently offers his love to the Father, humanity completely affirms – for the first time since Adam's self-inflicted wound – that God's generous goodness is the source of its own goodness.

Built into this understanding is a complex claim about how reality truly is. Despite appearances, humans and all of creation are intrinsically good; that is, good in themselves independent of how we think of them or how they please us, precisely because they are a gift from God and exist in relationship to him. As God affirms this goodness by assuming human flesh, as Jesus in his humanity affirms this goodness and its source by remaining steadfast in love and obedience to the Father even unto death, so Christians affirm it, because of Christ, through the worship of God and through intercessory prayer on behalf of the world. Through worship and prayer, we are made human again.

Christian worship, in other words, is neither mere ceremony nor an instrument of spiritual fulfillment, but a practice that affirms both God's goodness and the truth of who we are as creatures. It is a statement of truth precisely *because* it is an act of love. And, because it is both, it is a lifelong discipline, a training, with profound implications for how we understand and live in the world. This discipline stands in stark contrast to the source of so much of our contemporary confusion about what is good: the dominance of a managerial mindset that comes with the discipline of a capitalist economy. This discipline, too, performs a truth claim about the nature of reality. On the basis of the Christian discipline that I have just sketched, I want to diagnose market and managerial discipline and its effects, both in the culture where it is pervasive and in our souls as we undergo its rigors, before finally considering in more detail how Christian worship in general and intercessory prayer in particular provide an alternative.

Several Habits of Highly Effective People

It may seem odd to call the capitalist economy a habit and a form of discipline, since it is as pervasive as the air we breathe and seemingly just as natural. But this is what true habits are like; that is why they have been called "second natures." Once learned, we wear them like our skin. Now when we think of habits we tend to think of things like smoking or repeating yourself, but the ancient sense of the term – while it does not exclude these – is much more profound. A habit is a pattern that you *inhabit*, and it is not so much something you see as something through which you see everything else. In this sense, language, even, is a habit. We all must learn our native tongue; yet if you speak English as your first or only language, the world simply comes to you in English. Moreover, the meaning of English words will change over time as they are used differently, and, when they do, this will affect how English-speakers see and act in the world.

All of this is why this book insists that Christian ethics is more fundamentally about habits, and thus about producing certain kinds of people, than about decisions, or producing certain kinds of consequences. Because habits determine what choices you think you have to decide from. For example, it would be odd to say that I wake up each day and *choose* not to kill my nextdoor neighbor. Rather, my way of life prevents that from ever becoming a real choice, and so, in reality, I never think about it at all. What is more, it only could become a real choice if it somehow engaged my desire, and, to engage my desire, something about this option must seem good. Otherwise, there is no way to account for why I might ever consider or do it. So, in order for killing my neighbor to engage my desire and thus become a real choice for me, I must already be confused about the difference between what is good and what seems good.

This confusion could take several forms. It could happen that I think murder is genuinely good in this case, which means that I don't understand the meaning of the word "murder." But it might also be that the meaning of the word murder had changed, that what formerly counted as murder no longer does. Or one might employ a new term – "pruning the neighborhood" perhaps. Indeed, such transformations in language happen all the time, in all sorts of cases, under the influence of new cultural habits. New habits produce new ways of speaking and describing the world, and these new ways of describing the world dictate what we think our choices are. Yet since we can only choose from among things that provoke our desire, a discipline not only teaches us what to know, how to describe the world, but what to want, or, in more traditional Christian terms, what to love. Hence these two, what is good and what is true, what we know and what we love, can never be separated.

At one level, the discipline administered by the invisible hand of the economy may now seem a little more obvious. Concern for future economic success, after all, has long dictated issues of war and peace. Nations are more willing to go to war when resources like oil or a trade route are at stake, and the desire for oil, power, or cheap exchange implies a certain commitment to what is ultimately good. But, at its most basic level, this discipline is subtler than that. The economy is, among other things, a pattern or a rhythm that structures time. For vast numbers of us, these rhythms determine when we wake and when we sleep, when we play and when we (mostly) work, even what and how we eat. Increasingly, they determine which days are to be consecrated and set apart as holidays (a term derived, incidentally, from the Christian "holy day"). This discipline transforms our language, giving us terms like "human resources," "worker flexibility," "downsizing," and "care-provider," terms that redefine the things they describe, shape our ideas about ourselves and others, and, ultimately, transform our choices.

Like all disciplines, the market aims for a goal: productivity and wealth. Now this may seem the obvious place to denounce wealth and the greed with which we strive for it, but such denouncements fail to get to the depths of how this discipline transforms our vision and our actions. Since productivity and wealth are the ultimate goods in market discipline, things are good insofar as they are useful; that is, insofar as they can be employed for the sake of attaining these ultimate goods. Goodness, in other words, is not intrinsic, but rather is derived in relationship to an external goal which may or may not be compatible with what makes a thing excellent on its own terms. A thing's goodness is the goodness of an instrument or tool.

Here again there are more and less subtle manifestations of this understanding. Education is now prized not because the culture values truth and wisdom, or views scholarship as a lifetime vocation, but because it is the means to economic success. So the study of science, engineering, and business takes precedence over theology, philosophy, literature, and history, as the ultimate questions raised by these disciplines become unimportant. Schools and universities, forced to justify their utility in the market's terms, employ the latest technology to "measure" the immeasurable and to ensure the production of better workers. Students elevate grades over ideas, and either feel the pressure to forgo what interests them or never ask themselves what interests them in the pursuit of a marketable skill.

Under the influence of this discipline, land ceases to be either common or sacred, and is transformed in its essence into potential real estate, awaiting "development" which usually does nothing to improve it. So common, public spaces come under constant assault, while those who defend them either find themselves deprived of a publicly recognized rationale for doing so, or justifying conservation in the same utilitarian terms as those who attack them – as if preventing environmental disaster were the only good reason to leave a field fallow. Much of our architecture is efficient, spare and ugly, and malls, superstores – even whole suburbs – are now often derelict within a generation or two of their founding. Rare is the building built with the intent of being serviceable for centuries. Art at its best is created, not for the sake of beauty, but as political protest. At its worst, it is concocted primarily to sell as "entertainment," as beauty has ceased to be a publicly recognized standard and become an arbitrary private taste and as people alienated from their work seek to escape through amusements (Aristotle, 1998: 228–34). And skilled work of the kind once passed down through a family or a craft for generations has either long given way to industrial efficiency and planned obsolescence or been repackaged as a fetish for those who can afford it. The irony is that rich people now eat the good, fresh produce from the land that working people once did, while working classes remain in the grip of corporations peddling slow, shrink-wrapped poison. Consequently, rich people are typically thin and poor people are fat – surely a perverse historical first.

More profoundly still, market discipline affects people's relationship to time beyond the eight-to-five rhythms of an average working week. From the market's perspective, only the ever-elusive future has any real value; indeed, "futures" are now commodities that can be traded. As a consequence, the present, like everything else, derives its meaning only from its relationship to something besides itself – the promise of future benefits – and the past only has meaning as an obstacle to be overcome in the search for greater efficiency. It confers no gifts and creates no obligations. Memory becomes dangerous, for it can oblige people to honor their past. So we are encouraged to embrace the young, the new, and the innovative, and, in so doing, to become amnesiacs.

This compression of time coincides with the obliteration of bodily and social space. Since the market considers you good only as a unit of production or consumption, it recognizes no fixed identities, no commitments to vows, to vocation, to place. From its perspective, we only "are" in the moment that we consume or produce. To the extent that this discipline dominates, we cease, in other words, to be human beings at all. We become disembodied spirits instead. (Virtual Internet communities and friends are the perfect expression of this; Ward, 2000: 244–60.) Since they reproduce their kind, become ill, and die, our bodies, too, are like the past. They are obstacles which the market must overcome by subordinating them to its brutal demands (Boyle, 1998: 13–67).

Since God has affirmed human goodness by lovingly assuming human flesh, and since our present does come to us as a gift from our past, these reductions are both deceptive and dehumanizing. This is evident in their social effects. As the past is reduced to an obstacle, as goodness is reduced to usefulness, and as humanity is reduced to a collection of spiritless spirits, mundane and unprofitable tasks such as rearing children, caring for the elderly, the sick and the dying either lose their rationale, are met by new industries operated by strangers, or are justified on the tenuous and manipulative grounds that a happy worker, one unburdened with guilt over the neglect of a child or a dying parent, is a productive worker. Commitments, which claim our time and our bodies, thus prove very difficult to sustain, both because the demands placed on us as producers require us to be infinitely "flexible," and because our training as consumers teaches us to evaluate all of our commitments according to criteria of customer satisfaction. Why should I faithfully sustain a commitment if it does not satisfy me? Moreover, this situation is now so developed that it has become unclear why such commitments might be desirable, and there is now widespread distrust of people with commitment – to truth, to an unproductive way of life, to friends – as dangerous. And, indeed, they are dangerous, not simply because perverse commitments result in violence, but because commitments disrupt the smooth machinery of the market, which thrives on destroyed commitments. It is no coincidence that many of the traditional institutions that have bound people together as friends and companions – the craft, the neighborhood, the village, the farm, marriage, the family, the parish – are in shambles. For mammon, like any god, demands its sacrifices.

Under the impact of this discipline, people, too, come to be defined by their usefulness as "human resources." Thus lives that "drain valuable resources" and appear to have no reasonable chance of success also lose *their* rationale. This fuels the spread of abortion and euthanasia, which are extended to ever-growing classes of people now deemed unproductive and unfixable. Though such actions arguably result in greater brutality, both to their victims and to the souls of a people who accept such things as normal, they are justified, ironically, in the name of compassion, on grounds that they eliminate suffering. Given that the original root meaning of "compassion" was "to suffer with," such justification is evidence both that habits transform our language and our choices, and that they produce confusion over the difference between real and apparent goodness.

Every discipline embodies and promotes a manner of thinking appropriate to the goals of that discipline, and these forms of rationality transform the people who acquire them. If you decide to become a surgeon, a Broadway stage actor, or a baseball player, you will have to give yourself over to a craft whose standards you do not define. As you do, you will be changed, and you will eventually think and live, if the training has been successful, like a surgeon, a stage actor, or a baseball player, and each of these is quite different from the others. The same is true of market discipline, but with a difference. This discipline, rather than being confined to one "craft," transforms every craft it touches into an image of itself, as the conversion of land to real estate and people to human resources demonstrates. One need only think further of how medicine, the theater, and baseball are constantly being distorted by bottom-line criteria of economic success to see how this is so.

The manner of thinking generated by market discipline is the art of management, not a particular set of skills appropriate to baseball or surgery, but a set of abstract procedures that purport to be adequate to any endeavor. The art of management has its own understanding of wisdom, in accordance with its view of the good. A wise person on these terms is a person who is thrifty or efficient and thus able to maximize his or her resources. Adam Smith said such a person has the virtue of parsimony (Smith, 1937: 321ff).

Now managerial technique is not entirely of the devil. There are vast numbers of ordinary projects, such as highway construction or running a non-profit organization, where we rightly value such efficiency and expertise. However, managerial technique makes a much better servant than master, and the abstract nature of its procedures, the presumption that they are applicable in every field, gives these techniques an internal tendency toward domination. So it is not surprising to discover, in the work of early "scientific management" gurus like Frederick Taylor and Harrington Emerson, the equation of management principles with a moral wisdom "applicable to all kinds of human activities" and to see in them a means to "infinite goodness, infinite wisdom, [and] infinite power" (Emerson, 1909: 15; Taylor, 1911: 26; McCarraher, forthcoming). And it is equally unsurprising to see, in our own time, and in the transition from "scientific management" to "human relations," that the corporation has become the putative site of social unity, furnishing the language for our moral imaginations (McCarraher, forthcoming).

Yet the art of management never ceases to be about control and profit, and there are at least three problems with its predominance. The first we have already seen. This art does violence to its objects because it aims, not for the intrinsic good of the craft – not for excellent medicine, or strong marriages, for instance – but for goods external to the craft. In so doing, it sacrifices excellence for efficiency (MacIntyre, 1988: 30–46). Secondly, management is about the efficient manipulation of means to ends. Because its techniques purport to be universal, it never asks whether the ends – maximum profit or emotional satisfaction, for instance – are appropriate to particular disciplines like medicine or marriage. A good medical practice might forgo some profits to order extra tests for a patient or to care for the poor. A good husband might forgo the emotional satisfaction of a job promotion or a mistress to care for an ailing wife.

The third problem is a little more subtle. It concerns not the effects on management's objects, the things it manages, but its effects on our souls when we are trained to view the world in managerial terms. In short, when this discipline dominates us, it affects not only how we relate to others, but how we relate to ourselves, causing us to treat ourselves and our passions as things to be managed efficiently. Happiness, health, or well-being becomes the psychological analog for industrial productivity and wealth, and therapeutic or pharmaceutical techniques for managing our emotions become the analog for managerial techniques in the world of business (MacIntyre, 1981: 30). Yet just as management procedures fail to ask whether their economic goals are compatible with the intrinsic excellence of medicine or marriage or baseball, so too we often fail under the influence of these techniques to ask whether our notions of happiness and mental health are appropriate.

For instance, a common definition of mental and emotional well-being goes something like this. Someone is mentally and emotionally healthy when he or she is content, functional, productive, socially well adjusted, and reasonably happy, and there are a glut of therapeutic, pharmaceutical, and self-help industries whose purpose is to help you achieve this state of well-being. (Just go to any bookstore!) These industries have produced terms like "grief process" and "closure" whose widespread use testifies to their prominence in our culture and to their influence on our view of ourselves. By their very existence, these industries assume that such qualities of contentment are "naturally" the qualities of a "healthy" human being, and this notion of health is largely independent of the circumstances in which human beings find themselves. In other words, a healthy human being looks pretty much the same wherever we find her, and the same techniques should help her to achieve this contentment, regardless of her culture, its view of the world, or her own.

Suppose now that you lived in Nazi Germany in the 1930s and 1940s. Your country is preparing to sacrifice a generation of its young in war, to wreak havoc on the rest of the world, and to call ruin upon itself. Whole classes of people are being harassed, rounded up, and executed in the most brutal fashion. Everyone is under heavy surveillance. All the energies of the culture are being marshaled to promote this way of life and its regime as wholesome and good. Now, who is "healthier": someone who fits the portrait of mental and emotional well-being that we just painted, that is, someone who can successfully negotiate the terrain of this culture on these terms, or someone who is so miserable, and who so despairs of the state of this culture, that she cannot "function" on its terms at all (Percy, 1991: 251–62)? Isn't the person whom we would normally call healthy not only profoundly unhealthy, but deeply confused – unable to recognize the true nature of her surroundings?

The dominance of therapeutic techniques prevents us asking just this question. Assuming instead that we "ought" to be happy, they help us to "manage" loss, to put it where it no longer exists, namely, "behind us" in the past. This is to say that the managerial mindset, in its therapeutic guise, creates in our souls the same relationship to time and to the past that it produces in our bodies in its industrial guise. Grief and loss are best avoided, but, failing that, they are obstacles to be managed and overcome. So we institute psychological strategies to emancipate ourselves from the past just as our hyper-mobility as workers drives us from home and from those institutions – like friendship, marriage, and child-rearing – through which we make bodily commitments.

This distorted relationship to time and loss disfigures our grief when loss inevitably comes. In earlier times, people had a vivid sense of living with their dead, and thus, with their past. This created an obligation to honor that past, to grieve its loss appropriately. There are numerous examples of this. There were the proverbial seven years of mourning, during which time it was considered indecent and dishonorable for the widowed to remarry. Survivors often labored for years to procure masses and prayers on behalf of their dead, honoring their memory and contributing to the work of their salvation. Rather than assuming we "ought" to be happy, people found it desirable to *remain* in grief in order to honor their loved ones appropriately. In our time the question of whether someone grieves "appropriately" not only makes no sense, it would be taken as a violation of the mourner's autonomy, and of the "natural" mechanisms of the "grief process."

This does not mean, of course, that there are not pre-given cultural scripts determining the shape of our grief. We just don't notice them. People whose grief is made public generally all speak a common language and experience their pain in the therapeutic lexicon of our culture, often describing their stage in the "grief process" and the techniques that help them "move on." Yet our inability to question the character of our grief calls its character into question.

Because grief and loss, like the past, are obstacles to be overcome, we tend to employ "managerial" strategies to minimize them. The ease with which we assure ourselves that our deceased are in a "better place," regardless of any other religious conviction, is one example. Such strategies are especially apparent during great national tragedies, such as the events of September 11, which is to say that distorted grief, like any distortion of soul, is not without political consequences. Unable to confront pointless suffering and death, we rationalize them by turning the dead into sacrificial victims, and we declare ourselves a stronger, more glorious people as a result of their sacrifice. We valorize those we mourn by making their loss a moment in the realization of a greater good.

Yet if God's creation is good, evils can be nothing but senseless, nothing but lamentable, even though God mysteriously works good from them. There could have been no *good* reason to kill Jesus, for instance; this would make Judas the hero of the crucifixion. Jesus's death is the height of audacity and injustice, and his resurrection refuses this injustice. Christian worship acknowledges this by including grief, even guilt, within its joy. Ours is the "sacrifice of a broken spirit" (Psalms 51: 18). Christian time reflects this, with Advent and Lent dedicated to fasting and other practices of self-denial, acts of charity, and penitence. This sacrifice culminates on Good Friday, as we contemplate this injustice with great lament. During Easter we rejoice that God has generously refused it. But we must do both – weep and rejoice – and worship, uniquely, encompasses both.

Our unwillingness to suffer the past with patience, our desire rapidly to assimilate loss to a greater good, takes neither evil nor goodness seriously. In other words, it fails either to be genuinely grateful or genuinely mournful, in part because it fails to be sufficiently penitential. Whereas Christian worship grieves over the senselessness of evil, this managerial strategy implicitly rationalizes evil by giving it purpose and makes it the occasion for the worship of something we truly love: our own power. And this merely stores up wrath for another day.

No one recognized this tendency more clearly than St Augustine, who experienced it both within his own soul and in the politics of his day. Augustine was suspicious of pity. He understood how we often need, and love, another's misfortune as the occasion for exercising our own pity, for celebrating ourselves (Augustine, 1992: 35–7). Similarly, he understood that great powers, in celebrating their own greatness, secretly needed and loved the injustice of their enemies as the occasion for exercising and magnifying that power (Augustine, 1984: 154). Precisely to the extent that they celebrated this power rather than lamented it, appropriated it rather than relinquished it, they praised the evils that made it possible. Distorted grief, therefore, manifests itself in a distorted form of public worship which calls forth continual blood sacrifice from the citizenry.

This conclusion demonstrates another crucial truth. Every discipline is an order of sacrifice, and every sacrifice is a profound indication of what we have been taught to love. Inasmuch as market discipline and managerial rationality reduce the good to the useful, obliterate time and space, and subordinate the intrinsic goodness of people, places, and things to the goal of efficiency, they perform a sacrifice whose real object of devotion is ourselves and our own power. This discipline, in other words, becomes the vehicle of our own self-love. Yet not even this self-love is genuine. For we are not just consumers, but also producers, not just managers, but are also managed; we do not simply dominate, but are also dominated, as we are called upon to sacrifice our time, our loved ones, our bodies, and our blood. Sacrificing to the gods of power, rather than to the God in whom we find our goodness, our sacrifice does not finally enlarge us, but rather destroys us (Augustine, 1984: 5).

Christian sacrifice does not deny the past, but brings it forward through our collective memory and God's continuing action into his eternal present. Through it we celebrate not our own power, but the peculiar power of God – which appears for all the world as weakness. In it we "offer and present unto [God] our selves, our souls and bodies, to be a reasonable, holy, and living sacrifice" (Episcopal Church of America, 1979: 356). But, unlike the sacrifice of economic discipline, this sacrifice does not defile our bodies by denying them or by turning them into something else. Rather this sacrifice fulfills the destiny of our bodies as creatures by uniting them to God's Body in the Body of Christ.

The Habit and Hope of Worship

In the previous section I argued that much of what is problematic about the sacrificial order of capitalist discipline stems from how it forces us to relate to time. Christian worship, too, has a particular way of understanding and inhabiting time, and there are several senses to this.

The Church traditionally has prescribed prayers for all hours of the day, called the "Daily Office" or the "Liturgy of the Hours," and the principal Sunday liturgy is simply the highest expression of the vigil of prayer that the Church keeps around the world and around the clock. Together these "hours" make up the Christian year, in which the Church claims time for God by living out Christ's life in the seasons of Advent, Epiphany, Lent, Easter, and Pentecost. Through this continual prayer, which is always a response to God's prior gifts to us, God makes the Church. Conversely, through these rhythms, the Church brings the time of creation more deeply into the life of God. The more we inhabit this time, the more this prayer claims our time, the more profoundly we are shaped by it.

The liturgy structures our relationship to time in another, arguably more profound sense. I said before that worship performs a truth claim; it is important not simply for *what* we say, but *because* we say it. It is something we do, an act that performs what it says. As an act, it is necessarily an act of love, and as an act of love it *performs* the truth that we are the creatures of God in Christ. Similarly, it performs a relationship between past, present, and future that stands in stark contrast to the market's denial of time. As a consequence, liturgy forms the worshiping soul and Christians, as Christ's body, in quite a different shape than does the discipline of the market.

The principal act of worship within most Christian traditions is the Holy Eucharist, and all of its principal movements involve a relationship to time. The reading of the

Word is an act of memory recalling God's deeds in history; yet with the sermon and the Creed, the tense shifts. The sermon interprets these deeds and conveys them to the present, eliciting the Creed in response. These acts make us owners of our past, provoking the Confession, where, in the words of Stanley Hauerwas, we learn to be sinners (Hauerwas, 1983: 30–4). The same logic that places Lent between Advent, Epiphany, and Easter places the Confession after the Creed. It is only against the backdrop of God's gifts and our identity as God's creatures that the notion of "sin" makes any sense. And it is only in lamenting our misuse of these gifts, often in things like the "grief process" which we take for granted, that we can faithfully receive them.

Our celebration of God's generosity thus makes a certain grief, a certain ownership of the past, integral to wisdom and to joy. Only by this grief, which is also integral to our reconciliation to God and one another, can we be the Body of Christ. Grief is not the last word, however, and in the absolution the priest announces God's forgiveness, God's commitment to us in spite of ourselves. It is this commitment, ultimately, that binds the members of the Body, moves our prayer, and grounds our hope. And, because of it, we are able to make the unity of the Body visible through the passing of the Peace.

Ownership of our past is crucial to the commitments, divine and human, binding together the members of the Body of Christ in the present. But this recuperation of the past is only one aspect of how Christian worship reconfigures the nature of time. Earlier we saw how capitalism compressed time into the moment of consumption or production, and how this denied the past, distorted the present, and destroyed bodily and social space. In the Eucharist, too, past, present, and future are conjoined in the eternal activity, the self-giving love, of God's present. The priest, standing before the bread and wine, asks God to "send your Holy Spirit upon these gifts that they may be the Sacrament of the Body of Christ and his Blood of the new covenant. Unite us to your Son in his sacrifice, that we may be acceptable through him, being sanctified by the Holy Spirit" (Episcopal Church of America, 1979: 369). Yet unity with Jesus and the Spirit does not deny the past or destroy space, but rather affirms space, by drawing the members of Christ's Body into a union which requires their continuing, bodily commitment to one another. Thus, at the close of communion, we praise God for "assuring us in these Holy Mysteries that we are living members of the Body of your Son," asking him to "send us out, to do the work you have given us to do" (Episcopal Church of America, 1979: 366).

Life within the Body of Christ occurs within the context of this dual movement into both the time of creatures and the eternity of God. And it is within the context of this Body and these movements that I wish to consider the practice of intercession, the prayers Christians pray on behalf of others and the world, as an alternative to managerial discipline that recovers time and bodily and social space. Since "intercession acknowledges the reality of the need of others and one's own powerlessness in respect of their future," it is the very opposite of managerial discipline, which is about the efficient use of power (Williams, 2000: 12). Truthfully naming and waiting amidst the reality of pointless suffering and death, intercessory prayer has a share in the grief and powerlessness that inevitably attends our lives in time. Yet in commending this powerlessness to the eternity of God, this prayer has a share in the hope that God offers in offering himself. This grief and this hope, which are denied by managerial discipline, then characterize how we most fully live out our identity as creatures and how, as creatures called to witness to the goodness of both God and the world, we embody God's commitment to the world in Jesus.

In earlier times, when monks withdrew from the world, they did so not because they hated and rejected the world, but because they loved it and wanted to commit the world to God through their prayers. To most modern minds, such activity seems pointless, and it is in several precise senses. Though we pray for what we want for the world, for our friends, for our brothers and sisters in Christ, we also hope and pray that what we want accords with God's desire for his creatures – "Thy will be done" – knowing full well that our prayer is often likely to be met with the same apparent silence as Jesus's prayer in Gethsemane. To acknowledge this is to acknowledge that we are not God, to be dispossessed of our pretensions to domination and control, to relinquish the power of our own hands and to place ourselves in the hands of another. We do not pray, in other words, in the hope of "manipulating" God into giving us what we want. Prayer does not have that kind of "point," for prayer is not a means to an end. It is, in this sense, pointless. It is an end in itself; for "it is right to give him thanks and praise" (Episcopal Church of America, 1979: 361). Yet it is precisely this "pointlessness" of prayer that affirms both the intrinsic goodness of God and of those for whom we pray; it is precisely in this powerlessness that we discover ourselves and others as creatures. And it is precisely by our abandoning the pretension to be God and thus acknowledging our difference from God, that we most fully embody God's commitment to the world and most fully learn to live in the hope of that commitment.

In one congregation that I know, a relatively young man who was a much-loved member of the community was diagnosed with cancer. His decline was rather rapid, and when it became clear that he was going to die, some of the members of the congregation organized a vigil of prayer by his bedside. They took turns, sometimes individually, sometimes in small groups, offering prayers on his behalf for relief from his suffering, forgiveness of his sins, and rest for his soul, commending him to God. They remained there, well after he lost consciousness, praying for several days until he finally died.

Such practices were once quite common. Yet a world dominated by managerial rationality conspires to render such suffering invisible and such activity either sentimental or incomprehensible. As a consequence of this invisibility, many of us and those we love will die an inhuman death, alone, attached to a machine. From a sentimental perspective, such pointless prayer is explained (or explained away) as psychological salve for the troubled souls of the mourners, as if praying in the presence of the dying were more pleasant than forgetting them. But perhaps the most common reaction is incomprehensibility. Why should a people pray at the bedside of someone whose death is imminent, who is not even aware of the gesture?

As I have repeatedly argued, the cost of managerial discipline is all too often the elimination of time, space, and, ultimately, our humanity. "Pointless" intercessory prayer, by contrast, affirms all these. To the extent that these prayers are offered in the lament of apparent powerlessness, to the extent that they are indeed "pointless," they honor the dying brother as good in himself, with an identity independent of his (or our) perception of it. To the extent that they are an expression of hope in God's mercy, they acknowledge God as the source and end of his goodness, and the ground of a corporate bond that we do not create but can only receive, a bond of unity that does not end in death (Augustine, 1992: 58).

Intercessory prayer, therefore, is the manner in which God binds the living and the dead, the past, present, and future, into one Body and into a common social space sustained by God's own self-giving. Past, present, and future intersect in the presence of this Body. They are not denied, distorted, and managed, but lamented, suffered, and awaited in a hope that is both longing and joy. To the extent that this prayer becomes our habit, our language, our manner of inhabiting the world, it becomes impossible for us to treat others either as means, as "human resources" to be distorted and misused for an alien purpose, or as ends in themselves, as self-determined atoms with no meaning beyond those they define for themselves. The former is a distortion imposed upon our identities by our economic function as producers, the latter by our role as consumers. Neither is the identity of a *creature* that exists in time, inhabits a physical or social body, or has a soul.

The practice of intercessory prayer affirms our identity as creatures and our hope in God, but it cannot do so without a virtue, out of place in the discipline of the market, without which there is no commitment, humanity, or hope. That virtue is patience. Patience acknowledges and inhabits time. It waits with expectation. It suffers with hope.

We hope not to suffer because suffering is good – it detracts from the goodness of God's creation – but to suffer well because God has found that creation worth suffering for. Patience therefore helps us sustain commitments unto death; hope assures us that death is not the last word. Commitments like marriage and prayer require time, and they require physical and social bodies. This patience is therefore hopelessly "uneconomical." It refuses to sacrifice the intrinsic goodness of others, the goodness of ourselves, the goodness of our commitments and our prayers to the goods of effectiveness, efficiency, and productivity. This patience makes us poor managers. But it might just make us human.

And that, surely, is good.

References

Aristotle (1998) The *Politics*, trans. C. D. C. Reeve (Indianapolis, IN: Hackett).

Augustine (1984) *City of God*, trans. Henry Bettenson (London: Penguin).

—(1992) *Confessions*, trans. F. J. Sheed (Indianapolis. IN: Hackett).

Boyle, Nicholas (1998) *Who Are We Now? Christian Humanism and the Global Market from Hegel to Heaney* (Edinburgh: T. and T. Clark).

Emerson, Harrington (1909) *Efficiency as a Basis for Operation and Wages* (New York: The Engineering Magazine).

Episcopal Church of America (1979) *Book of Common Prayer*.

Hauerwas, Stanley (1983) *The Peaceable Kingdom* (Notre Dame, IN: University of Notre Dame Press).

MacIntyre, Alasdair (1981) *After Virtue* (Notre Dame, IN: University of Notre Dame Press).

—(1988) *Whose Justice? Which Rationality?* (Notre Dame, IN: University of Notre Dame Press).

McCarraher, Eugene (forthcoming) *The Enchantments of Mammon: Corporate Capitalism and the American Moral Imagination*.

Percy, Walker (1991) *Signposts in a Strange Land*, ed. Patrick Samway (New York: The Noonday Press).

Smith, Adam (1937) *The Wealth of Nations* (New York: Random House).

Taylor, Frederick W. (1911) *The Principles of Scientific Management* (New York: Norton).

Ward, Graham (2000) *Cities of God* (London: Routledge).

Williams, Rowan (2000) *On Christian Theology* (Oxford: Blackwell).

CHAPTER 19

Being Baptized: Bodies and Abortion

Frederick Christian Bauerschmidt

Abortion and Perplexity

Anyone with a passing acquaintance with the abortion controversy knows that it is largely framed in terms of competing rights: the fetus/child's "right to life" and the woman/mother's right to "control of her own body" or "procreative choice" or some other similar formulation. It is also evident that the debate is one that has, on the whole, gone nowhere, except toward a further hardening of positions on both sides. One might expect that the shared commitment to human rights would provide common ground upon which the issue could be discussed. Yet, what seems like common ground – human beings as possessors of rights, government as the protector of those rights – yields virtually nothing by way of agreement on the question of abortion. Whatever the merits of "rights talk" in other contexts, in the context of abortion it has proved perplexingly unfruitful.

Attempts to shift the basis of the debate seem always to end up back in the same place. For example, Ronald Dworkin discusses abortion in terms not of rights to life or choice, but of differing views on life's inviolability or "sanctity." In the end, however, Dworkin's argument turns out to be another argument about rights, only in this case it is an argument about the right to freedom of belief. He argues that, since differences on the question of abortion are differences about life's "sanctity," these are quasi-religious differences, and therefore ought to be removed from the realm of governmental control: "the critical question is whether a decent society will choose coercion or responsibility, whether it will seek to impose a collective judgement on matters of the most profound spiritual character on everyone, or whether it will allow and ask its citizens to make the most central, personality defining judgements about their own lives for themselves" (Harris, 2001: 203). What appears at first to be a move away from the rhetoric of rights turns out instead to be a move from the language of right-to-life versus right-to-choice, to the language of the right to freedom of religious or quasi-religious opinion.

Dworkin's argument is instructive. Perceptive interpreter of liberalism that he is, he sees that shifting the focus from a "right to life/choice" to a "right to (quasi-religious) opinion" gives a much stronger foundation to abortion rights, for if there is a real thread running through the fabric of liberal democracy, it is freedom of opinion. Pierre Manent has argued that freedom of opinion, specifically opinion about what it means to be human or, in Dworkin's language, what makes life "sacred," is absolutely central to the project of liberalism. Modern democracy seeks "to construct a rigorous moral and political doctrine without inquiring into the nature, essence, or substance of man, and even by rejecting any affirmation regarding human essence as presumptuous or idle" (Manent, 1998: 124). Having come to the conclusion that there is nothing that defines the human, or, which amounts to the same thing, that one cannot objectively know what defines the human, modern liberal democracies establish themselves on the right of individuals to define for themselves what defines the human. Thus a human being comes to be defined – paradoxically? incoherently? – by a right to self-definition.

The perplexity that attends the abortion debate points to a perplexity at the heart of liberal democracy. In maintaining that we have no right to define for another what the happiness of the human animal consists in (or, in Dworkin's terms, what makes life sacred), the law brackets the question of what it is to be a human. But, in order to speak of human rights, as liberal democrats do, you have to have some idea of what human beings are. In order to defend human rights, as the laws of liberal democracies seek to do, one must adopt some position on what Manent calls, "the nature, essence, or substance of man." Yet this is precisely what the laws of liberal democracies *cannot* do because the right to opinion, the right to decide for oneself what constitutes the sacredness of life, is foundational to liberalism.

The abortion debate is the corrosive that reveals this perplexity, precisely because it raises so pointedly the question of the nature, essence, and substance of the human animal. Obviously, the issue of the status of the fetus raises this question, and most pointedly. But even in cases where a writer leaves aside this issue, or grants his or her opponent's view, questions of the nature of human beings constantly resurface in other forms. What is the relationship of "self" and "body"? What are the boundaries of personal identity? What does one owe to other people? These, no less than questions about the status of the fetus, are questions about what it is to be human. In the abortion debate, they are questions that seem to demand an answer. And they demand not only an answer in the privacy of one's conscience (where liberals are quite happy to have them answered), but a *political* answer. For these questions are inseparable from other questions: What are the boundaries of the body politic? What substantive virtues sustain this body and what vices destroy it? But these are precisely the questions that liberal democracies cannot answer. My suspicion is that the resolution of the abortion question in liberal democracies awaits the (infinitely deferred?) resolution of this perplexity.

Bodies and their Virtues

Part of the poverty of "rights" as a language for moral reflection, and part of the attraction of "virtue" ethics in the past few decades, is that moral questions are not simply questions of what one should *do*, but also questions of who one should *be*. Our actions not only affect others, granting or denying them certain rights; they also affect us, shaping our identity or character. In the specific case of the debate over abortion, much attention has focused on the rights of the fetus and the rights of the mother, but rather less attention has been paid to the question of how abortion, as an activity, shapes the character of those involved in it. Put somewhat differently, the problem with reducing the issue of abortion to the question "is the fetus a human being with a right to life?" or to the question "should the interests of the mother outweigh those of the fetus?" is that such questions only address what impact certain actions have outside the doer of those actions. They miss entirely the question of the impact of the action on the agent.

A further difficulty with the language of rights is its tendency to abstraction; possessors of rights are disembodied entities, seemingly without history or location. One of the points that has been pressed by some pro-choice advocates is the need to take human embodiment seriously: human beings are not simply minds temporarily rattling around in material vessels; we quite profoundly *are* our bodies and this must be taken seriously in discussions of abortion. What is the somewhat abstract right to life of an embryo compared to a woman's bodily well-being? Beverly Harrison and Shirley Cloyes claim: "One of Christianity's greatest weaknesses is its spiritualizing neglect of respect of the physical body and physical well-being . . . [W]e have no moral tradition in Christianity that starts with body-space, or body-right, as a basic condition of moral relations . . . In any social relation, body-space must be respected or nothing deeply human or moral can be created" (Steffen, 1996: 332).

In focusing on embodiment, Harrison and Cloyes help to make the question of abortion more concrete. However, I think that they are profoundly mistaken in saying that there is no moral tradition in Christianity that starts with "body-space" as a basic condition of moral relations. In fact, as I shall argue in the rest of this chapter, the moral world of Christianity, seen through the prism of the practice of baptism, is *nothing but* a reflection on "body-space." Harrison and Cloyes seem to miss this because their commitment to liberalism makes their understanding of embodiment a thoroughly individualistic one, in which, as John Locke argued, the body is something "possessed" by the individual: hence their identification of "body-space" with "body-right." The Lockean body, the liberal body, is one with self-evident boundaries, like a well-surveyed, clearly demarcated piece of land. It is a "space" that one has a "right" to, presumably because of the time and labor one has invested in it. From such a perspective it is clear that, in the case of abortion, one has a right to decide who can occupy this space.

The moral reflection that grows out of baptism, on the other hand, begins not with the theoretical body possessed by an individual, but with the concrete embodied person and the social body into which people are initiated in the waters of baptism. From the perspective of such a baptismal body, issues of "body-space" and "body-right" look quite different from the way they look viewed from the perspective of the liberal body. As we shall see, its virtues are not powers of self-control and self-containment, but powers of self-donation, the perpetual dynamic in which virtue is "exteriorized" through enactment.

Yet it is not simply liberalism that blinds us to the moral significance of baptismal bodies and the virtues or powers that course through them, defining their character.

Much Christian thinking about baptism focuses on the individual and the spiritual rather than the corporate and the material. Baptism is seen as the way in which individuals have the stain of original sin washed from their souls or, alternatively, as the way in which individuals publicly profess the inner, spiritual transformation by which they have been born again. Such visions of baptism present at best a very stunted version of the Church's rich theology of baptism as the rite by which God "has rescued us from the power of darkness and transferred us into the kingdom of his beloved Son" (Colossians 1: 13).

With our demythologized imaginations, we modern people, Christian and non-Christian alike, have difficulty appreciating fully the realism with which early Christians spoke of the body of the baptized as "spirit-filled" and incorporated into the Body of Christ. But if we take seriously the notion of human beings as ensouled or en-spirited bodies, then the body is not simply an inert object that the mind somehow possesses and operates; rather, the body is "constructed" by the spirit: our identities are shaped by the various spirits and powers that act upon it.

From the perspective of baptism, the body is a contested area, over which different "spirits" seek control, fighting to subject the body to their powers, to mark it with particular virtues and vices. Dale Martin's characterization of the common ancient perspective, shared by Christians and pagans alike, captures this well:

> In the absence of such ontological dualism, for most people of Greco-Roman culture the human body was of a piece with its environment. The self was a precarious, temporary state of affairs, constituted by forces surrounding and pervading the body, like the radio waves that bounce around and through the bodies of modern urbanites. In such a maelstrom of cosmological forces, the individualism of modern conceptions disappears, and the body is perceived as a location in a continuum of cosmic movement. The body – or "the self" – is an unstable place of transition, not a discrete, permanent, solid entity. (Martin, 1999: 25)

Though such a view might sound suspiciously postmodern, it is already implied in Aristotle's term *eudaimonia*, usually translated "happiness," but literally meaning possessing (or being possessed by) a good *daimon* or guardian spirit. It is also the context of Paul's concern over pollution (which is Martin's focus), Jesus's ministry as an exorcist, and claims, like that found in the letter to the Ephesians, that "our struggle is not against enemies of blood and flesh, but against the rulers, against the authorities, against the cosmic powers of this present darkness, against the spiritual forces of evil in the heavenly places" (Ephesians 6: 12).

Further, if politics is a shared pursuit of *eudaimonia*, then we might think of social bodies as achieving their ultimate unity through common possession of and by one *daimon*. Social bodies, no less than individual bodies, are subjected to spiritual forces. In baptism, our individual bodies are drawn by the Spirit into a single corporate body, so that we, "like living stones," may let ourselves "be built into a spiritual house, to be a holy priesthood, to offer spiritual sacrifices acceptable to God through Jesus Christ" (1 Peter 2: 5). Through baptism, "there is one body and one Spirit" (Ephesians 4: 4); we might even say that there is one body *because* there is one Spirit.

Such a description of our existence, far from needing to be demythologized, is in fact *more* realistic, less "mythical," than the liberal account of the self. The freedom of choice that is, as Slavoj Žižek notes, "at the very nerve center of the liberal ideology," depends on a ludicrous, yet somehow very believable (because so desirable), myth of "the 'psychological' subject endowed with propensities he or she strives to realize" (Žižek, 2001: 116). This psychological subject possesses sole right to its body, which is the domain in which it realizes its potential. The liberal myth blinds us to the way in which the spiritual forces of Church, market, state, media, family, angelic and demonic powers operate upon our bodies, our selves. So the *real* myth is of an irreducible, dis-embodied core of selfhood, magically protected by a freedom that is not subjected to external powers. The virtuous liberal self would be one that possesses the habits and dispositions necessary to police its body-space in such a way as to attain the "propen-sities he or she strives to realize."

Baptism requires a different account of the self and its virtues because it requires a different account of bodies – both individual and corporate. The baptismal "body-space" is not a self-inclosed private domain. It is something shared because it is some-thing surrendered to the Spirit of God.

Building a Temple for the Spirit

If we want a clearer idea of what sort of body is bestowed in baptism, we ought to look at the event of baptism itself. Of course, baptism takes place in many different ways, according to many different rites, at many different ages. The essential rite, involving water and the triune name, is largely agreed on, but in all traditions this is located within a larger complex of words and gestures that serve to bring out more fully what that tradition understands to be taking place in baptism. In what follows, I will look at one particular rite from my own tradition, the Roman Catholic rite for infant baptism, with occasional side glances at other rites and traditions.

Touching and claiming

In the baptism of an infant, the rite begins with the claiming of the candidate's body-space by God and the Church. The priest says, "I claim you for Christ our Savior by the sign of his cross," and traces the cross on the child's forehead, inviting the parents and godparents to do the same. This claiming is the beginning of the construction of the baptized body, and as such it must involve touch of a particular sort. This touching is cruciform and communal. It is not a grasping touch that seeks to control or dominate or abuse, but a touch that welcomes. It is touching in the shape of the cross, the sign of the renunciation of control. And it is not an isolated and isolating touching, as if the cultic figure of the priest were gaining some unique, even magical control over the can-didate's body. Rather, the candidate is also touched by parents and godparents, those within the ecclesial community who will have special care for day-to-day formation of the child. In baptism, the Spirit invades the candidate's body through the touch of the ecclesial community.

Repeatedly, in the rite of baptism, the body of the candidate is touched, so that through touch it may be incorporated into the ecclesial Body of Christ. The body of the candidate, whether child or adult, is handled in such a way as to make clear that the candidate has no "body-right." It is a body caught in the midst of what Dale Martin calls a "maelstrom of cosmological forces." The potential for abuse here is clear. What is to prevent those who handle the candidate's body in baptism – the priest, the parents, the godparents – from using this as a justification for *mishandling* the candidate's body, for claiming authority over it in the name of God? Recent events have made clear that the potential for such abuse is more than a theoretical possibility. Of course, it is not clear that Lockean bodies are any less subject to abuse, and the excessive privatization of body-space might have its own contribution to make in increasing the chances of abuse. But, ultimately, the only guard that the baptized body has against abuse is the cruciform and communal character of the baptismal touch. The cross and the community make it clear that the baptized body is a body subjected not to any human individual, whether priest or parent, but to God and to God alone. In seeking to claim the candidate's body for Christ and the Spirit, and thereby to free it from other spirits, baptism paradoxically seeks to give the candidate a kind of self-possession. "For all things are yours . . . all belong to you, and you belong to Christ, and Christ belongs to God" (1 Corinthians 3: 21–3).

The baptized body is entrusted to the entire community, which must constantly ensure that the body is treated with the dignity of a temple of the Spirit. In order to do this, the hands that touch the candidate must belong to those who understand their own body-space as defined by baptism. One of the most dramatic challenges that early Christianity posed to the traditional Roman understanding of family and authority is that it removed the human body from the authority of the *pater familias*, to whom newborn children were presented for acceptance or rejection, and placed it under the authority of God. In that sense, the baptismal community is one without "fathers." The hands that touch the candidate cannot be "fatherly" hands: they cannot be hands that claim the power of life and death, for such power belongs to the "one Father – the one in heaven" (Matthew 23: 9).

Story

The Roman Catholic rite of infant baptism then continues with the liturgy of the Word, which is a sort of compression of the extended catechesis that precedes adult baptism. In baptisms celebrated outside of the Eucharist, this may consist of only a brief reading from one of the Gospels, but ritually the point is clear: baptism is incorporation into the narrative of Christ. In baptism, the candidate is inserted into the story of Israel, Jesus, and the Church, like a seed that is put into soil. It is that story that will, through constant rehearsal in the Sunday eucharistic gathering, nurture the candidate, so that he or she can constantly appropriate anew the significance of the cruciform sign with which they were signed. It is through the biblical narrative, rehearsing the words and deeds of God's people and God's Messiah, that the candidate will learn the ensemble of corporeal and spiritual gestures that define God's people in the world. One might say that through the proclamation of the biblical narrative, the Word, as word, touches the baptized body.

Petition and epiclesis

The intercessions that follow, which culminate in the litany of the saints, are an indication of a fundamental characteristic of the baptized body: its neediness. This neediness is not simply the neediness of the candidate's body. True, the person being baptized needs the prayer of the community. But the communal body is also a needy one. The construction of the baptized body is not a human project, but the work of Christ's Spirit. If the Church is to share in this task, then it can only do so in the context of prayer, whereby it calls upon the Spirit. Therefore, in the intercessions, the community does not simply pray for the child and its parents and godparents, but it also prays, "renew the grace of our baptism in each one of us." The child depends on the prayers of the community, but the community itself only dares to pray on the basis of the Spirit's unceasing renewal of the baptismal gift to each and every member. This complex network of dependence, displayed in the intercessory prayers, constitutes the freedom of the baptized bodies: "you were called to freedom, brothers and sisters; only do not use your freedom as an opportunity for self-indulgence, but through love become slaves to one another" (Galatians 5: 13). Freedom is not the ability to dispose of one's body as one wills, but rather the freedom to give one's body to another in loving service.

There then follows an exorcism. To some, no doubt, this seems like a superstitious hold-over from primitive times, and it is in fact optional in the reformed Roman rites. Indeed, modern baptismal rites seem a bit embarrassed by the exorcistic character of traditional baptismal rites and tend to tone these elements down. But exorcism is fundamental to baptism, and in the Roman rite it follows logically upon the prayers: only after having called upon the Spirit do we dare to join the battle with the spiritual forces of oppression. The prayer of exorcism, after recalling that God "sent [his] only Son into the world to cast out the power of Satan, spirit of evil," asks for the candidate: "set her free from original sin, make her a temple of your glory, and send your Holy Spirit to dwell with her." Once again, the priest, having anointed the child with oil, lays hands on it. Once again the body is touched, freeing it from the illusion of self-possession, which is perhaps the chief spirit that must be cast out. And once again, this touch must come from a community that itself is being freed from this same spirit of self-possession, a community of those who view neither their individual bodies nor their collective body as a space that they control, but as a space for the radical hospitality of the Spirit.

The baptismal water is then blessed in a prayer that, through the logic of typology, identifies it with the role of water in God's saving actions. The water of the font will become the waters over which the Spirit moved in creation, the waters of the Red Sea, the waters of the Jordan in which Jesus was baptized, and the water that flowed forth with blood from the side of the crucified Jesus. Perhaps this last is the most startling: it is through the sacramental blood and water that we are drawn into Christ's welcoming body. By entering into the water that flows from Christ's body, the candidate will become one with that body, as if the baptismal water will erode the boundaries between the candidate's body and the body of Christ. This erosion of boundaries is inherent in the typological sensibilities of the prayer; there is no division between the waters that flow through the Red Sea, the Jordan, and *this* font, here and now. The story of the Church, and of this individual being baptized, flows into the stories of Israel and Jesus.

Turning

The water having been blessed, the parents and godparents renounce Satan and profess faith in the triune God, through a variant on the Apostles' Creed. Renunciation and profession go together: the only way we can renounce Satan is to profess faith. There is no gap between the two, where we achieve some sort of neutral stance between the Spirit of God and the powers of this present age. It is not as if we renounce evil and then achieve the status of the mythical liberal subject, who is free to choose whether or not to follow Christ. To turn away from evil is always already to be turning toward Christ. In the Eastern liturgy this is dramatically symbolized by facing West, the realm of darkness, for the renunciation and then, after spitting at Satan, turning to face East, the direction of the rising sun, to profess faith in Christ.

In contrast to the pre-Vatican II rites, the parents and godparents do not speak in the name of the child; the questions of renunciation and faith are addressed to them, not to the child. There is no fiction of an implicit faith in the child; rather the child is entirely dependent upon the Church's faith that the parents and godparents profess. Thus at the conclusion of the profession of faith the priest says, "This is our faith. This is the faith of the Church. We are proud to profess it, in Christ Jesus our Lord." Again, the candidate is planted in the Church like a seed in the soil or a child in the womb.

Washing and anointing

Immediately upon the profession of faith follows the baptismal washing. In both the Roman and Eastern rites, the normal mode of baptism, even for infants, is a threefold immersion in the name of the Trinity. These two elements – immersion in water and the triune name – constitute the core, if you will, of the sacramental action and it is worth looking at them both in turn.

The Eastern liturgy presents a vivid picture of the waters of baptism as a site of spiritual combat, praying in the blessing of the water: "do not let a demon of darkness hide itself in this water, and do not let an evil spirit, bringing darkening of thoughts and disturbance of mind, go down into it with the one who is being baptized." Water is not simply the humble servant of God, a useful substance for washing. It is a chaotic place, a liminal place of transformation. Patristic commentaries, inspired by John 3: 3–8, liken the waters of the font to the waters of the womb. It is in the womb of the font that the baptismal body will begin to be knit together. These waters effect the final dissolution of the old self, which has been persistently sought throughout the rite, so that the new self can be born. As such, they are a place of danger, because in entering them we run the risk that the self will dissolve without resolving into a new self.

The speaking of the triune name of Father, Son, and Spirit is what brings the danger of the water to resolution. We might think of the names "Father, Son, and Holy Spirit" as a highly compressed form of the entire scriptural-ecclesial narrative, which is to impress itself upon the one being baptized. This is even more dramatically expressed in the baptismal rite in Hippolytus's *Apostolic Tradition*, which dates perhaps from third-century Rome. In this rite, the baptismal washing accompanies the profession of faith itself: the candidate is immersed after each of the three sections of the Creed. We can see an analogy in the practice prescribed in the *Babylonian Talmud* for converts to Judaism, in which, after circumcision in the case of men, they would be immersed in water while two teachers of the community stood by their sides and recited "some of the lesser commandments and some of the greater ones" (*Yebamoth* 47 A–B in Stewart-Sykes and Newman, 2001: 22).

The story of the Father who hands over his Son to his people so that they may live through the Spirit is for Christians the "law" that structures their identity; it is the sign inscribed on their hearts (Colossians 2: 11–12); one might even say that it is the genetic code of Christ's body. Unlike circumcision, the rite of Christian initiation itself leaves no visible mark on the body. Yet the marking is not "spiritual" in the sense of unrelated to the body. The transformation that the body undergoes is to show itself by walking in love, light, and truth (Romans 14: 15; 1 John 1: 6; 2 John 1: 4). More particularly, the baptized body must live out the radical welcome it has received from God in the waters of the font by extending that welcome to others. The baptized body now lives the story with which it has been marked. From the chaos of the waters a new self is born.

The anointing with the perfumed oil of chrism that follows in the Roman rite has a complex and contested history, particularly its relation to the sacrament of confirmation. Here it shall suffice to say that the spoken formula that accompanies this anointing, while mentioning the Holy Spirit, interprets it as primarily "christic." It draws out the consequences of the baptismal washing, underscoring the new identity of the baptized body as a participant in the body of Christ, who was anointed as priest, prophet, and king. The candidate, now called a "neophyte," has become part of God's messianic community. As such, the neophyte is an *alter Christus*: one whose identity is no longer separable from the identity of Christ.

Clothing in glory

After the anointing, there follow two rituals that ought to be understood as closely related to each other. The neophyte is first clothed in a white garment, which is described as "an outward sign of your Christian dignity." Then the parents and godparents are given a candle lighted from the Easter candle and told, "This child of yours has been enlightened by Christ. She is to walk always as a child of the light." These two rites are intended, like the anointing with chrism, to make clear what has happened in the baptismal washing: the neophyte has been clothed in the messianic glory of the risen Christ. This theme is especially prominent in the ancient Syrian tradition, which conceives this clothing in bodily terms: the body, which lost its glory due to Adam's sin, is re-clothed in the glory that Christ himself deposited in the baptismal waters at his own baptism in the Jordan (see Anderson, 2001: 129–32). Baptism is not simply a "spiritual" renewal, but in fact the neophyte's body has been transformed, re-knit in the womb of the font and re-clothed in the light of glory, so as to be conformed to the glorified body of Christ. The Eastern liturgy makes the connection of clothing and light quite explicit, singing at the clothing of the neophyte, "Grant to me a robe of light, O most merciful Christ, our God, who clothe yourself with light as with a garment." Not only are the boundaries between baptized bodies blurred by their common inclusion in the one body of Christ and their animation by the one Spirit of Christ, but the boundary between the baptized and Christ himself is also blurred. The neophyte's "robe of light" is a participation in the glory of Christ's risen body.

Eating

The rite culminates, at least ideally, in the celebration of the Eucharist. The traditional restriction of the Eucharist to those who have been baptized is not because baptism is a prerequisite that makes one worthy to receive the Eucharist. Rather, the Eucharist is the continuation of what was begun in baptism; it is the weekly reconstitution of the baptized body. It is the place of growth for the seed that has been planted in Christ's body.

In Justin Martyr's account of baptism, the "hinge" between baptism and the Eucharist is the neophyte's first exchange of the kiss of peace with the gathered community. Edward Phillips has suggested that for the early Christians the ritual kiss had a pneumatological significance; it was, "a ritual enactment of the sharing of the *pneuma* [spirit] among believers that delineated the boundaries of the community, much in the way that the kiss could delineate family boundaries." The Church was the new family, whose Father is God. Phillips pushes this further, arguing that for the early Christian communities the Spirit was "communicated through the mouth of one believer to another" (Phillips, 1996: 12). In the exchange of the kiss and the ritual meal that follows a "network of the Spirit" is set up; a Spirit-filled body is constituted.

The culmination of the unrepeatable initiation in the constantly repeated Eucharist casts light back upon the nature of this Spirit-filled body. The Spirit is known by the name "Gift," and to live by the Spirit is to live as gift. The Eucharist is the Church's proclamation that the baptized body is a body that is "given for you": it is given to the Church so that the Church may be what it receives, and the Church in turn gives its body for the life of the world.

Baptized Bodies in the Midst of the Nations: Beyond the Minimally Decent Samaritan

What, you might reasonably ask, does all this have to do with abortion? More specifically, what does this tell us about the sorts of laws nations should have concerning the regulation, if any, of abortion? Does not such an account merely reinforce the impression that Christians speak an arcane language that is unintelligible and irrelevant to the rest of the world? Can baptism, so understood, be anything more than a purely private affair?

If this were the case, then I would have fundamentally misrepresented Christian baptism. As Louis-Marie Chauvet writes: "The difference inscribed on the body of every person through Christian initiation is so important that, far from imprisoning one into a clan or cultural group, as some other rites of initiation do, it opens onto the universal: by their baptism, Christians do not become members of a ghetto, but sisters and brothers of all humans in Jesus Christ" (Chauvet, 2001: 111). This point cannot be underscored too strongly. The Church is salt and light; it is a sign to the world of the world's own true identity as God's creation. If the divine glory in which the baptized body is clothed blurs the boundary between the baptized body and Christ's body, that same divine glory, refusing to be contained, also blurs the boundary between baptized bodies and unbaptized bodies. As Origen wrote, "Christ has the whole human race, and perhaps even the totality of creation, as his body" (in von Balthasar, 1984: §791).

We might say that the baptized body is simply the ordinary human body illuminated by the divine glory that appeared in the life, death, and resurrection of Jesus Christ. But this "illumination" – an ancient term for baptism – makes all the difference, for it reconfigures our entire self-understanding. It will not help us resolve the conflict between the standard "pro-life" and "pro-choice" positions, not least because both of these positions presume that bodily life is like some sort of object that human beings *possess*, rather than that which they *are*. The light that baptism casts calls precisely such an assumption of ownership into question. Put differently, it shifts the relevant question from "who owes what to whom?" to "who is my neighbor?"

This question is, of course, the self-justifying question that the lawyer asks Jesus in Luke's Gospel, to which Jesus replies with the parable of the Good Samaritan. This parable features in Judith Jarvis Thompson's classic essay, "A Defense of Abortion," which offers the famous thought experiment in which I am asked to imagine myself awakening to find that my circulatory system has, while I was sleeping, been linked to that of a famous violinist, whose kidneys have failed and who needs my body for the next nine months to sustain his life. Thompson asks, "Is it morally incumbent on you to accede to this situation?" (Harris, 2001: 26). In arguing that one need not accede to such a situation, and therefore need not accede to letting a fetus use one's body for nine months, Jarvis quotes the Gospel of Luke, and proceeds to distinguish the kind of Good Samaritan that Jesus depicts from what she calls the "Minimally Decent Samaritan." Members of society have a right to expect "minimal decency" from each other, but no one has a right to expect of me the kind of sacrifice that the violinist – and the fetus – places on me. I may *choose* to accept such a sacrifice, for religious or other reasons, but no one can expect it.

But, of course, Jesus uses the parable to different purposes. By offering it in answer to the question "who is my neighbor," Jesus presents the Samaritan neither as some sort of extraordinary moral hero, nor as someone who exercises an optional virtue as part of a personal life project. Rather, he is someone who acted as a neighbor, doing the "minimally decent" thing that is required to make life together – neighborliness – possible. The parable seems to say that the minimal decency required for human beings to live together might be something more robust than non-interference. Jesus offers the parable as showing what it means to love your neighbor as yourself, something that he says one must do in order to "live" (Luke 10: 28). Put differently, the moral achievement of the Samaritan was not the decision to help the wounded stranger, but the ability to recognize that he had no choice but to help this wounded and vulnerable one. In terms of Thompson's thought experiment about the violinist, we might say that the Samaritan is one who recognizes that his body is *already* linked to the body of the needy neighbor, and always has been.

The parable is an exemplary depiction of the action of the baptized body. Paul writes, "Do you not know that your body is a temple of the Holy Spirit within you, which you have from God, and that you are not your own? For you were bought with a price; therefore glorify God in your body" (1 Corinthians 6: 19–20). In other words, the baptized body must display the glory in which it has been clothed. What it means to display this glory is indicated by Jesus's words at the end of the parable: "Go and do likewise" (Luke 10: 37). The kind of care shown by the Samaritan to the wounded stranger constitutes minimal decency; it is simply what it means for a baptized body to live.

But this decency is itself something quite extravagant: it is a revelation of glory that involves touching the open wounds in the other's body, putting one's possessions at the disposal of the other, promising to return to the other. In a sense, it involves seeing the wounded stranger's otherness breached by the commandment to love the neighbor "as yourself." It involves seeing the wounds of the neighbor in light of the wound of love inflicted upon oneself in baptism. It is important to the story that the Samaritan is outside of the bounded group of the wounded Jewish traveler. The wounded man is not simply a stranger, but an enemy. But the body clothed in glory is an open body. It is a body that has been pierced by the Spirit. It is a body that can no longer clearly distinguish between self-love and love of neighbor, or even love of enemy. It is a body that cannot help but be at the disposal of the neighbor in need.

Perhaps the most important task of Christian theology is to convince Christians that the light cast by baptism enables them to think beyond "pro-life" and "pro-choice" in order to see nascent human life not as a being with rights, but as the needy neighbor to whom we must respond in order for our baptized bodies to live. One might even go so far as to say that it is in welcoming the valueless, powerless life of the unborn that we most vibrantly replicate God's baptismal welcome of us (see 1 Corinthians 1: 28).

Of course, one might ask how this will help in public policy debates over abortion laws. I am not sure that it will, given the rules of the game in liberal democracy. But Christians believe that the kind of extravagant openness displayed by the Good Samaritan and engendered by baptism is something that is fundamental to living as a human being. If the body clothed in glory by baptism is simply the living human body in its fullness, then Christians ought to trust that others will be drawn by this glory, drawn by the promise of life in its fullness.

I do not pretend that Christian witness will necessarily be any more consensus-building than the language of rights. It is not likely to produce a judicial or legislative solution to our societal perplexity over abortion. But while it would certainly say something sad about a polity if it could not enact laws to protect the needy neighbor, we cannot as Christians let concerns about legislation distract us from our primary task of living so that the radical welcome we have received and the glory in which we have been clothed manifests itself to the world. Christians, both as individuals and as groups, already do much to help women who are pregnant in difficult circumstances. But more than this is needed. Without ceasing to welcome and value the lives of the unborn, Christians need also to welcome and value the lives of pregnant women. They need to be honest about the pain – sometimes continuing for a lifetime – that women who surrender their children for adoption feel, and not offer adoption as a "simple" solution. They need to reflect more deeply on what it is that makes a pregnant woman's circumstances "difficult," what societal structures and cultural patterns make childbearing a liability.

Perhaps most important is a need for Christians to practice a radical openness that can model for others how a life of "difficult circumstances" can be a life of glory. Christians ought not to minimize the kind of radical demand that pregnancy and motherhood put on women. But Christians, who, like the Samaritan, extend the cruciform touch of baptism, may be able to take some of that demand upon themselves, and in doing so make credible the claim that the life of self-gift, not the life of self-possession, is what it means to have life at all.

References

Anderson, Gary A. (2001) *The Genesis of Perfection: Adam and Eve in Jewish and Christian Imagination* (Louisville, KY: Westminster/John Knox).

von Balthasar, Hans Urs (ed.) (1984) *Origen: Spirit and Fire. A Thematic Anthology of his Writings*, trans. Robert J. Daly (Washington, DC: Catholic University of America Press).

Chauvet, Louis-Marie (2001) *The Sacraments: The Word of God at the Mercy of the Body* (Collegeville, MN: The Liturgical Press).

Harris, John (ed.) (2001) *Bioethics* (Oxford: Oxford University Press).

Manent, Pierre (1998) *The City of Man*, trans. Marc A. LePain (Princeton, NJ: Princeton University Press).

Martin, Dale (1999) *The Corinthian Body* (New Haven, CT: Yale University Press).

Phillips, L. Edward (1996) *The Ritual Kiss in Early Christian Worship* (Cambridge: Grove Books).

Steffen, Lloyd (ed.) (1996) *Abortion: A Reader* (Cleveland, OH: Pilgrim Press).

Stewart-Sykes, Alistair and Newman, Judith H. (2001) *Early Jewish Liturgy: A Sourcebook for Use by Students of Early Christian Liturgy* (Cambridge: Grove Books).

Žižek, Slavoj (2001) *On Belief* (London: Routledge).

CHAPTER 20

Becoming One Body: Health Care and Cloning

M. Therese Lysaught

The right side of a young boy's face stares from the cover of the June 2002 issue of the *Atlantic Monthly*. His large, dark eye arrests and holds the viewer. His expression is somber – innocent yet veiled in sadness. The lighting in the photo draws one's eye to the perfect beauty of his toddler cheek, his tousled hair, his exquisitely youthful features. One cannot help but stare at his face. Even so, words dance in the periphery of one's vision: "Save their son's life." "Desperate." Finally, the reader's eyes are drawn downward to the title of the story that attends this face: "Cloning Trevor."

Trevor's story is poignant and deeply moving. At two years old, he suffers from X-linked adrenoleuko-dystrophy (ALD), a relatively rare genetic disorder that will ravage his young brain and take his life before he reaches his teens. Trevor joins a growing community of other children who play a particular role in the public debate about health care. Time and again, developments in biotechnology present us with an ethical "dilemma." Arguments are made, analyses offered, panels are commissioned. But often, into the rancorous debates, a silent image rises. It is the face of a child, a child like Trevor, sick and perhaps dying.

These faces silence the discussion. Wordlessly, they appeal: permit the research to go forward, allow federal funding, eliminate public oversight. Without argument, they persuade. These images of children function to forestall critique, to displace argument, to garner public support – and public monies – for research at the cutting edge of biotechnology. The challenge they present brings argument to an end.

But why? Why do they bring argument to an end? Or, more precisely, how do they do this? They do so because children have become icons of biotech research. Like religious icons, these images of sick and dying children provide a window to what our culture considers to be transcendent. They transport us – however briefly – to a promised land, shaping our attitudes, dispositions, and actions to comport more closely with this transcendent world. They powerfully distill the fundamental story and practices that shape our culture. This story and its practices are so much a part of who we are, of how we have been shaped to understand the world, that we take them as givens, as self-evident, as true. Immersed in them as we are, it is difficult to find a vantage point from which to critique them, from which to respond. We are silenced.

In the face of such a silencing power, where might Christians regain the power to speak? When, face to face with Trevor, how ought Christians to respond to cloning? Fifteen years from now, Christians may well find themselves faced with this very question: cloning may be offered to them as a successful therapy for their own child, sick or perhaps dying. Where might they begin to discern the way forward?

One answer to this question lies in the decidedly peculiar way that Christians treat their children: they baptize them. What is the significance of baptism for how Christians think about the relationship between their children and health care? What is the significance of baptism for how Christians think about the meaning of even having children? The significance, I will argue in this chapter, lies in the ways in which the practice of baptism challenges the very presumptions that drive the desire for cloning and the subtle rhetorical framework that makes stories like Trevor's so difficult to resist.

Cloning and its Ends

Cloning emerged on the scientific scene in the 1950s. Yet, until recently, it has only sporadically engaged public attention. Gina Kolata (1997) suggests that cloning was used by the early developers of the nascent field of bioethics to draw attention to their field. Important figures like Leon Kass (1967) and Paul Ramsey (1970) were the first to provide a critical moral analysis of human cloning.

Until Ian Wilmut created Dolly the sheep in 1997, however, neither public nor bioethics "experts" took notice. Recent technological developments, therefore, meet a public singularly unprepared to meet the well-orchestrated pro-cloning lobby. Notwithstanding occasional news flashes, no one has yet succeeded in cloning a human being. Yet were human cloning to work, what would it entail?

To clone, researchers remove the nucleus (which contains most of the genes and directions for function) from an oocyte (a woman's reproductive cell). Imagine taking a chicken egg and, without destroying the egg, removing all of the yolk, leaving only the egg white within the shell. Then researchers obtain a cell (say, a skin cell) from the body of an adult. Since it comes from the body it is referred to as a "somatic" cell. The researchers likewise remove the nucleus from this skin cell; they inject or "transfer" that nucleus into the en-nucleated oocyte. This would be like injecting it into the de-yolked chicken egg, only on a much, much smaller scale. The researchers would then stimulate the oocyte with an electrical charge, causing the combined materials from the two different cells to fuse. The oocyte now begins to divide and grow. It becomes an embryo in (almost) the exact genetic likeness of the original somatic cell.

Critics and advocates alike argue their position based on important goods that cloning might violate or promote. Some reject reproductive cloning because it presents a threat to the good of physical or mental flourishing. On simple utilitarian grounds, the National Academy of Sciences, for example, found reproductive cloning to be "unethical at this time." Given how many attempts at cloning fail in order to create mammalian clones and the unknown risks of cloning to the cloned being, they argue that the risks of the procedure outweigh the potential benefits. Were the technical risks of the procedure to diminish, reproductive cloning might then become acceptable.

Others are concerned about the good of being an end-in-oneself. What would it be like, they ask, to know yourself to be an "imitation"? What would it be like to know that you were brought into being in order to replace a dead sibling? Would the clone feel pressured to be "just like" the other? How might parents, even unwittingly, attempt to shape the lives of their cloned children to either replicate their strengths or compensate for their deficiencies?

Further criticisms concern the good of individuality. Each child, they argue, has a right to a unique genetic identity. In many ways, what society values most about each person is their uniqueness. Related to one's parents but distinct from both of them, one's identity is a gift, a mystery that orients the individual toward an open, undetermined future. Beyond being valuable in itself, uniqueness is rooted in biology, in one's very DNA. These critics rightly critique a "person–body" dualism that underlies the practice of cloning, calling to mind the importance of embodiment for personhood.

Yet, at the same time, cloning promises to help people achieve very important goods, goods long considered central to human flourishing. A first of these would be the good of procreation. Many couples or individuals find themselves unable to conceive, or they know that they are at risk of transmitting a serious genetic disease to their child. The spectrum of reproductive technologies promises to overcome these obstacles. Roughly 80 percent of the time, however, reproductive technologies fail. Many couples desire that their child will be biologically linked to at least one of them. Cloning, it is argued, offers many couples their "only hope" as they have exhausted all other means of having "their own" children.

In so doing, cloning provides a way for individuals to maximize the good of freedom. As an infertility treatment, cloning becomes a question of reproductive freedom and autonomous choice. The Human Cloning Foundation argues that to ban cloning would violate the human and constitutional right to reproduce in the manner of one's own choosing, without undue government interference. As long as the adult consents to be cloned, advocates argue that no one is harmed. Moreover, cloning would open an avenue of reproduction to those who are not married but who wish to have a child to nurture, individuals who fear the death of their genome.

For others, cloning promises the good of resurrection. Many of those who have funded cloning research or who have appeared in newspaper stories desperately wish to see human cloning succeed so that they may bring back to life someone who has died. Most often, the stories surround the death of a child. While they acknowledge that the clone would be a different person from the loved one they have lost, the clone's genetic identity with their child promises to resurrect his or her beauty and perfection, to assuage the unfathomable pain that the tragic death of a child brings.

Relatedly, the Human Cloning Foundation and the quasi-religious group the Raelians champion cloning as a route to the good of immortality. As the founder of the Raelians claims:

> Cloning will enable mankind to reach eternal life. The next step, like the Elohim do with their 25,000 years of scientific advance, will be to directly clone an adult person without

having to go through the growth process and to transfer memory and personality in this person. Then, we wake up after death in a brand new body just like after a good night sleep! (Clonaid website: www.clonaid.com)

Others have similarly argued that cloning provides us with a way of becoming "like God" and thereby fully growing into "God's image."

Most "mainstream" commentators have serious reservations about using cloning techniques to reproduce people. Nonetheless, they enthusiastically support cloning as a way to pursue the good of healing. In what is (euphemistically) referred to as "therapeutic" cloning, researchers would clone embryos and grow them just long enough for the embryos to generate a sufficient number of stem cells. These stem cells could be used to grow tissues that could be used therapeutically to treat a wide array of diseases. Cloning, researchers argue, would provide a way to grow stem cells that match the tissue type of the patient, therefore reducing the risk of tissue rejection. Researchers cite a laundry list of conditions such tissues could theoretically be used to treat: from Parkinson's and Alzheimer's, to juvenile diabetes and heart disease, to the tragic frailties of the human body that result in spinal cord injuries. Trevor's story is one that dangles before the readers the unfulfilled promises of "therapeutic" cloning.

Moreover, by potentially offering an unlimited supply of replacement tissues to treat the inevitable physical declines that come with time, stem-cell research and cloning ultimately aim at another good, a different form of immortality, namely, the defeat of aging. Michael West, CEO of Advance Cell Technology, a biotech company at the forefront of human cloning research, captures this piece of the vision remarkably well. West exclaims:

"I don't think what's properly weighed in the balance is the amazing breakthrough that this is. I mean, the idea that you can take a person of any age – a hundred and twenty years old – and take a skin cell from them and give them back their own cells that are young! That's such an incredible gift to mankind! For the US Congress to spend two hours and debate this and say, 'Oh, we'll make this all illegal,' to me is unbelievable. They don't understand." He shook his head. "We've never been able to do anything like this before." (Dunn, 2002: 46)

Following the well-trodden path of many other biotech innovations, cloning promises to be the Holy Grail, that which will perfect human life.

Cloning and its Bio-utopia

West's claims suggest that more is at stake with cloning than simply therapy or reproduction. Indeed, goods, while ends in themselves, also point us to more ultimate ends, namely, what one believes to be transcendent or ultimate. Cloning, one might argue, trades on a powerful set of stories and assumptions that deeply shape our culture. To make sense of cloning requires understanding this story and assumptions.

The central story of this vision is the myth of scientific progress. By "myth," of course, I mean not "untrue" but basic, formative narrative. This story of science is well known. It is one of triumph, of salvation. It is first triumph over nature. Nature, for modern science, is not "creation" with its own inherent value. Rather, it is either raw material to be examined, explored, and exploited for human interests and ends (think of human embryos), or it is chaotic and threatening, a power which likewise must be conquered and harnessed so that it does not threaten human well-being (think of disease). Science is that mode of human agency that harnesses, directs, and domesticates that power. It is that higher power that saves us from the chaotic threat.

That the myth is one of "progress" points to an essential component of the narrative. For scientific and medical progress can only count as progress if measured against a goal toward which it strives. Belying its method, the fundamental conception of science is teleological. The ultimate goal of this progress is nothing less than a promised land (an "eschaton"), or in the words of Joanne Finkelstein (1990), a "bio-utopia."

That there is a relationship between technology, medicine, and the social order will come as no surprise to historians of medicine. Even the most cursory review of the history of eugenics illustrates this. Today, biotechnology and cloning – with their promises to defeat illness, aging, and death – posit a utopia which shapes society's actions now. As in Michael West's vision, in this utopia debilitating diseases and aging will have been effectively eliminated. Each new discovery promises the end to disease as we know it – to be, as mentioned earlier, the Holy Grail. Biotechnology, through technologies of surveillance, elimination, and cure, promises the perfection of human life.

Others have named this eschaton "the peaceable moral community." This community is comprised of "persons." While different criteria are put forward by different philosophers, the most representative might be the position outlined by H. Tristram Engelhardt (1986). Drawing on Kantian moral theory, he maintains that those creatures are persons that are rational, self-conscious, autonomous, and possess a moral sense.

In this utopia, the human community has attained perfect peace. It can do so because it is only comprised of "persons," creatures whose rights must be respected and who have obligations to respect the rights of others. It also comes as close as possible to eliminating illness and disability. For individuals with impairments – the developmentally disabled, elderly people with dementia – clearly do not display certain key characteristics and are therefore deemed "non-persons." As non-persons, they are not bearers of rights and therefore have no rights to be abrogated. As such, they are not members of the moral community; they have no right to its protection. No one is obligated to them. No intrinsic *moral* barriers stand in the way of their being, as Engelhardt notes, "killed painlessly, at whim" (1986: 116).

At the same time, no moral barriers prevent other human non-persons from being used therapeutically in the service of persons. Embryos, clearly, would count as non-persons. Without rights, they cannot be harmed by being used or by being destroyed. Consequently, there is nothing in the realm of morality that protects them from being "killed painlessly, at whim," as they would be in "therapeutic" cloning. They are "things" that can be used as a means to others' ends.

How does one get to the promised land? What will usher in this eschaton? The vehicle for this journey is the practices of the market. In a technologically mediated society, interests, values, and desires are cultivated by those who control technology. Most often, those interests are driven by desire for profit. Once technologies become available, applications must be found. It is the job of the biotech company to cultivate in the general public the desire for the possible outcomes such technologies can achieve. Revenues, it is argued, are necessary to fund research and development which is crucial to the discovery of new cures. Thus, the capitalist character of the new biotechnology becomes justified by appealing to the overarching story. Without the infrastructure of market economics, the promised land will remain just a promise.

A final component of this story is the eclipse or exorcising of religion. A central piece of the myth of scientific progress is not only science's triumph over nature but its triumph over the strictures and primitive irrationality of religion and morality as well. Well known are the stories of saints like Galileo and Vesalius, who persevered in truth against the censure of religion and archaic moral concerns about the treatment of dead bodies.

Science's continuing conflict with religion remains a stock piece in the contemporary narrative. In the debate surrounding human embryonic stem-cell research, it is remarkable how often iconic children are described as "Roman Catholic." A clear subtext in these examples is the claim that entry into this promised land requires one to renounce the authority of any alien traditions. In Trevor's story, the author literally characterizes the Human Cloning Prohibition Act passed by the US House of Representatives in 2001 as "politics and religion . . . trumping science." Religion is equated with "religious fundamentalists." Those who oppose cloning do so only emotively – with "shock, indignation, and horror." No indication is given that they might have reasons or arguments. Here and elsewhere, scientists are portrayed as stock characters – lone, youthful heroes, acting autonomously in conscience against brainwashed bureaucrats, mavericks, innovators. Servants of reason, they bear "the burden of moving scientific research forward."

That Peculiar Practice Called Baptism

In many ways, cloning claims to simply be one technique by which responsible parents care for their children – either by bringing them into being or healing them when disability and death threaten. Might cloning be one way the Church might care for the well-being of children as well? Or does cloning entail a set of presumptions that are fundamentally at odds with who Christians understand themselves to be? To answer these questions, we must first reflect on how Christians care for the well-being of their children generally. This leads us, as mentioned at the outset, to the practice of baptism.

I begin with a story of an admittedly unusual baptism – the baptism of my own twin children. As multiples often do, they arrived eight weeks early. Being born early is not ideal. Babies gestate for nine months for a wide variety of reasons, so when the process short circuits, those of us who are fortunate enough to live in a land wealthy enough to sustain neonatal intensive care units can turn to modern medicine to assist our children through the crisis that prematurity presents. This my husband and I did, grateful for the expert tending of nurses and the highly specialized skills of physicians who nurtured the babies during the month they spent in the hospital.

We did not think twice about tending to their health through medicine. Yet it also seemed right that they should be baptized. This was no deathbed grabbing them into heaven. They needed health care, but they were not dying. Rather, in our joy in welcoming them into the world, we wished to welcome them into the Church. A whole army of people were praying for them, so it seemed fitting that they be baptized into this company of saints who were lifting up their voices on their behalf. We could not take them to Church, but we could bring Church to them.

So they were baptized in the hospital. Our priest arrived at the neonatal nursery late in the afternoon of their second day. The lights in the nursery were low. Monitors beeped, nurses quietly went about their work. He unpacked the familiar baptismal items – his prayer book, a cross, a white cloth, a candle, the oil. In the course of setting up for the sacrament, he asked "and who will be the godparents?" Truth be told, my husband and I had not gotten that far down our list of "things to do before the babies came." In the chaos attending the babies' birth, we had forgotten this crucial step. We were godparent-less.

But God gives us the gifts we need when we need them. One of the nurses volunteered to stand in as godmother. A woman of rapid conversation and non-stop humor, she had already (in their short time there) festooned the babies' beds with pink and blue rosaries and prayer-cards from her children's school. Only God could produce such a godmother on a moment's notice! Our priest volunteered to be the godfather.

With godparents in hand, we proceeded. In the dim light of the neonatal intensive care nursery, fitted with IVs and nasogastric tubes, Mary Margaret and Samuel Alexander were baptized into God's Church and anointed with the oil of gladness. Months later we held a "welcoming mass" for the babies. A rite for this is included among the Roman Catholic rites for baptism. There we celebrated, in proper communal style, their entrance into the Church. It was a festive affair. The nurse-godparent, who has since become our friend, informed us that day that ours was the first baptism that had ever been performed in the intensive care nursery of that particular Adventist hospital. What had seemed so natural to us to do was in fact novel.

As with many true stories, this story of baptism was not quite the ideal. Nonetheless, this particular event points to a radically different set of presuppositions than that required by the practice of cloning; it demonstrates how Christian practices provide practitioners with skills for living differently in the face of tragedy.

Why do Christians baptize babies anyway? Is this not a peculiar thing to do? Many Christians *do* think it is a peculiar thing to do. Certain Christian communities defer baptism until children are older – some wait until they are seven years old, some until they are in their teens, while others believe that consent to baptism requires adult status. Yet infant baptism is an enduring practice. The Church has baptized infants from very early in its history; it remains a central practice of most Christian communities today.

Moreover, Christians are not of one mind on how baptism ought to be performed. Pentecostals and Baptists immerse their candidates; Catholics are often accused of just "sprinkling" theirs. Even within the Roman Catholic Church, the way one baptizes infants differs significantly from the rites for the Christian initiation of adults. I will structure my reflections according to the Catholic rites but will highlight key aspects of baptism that speak to the question of cloning.

Baptism is an especially peculiar thing to do to babies, given what Christians believe happens in the sacrament. Contrary to the way it is often understood, baptism is not simply a naming ceremony, a way to mark and celebrate the birth of a child. In fact, in baptism, the joy and miracle of birth is relativized. For Christians, as the trenchant patristic theologian Tertullian noted, "are made, not born."

How is it that baptism might "make Christians"? For the Church, the first step is to become "children" of God. Christians do not understand this claim as mere metaphor. The Church believes that those who are baptized – whether babies or adults – literally become part of the Body of Christ, the Body of God's Son. Becoming part of God's Son, they become God's children. Certainly in our own case, we baptized our children in the hospital in part because we wished to share with God our joy in their presence; knowing how deeply God had gifted us, we wished to share with God our greatest treasure. We wanted these children to be God's children too.

Through the sacrament, one's identity as children of God becomes primary, taking precedence over any other identity; for example, a member of a particular family, children of particular parents, citizens of a particular country, and so on (Galatians 3: 27–9). Whether adult or infant, baptism renders Christian identity fundamental.

Christians understand that being "incorporated into Christ's body" means not just entering into the life, death, and resurrection of Jesus. It means entering into Christ's body, the Church. The Body of Christ (that is, the Church) is the People of God. Thus, to be incorporated into Christ's Body is to be incorporated into God's People – it is to become one of them. In baptism, the People of God welcome into their midst yet another one of their company. As mentioned earlier, we desired baptism for our children to connect them more concretely to God's people, especially those we knew who were praying for them and lighting candles. Though physically separated from the community by the isolation of neonatal intensive care, the sacrament brought the community to the children. In it, they entered a larger company than that of simply their nurses and frazzled parents.

Children, of course, need parents. Here, however, the Church turns not to one's biological parents. Rather, it fosters a far more radical practice – it designates godparents. Godparents are required both for infant baptism as well as for baptizing adults. For, through baptism, adult converts become not only children of God but "baby Christians" (1 Corinthians 3: 1; 1 Peter 2: 2). For infants and adults alike, godparents accept the new child of God as their own, with the sobering yet joyful responsibility of raising them in the life of faith.

That the Church designates some of its members to be godparents also conveys certain anthropological claims. Some theologies of baptism stress the importance of personal conversion, personal acceptance of the fundamentals of the Christian faith, a demonstrated change in lifestyle before initiating a person into the Christian community. Because children cannot voluntarily consent to the faith, some Christian churches reject the practice of infant baptism. (Nevertheless, most of these communities "dedicate" their babies to the Lord. Such a practice is quite analogous to infant baptism – an act by which the community welcomes the child into the community, recognizing it as a child of the community rather than as property of the parents.)

Nonetheless, most Christian communities still baptize their children, even though they cannot speak for themselves. Instead, the parents and godparents speak for them. In the rite, they request baptism for the child. They commit the child to the path of discipleship. The child is anointed, marked with the sign of the cross, and baptized in the name of Father, Son, and Spirit. In practicing baptism in this way, the Church reminds us that particular characteristics – like autonomy and rationality – are unimportant for what it means to be a child of God. The Church reminds us that it is not we who choose God but we who are chosen by God (Galatians 4: 9). Faith is not a choice – it is a gift. Identity resides not in the ability to choose. It resides in the fact that before we are able to choose we are chosen. It reminds us that the Church is not simply one more voluntary association; it is rather a community that particularly welcomes into its midst those who are vulnerable, marginalized, those who cannot speak for themselves, those often whose ability to freely exercise their will is compromised.

Beyond the parents and godparents, baptism is a celebration of the community. Certainly, in the past, baptisms were often conducted quietly and "privately" in the back of the church. Still, today, it is not uncommon to attend a baptism which is an afternoon affair, attended only by family and friends. But baptism is a celebration – the welcoming of a new member! As the People of God in baptism welcome a new member into the Body of Christ, the People of God need to be there to do the welcoming! The congregation welcomes the new member, witnesses their initiation, prays for them and with them, and pledges to teach the child the ways of discipleship, how to live into Christ's likeness.

As such, baptism is not just "one more thing" inserted between the homily and the offertory. It reshapes the entirety of the service, changing the choreography, recasting the prayers, readings, and homily into baptismal mode. In the liturgy of the Word, the community encounters the Word of God. In the Scripture readings, the congregation hears of God's acts among his people. In the Gospel reading, the community encounters the Word of God himself, Jesus Christ. The readings proclaim for the community and the initiate the fundamental story and truths that shape Christian lives.

Importantly, the baptismal rite itself is not the end of the story. The rite points forward to the liturgy of the Eucharist, where those present encounter the Word of God in the elements of bread and wine, in the celebration of the paschal mystery of Christ's death and resurrection. And point here it must, for the paschal mystery is the full meaning of the immersion into the baptismal waters. For to be incorporated into Christ – literally, to become part of Christ's body – means to enter into Christ's life. For Paul, that means to enter into his death (Romans 6: 4–5). Nowhere do Christians more powerfully enter into Christ's death than when the Church celebrates the paschal mystery at the Easter vigil and the Sunday liturgy, and thus it is here that baptism ideally occurs.

Being buried with Christ in baptism gives the Church hope that it will be united with Christ in the resurrection. This side of the eschaton, however, this necessarily remains a hope. And so the first virtue newly baptized members embark on upon entering the Christian life is the virtue of hope.

Baptism: The End of Cloning

Those, then, who mean what they do when they baptize their children must find cloning deeply incongruous. Not only does baptism radically challenge the narrative of parenting that drives some couples to see reproductive cloning as unobjectionable, it also locates the goods of healing at which cloning aims in a very different narrative and vision of the transcendent, thereby giving Christians an alternative way of pursuing those same goods.

Baptism complicates the narrative of parenting that so greatly privileges biological relationship. It reminds us that the most important thing about our children is that they are not our own. Shortly after they are born into the world, amidst awe and joy, Christians bring their children to baptism and turn them over to others. First, we turn them over to God. "Procreation," one must remember, is not "reproduction." Etymologically "procreation" means "creation for," which means first of all creation for God. In baptism, Christians give up their claim to "ownership" and give their children to God.

At the same time, we turn them over to other Christians. The practice of godparenting further distances the claims of biological parents *vis-à-vis* their children. "Natural" parents invite others to become co-parents with them, admitting that they alone are not sufficient for the most important task in this child's life, the task of rearing the child in the faith of the Church.

Godparents likewise accept spiritual responsibility for a child often biologically unrelated. So seriously did the medieval Church take the role of godparenting that, as Joseph Lynch (1986) notes, natural parents were often excluded from the baptismal ceremony. Godparenting established networks of spiritual kinship that united families in bonds more sacred than ordinary kinship. The child–godparent relationship was often perceived as close enough to prevent marriage between members of the two families.

Our own story is a case in point. Our children's godparents were not chosen for some honorary reason or family ties. Our children's godmother was a stranger to us. Yet, at the same time, she was not – she was a member of our community, the Body of Christ. Deeply formed as a member of the Church, when called, she did not blink. She simply responded, as a member of God's people, to parent these two small children in the life of faith.

Thus, in baptism, Christians become people who know spiritual kinship to be more fundamental than biological kinship. Baptism grants us a greater range of procreative freedom insofar as it frees us to be related to others beyond the constraints of biology. In becoming brothers and sisters to each other, "members of Christ and severally of each other" (Romans 12: 5), Christians become parents to the community's children, both those who are welcomed as infants and those adult converts welcomed as "baby Christians."

Cloning, from this perspective, then represents not simply one more technique that promotes reproductive freedom. Rather, it represents a form of bondage to a narrow notion of relationship. It is not unimportant that stories of parents and individuals who wish to pursue cloning as a form of reproduction are often described as "desperate."

For this reveals, though unintentionally, how deeply our culture constrains our imaginations. When something that is a good leads us to desperation rather than freedom, then it has become for us an idol.

Indeed, many of the arguments both for and against cloning are predicated upon idolatrous claims. They seem persuasive to us insofar as they invoke real goods as their justification. But even good ends can become vices. As Stanley Hauerwas and Joel Shuman note, "We cannot then speak of the body's goods – including the physical health of any one individual body – apart from its Good; for to do so is to attenuate the body's health, which cannot be properly considered apart from its relationship with other bodies" (Hauerwas and Shuman, 1997: 64). Echoing Augustine, Hauerwas and Shuman remind us that the goods of procreation and freedom, as well as others, must be ordered rightly.

At the same time, baptism challenges traditional anthropological claims. On the one hand, it reminds us that identity is not first and foremost about individuality and uniqueness. In baptism, one's individuality becomes subsumed into a greater identity, as the baptized are made members of a Body. Christian identity is determined not by a unique genome; Christian identity is determined by him whose body we become a part of. Identity, then, is located beyond the self, not within. Nor is identity and value assigned on the basis of philosophically derived attributes. Autonomy, rationality, and the ability to choose are irrelevant for inclusion into the community of God's people. In baptism, children are reborn as children of God before they have the ability to "choose" this for themselves.

Finally, infant baptism reminds us that our identity as members of Christ's body is not simply an intrinsic possession obtained by ontological fiat; it is an identity one must grow into. Made Christians in baptism, children then must learn what it means to be in the likeness of Christ. Christians believe that their task is to become, in the words of Thomas à Kempis, "imitations of Christ." For Christians, then, the issues of imitation raised by cloning are not so deeply troubling. What directs our lives is not a sort of fate trapped in our DNA. Rather what directs our lives is he who Christians follow, he whose life Christians imitate.

Many Christians may readily see how reproductive cloning fails to fit with lives shaped by the practice of baptism. Yet therapeutic cloning may seem harder to resist. Might not cloning represent an important way by which Christians care for the well-being of our children? Certainly, to watch a child suffer a devastating and eventually fatal disease brings grief unmatched to that child's parents and community. Healing is certainly to be desired and ardently prayed for. Christians rightly celebrate healing as an in-breaking of redemption. It is a concrete instance of God's work in the world and a promise of the fullness of redemption that we await with fervent hope. That healing is part of God's work is captured in Jesus's injunction to his disciples. As he sent them out, to witness to the Good News he made clear that healing is central to discipleship: "Into whatever city you go, after they welcome you, eat what they set before you, and cure the sick there. Say to them, 'The reign of God is at hand'" (Luke 10: 9). The cure of the sick is one of the wondrous signs that God reigns over the powers of this world. A central element of Jesus's own life among us, healing remains a fundamental commitment for the Body of Christ in the world.

Yet for Christian communities, healing cannot be an end in itself, pursued at all costs. While dearly valuing the skills and technology of medicine, Christian pursuit of healing must proclaim God's reign. If it does not, then the goods of technology, healing, and life have become idols.

In the case of cloning, they have. Cloning is a practice that seeks not the reign of God but the in-breaking of a different eschaton, a bio-utopia. It proclaims not the reign of God but the triumph of science. It seeks to incarnate in the world a bio-utopia, a vision of the future that parodies Christian eschatology, promising a world without illness and death but also without God. And like all false gods, it requires sacrifice – in this case the sacrifice of life to preserve life. Ironically, the life sacrificed is the life (in cloned form) of the very person to be "saved."

Spirits are also known by their fruits. One dominant motif of the bio-utopic narrative is that of desperation. Parents are repeatedly configured as desperate for some way to save their children's lives; technology is their last and only hope. Beyond technology, there is nothing. This hopelessness stems from the fact that as much as science proclaims a vision of a world without illness and death, that vision will not come true in our lifetimes. The bio-utopic vision is not a promise for people living now – it is for future generations. Thus, should disease imperil us, all that biotechnology can promise is to try to save our biological life. In a world that no longer acknowledges God, hope is restricted to physical healing. Trevor's death, therefore, can be only a tragedy.

For Christians to enmesh their children in forms of idolatry that engender the vice of desperation hardly seems to be a form of care. Furthermore, the practice of baptism helps train parents to resist the tyranny of these idols and seeks to foster contravening virtues. Baptism first provides a way of resisting this idolatry by acknowledging the reality and inevitability of death. Not only in baptism do Christians give their children over to God and other parents. Centered on the paschal mystery, they give their newborn children over to death. Children become members of Christ's Body not by being born into his incarnation but by being baptized into his death (Romans 6: 3–4). In baptism, newborn children die with Christ. In baptism, parents rehearse or practice separation, loss, the giving over of our deeply cherished children.

This, of course, is no easy task. Christian parents can only do this insofar as they are formed by a fundamentally different narrative than that of the myth of scientific progress. Christians know themselves to be located in a history that tells not the story of the triumph of science over nature, authority, and religion. Rather, the Christian narrative is the story of God's constant presence and care, ultimately triumphing over the powers of sin and death. In believing that Christ has truly risen from the dead, Christians have hope that their children's death will not be the end for them. Baptized into Christ's death, with him they will rise. Death will never be the final word. As Augustine counsels, "life is changed, not ended."

This is the end to which healing points. Any attempt to heal our bodies this side of eternity must be read in light of the redemption that is to come. But, clearly, the fullness of redemption is to come. This side of eternity, the pain felt upon the death of one dearly loved reminds us that the Christ followed is Christ crucified, the one who emptied himself for our sakes, and who exercised the greatest power – the triumph over sin and death – through becoming weakest.

Located within the practice of baptism, then, Trevor's story would read differently. Baptism would remind us that, for Christians, death, though very real and painful, does not have the last word. As such, it ought not necessarily silence us. Instead, baptism frees us from the power illness and death threaten to exert over our lives, a power that would drive us to cloning as a way of avoiding the death of our loved ones or of our genes.

Practiced well, baptism helps to shape Christians into people who know their lives to be oriented toward a different transcendent, a land different from that promised by biotechnology. By incorporating us into the Body of Christ, baptism requires that Christians understand their relationship with their children (and others!) in a way radically different from that championed in our culture. Practicing baptism faithfully is one exercise through which Christians gain virtues necessary for resisting the ways in which culture would shape us. The story that Christians learn through baptism provides a language by which to redescribe what is taken to be true or given. In these ways, baptism provides a framework for helping Christians to critique what is at issue behind the question of cloning and its place within the life of the Body of Christ. More importantly, baptism enables Christians to resist the silencing that attends the shaping of public discourse.

References

Dunn, Kyla (2002) "Cloning Trevor," *Atlantic Monthly*, June: 31–52.

Engelhardt, H. Tristram (1986) *Foundations of Bioethics* (New York: Oxford University Press).

Finkelstein, Joanne (1990) "Biomedicine and Technocratic Power," *Hastings Center Report*, July/August: 14–16.

Hauerwas, Stanley and Shuman, Joel (1997) "Cloning the Human Body," in *Human Cloning: Religious Responses*, ed. Ron Cole-Turner, pp. 58–65 (Louisville, KY: Westminster/John Knox).

International Commission on English in the Liturgy (1970) *Rite of Baptism for Children* (English translation) (New York: Catholic Book Publishing).

Kass, Leon (1967) "Letters to the Editor," *The Washington Post*, November 3: A20.

Kolata, Gina (1997) *Clone: The Road to Dolly and the Path Ahead* (New York: Morrow).

Lynch, Joseph H. (1986) *Godparents and Kinship in Early Medieval Europe* (Princeton, NJ: Princeton University Press).

Ramsey, Paul (1970) *Fabricated Man: The Ethics of Genetic Control* (New Haven, CT: Yale University Press).

Searle, Mark (1980) *Christening: The Making of a Christian* (Collegeville, MN: The Liturgical Press).

CHAPTER 21

Becoming One Flesh: Marriage, Remarriage, and Sex

David Matzko McCarthy

Predominant forms of social and economic exchange have shaped modern practices of marriage and family. Divorce, for instance, has become a complementary institution to marriage, but the impermanence of modern love and utilitarian commitments is only a symptom of a more fundamental problem. Concerned citizens, economists, and politicians from the right and left praise the interpersonal goods of marriage and the social benefits of a strong family. They speak with earnest and depth of feeling about unconditional love and about the good life that is attained through the intimacy of the I and Thou. On a typical wedding day, a glowing bride and groom will be embraced and congratulated on the auspicious beginning of their new family. Invariably, they will greet this new beginning and its well-wishers with joy, even though they and everyone gathered understands that this starry-eyed couple, if they are in fact starting a new family, is being left alone on hard and unforgiving terrain. Only the strong or lucky will survive.

This reality of the wedding day should worry us, not simply because the promises of marriage are likely to die of exposure, but also, and more worrisome, because the tasks and ends we set before a married couple are misguided challenges for the Church. If only the lucky and strong survive, enduring marriages will surely be with us, but not necessarily because we share life in Christ. In our day, successful marriages must be whole and self-sustained in interpersonal and economic terms. For this reason, we hope for strength, grace, passion, and good luck on every wedding day. By and large, a person hopes to marry someone extraordinary and unique, and it is an embarrassment to settle for someone who would be merely a good husband or wife. However, good company among husbands and wives, not passion or a couple's self-reliance, is at the center of Christian practices of marriage. When we, who gather in God's name, are able to sustain mediocre and fragile marriages through misfortune, we will know that we are living as the people that God has gathered as the Body of Christ. This is the calling of marriage in the Church: when two are bound together, they are more deeply bound in the household of God.

The central claim of this chapter is that Christian practices of marriage make sense only when the Church understands itself and lives as a social body – as a polity of God's good news. The wedding day does not mark the beginning of a new family; indeed, it is a consequence and outgrowth of a kinship and community of faith. Christian marriage is not a whole communion of two, but a particular kind of grace-filled friendship within the fellowship of the Church. This claim will be spelled out in the second and third sections of the chapter in relation to practices of discipleship, baptism, and Eucharist. The first section will set the context, by way of contrast, through a discussion of marriage in contemporary social life. I will conclude with a proposal about sex and embodiment in marriage.

The Tie that Unwinds

In his *Spheres of Justice*, Michael Walzer characterizes marriage as a contractual agreement that binds its partners in love, in order to secure access for each to a reliable source of love (1983: 227–42). Marriage (along with family) constrains and administers affection and preferential regard. It is an agreement that is patterned after the logic of the social contract, but in the emotional sphere. In Walzer's view, marriage stabilizes and maintains a fair exchange of affection, for the mutual self-interest of the partners in a chaotic and competitive market of love. Walzer's theory is not cynical. He proposes that love is a precious human asset and essential good. He knows that kinship and affection cannot be sectioned off entirely from social life. He is aware that familial connections will impinge upon a society's distribution of wealth and power. Yet, as a modern political philosopher, he recognizes that marriage and family have no legitimate role in the political and economic spheres. His strategy is to limit the social purview of kinship, and in the process, defend marriage and family as the appropriate sphere of affection and preferential care.

According to Walzer, the role of family must be limited because it reproduces social, political, and economic injustice. Progeny of the rich inherit wealth and influence. They attend exclusive schools, and they are trained with the advantages of power. The poor, on the other hand, reproduce habits of poverty. For this reason, Walzer holds that the distributive aims of democratic life must continually work against family, through, for example, taxation and public schools. Like Plato's guardians, all of us, as members of a democratic state, must disabuse ourselves of the influence of family. Unlike the guardians, however, each of us must enter social life as an individual, not with disinterest, but with our own individual interests.

More conservative defenders of the family agree. Unlike Walzer, they merely hold to the Enlightenment view of the family as a natural domain outside the social contract. Differences, which Walzer thinks arbitrarily based on family relations, are believed to be natural to the individual, who is free from the constraints of family when he (the Enlightenment philosopher's he) enters public life.

Likewise, the history of modern marriage and family is a process of detachment. Edward Shorter, in *The Making of the Modern Family* (1975), offers a suggestive description of the modern family as a free-floating twosome. The description highlights two important elements. First, family is now free from ancient and medieval controls of the household economy, social and political alliances, and one's station in the social order, tradition and intergenerational relationships. Second, family is joined instead to the relationship of two individuals. A couple makes a family. As a twosome, the free-floating family is not entirely free, but moored to the utility of interpersonal love. In this regard, Walzer notes that marriage and family are a source not only of political and economic inequity, but of emotional inequities as well.

Interpersonal love is a precious commodity, which is distributed unevenly and haphazardly when open to the liberty of individuals. Love is a valuable resource, particularly insofar as interpersonal exchange has become the basic means of forming necessary attachments in an otherwise disinterested economic and social world. "Love as passion" is the mechanism for disenchanted moderns and postmoderns to form what Niklas Luhmann calls a close (as opposed to impersonal and unpredictable) world. This form of love is new to our age; it is grounded in a desire for intimacy itself, not on any external aim or conception of the good (Luhmann, 1986: 129–54). In other words, the process of detachment from family, economy, and social station is essential to contemporary conceptions of love. The goal of a loving relationship is to have a relationship founded only on the interpersonal coupling of freely chosen partners.

In this context, modern intimacy is essentially romantic; that is, its purpose is set over against the actual world of social and economic exchange. Spontaneity and novelty are thought to be love's true nature, over against work and routine. Popular conceptions of love and marriage fit with modern conceptions of social life as a whole. They are structured according to a Humean relationship between sentiment and social institution, between natural feeling and the social contract (Hume, 1965). As a sentiment, love springs from us without reason, and because prior to reason, it is the reason (impetus and force) for the contract or covenant of marriage. Love binds us together, and marriage, like any reasonable institution, protects the interests and desires of those who bind themselves to it. The reason for marriage is its usefulness for the individual members of the contract, and, without the balance of interests and desires, the rationale for marriage is arbitrary and oppressive.

The unassailable ground of love-as-passion is free choice (rather than the good). It is a procedural instrument. Walzer calls freedom the distributive principle of love, and he points out that the paradigmatic mechanism for the circulation and allocation of love (and therefore for courtship in the West) is the date. He notes an historical progression of mechanisms for finding a partner, from the arranged marriage – the class-conscious cotillion, public promenade, and a visit to the family parlor – to the date. On a date, individuals are not restrained by the influence of family, community, or marriage as an end. In the private sphere of the date, men and women are free to negotiate investment and return. "Love, affection, friendship, generosity, solicitude, and respect [as well as the meanings of commitment and sex] are not only initially but also continuously, at every point in time, matters of individual choice" (Walzer, 1983: 238).

On the date, the couple wants to be left alone, free from outside intrusion. This is the landscape where their love is cultivated and where they are joined as one. Freedom from social and economic constraints is required to be sure that love is founded on nothing but interpersonal intimacy. For this reason, many sincere and well-intentioned couples are dumbfounded when they discover that priests and ministers do not conceive of the wedding ceremony as a service to them. Many desire to be married in the Church, but they find that clergy are surprisingly unwilling to negotiate terms. Clergy seem to want to impose a one-size-fits-all ritual, when spontaneity and liberty are the logic of love. Some engaged couples are able to see that they are not entering their own private marriage, but are taking on a way of life in the community of faith. Other couples resist to the end. They will surely conclude that their pastor is much less Christian than the caterer, who certainly would have allowed the couple to write their own vows. For them, the marital commitment continues to be a form of market exchange.

In Walzer's view, the promises and vows of marriage bring an end to the constant bargaining and vulnerability of the market. Sooner or later, a "love life" of interminable "relationship" after "relationship" becomes simply too exhausting to maintain, even though the private bond of lovers remains the interpersonal ideal. Marriage is likely to be conceived as a good deal, not in a cynical sense of "this is the best I can do," but in a romantic sense of "this one is perfect for me . . . We will always be lovers." At this stage, settling down in marriage or living together is a welcomed restraint. Here, as Walzer points out, there is a dramatic shift from a market framework (the date) to the language of unconditional love. Unconditional love must be the logic of marriage, if it is going to be sustained as a viable alternative to the date, the affair, and love as a commodity. However, if freedom is the distributive principle of love, then the constraints of the unconditional relationship are likely to become intolerable, and the very form of marriage, as a binding in love, is always a threat to love itself.

If Walzer's analysis is correct, the threat of binding and constraining love is at least one reason why living together has become a prominent option in liberal societies. Without the formal bond, a couple hopes to dodge the hazards (or the shock) of marriage. For decades, living together has been conceived, both popularly and among sociologists, as an opportunity for a trial marriage. According to this logic, those who "live together" will be better suited to make formal marital vows. However, recent evidence suggests the contrary, and we should expect the contrary if cohabitation is an attempt to avoid marriage and maintain the formative experiences of romance and dating. Those who live together "are as likely to return to singleness as to enter marriage," and cohabiters who do marry are more likely to divorce than those who enter marriage from a single state (Thatcher, 2002: 7, 23–4). Those who cohabit while raising children are more likely to separate, and one study claims that cohabiting couples, on average, report a lower quality of interpersonal relationship, judged on criteria of "disagreement, fairness, happiness, conflict management and interaction" (Brown and Booth, 1996: 673, cited in Thatcher, 2002: 15).

Ironically, the dominant forms of social and economic exchange that make the ideal of interpersonal marriage (or living together) prominent also make its success unlikely. The modern social contract and market capitalism, as they are based on self-interest and consumption, do not cultivate the attitudes and skills necessary for sustaining common life. Marriage is thought to be useful for the pursuit of interests determined by the individual members. Typically, pastors who prepare couples for marriage confront a twofold set of problems. Young men and women who are immature in their faith also lack skills of interpersonal communication. They have great difficulty grasping what it might mean to make a public commitment of marriage as part of a community of faith, and they have a superficial relationship and risk very little self-revelation. Few couples have dared to broach discussions about what each expects of married life.

Those deeply imbued in a culture of market consumption have to be trained, not only about their faith and marriage, but also about how to raise important questions about shared life, how to introduce disagreements and deal with conflict, and even how to approach the subject of sex. A twenty-six year old man and woman might be sexually active, but each has little sense of what the other partner thinks or feels about their own sexual relationship. Most congregations and parishes have marriage preparation programs that attempt to impart an understanding of discipleship, worship, prayer, and marriage as vocation in the Church, but the programs also must introduce questions about finances, housework, career, domestic abuse, and expectations of lifestyle and family size (Office of Family Life, 1997). Marriage preparation courses do good work as they attempt to initiate the process of sustaining a household and a couple's friendship (Markey et al., 1985). This is an appropriate task for the Church, but it also shows the profound failure of modern courtship, "love as passion," and Walzer's attempt to create a sphere of love through our dominant social and economic languages of interests and utilitarian exchange. Inevitably, the useful marriage will be of little use.

The Tie that Binds

Interpersonal intimacy is not the foundation and purpose of marriage. Although communion between husband and wife is considered the center of marriage by the mainstream in contemporary theology and Church life, this focus is a well-meaning mistake. It is well meaning because self-giving, in imitation of Christ, is the Church's contrast to marriages of utility. In view of this contrast, highlighting a couple's whole, self-sustained, and romantic communion is thought to be a great historical advance and the solution to enduring problems of marriage (Hill, 1996). But this solution is usually based on the misjudgment that the interpersonal "I and Thou" *is* the center, rather than simply *at* the center of marriage. The practices of common life in the Church and the virtues of discipleship are the foundation and purpose of marriage, which then form a fertile place for the cultivation of interpersonal intimacy. Intimacy is *at* the center in the way that fish thrive in the environment provided by a reservoir, which is fed by a flowing stream and has the purpose of supplying a community with water. Likewise, interpersonal communion is likely to flourish in Christian marriage, but it is not the linchpin.

The virtues and practices of a good marriage are not specific to it. The ancient and medieval priority of virginity over marriage has been almost universally rejected (even by those who take vows of celibacy). However, the early tradition of the Church is correct insofar as it does not consider marriage necessary for a whole, contented, and complete Christian life. If the ancient emphasis on virginity is too severe, then the recent idea that husband and wife complete each other is misplaced rigor at the other extreme. Either by the luck of a good match or through Herculean "relationship skills" a couple might experience wholeness in their exclusive "I and Thou," but such a relationship is not an interesting task for the Church, nor is it the promise of grace. Marriage is a particular kind of relationship within the purview of our baptism and in the company of the Church.

Marriage and family constitute a set of practices that Christians, at first glance, seem to share with their neighbors and fellow citizens in various secular communities. For this reason, family has become a particularly important point of contact for the Church's witness and efforts for social reform (McGinnis and McGinnis, 1990). Family in the Church is understood to be a counter-polity and a key site for the cultivation of common life, over against the dominant polity of individualism and utilitarian self-interest. With this stress on the social character of marriage and family comes the clear awareness that wider culture cannot support the polity of family, and that preparation or suitability for marriage requires the full measure of Christian catechesis and training in the practices of discipleship. Preparation for marriage is not just a matter of instruction on the particular duties of the spouse and parent, but more importantly formation in the practices of the Christian life (John Paul II, 1981).

According to the Pontifical Council for the Family, preparation for marriage begins with baptism and is carried on in the parish and other forms of Christian association where "living together as a community is learned" (1996: no. 29). In other words, the basic practices that make for a good marriage are the same for clergy, single people, and cloistered contemplatives. Prior to conceptions of love between husband and wife, God's love is already the center of the Christian life (1996: no. 25), and to speak of marriage in terms of Christ's love for the Church is meaningless apart from the gathering of a people who worship. It is in worship where we learn the gestures of God's love and are called to God's way of reconciliation and peace in a world of violence and estrangement. We are being prepared for marriage when we begin to learn the habits of communion, and when we begin to "acquire a critical ability with regard to [our] surroundings and the Christian courage of those who know how to be in the world without belonging to it" (1996: no. 27).

Marriage, in the New Testament, provides a context for witness to life in Christ. It is not merely an interpersonal endeavor. In fact, the Gospels, and the letters of Paul, have little to say about the relationship between husband and wife except that men and women are bound to stay united if married and advised to stay single if they have been given such a gift (Matthew 19: 1–12; 1 Corinthians 7: 1–15). The main concern is not marriage *per se*, but discipleship. Elsewhere in the New Testament, instructions are given on the duties of household members to one another (Ephesians 5: 21 – 6: 9; Colossians 3: 18 – 4: 1; 1 Peter 2: 18 – 3: 7). Ephesians 5: 21–33 is commonly interpreted as a celebration of mutual love between husband and wife, when, in fact, the marital framework that is assumed is typical of the ancient world. It is asymmetric, hierarchical, and nothing like what Walzer might call an egalitarian distribution of love. Instead, husbands are called to love their wives (as inferiors), and wives to respect their husbands (as superiors). The symmetry of Ephesians 5 is not interpersonal love, but a mutual subordination for the purpose of fostering holiness, which in turn serves as a witness to Christ (cf. 1 Peter 3: 1–7). This imitation of Christ (not the hierarchical ordering of the ancient household) is the key purpose of marriage.

The witness of common life, for example, is the underlying theme in Matthew 5: 31–2, where Jesus denies the legitimacy of divorce except in cases where the marriage is already illicit or broken (Hays, 1996: 352–7). Jesus's Sermon on the Mount in Matthew 5–7 is not a program for the good marriage, but a way of life for disciples (and Israel as a whole) who are called to be the salt of the earth and light of the world (Matthew 5: 13–16). However, the character of a good marriage is obvious in the outline for discipleship. Reconcile with your brother or sister (husband or wife) before you lay your gifts on the altar (5: 23–4). Settle your disputes. Do not look with lust at a woman (5: 27–30). Here, it should be noted that "looking with lust" is not an internal state but a public act (and in our world a thriving industry) that, like adultery, divides rather than unites. Discipline your eyes. Discipline your words, and be bound to them. "Let your 'Yes' mean 'Yes', and your 'No' mean 'No'" (5: 37). We should add: be faithful with ordinary words in ordinary matters of family and home. Do not retaliate against wrongs done (5: 38–41), but go beyond your duty to serve others. Love your enemies (5: 43–8) and show hospitality to your adversaries (especially when you share a bed).

In the middle of these disciplines of Matthew 5 stands the teaching on divorce (5: 31–2). The disciplines are a program of reconciliation. They are not a private or personal code, but a way for gathering and sustaining a people who witness to God's way. The interpersonal skills of Christian marriage are carried by these practices of discipleship. Other practices should be added as well, such as sharing material resources, table fellowship, mutual correction, forgiveness (Matthew 18: 15–35), and the works of mercy (Matthew 25: 31–46). We should not forget that Matthew's Gospel is deeply concerned with the gestures of prayer (6: 1–18) and conceives of the kingdom, not as a wedding or marriage, but as the wedding feast (9: 15; 22: 1–14). The wedding is the occasion for the gracious hospitality of the host and the gathering of uninvited guests. These are the ties that bind.

One Bread, One Body

In the Catholic Church, the sacrament of marriage is set within the sacrament of the Eucharist, "which above all is the source of love and lifts us up into communion with our Lord and with one another" (International Commission on the English Liturgy, 1990: 721). God's offer of grace transforms our love. In modern times, a man and woman go to the altar with profound love and passion. The two desire steadfast union and feel the great joy of self-giving love. Their promises of fidelity, enduring love, and mutual care express the fullness of their desires to love each other as we are loved by God – free, gracious, constant, and unwavering. We are willing to love each other in the delight and richness of our lives, and through the struggles of our material and spiritual poverty. Our human loves are deep and rich in expectations, but they are fragile as well. We Christians profess our marriage vows before God and the Church in the hope that our promises will be made complete. In faith, we hope that our loves will be lifted up and fulfilled through God's grace and God's love as it radiates through our lives and the whole life of the Church.

In a life of faithfulness, our deep feelings of love can be transformed by the friend-ship of God. When we announce our intentions for marriage and take our vows before the Church, we are able to celebrate and to see the great wonder of married life. This very celebration is a witness of faith. This great joy is ours because we are not alone; we are part of a people, a body, and a counter-society that sets itself to the task of living in light of God's self-giving love. In this regard, it is important to live out the union of marriage within the habits of the Eucharist and the continuing life of the Church. The promises of self-giving love are not our private possessions, but shared in the worship and works of the Church.

When a couple is disengaged from the habits of communion and thanksgiving, the meaning of the sacrament of marriage is set on edge. It is hard to be married without also participating in the common life of the faithful. This statement is a counter-cultural claim. In the United States, many couples, who have been baptized, seek to be wed in churches (as well as have their babies baptized) through a ritual that they con-sider independent of day-to-day life in the Church. They make sense of a church wedding, it seems, with a notion of "spirituality" that is indistinct and shallow enough to be attached and detached from life in the community of faith. However, apart from the life of the Church, from the gathering of the faithful and from baptism and Eucharist, the rite of marriage will be disjointed. Although a couple's intentions may be genuine, they are not likely to acknowledge the sacrament in its fullness as a gift of God's grace.

A thin, but popular spirituality fits with a free-floating romantic ideal. If true love is spontaneous and wells from within, if it is free over against the routines of everyday life, if a couple expects an exotic honeymoon to provide the ideal and ultimate expres-sion of their love, the fact that they do not make a habit of church attendance makes their wedding in a church all the more extraordinary, remarkable, and "meaningful." When they plan their wedding, they are likely to need all the imagined accoutrements of tradition: colorful vestments, flowing veil, morning coats, and perhaps a horse-drawn carriage. All these will make perfect sense, while the words of Scripture and the eucharistic prayer will present annoying but tolerable puzzles. Some couples might experience more discomfort than this, but the general notion that a wedding ceremony is a whole unto itself will overcome uneasiness with the ritual or guilt about not wor-shiping regularly.

Solutions to contemporary problems of marriage in the Church are not easy to put into practice. Pope John Paul II, in accordance with the 1983 Code of Canon Law, holds that the sacrament of marriage is available to non-believing but baptized persons when they acknowledge and agree to the Church's intention for their marriage, that is, when they accept its indissolubility, fidelity, and place as a witness to God's steadfast love (John Paul II, 1981: 68; Heaney-Hunter, 1996: 110–12). Although the Pope's position might be seen as a surprising or disturbing concession, his astounding evangelical claim is that the sacraments of the Church do indeed bestow grace regardless of the sub-jectivity of the recipient.

The worship and thanksgiving of the Church is a real source of grace and the true ground of marriage. Believer's baptism has become the theological paradigm for enter-ing the Catholic Church and is the model for the Rite of Christian Initiation for Adults

(RCIA). However, infant baptism takes the lead, theologically and in practice, for a variety of reasons. Infant baptism makes clear that our relation to God and our active faith are always gifts. It makes clear that we do not make ourselves or will ourselves to have faith. Infant baptism makes clear that the presence of God in the world is mediated through the gathering of a people, who worship him and are called to be holy as God is holy.

In this way, baptism – the received grace communicated clearly in infant baptism – is the basis of the sacrament of marriage (as the Eucharist is the tie that binds). Those who have been baptized have been adopted as sons and daughters of God. Grace is given, and we need only respond. As baptized, we are no longer strangers. Even when we sojourn in a far off land, we are always still members of God's house. We do not need to find God; we need only turn our face toward home where we will be greeted as the prodigal and treasured son (Luke 15: 11–32). The feast is in our honor. It may be that our return is twenty, thirty, or fifty years after our baptism. Nonetheless, the grace of baptism has had a grasp upon us, and we have come to see, in retrospect, that its mark has been on our lives.

The same holds for the grace of marriage as a sacrament of the Church. In acknowledging and accepting the Church's purposes for marriage, and by receiving the grace of sacrament, we are marked. It may be that we do not respond to the grace of married life until ten or twenty years after the wedding. We may live far from the habits of community and prayer. Most of us try to make our marriages work on our own, just as the prodigal son tries to make his way in a distant land. But grace has a hold on us, and we need only turn our lives toward God and take our place at the table in worship. This view of marriage is almost unthinkable in our age of self-reliance, but the heart of marriage in the Church is the grace that we do not make or break our loves by our own will. Marriage is a gift.

The wedding day brings great hope because marriage in the Church mediates the love of God. Bride and groom, family and friends gather to celebrate a new beginning and new prospects for love and shared joy. Weddings are grand events that bring a community together. They ought not to be austere. The fullness of joy on a wedding day is that God is with us, that the company that gathers in God's name is not merely a witness or audience to the event, but is a key actor in the event itself. We are not alone. In marriage, it is also to the Church and way of discipleship that we are bound. The newly married couple is called to a life of love, faithfulness, and service. This call is indeed the fullness of matrimonial grace.

Indissolubility, Dissolution, and Remarriage

Christian marriage forms a permanent union. Long before marriage was considered a sacrament, Augustine refers to marriage in the Church, both monogamous and indissoluble, as a sacramental bond. Marriage is a sacred sign of the "unity of all of us subject to God which is to be in one heavenly City" (Augustine, 1955: 21). It is interesting that, on this point, Augustine does not cite Ephesians 5: 21–33, where marriage is a sign of the relationship between Christ and the Church. Instead, he thinks of marriage in terms of the steadfast union among us that is now possible because we have life in Christ. An analogy with procreation may be at work. Augustine holds that the procreative character of marriage certainly binds husband and wife, but given that God could make men and women out of dust, our role in the generation of race is the source of a special affinity among all human beings. The union of a man and woman (which for Augustine is primarily procreative) is the consequence of God's plan for a greater human unity. In the same way, marriage is a sign of unity of human community that is now possible through our redemption in Christ.

If marriage is a grace-giving sign (even if not a formal sacrament for some churches), then it will not be dissolved by a couple's own self-determination. In marriage, a man and woman have entered a union that is not just their own, but is received in participation with Christ and properly lived out in unity with the Church. Many marriages, in fact, do end in separation and dissolution, and some rightfully so. However, one form of dissolution can be excluded by the nature of marriage in the Church. The goods of marriage are contradicted when a couple ends their marriage privately for private reasons, or if they make their appeal for public dissolution only in the courts (1 Corinthians 6: 1–11). Marriage is not contingent on the whim of the partners or the usefulness of one spouse for another. This is both the hard teaching about marriage in our time and the incredibly good news. Christian marriage has purposes beyond the pleasure and contentment of the partners; yet, it promises the joy of steadfast love. Many marriages lack affability and companionship; nonetheless, it is assumed that communion in the Church and growth in the ways of discipleship will cultivate friendship, affection, and intimacy between husband and wife. Marriage promises love because it is a context for endurance, patience and hope, conversion and renewal, forgiveness and reconciliation.

The communal nature of Christian marriage is intrinsic to it. It seems to be common practice that we learn to see and understand our own marriages within the context of wider friendships, among communities of young and old, single and married. Couples befriend couples; husbands encourage husbands, and wives stand by wives. Through these friendships in the Church, we are able to make judgments and seek wisdom. We are given a perspective to see the difference between a difficult time and a hopeless situation. On the one hand, an older couple might tell a younger one about long dry spells or years of discord that have been redeemed. On the other hand, a woman might be encouraged to leave her abusive husband. It is part of the pathology of domestic violence that the victim is isolated, blames herself, and has unrealistic expectations about fixing the problem by herself. What is needed is communal intervention and a public process of repentance by the abuser, treatment, and change. By processes such as these the goods of marriage are sustained.

In this regard, the process of annulment in the Catholic Church may be instructive, for both its successes and its shortcomings. It should be noted, at the start, that the process does not pertain to the dissolution of a marriage. It is not equivalent to divorce. Annulment deals with the validity of the marriage at its inception, as a covenant established by the consent of the partners. If a marriage is annulled, it is not erased (as though it had not existed); rather, it is retrospectively understood to be faulty or invalid as permanent covenant, precisely at the point where a couple formed the union. If a marriage is annulled, a person is not bound by the vows of indissolubility and is free to remarry. It is a process subsequent to separation or divorce.

Marriage vows may be annulled because they lacked proper form, as when an unbaptized person receives the sacrament of marriage. Or, the consent of the partners may be invalid, as in the case, for instance, when an alcoholic makes a vow even though her illness obstructs her choice to be a spouse and parent. The alcoholic, of course, is likely to think that her use of alcohol is not a problem. This is the heart of the problem (and the marriage of a recovering alcoholic will present a different case). Likewise, the abusive husband, noted above, lacks knowledge of what marriage entails so that his consent to marriage is faulty from the start. Annulment does not decide that these marriages should end, but when they do end, it is a determination that they lacked valid form (particularly in terms of the sacrament) or lacked valid consent.

The process of annulment is criticized for a variety of reasons, but it is exemplary to the degree that it provides a set of procedures in the Church where former husbands and wives, along with family members and friends, are able to give an account of marriages gone wrong. The process is criticized by many because it is juridical in form. It pertains to the legal validity of the marriage contract. Often annulment is misunderstood to mean that the marriage did not really happen and children are illegitimate. This is not the case; the determination is that the form or consent to the goods of marriage was invalid and therefore not binding. In effect, the process of annulment is an attempt to protect the coherence of marriage. If people enter their vows in good form and with proper intent, then the vows must hold.

Some criticize the process because annulment is granted too readily, but most criticisms come from the other direction. Most claim that the system is too complex, takes too much time, requires too much institutional support and drains resources. In this sense, the process of annulment speaks of Christian marriage as a whole. In a world of utilitarian contracts, marriage requires too much of us, too much patience and hope, and too much openness to common life. In these terms, no marriage is possible without grace and the good company of those who, in faith and hope, are also along the way.

Conclusion and Sex

Infamous in our time, Augustine is known for the claim that marriage and sexual intercourse are not goods in themselves – not like wisdom, health, and friendship, which are sought for their own sake. Rather, marriage and sex are goods sought for the sake of friendship and the human affinity that comes with sexual generation (Augustine, 1955: 9). Augustine is a man of his times. He assumes that friendship, in its highest form, is known through friendships among virtuous men. If we depart from his assumptions about gender, and if we assume a connection between the love of friendship and erotic love, it is even more important to understand marriage as a relative good and to think about friendship in the plural, that is, as social and productive of other mutually supporting friendships. Marriage is not equivalent to the good of friendship; rather, we should say that marriages are in good working order when they are cultivated within and also foster and enhance an expanding circle of friends. Prayer, corporate worship, reciprocal care and obedience, hopeful patience and trust, mutual correction, non-retaliation, forgiveness, and reconciliation make friendship in marriage a promising and wonderful prospect. These practices make the single life and unexceptional marriages wonderful prospects as well.

Sex will serve as a concluding example. When the topic is introduced in contemporary theology, it is usually set within the context of marriage as a complete and complementary communion of two people (Genovesi, 1996: 151–71). The popular assumption (and fear) is that marriage needs to be considered as the apex of interpersonal communion; otherwise, it threatens to be considered merely functional and ordinary. Few in our time would dare to claim that marriage is, in essence, simply an everyday life of household management, common work, companionship, and training in neighborly love (McCarthy, 2001: 33–64). But this is, in fact, the case with marriage, except that we can invest the sexual relationship between husband and wife with a unique intimacy of total self-giving and unity. With this romantic investment, the hope is that we can counter the routine and everyday of married life with a timeless account of finding ourselves at the moment of sexual union. This idealized account of sex is attractive if married couples must make their marriages meaningful on their own.

Sex in Christian marriage is surely a profound bodily self-giving. Certainly, there are times when we give ourselves over to the other totally. Without a doubt, sex provides a way for married couples to sustain intimacy. Undoubtedly, however, there are as many times when we are simply fulfilling a marital duty (1 Corinthians 7: 3–5). Whether in marriage or not, sex is often routine, usually ordinary, and on occasion prosaic. Sometimes it is demanding and manipulative. Still Christian marriage (in the context of practices of forgiveness and reconciliation) can make sex into something truly good. In the Church, our marital intimacy does not depend upon the heights of sexual union. Joined by the friendship of God, we can face our spouses without fear of the ordinary, or fear of our aging bodies, pains, shortcomings, and unattractiveness, imagined or real. We need not perform in bed. The practices of discipleship among the company of friends promise to make rich marriages out of mediocre sex. This kind of bodily self-giving is profound. Sex is intimate because husband and wife share bodily presence over time – sharing a bed, suffering, hopes, worries, joys, sickness, and health – in community with those who have been gathered by God and, in response, pledge that their presence will endure as well. This is indeed good news for our time.

References

Augustine (1955) "The Good of Marriage," in *Saint Augustine: Treatise on Marriage and Other Subjects*, ed. Roy J. Deferrari, The Fathers of the Church New Translation, vol. 27, pp. 9–51 (New York: Fathers of the Church).

Brown, Susan L. and Booth, Alan (1996) "Cohabitation versus Marriage: A Comparison of Relationship Quality," *Journal of Marriage and Family*, 58: 3 (August 1996): 668–78.

Foster, Michael Smith (1999) *Annulment: The Wedding That Was* (New York: Paulist).

Genovesi, Vincent J. (1996) *In Pursuit of Love: Catholic Morality and Human Sexuality* (Collegeville, MN: The Liturgical Press).

Hays, Richard B. (1996) *The Moral Vision of the New Testament: A Contemporary Introduction to New Testament Ethics* (New York: HarperCollins).

Heaney-Hunter, Joann (1996) "Living the Baptismal Commitment in Sacramental Marriage," in *Christian Marriage and Family*, ed. Michael G. Lawler and William P. Roberts, pp. 106–24 (Collegeville, MN: The Liturgical Press).

Hill, Brennan R. (1996) "Reformulating the Sacramental Theology of Marriage," in *Christian Marriage and Family*, ed. Michael G. Lawler and William P. Roberts, pp. 3–21 (Collegeville, MN: The Liturgical Press).

Hume, David (1965) *A Treatise of Human Nature*, ed. L. A. Selby-Bigge (Oxford: Clarendon Press).

International Commission on the English Liturgy (1990) *The Rites of the Catholic Church*, vol. 1, Study Edition (Collegeville, MN: Pueblo/The Liturgical Press).

John Paul II (1981) *Familiaris consortio, Origins* v. 11, nos. 28–9 (December 24, 1981): 438–66.

Luhmann, Niklas (1986) *Love as Passion: The Codification of Intimacy*, trans. Jeremy Gaines and Doris L. Jones (Stanford: Stanford University Press).

McCarthy, David Matzko (2001) *Sex and Love in the Home: A Theology of the Household* (London: SCM).

McGinnis, Kathleen and McGinnis, James (1990) *Parenting for Peace and Justice: Ten Years Later* (Maryknoll, NY: Orbis).

Markey, B., Micheletto, M., and Becker, A. (1985) *FOCCUS: Faciliating Open Couple Communication, Understanding and Study, Facilitator Manual* (Omaha: Family Life Office, Archdiocese of Omaha).

Office of Family Life (1997) *Pre-Cana Manual* (Baltimore, MD: Division of Religious Education, Department of Catholic Education Ministries, Archdiocese of Baltimore).

Pontifical Council for the Family (1996) "Preparation for the Sacrament of Marriage," *Origins* v. 26, no. 7 (July 4): 97–109.

Shorter, Edward (1975) *The Making of the Modern Family* (New York: Basic Books).

Thatcher, Adrian (2002) *Living Together and Christian Ethics* (Cambridge: Cambridge University Press).

Walzer, Michael (1983) *Spheres of Justice: A Defense of Pluralism and Equality* (New York: Basic Books).

CHAPTER 22

Sharing Peace: Discipline and Trust

Paul J. Wadell

Hardly anyone sees what a risky gesture it is. There is a moment in the Christian liturgy when those present are invited to share with one another the gift of Christ's peace. Some do it with a handshake, some with an embrace. But few grasp the commitment that they are making when they pledge to conform their lives to the rigors of the peace of Christ in a world that not only seems more skilled at alienation and dissension, but which also lacks the courageous truthfulness that living the peace of Christ demands. Nothing is more hopeful than to be part of a community committed to embodying the merciful peace of Christ in a world too often trapped by the seductions of violence. But neither is anything more demanding because promising to live by the peace of Christ means being initiated into a way of life where one learns that God's order is established not through coercion, but through patient, suffering love.

The practices of peace are not easily learned, and surely not easily sustained. But they are crucial in a world where people often seem better at contributing to one another's dying than to offering each other life. Narratives of death can appear sovereign, but Christians believe that these sagas of diminishment will not prevail because the life, death, and resurrection of Jesus make possible a new way of life in which the logic of violence is exposed and overcome. This life-giving narrative entered the world in Christ and should continue to be told by all those baptized in his name. In this story, people build one another up, support and care for one another, seek the best for each other, and offer forgiveness when they fail. In this story, people acknowledge the things that foster division and nurture breakdowns in love, but commit to cultivating instead the demanding but truly hopeful disciplines of love, truthfulness, patience, and forgiveness. They pledge to be a people of peace.

The gift of peace witnesses the life Christians promise to live. This chapter will explore what it means to live the peace of Christ by showing first how Christians' commitment to peace is founded on their understanding of a Trinitarian God, and why such a theology of God calls the Church to embody a particular way of life in the world. Second, it will examine how the Eucharist continually initiates Christians into a new way of life where the practices of peace are learned. Third, by looking at how the medieval theologian Thomas Aquinas understood the communal life of charity, it will probe the specific requirements of living together in the peace of Christ, especially why flourishing in this peace demands a truthfulness and trust without which authentic community cannot exist.

The Church: Called to be an Icon of the Trinity

The most fundamental Christian claim about God is that God is a community of persons bonded together in love. God is not three isolated, disconnected individuals, but a partnership of love in which each person's love gives life and identity to the others, the result of which is the perfection of happiness and joy. God's very being is relational because at the heart of God is not solitude and isolation, but a trinity of persons united in perfectly intimate love. There are no divisions in God, no alienation in God, and no breakdowns of love in God. God is the true peaceable kingdom because in God relationships are characterized by generous, affirming, mutually edifying love.

What does this mean for the Church? The Church is to be an icon of the Trinity, the community whose members, however imperfectly and incompletely, share in and conform to the love, joy, and peace revealed in God and who witness this peace to the world (Forte, 1991: 23). As an icon of the Trinity, the Church should be the people who show the world that human beings are fulfilled as persons and know happiness not by accumulating possessions, becoming celebrities, or savoring power, but only in relationships and communities characterized by affection, trust, faithfulness, and care. Put differently, Christians should resist settling into relationships marked by domination, fear, jealousy, distrust, or manipulation. All these lead to breakdowns in love and the loss of peace. The Church is no stranger to breakdowns in love but, as an icon of the Trinity, refuses to surrender to them because it knows that the unity, love, and peace seen in God is prior to, and ultimately more powerful than, anything that divides us.

But this unity and peace are violated all the time. In many societies today, men and women are not initiated into the virtues and practices of peace, but into what Johann Baptist Metz calls an "anthropology of domination" (1981: 35). They are taught that they gain their identity not through relationships of friendship, love, truthfulness, and justice, but by dominating and subjugating others. On this understanding of the self, one exists to the degree that one exercises power over others, and flourishes in the measure that others are diminished. In the anthropology of domination, human beings are essentially disconnected, antagonistic beings living in a crushingly competitive world where everyone looks out for oneself.

There is something inescapably violent in this understanding of the self because it argues that identity requires oppression. It is a vision of life that sees human beings locked in ceaseless competitive struggle as everyone seeks to dominate everyone else. It is a world in which people come to life through self-love and self-assertion, not gentleness, mercy, compassion, or peacemaking. Here people grow not when they support others, raise them up, and love them in joyful self-forgetfulness, but when they are able to manipulate and exploit. This is not a world in which people can live together in genuine peace because the only peace possible is the false and shaky peace that comes when the strong subdue the weak.

The anthropology of domination permeates life. It is seen in the business world where corporate executives believe the only way to succeed is by continually growing bigger, and where large corporations thrive only by absorbing smaller ones. It is seen in the humor of movies and television where clever, sexy people shine by ridiculing anyone not so fortunately endowed. It is seen in everyday interactions where individuals are quicker to assert their rights than they are to inquire about the needs of others. It is seen in politics where people are taught to view themselves as competing individuals who must see other individuals and groups as adversaries fighting for the same limited resources, influence, and power. In such a drama, the purpose of politics is not to ensure justice for the human community, but to promote self-interest and to arbitrate differences between inherently hostile groups.

In a culture where power has become the ultimate idol, there has to be a people committed to the life-saving disciplines of peace. This is the call of the Church. The Church is the community summoned to write a history counter to the narratives of violence, domination, and diminishment. Christians, through baptism, have been entrusted by God with the task of working for the unity and peace of all human beings, a unity and peace attained by Christ that is to be "realised historically in the Church" (Forte, 1991: 23). Living from the memory of having been reconciled to God and to one another through the Cross and resurrection of Christ, the mission of the Church is to be the visible, historical sacrament of "God's plan of unity" for the world (Forte, 1991: 24). All people are called to this peace, and the vocation of the Church is to live in God's peace now.

In a world riven by hostilities and divisions, the Church becomes not a place of refuge and retreat, but a new polity, a distinctive, visible, concrete society modeled not on an anthropology of domination, but on the politics of truthfulness and peace made possible by the life, death, and resurrection of Jesus. Committed to the new way of life envisioned in Jesus's proclamation of the reign of God, Christians constitute a community where people take care of one another, are patient with one another, and seek the well-being of one another. In their pledge to live according to the disciplines and practices of the reign of God, they show the joy and freedom that come from renouncing retribution and embracing reconciliation and peace instead. It is this commitment to follow the new way of life begun by Christ that makes the Church a true instrument of salvation for the world.

This commitment to peace does not make the Church an elitist community that turns its back on the world. It makes the Church a "contrast-society" whose very willingness to risk the way of Jesus constitutes it as a gracious, transformative presence in the world – the biblical "city on a hill," "light of the world," and "salt of the earth" (Lohfink, 1984: 66). Christians practice the disciplines of truthfulness, reconciliation, and peace not because doing so is easy, but because it is the way of life to which Christ has called them and the only way they can be God's holy people in the world and for the sake of the world. As a people of peace, the presence of the Church may be a judgment on the world's politics of violence and practices of domination. But the Church exists not primarily to judge the world, but to fascinate it with a much more attractive possibility: the possibility of lasting intimacy, friendship, and love in a community that refuses to let enmity and vengeance prevail. The Church contradicts the world's understanding of reality in order to show the world an immensely more human way of life made possible by Christ, and one that conforms to the joyous, unifying love that is God.

This new social order and new way of life are formed through the prayer and worship of the Church. Consider the structure of the Eucharist. The Eucharist begins with the minister or priest greeting those assembled – "The grace and peace of God our Father and the Lord Jesus Christ be with you" – and the community responding: "And also with you." In this way, Christians know that they are receiving the gift of the peace of Christ in order to be the peace of Christ. Christ's peace should be the quintessential mark of the Church, the distinctive sign of its faithfulness to the reign of God. This is why the Eucharist cannot proceed – cannot truly be celebrated – unless anything that might divide the members of the community is first addressed. In the Sermon on the Mount Jesus set forth the attitudes, virtues, and practices that would constitute the new social order of the reign of God. There he instructed anyone wishing to be his follower: "If you bring your gift to the altar and there recall that your brother has anything against you, leave your gift at the altar, go first to be reconciled with your brother, and then come and offer your gift" (Matthew 5: 23–4).

I once belonged to a faith community that strove to shape its life according to Jesus's instruction. For a few years we followed a practice designed to help us deal with the conflicts, tensions, failures, and misunderstandings that, if not addressed, erode community life and weaken the peace of Christ. Once a month we would gather to explore what might be hindering the unity and peace that we wanted to characterize our lives together in Christ. We would begin those evenings with half an hour of silent prayer. During that time we would place our lives before God and pray to recognize any attitudes or behavior whose sinfulness weakened our community and violated the peace of Christ. We knew we could not be a true eucharistic community without honestly addressing those things that can be toxic for any community's life.

This time of prayer was followed by an exercise in which we would write down some fact we wanted to bring before the community. It could be a special grace someone had received, but normally it was a fault one wanted to bring to the community in order not only to seek healing and to ask forgiveness, but also for guidance in changing one's behavior. Each of us would read what he had written and the other members would respond. Such evenings of "fraternity" were not easy for no one likes his life to be so carefully scrutinized by another. But we knew that the only way we could sustain the peace of Christ in our midst was if we regularly acknowledged the sinfulness that could make its possession so precarious. That confession of fault was the "gift" we brought to the altar, for, having been reconciled to one another and to God, we concluded the evening by celebrating the Eucharist and reaffirming our commitment to live in the peace of Christ.

This does not mean that Christians must live in such intimate, intentional communities in order to practice the peace of Christ. It does mean, however, that there is no way for any Christian community to be a sacrament of Christ's peace unless it regularly reckons with, and works to overcome, the manifold toxins that destroy that peace.

The forces of division are legion and the Church is no stranger to them. Pettiness, bitterness, resentment, and vindictiveness can find a home in Christian communities as quickly as anywhere else; indeed, they can be harder to detect because of what these communities pledge to be.

For example, a friend of mine was once pastor of a small Christian church in Pennsylvania. Convinced that she was called to ministry in the Church, she devoted herself unstintingly to helping her congregation move to a deeper life in Christ. But her service in the Church almost killed her spirit because her efforts to lead were met with such resistance. Instead of a community characterized by faithful discipleship, she found herself enmeshed in webs of divisiveness, petty jealousies, and lies. In this congregation, the sign of peace represented not the truth of the community, but an almost blasphemous self-deception. How could they offer Christ's peace to one another in worship when they conspired to destroy that peace in their lives together? If the celebration of the Eucharist is not to deteriorate into sham and pretence, Christians must find ways to be reconciled to one another before they bring "their gifts to the altar." Otherwise, the Church only mirrors the world's despair instead of contrasting it in hope.

Eucharist: Learning and Living the Practices of Peace

The sign of peace Christians offer one another at worship is not an isolated gesture, but a symbol of a whole way of life that begins with baptism and is nurtured and sustained through the Eucharist. Baptism and the Eucharist are rightly called sacraments of initiation because through them Christians are formed in the practices, virtues, traditions, and disciplines of a new way of life. This emphasis on being reborn into a truly new kind of existence is captured in Paul's baptismal catechesis to the early Christian community at Rome. Paul reminds them that through baptism they have participated in the death and resurrection of Jesus and, therefore, are called to "walk in newness of life" (Romans 6: 4). Similarly, Paul's use of the images of "light" and "darkness" illustrates the sharp contrast between who Christians once were in their unredeemed existence, and who, thanks to God's mercy, they now are in Christ: "There was a time when you were darkness, but now you are light in the Lord. Well, then, live as children of light" (Ephesians 5: 8).

Baptism and the Eucharist must be seen in partnership because the Eucharist is meant to continue the configuration of one's life to Christ begun in baptism. Baptism is not a singular past event, but a continuing, unfolding grace to which Christians are challenged increasingly to conform their lives. Christians never "finish" their baptisms; rather, they grow more deeply into them through the Eucharist and the distinctive way of life it engenders.

How should this new way of life be understood? First, it is a way of life characterized by unity. This can be seen in three ways. The Eucharist is the sacrament of unity because it symbolizes that the new life to which Christians are called is not a purely individual affair, as if the Church were nothing more than an assembly of disconnected individuals. On the contrary, the Christian life is inherently social and communal because the Eucharist, like baptism, articulates that every Christian is foremost the member of a body. The Eucharist erases any notion that Christians can journey to God alone. As Philip Kenneson notes,

> According to the Scripture, Christians have no separate identity apart from the body of Christ. Becoming a Christian and becoming engrafted into the body of Christ are the same thing. This is why Paul can insist that we belong to each other, that we are "members of one another" (Romans 12: 5; Ephesians 4: 25) . . . We belong to each other because God has brought us together, connecting us to one another through and in Christ. (1999: 148)

There is a second sense in which the Eucharist can be rightly called the sacrament of unity. In perhaps the earliest Christian reflection on the ethical significance of the Eucharist, Paul chides the Christians of Corinth for the divisions and hostilities among them. He reminds them of the deeper unity and peace to which they are called in Christ, a unity and peace symbolically enacted through the Eucharist. "And is not the bread we break a sharing in the body of Christ? Because the loaf of bread is one, we, many though we are, are one body, for we all partake of the one loaf" (1 Corinthians 10: 16–17). Because of the Eucharist, Paul argues, Christians should stand against the world's legacy of fragmentation and brokenness, not reinforce it. Paul's testimony endures as an unassailable reminder that Christians are no strangers to hostilities and division; however, they should recognize that the hostilities and divisions, no matter how real, should never prevail.

Christians should never grow comfortable with all the things that fragment and divide, but work to overcome them in order that the peace of Christ be restored. As Robert E. Webber and Rodney Clapp write, "In a fragmented, dis-membered, rootless world, the church serves a crucial service in coming together for the Eucharist, learning to be a whole body, re-membering and rerooting its identity and vision" (1993: 79). The Eucharist flows from and articulates the foundational unity of all things in God and, as an eschatological banquet, anticipates the final reconciliation of all creation in Christ, a restoration made possible "through the blood of his Cross" (Colossians 1: 20). Thus, even though there is brokenness and alienation in the world, in societies, in families and relationships, and, yes, sadly, in the Church, the Eucharist should prompt the Church to be an agent of reconciliation and healing not only among its members, but also for the world.

A third way in which the Eucharist is a sacrament of unity and fosters the peace of Christ is that it brings people together in a way that transcends the normal ordering of our world. The amazing thing about the Eucharist is that it gathers together for a meal people who might never invite one another into their homes for dinner. This strangeness of the Eucharist should not be overlooked: the table of the Lord is different from other tables, just as the Lord's Supper is different from our ordinary ways of eating. Normally people sit down at table with those with whom they are familiar, people they like and whose company they enjoy. But at the Eucharist one's table companions may be strangers, misfits, malcontents, or even an assortment of enemies. There is no guarantee that in celebrating the Lord's Supper Christians will be surrounded by like-minded friends; indeed, they may pass the cup to someone whose presence makes them deeply uncomfortable. What accounts for such strange behavior?

At the Eucharist Christians are educated in the "table manners" of the reign of God (Lohfink 1999: 183). Jesus embodied the unsettling table manners of God's reign in the table fellowship he practiced in his life. Much like today, at the time of Jesus to sit down at table with someone was to acknowledge kinship with them. To share a meal indicated not only affection and care for another, but also a bond of fellowship. Jesus scandalized his contemporaries because he constantly violated the prevailing understandings of who should be included in fellowship. He welcomed to the table all the people who were judged to have no place in the community: tax collectors, lawbreakers, prostitutes, sinners, the sick, the strange, and the poor. In sitting down at table with these discarded, forgotten members of society, Jesus was not only challenging the prevailing customs of society, but was also creating a new kind of community that was no longer governed by practices of exclusion. As Donald W. Shriver, Jr, observes, "If the mealtime events recorded in the Gospels were remembered with accuracy, they were often occasions on which social boundaries were broken and then redrawn inclusively by the chief guest" (1995: 40). This same dynamic of recreating community through a politics of unity and inclusion, instead of our customary practices of division and exclusion, ought not only to guide how Christians celebrate the Eucharist, but also to inform their understanding of what it means to live a truly eucharistic way of life.

A second characteristic of the way of life formed through the Eucharist that contributes to a life of peace is giftedness. At the Eucharist the Church brings to the table of the Lord the bread and wine that will become the body and blood of Christ. Those gathered recognize that the bread and wine they offer are themselves gifts of the Creator, expressions of God's generous goodness and ever-abundant love. At that moment, the Church prays: "Blessed are you, Lord, God of all creation. Through your goodness we have this bread to offer, which earth has given and human hands have made. It will become for us the bread of life." The Eucharist teaches Christians that everything is a gift and that the whole of creation never ceases to live from the inexhaustible generosity of God. The Church is the people "awakened to the fact that to know the world is to know a gift" (Webber and Clapp, 1993: 58).

This awareness shapes the lives of Christians in important ways. As a community of giftedness, Christians realize that peace is a real possibility because their lives are not their own possession, but belong to God. Violence and conflict accrue when people believe that their self is something they have uniquely created and to which they must feverishly cling. But Christianity teaches that the self is a gift of God's love, not one's personal achievement, and that this gift is not to be aggressively protected but to be given away. Through the Eucharist Christians learn to yield their privacy and their possessiveness in order to become part of a story larger than themselves. A life of discipleship is "extended training in being dispossessed . . . of all that we think gives us power over our own lives and the lives of others" (Hauerwas, 1983: 86). The Eucharist teaches Christians that they do not own themselves and, therefore, are free not to be in control. Peace is possible when people surrender to the fact that their lives are in God's hands and that their ultimate security lies not in wealth or weapons, possessions or power, but in God's love. Knowing that their lives are not theirs to possess and control, but gifts to share with others, frees Christians to open themselves to the unexpected, gracious surprises of God, whether that surprise come through a friend, a family member, a curious child, or a memorable stranger.

Second, as members of a community of giftedness, Christians know they have been given one another as gifts to watch over, nurture, and respect. As members of the Body of Christ, Christians are not only in abiding and unbreakable relationship with one another, but are also entrusted to one another and responsible for one another. In his *Jesus and Community*, Gerhard Lohfink describes the solidarity among Christians as the "praxis of togetherness" (1984: 99). Working with Paul's admonition (1 Thessalonians 5: 11) that Christians are to "build one another up," Lohfink says a life of such mutual edification demands that Christians learn to be responsible for one another, look after one another, encourage one another, and care for one another. The Church should be an edifying community, a community that inspires because in it people find women and men who know how to live together in charity, truthfulness, joyfulness, and peace. Such peace is not the counterfeit tranquility that is the result of leaving one another alone; rather, it characterizes a community in which people honor one another, bear with one another patiently, admonish one another, console one another, and forgive one another.

A third quality of the new way of life into which Christians are initiated through the Eucharist is that it is a transforming way of life. This is symbolized most vividly at the consecration of the bread and wine into the body and blood of Christ. Just as the gifts of bread and wine are transformed, so must the lives of Christians be continually transformed if they are to live the peace of Christ. The pattern of this transformation is the Cross. Through his death and resurrection Jesus disarmed the powers of violence and exposed their ultimate futility. On the Cross Jesus demonstrated that one of humanity's most abiding illusions is the conviction that threat and violence must rule the world. The death and resurrection of Jesus testify that the power that moves the world is the power of God's non-violent, suffering love, and it is to this that the Church is called.

But the Church cannot be the community of God's peace unless Christians first encounter the violence in themselves. On the Cross Jesus showed that violence could not contain him because God's love is stronger than all the forces of darkness. But too often violence can contain and control the hearts of Christians. Thus, the initial transformation that must occur to people pledged to an eucharistic way of life is to unlearn the attitudes, dispositions, habits, and practices that nurture hostility, bitterness, and violence in the self. This is a continuing discipline that requires humility, self-scrutiny, and the guidance of others precisely because habits of violence can be so deeply ingrained. Indeed, an integral element to sanctification is recognizing "how much violence I have stored in my soul, a violence which is not about to vanish overnight, but which I must continually work to recognize and lay down" (Hauerwas, 1983: 94).

An essential mark of the transformation that ought to be worked in the Church through the Eucharist is reconciliation. What does worship do for the Church? It ought to make it the community in which habits of discord and self-righteousness are replaced by practices of reconciliation and peace. A way of life patterned on the Cross is inescapably a reconciled and reconciling way of life because the everlasting power of the Cross is to reunite what sin has scattered and splintered. As Colossians 1: 19–20 testifies, "It pleased God to make absolute fullness reside in him and by means of him, to reconcile everything in his person, both on earth and in the heavens, making peace through the blood of his cross." The Cross testifies that human beings can live at peace and can overcome the poisons of violence and vindictiveness because they have been reconciled to one another and to God through the death and resurrection of Jesus. The Cross not only makes all things new, but indeed makes the once unthinkable possible: all the walls that divide us, all the hostility that thwarts us, and all the bitterness and pain that diminish us, need not and ought not prevail. In Christ, those who had been scattered, broken, and divided are healed and reconciled so that they can live the "gospel of peace" (Ephesians 6: 15).

Living the gospel of peace is a fourth and definitive quality of the new way of life nurtured in the Eucharist. Peace is the gift of the reconciling work of God and ought to be the cornerstone of the edifying community the Church is called to be. But the peace Christians are called to live is strikingly different from customary understandings of peace. People are taught to think of peace as little more than the absence of conflict. Or else they equate peace with the fragile tranquility that comes when, in the name of freedom of choice or individual rights, people agree to tolerate almost anything. In such a landscape, peace is little more than the loneliness that results when people have agreed to leave one another alone.

God's peace, however, is defined not primarily by the absence of violence, hatred, and conflict, but by the substantive presence of a community that embodies the virtues of justice, truthfulness, humility, patience, and genuine fraternal affection. When Christians offer one another the peace of Christ at worship they go public with the pledge not to leave one another alone, but to be the kind of community where misunderstandings, conflicts, and divisions are overcome through the hard discipline of love. Love is a matter of attending to the other, and Christian love is the practice by which one promises to attend to the other not only when doing so is easy, but also in those moments where it seems reasonable to reject and revile another. Such peace is far more than flaccid sentimentality or superficial cheerfulness; rather, it is the fruit of a love characterized by patience, meekness, imagination, and hope.

No Christian community ever embodies the peace of Christ in its fullness. The Church is a people on the move, a people on a journey to a new heaven and a new earth. As the Church journeys to the fullness of the kingdom of God, it strives to live according to the justice and peace of that kingdom, all the while confessing the numerous ways it falls short. Nonetheless, it is exactly Christians' belief about the final victory of Christ over the power of violence that enables Christians to live in Christ's peace now. The sign of peace is an eschatological gesture. Christians promise peace to one another not in the misguided illusion that their relationships will never be tarnished by animosity, but in the belief that their convictions about the future free them to live more hopefully and creatively today. Christian eschatology maintains that the world ends not in violence and death, but in life, love, and peace because evil and death are defeated by the "blood of the Lamb" who was slain (Revelation 6: 12). And so the gift of peace Christians offer one another symbolizes how the Church looks to the future in order to know how to live in the present. Allowing God's future of justice and peace to be the measure of their lives now, Christians pledge "to be a community where the peace of God's kingdom begins" (Webber and Clapp, 1993: 60).

This is why I have never forgotten the day that I was refused the gift of peace. It happened several years ago when a colleague and I were giving a workshop for priests in Missouri. Most of them were cordial and hospitable. But there was a group of younger priests who were smug and supercilious. Still, I was not too discouraged because at the end of each day we gathered for the Eucharist, a reminder, hopefully, that our unity in Christ was deeper and stronger than whatever might divide us. I thought being able to gather around the table of the Lord would make any disagreements among us secondary. But I was wrong. On the last day of the workshop I stood next to one of these younger priests at the Eucharist. When it came time to offer one another Christ's peace, I extended my hand to him but there was no response. With his hands folded and a look that clearly did not wish me well, he refused to extend to me the gift of Christ's peace.

The Eucharist continued and both of us received communion but that, I now believe, was wrong because there was no communion between us. The sign of peace should symbolize unity and peace between one's self and others, but his refusal of Christ's peace from me signaled that the "gift" he had brought to the table was not peace, but division. If this had been acknowledged and addressed, the very meaning of the Eucharist as a sacrament of unity would not have been violated that day. As I recollect this moment, still painful to remember, I believe the mass should have halted then so that the community could have helped us deal with the barriers between us. Those present could have reminded him that we are obliged to offer one another Christ's peace and to overcome whatever hinders it because peace is a defining characteristic of a life of discipleship.

I remember that day vividly because the young priest's refusal not only stung, but also stood in glaring contradiction to the relationships Christians pledge to have among themselves and to the kind of community the Eucharist should create. Even though the Eucharist continued that afternoon, his rejection of fellowship with me in Christ transformed that liturgy into a ritual of mourning, a sad reminder of how anger, pride, and self-righteousness can overpower the peace that should govern our lives. Nonetheless, hopefully for him the memory of my outstretched arm abides not as a symbol of futility, but as sign that the gift of Christ's peace is always being offered, can always be received, and ultimately will prevail. Even in our refusals, the offer of Christ's peace testifies to a love that is stronger than the sin that can often rule our hearts.

The Communal Life of Charity: Living in the Peace of Christ

In her novel *Evensong*, Gail Godwin describes the Eucharist as "eternal companionship" (1999: 11). Perhaps surprisingly, she echoes Thomas Aquinas, the great theologian of the thirteenth century, who spoke of the Eucharist as the sacrament of charity, the sacrament of lasting concord, peace, and friendship with God and one's neighbors. But Aquinas knew that there could be no "eternal companionship," no true charity, trust, and peace in the Christian community unless the Eucharist was envisioned not only as a particular sacrament, but also as the portal to a way of life characterized by specific virtues, practices, and dispositions. It is in acquiring and practicing the virtues of a life of charity that the peace of Christ can be nurtured and sustained in the Church. Among the array of virtues necessary for living together in the peace of Christ, Aquinas spoke of gentleness, humility, patience, truthfulness, and fraternal correction.

Gentleness is necessary for living in the peace of Christ because gentleness subdues anger, lessens bitterness, restrains one's desire for revenge, and helps one move beyond resentment (Aquinas, 1975: II-II, 157, 1). Similarly, humility safeguards the peace of Christ because it teaches reverence for others and trains one to look for the good in others rather than zeroing in on their shortcomings (1975: II-II, 161, 3). Humility teaches one to yield to others instead of insisting that the self's desires, opinions, and preferences must always prevail. And, Aquinas knew, there could be no peace without patience because it is only with patience that one can deal not only with the hardships, setbacks, and disappointments of life, but also with the nagging imperfections and shortcomings in others as well as oneself. Without the ability to be patient with the sin in oneself as well as in others, one can easily conclude that living together in peace is not possible after all (1975: II-II, 136, 1).

Of all the virtues Aquinas identified as essential for a community committed to the peace of Christ, none demands attention more than truthfulness and fraternal correction because both have become such rare practices in our world today. Many people mistakenly believe that truthfulness is incompatible with love because they think that love must always be affirming. But if the essence of Christian love is to seek the good of the other and to call another to a deeper imitation of Christ, love must involve admonition as well as affirmation. To love someone is not to be afraid to challenge him or even to correct him because, as Josef Pieper observed, to love another is "to wish that everything associated with him may be truly good" (1997: 190). Such truthfulness honors a person because it recognizes in her a capacity for goodness and holiness she may not yet see, but which she needs to see if she is not to despair of the glory to which God calls her.

By offering and receiving the gift of Christ's peace at worship, Christians give each other permission to be truthful to one another, especially if they see a member of the community slipping into behavior that is harmful for him or her and, therefore, harmful for the community. This commitment to be truthful is a sign of the community's faithfulness and love for one another. But it also reflects the community's realization that living together in the peace of Christ is impossible unless people are confident that they will be truthful to each other. As Aquinas noted, "People could not live with one another were there not a mutual trust that they were being truthful to one another" (1975: II-II, 109, 3).

In the communal life of charity, truthfulness must sometimes take the form of fraternal correction. Aquinas saw fraternal correction as a true expression of love because if one wants what is best for another one must be willing to call attention to attitudes or behavior that are destructive both for the individual and the community. "Ridding someone of an evil," Aquinas wrote, "is really the same as doing him good, and is, therefore, an act of charity, for it is charity that makes us will our friend's welfare and do our best to bring it about" (1975: II-II, 33, 1). In fact, Aquinas viewed fraternal correction as such an indispensable requirement of love, that not to call a sister's or brother's attention to acts that were detrimental to their spiritual well-being was a sin (1975: II-

II, 33, 2). Aquinas realized that the bonds of community are weakened if its members are unable to address behavior detrimental to their lives together.

There is a scriptural precedent for Aquinas's position in Matthew 18: 15–18. Jesus addresses the need for fraternal correction if any community of disciples is not to be undone by the transgressions of its members. He envisions a community where people hold one another accountable and deal openly with behavior that damages the community: "If your brother should commit some wrong against you, go and point out his fault, but keep it between the two of you" (Matthew 18:15). Jesus's words indicate that the purpose of fraternal correction is for reconciliation with the wronged party and restoration of the relationship. However, if someone consistently refuses to accept responsibility for his behavior, the well-being of the community demands that he be removed from its midst until he is willing to accept the correction and amend his behavior: "If he ignores even the church, then treat him as you would a Gentile or a tax collector" (Matthew 18: 17). To many, Jesus's words sound harsh. But if the Church is to live the peace of Christ it cannot afford to tolerate behavior that is consistently at odds with the life and example of Christ.

Similar attention to the importance of fraternal correction is seen in the writings of Paul to the early Christian churches. As Romans 15: 14 illustrates, Paul knew that mutual admonition was absolutely necessary for the continuing vitality of the community. Unlike many who think that their behavior, including the wrong they do, is nobody's business but their own, Paul saw that everything one does affects the common good. The good one does builds up the community, but the wrong one does surely weakens it. This is why in any community dedicated to the peace of Christ conflicts cannot be "suppressed or artificially concealed. The courage to admonish others fraternally and the humility to let oneself be corrected are among the most certain signs of the presence of authentic community and of consciousness of community" (Lohfink, 1984: 106).

This chapter has explored what it means for the Church to live the peace of Christ. There may be no riskier and more demanding act than for Christians to offer one another Christ's peace at worship, and see in that gesture a sign of their pledge to allow Christ's peace to reign in their hearts. Promising to conform their lives to Christ's peace implicates Christians in practices and disciplines that will ceaselessly call them to greater conversion of heart and remind them of how imperfectly and incompletely they embody God's ways in the world. Nonetheless, in a world that knows narratives of death all too well – and is tragically adept at practices of violence – there is nothing more promising and nothing more hopeful than a people whose greeting, even to their enemies, is always: "May the peace of Christ be with you."

References

Aquinas, Thomas (1975) *Summa theologiae* (New York: McGraw-Hill).
Forte, Bruno (1991) *The Church: Icon of the Trinity* (Boston: St Paul Books and Media).
Godwin, Gail (1999) *Evensong* (New York: Ballantyne).

Hauerwas, Stanley (1983) *The Peaceable Kingdom: A Primer in Christian Ethics* (Notre Dame, IN: University of Notre Dame Press).

Kenneson, Philip D. (1999) *Life on the Vine: Cultivating the Fruit of the Spirit in Christian Community* (Downers Grove, IL: Intervarsity Press).

Lohfink, Gerhard (1984) *Jesus and Community: The Social Dimension of Christian Faith* (Philadelphia: Fortress).

—(1999) *Does God Need the Church? Toward a Theology of the People of God* (Collegeville, MN: The Liturgical Press).

Metz, Johann Baptist (1981) *The Emergent Church: The Future of Christianity in a Postbourgeois World*, trans. Peter Mann (New York: Crossroad).

Pieper, Josef (1997) *Faith, Hope, Love* (San Francisco: Ignatius).

Shriver, Donald W., Jr (1995) *An Ethic for Enemies: Forgiveness in Politics* (New York: Oxford University Press).

Wadell, Paul J. (2002) *Becoming Friends: Worship, Justice, and the Practice of Christian Friendship* (Grand Rapids, MI: Brazos).

Webber, Robert E. and Clapp, Rodney (1993) *People of the Truth: A Christian Challenge to Contemporary Culture* (Harrisburg, PA: Morehouse).

PART V
Re-enacting the Story

CHAPTER 23

Offering: Treasuring the Creation

Ben Quash

Inside my church, at every Eucharist (and in other ways at other times) practices of offering go on. These are many and various. They include the members of the congregation offering their time, their physical presence, and their attention (as far as they can manage it) to Scripture readings, sermons, liturgical words and actions, and each other. The gathered congregation offers prayers. They offer to God and one another a public declaration of repentance. They offer hands, embraces and words of greeting at the sharing of the peace. The consummate moment of offering, however, is immediately before the beginning of the eucharistic prayer, at what is often called the "offertory." At this point, the gifts of the people (usually money) are brought up to the altar, prayed over and dedicated to God's work. And with them, bread and wine ("fruit of the earth, and the work of human hands") are handed over to the priest to be consecrated.

Outside my church, something in the order of a mass extinction of plant and animal species is underway across the globe. This is the latest of several mass extinctions in the earth's history, but it is distinctive in that an animal – *Homo sapiens* – is playing a key role in bringing it about. The philosopher Stephen Clark has been observing what has been going on outside my church (and outside his own) for a longer time and with more scientific knowledge than I have, and he describes it as follows, drawing in this passage on the work of the scientist E. O. Wilson:

the rate of species loss is between a thousand and ten thousand times the usual. We do not know – and probably will not know until it is far too late – if too many key species are being eliminated for the whole to survive in any form hospitable to us. "One planet, one experiment." . . . Sometime in the next century, we will have pulled so many threads out from life's tapestry that the whole begins to fray. We have already made inevitable a climate change that is likely to drown millions and starve millions more. The bacterial and invertebrate population of the planet will no doubt adjust. Human beings have been trying to live "at the top of the food chain," as if they were large carnivores, despite the obvious truth that carnivores are always scarcer than their prey. We have been trying to secure things for ourselves despite the obvious truth that everything we have and relish is the product of a system that we do not understand and cannot replace. The only sort of species that has much hope of survival is one without delusions of grandeur . . . (Clark, 2000: 96, 114)

I said that this is a description of what is happening "outside" my church, but of course my church, like the whole Church in all its parts, is thoroughly embedded in the situation. It is affected by it and contributes to it. This chapter, then, will look at some of the ways in which what goes on inside my church may address, judge, and offer resources for repairing the relationship between human agents and their natural environment.

Issues

Speaking of the "natural world" as something over against us, and the "non-human creation" as something from which we are by definition distinct, can seem to reinforce a dualism between humans and something we have chosen to call "nature." Mean-while, speaking of the "environment" seems to play into an anthropocentrism that denies proper respect to other living things and complex systems in their own right. Whose "environment" is "the environment"? The answer is inevitably: human beings. Talk of the environment can make it sound as though everything in the world exists merely as the scenery for human activity. How do we decide whether that is true or not? How should the human relationship to nature be construed? What policies and prac-tices ought to be developed not only to meet immediate crises but also to foster longer-term visions of flourishing? Many of the "stories" which purport to help us orient ourselves in relation to these issues leave much to be desired. I will outline some of these "stories" in this section.

The tension between freedom and determinism

The dominant story in the West, perhaps, is that of Enlightenment and post-Enlightenment thought about the human subject. We can isolate two key moments in this story. The first is the moment at which a claim was made for the radical and inalienable freedom and self-possession of the human subject. The human being belongs to himself, according to this claim; he is a center of self-governing rationality and will, and no one and nothing else governs him. (As Joan Lockwood O'Donovan, 1998: 20–1, 23, has pointed out, there were pre-Enlightenment theological roots to this claim, but the Enlightenment tradition of Hobbes, Locke, and Kant gives it defini-tive expression.)

Then, principally in the nineteenth century, there came what might be called the second moment of modernity, in which modernity woke up to a whole series of what it perceived as *threats* to this freedom and self-possession. Each of these in a slightly different way was located in the sphere of "nature." Broadly, Darwinian theory suggested that our subjectivity was the product of biological processes – *animal* processes. Freud indicated the many ways in which the human mind was neither rational nor self-transparent, but subject to dark promptings, drives and taboos that were part of the common inheritance of our species. Marxian theory emphasized the way in which the human subject was determined by *material* forces (social and economic) well beyond itself. The self-determination of the individual human subject did not seem so obvious any more.

Thought about the human relationship to the natural world tends to work itself out in the tension between these two modern perceptions: the freedom and self-direction of human agents, on the one hand, and the existence of determining forces outside our control on the other. The former emphasis tends to enforce the idea that we are "not-nature"; it is perhaps corrected by the latter's reminder that in crucial ways we *are*. But there can be distortions the other way too. The latter emphasis can enforce the idea that we are not free (and therefore not responsible), and needs its own correction by the former. This dialectic does not dissolve the tension between freedom and determinism: it may not be soluble in the terms currently available within the modern story. But managing this tension presents modern thinkers with some of their most acute problems – and this is certainly so in the area of environmental ethics. The tension is characteristically present in one of the most recent publications of the United Nations Environment Programme, *Global Environment Outlook 3*, as it attempts to anticipate what lies ahead for the environment: "Uncontrolled forces, both human and natural, will contribute to the course of events. But informed decision-making also has a real and vital role to play in the process of shaping the future . . ." (United Nations, 2002: 320).

The dominance of management models and the lure of "sustainability"

Inheriting the terms of the freedom–determinism dialectic, much environmental decision-making operates with the idea that the natural world needs "management." This may not imply so strong a view of what the United Nations calls nature's "uncontrolled forces" as to call them a *threat* to the self-constitution of human freedom (though they may well be), but it at least views them as a *problem*. The management model of response can take a variety of forms (I am grateful to the ethicist and theologian Rachel Muers for some of what follows here).

One model is fatalistic about the impossibility of changing the voracious and destructive human demand for more and more goods and services, whatever the cost to ecosystems and the species that depend on them. The best hope humans have is to trust that their technological skills will permit them to adapt if and when they make the planet a desert. Human beings may, in other words, have to make for themselves artificial environments when they have destroyed their "real" one. Perhaps these will be in space, or in carefully sealed bubbles on the earth. The prospect seems unappealing. A side-effect of this imagined future might well also be gross inequality between those who can afford to inhabit these carefully engineered spaces and those who must face the worst consequences of a consumption they barely, if ever, had a chance to participate in. Like the residents of present-day "gated communities," only the relatively powerful and wealthy will be able to afford the security and privilege of comfortable survival.

A relatively more optimistic version of the management model hopes that policy interventions by benign governments, and the introduction of internationally agreed regulatory frameworks and planning processes, will temper human greed and avert the worst consequences of our current excess. This depends on governments actually sticking to the frameworks they agree, and being prepared to accept the consequences of electoral unpopularity for measures that restrict consumer freedom. It also risks a more bureaucratic and state-interventionist world.

Finally, there is a utopian vision, with all its attendant implausibility, that foresees a new visionary state of affairs in which there are radical changes in the way that people treat each other and the world around them, and large corporations behave with impeccable ethical accountability. A few environmentalists hold to this paradigm as realizable, at least in principle; but, as more and more people in some of the largest countries in the world (China and India, for example) seize with enthusiasm their first opportunities to *drive* their children to and from school, thus at long last tasting the way of life so long envied in the developed West, the odds seem stacked against a sudden, worldwide change of heart. Corporations anxious to market the products associated with such a "successful" way of life simply and ruthlessly exploit such desires.

The contemporary concern with finding a Holy Grail called "sustainability" dominates the discussions of environmentalists and government planners as they hold before themselves these various possible scenarios. Ideally, sustainable practices will balance the requirements of development (by which wealth is created), equity (by which injustice is avoided, and the few do not benefit at the expense of a disadvantaged majority), and protection, or conservation, of the environment. At best, a way will be found to enable these three concerns actually to *serve* one another. The fact remains, though, that this model is still a management model, and so still implicitly reinstantiates a dualism between human beings and the natural world which it is their principal task to control.

Management models in all their forms, even in their best form, are vulnerable to criticism in two ways. They objectify the natural world – even instrumentalize it – and they depend on a human capacity to predict the future and the consequences of human interventions and plans. This capacity is highly questionable, given the extraordinary complexity of what is being dealt with. The truth is that the detail of the universe is largely beyond our grasp, and the extraordinary combination of factors and relationships that holds the ecosphere in shifting balance is not something we have a secure hold on.

Meanwhile, we are not free, when in management mode, of the risks of over-manipulating the living things for which we have assumed responsibility, as though they had no countervailing interests. As John Milbank points out, "The danger is that claims to have identified 'optimum' environments, the most 'natural' and 'sustainable' balances, will often mask the ruses of human power and ambition" (Milbank, 1997: 262). We are prone to elevate function or utility over relationship; in other words, to accord respect to aspects of the natural world for "what they have done for us" (or might yet do), not because we are related parts of a single whole, the other parts of which have their own moral standing. One of the most vivid examples of this tendency on the part of humans is the no doubt efficient (in a limited, technical sense), but at the present time utterly brutal and ugly, mass production of animals for food.

The assumption of manipulative hegemony over the things of the earth is one form of the anthropocentric strand in attitudes to the environment (the natural world has status only and precisely as "our environment"), a position variously countered in the name of zoocentrism, biocentrism, and ecocentrism (and even, occasionally, in the name of theology). Zoocentrism claims that the higher animals are also, alongside humans, proper objects of moral concern; biocentrism extends this concern to all living things; and ecocentrism to whole ecosystems. (Michael Banner treats these alternatives at greater length in Banner, 1999: 174ff.)

Arguing that the brutal, instrumentalizing use of non-human life for the satisfaction of human wants has to be checked, however, may not necessarily lead one to the complete abandonment of an anthropocentric position – or at least a position that recognizes that we have no other perspective from which to attribute value and make ethical judgments than one grounded in our humanity. The truth is that it is *as humans* that we do our valuing; even the most sympathetic and "selfless" valuing of the non-human world is such *as human* valuing. Even if we admit that other animals (snakes, for example) have interests, and value aspects of *their* environments in ways that have no reference to humanity, we cannot step out of our own natures.

Immanentism

Another dominant "story" by which a non-theological environmental ethics frequently tries to orient itself is what we might call the immanentist one. On this account, no evaluation of natural goods or natural rights is permitted to make appeal to anything outside the material world itself.

Immanentist stories can assume variously scientific and mystical guises, and sometimes represent a mixture of the two. This is true to some extent of certain "holistic" approaches to nature. The moral claims of "nature-as-a-whole" are argued on the basis that it is "a creative, life-sustaining process, the well-functioning of which is not only vital to but constitutive of human and non-human well-being" (Fern, 2002: 3; Fern calls nature-as-a-whole "sentiotic" on the basis of this description of it). "Affirming the sentiotic goodness of nature does not depend on a belief in God, let alone a theodicy. All that it requires is a belief that wild nature has an inherent proclivity to well-being" (Fern, 2002: 60–1). The more hard-line scientific versions of immanentism are well known and often polemical (Richard Dawkins and others); the more mystical extremes echo the habits of mind of the Romanticism of a previous era, and counsel an effacement of human concerns before the oracular, self-regulating wisdom of Mother Nature. Her "utterances" represent the only viable source of both spiritual and aesthetic value for contemporary humanity.

That these latter appeals are flimsy and intellectually unsustainable should be clear. We cannot have it both ways: both denying any transcendent source of value, form, meaning, and at the same time wanting to keep goodness, beauty, and truth in play.

And there cannot be presumed to be a secure basis for honoring human beings (and individual creatures) and their projects and desires when ultimately everything is "world-process" inexorably unfolding toward its own end. Rather, the honest logical conclusion of this immanentism must be what is sometimes called "eco-fascism": even if we are the strongest and cleverest of animals, we are bound "to gloriously submit ourselves to the yet stronger, the planet as such, the self-maintaining totality" (Milbank, 1997: 262). "Believing that we are all 'one', that there is only a single, turbid stream of being, life and consciousness, we transform everything into material" (Clark, 2000: 316) – ourselves included:

> The dangers of pure immanentism seem obvious: resignation to death and redundancy, to the "natural law" of competition. Exactly what, for such an outlook, inhibits an ecological fatalism of the kind which assumes that humanity's gloriously natural self-vaunting is doomed to an equally natural demise, although the planet will continue, at least for aeons? (Milbank, 1997: 261)

It is now time to go back to church.

Liturgical Offering

In the service of Holy Communion in the Anglican *Book of Common Prayer* of 1662, still used at many of the services in my church, the offertory unleashes an extraordinary wealth of scriptural texts into the liturgy. Directly after the recitation of the Creed and the preaching of the sermon, and before the prayers of intercession, the rubric instructs: *"Then shall the Priest return to the Lord's Table, and begin the Offertory, saying one or more of these sentences following, as he thinketh most convenient in his discretion."*

No less than twenty sentences then follow, all of them in various ways inviting the congregation to make offerings. The majority of them urge a special consideration of the ethical claims of the poor on those who have much. A few remind the people that they must support the ministers of the gospel in their work. Some, importantly, place in the foreground a reminder of the final judgment, and the reckoning of what we have done with what we have been given. A repeated emphasis, both in these and the other sentences, is on the importance of gladness and love in giving. The generosity ought not even to feel like an effort: "not grudging or of necessity; for God loveth a cheerful giver" (2 Corinthians 9). In other words, it belongs to an "economy" beyond that of utilitarian calculation. There is a stark reminder (also present in the service for the Burial of the Dead) that the goods we have we have as a loan not as an entitlement: "Godliness is great riches, if a man be content with that he hath: for we brought nothing into the world, neither may we carry anything out" (1 Timothy: 6). And, overlapping with this reminder, there is a vivid picture of how, when we use "our" resources well, even in the service of creaturely recipients, we are in fact entering a relationship of reciprocal blessing with *God*, and we are promised that our *giving* is a preparation for *receiving back*: "He that hath pity upon the poor lendeth unto the Lord: and look, what he layeth out, it shall be paid him again" (Proverbs 19).

The rubric then states:

Whilst these Sentences are in reading, the Deacons, Churchwardens, or other fit person appointed for that purpose, shall receive the Alms for the Poor, and other devotions of the people, in a decent basin to be provided by the Parish for that purpose; and reverently bring it to the Priest, who shall humbly present and place it upon the holy Table. And when there is a Communion, the Priest shall then place upon the Table so much bread and wine as he shall think sufficient.

Modern liturgies are, on the whole, more similar to one another than they are to this Prayer Book practice, but the link between the giving of alms (in the form of a collection) and the presenting of bread and wine for eucharistic use is, if anything, stronger. In many churches now, the bread and wine are brought to the altar in procession, from amongst the people, in the same way that collection money is. This liturgical action stresses that fact that bread and wine are also, like money, the product of human labors in the context of God's gracious provision (his provision of the conditions we need for the work of our hands to prosper). The words said over the bread and wine make this even more explicit:

Blessed are you, Lord God of all creation; through your goodness we have this bread to offer, which earth has given and human hands have made. It will become for us the bread of life.

Blessed are you, Lord God of all creation; through your goodness we have this wine to offer, fruit of the vine and the work of human hands. It will become for us the cup of salvation.

And in each case the people respond: "Blessed be God for ever." In these liturgical exchanges the congregation learns to think about the whole creation (in connection with these specific gifts of the creation) as belonging to God ("Lord God of all creation"). It learns in appropriate humility (without what Clark would call "delusions of grandeur") to acknowledge that it "has" these gifts only because of life-giving forces wholly in excess of its own control ("through your goodness"; "which earth has given"). It learns to make its offering in the trust that God's goodness will reciprocate in ways that amaze it and confound normal expectations ("it will become for us the bread of life"; "it will become for us the cup of salvation"). And it learns to set this whole interaction in the context of divine praise ("Blessed be God"), so that the focus is never on the objects of exchange in their own right, but on the subject of this giving and receiving.

The Orthodox theologian Dumitru Staniloae is alert to the danger of focusing only on the objects and not their source. It threatens to affect the way that human beings handle all the things of the earth:

The world is a gift of God, but the destiny of this gift is to unite man with God who has given it. The intention of the gift is that in itself it should be continually transcended. When we receive a gift from somebody we should look primarily towards the person who has given it and not keep our eyes fixed on the gift. But often the person who receives a gift becomes so attached to the gift that he forgets who has given it to him. (Staniloae, 2001: 1)

The offertory is a powerful antidote to this tendency to forget the giver.

Perhaps more than anywhere in Christian liturgy, this moment of the "presentation of the gifts" highlights the wondrous possibilities latent in material things – the things of the earth, God's non-human creatures. They are themselves to be the vehicles of "life" and "salvation." They are treated with reverence (carried in procession, no less) and placed on the altar. And the overriding emphasis is that they are not our servants, they are God's blessings, and it is by his relation to them (not our manipulation of them) that they bring life. The handing over of created things at the offertory is thus a way of letting them be what God wants them to be, rather than what human beings wish to make them.

This highlighting of the importance of God's inalienable relation to his non-human creatures may trigger associations with other deeply rooted strands in the Christian liturgy, and in the words of Scripture. In the canticle *Benedicite, Omnia Opera*, for example, in verse tumbling over verse, the panoply of created things (zoo-, bio-, and eco-) is addressed directly, as though possessed of its own subjectivity: "O all ye Works of the Lord, bless ye the Lord: praise him, and magnify him for ever." The sky, the rain, the sun and the moon, stars, winds, fire and frosts, night and day, light and darkness, mountains, hills, green things upon the earth, seas, whales, birds, beasts, cattle, and finally human beings – all are summoned to do exactly the same thing: "praise him, and magnify him for ever." Like the bread and the wine, they are shown to be oriented to the disclosure of the glory of God. And they are shown to be known and loved by God in a way that does not always need to make reference to human beings, though we *are* encouraged to see ourselves as in relationship (in *fellowship*) with them. They can speak to God, and be spoken to by God, directly, just as we can. "[L]iving creatures are not only part of our metaphysical being nor, simply, 'love letters' from God to us, they themselves are the objects of and in their own way responsive to the love of God" (Fern, 2002: 204).

When God made the things of the earth, he spoke to them: " 'Be fruitful and multiply and fill the waters in the seas . . .' The verb in the imperative form belongs not to reference, nor to action, but to the language of address. By speaking to his creation in this way, God grounds the priority of divine command and establishes the possibility of reciprocal address" (Davies, 2001: 267). In short, if there is to be a serious recognition that the *lex orandi* should be allowed to shape the *lex credendi*, then the liturgy ought to teach Christians that they should not seek to shape and direct the ends of other creatures unless there is first a recognition that they are fellows in relationship to God (even, potentially, friends). "The Church has been singing and praying for centuries in terms that clearly specify that all things have a voice; why not take that seriously?" (Clark, 2000: 227).

How Christian Practice in Relation to the Environment Might be Shaped by Worship

The story God tells about himself and his world – a story rehearsed in Scripture and through the Church's worship – differs from the various stories that guide much contemporary thinking about the environment. It offers special ways of approaching the subject.

The Christian story contrasts with the immanentist one, as has already begun to be clear. The immanentist has no reason to anchor the truth, goodness, or beauty of any individual being (or relation) anywhere other than in the immanent processes and struggles of the "world-system." This means that the immanentist can only believe in particular interests, not in absolute value. Inasmuch as there is any arbiter of value, it is the "world-system" itself, but this is only to say that what will be will be (to enthrone fate – a Stoic policy). Human perceptions of what is right or glorious, human loves and attachments to things of the creation, can be no different from the interests of any other life-form competing to survive. So the immanentist's enjoyment of material goods is shadowed by the acute sense of their transitoriness, and the belief that the enjoyment itself is at best a "phenomenon" generated largely accidentally by a process that has not the slightest regard for the happiness of people.

Christians see that all living things have an origin in God's goodness and a direct relationship with God. Their value is real, and irreducible, inasmuch as it springs from God's love and regard. In the liturgy of the Church of England, the following words are used as the collection is brought to the altar. They serve to set the creaturely gifts in their right context: "Yours, Lord, is the greatness, the power, the glory, the splendour and the majesty. Everything in heaven and on earth is yours. All things come from you, and of your own do we give you." The things of the earth are known and recognized as gifts; they do not become just things in themselves as they are for the immanentist, having lost their meaning as signs of God's love. Nor are the things of the earth valued for the mere usefulness which human beings have from them.

If the Eucharist as a whole is a great display of God's ordering of all things in Christ, then the offertory most particularly shows his ordering of the natural world of which humans are a part. The Eucharist helps humanity to see how the real secret of the world's ordering is Christological and therefore also eschatological (for Christ is the one in and for whom all things exist *ultimately*). To participate in the Eucharist is like being able to watch the Big Bang: the dramatic event by which the universe is disposed. It is to see, in the face of other descriptions of what orders the universe, that in the Alpha and Omega the created world has a more than immanent point to it. In the offertory, there is a very special disclosure of the truth that the way the world is (bread and wine) is in motion toward what the world becomes in Christ. There is a display of what it was that Christ assumed in the Incarnation – the things of earth in their real earthliness. As a consequence of what the offertory does with them in the Eucharist Christians look at them again as "God-bearing." The mere fact that they are things God chose for existence, just as he chose humanity, would be a good enough reason not to despise or hurt them (Clark, 2000: 300). But the fact that the creation and all its fruits – offered on the altar in bread and wine – have been chosen to "bear" the weight of the Savior means that they are blessed even as Mary was blessed when the angel came and spoke to her.

Of course, like immanentists, Christians know that in time all creatures are transitory. But in the light of the Eucharist this does not shadow the Christian's enjoyment of them, because Christians know from the Eucharist's proclamation of Christ's resurrection that God's power can transform and restore his creatures in a life that does not end, and they rejoice that this hope has been bestowed on all matter.

There are other stories to which the Christian story offers alternatives, especially in its eucharistic celebration. The Christian story contrasts with what might be called the "Manichean" character of many contemporary approaches (to borrow a phrase from another era). The perceived tension between freedom and nature outlined above is Manichean, in that it supposes an irreconcilable opposition between the human spirit and a natural world *to which that spirit does not ultimately belong* but in which it is trapped. This is a doctrine that denies the oneness and the goodness of God, positing instead primal conflict between two principles. The best a Manichee can hope for is to control the small part of her threatening and hostile environment (because nature in the end is just a threat to the freedom of the spirit) until release comes. So Manichees have their own quite persuasive reasons for wanting to embrace the management model of dealing with the environment, though they are not optimistic about its success on a large scale. Their aim is probably to live in one of the artificial bubbles of the future (the post-desertification "gated communities"), as they have little reason to hope for any better outcome.

Christians, meanwhile, trust in the basic goodness of creation. Of course, they recognize that it is a fallen creation – even the non-human parts. This means that they do not look at the way the creation is now and assume that all is exactly as it should be. They admit very often that they cannot see or imagine how the created order as it now stands could be wholly compatible with human blessedness and flourishing – indeed, the blessedness and flourishing of all created things in their many interrelations. But it is precisely here, again, that the Eucharist helps them, inasmuch as this sacrament of Christ's incarnation, sacrifice and resurrection displays the ordering of creation in relation to its origin and its end. When Christians don't know what a thing is, or what to do with it, they go back to where it figures in the Eucharist to find out. In this case, *contra* the Manichees, they learn that because of God's direct and loving relationship to his creation, both human and non-human, and because Christ is present by the power of the Spirit in the communion of all created things, they must have the same sort of hope for it as they have for themselves. They are not permitted to think of themselves as "not-nature," and of nature as "not God's." Believing that all things have their origin and end in the goodness of the one God, and that Christ has made them his dwelling place, they abide with the creation, and seek appropriate solidarity with it. Where others see only rubble, they look in the expectation of seeing beauty (the beauty that belongs to all God's gifts, which will be made perfect in the *eschaton*).

The Christian story contrasts, too, with what could be called the "Promethean" attitude that holds that human ingenuity alone can solve all the difficulties we face now and will face in the future. This Promethean attitude is present in the "strong" form of the management ethic (more optimistic than the Manichean attitude in believing it can solve *all* the world's problems), and also in certain forms of anthropocentrist approach which regard the natural world as in principle endlessly manipulatable and without its own moral integrity. The Promethean thinks that he has at least all the relevant information at his disposal to make appropriate plans on behalf of the environment, and regards any natural thing as available for his unrestricted use (as orientated to *him* rather than to some *telos* of its own, or of God's).

Christians are not free of an anthropocentric habit of mind, in that they believe that God has entrusted human beings with special responsibilities, and that he spoke his Word definitively in a human person. The human mind has a particular power of recognition and reflection in relation to other creatures, as witnessed in the story of Adam's naming of the animals. Christians do not seek to obliterate the responsibilities of moral judgment and action by some passive self-abasement before the "forces of nature." Their liturgical practices teach them to trust that God means them to make decisions about created things, and to use them in the service of life and salvation. They will often have to accept that they have to destroy some forms of life in favor of others (perhaps their own), but their concern is to do so for the right reasons. "Preferences" (greed, covetousness, desire for power, fear of the future, fear of death) are not enough of a justification for the appropriation of created things to oneself.

If God's work in Christ, made present in the Eucharist, is a work of reassembly – the display, as I have argued, of a surprising ordering of things – then just as at Christmas God reassembles man and woman, kings and working people, stars and animals, heaven and earth in a way that makes Christmas thoroughly eschatological, just so in the Eucharist God reassembles the dispersed characters of his creation in a way that shows their true relations in the light of their ultimate end. In the Eucharist's ordering of creation, humanity is shown to be that part of creation that does not wield supreme manipulative mastery over it, but that brings its fruits to the altar in a eucharistic act that is its highest calling (the offering of praise and thanksgiving). Humanity has to nurture, foster, care for the creation precisely so that it can fulfill this specially human task in the context of the creation's whole ecology of praise – the task of offering creation at the altar to be blessed. In this perspective, humanity does not nurture, foster, and care for the creation because otherwise humanity would die out; it does so because otherwise humanity (and through it the world) could not fully realize its eucharistic calling – could not fully celebrate the Eucharist.

There is a particular sort of humility to be learnt in seeing oneself as part of such an ecology – a humility absent in the Promethean. Moreover, Christians (unlike Protheans) are cautious about making claims about their own knowledge of the future. As we have noted, God lets Christians live with a strong awareness of where things have come from originally (from God's goodness) and of what their "end" is (God's glory), but they are ready to be surprised by what happens in the interim. What God does with the gifts placed on the altar is not a function of cause and effect, it is an act of grace. What God will do with the creation, even in the manifest crisis in which it is now embroiled, is not wholly predictable by the faithful believer. Christians are ready to live with uncertainty, though not with despair, about specific outcomes in relation to the immediate or even medium-term future of the environment. They can be realistic about the seriousness of present circumstances and the limits of their ability to change them (we are humans not deities), yet deeply hopeful that God can make all things new, and utterly committed to doing what they can to make that hope visible in the present. This is why the offertory sentences in the *Book of Common Prayer* are so saturated with eschatological anticipation, and make the link so strongly between our present offering and God's final bringing in of the Kingdom.

What, in conclusion, will it look like to "make that hope visible in the present"? It will look a bit like the Church at worship, and living out of its worship. Part of the problem afflicting present environmental decision-making is a crisis of *how* to value the environment – before any particular practical decisions are made about what to do in this or that situation (Banner, 1999: 163–203). There is genuine confusion at present about where complex values derive from and how they are to be measured. This is part of a larger modern debate, and a variety of matrices for the attribution of value have been put forward (cost–benefit analysis being one particularly unsatisfactory one; an earlier one was Marx's, in which labor determined all value). For Christians, values are identified and attributed in the activity of *worship*. They thus model with a certain confidence their distinctive evaluation of created things, and for them the crisis in *how* to value the environment proves not to be incapacitating. Knowing that the environment is to be valued as the object of God's love and regard, as enjoyable and usable by humans (without fear, acquisitiveness, or violence) in the service of life and salvation, permits a less paralyzed though certainly more modest approach to the assessment of any particular "issue."

The Church will also model out of this a very particular and extraordinary form of "dominion." This is a word I have avoided so far because it is too often bandied around as the mark of a Christian high-handedness and proprietary arrogance toward the natural world. And, indeed, in its roots as a Roman legal term, *dominium* means precisely full *ownership* (see O'Donovan, 1998: 31). Joan Lockwood O'Donovan has shown in a fascinating historical study how, in the early fourteenth century, the radical Franciscan ethic of poverty (or non-proprietorship) was countered by a papalist move to justify enforceable legal property rights on the basis that rule over the human and non-human creation was part of Christ's perfect humanity. Both sides appealed by analogy to the *divine life* to make their case: for the Franciscans, the rejection of all possessions was an *imitatio Christi*, and, for the papal side, the ownership with which Adam was endowed at the moment of his creation was in the image of God's own *dominium*, and subsequent exercise of such ownership could be legitimized by "Christ's purported exercise . . . of universal and immediate lordship over property" (O'Donovan, 1998: 32).

The trouble with the papalist position (apart from its influence on a subsequent secular tradition of natural rights theory and its exaltation of the proprietary will) is that it obscures the fact made so clear by the offertory that human "lordship" is to be wholly set in the service of God and the neighbor. The trouble with the Franciscan position is surprisingly similar in that it, too, is *individualistic*. The Franciscan ethic of poverty is not the complete theological alternative to the natural rights tradition:

> For Bonaventuran, as for all Franciscan theology, the communal features of the Minorite life were incidental to, indeed in tension with, the practice of evangelical poverty. The latter was inseparably wedded to the eremitical pattern of the wandering apostle . . . and to the towering figure of St Francis . . . Thus did St Bonaventure fail to place his idealistic and Christological epistemology and his Augustinian ethic of ordered love directly in the service of elaborating apostolic community as distinct from the apostolic "way." (O'Donovan, 1998: 34)

In other words, for both positions, there was not enough account of the *Church* (and O'Donovan herself turns to the writings of John Wyclif for the corrective to this imbalance).

In the Church, Christians learn that *real* gospel dominion in the tradition of the first apostolic communities in the Book of Acts is "communicating and communicable possession" (O'Donovan, 1998: 34). The gifts of the offertory are always distributed afterwards. This shows that, in the community of the Church, such "possession" as there is of the non-human creation is shared "possession," and intended for further sharing. "Communicating and communicable possession" represents a recovery of an original and good use of the earth's bounty, mediated by participation in Christ through the power of the Spirit (who also ecclesially "shares out" all the goods that are in Christ). "Evangelical dominion is, therefore, the just communal possession and use of earthly goods that, shadowing God's own dominion, conserve their being and assist them to realize their divinely appointed purposes" (O'Donovan, 1998: 35). Being thus a "possession" in the image of God's own dominion, it is far from being the exercise of a lonely proprietary will, and therefore far from the notion of dominion that has dogged much modern use of the term. God's dominion is generously distributive, and "makes room" for being. It is inherently to do with establishing relations of mutual love. (This, incidentally, makes the language of stewardship problematic in the context of Christian discussions of how to treat the non-human creation, for as Fern puts it, "what makes stewards 'stewards' in the first place is their responsibility for managing another person's . . . chattels" (Fern, 2002: 212–13), and to view the world as God's chattel is to distort the personal relationship he has with his creation.)

In the Eucharist, Christians learn how to make their "possession" and use of earthly goods a faithful image of God's dominion. Recognizing that they share being with other creatures whom God has also chosen for existence, their imitation of God's dominion leads them to try to conserve the being of non-human creatures and help them to occupy and fulfill their God-given place in God's purposes. In the Church, the space opened by Christ's reconciling work, this "possession" can be learnt and practiced together. Thus, in the Church, "the non-proprietary nature of humankind's original possession of the creation" finds itself "brought to an even higher fulfillment by Christ's redemptive and sanctifying grace" (O'Donovan, 1998: 37). Christians learn that coming to know and share in the love of Christ means (indivisibly) coming to know and share in the fellowship of the Holy Spirit: fellowship with all the other objects of Christ's loving regard.

An acute part of the difficulty facing environmentalists at the moment is the near impossibility of taking decisions that are in common. The uniting factor is often little more than "a mere agreement to survive" (Milbank, 1997: 265). Yet it is only with such a common mind that humans can approach the physical environment in a coherent way, shaping it for justice and beauty and convenience. Justice, beauty, and convenience "reflect and embody a common civic life: constitute, materially, a mode of human reciprocity collectively affirmed" (Milbank, 1997: 265).

By God's grace, wonderfully, Christians have this common life in the form of the Church, and should seek to foster it there for the sake of the world's salvation. God has given the Church a form of life whereby it can identify objectives and goods "which technocratic and expert thinking cannot themselves determine" (Banner, 1999: 203). Christians have in common the awareness that their first task is not to cling to, hoard, or manipulate creaturely things. Their hope in the resurrection means that they are less bound in their attitude to the environment by a determination to survive at all costs or to grab what can be grabbed ("attachment to the things of this world is felt particularly strongly by those who do not believe that there is any further transformation of this world after the life which we now know" [Staniloae, 2001: 1]). At the same time, they have in common an alertness to their "dependence on a fruitful world" (Clark, 2000: 256), which is not an *alternative to* but *part of* their dependence on the grace of God.

   Their form of life in the Church, and especially the habits learnt in the offertory, enable them to have in common this vision, which is in the end a vision of the dominion of God, the hope which is in Christ, and the fellowship of the Holy Spirit. Their form of life, and especially the offertory, help them to realize that the whole world belongs to God, not as property, but as something intrinsically communicable and communicating: part of the fellowship of all created things which is made visible in the Eucharist. By the power of the Holy Spirit the whole world can "belong" to Christians in the same communicable and communicating way, so long as they let their practices teach them that they are in common possession of themselves, of one another, and of the rest of creation only because all these things are first and last in Christ.

Acknowledgment

I am grateful to the British Academy for financing the period of research leave during which this chapter was written.

References

Banner, Michael (1999) *Christian Ethics and Contemporary Moral Problems* (Cambridge: Cambridge University Press), esp. pp. 163–203.

Barth, Karl (1936–69) *Church Dogmatics*, ed. G. W. Bromiley and T. F. Torrance, 13 vols (Edinburgh: T. and T. Clark), esp. vol. 3, part 2.

Blond, Phillip (2003) "Prolegomena to an Ethics of the Eye," in *Studies in Christian Ethics*, 16:1 (London: T. and T. Clark).

Clark, Stephen R. L. (2000) *Biology and Christian Ethics* (Cambridge: Cambridge University Press).

Davies, Oliver (2001) *A Theology of Compassion: Metaphysics of Difference and the Renewal of Tradition* (London: SCM).

Fern, Richard L. (2002) *Nature, God and Humanity: Envisioning an Ethics of Nature* (Cambridge: Cambridge University Press).

Milbank, John (1997) *The Word Made Strange: Theology, Language, Culture* (Oxford: Blackwell), esp. pp. 257–67.

O'Donovan, Joan Lockwood (1998) "Natural Law and Perfect Community: Contributions of Christian Platonism to Political Theory," *Modern Theology*, 14: 1.

Staniloae, Dumitru (2001) *The Victory of the Cross*, 2nd edn (Fairacres, Oxford: SLG).

United Nations (2002) *Global Environment Outlook 3: Past, Present and Future Perspectives* (United Nations Environment Programme: Earthscan).

CHAPTER 24

Participating: Working toward Worship

R. R. Reno

A Christian ethic of work must always reflect the fact that our labors lead to the Sabbath. The work-a-day world of earning a living and taking care of a household finds its proper end in the divine work of worship. Planting and harvesting certainly serve to sustain life, but it is the bread and wine, offered in the Eucharist, that fulfill and complete this labor. Teaching children to read and write is a basic duty, and such work prepares young people to participate fully in society, but reading the Scriptures and reciting the liturgy complete such efforts.

That work should serve the Sabbath is expressed by Augustine's well-known observation about use and enjoyment: we should enjoy God, and others in God, and we should use everything else in such a way that we might enter ever more fully into that enjoyment. In a great deal of the theological tradition, this proper ordering of worldly activity and love of God is expressed in terms of the ancient priority of the *vita contemplativa* over the *vita activa* (for a contemporary restatement, see Pieper, 1963). Beatitude is our proper end. Neither the tinkering of the tinker nor the tailoring of the tailor brings us to the heavenly feast. Our joy is in the Sabbath, and we live well when we work toward that end.

The clear subordination of work to the enjoyment of God in worship is crucial, but we should not be deceived by the Christian tradition's use of the philosopher's ideal of contemplation. Both Plato and Aristotle clearly reflect the ancient Greek dismay over the worldliness of work. Plato reports and endorses Socrates' rejection of practical expertise (*techne*) in favor of a philosophical knowledge (*episteme*) that is receptive rather than active. For Aristotle, the highest good is contemplation (*theoria*), and this pursuit of the highest good requires us to separate ourselves from the activities of life (*praxis*) that bind and limit us, not only the servile arts of the laborer, but even the noble arts of political life (Aristotle, 1995: 1333a; see also Aristotle, 1980). For a Christian work ethic, this presumed antagonism between the necessities of work and the highest good must be rejected. To recall Augustine's distinction between use and enjoyment, a Christian work ethic recognizes that the life of discipleship rightly accepts the necessity of work as a providential imposition that we can use, not only to ensure survival, but also to prepare the soul for enjoyment of God, and others in God.

In this sense, it may be more appropriate to say that God "uses" work so that we might enjoy him. This shaping is not theological in an immediate sense. God does not put down a eucharistic template onto human life. Instead, the ordinary conditions of human work have common features that make the act of Christian worship a fitting fulfillment. I wish to develop an account of the providential ordering of work, highlighting ways in which labor prepares us to enter the sanctuary of prayer with dispositions suited for worship. Three aspects are crucial: (1) The disciplining necessity of work prepares us for discipleship and the demanding requirements of a life of prayer; (2) the bitter necessity of work reminds us of our sinfulness and our need for divine grace; (3) the humanizing role of work awakens our desire for the divinizing power of worship. To these three characteristics of work I now turn.

Disciplining Necessity of Work

How should work be defined? In complex industrial and post-industrial societies, work usually means employment and being paid. The bartender may expend as much energy lifting the beer mug from tap to table as I do lifting it from table to lips, but that is his "job," while I am relaxing. Yet, wages do not define work. I do not pay my son to clear the table after dinner, but I can report with confidence that he regards the chore as work. Furthermore, the exchange of money for work, as well as the bright line that separates workplace from home, is an historically recent development. Thus, work extends beyond wage earning.

But how far does work extend? Establishing clear boundaries is difficult. One could say that work is any purposeful activity that seeks to satisfy human needs, or, in the case of a complex modern society, purposeful activities that either satisfy human needs or sustain social institutions that support those purposeful activities (Volf, 1991: 10–14). This definition narrows the field helpfully, but not entirely satisfactorily, for many pleasant diversions contribute to purposeful activities. Think of an afternoon tennis match and the clear human need for leisure. Thus, to establish a boundary, I want to focus on the necessity of work. Work is a purposeful activity that we must undertake, even when we wish to do otherwise. The element of compulsion has external and internal aspects, both of which help separate work from other human activities, and both of which prepare us for the Sabbath.

The external aspect rests on our need for survival. At a basic level, unless we rouse ourselves to work, we will not eat. Had no prehistoric being stalked animals or cultivated the soil, the human race would not have endured. Of course, for most people in industrial societies, the necessity of work is not driven by such an immediate need and subsistence no longer animates work. Instead, we respond to a cultural analog of the second law of thermodynamics. Unless we constantly add human energy to current social practices, they will decay and decline. We do not just need investors, managers, and factory workers to make a manufacturing company a going concern, we also need stockbrokers and floor traders and regulators and accountants and lawyers – and seemingly more every year. Productive social practices are not perpetual motion machines; they need constant infusions of human energy. For this reason, even amidst abundance beyond the imaginations of those who lived even a century ago, wealthy societies continue to put pressure on nearly all of their members to be "productive." The watch needs to be tightly wound in order to keep the gears of society functioning. Work is the pound of flesh that society extracts as payment for the debt of communal life.

The external demands of work are not always externally imposed. Work also has an internal appeal. Most people want to do something that will force them to do what they do not want to do. In spite of all efforts of escape, human beings actively desire the discipline of necessity that accompanies work. Work has to be serious; it must place demands upon us if it is really to count. To be sure, most need the pay check, and the extrinsic necessity of work can seem singular and dominating, but a desire to have a life characterized by more than desires and their fulfillment always operates below the surface. We strangely desire a necessity that will force us to wake in the morning when we would rather sleep, and, for all our dreams of leisure, the evidence is overwhelming that the freedom to do exactly what we want, when we want, brings no happiness. Thus, when a retired man says "I want to do something meaningful with my free time," he is asking for time that is not free. He is asking for an activity that has the sharp edge of compulsion.

Necessity, both external and internal, separates work from other purposeful activities. When training for a marathon becomes necessary – maybe because your family now depends upon the sponsorship money, or perhaps because you have developed an elaborate sense of the larger social importance of sport, which you now feel obligated to uphold and enhance – then it begins to become work. It is work rather than leisure when colored by coercive necessity. For this reason, in the background of all work are the bark of the foreman and the crack of the whip.

The disciplining necessity of work foreshadows the commandment to keep the Sabbath holy. It is not the case that worship is optional. As Paul teaches in his genealogy of morals (Romans 1), the question is not *whether* we shall worship, but only *what*. Promethean fantasies of a purely human-centered existence are as difficult to realize as fantasies of aristocratic indolence. We are propelled by an inner need to bow down, and, as a consequence, unless true worship is always before us, there is always the danger that we will work feverishly in order to propitiate Baal, whether in his bloody martial form or in the bloodless image of lucre. One need be no Sabbatarian to recognize that the Christian requirement of regular public worship is fundamentally important. Like marriage and sexual desire, this external necessity, rightly imposed by the Church on its members, wisely encouraged by any sensible social policy, ensures that our internal drive toward worship finds fitting rather than perverse expression.

Bitter Necessity of Work

The dark shadow of necessity has dominated traditional Christian reflection upon work. Drawing on a few Pauline passages that explicitly mention work (for example, 1 Thessalonians 4: 11; 2 Thessalonians 3: 10; 1 Corinthians 4: 12; Ephesians 4: 28), theologians have largely treated work as secular necessity, something we must do in order to maintain life. Thomas Aquinas is typical. When discussing the question of whether monks must do "productive" work (in the idiom of his time, "manual labor"), Aquinas allows that work is necessary for subsistence. Human beings cannot survive without food, and food requires work. For this reason, the obligation to work is a precept of natural law. All of us, then, must acknowledge the duty to submit to the necessity of this kind of work (Aquinas, 1981: II-II, 187, 3).

This focus on the Pauline texts and treatment of work as a precept of natural law is widespread in the Christian tradition. However, an assessment of work as a divinely ordained punishment has also influenced Christian attitudes toward the common life of labor. Attention typically focuses on Genesis 3: 17–19, in which the Lord God declares to Adam the consequences of his transgression:

> Because you have listened to the voice of your wife, and have eaten of the tree of which I commanded you, "You shall not eat of it," cursed is the ground because of you; in toil shall you eat of it all the days of your life; thorns and thistles it shall bring forth to you; and you shall eat of the plants of the field. In the sweat of your face you shall eat bread till you return to the ground, for out of it you were taken and to dust you shall return.

The main emphasis of Christian exegesis falls on the punishment of death ("to dust you shall return"), foreshadowed in the warning in Genesis 2: 17 ("of the tree of the knowledge of good and evil you shall not eat, for in that day you eat of it you shall die"), and definitely formulated in Romans 6: 23 ("the wages of sin is death"). Yet, for centuries, Christian interpreters have also linked the extrinsic and often bitter necessity of work to this passage. The necessities of life – "bread" – must be wrested from nature in sweat-soaked toil, and this life of work will be afflicted by the "thorns and thistles" of difficulty. And, further, as an early Christian commentator emphasizes, the downward gaze of the field worker reminds him that the fruitful earth will be the place of his burial (Chrysostom, 1986: 244). Our efforts may sustain and enhance human life, but never with any realistic hope of lasting success. Death will always nullify the labors of our hands. In this way, the bitter necessity of work is linked to the hard necessity of death.

The Protestant tradition of exegesis has exploited this link to develop a sophisticated view of work as punishment. Martin Luther's exegesis provides an important basis for this tradition. In his *Lectures on Genesis*, Luther discounts Genesis 2: 15 ("till and keep it"), picturing the fields of Eden as producing a bounty "unsown and uncultivated" (Luther, 1965: 206). Thus, for Luther, labor only enters the scene after the Fall. Here, Luther would seem to follow the ancient and medieval tradition of defining work as an extrinsic and unfortunate necessity. He does treat work as largely negative, but, by describing it as divine punishment, Luther draws the suffering caused by work into God's larger purposes. Work is divinely mandated, and, because God does not punish in vain, this mandate has positive, remedial consequences. In other words, as punishment, work has "supernatural" significance. However painful, work prepares us for the Sabbath joy of fellowship with God. As such, Luther enters into an extended reflection on the positive spiritual fruits of work, fruits that stem from the extrinsic and painful necessity of work.

The first aspect has to do with work and responsibility. Since the text suggests that God punishes Adam for wrongfully listening to the voice of his wife ("because you have listened to the voice of your wife"), Luther links the travails of labor with the need to rule over and provide for a family. "The husband," he writes, "endures his penalty in the management of the household . . ." (Luther, 1965: 205). A wife, he points out, can be very difficult to control, and the need for a family to function as a well-ordered unit constantly intrudes upon any pleasure the husband might take in his work. Indeed, because the social organization of labor in Luther's time was integrated into the daily functioning of the household, disorder in the home quickly translated into disorder and conflict in working activities. Thus, the primeval failure of Adam to exercise properly familial leadership translates into a continuing corruption of the harmony of family life. "It is the husband's duty to support his family, to rule, to direct, and to instruct; and [as a consequence of the Fall] these things cannot be done without extraordinary trouble and very great effort" (Luther, 1965: 203).

Whether or not we accept Luther's picture of familial harmony based upon male dominance, his insight into the relationship between responsibility and work is apt. One of the most frustrating and painful aspects of work is a disordered workplace characterized by conflict rather than cooperation. We can easily deceive ourselves about our own sinfulness and imagine ourselves rather good-natured. However, about others we tend to be more clear-sighted, and, in the workplace, we are forced to confront the reality of sin. We see the perversity of our common humanity when we try (and fail) to cooperate in work, and, for just this reason, work is often an affliction. In this way, work and its responsibilities can make for a keen apprehension of the reality of human sinfulness and the burden of Adam in which we all share.

The second punitive aspect of work, for Luther, is its sheer difficulty. We experience work as exhausting. For this reason, work is painful. Even if we like our jobs, there are always days when we are drained, either physically or emotionally. The evening Martini is an anodyne that testifies to the afflictions of work. For Luther, the bitter taste of the sweat of our face afflicts all of our efforts. The pain of work is a perpetual admonishment that helps us rid ourselves "of our smugness and walk in the fear of God" (Luther, 1965: 209).

Here, the contemporary reader tends to grimace. "How can a good and loving God inflict pain upon us?" This response ignores a simple reality. Encouragement and the promise of reward are not sufficient to motivate bad people to change their ways. Since God is not a modern liberal, he does what is necessary rather than what is nice. Given the fact that all of us are bad people (and some of us are so bad that we vainly and lazily think ourselves good), God wisely uses pain as a punishment to encourage us to think seriously about whether or not we need to undertake a fundamental change in the way we lead our lives. And since we would rather not think seriously and we certainly do not want to change, it is a good thing that God imposes work upon us as a painful necessity. We may dislike the bitter taste, but it gets our attention.

The third dimension of Luther's reflection upon the role of work concerns idleness, which comes to play a large role in the Christian tradition as a whole. Luther notes that while we would like to escape from the necessity of work, our inability to do so saves us from the temptations of idleness. Those temptations are great. The proverbial wisdom of the Old Testament warns that "idleness teaches much evil" (Ecclesiasticus 33: 27), and Paul's admonition that those who will not work shall not eat occurs in the context of a concern about the disruptive meddling of those who have too much time on their hands (2 Thessalonians 3: 10–12). To a great degree, the so-called "Protestant work ethic" emerges from the seriousness with which the Puritan faithful took the all-too-human insight that idle hands do the devil's work. If you spare the rod you will spoil the child – and if you do not keep him busy, you will need to use the rod more often than not.

For Luther and the Protestant tradition, work does not just prevent idleness. It also functions positively. Labor at a job one does not like (and all of us, at some point, do not like our jobs) builds up the virtues of patience and fortitude. In the face of the painful necessities of work, we must "teach our hearts to be patient," and we "ought to have courage and overcome these evils through hope . . ." (Luther, 1965: 214). Suffering afflictions in this world makes one sensible that there is no salvation in and through work. Thus, the pain of work offers a salutary reminder that one's hope should be in God alone.

Finally, Luther sees great wisdom in the universality of divine punishment. All experience work as an affliction. Luther draws attention to the fact that the powerful are no less burdened than the weak. "I have heard," he reports, "that Emperor Maximilian was so occupied with the affairs of state that he never had enough leisure for taking food" (Luther, 1965: 212). One is hard pressed to believe that the Emperor ate more poorly than his peasants, but Luther's hyperbole highlights an important truth. It is not the case that work is more fun or more relaxing or more enlivening for the rich and powerful. Indeed, the fantasy of early retirement among young entrepreneurs and professionals testifies to the universal experience of work as an affliction. The same holds for those whose lives are not defined by the marketplace. Against common fantasies about authors and artists and the blissful vocation of creativity, memoirs and biographies testify to the pain felt by those who were seemingly spared the tedium and futility of work-a-day jobs. One can regret this common condition; indeed, with repentant hearts, one should. Yet, justice is served by the fact that all must taste the bitter sweat of their brows.

While we may affirm or reject one or all of Luther's four punitive elements, his approach blocks two false ethics of work. First, to affirm work as punishment prevents us from romanticizing work. In many ways and for many reasons, we do not like to work, and, if we follow the basic line of Luther's reasoning, we have no reason to falsify or deny that experience. Second, since work is ordained by God as punishment, we are not tempted to fantasize about escaping from the pain of work. Short of the consummation of all things, we must endure the penalty of work. And this is a good thing. It is good for work to be bad because it serves as a reminder that our sinful existence is fundamentally disordered. Thus, work is a painful necessity – it is to be regretted without being avoided.

Luther's punitive view of work prevents us from romanticizing the work of sustaining a Christian community and fantasizing that we might dream up an ecclesial scheme in which worship will "just happen." Running a Church is hard work, and illusions to the contrary feed clerical sloth, anger, and despair. The same holds for lay people. I have often heard friends complain that their involvement in the Church is just "too much work." Or they complain about the regular routine of regular worship. They want Church to be a form of leisure or entertainment, something fresh and new that will be a deliverance from the all-too-human limitations of the working day. Yet, this is not the meaning of the Sabbath. The "rest" of Christian worship occurs in and not in spite of the world of sin and death. The joy of worship addresses the bitter cup of sin; it does not change the subject. For this reason, the punitive dimension of work, its burdening reality, its tiresome regularity, its ubiquity and universality, is present in the life of the Church. The bitterness forces worship onto the power of God, not of those who organize and coordinate. The regular routine prevents idleness and encourages patient endurance, a spiritual virtue much commended in the early Church. Thus, worship is tinged with the punitive dimensions of worldly work, not in spite of salvation in Jesus Christ, but because he comes to us in this way, for our sake.

Work as a Humanizing Activity

With increasing confidence, modern Christianity has emphasized the positive and humanizing aspects of work, drawing out the theological importance of our increasingly productive modern society. Instead of punishment, attention falls on the task God assigns to the man and woman: "Be fruitful and multiply, and fill the earth and subdue it" (Genesis 1: 28). When combined with Genesis 2: 15 ("The Lord God took the man and put him in the garden of Eden to till it and keep it"), the procreative emphasis expands toward the productive. Work creates and echoes divine creation.

In his encyclical on work, *Laborem exercens*, John Paul II offers one of the most extensive and optimistic meditations on these passages from Genesis. He treats the divinely appointed task as testimony to our fundamental drive toward purposeful work: "Even though these words do not refer directly to work, beyond any doubt they indirectly indicate it as an activity for man to carry out in the world" (para 4.2). Work, then, is constitutive of the human condition. Because we are created for work, John Paul II insists that "human work has an ethical value of its own" (para. 6.3). This value is twofold. In the first place, work is integral to our humanity. To work is to become more human. The second value of work is its capacity to draw us closer to God. "Man," John Paul II writes, "created in the image of God, shares by his work in the activity of the Creator" (para. 25.2). For this reason, according to John Paul II, work is properly "spiritual." Even amidst its inevitable pain and difficulties, "people come closer, through work, to God, the Creator and Redeemer, to participate in his salvific plan for man and the world and to deepen their friendship with Christ . . ." (para 24.2).

This theological exaltation of work certainly moves beyond the traditional Christian view of work as a natural duty. It also extends beyond the monastic ideal of *ora et labora*, which seeks to sanctify secular work in and through a life of prayer. Not surprisingly, then, such a positive attitude toward work has attracted criticism. Stanley Hauerwas offers a number of objections: this view of work is romantic and elitist; it is based on an implausible personalist philosophy rather than Scripture; it entails a Pelagianizing equation of human and divine work; and, finally, such a high view of work contributes to our already pervasive idolatry of work (Hauerwas, 1983: 42–58). Against the idea of work as participation in divine purposes, Hauerwas reiterates the limited affirmation of work that has characterized most of the Christian tradition. Work is necessary because it "gives us a means to survive, be of service to others, and, perhaps most important of all, work gives us a way to stay busy" (Hauerwas, 1983: 48). Work meets basic needs, contributes to the common good, and keeps idle hands busy and far from the devil's work.

Is John Paul II's work ethic romantic and elitist, unscriptural, Pelagian, and idolatrous? Answering such questions would entail extensive digressions into the modern view of work, biblical hermeneutics, and the history of Protestant and Roman Catholic debates about nature and grace. I cannot allay these concerns, and I will not argue for John Paul II's vision of secular work as a form of human participation in divine creativity. Nonetheless, the view advanced by Hauerwas seems inadequate. To say that work is just making a living is as implausible as saying that sex is just satisfying instincts. Work, like sex, seems to have a theologically important significance, and this prevents us from either "naturalizing" it completely or relegating its spiritual significance to punishment or distraction.

Furthermore, a humanizing view of work is not uniquely modern. Consider the Targum Pseudo-Jonathan. This Aramaic translation of the books of Scripture from the time of Jesus provides a haggadic expansion of Genesis 3: 17–19. Instead of having the Lord God pronounce the necessity of labor upon Adam, the Targum makes work a petition that Adam addresses to God. After the Lord God says that Adam shall eat the plants of the field, the Targum continues, "Adam answered and said, 'I beseech by the mercy before you, O Lord, Let me not be reckoned before you as cattle, that I should eat the grass of the surface of the field. I will arise and labor with the labor of my hands, and I will eat of the food of the earth; and thus let there be a distinction before you between the children of men and the offspring of cattle.'" It is on the basis of this petition, then, that the Lord God assigns to Adam the task of work. Clearly, in this haggadic addition, the Targum represents work as the crucial means by which men and women preserve and restore their humanity. As John Paul II wishes to emphasize, work is a divinely imposed necessity that ennobles and contributes to our spiritual lives.

How, then, does our work ennoble and upbuild? I will suggest four ways in which work edifies and fulfills. Discussion of these ways will not unveil the eschatological significance of work in a material way. On the day of the Lord, nearly all worldly work may come to naught, and this should chasten our sense of the importance of what we do day in and day out. Nonetheless, I hope that these positive aspects of work will clarify its role, however materially inconsequential, in shaping human sensibilities so that the life of discipleship can be inhabited more fully.

(1)   Work provides a social identity that goes beyond family, clan, and nation. This positive contribution of work is often hidden. It is with regret that we say a man is "defined by his work," and the term "workaholic" identifies a real diminishment of life. However, what is abused is not intrinsically bad. The ability of work to command our loyalty and consume a great deal of our time is often a positive good. For family, clan, and national identities are not always benevolent. They can diminish and constrict human life. To have a job, a place to stand in the world, an identity that is fashioned,

at least to some degree, by one's own agency and effort, helps to free one from the illusion that one's identity is simply a static, unchangeable fact. In this way, being "defined" by work opens rather than constricts.

In the Protestant tradition, the term "vocation" was expanded from a purely clerical and monastic use to express the sacred potential of secular work. We are "called" to our labors. We all must labor to inhabit our jobs – we must do the work. And for this reason, unlike nationality and family, the social identity found in work is not conferred or inherited. In this way, while work rarely reflects our freedom, it does contribute to our distinctiveness as people. I might be a good, bad, or indifferent son, but only the adjectives are in doubt. If I am an indifferent and haphazard bricklayer, then I am very likely to be fired, and am soon to be no bricklayer at all (if I ever was one in anything but name).

The way in which work both frees identity from the bonds of "blood and soil" and shapes human identity according to specific standards clearly foreshadows the call of the Gentiles into the fellowship of Israel. To be baptized is to be placed into a divine workplace in which family, clan, and nation do not define the practices and skills necessary for worshiping well. Moreover, this call, like so much of secular work, is something that shapes us to achieve its purpose. Much as being a bricklayer entails accepting the disciplines of laying bricks well, to be a Christian entails accepting the disciplines of the Christian life. In this way, secular work is a figure for sacred work.

(2) Work demands social interaction. Unlike the loyalties of family, clan, and nation, work is eccentric. It draws us into the company of men and women with whom we might not otherwise associate. In this way, the necessity of work exerts a benevolent influence upon our tendency to draw a narrow circle around our lives. In some jobs, this social interaction is limited, and in many jobs the interaction rarely rises to any level of personal intimacy. Furthermore, we segregate ourselves at work, and the hierarchies of the job can be ruthless. Yet, limitations aside, work forces men and women to stand shoulder to shoulder, and while this may not always lead to friendship, it often leads to respect for a person whom our families, clans, and nations train us to dismiss or despise.

The intrinsically social nature of worship intensifies this pattern, calling individuals to a common altar. However important are moments of solitude, the center of Christian worship, the Eucharist, cannot be celebrated in isolation. Even the Tridentine practice of the private mass presupposed a spiritually present congregation of the heavenly hosts. Thus, in worship, the respect for others that secular work can inculcate is pressed toward the divine commandment of love, and the figure for cooperation in pursuit of worldly ends is fulfilled in a common prayer that seeks the heavenly goal of glorifying God.

(3) Work requires us to develop self-discipline. Here, the necessity of work shapes our passions. We need to wake up early to get to work on time. We must resist the desire for a nap after lunch. We have to endure an incompetent boss. These are obvious instances in which work disciplines us, and Luther draws attention to the virtues of fortitude and patience that stem from such trials. But, more positively, our jobs have demands internal to the activity we undertake. If we are to sell cars, then we must train ourselves to smile winsomely and speak earnestly. If we are to lay bricks, then we must

learn to use the line and level. If we are to plant crops, then we must become proficient in agricultural techniques. If we are to grade papers, then we must internalize the rules of grammar and the arts of composition. In each instance, the specific task places demands upon us.

A Christian view of secular work should never confuse the demands of the workplace with the commands of God. However, a Christian work ethic should acknowledge that such demands can train the soul for the more severe and comprehensive disciplines of the Christian life. Bricklaying does not prepare one for the heavenly kingdom, but someone who has acknowledged and mastered the art of his or her trade may be better able to recognize that the practice of worship will entail accepting a discipline that is intrinsic to the task and not subject to our passing whims. One can no more play at prayer than one can dabble in plumbing. Doing it well requires doing it seriously, intelligently, and with an expertise born of accountability to the standards of a job well done.

(4)   Work provides scope for creativity. Modern philosophers and theologians can romanticize work because it does have an element of romance. The labor of our hands does, collectively, shape the natural world and the cultural forms we have inherited. A steel worker can look upon a skyscraper and with pride say, in full seriousness and without self-delusion, "I built that." Of course, he did not build it alone, and, of course, the steel is but a portion of the overall building, and, of course, such buildings could not be constructed without the vast resources of a complex modern industrial society. Yet the pride is proper. Nearly all human work is productive, even when it seems otherwise because the effects are so muted by the sheer scale of modern society, or because the labor takes place in the ethereal world of paper and pencil – or computer screen and fiber-optic line. The teacher who sees a class graduate witnesses the effects of labor. The fast-food server may rue the ubiquity of those golden arches, but they are a visible sign of the continuing conquest of the global palate. Nobody can guarantee that human creativity will always be for the best.

Two modern prejudices, originality and individuality, both legacies of modernity, obscure the creative dimension of work and often lead to protests that work cannot have this dimension, or, if it does, then discipleship must move in the opposite direction.

First, the notion of creativity tends to be restricted to the work of the artist or poet. They exercise "poetic license," and their work generates something distinctive and new. The greengrocer and espresso barista clearly do not. They purvey the work of others, or create the same thing over and over again. Hence, as Hauerwas objects, the idea that work is creative is a pious dream at best, and an anesthetizing ideology at worst. Yet, the objection concedes too much to romantic conceits. Earlier accounts of creativity treat the artist as oracle rather than originator. At the outset of *Paradise Lost*, Milton invokes the aide of the Heavenly Muse to raise and support the "great Argument" that is not his, but rather the very argument of Christian truth (Book I: 1–25). He cannot "create" a justification of the ways of God to men; he can only testify to the wisdom and righteousness of that which God has done. The fact that the greengrocer arranges apples to make them appealing to customers is actually closer to Milton's self-understanding than romantic fantasies of originality. Making rotten apples seem ripe is propaganda. Good poetry can do no more than lead our hands toward ripe apples most worth eating.

Second, many modern views place great emphasis on individuality in creative work, and, in contrast, nearly all ordinary work is collective in nature. Thus, one rejects the idea that work is creative. But, once again, the objection concedes too much to an ideology of art. Contemporary art historians now quietly allow that modern assumptions are not adequate to pre-modern practice. The old masters were quite willing for assistants to finish large canvases. Indeed, medieval art seems to have been produced in a nearly "industrial" fashion in order to meet the decorative needs of ecclesiastical building and the increasingly expansive palaces of the wealthy. And even amidst the great modern cult of genius, artists have clumped together for inspiration and mutual support as they push the limits of technique and vision. Individuality, then, has more to do with idiosyncrasy than creativity, and the collective nature of work in no way impairs our ability to experience work as generative and original.

The potential for creativity in secular work clearly prefigures the work of prayer, for in the life of the Church, the gathering of the people in worship is the creative act without peer. Social outreach is important; educational programs are necessary; budgets must be balanced and buildings repaired. All this work is quite real and contributes to the flourishing of the Church. Nonetheless, it is the work of worship that makes the Church a Church rather than a benevolent association. The act of worship makes the community into the people of God. Of course, it is God's work. He calls all people to himself in Jesus Christ. Yet, just as the steel worker is called to the heights of the skyscraper and is given the means to contribute to the completion of the project, every baptized person is called to heights of the Eucharist and is given the means to contribute to the completion of the divine project of redeeming the whole world. For, in the Eucharist, each person is called to join with angels and archangels and with all the company of heaven in praise. We are all called, and we are given the fitting words of the hymn of eternal praise.

Doing the Work of the Lord

Western Christianity has powerful antibodies that quickly move to attack any encroachment upon God's singular prerogative. Jesus alone saves. We may join our voices to angels and archangels and with all the company of heaven, but we are not to imagine that we can work our way toward the heavenly kingdom. Too often, however, these antibodies attack human agency in general rather than spiritual presumption. A positive appraisal of work is not equivalent to works-righteousness. Karl Barth was a great critic of spiritual presumption, but he offers an encouraging assessment of the theological significance of work. "Within its limits," he writes, "creaturely activity can take the form of correspondence to divine activity" (Barth, 1961: 482). When the bread and wine enter the sanctuary as the elements for the eucharistic offering, the labor of human hands enters as well.

As I have attempted to show, the limits that shape a theology of human work should be derived from the ways in which God has ordered our days of work toward a proper enjoyment of the Sabbath. This theological ordering of work toward worship is manifest in the Scriptures. Just as the Song of Songs utilizes conjugal joy as a figure for the joy of union with God, so also does Isaiah treat worldly work as a figure for eschatological joy. The new heaven and new earth of the age to come will fulfill the righteousness of God, and the "rest" of this great Sabbath will involve the work of our hands. The joy of Jerusalem will include the building of houses and the planting of vineyards (65: 17–21). The hands of work are transfigured into the hands of prayer.

The patristic tradition recognized the many ways in which the structure of ordinary human life prepares us for the gospel. Didymus the Blind offers an extended allegorical interpretation of Genesis 3: 17–19 (Didymus, 1976: 241–9). For Didymus, the hardships of work can be transformed into the godly grief Paul commends in 2 Corinthians 7: 10. Such grief is the entryway into joy. Didymus's exegesis defies summary, but across his wide-ranging allegory he continually returns to the theme of cultivation and work. The thorns and thistles of our sinful indifference can choke the gospel (cf. Luke 8: 14ff), but appealing to Hebrews 6: 7, Didymus observes that the soul committed to labor in the Lord's vineyard can bring forth a bounty of blessings. Doing the work of God brings the joy of solid food (Hebrews 5: 14). Here, the labor assigned to Adam is interpreted as prefiguring the labor we must undertake on behalf of the kingdom of God. It is not just the retributive labor that Luther envisions, although Didymus certainly includes that aspect. Instead, the worldly work assigned to Adam is capable of being elevated to spiritual and supernatural purposes. Like those who laid the stone of the Temple in Jerusalem, we are called to labor with Christ to build up the eternal and heavenly city.

This elevation does not happen in an apotheosis of worldly work, as if, somehow, the bricklayer can so spiritualize his labors as to divinize them. Here, the distinction between work and the Sabbath must be emphasized in order to avoid an idolatry of work. Instead, worldly work becomes supernatural when the habits, disciplines, and practices developed in and through worldly work are brought into the service of the Church. The necessity of work disciplines all human life. The bitterness of work punishes and turns us toward God. Work humanizes and fulfills. In all these ways, the end and purpose of work is to train us to become workers in the Lord's vineyard.

References

Aquinas, Thomas (1981) *Summa theologica*, trans. the Fathers of the English Dominican Province (Westminster, MD: Christian Classics).
Aristotle (1980) *Nicomachean Ethics*, trans. David Ross, revised by J. L. Ackrill and J. O. Urmson (New York: Oxford University Press).
—(1995) *The Politics*, trans. Sir Ernest Barker, revised with notes by R. F. Stalley (Oxford: Oxford University Press).
Barth, Karl (1961) *Church Dogmatics*, ed. G. W. Bromiley and T. F. Torrance, vol. 4 (Edinburgh: T. and T. Clark).
Chrysostom, John (1986) *Homilies on Genesis*, The Fathers of the Church, vol. 74, trans. Robert C. Hill (Washington, DC: The Catholic University Press).

Didymus the Blind (1976) *Sur la Genèse*, vol. 1, trans. and ed. Pierre Nautin, Sources Chrétiennes, no. 233 (Paris: Cerf).

Hauerwas, Stanley (1983) "Work as Co-creation: A Critique of a Remarkably Bad Idea," in *Co-creation and Capitalism: John Paul II's Laborem Exercens*, ed. John W. Houck and Oliver F. Williams, pp. 42–58 (Washington, DC: University of America Press).

Luther, Martin (1965) *Lectures on Genesis*, Luther's Works, vol. 1, ed. Jaroslav Pelikan (Saint Louis, MO: Concordia).

Maher, Michael (trans.) (1992) *The Aramaic Bible*, vol. 1b (Collegeville, MN: The Liturgical Press).

Pieper, Joseph (1963) *Leisure, The Basis of Culture*, trans. Alexander Dru (New York: New American Library).

Volf, Miroslav (1991) *Work in the Spirit: Toward a Theology of Work* (Oxford: Oxford University Press).

CHAPTER 25

Remembering: Offering our Gifts

D. Stephen Long and Tripp York

How do the gifts we exchange in worship illumine the necessary economic exchanges in our everyday life? Can they generate the social bonds that render those exchanges intelligible? These questions seem odd to those of us who received our education in the modern university; for the university divides disciplines such as theology, politics, and economics into distinct autonomous fields of study, assuming that each can give an account of itself without the need for the other. Politics and economics explain the facts of social bonds; their subject matter is the distribution of power and analysis of exchange. Whatever modern theology does, it does not seem to do that. It sets forth values or answers questions of meaning. It only indirectly relates to politics and economics.

Yet it was not always so. Eamon Duffy (1992) explains how Sunday ceremonies of the eucharistic celebration in sixteenth-century England were essential to social arrangements and the distribution of power. They both "promoted harmony" and "imposed hegemony." Where laity stood in the processional, who kissed the paxbread first, and who provided the eucharistic bread for the celebration were all matters that produced social harmony as well as division. In some places the bread itself was cut into varying sizes dependent upon one's social rank. In 1518 John "Kareless" was accused of the deadly vice of pride for "taking too large a piece of the holy loaf." Not only the reception of the Holy Loaf, but also the "gifts" that people offered to the Church for the celebration of the mass were causes for social harmony as well as hegemony. They were how people would be remembered at the great moment of the eucharistic celebration. As Duffy notes, "again and again one encounters bequests of linen for use in the Mass. Gifts of this sort gave those of modest means a way of perpetuating their personal presence at the heart of the community" (Duffy, 1992: 126–8). The "gift" of the Eucharist and the "gifts" church people brought to it – for better or worse – established social bonds of harmony and hegemony. The politics and economics of a sixteenth-century English village were inseparable from theological concerns.

We do not live in sixteenth-century England. Neither the Eucharist nor the Church gives our everyday social life its political or economic orientation. Yet even to have an "orientation" is to be residually affected by that other world, for it is to be directed toward some end. As Albert Borgmann notes, the term "orientation" arose from the way cathedrals once shaped daily life. They were built toward the east, bearing witness to where Christian hope was directed – toward the homeland of Christ who would one day return. They structured the time and space of everyday life, seeking to orient us by the virtues of hope and faith toward our true end, which was to be found in Christ (Borgmann, 1987: 72).

Most people still seem to have some orientation to their lives; we are not simply spinning on a little blue ball ride through a vast nothingness, "plunging continually, backward, sideward, forward, in all directions" (Nietzsche, 1983: 95). While the space and time of modern life are not so structured as to orient us to the end of Christ, our lives are routinely oriented. They are oriented by "interstate highways" that give access to malls and other major business attractions. The patterns and practices of our lives orient us in the world first and foremost as consumers. We are all consumers whose end is to buy and sell within the marketplace – twenty-four hours a day, seven days a week. This is the default position of our orientation, much as the orientation provided by the Eucharist was the default position in sixteenth-century England. If our lives can still be oriented by the gift of the Eucharist it will require a particular intentionality and attentiveness on our part.

What difference would it make to have our lives, especially the everyday exchanges that provide our daily sustenance, more oriented by the gifts one finds in the Church's liturgy than by the interstate highways that give us our direction? This chapter will address that question, working with the assumption that such an ecclesial orientation is still present – even if only residually so – in the Church's liturgical life. We do not need to invent something new to produce this other orientation. We do not even need some cataclysmic revolution. Instead, we need to be attentive to what God has already given us and learn to recognize the competing practices that orient our lives in directions other than that of this gift. In fact, we will argue, the distinguishing practices between a life oriented by the gift found in the Church's liturgy and one found on the interstate highways is the difference between "gift" and "contract."

Bringing our Gifts to the Altar

After sharing the peace and before praying the Great Thanksgiving, Christians are instructed to bring an offering to the altar. This practice occurs among diverse churches and almost always includes tokens of people's everyday livelihood. For instance, in Wesleyan churches in Haiti, this offering includes the basic produce of everyday life; vegetables, chickens, hogs, and even donkeys are brought to the altar. Worship proceeds amid the chaos of fluttering wings and braying beasts as all these gifts are received before the congregation shares together in the Lord's Supper. In most mainline churches the offering is more "civil." It is usually a collection of money brought forward with the elements – the bread and wine – to be used for the eucharistic celebration. Yet what are these gifts we offer at the altar? What is their purpose? Few people would be so crass as to think that the tokens we bring are presented to buy God's favor. They are not akin to economic transactions where an exchange occurs for the sake of goods or services rendered. Why then bring any "gift" at all?

The gift we bring only makes sense when it is brought along with the bread and wine that will represent Christ's body for us. The "gift" that the Christian Church offers at the altar is not the produce of our own labor; it is instead the gift of Christ's offering for us. It is this gift that we offer to God. It is why in the United Methodist Church we pray "in remembrance of these your mighty acts in Jesus Christ, we offer ourselves in praise and thanksgiving as a holy and living sacrifice, in union with Christ's offering for us . . ." Similarly, the Great Thanksgiving in the Anglican *Book of Common Prayer* states: "We celebrate the memorial of our redemption, O Father, in this sacrifice of praise and thanksgiving. Recalling his death, resurrection, and ascension, we offer you these gifts."

What are "these gifts?" They are the elements that will be for us the body and blood of Christ as we remember his deeds on our behalf. In other words, the gift that we offer to God is first and foremost the gift God himself has given to us. We offer him the gift of the Son's sacrifice for our sins; this gift renders intelligible all the other gifts we bring, including all the physical and intellectual "gifts" that we have and are – the bodily labor that sustains our daily life as well as our capacities for speech and thought that issue forth in praise and thanksgiving. For those of us who hope to find our orientation through Christian worship, this "gift" should provide it.

Is Such a Gift Possible?

What should be less controversial than the goodness of a "gift," which allows us to see all our lives within the context of God's gift to us? Although what is good has been, is, and probably always will be contested, a gift might be considered an unproblematic good. The very language of "gift economy" sounds preferable to an economy based on "contract." Would we not rather see our lives in relation to others in terms of "gifts" than "contracts?" To invoke the term "gift" is to rally people around something seemingly good. But is such a gift possible? Or is it a subtle and therefore dangerous form of manipulation, especially when that gift is proclaimed as God's own self? Is it "social harmony" that this gift seeks to provide for us, or is it "social hegemony?"

None of us asked Christ to give himself to redeem us from our sins. Such a "gift" happened to us, before we were born. We incur guilt because our forebears sinned, but God chooses not to impute this guilt to us. Instead, God for-gives us our sin if we receive the gift Christ offers. Those who refuse the gift risk eternal blessedness for the hell of life without God. Such inequality seems beyond being manipulative; it can easily appear tyrannical. Each person is eternally responsible for his or her reception or refusal of a gift for which he or she did not ask. As John Leonard (2002) has noted, this kind of inequality is precisely why the portrayal of Satan in Milton's *Paradise Lost* is so seductive. Satan refuses to be manipulated by the "gift" and rallies over one-third of the angels to make the same refusal through a stirring proclamation of liberty and equality:

> Will ye submit your necks, and
> Choose to bend
> The supple knee? Ye will not, if
> I trust
> To know ye right, or if ye know
> Yourselves
> Natives and sons of Heav'n
> Possessed before
> By none, and if not equal all, yet
> Free
> Equally free. (Milton, quoted in Leonard, 2002: 28)

Does not the reception of this "gift" force us into a burdensome situation of an eternally bended knee, constantly expressing our gratitude for a "gift" for which we did not ask? What could be more manipulative, hegemonic, and ultimately oppressive than this? We are eternally indebted for a gift we did not seek.

Perhaps "gift" should not be so easily celebrated, not only when it comes to God's gift of the Son poured out for us, but also when "gift" is asserted as the basis for political and social bonds. Gift economies can easily imply gross inequalities and burdensome obligations we can never forget. In a gift economy, there is no clear measure by which one can know that debts have been discharged. There is never a point at which the debt can simply be forgotten. The memory of the debt requires reciprocal gifts that never come to an end. The bonds of obligation remain in perpetuity.

Some anthropologists argue that pre-modern cultures were bound together by such a gift-exchange economy. In his book *The Gift: The Form and Reason for Exchange in Archaic Societies* (1990), anthropologist Marcel Mauss argues that the root of all economic exchange lies not in bartering, but in gift-giving. In a gift-giving community people are engaged in perpetual exchanges that bind one to another for the common good. To give a gift is to request that a gift be given in return; to accept a gift is to commit oneself to such an economy. In a culture constituted by this kind of politic everything is based on reciprocity. The gift-giving community is a social and political community that subsumes all dimensions of life. It is what Mauss calls the "potlatch" – the place of being satiated. The potlatch is the system of total services in which the legal, economic, political, religious, and moral can only be harmonized by the activity of gift-giving (Mauss, 1990: 5–7).

Though this economy appears to be premised upon a notion of voluntarism, it is actually an obligatory form of participation. There are no such things as free or pure gifts; there is only gift-exchange. As all are required to be donors, all are also required to be recipients. To refuse reciprocation places the act of giving outside any mutual ties; it relinquishes any future claims one may have on another. Donors who imagine themselves exempt from reception deny the *telos* of such an economy. Likewise, to refuse to receive is to refuse to give. Such non-participation is tantamount to declaring war as it rejects the bonds of commonality. It denies that the future recipient maintains any claims over the goods in question and obliterates the common relationship needed in order to sustain a gift economy (Mauss, 1990: 13). Nothing can be held in perpetuity and no one is ever exempted from the continuing process of recycling gifts. For this reason, the gift economy is a more visible economy than the free-market economy of late modernity. In the former, everything is for passing on; goods are *a* good because they are never alienated from the common life.

This kind of gift-giving may still be present in modern economic arrangements. In his *Sex and Love in the Home*, David McCarthy (2001) presents an economy based on "neighborly gift-exchange," which "has its foundation within the temporal structure of common life and the ad hoc currency of the non-identical gift" (McCarthy, 2001: 105). Daily exchanges, such as watching each other's children, providing meals, and shoveling snow, are not done in terms of the "contractual" exchanges of identical gifts that take place in malls, fast-food restaurants, and banks. Yet, as McCarthy points out, gift-exchanges are not without expectations. They bind us together through obligations, which are risky precisely because they are "non-identical." We are not certain where the obligation begins or ends.

Stock options and signing bonuses may be simulacra of a "neighborly gift-exchange." They, too, are non-identical exchanges that go beyond a bare exchange of identical proportions. A CEO who is given stock options is given a "gift" of a future possibility that ties his or her gift to the performance of the stock (not necessarily to the good of the corporation – and thus it is a simulacra of a neighborly gift-exchange). If the stock increases substantially, the CEO is able to purchase the stock at the contracted price when he or she signed on as chief administrator. The difference between the stock's increase in value and the stock price at signing seems to be a "gift" beyond the strict requirements of payment for services rendered. But has not this kind of "gift" exchange destroyed lives and corporations? Are not "gifts" inherently manipulative? Are they not merely concealed forms of privilege and power? Given the problematic nature of gifts, it comes as no surprise that in modern political arrangements where liberty and equality rule – like Satan in *Paradise Lost* – "gifts" are rendered apolitical. Instead of any gift economy, a strict notion of equality measured by contract seeks to define all our exchanges and thus orient our lives.

Liberal Redemption: Contract and Forgetting

Within the tradition of liberalism, social bonds are to be regulated by contracts so that we will know when our obligation begins and ends. Once the contract rules us, we are not bound to the "giver" beyond that to which we willingly consent. When I purchase produce at the local supermarket the only exchange presented to me depends upon the value of the produce before me. Once I have paid the requisite amount, no other obligation remains. I do not need to know how the vegetables I purchase were grown, harvested, and shipped. I am under no obligation to determine whether the price I paid can sustain the lives of those who make my consumption possible. I need to know one thing – what is the value of this product? If I find my agent-satisfaction increased by parting with my money in order to consume this product, then I will "rationally" choose to do so until it no longer benefits my agent-satisfaction. This form of rationality, known as "marginal utility," becomes the only form of rationality I need in order to engage in "reasonable" economic exchanges. I am an individual in the marketplace who has no other obligations than those that I choose, and I choose them solely based on whether or not I consent to the value of the product presented to me.

The exchange that occurs in the marketplace assumes liberal political society with its originating myth where, in order to secure my individual will from onslaught by unnecessary burdens, each individual gives the trust of her or his individual will to the sovereign authority that preserves us as individuals against each other. We primarily need protection from each other and this protection provides the bonds of society. The capitalist market is an extension of this notion of liberal political society. Each individual meets in the marketplace in order to buy and sell, based solely on his or her individual freedom to do so. As long as these exchanges do not fundamentally call into question the conditions of liberal society itself, they can be pursued. The notion of "contract" ensures that the exchange is consensual, based on the individual's will. Whether the exchange is for food, clothing, sexual intercourse, a mortgage, or education, an explicit or implicit contract defines the terms of the agreement such that the expectations of fulfillment are as clear and as precise as possible. We are all individual consumers engaging in mutually consensual transactions.

John Stuart Mill recognized that the political and social basis for the orienting power of individual consumption was "liberty." For Mill, individuals must be free to enter into any exchange they deem conducive to their own interest, including even exchanges of "fornication" and "gambling," which require the toleration of "pimping" and "keeping a gambling house." The only qualification to this liberty is that people should not be coerced. They enter into exchanges "either wisely or foolishly, on their own prompting, as free as possible from the arts of persons who stimulate their inclinations for interested purposes of their own" (Mill, 1975: 97). But each individual must be made free from any undue obligation imposed by another. Under such conditions, one can then enter into any exchange one desires for it will be freely entered into. Contracts are means by which such freely entered agreements can be protected and achieved.

This could potentially prevent the kind of abusive gift-exchanges noted above. Contracts are an attempt to ensure consensual exchanges. When I enter into an exchange with a mortgage company we have clear expectations of each other. They tell me how many payments I must give them, when I must make the payments and what the penalties will be if I am late. We are both clear when our relationship will come to an end. In fact, when that relationship comes to an end we no longer have reason to be in contact with each other. We can forget each other. I do not expect them to relate to me as in a "gift economy." They do not give me money and say "Here is the money, pay it back when you get the chance. If we need something from you, we will let you know." That would make us both nervous. How could they be certain I will not refuse to fulfill my debts to them without penalty? How could I be certain that what they need from me will be appropriate and will come at an appropriate time? If we do not have clear contractual obligations, then any "gift economy" will make us more dependent upon each other. Contracts are intended to protect us from such dependence. They provide the necessary distance from each other that prevents undue obligations.

Gifts: Outside Politics

Contracts seek to ensure that all our exchanges are consensual, based on the freedom of the individual will to consent. They free us from the possibility of burdensome obligations a gift economy imposes. However, once contract defines economic and political bonds, gift-exchange no longer has a political role. Gift is rendered apolitical, outside the city where, as Aristotle noted, only a god or a beast can survive. It comes as no surprise that, within liberal political and economic systems where social bonds are based upon clearly defined and precisely calculated exchanges, the notion of "gift" becomes defined as disinterested and unconditional. A gift does not function like McCarthy's "neighborly gift-exchange." Instead, a gift becomes that which is given without any expectation of return. "Gift" cannot orient our lives; it no longer has that kind of political power. Not even God's own gift can accomplish a political orientation once we are all individuals, bound by contracts of our own choosing that free us from each other. Contractual exchanges allow us to forget everything but whether or not we were free when we chose this rather than that. It is not surprising that Christology – especially Christ's resurrection from the dead – becomes problematic under such social conditions.

This depoliticized notion of gift has had tremendous influence on Christian ethics, particularly in modern interpretations of Christian love. For instance, Anders Nygren defines the essence of Christian love, which he terms *agape*, as a gift given without any thought of return. It is completely disinterested. In similar fashion, Søren Kierkegaard argues that the apex of Christian love is found in loving the dead because in loving the dead the lover's love cannot be reciprocated – it is purely selfless (Kierkegaard, 1995: 345–59). This agapic form of love from both Nygren and Kierkegaard influenced the work of many twentieth-century Christians, including the prominent Christian ethicist Reinhold Niebuhr. In Niebuhr, Christian ethics becomes self-sacrificial. My action is only truly loving when I do it solely with regard to someone else's benefit and not to my own. It must be "disinterested." For this reason, the truly loving action becomes characterized by crucifixion and death. The resurrection, especially the resurrection of the body, is rendered problematic. For it still smacks of a "return." But, of course, such loving actions are always apolitical; they take place "outside the city" where only fools and martyrs reside. They are to be applauded and celebrated, but they are apolitical.

If gift is rendered apolitical in modern society, might it return in a postmodern era? Insofar as postmodernity remains inevitably linked with the modern, we should expect that here, too, "gift" is at best a renunciation of all temporal political and social bonds for the sake of a superhuman act of unconditional sacrifice, one that can only finally assume death as its end. For only when my "gift" ends in my own death can I truly know that I did not reduce "gift" to a contract. Only then can I be certain that the gift is given "without strings," such that I truly did not expect return. It is no surprise then, that given the tight link between modernity and postmodernity, "death" becomes the greatest of all gifts – the only way to escape the temporal order and its inevitable generalities. This can be seen in Jacques Derrida's work where he writes "The absoluteness of duty and responsibility presume that one denounce, refute and transcend at the same time, all duty, all responsibility, and every human law. It calls for a betrayal of everything that manifests itself within the order of universal generality . . ." (Derrida, 1995: 66). Ethics assumes a singularity, an unconditioned givenness, that refuses everything that has come before, everything that has been measured, ruled, generalized into a law or tradition. Heresy becomes dogma. Everything else must be deconstructed for the sake of the unconditioned call to act in the moment with no expectation of return. Only such an act can truly "account" for a gift.

Surely "contract" is safer than "gift." It preserves our independence and equality. It prevents us from "bending the supple knee" before those who would seek our indebtedness, whether it be temporal or eternal powers who do so. Contract is a hedge against hegemony. The modern notion of contract seems preferable to the notion of gift. But has the reduction of exchanges to contractual–consensual relations given us the promised freedom? Are we yet "possessed by none" but ourselves, each equally free from the other? In fact, the opposite occurred in the modern era. The more we seek to be free from the other by social bonds determined by identical exchanges, the more these bonds take over our lives and force us into a single common orientation; we are all required to be individuals whose "reasonableness" depends on our will to consume. This increasingly defines every social relation – family, marriage, neighborhoods, friendships, university, and the Church. This squeezes out any possibility of seeing our lives and work as gift. Gifts provide no political orientation. The social bonds I inhabit are simply those of my own choosing – they are all "limited liability" relationships with clear and nameable endpoints, along with escape clauses to help me end them when my will so chooses.

A Different Kind of Gift: The Politics of Remembering

Perhaps we think of gift, including the gift of God's own self in the Eucharist, as separate from political and economic matters because our lives are more oriented by the practice of contract that a consumerist culture demands of us than by the liturgical offering present in the Eucharist. Christ's "gift" becomes a problem precisely because I did not consent to it before it was offered. Such a gift need not even be refused for it has no necessary hold on my will in the first place, unless I first give it such a hold. And, even then, I can tacitly recognize that any hold it has will be conditioned by my own choosing and not because I am somehow necessarily obligated by a gift given before my will even was.

But when we make this argument we find ourselves in accord with Milton's Satan, and perhaps that should cause us to pause. When we find ourselves trapped in this kind of perverse logic perhaps we have not yet understood the nature of gift (or the nature of God). As John Milbank argues, a genuine gift is neither unconditional nor disinterested. In fact, a genuine gift, like erotic love, "is most free where it is yet most bound, most mutual and most reciprocally demanded" (Milbank, 1995: 124). Gifts, then, are not the opposite of contracts. Like contracts, they assume a return, but, unlike contracts, the return never ends. My reception of a gift from another and the consequent return leads us more fully into the life of the other while also fulfilling my own life. For this reason, a gift economy is a virtuous economy. As Alasdair MacIntyre notes, virtues are not grounded in competitive practices where one person's excellence can only be had at the expense of another, but virtue implies a "cooperative social practice" where one person's achieving or fulfilling her proper function helps the other fulfill her excellence as well (MacIntyre, 1984: 187).

The virtues here are not simply means between a deficiency and excess. They are plenteous such that they can never be exhausted. The infused virtues of faith, hope, and love are inexhaustible because they are the very life of the Holy Spirit who is "Gift." Thomas Aquinas argued that the Holy Spirit is properly named "Gift." The Spirit is the Gift (*Donum*) who is the Love proceeding from the Father and Son. The Spirit is also the Gift-given (*Datum*) who makes possible our creation and redemption. Because the Spirit cannot be alienated from the Giver, the Spirit is given without any intention of a return (with no "*intentione retributionis*" according to Aquinas). Something that cannot be alienated cannot be returned in kind, even though it can be given to another and become his as well (Aquinas, 1981: Ia, 38). Whenever such a gift is received, it becomes conformed to our very being. Thus we turn to God and offer it in praise and thanksgiving. Such a gift-giving economy draws us closer into the life of God, a life that knows no lack. This is why the Christian doctrines of *creatio ex nihilo* and God's impassibility are so important for a proper understanding of a gift economy.

God did not have to create, nor become bodily present in Jesus. God does not create or redeem to satisfy some lack in God's own nature. It is not a return that satisfies something God does not yet have. God is already the fullness of being, given in God's own self through the processions of the triune persons. Thomas Weinandy (2000) notes that only God can truly be gift. All human giving is only "partial" for the person who gives "must do so only through mediating words (words of kindness and love) and actions (hugs, kisses, sexual relations, etc.) which express only a partial giving of oneself even if one's intention is to give the whole of oneself." But the triune processions are true gifts. "The persons of the Trinity are eternally constituted in their own singular identity only in relation to one another, and thus they subsist as who they are only within their mutual relationships" (Weinandy, 2000: 116). Our gifts are at best analogical participations in the Gift which is "the more excellent way" – the triune God. God is always already complete, the full actualization of being that needs nothing outside him in order to complete himself.

God is pure act and pure gift. The fact that creation exists bears witness to God's goodness as gift. It is not a contractual relationship where God and creation meet in the marketplace to bargain over debts. The gift of the Son, like the gift of creation itself, comes to us solely out of God's good abundance. This does not mean it is "unconditional." God gives to us what God is – the goodness of being. We are to participate in that goodness and this is the purpose for our being. We are called to reciprocate the gift of being by participating in its goodness. But this is always a non-identical reciprocation. We cannot create being *ex nihilo*; we participate in it by reciprocating God's good gifts with God and each other. The Christian recognizes, as fundamental to his or her narrative, his or her place as a contingent creature. Such a status reminds us that we exist as gift. Gifts do not end in death or disinterested love; rather, they end in a life returned to God.

Of course, as MacIntyre (1984) also reminds us, the cooperative internal goods of virtues only exist within institutional structures where some goods are competitive and therefore scarce. While the virtues of knowledge and wisdom are non-competitive, they are often cultivated in institutional contexts where funding is competitive. There are inevitable limits we discover even in our pursuit of non-competitive goods. When John "Kareless" takes too much of the Holy Loaf, less is left for others. Even though we need not capitulate to the basic premise of economists that every good is intrinsically scarce and thus the first task of the economist is the efficient distribution of scarce goods, we must nevertheless recognize that limits exist. To learn to live within those limits, even while pursuing limitless goods like God's own goodness, is to become a moral subject (see Williams, 2000: 139–54).

The Gift of Life

For the Christian, the contrast between living in God's life, which is an inexhaustible gift, and the limitations of inevitably sinful structures, means that the truly Christian life could end in martyrdom. This is not a self-sacrifice and should be distanced from any notion of *agape* as unconditional. In martyrdom, the believer's life is literally returned to God, and this is what makes such a witness possible. But not even in martyrdom do we offer a counter-gift equivalent to the gift of Christ's sacrifice for us. Though martyrdom is, in the words of Tertullian, Origen, and a host of other theologians, a perfecting of the Christian life (martyrdom itself is understood as a gift), the giving of Christ's sacrifice at the altar is the substance of the counter-gift in question. This is not to pit these two liturgical performances against one another – for neither is intelligible without the other. It is rather to say that what is given at the altar is the sacrifice of Jesus, which is not only his death, but even more importantly his resurrected life – a bodily presence that is no longer bound by the limitations of space and time. Death cannot overcome it. Jesus can be fully present in each person's bodily eating of the Eucharist and yet Jesus will never be exhausted.

Christians, therefore, reside in a constant state of thanksgiving – a perpetual Eucharist. In this continuing exchange of divine gift and human response is the "living through the offering (*through* the offering, through the *offering*) of the gift given to us of God himself in the flesh." The appropriate response is not one of spontaneous love arising out of one's own volition (as if communion can be sought without God first pursuing us); rather, the appropriate response is to "*repeat differently*, in order to repeat, *exactly*, the content of Christ's life, and to wait, by a necessary *delay*, the answering repetition of the other that will fold temporal linearity back into the eternal circle of the triune life" (Milbank, 1995: 152). By arguing that delay and non-identical repetition constitute a gift-exchange economy, Milbank is suggesting that for a gift to be a gift demands that a gift be given in return. Despite our best self-sacrificial sensibilities, a gift-*exchange* is the only kind of gift truly open to us as creatures. No anonymous relationships between donors and recipients can ultimately prevail. Who we are is determined by the gifts we receive and return – or fail therein.

To give a gift is to engage in a political act. It creates an economy predicated on mutual participation that narrates realities such as "independence" or "self-sacrifice" as fictions. This is not to say that the sacrifices one makes for others are an illusion, rather the sacrifices are only intelligible in the light of the social mode of being made possible by communal practices of gift-giving. Such practices do not originate within the will of an individual or a community; instead, they find their basis in that eschatological marriage between God and the Church.

Remembering our Debts

Being wed to God, of course, is no easy matter. The Church seems such an ineffectual and diseased vessel that it is easy to look elsewhere for our orientation – to forget a "catholic" Church in favor of a "global" market. The temptation toward adultery seems, at times, almost overwhelming. Much of our infidelity occurs because we forget to whom we belong as Church. There is an ancient Jewish aphorism that says: memory is the pillar of redemption; forgetfulness is the beginning of death. In a capitalist-consumer culture we are habituated in certain economic practices that train us in the art of forgetfulness and invite us to love death (Pickstock, 1998: 101–19). We are ever in search of the "new and improved" that comes to us only as we negate the old and outdated. We buy, we use, and we discard *ad infinitum*. This is not only the case with automobiles; it also becomes true of theology and Christian practices. The Church itself desperately searches for the right "niche" market to sell its wares, and we are all too willing to forget who we are for the sake of market shares. This is precisely why the repetition of the liturgical performance of the Eucharist and the bringing forth of our own offering can be a radical political act. It causes us to see our everyday lives in terms of the orientation Christ gave and gives us.

In an effort to guard against amnesia the Church performs particular liturgical rituals that function as story-telling devices reminding us as to who we are and how are lives are to make sense. The Eucharist is *the* reminder *par excellence*. This act of remembrance makes possible that form of Christ's body known as the Church. To say that the Eucharist is an act of remembrance is not to evoke images of a static event, for this memorial is a "living memorial." It reminds "the reminded" that certain practices can only make sense if Jesus has been raised from the dead. If this is true, that is, if Jesus has been raised from the dead, then in the words of Wendell Berry we too must "practice resurrection" (Berry, 1991: 62). If we forget Christ's resurrection, we will not be able to remember well what we ourselves are called to practice.

The gift that is the Eucharist is the gift that obligates its consumers to love one's neighbor as Christ loved us all. Just as Christ refused disobedience even to the point of the cross, so should we; as Christ shared food with others, so should we; as Christ dispossessed himself, so should we. Those believers who dine on the body of Christ become Christ's body as they pledge to imitate his love. Insofar as believers do this, they make Christ present to the world. As the Mennonite theologian John Rempel argues, in its role as the embodiment of the Church's daily exchanges, the Eucharist is the *sine qua non* of the Church (Rempel, 1993: 88). There can be no understanding of the gift that is the Eucharist that does not in some way shape how Christians are to live in a forgetful world. It renders possible – and necessary – the copious sharing of goods by which all are nourished and sustained. Our material goods generate friendship as the giving away of goods necessitates a reception of goods. Milbank claims that the Eucharist "positions each and every one of us only as fed . . . and bizarrely assimilates us to the food we eat, so that we, in turn, must exhaust ourselves as nourishment for others" (Milbank, 1992: 342). In consuming the flesh and blood of Christ we participate in the ultimate giving away: the giving away of Christ's body. In this act we become Christ's body, which, once it is in us, cannot be contained but must be shared. For it is not conformed to us, but we are conformed to it. To remember this gift as a gift-exchange is to participate in the divine economy whereby Christians are taken into the life of the triune God and become Christ on earth.

Participation in the divine life reorders our everyday exchanges. For embedded in the Eucharist is a "glimpse and foretaste of the ultimate good for God's creation, which is God himself" (Long, 2000: 235). This is the one "resource" that denies scarcity and rejects competition. At this table, all are satiated because after the Resurrection, there can be no shortage of Christ. (Thus historical quests for Jesus remain misguided attempts to discover a scarce commodity, which cannot be discovered through these means because it is not scarce.) Precisely because Christ is inexhaustible, language such as "consumption" assumes a different meaning. To consume a commodity is to be oriented toward a desire that is not finally satisfying. To have one's life defined by this kind of consumption is to be bound by what Tolstoy termed, "the gnawing agony of desire." It is to be bound by the fear that there may not be enough for all, so I must consume before it disappears. But to consume Christ is to know a different kind of desire, a non-competitive desire where I can consume without fear that my eating causes your hunger (Pickstock, 1998: 121–66). This is not to overlook the limits of competitive goods; it is to re-orient them. My everyday exchanges are to be made intelligible by my "consumption" of Christ's own life, and so we pray "Recalling his death, resurrection, and ascension, we offer you these gifts." Our gifts are to be re-ordered by this "recalling."

What does this mean concretely? It does not provide us with a blueprint for a global economic system. It does not tell us which global economic system the Church must support. If a theological ethic must do this, if it must teach us how to rule on a global basis, then our modest proposal will be dismissed as asocial. If Christian theology must address the "social problem" as defined by Ernst Troeltsch – "How can the Church harmonize with these main forces (State and Society) in such a way that together they will form a unity of civilization?" – then this act of memory, which the Eucharist is, will not be able to be viewed by theologians or ethicists as a viable "social ethic" (Troeltsch, 1981: 32). But that may say more about what theologians and ethicists think about the nature of the Church and God's relationship to it than about "social ethics." Our modest proposal is not a "social ethic" in terms of an application of social principles to something called "society" which will allow us to rule and order it. Far from such a "social ethic" (if such exists other than in the minds and books of social ethicists), this modest proposal draws on concrete, everyday practices to show how Christians might begin to think of their lives as oriented by Christ's offering for us rather than by the consumerist culture which receives its orientation from other concrete, everyday practices such as superhighways, malls, and food courts. To have our lives oriented by Christ is to become "friends" who "consume" in common, rather than individuals who consume in order to remain free from each other.

The logic of the contemporary market is not one of friendship and obligation. Instead, goods are alienated from the common life inasmuch as the only common life sustainable is the consumption of such goods. Goods are made possible by a contractual relationship that presumes that all exchanges are located in the disinterested will of the participating individuals. Such "disinterest" presupposes both sacrifice and alienation from such goods that, ironically, renders those goods nothing more than commodities, i.e. they are only defined by the subjective "commodious" character individuals attribute to them. Yet, gifts are neither commodities nor sacrificial acts. Gifts are marked by a social reciprocity that, within the Church, finds its greatest intelligibility. Gifts cannot be finally alienated from the giver because the gift extends through time and space in the lives of those who receive them. Goods are only goods if they are for something that is good. Goods, in order to be a good, must be directed toward an end, and in the Church that end is friendship with God. All of our goods, therefore, can only truly be good if they cultivate the habits and dispositions necessary to direct us to this end.

References

Aquinas, Thomas (1981) *Summa theologica*, trans. the Fathers of the English Dominican Province (Westminster, MD: Christian Classics).

Berry, Wendell (1991) "The Mad Farmer Liberation Front," *In Context: A Quarterly of Humane Sustainable Culture*, Fall/Winter.

Borgmann, Albert (1987) *Technology and the Character of Contemporary Life* (Chicago: University of Chicago Press).

Derrida, Jacques (1995) *The Gift of Death*, trans. David Wills (Chicago: University of Chicago Press).

Duffy, Eamon (1992) *The Stripping of the Altars: Traditional Religion in England 1400–1580* (New Haven, CT: Yale University Press).

Kierkegaard, Søren (1995) *Works of Love*, trans. Howard V. Hong and Edna H. Hong (Princeton, NJ: Princeton University Press).

Leonard, John (2002) "Did Milton Go to the Devil's Party?" *New York Review of Books* (18 July), 49: 12.

Long, D. Stephen (2000) *Divine Economy* (New York: Routledge).

McCarthy, David Matzko (2001) *Sex and Love in the Home: A Theology of the Household* (London: SCM).

MacIntyre, Alasdair (1984) *After Virtue: A Study in Moral Theory* (Notre Dame, IN: University of Notre Dame Press).

Mauss, Marcel (1990) *The Gift: The Form and Reason for Exchange in Archaic Societies*, trans. W. D. Halls (London: Routledge).

Milbank, John (1992) "Enclaves, or Where is the Church?," *New Blackfriars* (June).

—(1995) "Can a Gift be Given? Prolegomena to a Future Trinitarian Metaphysic," *Modern Theology*, 11: 119–61.

Mill, J. S. (1975) *On Liberty* (New York: W. W. Norton).

Nietzsche, Friedrich Wilhelm (1983) *Untimely Meditations*, trans. R. J. Hollingdale (Cambridge: Cambridge University Press).

Pickstock, Catherine (1998) *After Writing: The Liturgical Consummation of Philosophy* (Oxford: Blackwell).

Rempel, John (1993) *The Lord's Supper in Anabaptism: A Study in the Christology of Balthasar Hubmaier, Pilgram Marpeck, and Dirk Philips* (Waterloo: Herald).

Troeltsch, Ernest (1981) *The Social Teaching of the Christian Churches*, vol. 1, trans. Olive Wyon (Chicago: University of Chicago Press).

Weinandy, Thomas G. (2000) *Does God Suffer?* (Notre Dame, IN: University of Notre Dame Press).

Williams, Rowan (2000) *Lost Icons: Reflections on Cultural Bereavement* (Edinburgh: T. and T. Clark).

CHAPTER 26

Invoking: Globalization and Power

Timothy Jarvis Gorringe

Consider this very famous image, Hans Holbein the Younger's painting *The Ambassadors*, which hangs in the National Gallery in London. Two wealthy, superbly self-confident men stand looking out of the picture. They are clothed in all the trappings of luxury and power. On the left is Jean de Dinteville, French ambassador to England at the age of only 29, his gown lined with ermine, a gold medallion round his neck, his doublet of satin, a finely chased gold baton, perhaps his sign of office, in his right hand. Across the table is Georges de Selve, bishop at the age of 25, future ambassador to Venice. On the table on which they rest their elbows are the appurtenances of Renaissance learning and culture – a lute, flutes, a Lutheran hymn book, a guide to arithmetic, a sextant, compasses – and two globes, one for the earth and one for the heavens. The year is 1533 and we are in the opening years of globalization. Pizarro sacked the Inca capital of Cuzco and stripped it of its gold in the same year. Holbein has already gone to the heart of it: the movement from center to periphery, the base in a powerful elite, the confidence in science and technology, the crucifix, emblem of what was central for the old world, pushed to the extreme margin, hardly visible against the rich green brocade. But Holbein has enough of a stake in the old world to make his own theological comment. He includes, in anomorphic projection, the picture of a human skull, at once a demonstration of Renaissance skill in perspective but also *a memento mori*: "I gathered for myself silver and gold and the treasure of kings and of provinces . . . Then I considered all that my hands had done and the toil I had spent in doing it, and again, all was vanity and a chasing after wind" (Ecclesiastes 2: 8,11).

I agree with Vandana Shiva (1998) that globalization is a continuation and intensification of the colonial process. It began, then, sometime in the first few decades of the fifteenth century when Genovese shipwrights made small but vital changes to the rudders of their ships. It enabled their seamen to sail down the west coast of Africa and extend their trade. As the new technology spread from shipyard to shipyard around Europe Portuguese navigators rounded the Cape of Good Hope and found a way of circumventing the Muslim stranglehold on the Mediterranean, and therefore on the spice routes. Bent on the same quest, Columbus crossed the Atlantic, and the conquest of Latin America began, the start of the history of Western colonialism. The first circumnavigation took place between 1519 and 1522. We talk endlessly of the Copernican revolution but it was this process of discovery, conquest, and trade that fired people's minds and changed the social imaginary making "the globe" for the very first time something compassable, conceivable. Why else did Shakespeare choose this name for his theater? The name was a sign of the "new realities" in which he staged plays about ruthless power and the lust for gold (*Titus Andronicus* and *Timon of Athens*). Holbein's ambassadors could spin their globe, knowing that it was possible to sail round it. They already knew that such journeys and such conquests produced fabulous riches, gold beyond the dreams of avarice. Where did the gold for their medallions and ornaments, the silver for the crucifix, come from? In 1503 Columbus had written back from Jamaica: "Gold is a wonderful thing! Whoever possesses it is lord of all he wants. By means of gold one can get even souls into Paradise." "Modern society," wrote Marx, reflecting on this letter, "greets gold as its Holy Grail, as the glittering incarnation of the very principle of its own life." Earlier he cites the Book of Revelation: "These are of one mind and give over their power and authority to the beast . . . And no one can buy or sell unless he has the mark, that is the name of the beast or the number of its name" (Revelation 17: 13; 13: 17). The connection between globalization and idolatry, the power of money and ruthless greed, goes back to the very beginning.

We can take another text from Revelation. "Because you have kept my word of patient endurance," we read, "I will keep you from the hour of trial that is coming on the whole inhabited earth (*oikumene*) to test the inhabitants of the earth" (Revelation 3: 10). The Greek word "*oikumene*" is the nearest we come in the New Testament to the idea of "the globe." It was a political concept. Nero was savior and benefactor of the *oikumene* – just as today the World Bank and the IMF are supposed to be. Augustus ordered a census of the whole *oikumene* to raise taxes (Luke 2: 15). Wars are expensive. Legions or B52s have to be paid for somehow. Most significantly for this chapter, the mob in Thessalonica accuse Paul and Silas of having turned the *oikumene* – the whole accepted political order – upside down (Acts 17: 6). This activity, critics protest, threatens trade (Acts 19: 27). The "hour of trial" mentioned by the author of Revelation probably refers to persecution incurred by Christians because they were seen to constitute a threat to the imperial order. Here, then, is another thing that goes right back to the beginning – Christian challenge to imperial *realpolitik* and its economic basis.

The Four Faces of Globalization

"Globalization," the process by which the world is knit tightly together in the interests of trade, begins with merchant capitalism, but the word is coined to speak of the effect of a fourfold contemporary process, in which information technology plays a crucial role. These processes are development, trade, the rise of finance capital, and McDonaldization.

Development

There are no cut-off points in history, and even revolutions have roots deep in the past, but the Bretton Woods conference of 1944 is a convenient starting-point for thinking about contemporary globalization. The contest between European states and empires had generated two global conflicts within twenty-five years, and the need was recognized to develop a new world order. Analyzing the scene, the world was divided not just into capitalist and communist but into developed and underdeveloped. The desirability of trade, the theory of comparative advantage, was the axiom which underpinned all thinking. Trade is what secures prosperity, but only prosperous nations can trade. For trade to be maximized, "underdeveloped" nations must be brought to the level of "developed" nations, where development was measured by GDP, by levels of industrialization, and by basic indicators such as literacy rates, child mortality, and so on. The Bretton Woods institutions – the IMF and the World Bank – were set up to help this to happen.

By the end of the 1960s it had become clear that something had gone very wrong with the process. Poverty in the South was deepening and underdeveloped countries found themselves trapped in dependency. This situation got immeasurably worse in the next decade. When oil money came on stream, banks looked around to see what to do with it because idle money is wasted. Cheap loans were offered to Third World countries to allow them to "develop." When interest rates rose, these countries found themselves trapped, effectively debtors forever to the Northern banks, paying back the initial loans hundreds of times over, but never able to get free of the interest.

"Globalization" describes this whole process of financial relations, of debt dependency, but also the process by which Northern banks suck the blood of Southern nations, extracting gold just as Pizarro and Cortes had done four centuries before. "Conditionality" ties countries into a particular understanding of economics with huge political and cultural consequences. Ownership of their industrial infrastructure passes overseas. It is true that there are some measurable gains for some of the poor. On the other hand, the 1997 United Nations Development Report noted that "The share of the poorest 20 percent of the world's people in global income now stands at a miserable 1.1 per cent, down from 1.4 per cent in 1991 and 2.3 per cent in 1960. It continues to shrink." Development, it has turned out, is about the exercise of power, and of about making sure that power balances are not disturbed.

Trade

The goal of development is trade because, according to the theory of comparative advantage, everyone benefits by this process. Citizens in the Northern countries are familiar with the "global economy" from the contents of their shopping baskets, or by inspecting where the parts of their cars, radios, or televisions come from. The global economy is part of the fabric of our daily lives. When a Northern citizen sits down to eat it is likely that he or she is benefiting from the labor of people from almost every country on earth. This might seem a good thing – a world of mutual dependence. In fact, what we are doing is enriching, and strengthening the power of, the big corporations, impoverishing the poor countries, and destroying the environment.

In the early days of merchant capitalism, a new kind of organization emerged from the guild structures of the Middle Ages. This was the corporation. The very name implies its dependence on Christian thinking about "the body." Like the Church, it is "one body with many members." Unlike the Church, it does not exist for those who are not its members but in order to make profits for its shareholders. This is its legal and, in the view of some, its moral duty. We have had corporations since the late sixteenth century, but "globalization" refers especially to the extension of corporate power over world markets. Today, 40 percent of world trade is in the hands of the top 350 companies. The largest ten corporations control assets that represent three times the total income of the world's poorest 38 countries. Of the world's 100 largest economies, 50 are transnational corporations. The 48 least-developed countries, by contrast, account for less than 0.3 per cent of world trade.

Corporations are bodies owned by their shareholders. Unfortunately, less than 1 percent of the world's population owns any shares and this means that the assets of corporations – approximately a quarter of the productive assets of the whole world – are held under a form of absentee ownership for the primary benefit of a tiny fraction of the world's richest people. To make their profits, they need to chase cheap labor, relocating from one country to the next, wooed by governments with huge cash incentives, ready to move again as soon as the economic "logic" dictates. Between 1980 and 1993 the Fortune 500 industrial firms shed 4.4 million jobs and increased their assets 2.3 times. Their CEO income increased by 6.1 percent to $3.8 million. The results of this economic system are grotesque: the world's top three billionaires earn more than the world's poorest sixty million people; the richest Mexican more than the poorest seventeen million of his fellow Mexicans.

Free trade is the flag of convenience under which the ship of capitalism sails. In fact, both the European Union and the United States are highly protectionist, as we have seen in recent disputes about steel. The Multi Fiber Arrangement, which protects Europe and America against cheap imports from the South, is in force till 2005. Its overall cost to developing countries is estimated at about $50 billion a year, roughly equal to the total of development aid. The EU specifically excludes metals, agricultural products, and textiles from free-trade schemes, and discrimination against basic commodities remains the biggest weapon against the poor countries, even more serious than debt. This kind of unjust trade has a huge impact on the environment. It is no accident that it is the world's most indebted countries – Brazil, Mexico, Zaire, Bolivia, Indonesia, and Malaysia – that are responsible for half of the tropical forest lost between 1991 and 1995. And this destruction goes on apace.

Finance capital

We use the term "globalization," thirdly, to refer to the change from industrial to finance capital. This is bound up with the abandonment of the gold standard, but still more importantly with information technology. This makes it possible to speculate on stock markets all round the world more or less instantaneously. Speed is of the essence, leading one firm to spend $35 million to gain a two-second advantage in accessing the Tokyo stock market. The vast bulk of financial trading today takes the form of stock speculation, trade in interest rates, the purchase of bonds or currencies on one exchange to sell them at a profit on another. In effect, bets are placed on the livelihoods of nations. It is a virtual world that impacts on the real world. Huge rises and falls on the stock market correspond to nothing in the real world. On the one hand, when the New York Stock Exchange lost $1 trillion in two months, in 1987, there was no change in the world's productive capacity. This money, which could "feed the world," related to no facts in the world of production. On the other hand, when such falls happen and firms collapse, jobs are lost and millions unemployed.

The faith and trust of the heart make both God and idol, said Luther. The whole process is built on confidence, or, as we say in the Church, on faith, which is at the heart of the whole process. This was clear in the medieval practice of "crying up" a particular coin, so that it would pass for a higher value. Dependence on confidence is illustrated in George Soros's betting on the pound or the mark, which created a crisis of confidence in those currencies. He caused the devaluation of the mark first by placing bets against it, and then by publishing a letter in *The Times* saying that he expected it to fall against other currencies. It promptly did so. He became a billionaire by putting people out of work and causing the value of people's pensions to fall. The popular term for this is "daylight robbery." Confidence was also what was at issue in the collapse of Barings Bank, when one of the bank's traders bet on the Tokyo stock market, and tried to cause it to rise. This happens every day. The unfortunate trader got caught out by the intersection of the real world with the virtual reality of the stock market. Had it not been for the Kobe earthquake he would by now have had a knighthood "for services to banking."

McDonaldization

We use the term "globalization," finally, to talk about the cultural consequences of these economic processes. It is not just one economic model that is exported worldwide, but the rationality that goes with it and the crucial signifiers that go with it: blue jeans, Marlborough, Coke, McDonalds. The twin towers of the World Trade Center may be down, but McDonalds is in Mecca as well as in Moscow and Beijing and virtually everywhere else. "We do not just want to succeed," says the CEO, "we want to dominate." The power of the huge retail chains is only sustained by expansion. In Britain, Tesco needs to open one new store a day to stay in business. It is naïve to think that this process can happen and culture not be affected. Much of the Muslim criticism of "the West" is on account of the export of individualism. But, to the extent that Muslim countries adopt the economic system, they are buying the bureaucratic rationality Weber spoke of, which disenchants the world. "Modern" economies do not exist apart from a transnational class comprised of bureaucrats, politicians, and business people who all share the same ethic and worship at the same shrine.

Perhaps there are gains in this cultural process: after all, the extension of "democracy" (by which we might mean the election of a billionaire once every four years) is part of the process, as is modern medicine, food hygiene, and educational provision. On the other hand, healthy ecologies abhor monocultures. Monocultures spell death. The idea that such cultures may subtly differentiate themselves region by region, so that what we have is "glocalism" rather than globalization is a fantasy dreamed up by advertising agents. Fast food is fast food and Coke is Coke. It is a way of life that is sold, a new mutation on the imperial dream.

"Your struggle is not against flesh and blood," says the author of Ephesians, "but against principalities, against powers, against spiritual rules in high places" (Ephesians 6: 12). Today, these principalities and powers are the forces involved in globalization. As Walter Wink has helped us to see, we engage them by unmasking them, by opposing to their social imaginary the counter-imaginary of the gospel. I turn now from the global to the local, and from empire to Church.

Three Eucharistic Snapshots

Globalization is colonization of "the whole inhabited earth." But the whole inhabited earth is also where the Church lives and works. "You will receive power when the Holy Spirit has come upon you; and you will be my witnesses in Jerusalem, in all Judaea and Samaria, and to the ends of the earth" (Acts 1: 8). Witness constitutes communities of praise, eucharistic communities, groups opposed to imperial accounts of what it means to be human. "It shall not be so amongst you" (Mark 10: 43). Let us look at three snapshots of such groups.

First, the very earliest picture that we have. This is a community in the harbor city of Corinth, class divided between rich and poor. They meet to celebrate Eucharist in the house of one of the wealthier members of the congregation. "Chloe's people," who have been working all day in the docks, smelling of salt, sweat, and fish, arrive from work starving and want to eat their lunch packets before the Eucharist. Servants, meanwhile, serve the wealthier group with wine. Both groups complain to Paul. What! He says "Do you show contempt for the Church of God and humiliate those who have nothing?" (1 Corinthians 11: 22).

We learn some valuable lessons from this eucharistic community. We learn not to worry that we are not an ideal community: no such group ever existed. We learn that to witness to the *oikumene* is to be part of the *oikumene* at the same time, to learn only through struggle how resistance to the taken-for-granted standards of society is to be built. It is something that has to be negotiated over and over again. We learn, too, that the Eucharist relates to the practices of economics. It is intended to be, says Paul, not a school for scandal but a school for sharing. In his exposition it emerges as an educative practice in which a sign we call "body" mediates between the historical memory of the physical body of Christ, tortured to death, and the body of believers called to become an alternative community, a new inclusive body that challenges the bodily disciplines of society.

Paul seems to have had in mind Deuteronomy 15: 4 in his discussion, the promise that, if God's command is followed, "there will be no poor amongst you." The Eucharist, he says, is the instantiation of this Jubilee legislation, which, by remission of debt, sees that there will be no poor amongst you. If you maintain and even increase such divisions, he argues, then you turn Eucharist into its opposite, and bring judgment on yourselves. From the word go, when we first encounter the Eucharist in the Church, therefore, there is a direct link between debt remission, the elimination of poverty, and celebration of the Eucharist.

Second snapshot: the island of Hispaniola in 1514, early on in the moment of globalization. Bartolomeo de las Casas, former colonialist, now priest, finds he has to preach on Ecclesiasticus 34:

> Like one who kills a son before his father's eyes
> Is the person who offers a sacrifice from the property of the poor.
> The bread of the needy is the life of the poor;
> Whoever deprives them of it is a murderer. (Ecclesiasticus 34: 24–5)

Reflecting on the position of the Indians, reflecting on African slaves he had seen in Portugal, he comes to the conclusion that the colonial system is insupportable in the light of Scripture. It was, he said in his sermon on the passage, sinful to hold the Indians in service. Since the colonialists did not change their practice, las Casas took his struggle for their freedom to the King. Eucharist led to a struggle for freedom for those who had been enslaved.

This story, and its text, reminds us how, in 1979, Rigoberta Menchu's sixteen-year-old brother, along with many others, was tortured by having his body parts cut away, and burned to death before his family by government troops seeking to keep Guatemala safe for capitalism, to see that "development" went on properly. The captain who inflicted the wounds and ordered the petrol to be poured over the victims spoke of it as combating terrorism. He and his troops, and thousands of others, were, and still are, "Like one who kills a son before his father's eyes."

A third snapshot. I am a member of the Iona community, an ecumenical, dispersed community of women and men, committed to peace and justice, based mainly in Britain. We meet in family groups, usually monthly, discuss campaigns, discuss news from the wider community, read Scripture, decide on action, say the Iona office and celebrate the Eucharist. We have no shrines or altars, as Minucius Felix said in the second century, and we use no vestments. The "celebrant" (but we are all celebrants) may be lay or ordained, and, needless to say, there is no gender discrimination. The Eucharist takes up our political concerns, is the context in which we offer our despair and hopelessness to God, but is therefore the place where, nourished by our reading of, and argument about, Scripture, we take heart from the promises of God. We seek to learn from, be traditioned by, Paul and Bartolomeo de las Casas. We ask how, as middle-class Christians not likely to be murdered for our faith, we can respond to the cry of the oppressed people, murdered and impoverished day by day to keep the wheels of globalization turning. I shall return to this shortly, but first I want to elaborate the theology that lies behind globalization.

Two Theologies

Finance capital, I noted, is based on faith. In fact, a whole theology undergirds the operations of globalization, opposed to the theology of the Eucharist. I shall highlight just five tenets of it. First, we know that Adam Smith, skeptic that he was, replaced the doctrine of God's providence with the doctrine of the "invisible hand." According to the Christian doctrine, it is God who oversees, accompanies, and rules all things for wise and loving ends. God does this by working through Word and sacrament, and through my neighbor, to bring these about. Of course, this is no Panglossian take on reality: in Scripture it is the story of Joseph that is the paradigm for providence. "God sent me before you to preserve life" (Genesis 45: 5). God turns human wickedness against itself. Through this story we learn to understand the crucifixion. This view is very different from Smith's doctrine, according to which it is "the market" which allocates things to the best human advantage.

When Adam Smith wrote *The Wealth of Nations* the slave trade was in full swing. Smith was a social liberal who questioned the economic benefits of slavery, but he did not see that it could be justified on his own account of the providential action of self-interest. Those who swear by the doctrine today (which means all financial columnists in all major newspapers, bankers, politicians of every major party) overlook the death of two hundred thousand by extreme torture in Latin America to keep "the market" safe, the impoverishment of those pushed off the land by turning it over to cash crops, the hopelessness of those made unemployed, the sickness of those working in unsafe industries which Larry Summers assured us was the duty of the North to export to the South.

Relatedly, in a neat inversion of the doctrine of original sin, Bernard Mandeville anticipated Smith by pointing out that it was useless to go against the grain of human nature and that it was time to realize that it was human selfishness that produced the goods, and not virtue. All that struggle for virtue was really a waste of time if you judged it by the success of the economy. Centuries of attempts to shape economic practice by scriptural norms were swept away. Nobody, of course, said that morality was bunk. What they said was that it was about avoiding insider trading, not falsifying claims for profits, making sure the accounts were in order. Provided you did that, you could have a clear conscience. This meant that the effects of corporate policies had to be understood as fate. If the rich get the gravy, in terms of ecosystem resources, or luxuries, whilst the poor get the blame, that's the price of progress. If people are maimed by land mines – what to do? Nobody compels people to walk in mined areas, or indeed compels them to be laid. But business is business, and if I don't sell them someone else will. The system itself is neutral. The privatization of ethics here goes hand in hand with losing sight of the bigger picture, referred to in the New Testament in the language of principalities and powers, that sum of all wrong choices which structure and skew societies in particular ways, and therefore provide us with guidelines about what is normal or even thinkable.

Third, Jesus's very first act in his ministry is to call disciples. Discipleship means discipline. "Let your moderation be known to all," said Paul to the Christians in Philippi.

"Expand or die" say the prophets of the International Monetary Fund: at the rate of no less than 4.5 percent per annum! The global economy is predicated on infinite growth, and when parts of the system cease to expand, they die. Paul's advice sprang from millenniums of peasant wisdom about what it is that enables human societies to survive. The hubris that Holbein's ambassadors radiate saw no need for such advice. With the technology and world population of 1533 they could not possibly have foreseen the consequences. Today, we know that the staffs of life – fish, water, and grain – are all in increasingly short supply. In the medical world, growth for growth's sake is called cancer. Our economists do not see that there is any analogy in the body politic.

The ecological crisis, by which I mean, first, pollution, environmental degradation, and the loss of biodiversity and, second, the macro problems like the destruction of the ozone layer and global warming, stems from this idolatrous commitment to growth at all costs. Growth, in turn, is related to power. Global warming, for example, is bringing about potentially catastrophic changes in the earth's climate with huge implications for millions of people living on shorelines and a devastating impact on crop management. The major cause of global warming is carbon dioxide emissions, two-thirds of which are caused by the world's consumer class. Where the poor release one-tenth of a ton each year, the consumer class three and a half tons; the richest tenth of Americans are responsible for 11 tons each. Individual lifestyle has a global impact. As a matter of sober fact, we are all members one of another, but nowhere is this translated into political and economic action. The globalizers rely on the possibility of a technical fix, overlooking the fact that the globe is finite. Others argue for a lifeboat policy, arguing that only those in the North – and probably only some of them – can remain in the lifeboat. When we consider the horrors of the twentieth century, who can say what this doctrine might lead to?

The counsel about moderation applies also to our consumption. Discipline means the education of desire. Corporations, on the other hand, require the exact opposite. They need us to be "consumers." To consume is to destroy, to devour. Aristotle taught that the desires of the human heart are infinite, but the corporations do not want to leave it to chance, which is why they spend billions of dollars on advertising. The key question is not what people want but what they can be persuaded to buy. Exchange value has priority over use value. Christians, on the other hand, are called to what the old eucharistic rubrics called "reverent consumption," which is consumption acknowledging that everything is gift.

Finally, the Christian ethic is characterized by respect for life. Respect for life is not just about not killing: it is about nurturing, cherishing, celebrating. The global economy, on the other hand, is characterized by the pirating of life, the attempt to patent, and make money out of, seeds and remedies that have been known by peasant communities for millenniums. The arrogance of corporate lawyers in this regard is astounding – a claim to the right to life in the interest of mammon, which comes with a threat to sue if that "right" is transgressed. The whole process is an expression of ingratitude, disrespect, and contempt, a claim to domination inherent in the imperial worldview.

These are some aspects of the theology of the non-God – mammon. Jesus said categorically that it was impossible to serve both God and mammon. Since the Middle Ages

Christians have grown increasingly skilled at putting the serpent's question: did God say? Not impossible, surely. Difficult, yes, but not impossible. Possible provided I keep my hands clean – and so on.

Invocation

> Come Holy Ghost, our souls inspire
> And lighten with celestial fire.

This is Bishop Cosin in the middle of the seventeenth century, classically expressing the moment of invocation that, we know, is at the very heart of the Orthodox Eucharist. There are many beautiful versions of this moment, but I want to begin by putting a query by it. When we read the Torah it is striking that almost everywhere it is God who initiates encounter: "The Lord appeared to"; "God said to Abram"; "The Word of the Lord came to." Abraham, Moses, and the rest are not hanging about temples waiting to hear a word. They are going about their business when God addresses them, grabs them by the collar, and sends them off somewhere else. Exactly the same applies to the call of the disciples or of Paul. It is not until we reach what the Hebrew Bible calls "the former prophets" that we have the child Samuel in the temple waiting to hear the word of the Lord. The reason for that is disturbing: "Now the word of the Lord was rare in those days; there was no constant vision" (1 Samuel 3: 1).

Let us put this question: is the Church, with its epiclesis, assuming that this is the situation? We can think of moments in the twentieth century – Barmen and the South African Kairos document of 1984 spring to mind – that have the character of a word of the Lord, an address with absolute authority, which demands our assent and corresponding action. "Leave your father's house, if that is the Deutsche Kirche or the apartheid church." Leave it, and go elsewhere. Perhaps we should add Medellin to this list; and Christian feminists will have their own account. But is the assumption behind invocation that in our days "there is no constant vision"? The answer is not far to seek. Jesus calls his disciples as they go about their daily business – worried by the new net sizes employed by Gadarene fishermen, by the consequent fall in fish prices, by the threat to the industry represented by the new Roman trawlers, and so on. The same goes for all those instances in the Torah.

The problem comes, in the Christian Middle Ages, with the assumption of a split between sacred and secular, faith and politics, the world of the sanctuary and the world of work. Not for nothing do all those contemporary instances of "the word of the Lord" I mention reject that division. This is the first thing we have to realize in thinking about invocation: the Eucharist is placed in the midst of the hurly-burly of history. In taking the stuff of labor – bread and wine – for signifiers, it proclaims nothing that the Lord made unclean. The distinction is not between sacred and secular but between the world viewed in the light of God's word, and the world viewed outside of that word. If I assume that God is ordinarily absent, then, of course, I have to call God down. But we have no shrines and altars because the *oikumene*, the whole inhabited earth, is our shrine and altar.

Does this mean that we can dispense with the idea of invocation? Not at all. Invocation is not about e-mailing an absent deity but about our awareness of absolute dependence, to use Schleiermacher's phrase. The Eucharist, the giving of thanks, stems from the whole of Jesus's practice, the way he was known for "blessing," which in Jewish practice means giving thanks to, God. We know that Jesus was, in the view of the moral majority, "a glutton and a drunkard." He dined with tax collectors and sinners: once again that "word of the Lord" in the midst of daily life. "Hey, Zacchaeus! Go and put the kettle on! I'm coming to your house." At these meals, at the great feedings, he always took bread, gave thanks, and broke it. This was why it was at the moment of the blessing that the disciples at Emmaus recognized Jesus. Everything else might be obscure but that action was absolutely characteristic. In line with the Scriptures, Jesus blessed God, gave thanks, expressed his sense of dependence and gratitude. This was his hallmark, and he bequeathed it as a hallmark to his disciples. It is quintessentially the opposite to the attitude of the ambassadors who are, as Descartes described them in the next century, "possessors and masters of creation" in virtue of their knowledge, power, and, ultimately, force of arms. Invocation is acknowledgment of our recognition that all reality, beginning with our own lives, is gifted, and, since dogmatics and ethics are necessarily interrelated, a whole political and economic practice follows from that. It cannot but be opposed to the practices involved in globalization that are essentially and at their heart an expression of imperial attitudes.

Invocation, then, is acknowledgment of grace, and grace is the soul of politics. This has major implications for our understanding of power. When you look at Jean de Dinteville in Holbein's picture you can see the shadow of his sword as it hangs from his left hip. The United States, says Thomas Friedman (2000), at a much more advanced stage of globalization, is "not just a country" but a spiritual value, a role model, a beacon for the whole world. It is "the ultimate benign hegemon and reluctant enforcer" and needs to recognize that "The hidden hand of the market will never work without a hidden fist . . . And the hidden fist that keeps the world safe for Silicon Valley's technologies to flourish is called the US Army, Air Force, Navy and Marine Corps." This is just an updated version of Dinteville's sword, the sword of Pizarro and of Cortes, which brought back gold from the Indies, finally undermining the Spanish economy.

The Eucharist, based on the absolute dependence acknowledged in invocation, has a different understanding of power. Power means effective agency, agency that attains its goals. When, in Scripture, God is vested with power, power is viewed as *ultimate* agency, the accomplishment of creation and redemption, the gifting of life. There are places in the Hebrew Bible when the authors, impressed by the power brokers in their contemporary world, obviously use the analogy of imperial power to think about the power of God. In the Isaianic school, in particular, there must have been some very lively debates about the true nature of power. Jesus and Paul were both traditioned by that school, and came down firmly on the side of the author of the so-called Servant songs. Taught by the crucifixion Paul writes:

> Jews demand signs and Greeks desire wisdom, but we proclaim Christ crucified, a stumbling block to Jews and foolishness to Gentiles, but to those who are called, both Jews and

Greeks, Christ the power of God and the wisdom of God. For God's foolishness is wiser than human wisdom, and God's weakness is stronger than human strength. (1 Corinthians 1: 22–5)

Uniquely in world literature, someone speaks of the weakness of God, and ventures a dialectical account of power. Power remains agency, but not that of one who is stronger than anyone else, but a power that overcomes through weakness. The crucifixion of Jesus reveals the illegitimacy of the power of the strong. Since the divine promises cannot fail, and since these are fulfilled in and through crucifixion, this must mean that this exercise of agency is stronger than what conventionally passes as power, the not-so-hidden fist of the army, navy, and air force. In virtue of the promise, there must be a way of understanding the power of the powerless. Following Jesus's own teaching, meditating perhaps on the story of the crucifixion as we have it in Luke, Paul redefines power in terms of forgiveness, of *agape*, love of the enemy. This kind of power is ultimate because it refuses alienation, refuses the last word of violence.

Let me return to that Iona community Eucharist. From that Eucharist comes a protest against Britain's murderous, idolatrous Trident missile program, the expense of which ensures that we do not have enough money for health and education. From the Eucharist we go and sit down at the base of these weapons of mass destruction, are arrested and charged, sometimes imprisoned, protesting this idolatry in the name of the word of the Lord. Futile? A waste of time? When people tell us this we remember that they told us exactly the same about the anti-apartheid campaign. Did Judas, as is now widely supposed, urge on Jesus the futility of non-violent action, the need to repay in kind, the likelihood of success given levels of resentment? Was that kiss intended finally to galvanize him into "action" – what is understood to be action in the globalizers' understanding?

Power is effective agency and it is vested in "the body of Christ" – the Church as composed of all of its members. In this "body" different parts play different roles (1 Corinthians 12). Paul does not draw the implication that there must be a head amongst the members, which must be obeyed, but follows up his earlier insight about weakness: "God has so arranged the body, giving the greater honour to the inferior member, that there may be no dissension within the body, but the members may have the same care for one another. If one member suffers, all suffer together with it; if one member is honoured, all rejoice together with it" (1 Corinthians 12: 24–6).

"Greater honour to the inferior member." This is a unique cultural politics that teaches us that it is from those who have suffered subjugation and domination that we learn our most enduring lessons for living and thinking. That must have been a very hard thing for Stephanas and Erastus to swallow. It is still hard for us. It calls in question all those six, seven, or ten-figure salaries pronounced as "necessary" for company CEOs. It asserts an alternative social imaginary, a different way to run the world.

"You are a kingdom of priests" says the author of 1 Peter. The Church is, in virtue of its founding charter, an egalitarian institution, a body, in which the first is the slave of all. It is a listening community or, as it came to be called, using terms from Greek political discussion, a democracy. At the heart of globalization, on the other hand, is the voiding of democracy by the power of money, its effective replacement by corporate power, the organization of the global economy in the interests of the rich.

Medieval theologians, in the situation of Christendom, drew up guidelines for the running of the economy on Christian principles. The very idea of Christendom, we have come to realize, is problematic, and in any case we cannot have it back. We have to live side by side with other faith communities, and we want to preserve and sustain, not eliminate, a multicultural world. Pentecost is not a return to a pre-Babel situation; it is the announcement that the gospel can be inculturated everywhere, heard in every tongue. It is not a warrant for McDonaldization, but for the preservation and appreciation of difference. At the same time, the forces which are dominating the world, in the processes which we refer to as globalization, have to be opposed because they are destroying it: destroying cultures, communities, ecosystems, and life itself if the process is left to itself. In Scripture the forces that destroy life, and that evoke worship because of their fascinating power in this regard, are called idols. At bottom, globalization is a process based on idolatry, as Marx realized in his citation of the book of Revelation.

Rooted in the Eucharist, in invocation of the God of life, Christians oppose this process, urging in its place policies of mutual accountability, of just sharing, of common ownership and of non-hierarchical forms of power. Here and there, hostile reaction shows that this opposition is beginning to tell. They must continue in joy, in the power of the word until, as in the first century and in seventeenth-century England, we hear the cry: "these people have turned the world upside down . . . this is bad for trade!" Not bad for trade, we reply, because trade is that sharing of resources, that giving from each according to his or her ability to each according to his or her needs, which the first disciples practiced as a world made conform to the God of life.

Bibliography

Bauman, Z. (1998) *Globalization: The Human Consequences* (Cambridge: Polity Press).
Beck, U. (1999) *What is Globalization?* (Cambridge: Polity Press).
Burgos-Debray, E. (ed.) (1984) *I Rigoberta Menchu* (London: Verso).
Cavanagh, D. Wysham and Arruda, M. (1994) *Beyond Bretton Woods: Alternatives to the Global Economic Order* (London: Pluto).
Duchrow, U. (1995) *Alternatives to Global Capitalism, Drawn from Biblical History, Designed for Political Action* (Utrecht: International Books).
Friedman, T. (2000) *The Lexus and the Olive Tree* (London: HarperCollins).
George, S. (1999) *The Lugano Report* (London: Pluto).
—and Sabelli, F. (1994) *Faith and Credit: The World Bank's Secular Empire* (Harmondsworth: Penguin).
Gorringe, T. (2000) *The Education of Desire* (London: SCM).
Gutiérrez, G. (1993) *Las Casas* (Maryknoll: Orbis).
Kneen, B. (1999) *Farmageddon: Food and the Culture of Biotechnology* (Philadelphia, PA: New Society).
—(2002) *Invisible Giant: Cargill and its Transnational Strategies*, 2nd edn (London: Pluto).
Korten, D. (1994) *When Corporations Rule the World* (Connecticut: Kumarian).
—(1999) *The Post Corporate World* (Connecticut: Kumarian).

Mander, J. and Goldsmith, E. (eds) (1995) *The Case against the Global Economy* (Sierra Club).

Marx, K. (1954) *Capital* (Moscow: Progress).

Monbiot, G. (2000) *Captive State: The Corporate Takeover of Britain* (London: Macmillan).

Rowbotham, M. (1998) *The Grip of Death: A Study of Modern Money, Debt Slavery and Destructive Economics* (Charlbury: Carpenter).

Shiva, V. (1998) *Biopiracy* (Totnes: Green Books).

Wink W. (1984) *Naming the Powers: The Language of Power in the New Testament* (Philadelphia, PA: Fortress).

—(1986) *Unmasking the Powers: The Invisible Forces that Determine Human Existence* (Philadelphia, PA: Fortress).

—(1992) Engaging the Powers: Discernment and Resistance in a World of Domination (Minneapolis, MN: Fortress).

CHAPTER 27
Breaking Bread: Peace and War

Gerald W. Schlabach

On December 24, 1914, the first Christmas Eve of World War I, peace broke out spontaneously, up and down the front that divided Europe. The trenches that sliced through Belgium and France had left professed Christians brutalizing one another across a no-man's-land of corpses and mud. But now the strains of *Stille Nacht / Silent Night* drew soldiers together in a makeshift truce, celebrating Christ's birth. Perhaps no chaplain offered the Eucharist or Lord's Supper, but some offered prayers. And soldiers did spread a kind of table, as they exchanged chocolates, cigarettes, a sample of their rations, and the ritual of improvised soccer. Then, a few days later, the killing resumed (Weintraub, 2001).

On another Christmas Eve in the 1980s in Chile, members of the Sebastian Acevedo Movement Against Torture quietly attended mass in an upper-class neighborhood. They shared the Eucharist with supporters of General Pinochet's military dictatorship, people who either refused to believe or rationalized away the government's systematic use of torture as a tool to stifle dissent. After mass, on the steps of the church, they handed out Christmas cards with a simple and conciliatory message: "For a Christmas without violence and a New Year without torturers." The reaction? Fellow Catholics, despite having just shared the table of the Lord, turned upon them, knocked them around, and turned them over to security forces (Vidal, 1986: 238; Cavanaugh, 1998: 261–2). How can Christians who share the table of the Lord harass, torture, or kill each other?

One answer appeared on a poster circulating in various languages around the world during the 1980s. Its answer was its alternative: "A modest proposal for peace: let the Christians of the world agree not to kill each other." However simplistic, the poster made an arresting point about the Cold War. To aim thousands of nuclear warheads at "those Godless communists" in the Soviet Union meant to target millions of Christians as well. Translated into Spanish for Central America in the 1980s the poster also made sense, as Christians fought against each other on behalf of dictatorship, revolution, then counter-revolution. But how, in the early 1990s, could the poster be translated for the former Yugoslavia? Would this "modest proposal" encourage Orthodox Serbian Christians and Catholic Croatian Christians to abandon their own genocidal conflicts precisely by ganging up on Bosnian Muslims instead?

Clearly, when Christians gather around the table of their Lord, there are many ways they "just don't get it." Still, in each of these cases, one can readily recognize an anomaly. Somehow the Eucharist keeps burrowing its steady way into the Christian conscience. Perhaps that is why, despite centuries of debate about whether Christians may appropriately participate in war, a nagging sense of doubt remains, even among those who have argued that they may – even must – participate in wars they deem just.

The Christian Presumption against Violence

All of salvation history converges and is continually made present in the Eucharist, argues Raniero Cantalamessa, preacher to the papal household (1993: 6–15). In breaking bread and sharing wine together, Christians commemorate and make present the central event of their faith. Jesus Christ has suffered and died, at the climax of a life and ministry inaugurating God's reign, giving God's life to others, but provoking the wrath and exposing the injustice of all the powers who array themselves in a vain illusion that we can secure our lives in some other way. Yet God has vindicated the way of this very Jesus by raising him from the dead, and now he is present in the Church, in the world. Looking back, Christians believe that Jesus's life and death was the fulfillment of God's faithfulness to, liberation of, covenant with, and witness through the people of Israel. Looking forward, they see all Jesus did as anticipating a great "messianic banquet" at the culmination of history, when God will regather a fallen humanity and heal a scarred creation through the eternal communion of God's reign. Looking around, they still see the brokenness of the world, but see it with renewed compassion and hope. For, as bread is broken before them in the Eucharist, God has entered bodily into human brokenness itself, thus opening space, in time, to rejoin God and one another in healing communion.

To break bread and share wine in the Eucharist has serious implications, therefore. In the words of moral theologian William Spohn, those who participate are quite literally "implicated in its dynamics" – implicated in Jesus's "way of ushering in the reign of God" (Spohn, 1999: 166). As Jesus gathered a community of disciples and friends around this common table, after all, he was not promoting the justice of God's cause, nor forging the identity of God's people in the way that most movements and peoples seek to secure themselves. Instead of keeping outcasts at a distance, he invited them to dine. Instead of getting his way by threatening to take the lives of others, he showed God's way by offering his own life for others. Instead of demonizing foreigners, he loved enemies. He offered security through generosity not hoarding, through risk but not through fear. Thus he died, but did not kill – yet he lives.

So Christians profess. But to eat from *this* table, to find life in *this* life, and to call this life *the* very life of the triune God (together with the great creeds of the Church) is to implicate themselves in God's way of non-violent love. Like it or not. Acknowledge it or not.

In the centuries-long debate among Christians over the stance they should take toward warfare, the core argument for *Christian pacifism* (from Latin words for peace-making) is that in Jesus Christ God has shown that the deepest and widest reality of the universe is God's own generous, self-giving life of mutual love. Despite the negative accent in "*non*-violence," the best definition of Christian pacifism begins in God's own life-giving positive: it is the patient and consistent discipline of discovering creative, life-building responses to unjust human conflicts. Pacifists reject violence because it is simply incompatible with such a discipline.

Pacifists certainly have pragmatic arguments for their stance too. Twentieth-century non-violent movements for Indian independence, civil rights for African Americans, an end to apartheid in South Africa, democratization in the Philippines, release from Soviet totalitarianism in Central Europe – and on and on – have shown non-violence to be not simply an admirable personal ethic but a potent political strategy. On the other hand, recourse to violence tends to provoke cycles of further violence, even when causes seem just and intentions pure. Furthermore, simply by preparing for war, societies pay the price of what economists would call "opportunity costs." Military preparation siphons resources away from productive economic activities; military options tempt politicians and diplomats with short-cut solutions to complex social problems.

For thoroughgoing Christian pacifists, however, these pragmatic considerations are encouraging but not decisive. What constitutes the core of their position is the life, death, and resurrection of Jesus Christ. Through him, God has shown the redemptive righting of wrong to proceed not through a predictable calculus of cause and effect, but through the unexpected logic of cross and resurrection (Yoder, 1994: 203–4). In the end, therefore, Christian pacifism does not stand upon a naïve confidence that every last struggle for justice is winnable through non-violent means. Nor does it stumble when the latest "bad guy" turns out to be a lot nastier than anyone expected. Rather, it trusts in the One whom Christians learn about in the Gospels, encounter through the miracle of his "real presence" in the Eucharist, and thus find training them to expect the incalculable. Implicated in the unexpected way that Jesus has inaugurated God's reign, they are freed to risk living according to that reign, already.

Admittedly, in most centuries and in most Church communities pacifism has hardly seemed to win the debate among Christians about the stance they should take toward war. Sometimes, Christians with access to political power have persecuted Christian pacifists outright. More often, they have made pacifists feel that they were the ones who must prove they were orthodox, patriotic, or not "irresponsible." Along the wide arc of Christian history, however, pacifism is the position that initially set the agenda for debate over warfare, and continues to leave Christians who would justify warfare per-petually bearing a certain burden of proof.

During the second half of the twentieth century, many representatives of the second major position in this debate, the *just-war tradition* of moral deliberation, have come to consider pacifism the historical and conceptual starting-point for their own position. Although Christians of the first three centuries may not have been pacifists in exactly the same way as modern Christian pacifists, historical evidence is compelling that they considered all bloodshed a sin, consistently refused military participation, and believed prophecies in Isaiah 2 and Micah 4 – concerning a time when nations would cease making war and beat their swords into plowshares – were being fulfilled through the very life of the Church (Hunter, 1992; Kreider, 1999: 27).

Conceptually, too, many interpreters believe the just-war theory begins with commitments that its advocates share with pacifism. Certainly, there are others who ground just-war theory in the need to structure human life with a basic order of justice, preserved through force. Yet even these have sometimes explained this ordering work as an act of love for neighbor (Ramsey, 1968: 142–3). At a time when most Christians have long since changed their mind about warfare and military service, the most convincing reason many can find for the taking of life is to preserve still other lives – particularly innocent life – against threats from criminals and aggressors (John Paul II, 1995: §55). This means that violence can never be the norm for Christians, but always an exception that requires justification. Even if war is justifiable, therefore, Christians can only approve it cautiously, reluctantly, with regret and without any spirit of revenge. In this way, a *presumption against violence* continues to work its way not only through Christian pacifism but through the just-war tradition (cf. NCCB, 1983: §§70, 120).

Christian pacifists sometimes point out less noble reasons why just war rather than pacifism has become the dominant position among Christians. Already in the New Testament, Christians needed reminders that their highest loyalties belonged to Christ and the Christian community (e.g. Philippians 3: 12–20; 2 Timothy 1: 6–10, Revelation 3: 14–22). As generations have passed, it is not surprising that the loyalty of Christians has easily reverted to family, tribe, or nation, whose claims again trump the claims of Christ. Even more seductive has been the temptation to confuse the cause of Christ with the cause of nation. That becomes all the more easy whenever the people called Church becomes so closely identified with a people called Greek, German, Ukrainian, Mexican, or American that national or ethnic identity becomes confused with Christian identity.

In this regard, many interpreters see the events of fourth-century Christianity as prototypical and trend-setting for later centuries. The trend sometimes bears the name of *Constantinianism* because a crucial moment came near the beginning of that century, when the Emperor Constantine legalized and patronized the Christian Church. By the end of the century, the Emperor Theodosius had made Christianity the official religion of the Roman Empire. Meanwhile, from the fourth century on, Christians with closer ties to governmental authority became suspiciously mute in their teachings on war. Medieval Christianity did keep alive a vision of Christian internationalism, whereby Christian culture and peoplehood always transcended national boundaries. But it did not prevent Christians from loving their European neighbors in the exclusive and sub-Christian way (cf. Matthew 5: 46–7) that meant joining forces for a series of crusades against Muslims (Cahill, 1994: 127–35, 146–7). Later, when Protestant Reformers attempted to correct the abuses of medieval Christianity, the mainstream Reformation actually complicated problems of war and nationalism. Relying on the support of princes, the Reformation identified churches all the more tightly with limited political territories. Looking back on the legacy of both medieval Catholic and Reformation Protestant developments, the operative war ethic of most Christians turns out to be *neither* pacifism *nor* just war, but combinations of crusade, machismo, and nationalism that permit warmaking to proceed by a logic of its own, largely unconstrained by moral concerns (Yoder, 1996: 1, 68–9).

Still, at every step of the way, some proponents of just-war thinking have sought to use the tradition not so much to justify as to limit violence. After all, the tradition demands that all who consider launching a military action must first pass the muster of a series of criteria. And then, as military action proceeds, a second set of criteria speaks to how they wage the war. Criteria for going to war are often listed under a Latin phrase with roughly that meaning, *jus ad bellum*:

1   The cause must be just; in other words, responding to a grave public evil, such as unprovoked aggression or threat to the human rights of entire populations.
2   The authority waging the war must be legitimate, duly constituted in service to public not private goods.
3   The intention motivating the war must be right, objectively aiming to promote the common good, not a hidden agenda.
4   Success must be probable, not a futile effort that does little more than destroy lives and resources on both sides.
5   The overall war effort must be proportional; in other words, the achievable good must outweigh the destruction that the war itself causes.
6   War must be the last resort, coming only after exhaustive attempts to resolve the conflict by peaceful means.

Even if all these criteria have been met, additional criteria apply to the conduct of warfare (*jus in bello*):

7   Non-combatants are to be immune from harm, military forces may never target civilians directly, and must make every effort to avoid indirect harm as well.
8   Specific military campaigns must also be proportional, employing no more force than necessary to meet military objectives.
9   Intention must continue to be right, subjectively motivated by a desire for peace with justice, not vengeance or hatred.

Astute students of these just-war criteria will notice that they appeal far more to so-called "common sense" than they do to any specifically Christian insights or convictions known through Jesus Christ. For some Christian thinkers, however, this points to solid reasons why the just-war theory developed and continues to be useful, not to reasons for suspicion. Christians must fulfill the gospel call to love their neighbors within the world as they find it. That world is fallen, sinful, and does not yet constitute the reign of God. Jesus's life and teachings offer the standard by which to measure all human action, and thus underscore the presumption against violence already evident in the law of Moses, but the fallenness of our world may nonetheless require exceptions to the moral norm. Christians live in a meantime, after all, a time between the "already" of God's reign as Jesus has inaugurated it, and the "not yet" of its fullness. The resurrected Christ is present with them through the Holy Spirit and in the Eucharist, but they still live in the meantime between Jesus's resurrection and the final resurrection whereby God will create a new heaven and earth (Isaiah 65: 17; Revelation 21).

In a complex world where our duties and loyalties are also complex, just-war theory proposes a way to maintain core Christian commitments to sustain life, love one's neighbors, and perhaps even love one's enemies by respecting their human dignity amid warfare. Complexity begins as soon as we must love two or more neighbors simultaneously, and one is attacking another. To many, Christian love itself would seem to require intervention to preserve innocent life, with the unintended possibility – though never the direct intention – of lethal violence. By extension, military action seems a way to defend the lives of many neighbors and whole societies.

Christian pacifists may believe that lethal violence is never so "necessary" as it seems, that more creative responses to threats are always available, and that until societies do far more to explore such alternatives they will not even have begun to fulfill the just-war criterion of last resort. But notice that as soon as a pacifist makes this kind of point, she concedes at least one other one: pacifists themselves often find it helpful to cite just-war criteria in their own efforts to resist war and limit violence. In the public forum where neither Christian faith nor Christian unity can be assumed, the just-war tradition of moral deliberation often serves to provide a common language for examining the justice of particular wars. Offering a common idiom that does not rely on specifically Christian beliefs therefore seems to some a strength not a weakness of the just-war framework.

In fact, increasingly lethal warfare in the twentieth century has made it more and more urgent for Christians to relearn the just-war criteria in order to scrutinize war more stringently. As they have done so more deliberately, many have found new reasons to rethink their stance toward war altogether. Take, for example, the indiscriminate effects of modern warfare on civilians.

Non-combatant immunity is in many ways the linchpin of the entire just-war theory (Ford, 1944; Ramsey, 1961). The prohibition against any direct targeting of civilians, after all, provides at least one moral absolute to keep what is otherwise a series of judgment calls from sliding into a morass of rationalization that merely provides cover for ulterior motives and sheer expediency. Modern warfare, however, has blurred the line between combatants and non-combatants in at least two ways. First, large nations and small guerrilla forces alike have found it advantageous to mobilize entire populations in support of their war efforts, thus turning their own non-combatant populations into military targets. Second, firepower has so increased that the most tempting weaponry available to many nations is too powerful to discriminate between military and civilian targets at all. Nuclear weapons are only the most dramatic example of what is now true of much "conventional" weaponry as well. Though high-tech "smart bombs" with computerized targeting may herald an end to this trend, for now these weapons comprise only a fraction of the world's arsenals. In any case, "smart-bomb" technology has its own tendency to depersonalize the humanity of its targets and obscure the real toll of war, video-game style. All of these developments have led some proponents of a just-war approach to wonder whether any modern war can possibly meet the criteria needed for a war to qualify as just.

Still, other modern developments also give pause, in other ways. Cases of egregious human rights abuses and genocide certainly provide one of the strongest arguments for the possibility of just and humanitarian military intervention. Christian pacifists would find the just-war approach far less objectionable if it were to establish a track record of limiting military action to something more like police action, done within the framework of international law and courts, to stop these crimes against humanity. If the "just-war" approach were "just policing," then war would be far less of a source of division between Christians.

To be sure, massive human rights abuses rarely happen without years of militarization, fueled by arms trade and military assistance from world powers (Renner, 1997: 7–8, 34; Stassen, 1998: 170–1). That raises the question of whether reliance on short-term military "solutions" will not perpetuate long-term cycles of violence. The need to stop a regime such as Nazi Germany, which was both systematically murderous and bent on world domination, seems to many an open-and-shut case for the legitimacy of just wars. Yet Hitler was the product of a previous century of European militarization, guided by ideologies celebrating strong and competitive nation-states as bearers of reason and civilization, which culminated in World War I but left Germans humiliated. In turn, Hitler's defeat involved alliances that consolidated Soviet power, launched the Cold War, and issued in an age of nuclear terror. Pacifists certainly cannot avoid the challenge that genocidal regimes represent, but to dismiss pacifist claims and proposals because they did not have an immediate response to Hitler in 1939 is like blaming a physician for failing to cure a recalcitrant chain-smoker of emphysema.

On the more positive side of the modern scene, active non-violence has demonstrated its practical political power well enough in the twentieth century that some theorists have put together strategies that would allow nations to begin a process of "trans-armament" toward non-military, civilian-based defense (Sharp, 1985). Meanwhile, amid the complex process of economic and cultural integration known as globalization, one clearly positive development is this: as nations recognize their interdependence they notice many new incentives to resolve their conflicts through peaceful means.

Finally, did the devastating attacks on New York and Washington, DC on September 11, 2001 "change everything" in this debate, too, as many Americans felt at the time? Though "9/11" made some pacifists reconsider their position, it also raised fresh questions about the efficacy of war in the modern era. Forceful police action to apprehend the perpetrators and try them as war criminals might be acceptable to some pacifists if done within the framework of international law. Yet the prospect of an unlimited "war on terrorism," which even its advocates admit may never really end, also gives pause. The Orwellian prospect here (as in George Orwell's classic novel *1984*) is a war that no military can decisively win, but that is perpetually available for politicians to use for rallying popular support and stifling dissent. As it stretches on, such a "war" promises to force non-pacifists to take their own second look – and reconsider the likelihood that terrorism can *only* really be overcome through non-military means.

The Eucharist: Our Peace at God's Lavish Table

What most regularly and quite literally prompts Christians to pause and to keep rethinking the question of war, however, is the proclamation of the gospel and its celebration in the Eucharist. The Eucharist and the Jesus whose "real presence" it invites into the gathering of believers are not just one reason among many for staying unsettled about Christian participation in warfare. It is the core reason, and the one that simply refuses to go away. The Eucharist is an offer of life, a promise of hospitality to strangers, a sharing of peace, a taste of God's generosity, a breaking that opens space for healing. It commemorates God's victory over every cosmic and historical force of evil by a lion – no, of all things! – by a lamb who was slain and by the blood of the martyrs who follow this lamb (Revelation 5 and 12: 11; cf. Weaver, 2001: 20–33). As Christians now celebrate the Eucharist around the globe, it makes more real than ever what was already clear when the God of Israel offered new life to Gentile nations through Jesus Christ: this is a gospel that bursts the confines of even the most sacred nationalism.

"Lord, I am not worthy to receive you, but only say the word and I shall be healed," say Roman Catholics in every mass. Paul has warned Christians not to partake unworthily of Christ's body and blood (1 Corinthians 11: 27–8). And yet knowing that they are *always* unworthy – never at the table except through God's generous and trans-forming forgiveness – Christians learn and re-learn the practice of generosity toward others. Thus, even those who cannot quite imagine how they will cease their own dis-putes, extricate themselves from systems of greed, and undo their complicity in killing (cf. James 4), find themselves quietly disquieted when they fail to show others anything less than the generous non-violent love that God has shown them.

In other words, if tension is evident at the very table that is the pre-eminent Christ-ian sign of human community and ultimate communion with God, the Eucharist is doing its work. Christians who participate regularly, mindfully, and bodily in the Eucharist testify that the ritual is powerful in part because it works on them at many levels. At each, there is a *proper* tension.

Already and not yet

As we have already noted, Christians live in a meantime between Jesus's resurrection and a cosmic resurrection – between God having *already* made the reign of God present in Jesus Christ, and God *not yet* having brought the fullness of that reign at the culmi-nation of history. Theologians and biblical scholars refer to this meantime as a period of "eschatological tension," a term based on a Greek word for that final culmination, the "eschaton." Christians impressed with the "not-yet" tug of this eschatological tension are more likely to argue that they have a responsibility to live out their Christ-ian faith amid the constraints and complexities of the world as it is, which is what seems to require a reluctant use of violence. Christians impressed by the "already" tug of this eschatological tension are more likely to argue that "the world as it is" is one in which God's Spirit is always offering new possibilities, and empowering people of faith to live now according to the future.

Cantalamessa's (1993) observation, that all of salvation history converges and is made present in the Eucharist, reconfigures this eschatological tension, however. All that God has "already" done through Israel, Christ, and the Church universal is acces-sible in every Christian community as it practices the Eucharist. What's more, the "not yet" of God's future heavenly banquet is already present in the mundane Eucharistic banquet that Christians celebrate now. Active participation in the Eucharist should not obscure the tragic realities of the world as currently structured. By making God's promised future so present one may taste it already, the Eucharist actually makes the Christian's sense of eschatological tension into an all-the-more excruciating tension. As the Eucharist pulls us toward God's future, the realities by which the world most decidedly is "not yet" the reign of God should move Christians not toward accommodation with "the world as it is," but toward a more poignant sense of holy dissatisfaction and urgency.

The end and the beginning of sacrifice

In the most important and decisive sense, the Eucharist re-presents the end of every sacrificial system by which humans seek to undo sin and violence through "just a bit" more violence. In analyzing the myths of many ancient and contemporary societies, René Girard has traced the deep instinct in human civilizations to maintain social harmony by transferring their own internal violence onto outcasts in their own midst and strangers beyond. The ritual sacrifice of animals may have served to reduce the shedding of human blood, but has hardly eliminated the scapegoating of other races, the handicapped, homosexuals, and dehumanized enemies. When Christ accepted the role of the perfectly innocent victim, according to Girard, God exposed as only God could the injustice of every sacrificial system, religious or sociopolitical. Because of Jesus Christ, human beings need no longer sacrifice (Girard 1996: vii–x, 9–19, 177–88).

In another way, however, Christ's true sacrifice has now made it possible for *true* sacrifice to begin. Sacrifice does not simply mean suffering. It also means offering, self-sharing, the giving over of life, and not just the giving up of life. Because Christ has secured human life and future in a way that the myth of redemptive violence always claims but fails to do, we are free to give ourselves to God and to others. When Christians place bread and wine on the altar, they have ceased to sacrifice with the flesh and blood even of animals. Yet when they do still offer God the ordinary grain and grape, transformed through the ordinary labor of their hands, they practice their gratitude. And they do so in trust that the one final bloody sacrifice that God offered in Christ is now repeatedly filling the living gift of ordinary lives with the very life of God.

That Christ is the end of all sacrifice is crucial if we are to understand the Christian response to war. War is a sacrificial system. Those who go to war as well as those who support them not only risk their lives, but they also sacrifice their normal unwillingness to kill. War has a powerful hold on our imaginations; that is, we find it hard to imagine living without the possibility of war because of the sacrifices war offers. The exposure to killing and being killed becomes for many the most decisive moral experience they can or will ever have. War creates camaraderie, a sense of community that is unique (Hedges, 2002). As a result many cannot imagine a world without war because war is the most morally intense experience many can have. Accordingly, many assume we must be ready to wage future wars if we are to be worthy of the sacrifices made on our behalf in past wars.

But the Eucharist is the counter-sacrifice to the sacrifices that war seems to require. The fraction, the breaking of the bread, is the sacrifice that ends the sacrifice of war. The Eucharist is not a sacrifice to appease an angry God, but rather is God's gracious action that makes us participants in Christ's sacrifice on our behalf. Christians, by sharing in the body and blood of Christ, are made part of God's life and thus become an alternative to the story of war. Through the Eucharist, Christians become God's time for the world, making possible a patience that no longer requires violence to sustain the waiting, the stillness that is worship.

Celebrating unity, recognizing disunity

Through God's work in Christ, that heavenly banquet is already present in the gathering of disciples who live in believing trust not fear. In communion with God, true human community is possible. The body of Christ made present at the table also makes the Church into the Body of Christ. In re-presenting the work of Christ, the Eucharist is a living sign of the Church's unity.

Yet here, too, Christians live in tension. Just as the tug of God's future accentuates pain at humanity's present, partaking of this sign of Christian unity accentuates a painful sensitivity to Christian disunity. As Spohn (1999) suggests, the scandal of division between classes, races, factions, and ethnicities is evident already in the tables of disunity that the New Testament records (Corinth, Letter of James, Jesus's Last Supper itself). Yet there is something "entirely appropriate" about the way that the Eucharist teaches Christians to recognize these divisions precisely as a scandal. "Like Southern Christians [in the US] who realized that praying 'Our Father' did not fit with segregation, those who share the Lord's table have to be in solidarity with the hungry of the world or they should stop coming to the table." Whether the scandal that Christ seeks to heal is the gap between rich and poor, enmity between nations, or division in the Church itself, "sharing the Lord's Supper commits [Christians] to go and do likewise." (Spohn, 1999: 165–84).

As Eucharist in the Church, Church in the world

Cantalamessa (1993) does not draw back from the ethical implications of all this. His Roman Catholic "high view" of the Eucharist as the real presence of the body and blood of Christ actually leads to more not less radical conclusions. The Eucharist is at the very center of the Church's life, he says, and thus constitutes the Church as the very body of Christ. Cantalamessa asks readers to envision three concentric circles. The outer one is the entire universe, the smaller is the Church, and the smallest is the "host" or eucharistic bread. Just as the Eucharist leavens and makes the Church into bread for the world, the Church is to leaven and nourish the world. Citing Paul's appeal that Christians "present their bodies as a living sacrifice" to God (Romans 12: 1), Cantalamessa hears nothing less than a call for Christians to *be the Eucharist* in the world: "You also do what Jesus Christ did; you also be a Eucharist for God!" (Cantalamessa, 1993: 16–17).

To "do this in remembrance of me," as Jesus told his disciples when he broke bread with them one last time, does not merely mean to repeat a ritual. "He was also saying: Do the essence of what I have done, offer your bodies as a sacrifice, as you have seen me do!" To be the Body of Christ, then, is to abandon ourselves to the will of God as Jesus has done, and to give God's gifts of life back to God in love. But it is also to allow ourselves to be " 'eaten' " by brothers and sisters who do not reciprocate one's kindness, to live what the world considers a "useless life," to serve the poor, to renounce authoritarian patterns of relationship, and to become defenseless together with the Incarnate One who thus became vulnerable (Cantalamessa, 1993: 17–19, 23–4, 66–76).

Mark of identity, marked for hospitality

With roots in the Jewish Passover and words of institution that speak of a new covenant, the Eucharist is a ritual of community formation and commitment that serves to mark the identity of the Christian within the Church. Christian traditions that practice what is known as "closed communion" and only invite full members of their churches to the table thus do so for entirely legitimate reasons, biblical and theological. In a consumeristic culture that encourages people to try out endless products and new experiences without making any commitment except a monetary one, it may be all the more important to guard the Lord's table from the cheapening effect of open supply with few demands.

Yet Christian traditions that practice "open communion" and invite all baptized Christians to the table also have legitimate reasons. If the Eucharist or Lord's Supper is what sociologists call an "identity marker," the identity that it marks is fruitfully paradoxical. One cannot properly identify with Jesus without identifying with his own hospitality toward outcasts, women, strangers, and sinners. The roots of the Eucharist include not only the covenant-ratifying meals of Israel but the hosting that Jesus himself did throughout Palestine, among crowds still wondering whether to follow him, and disciples who stumbled when they tried.

How to hold these two dimensions of the Eucharist together in actual practice is a nettlesome problem. What should be clear in every Christian tradition, however, is that, as guests at Jesus's table, Christians are called to become generous hosts. Even the most hospitable families need intimate meals just to themselves. Whether or not a Christian community decides to open its table to visitors, the Eucharist should issue in lives of generous Christian hospitality in the world. Perhaps the way to solve the dilemma of closed or open communion is for the Church's preaching and practice to "implicate" communicants far more starkly in lives of costly discipleship, loyalty to Christ and Christian community over nation, generosity toward the poor, and love of enemy. That way, none will even imagine coming casually to the table.

"Do not eat or drink unworthily," but "I am not worthy"

Yet who then would dare come to the table at all? To a Corinthian Church so insensitive to its factions that the rich could barge ahead of the poor to eat, Paul warned that anyone who ate the bread or drank the cup unworthily would be "answerable for the body and blood of the Lord." Thus, he told the Corinthians, "Examine yourselves, and only then eat of the bread and drink of the cup" (1 Corinthians 11: 27–8). Is it possible to do this and *ever* find oneself worthy?

What the Corinthians were to see as they examined themselves was the very body of Christ not only in the bread but in one another (1 Corinthians 11: 29). Strange as it sounds, the only way to come worthily to the table is to look around the assembly and recognize that *none* are worthy. "See," Paul had written in the same letter, the body of Christ is made up of fools and failures and commoners with no celebrity and nothing to boast of in God's presence – except Christ Jesus, the source of our lives (1 Corinthians 1: 26–31). To take one's place in such company is to forgive them all. They are no more but no less worthy than I. For all Christians are there solely by grace. Yet none is there through the "cheap grace" that would leave relationships unchallenged, unchanged, or unreconciled. To dine in such company, after all, is change and reconciliation already.

The generosity of God, for us and through us

In summary, God has set a lavish table, hosting outcasts and enemies, feeding all with God's own life. Incarnate in Jesus Christ and embodied still in bread and wine, God offers life to the world by a further miracle of incarnation through all these sinful, bumbling, short-falling Christian lives which yet become Eucharist in and for the world.

Anti-Eucharist: Arms Trade as the Distribution of Scarcity

If only that shortfall were at least not so lethal. For what too many Christians continue to offer the world is an anti-gift, an economy not of salvation but of death. Called to offer their own lives and bodies to feed the hunger of the world, they are complicit in arms trade and military "aid" that only leaves the world hungrier. Surely this scandal is one that pacifist and just-war Christians must feel and act upon together.

Military "aid" and arms trade is a gift that keeps on taking. Imagine that someone were able to distribute small versions of what physicists call "black holes." The actual astronomical kind suck into themselves all nearby light, energy, and matter. To distribute our imaginary mini-variety would be like distributing Eucharistic hosts, but in reverse. For instead of offering grace, empowerment, and generosity to the world, they would deplete life, energy, and resources in a kind of anti-Eucharist. Something like this is already happening.

In the late 1980s and early 1990s, as the Cold War came to an end, policy-makers on both sides of the Atlantic spoke of a possible "peace dividend." Military budgets could shrink and resources long dedicated to the arms race could now be dedicated to economic development at home and abroad. Deficit spending might eventually give way to surpluses. The surplus that North Atlantic nations began to share, however, was their new weapons surplus.

The Cold War had often been quite hot for the nations around the world through which the United States and the Soviet Union competed for geopolitical influence in proxy wars. After the Berlin Wall fell in 1989, the early 1990s initially saw a declining arms market, but then at least four events and trends set in:

1   Fearing the loss of markets and arguing that lucrative arms sales would shore up trade balances, the US and competitor nations sought to promote arms production and sales.
2   Quick victory by the US and its allies in the Persian Gulf War served to advertise the superiority of American weapon technology over Soviet arms that Iraq had borne.
3   Budget-minded governments realized they could upgrade their own militaries at a reduced cost to taxpayers or even for "free" by selling aged weapons to poorer nations.
4   Lower down the military food chain, deals sometimes turned on the offer of outright giveaways on still-older, still-smaller, but greater-surplus arms (Sivard, 1997: 12–13, 16; Stassen, 1998: 171–3).

So the 1990s may have looked like a period of disarmament for citizens of Europe and North America who were relieved to see a nuclear stand-down at last. But any drop in global spending on arms was misleading, since it came with the worldwide proliferation of small arms. Not only did hot and brutal regional wars continue in nations such as Mozambique, Angola, Somalia, Sudan, Afghanistan, and the former Yugoslavia. Even nations who achieved celebrated peace accords – South Africa, Nicaragua, El Salvador, Guatemala – awoke to find vast quantities of left-over arms circulating in the civilian population, fueling crime rates, and undermining prospects for revitalized civil society. Meanwhile, favored allies such as Turkey and Bahrain continued the Cold War practice of turning official military aid into tools for repressive policies against their own populations. And then there were the weapons that lay immobile in the ground – land mines – waiting for decades like those imaginary black holes, rendering fields unproductive for farmers and lethal for wandering children (Renner, 1997: 11–13, 19–30; Stassen, 1998: 173–4).

Obviously, the most serious drain from this anti-Eucharist of arms trade is upon the lives and health of those who suffer attacks upon their human dignity, and upon the vitality of civil societies rife with endemic violence. Food supplies, health care, safe drinking water, and environmental integrity all suffer as societies continue to divert resources into the dubious security of weapons procurement.

But there are consequences, too, for the sellers and "donors" of this false generosity. Wealthy societies – and the Christians within them – are tempted (at worst) to think of other peoples as problems to be suppressed. Or they are tempted (at a lowly best) to offer them solutions that do not require the donors to share their bodies through authentic cross-cultural exchanges of gifts and wisdom over time. Instead, even non-military "aid" is less generous than it appears, for it often comes with strings attached, requiring recipient nations to buy products from donor nations alone, thus indebting them.

Finally, trust in military solutions depletes the incentive to develop non-lethal ways of protecting ourselves and others from criminals and aggressors. God's generosity in the Eucharist would train our eyes to see far fewer threats than our fears and ideologies of scarcity would have it, but in a fallen world there will always be some criminal threats. God has given the Church its own non-violent practices of discipline and sanction, however (cf. 1 Corinthians 6: 1–8, Matthew 18: 15–18). The more Christians do to develop these, the more they will have to offer our violent world to develop analogous practices of non-violent direct action, non-lethal community policing, and civilian-based defense (Yoder, 1992). When Christians let these languish they implicate themselves in attacks upon the global Body of Christ.

The Right Way to Stay Hungry

For this body, too – the Body of Christ spread throughout many nations, embracing the best values of every tribe and nation by refusing captivity to any one culture – is God's gift to each Christian. To identify with all God's people is to identify with their joys as well as their pains (1 Corinthians 12: 26). To feed on the bread of the Eucharist is to be filled "with finest wheat." But, in another sense, to feed on this bread and to drink of this wine is also the *right* way to stay hungry.

In solidarity with sisters and brothers around the world, the Eucharist should fill Christians with the joy of worldwide communion, even as it accentuates their pain at disunity. In providing a taste of the fullness of God's reign, the Eucharist whets their hunger and thirst for God's justice. In taking the very body and blood of Christ into their own bodies, the Eucharist turns the bodies of all Christians who partake across enemy lines into sanctuaries one dare not attack. Thus would it train Christians to love every other enemy too as God's beloved creature, made in the image of the Trinity, created for communion not competition.

So how can Christians who share the table of the Lord kill each other – or anyone else? How indeed?

References

Cahill, L. S. (1994) *Love your Enemies: Discipleship, Pacifism, and Just War Theory* (Minneapolis, MN: Fortress).

Cantalamessa, R. (1993) *The Eucharist: Our Sanctification*, trans. F. L. Villa (Collegeville, MN: The Liturgical Press).

Cavanaugh, W. T. (1998) *Torture and Eucharist: Theology, Politics and the Body of Christ* (Oxford: Blackwell).

Ford, J. C., SJ (1944) "The Morality of Obliteration Bombing," *Theological Studies*, 5: 261–309 (September).

Girard, R. (1996) *The Girard Reader*, ed. J. G. Williams, (New York: Crossroad).

Hedges, C. (2002) *War is a Force that Gives us Meaning* (New York: Public Affairs).

Hunter, D. G. (1992) "A Decade of Research on Early Christians and Military Service," *Religious Studies Review*, 18 (2): 87–94 (April).

John Paul II (1995) *Evangelium vitae* [*The Gospel of Life*], encyclical letter (March 25).

Kreider, A. (1999) *The Change of Conversion and the Origin of Christendom* (Harrisburg, PA: Trinity).

NCCB (National Conference of Catholic Bishops) (1983) *The Challenge of Peace: God's Promise and Our Response* (Washington, DC: United States Catholic Conference), May 3.

Ramsey, P. (1961) *War and the Christian Conscience: How Shall Modern War be Conducted Justly?* Published for the Lilly Endowment Research Program in Christianity and Politics (Durham, NC: Duke University Press).

—(1968) *The Just War: Force and Political Responsibility*, introduction by Stanley Hauerwas (New York: Scribner).

Renner, M. (1997) *Small Arms, Big Impact: The Next Challenge of Disarmament*. Worldwatch paper, no. 137 (Washington, DC: Worldwatch Institute).

Sharp, G. (1985) *Making Europe Unconquerable: The Potential of Civilian-based Deterrence and Defence* (Cambridge, MA: Ballinger).

Sivard, R. L. (1997) *World Military and Social Expenditures 1996*, 16th edn (Leesburg, VA: WMSE).

Spohn, W. C. (1999) *Go and Do Likewise: Jesus and Ethics* (New York: Continuum).

Stassen, G. (ed.) (1998) *Just Peacemaking: Ten Practices for Abolishing War* (Cleveland, OH: Pilgrim Press).

Vidal, H. (1986) *El movimiento contra la tortura "Sebastián Acevedo": derechos humanos y la producción de símbolos nacionales bajo el fascismo Chileno* (Minneapolis, MN: Institute for the Study of Ideologies).

Weaver, J. D. (2001) *The Non-violent Atonement* (Grand Rapids, MI: Eerdmans).

Weintraub, S. (2001) *Silent Night: The Story of the World War I Christmas Truce* (New York: Free Press).

Yoder, J. H. (1992) *Body Politics: Five Practices of the Christian Community before the Watching World* (Nashville, TN: Discipleship Resources).

—(1994) *The Royal Priesthood: Essays Ecclesiological and Ecumenical*, ed. M. G. Cartwright, with an introduction by R. J. Mouw (Grand Rapids, MI: Eerdmans).

—(1996) *When War is Unjust: Being Honest in Just-war Thinking*, rev. ed. D. Christiansen, with a foreword by C. P. Lutz (Maryknoll, NY: Orbis).

CHAPTER 28

Receiving Communion: Euthanasia, Suicide, and Letting Die

Carole Bailey Stoneking

The term "euthanasia" has Greek roots and literally means "good death." While the term implies that there can be a good death, in itself it does not tell us when or under what conditions death is good. Is a good death one that we know is coming and over which we have control? If in certain circumstances, death is no greater an evil than the patient's continued existence, do the usual reasons for not wanting to be the cause of someone's death, even our own, simply not apply?

The aim of not starting or discontinuing certain types of treatment is often to spare the patient additional and unjustifiable pain, to save the patient from the indignities of hopeless manipulations, and to avoid increasing the emotional and financial burdens on the family. If, for these reasons, death is deemed the "best possible outcome" for certain patients, what moral distinctions separate allowing death from causing death? Is it better still if death takes place through the action of the patient, "assisted" by a doctor? A continuation of the logic of much public discourse would train us to prefer physician-assisted suicide, for thus the patient's right to privacy is upheld, while at the same time we honor that barrier that prevents doctors from actually doing something that will cause death in an immediate or direct way. Physician-assisted suicide seems the best way to claim some control over death, a final and ultimate exercise of autonomy.

It is interesting here to recount a little of the recent history of the practice of physician-assisted suicide. The most well-known advocate and practitioner has been retired pathologist Jack Kevorkian. His activities in assisting suicides have been much publicized. Many of the families of people he has assisted to die speak highly of Dr Kevorkian. In the videotapes that he made before each death, the individuals who died were seen pleading to be allowed to die. He is depicted as the savior-physician, the good doctor who receives them and provides them with the means that would end their suffering.

However, his critics point out that at least some of the people who wanted to die might not have done so if they had been rightly helped – if their pain had been adequately treated, for example. Some of the people Dr Kevorkian assisted were not terminally ill. One was in the early stages of Alzheimer's disease, and another had multiple sclerosis. The primary physician of another who claimed to have multiple sclerosis said the patient showed no evidence of this; the patient did, however, have a history of depression. In one case, a woman had chronic fatigue syndrome and a history of abuse by her husband. The people Kevorkian assisted to die were predominantly women who may have been worried about the impact of their disease on others as much as the difficulty of the disease itself or its prospects for them. In fact, three times as many women as men attempt suicide, though men succeed more often than do women. Some suggest that death may appear different to women. Stephanie Gutmann (1996) writes: "If it is given a human face by a soothing physician/assister there is all the more reason why the super-altruistic woman with a life spent serving others would want to put down her burdens, and succumb."

What does the case of Dr Kevorkian tell us? Is something not terribly awry when killing is described as caring? There is a gap between these stories and the Church's stories and practices, a gap which must be examined if we are to understand what has gone awry. One might say that the savior that advocates of physician-assisted suicide embrace is a soothing physician/assister, one who promises to save us from ambivalence, from all anguish and suffering, by shaping a vision and adopting a discourse distorting and disregarding of a genuine human identity, but tightly joined to the choices of "rational individuals" under universalizing conditions. The performances of these icons cannot tolerate moral ambivalence or recognize meaning in suffering; the performances of these icons are the customary repair worked upon a cultural discourse that cannot account for the practices of caring-for or caring-from either within or over time. Here lies the gap, one that we cannot afford not to examine.

The lack of conceptual clarity about the practises of a Jack Kevorkian, practises which progressed from assisted suicide to active euthanasia, conceals the way in which his performances deepen our alienation and blind us to the significance of attending to lived lives, of focusing on the practices of life and of faith that we are already engaged in. In this chapter, I try to imagine a different posture for the Church, a posture that speaks the grammar of its own normative story, a posture less abstracted from the wellsprings of Christian commitment. What does receiving the cup of Christ commit us to? What does the practice of receiving communion teach us about patience and caring, living and dying? Rather than a systematic exposition in the traditional mode, i.e., an exposition in words that ordinary people do not recognize and cannot understand, I turn first to an imaginative story of ordinary people, to try to say what matters, in a way that matters, about what these practices mean.

The story begins in a room chilled by the approach of death, where an old woman and her grieving daughter are saying goodbye in silent, urgent conversation. In the next room, a young boy waits with his father, remembering the tales his grandmother and mother have passed down, an inheritance rich in language and music and imaginative teaching, told by women to a child who will one day find such wisdom needful. The boy describes the night:

> The wind has got into the clocks and blown the hours awry. It was an unsteady wind, rising to a wail at the eaves and corners of this big brick house of my grandparents, then

subsiding to insistent whispers that rustled inside the room. My father and I listened to the wind and tried to talk to each other, but it was difficult and we fell silent for long stretches, forced to attend the wind we feared so much . . . On our right-hand side loomed the door we were not going to open. It entered upon the long dark hall that led to the back bedroom.

In that room my grandmother lay dying while my mother kept watch beside her. A doctor had been called for, but long hours had passed since my father had telephoned, choking back his sorrow and speaking, in a strained hoarse voice . . .

My father and I sat in our chairs and stared at the clocks on the mantel behind the wood heater. A tall wooden clock stood in the middle; behind gilt-filigreed glass it showed a dingy face with sharp Roman numerals and suspended below that an ornate gilt pendulum. Beside it sat a fancy clock Uncle Luden had brought from Memphis; it had four brass balls that circled below a small face, and the whole was inclosed in a spotless bell jar. There was a dull electric clock in a black housing; my father had brought it here last week because he didn't trust the other clocks to keep good time. Then there was a large silver watch encased in a velvet box with its face open to display the hour its owner – my grandfather – had died; it always read 12:12.

Only now it didn't. Now it read 2:03 or 11:00 or 6:15. The wind had got into it and blown the hours awry. Under the bell jar the four brass balls of Uncle Luden's clock turned one way and then another, whirling swiftly or barely moving. The pendulum in the gilt clock was as irregular as a cork bobbing on a fishing line. The wind had got into the electricity also and the hands of that clock pointed where they pleased.

When I told my father what was happening, he said, "Yes, time is getting ready to stop."

"Stop?"

"Yes. For our family at least. Time will have to stop for us and it's hard to think how it can start up again."

"I don't understand," I said.

"If we lose your grandmother, if Annie Barbara Sorrells dies, a world dies with her, and you and I and your mother and little sister will have to begin all over. Our time will be new and hard to keep track of. The time your grandmother knew was a steady time that people could trust. But you can see for yourself that we are losing it."

The clocks read 10:21, 3:35, 9:06, 4:06.

"Yes, I see," I said, "but I still don't understand."

He seemed not to hear. "This is a solid house, " he said, "as solid as your granddaddy ever built. But can't you feel it trembling in this awesome wind? If the wind that has come upon us can make this house unsteady, it's no wonder what great damage it can do to time. Time is so flimsy, it is invisible."

"Is grandmother going to die?"

"Your mother thinks so."

"What do you think?"

"I can't bear to think."

"Neither can I," I said, "but what are we going to do?"

"We will watch the clocks at their strange antics," my father said. "We will listen to the wind whisper and weep and tell again those stories of women that your mother and grandmother needed for you to hear. We will hope that this house stays rooted to its earth and is not carried away by the wind into the icy spaces beyond the moon."

"Do you think that can happen?"

"I don't know," he said, "but I am going to hang on here as tight as I can." (Chappell, 1996)

The father's anchor, as it turns out, is a chorus of women's voices telling stories that build and weave in a counter play as intricate as that of fiddle and bow. In the novel *Farewell I'm Bound to Leave You* (1996), Fred Chappell assembles a chorus of voices that raise and share and celebrate the common song of life. Stories of the traveling women, the shooting woman, the figuring woman, the fisherwoman, the madwoman, the shining woman, the helpinest (*sic*) woman, the remembering women, all call upon us to listen patiently, to reflect deeply, to desire rightly; these are stories that root us to this earth, in ordinary time, even as father and son patiently wait upon death.

Patience, however, is not a modern virtue, and waiting upon death is an increasingly uncommon practice. Perhaps patience is uncommon because it does not have its beginning in discrete decisions about what to do, the focus of much modern medical ethics; rather, patience has its beginning in the formation of our bodies as we live in certain kinds of relationships with others. Patience, then, is critical for approaching and taking seriously the ways patients have learned to understand what it might mean to *be* bodies. It is critical for caregivers, even as it is also critical for the sick, for the performance of illness. But to be patient when we are sick, or when we are caring for the sick, requires first that we learn how to be patient when we are not sick, training in the flesh, in the company of others. Where do we turn to learn such patience, where do we turn for training in the flesh?

Christians can turn to the distinctive practices that body forth the Christian story, namely the liturgy. Christian worship trains us to see that positive descriptions of euthanasia and suicide are based upon false and destructive accounts of human life, that euthanasia and suicide are material displays of the impatience that derives from placing trust in the wrong narrative. This false narrative informs the conviction that it is better to do something to ensure the "best outcome possible" than to passively await the inevitable. The Christian community has too often participated uncritically in a medical system based upon the false narrative spun by modernity. Yet at the heart of Christian tradition are the resources for offering substantive alternatives for the patient receiving and giving of care. The patience embodied by Christ in receiving the cup, an action Christians ritually imitate, shape us into the kind of people capable of understanding that patience is anything but passive.

How Patient Care Becomes Christian

> Then he took a cup, and after giving thanks he gave it to them, saying, "Drink from it, all of you; for this is my blood of the covenant, which is poured out for many for the forgiveness of sins." (Matthew 26: 27–8, NRSV)

The kind of patience displayed for the boy through the company of the women is also distinct from passivity. It is of the kind Yearley (1990) ascribes to Aquinas in his book, *Mencius and Aquinas*: patience born of fortitude. Patience born of fortitude is not the indiscriminate acceptance of any and every evil. The patient person is not the one who does not flee from evil, but the one who does not allow him or herself to be made inordinately sorrowful. Patience born of fortitude keeps us from the danger that our spirit may be broken by grief and lose its greatness. Such patience has its beginning in God, in God's own endurance of human failings; it is exemplified in Christ's life, in Christ's patient restraint, even though, had he willed "legions of angels would at one word have presented themselves from the heavens." Christ exhibited patience in his body.

Yet, the narrative logic of waiting upon death, with the courage to be rightly sad-dened, and without succumbing to the temptation to give up hope, cannot be grasped within the context of a society that authorizes a form of medicine that in the name of relieving suffering, kills. Physician-assisted suicide and euthanasia can only be under-stood as resulting from certain attitudes toward life, even as waiting upon death and patient restraint can also only be understood as resulting from certain attitudes about life. Our attitudes, our descriptions, our very actions are held fast by stories, by the nar-ratives which are our context for meaning, the wisdom which we will find needful. Certain stories sustain certain descriptions.

For example, it is often assumed that a lack of restraint and unwillingness to wait upon death, as manifest in physician-assisted suicide and euthanasia, derive from the notion that such acts represent positive moral goods or rights, particularly as these acts are cast as humane. The story that underlies an understanding of physician-assisted suicide and euthanasia as humane would have us believe that we are the determiners and possessors of our own life, that our time is something to be lived through, and thus that death, when it can no longer be avoided, can be hastened through our own power. This is a widely held story. It is one that is incompatible with and even subversive of some fundamental elements of the Christian story.

Christians' reasons for living begin with the understanding that life is a gift. We are not our own creators. Our desire to live should be given shape in the affirmation that we are not the determiners of our life, but God is. The logic of the Christian narrative teaches us that life allows us the time and space to live in the service of God. This is the logic of the claim made by Hauerwas and Bondi in *Truthfulness and Tragedy* (1977) that Christians see life as the gift of "time enough for love." This claim stands in stark con-trast to the claim that our time is something to be lived through. The claim that our time is something to be lived through is the ground of a will to die. The story of moder-nity fashions a will to die, a means of escaping the anguish of death, if not escape from death. We are given to imagine that we can control our destiny; and so in an act of com-mittal to the god of autonomy, a god fashioned on the boundaries of medicine, many would call upon the practitioners of medicine to forgo restraint, to kill those whom they cannot cure.

Yet Christ exhibited patience in his body. Christ never willed to die. " 'Father, if you are willing, take this cup from me; yet not my will, but yours be done.' An angel from heaven appeared to him and strengthened him. And being in anguish, he prayed more earnestly, and his sweat was like drops of blood falling to the ground" (Luke 22: 42–4, NRSV). Jesus's desire is directed not toward life as an end in itself. Rather Jesus's desire is directed toward God's will, both in his living and in his dying. Jesus commits himself into God's hands. Likewise, Christian participation in the Lord's Supper is an act of com-mittal. It is deadly work.

Receiving the cup of Christ is deadly work because it forms our lives not in terms of what we will do with them, but what God will do with our lives, in our living and our dying. Receiving the cup of Christ is deadly work because it forms us into a people ready to die for what we believe. Thus when Christians use the language of the "gift of life," that language is not meant to direct our attention to the gift, but rather to the nature of the giver and the conditions under which that gift is given. Life is a gift exactly because the character of the giver does not require that the gift be given at all. At the very least this means that accepting the fatedness of our ending is a way of affirming the trustworthiness of God's care for us. It means that we will not fight our own death or the death of others when it cannot be avoided. Dying itself is not the tragedy; rather dying for the wrong thing.

Indeed, when we receive the cup of Christ, we commit our spirits to God, and we commit ourselves to dying in a manner that makes it possible for us to be present in memory. For it is a harsh truth that suicide eradicates the presence of the other and results in the other's loss in our memory. In this regard, Hauerwas and Bondi (1977) are right to suggest that our very existence – that is, our willingness to be present (perhaps especially in memory) – has a moral significance that we seldom notice. Chappell's (1996) characters embody this willingness. The physical presence of the boy and his father during the mother's and grandmother's hours of grief, display the power and support generated toward those we love by our "mere" presence. Though the boy and his father search for what to say or do, they know with certainty that they should be there. In the same manner, the women's presence speaks, without words. The grandmother and all the women whose voices are assembled are re-membered; their wisdom lies precisely in this nearness.

Significantly, the willingness of the grandmother to die in a manner that will make it possible for her to be present in her family's memory does not remove the anguish of her death. Christians know that committing our spirits to God will not remove the anguish of our deaths, nor will it remove the anguish that is part of life. In other words, committing our spirits to God has serious implications not only for our care of the sick and dying, but our performance of illness. Receiving the cup of Christ, receiving communion, is for Christians the source of truthful habits of speech and gesture. As Christ exhibited patience in his body, Christians must be trained in patience of the flesh. Thus we do not take communion, we receive communion. Celebrants who give the cup to each worshiper, and likewise give the bread to each worshiper, rightly recognize the significance of training the people of God in the bodily habit of receiving the cup and the bread. These habits help us understand why we should neither seek death, nor invite it prematurely; rather, we should learn to bear all patiently than to dare death impatiently.

As noted earlier, however, patience should not be confused with passivity. The patient performance of illness should not be confused with a passive performance of illness. The sick and dying have a potentially profound effect on their caregivers and others to whom they are present. The grandmother's dying in *Farewell* is anything but passive. She is fully present to those around her, her presence a gesture of both resistance and witness to a world characterized by loneliness and isolation. It is this patient presence that keeps her from being severed from her family, even though she is bound to leave them.

Aquinas not only noted the difference between patience and passivity, he maintained that true patience comes from God and is shaped by an appropriate sadness and joy.

The background belief of this sadness and joy is an understanding of our place as creatures, an understanding shaped by an insuperable sadness and dejection about our condition. Christ's own suffering on the cross exemplifies the sorrow that must be present in every Christian's life. Here the claims of Hauerwas and Pinches in *Christians Among the Virtues* (1997) are quite instructive: Christians are "saddened by their own frailty, by the suffering present in the world, and by their inability to change either fundamentally." Indeed, Christians may be called upon to let the body be the body, to allow others to care for us, to allow death. Allowing death requires strength from God, specifically that strength that comes from hope, yet even an allowance of death does not remove its anguish.

Indeed, the challenge is that the sadness which one appropriately feels should not become depression, despair, or apathy. This task falls to patience, and is marked by an unwillingness to relinquish hope. Christian hope unravels the knot that ties us to needing and wanting more for ourselves; Christian hope makes caring intelligible and waiting possible. Christian hope is not an unreflective or inappropriate optimism, reflecting only dullness or presumption. Rather, Christian hope and Christian patience are shaped and sustained by stories and practices that see our misfortunes, even the misfortune of our illness and death, as part of our service to one another as God's people.

In other words, our belief in a God who suffered in the flesh calls upon us to care patiently for patients for whom there is no cure, and to practice patience when we are sick. The gift of our own bodies is a resource for learning to practice patience. As Hauerwas and Pinches (1997) argue, our bodies will not let us do whatever we think we should be able to do. "We are our bodies," they write, "and, as such, we are creatures destined to die. The trick is to learn to love the great good things our bodies make possible without hating our bodies, if for no other reason than that the death of our bodies is our own death." Our bodies remind us that we are not our own creations.

God also gives us a resource for learning patience in giving us one another. Again, Hauerwas and Pinches write:

> To learn to live with the unavoidability of the other is to learn to be patient. Such patience comes not just from our inability to have the other do our will; more profoundly, it arises with the love that the presence of the other can and does create in us. Our loves, like our bodies, signal our death. And such love – if it is not to be fearful of its loss, a very difficult thing – must be patient. Moreover, patience sustains and strengthens love, for it opens to us the time we need to tell our own story with another's story intertwined and to tell it together with that other. So told, the story in fact constitutes our love. (Hauerwas and Pinches, 1997: 176–7)

Though separated by time and space, the nearness of the women to the boy and the father in Chappell's novel lies in the nearness of the stories and the time needed to tell their stories intertwined with the boy's, and tell it together with the boy. We are all needful of such wisdom.

Finally, the time to share these stories is itself a resource and a gift. We are given the gift of time enough to acquire those habits that come from the ordinary, worthy, and, as important, *shared* activities of everyday life, activities such as storytelling. This practice in particular not only takes but creates time, especially when time "goes awry." When time goes awry we can only depend upon the stories we have learned, the wisdom we have gained. The women in *Farewell* had the patience to share their stories with the boy; the boy in turn was not only worthily entertained, but rightly trained. In that regard it is important to note that the women's stories, reminders of the joy and sadness that form our lives, do not train the boy in a false courage; rather, the stories sustain both father and son through the sadness of the night when time went awry. In essence, the stories start time up again, binding the grandmother's past and the boy's future, and providing the anchor that is needed in the present.

From the View of God's Patient Care

Christians learn such patience first through God's stories and the recognition of God's patient care of God's creatures. Indeed, it is only as we learn to follow a savior who embodies God's patience that we can make that same patient care which surrounds us more fully ours. It is God's patient care and the story we hold about life that provides us with the skills to approach the context that sustains any account of euthanasia and physician-assisted suicide in what must seem to others a peculiar way. Who we are determines how we view context, seeing it in this way rather than another. Christians are a people who, rightly trained, see euthanasia and physician-assisted suicide as material displays of the ways we have failed God.

Euthanasia and physician-assisted suicide are material displays of our failure to acknowledge our creaturely limits and the sense in which most things in our life remain out of our control. Our society is so captive to the notion of control that we imagine we ought to control our own deaths; thus physician-assisted suicide is nothing if not co-operation born of the desire to secure the "best outcome." Belief in human autonomy, rather than belief in God, is the background belief that makes a positive description of suicide or euthanasia possible. Autonomy has become an imperative; that which we cannot control, our belief in autonomy teaches us to hate. Thus we learn to hate our aging bodies; and we learn to hate those others who are sick and dying. We even learn to hate those we would define as "permanently dependent," exactly because they will always need our care.

This "hatred" is tragically displayed in those cases of a Down's syndrome child born with duodenal atresia whose parents refuse, or are advised to refuse, the surgery necessary to stop the child from starving to death. More difficult cases involve questions about how much should be done or how much parents should do to keep alive children suffering from spina bifida. Many assume the parents of the Down's syndrome child to be clearly in the wrong not to secure adequate medical attention for their child, but when confronted by the multiple and severe problems often associated with spina bifida, the "choices" are not so clear.

Similar concerns arise when one examines the moral implications of our attempts to prevent retardation through prenatal diagnostic procedures, i.e., amniocentesis. Does a prenatal diagnosis imply that we should only welcome "perfect" children?

Raising these issues points out the power of autonomy, its descriptive as well as normative control. The god of autonomy creates a tyranny of "normality"; i.e., certain "abnormalities" would justify an allowance of death, though for very different reasons from those set forth and grounded in Christ's acceptance of the cup of sorrows. These are material displays of how accounts of our commitments to one another that are based upon autonomy are destructive accounts. Neither the language of autonomy, nor the language of rights, nor even the language of equality, can sustain our commitment to care for such profoundly different children.

It should come as no surprise then that the language of autonomy is likewise destructive of our commitment to care for profoundly different adults, not only the sick and dying, but the mentally ill; the mentally ill are, after all, in some ways not that unlike Down's syndrome children. Like Down's, mental illness is one of the innumerable contingencies of human life. The language of autonomy would suggest that those who suffer mental illness ought be treated with efficiency through professionals and institutions, but all too often efficiency is code for isolation and abandonment. The language of autonomy cannot value or esteem those who cannot exercise the ability to be self-ruling. But the language of communion can. The conviction that we are all God's creatures, that we are together for one another, through the grace of God, in offering to God, is a conviction substantive enough to teach us not to fear our differences and, indeed, to see that we would not be whole without the other being different from us.

The language of communion gives rise to the recognition that the Church is Church in mutual work and ministry with those who are in many ways alike, and in many ways profoundly different, those whom the world would hate or fear, or even kill. The Church that is rightly formed by its own narratives, offers asylum, a peculiar kind of zone of safety, where compassion displays dissent, and patience is embodied in a people who are a sign of hope in a world without hope. The form of life to which Christians believe they have been called by Christ is found in many places and bodied forth in many stories. It is found in places like Cornelius, North Carolina where the people of Mount Zion United Methodist Church are raising funds to build on their church grounds a UMAR (United Methodist Agency for the Retarded) group home; significantly the people of Mount Zion also envision building on the same grounds, an assisted-living facility. Mount Zion's vision is a priestly vision of a community gathered in mutual work and ministry.

The Church that receives Christ's own passion forms not only a patient people, but a compassionate people, a people made whole by otherness; that is, a people whose encounter with otherness is constructive rather than destructive. Reverend Michael Bailey, who now serves Mount Zion church, previously served an international church in Europe. At the beginning of his ministry there he was introduced to two members of the congregation, "William" and "Miss Ida." These two were an unlikely pair. William was a thirty-nine year old mentally retarded man who every Sunday sat with the choir and recorded the service, while methodically rocking in time with the music. Miss Ida was an elderly matriarch of the congregation, a sophisticated senior who had traveled all over the world; every Sunday she sat straight-backed and still near the front of the congregation, lips pursed, hands folded neatly in her lap.

Sadly, William's elderly mother had died the very day his family moved into the community. William, knowing his mother loved sacred music, began coming to this church composed of people from forty different nations, people who bodied forth difference. Initially, he also sat near the front of the congregation, not far from Miss Ida, clicking his recorder on and off, rewinding, fast-forwarding, sometimes mumbling, and all the while rocking back and forth, back and forth. After a few Sundays, someone told William he was making too much noise. If he insisted on bringing the recorder and pushing the buttons, he would need to sit in the narthex and listen to the service over the speakers. That is what William did for the next three Sundays. On the fourth Sunday, Miss Ida arrived uncharacteristically late and asked William why he was sitting in the narthex and not in the church. William told her: "the people in there said I was making too much noise. I have to sit out here." In a quiet act of compassionate dissent, she sat with him. He rocked and she was still. The next Sunday, five others joined them. On the following Sunday, thirty people sat in the narthex. Today, William sits with the choir. He is the "assistant sound man." Every Sunday he records the service, clicking his buttons, mumbling and rocking. After each service, William walks several miles to the cemetery and leaves the cassette on his mother's grave with these simple words, "Here's church, Mama." William understood communion; his ministry was to help others understand.

Time Enough for Love

Christian love arises not in isolation or abandonment, Christian love arises in the presence of others, it arises in spite of our inability to control. Love arises in the flesh. It occurs or fails to occur in particular relationships. There are, in other words, theologically virtuous ways of being ill, of dying, and of caring for the sick and dying, that are determined by our particular beliefs and our membership in the Body of Christ, ways that faithfully display to the world the reality of a Christ who suffered in the flesh. Significantly, we Christians enter into those relationships that train and enable us to live well as the Body of Christ through regular participation in worship. In worship we learn to make God's story our own. God's story is a gift, often reluctantly accepted, if at all, demonstrating that, indeed, we need one another to learn to live that story well. We need the distinctive practices of the liturgy in which our identity and morality are grounded, to re-member Christ's story, his willingness, in spite of his own reluctance, to receive the cup. Receiving communion, the physical movements of the body, receiving rather than taking, train us not only in word and thought but in action; receiving communion trains us in the truth it confesses, we are together for one another through the grace of God, and in offering to God.

In this regard the boy's initial characterization of the night of his grandmother's dying as the night that time went awry is instructive. Chappell's novel recognizes that dying is not only threatening, it literally takes time from us. In the midst of the anguish of confronting the end of his grandmother's time, the storied presence of the women, and the literal presence of his mother and grandmother, give the boy a resource for living in the reality of time present, as well as a resource for valuing the grandmother for who she is in the midst of her experience of death. Still, Chappell does not back away from the demands this places upon the boy and the need it creates. Ostensibly, the boy and the father are there to care for the mother and grandmother, but the reader quickly realizes the impossibility of a clear distinction between caregivers and cared-for. The relationships between the characters are organic in that patient presence becomes for all a purely natural expression of membership in that family; for Christians such presence is likewise an expression (if not a "natural" one) of membership in the Body.

This notion of an "organic" membership in the Body is also instructive, for it gives us to understand that a patient performance of illness is not finally dependent upon modern medicine's assumptions about performance, language, meaning, and humanity itself. In *Farewell I'm Bound to Leave You*, it is never clear that, on the night of her death, the grandmother utters even one word, yet her presence speaks. It is never clear that she is conscious, yet her person witnesses to the fundamental question of whose she is. As dawn breaks and death is imminent, Chappell (1996) returns the reader to the room where the boy and his father wait:

10:17, 4:44, 8:20, 1:28

The clocks were as crazy as ever, yet there we sat, my father and I, patient before that cold wood heater, watching the wild hands as if they might point to the true time if only we mustered the courage to wait them out. But the wind was too mischievous in their works. The minutes and seconds got lost among the years and dropped away to wander eternity.

Outside this too-large house, the wind would rise to a fury and then subside, no more predictable than the times the clocks were telling. To the window behind our chairs it brought weathers of every sort – drought and tempest, spring rain and early snow, Sahara-like sunshine and melancholy fog. This old house had always stood steady before, but now the time this wind had so distressed was rocking the structure with dread power. We could feel the foundations clinging to the ground with desperate fingertips.

"All right," I said. "Now I'm scared. Pretty much scared, I'll tell you."

"I can't blame you, Jess," my father said. "I'm scared pretty tight myself. It's a good thing we let your sister sleep over at the Williams place tonight. We didn't think she should be here, you mother and I. Mitzi's too young to understand."

"Neither do I," he said. "I know that the way time and space and matter are built together makes death inevitable. But I don't understand."

"Maybe they're built wrong," I said. "Maybe it was a bad plan to begin with."

"Maybe so. Have you got a better one?"

"It's hard on Mother."

"Yes," he said.

"It's just too hard. I can tell. I can hear them talking together or thinking together all the way from the bedroom."

"Yes. So can I."

I hung my head and closed my eyes to hear.

And so farewell I'm bound to leave, All away you rolling river, I'll be gone when dawn is breaking.

O Mama, don't say so. Not this dawn or the next or the next. It is too soon for you to go.

I wish that song would quit me. I am trying to think of Jesus, but that old song is in the way . . . I must think of Jesus . . . I have been mostly good with my thoughts, but now I can't.

You mustn't blame yourself Mama. Thoughts come and go — you can't help that.
I need to be steadier in mind. If I am steady, Jesus will come to me.
O Mama.

"Now they are thinking or saying the same thing," I told my father.

"Sometimes they split off from one another like a little creek up high in the mountains that will divide around a big rock and then come back to meet itself."

"Yes," he said.

"I don't understand how we can hear them all the way down that dark hall with the doors shut."

"We can't hear them," he said. "We only know what they are thinking or saying. We are not hearing with our ears."

"How, then?"

"It is the way of families," he said. "But only at special times."

"What kind of special."

"Hard, mostly," he said.

"I still don't understand."

"Be quiet and I will tell you something," he said. "Not long from now there will come an icy cold into this room. There will be a darkness like we were trapped inside a vein of coal. I want you to be brave and show me what you are made of, and I will try to be brave, too. Then it will pass on like a slow and painful eclipse of the sun and moon and stars. It will be terrible . . . So hang on tight, Jess. It is coming soon."

"It is already here," I said. "It is in the hallway, making the darkness darker. And it is already cold in here and getting colder. It is just outside the door, ready to come in. Don't you feel how close it is?"

"Yes," he said.

Then the shadow was upon us and within us and was as bad as he said it would be. I don't know how many eternities we suffered there, my father and I, but they were motionless with despair. Yet the shadow lightened a little at last; the windows went quiet with predawn light. We knew that the final thing my grandmother said or thought was, Farewell, daughter, it is Jesus at last, and that the final thing my mother said or thought was, Don't leave me alone in this world without you. And then there was light enough in our front room to read the clocks. My grandfather's watch in its case read 12:12 and the other three said 5:11. Time had started up again, but I could tell my father was right: It would be a different kind of time we had to live in now; it would not be steady in the least and the winds would be cold in our faces against us all the way.

"Cora is trying to come down the hallway," my father said. "But it is dark and she can't find the switch and she is frightened. If you and I don't go to meet her halfway, she may not make it back to us. Are you ready to go with me into that dark hallway and bring your mother back here into the light?"

"No, I am not ready," I said. "But I'll go with you anyhow."

"Good," he said. "She's going to need us."

"We're going to need her, too." I said.

When we receive communion, we not only acknowledge whose we are, we receive into our lives the truth that we are, all of us, the living and the dying, the caregivers and the cared for, in some ways alike and in many ways different, *together for one another*, through the grace of God, in offering to God. Thanks be to God.

References

Chappell, Fred (1996) *Farewell I'm Bound to Leave You* (New York: Picador).

Gutmann, Stephanie (1996) "Death and the Maiden," *The New Republic* (24 June): 20–8.

Hauerwas, Stanley, with Richard Bondi and David B. Burrell (1977) *Truthfulness and Tragedy: Further Investigations into Christian Ethics* (Notre Dame, IN: University of Notre Dame Press).

—and Pinches, Charles (1997) *Christians Among the Virtues* (Notre Dame, IN: University of Notre Dame Press).

Yearley, Lee (1990) *Mencius and Aquinas: Theories of Virtue and Conceptions of Courage* (Albany, NY: State University of New York Press).

CHAPTER 29

Sharing Communion: Hunger, Food, and Genetically Modified Foods

Robert Song

The following account of the experience of starvation was written by a British journalist visiting a refugee camp in Ethiopia in 1985:

> This is what happens when you starve to death: at first there is hunger and a craving inside which after two or three days turns to a pain. But the obsession with food does not last long. After four or five days the gnawing pains subside and the stomach wall begins to shrink. This is a process which can happen repeatedly in situations where food arrives only at rare intervals.
>
> Even the thinnest person has just beneath the skin layers of subcutaneous fat. At the next stage the body begins to live off these reserves. How long they will last depends on how healthy you were to start with. In the affluent countries we often try to reach this stage by design; we call it slimming. If you are an African whose body has been weakened by years of poor diet and intestinal parasites this stage may last three weeks, or four perhaps. If you are getting a little food, no matter how meagre the supply, this could spin out the process for many months.
>
> Eventually though your body runs out of fat and begins to live off the substance of the muscles in your thighs, buttocks and upper arms. In a desperate attempt to stay alive you are consuming your own body. As if in revolt at this unnatural act, your body erupts in all manner of warning symptoms. Your tongue begins to ache, sores appear at the corner of your mouth, your gums start to bleed or your hands and feet begin to swell. So does your stomach: in children, often aggravated by parasites, it becomes huge.
>
> At this stage the hunger begins to eat into your brain. You have become too tired to work or make much effort to search for food. You have, by now, lost all interest in the idea of food anyway. You become irritable. Occasionally, you fly into a real rage, for no reason at all. You find that you are unable to concentrate. You are becoming a different person.
>
> About now, if you are a woman, you stop menstruating. Your body can no longer consider the possibility of reproduction. In any case you long ago lost interest in sex. There is little milk left now in your breasts for your infant.
>
> Now your hair loses its color and sheen. It goes soft and falls out in handfuls. Your skin begins to take on a piebald texture. A stranger could now count your every rib from ten

yards away, and the TV cameras come much closer than that. Your upper arms have shrivelled to the width of your forearm, in which you can now see the two parallel bones and
the ligaments which join them. Your elbows and wrists stick out like huge comic bulges in
comparison. So do your knees, on legs which look like broomsticks covered in skin. Now
you really know what is meant by the expression "skin and bone." It is all you are. Not that
you care much. Your mind has gone past the stage of irritation now. You are overcome
with an indefinable sadness. Your eyes have become glazed and a seductive apathy has
seeped through every fiber of your body. As starvation takes its final grip you lose interest
in everything, even in your own baby who is dying on your lap as you sit motionless, on
the ground.

The aid workers who arrive do not seem to understand this. They keep trying to force
you to eat the milky porridge they offer. They keep putting the spoon in your hand
and guiding it to the baby's mouth. When they turn to the next sufferer you let it fall from
your fingers. It falls to the dry soil and the flies buzz around; it does not enter your mind
to wave them away. You do not even notice that they are crawling around the baby's eyes
and over his face, which is shrivelled now like a little old man's. You sit and stare at nothing.
All about you the world goes about its business. You watch through an impenetrable
window. You will probably not actually die from malnutrition itself but the wasting has
lowered your body temperature and increased your vulnerability to the most minor of
infections. Death, when it comes, will be a blessed release. (Paul Vallely, in Blundy and
Vallely, 1985)

When one is touched by a reality like this – here I take it that the vast majority of
those who read this chapter will, like myself, not be amongst those who have experienced real hunger – the initial sense of shock can easily turn into the search for
someone to blame. And there is no shortage of potential targets. Corrupt political
leaders who are only interested in enriching themselves and their cronies. Or murderous warlords whose lust for power mires their countries in endemic civil war. Or greedy
multinational corporations that strip wealth from poorer nations but give little back.
Or an international banking system that is bent on extracting debt repayments from
countries that can ill afford them. Or oil companies that lobby for policies that exacer-
bate global warming, resulting in decreased rainfall and poor harvests. Or HIV/AIDS
that is robbing countries of their economically most productive age groups.

Whatever the truth in each of these cases, behind the increasingly frenzied impulse
to blame lies a sense of guilt. Part of this feeling of guilt can be traced to the vast disparities of wealth and poverty: at the same moment as some are enjoying the finest
foods from around the world, others are scratching for roots and berries. It may not be
very clear whether there is a direct causal relationship between the two. Indeed, those
who are rich may even believe that the long-term solution requires them to consume
more: for by doing so they will create greater wealth for everyone, since they are buying
goods that others have produced, which allows them to buy goods that still others have
produced, which means that those others in turn . . . and so on. But this does not erase
the sense of guilt. After all, whatever the best long-term route to equitable distribution
and prosperity for everyone across the globe, there are people suffering at this very
moment; aid agencies are putting out appeals even now for financial assistance; and
the more who respond to those appeals, the more who will benefit – and perhaps even

live – that will not otherwise do so. Somehow the failure to attend to this suggests the lack of the purity of heart to give one's love entire and free.

In truth, most of us are not very well suited to addressing the reality of hunger on the scale it presents itself – we cannot bear very much reality. It is not surprising that most people turn back to the press of their everyday lives, feeling overwhelmed, inadequate, defeated, and psychologically unable to do much except perhaps resolve to give more the next time a humanitarian crisis makes the news. Or, if individuals do make it a focus of their lives with the intention that, insofar as it lies in their power, it shall never happen again, they may find themselves caught in another cycle of attitudes and emotions, starting in anger and determination, passing through depression and indifference, and ending in despair. Maybe their outrage causes them to turn to violence . . .

In the face of hunger, it is an awesomely courageous, even shocking, undertaking to participate in the Eucharist. For the Eucharist proclaims that hunger and poverty, disease and death, are not the last word about the human situation. Despite the temptation to regard them as the ultimate reality, as brutal and ever-present reminders of the mocking hostility of the universe, the Eucharist asserts that they are embraced and held within a greater story, greater even than the wild facts of famine and starvation.

The idea that there is a greater reality to be found in the Eucharist than the satisfaction of physical hunger is shown by the miracle of the feeding of the five thousand and Jesus's discourse on the bread of life found in John 6, a chapter suffused with intimations of a eucharistic theology. Drawing out the meaning of the feeding of the five thousand, Jesus rebukes the crowd for eating their fill of the loaves, but failing to see the miracle as a sign. He contrasts the food that perishes with the food that lasts for eternal life, the manna in the wilderness with the true bread from heaven. Christ himself is the bread of life, he declares, and those who eat of this bread will never die. Through a series of clearly eucharistic references, we are invited to understand the bread and wine as pointing beyond their immediate visible appearances to eternal life (verses 51–8). The human need for physical food is subordinate to the human need for the true bread given for the life of the world.

The chapter poses a further challenge to the assumption that scarcity and death are the truth of things. For the miracle of the feeding of the five thousand indicates also how eternal life is to be characterized: namely, in terms of the messianic feast, a vision of divine abundance that sweeps aside the assumptions of scarcity with which the disciples operate ("There is a boy here who has five barley loaves and two fish. But what are they among so many people?": verse 9) and multiplies food such that even after the hungry are satisfied, more remains. When the people offer all that they have, Jesus takes, blesses, breaks, and shares it – and they find that there is more than enough. A similar message of abundance is conveyed by the miracle of turning water into wine at the wedding feast in Cana (John 2: 1–11).

But this eschatological banquet is not prefigured as a purely future salvation, as if people's lives now are of no spiritual significance. Eternal life for John is also a present reality into which those who hear and believe have already passed (cf. 5: 24). The miracle is not just a sign that shies away from itself, a sermon illustration that can be dispensed with once the point has been grasped. It also embodies that which it signifies: the feeding of the five thousand could not be a sign of the bread that gives eternal life if the five thousand had not been fed. The Eucharist, this suggests, is not related to the vision of messianic abundance as a mere symbol of it: somehow the relations of the two are more substantial.

We can explore this further by discussing how the sharing of bread is intimately connected to the unity of the Body of Christ and, if so, how this might be embodied in a hungry world.

One Bread, One Body

Eating together was a central feature of the early Church's life. This was no doubt in part a continuation of the table-fellowship they had enjoyed with Jesus, at which he had been the head: it is no accident that it is at the moment of the breaking of the bread that the disciples on the road to Emmaus recognize the risen Lord (Luke 24: 30–1), or that other resurrection appearances feature Jesus eating with the disciples (Luke 24: 41–3; John 21: 9–14). But the shared meal is also at the heart of the vision of the early Church pictured in Acts 2: 43–7, the body of believers formed by the descent of the Holy Spirit at Pentecost. Of the nine key acts performed by the believers that are listed in these verses, breaking bread together in their homes is the fifth and central one. This is not a community in which eating was an incidental activity, but one in which the shared meal forms the basis for communal life: thus the first major organizational development in the Church's life is a result of problems that arise out of the daily distribution of food, an activity that is taken for granted as intrinsic to the Church's practice (Acts 6: 1–6; Yoder, 1992: ch. 2).

The centrality of the common table to the early Church's identity was inseparable from the unity of the body of believers and the satisfaction of the needs of all. The result of the coming of the Holy Spirit is a community in which all of those who believed were "of one heart and soul" (Acts 4: 32), the natural outworking of which was a spontaneous generosity whereby all things were held in common. There was not a needy person among them, we are told, as those who owned property sold it, the overflow of goods spreading out to all who had need (4: 34). This is also the central theme of Paul's discussion of the Eucharist in 1 Corinthians 11: 17–34, occasioned precisely by the failure of the Corinthians to recognize the relation between the Lord's Supper and the unity of the body. Evidently, when the Corinthians met to eat together, their accommodation to discriminatory social conventions meant that some were getting drunk while others were going hungry. In contrast to this, Paul declares the fundamental principle that "we who are many are one body, for we all partake of the one bread" (10: 17). Failure to discern the body as that which is constituted by sharing the bread would incur the Lord's judgment.

In this passage, Paul also makes clear that, in eating the bread and drinking the cup, Christians are proclaiming the Lord's death (11: 26). This is important for understanding the nature of the unity that is celebrated at the common table. Communion is fundamentally participation in the death and resurrection of Christ, before it is the fellowship of the Church: it is through Christ's death that we are reconciled to God, and thence we find reconciliation with one another (cf. Ephesians 2: 13–14). Abstracted from that prior identity in Christ, the reconciled community of the Church becomes the merely horizontal sociality of a group of people that get on together (or at least have learned to endure their differences). Rather, it is the Lord's Supper, and Christ is the host that invites us to participate.

Without this recognition, Christians can be deceived into thinking that they are the ones showing hospitality at the Eucharist. As a result, if they are rich, their relations with the poor may become corrupted by a mentality of "charity," in which "those less fortunate than ourselves" become the target of philanthropic efforts, whether these take the form of financial giving, social action, political campaigning, or whatever – activities which are liable to insinuate attitudes of self-righteousness and condescension on the part of the donor, matched by resentment should the recipient show insufficient gratitude. Depicting the role of the rich in terms of unilateral acts of virtue also fails to recognize that behind hunger, as a matter of a lack of food and access to resources, lies a breakdown of relationship between the rich and the poor, so that the hungry become objects of the distanced televisual gaze of the well fed. Against this modern notion of charity as benefaction toward needy others lies an earlier, medieval understanding of charity as a state of social friendship, in which giving took place within a network of reciprocal relationships. These relationships were certainly noncommensurate, but they at least allowed for the possibility that someone might be a recipient as much as a donor – and a donor as much as a recipient. Set within the sacramental context of Christ as the ground of social solidarity, this notion of charity preserved the idea of love as a form of mutuality shared by all, and not just as the prerogative of the powerful.

Eucharistic community is therefore always the response to Christ's own hospitality at the Lord's table. While it opens up the horizon of a radical economic sharing of goods, it is not "communism," a merely horizontal commitment to egalitarian community. Rather, it is about unity in Christ, in which hospitality and care for the other are not the occasion for subterranean attitudes of superiority, but flow from the joint and mutual acknowledgment that all are dependent on grace – rich as well as poor, poor as well as rich.

Corrupted understandings of hospitality are not the only way of compromising the unity of the body. 1 Corinthians 11 connects divisions within the body with the greed of certain groups that led them to be blind to the needs of others in the Church. But such selfishness and myopia should not be seen as simply individual moral failure, although individuals were no doubt at fault. They were also the result of importing into the Church the inequitable social structures of the surrounding world. The Corinthians had failed to see their need for a corporate solidarity over against the social forces that would divide them.

At the individual or group level, it may be less easy to recognize the structural dimensions of sin for what they are. At a global level, by contrast, the systemic sins that separate rich from poor are manifest. They are found in destructive economic assumptions, corrupt political institutions, socially discriminatory practices, and inequalities of access to power on grounds of gender or race, or simply networks of expectations that ensure that the poor remain poor. These contribute to poverty and hunger, but are not simply a matter of individual wrongdoings that can be resolved by individual repentance and reconciliation – even if individuals reinforce the sway of these through their choices, as well as being influenced in their choices by them. And their combined effect for those who remain hungry can seem so monstrous, so all embracing, so inescapable, as to extinguish any last flickers of hope for change.

The New Testament describes structural sin in the language of the principalities and powers (Berkhof, 1977; Wink, 1984, 1986, 1992; Yoder, 1994: ch. 8). These are corporate entities that are at once earthly and heavenly, material and spiritual, visible and invisible – for example, as "forces of evil in the heavenly places" (Ephesians 6: 12) they are clearly spiritual, while elsewhere the authorities instituted by God refer to the earthly rule of Rome (Romans 13: 1). Originally created good, the powers are an essential part of human existence, and therefore are not to be regarded as simply evil (Colossians 1: 16). But they are fallen and have become "cosmic powers over this present darkness" (Ephesians 6: 12). Yet for all their awesome strength they have been disarmed on the cross, Christ making a public spectacle of them (Colossians 2: 15). As a result, God has put them under Christ's feet (Ephesians 1: 20–2).

If the powers work to divide the body, Christ's victory over the powers is celebrated in the eucharistic enactment of the unity of the body. The company of people gathered round the table receive communion as a body, not simply as an aggregate of individuals: it is customary to receive communion even if one has arrived late and missed the confession, for example, since others have said it on one's behalf. Moreover, by partaking in the one bread, the gathered congregation represents an alternative to the bodies that incorporate systemic sin: transnational corporations, for example, etymologically are "bodies," but ones which have too often become parodies of the body. From this may flow a witness to a different way of being which refuses to grant the aura of necessity to what otherwise may seem unavoidably to fracture the body – whether this be "the logic of the market," the power of international institutions, the history of colonial oppression, the grip of civil war, the gender inequalities of poverty, or the myriad of other interlocking forces that serve to subjugate the poor. And because the eucharistic witness is a materially embodied practice, it suggests that resistance to these forces is not a quasi-gnostic display of meaningless handwaving, but can be intelligibly pursued as the (albeit fragile and vulnerable) anticipation in the present of the messianic future.

Embodying the Eucharist: Eucharistic Practices in a Hungry World

How should Christians embody the Eucharist in a hungry world? The first answer is in terms of immediate liturgical practice. For example, if the unity of the body is of prime importance, it is worth considering whether those churches which share communion "in the round" may represent this insight more effectively than those in which individuals queue to receive what may too easily become a private religious blessing. Those churches which use small individual cups may increase this sense of unity still further if all communicants can drink simultaneously.

Surrounding the liturgy are a number of other practices which might be retrieved. Given the centrality of common meals in the early Church – in a substantial and not merely token form – perhaps the most obvious of these is recovery of the *agape*. The New Testament assumption is that the eucharistic actions took place in the context of a shared table-fellowship (cf. 1 Corinthians 11: 20, "when you come together"). While the Eucharist was open to the kind of Corinthian corruption condemned by Paul (and was subsequently to become a token meal separated from the fellowship meal), this is better understood as a reason for ensuring that the Eucharist truly embodies hospitality, rather than a reason for abandoning its *agapic* elements. Even if it need not be a feature of every communion service, Eucharist in the context of a shared substantial meal should be a regular part of the Christian experience of worship.

Another practice historically associated with the Eucharist is that of fasting. This is often undertaken as an act of penitence or as a spiritual discipline that nourishes prayer. But it can also be an act of solidarity with those who are in need: although it can never replicate the experience of involuntary hunger, it at least demonstrates a willingness to share vulnerability to physical need. (It may also have the additional effect of alerting Christians to the role of food and mealtimes in their everyday life, and therewith the potential for enslavement to particular patterns of eating.)

If hospitality is central to the Church's definitive mode of being, the spontaneous generosity shown in almsgiving also needs to be reclaimed. Almsgiving has fallen into disrepute because of its association with the idea that addressing poverty is a matter of patronizing and arbitrary "charity" rather than "justice." Yet it is misunderstood if it is regarded as inadequate social service. Rather, it is fundamentally about friendship and personal encounter between rich and poor. Indeed, because it is about the call to fellowship, for Christians it comes before the setting up of social-security systems, and forms the context within which more elaborate forms of social care are to be understood (Attias, 2001: 15–16). This also suggests a renewal of the distinctive office of the deacon. While the diaconate has in many churches become a temporary stepping stone to the presbyterate, the New Testament never loses sight of the connection of *diakonia* with practical service (e.g. 2 Corinthians 8: 4), a ministry which would have been intimately involved with the collection and distribution of tithes (cf. Acts 6: 1–6).

There are, of course, many other disciplines for Christians to embrace, from options for simple lifestyles and thinking about the use of money to Church hospitality on a broader scale. One form of action I want to consider at greater length centers on the "fair trade" initiatives that have emerged since the 1970s, often pioneered by Christian organizations. Fair trade in this context does not refer to international trade that is freed from unfair tariffs or import duties and so offers a level playing field to different trading nations. Rather it is an organized effort on a much smaller scale to ensure that individual producers in developing countries are paid a fair price for what they grow.

Fluctuations in global commodity prices mean that the price paid to producers can be unpredictable and can in certain circumstances dip even below the cost of production. The global trade in food commodities such as coffee or bananas, tea or cocoa, is often in the hands of a few multinational companies, who, of course, have an interest in purchasing at the lowest price available. By contrast, fair-trade purchasers, who typically deal directly with producer cooperatives rather than working through a series of intermediate traders, agree a guaranteed minimum price that is paid should the prevailing market price drop below this level, while a premium is added should the prevailing price be above it. Furthermore, a small percentage is added to enable local communities to improve their educational, health, and welfare facilities.

How can this be understood as part of Eucharistic witness? Fair trade has been criticized in a number of ways. Some point out that it lends itself to tokenism, consumers in the wealthy North buying the occasional jar of fairly traded coffee as a relatively painless sop to a guilty conscience. It is small scale, turns on charitable feelings, and is wholly inadequate to meeting the vast challenges posed by the inequities of the global trading system. Others note that fair trade typically does not reach the poorest of the poor or those who are actually hungry, or wonder whether in the long term it reinforces the power of international capitalism. Still others are worried that buying and selling goods in church on Sundays (in the UK a significant proportion of fair trade is conducted in this way) is a misuse of God's house.

In response to this, we can interpret fair trade as economic partnership for mutual benefit, which emphasizes the relationship of purchaser and grower (for example, fair-trade products often carry pictures and small profiles of individual farmers), by contrast with the objectified and instrumentalized relations of producer and consumer reduced to the impersonal exchange of goods and money. In other words, it is possible to engage in fair trade as a witness to a new economic order, one that expresses the nature of eucharistic community and is not defined by the imperatives of market exchange. Against legalistic sabbatarianism, this implies that, far from it being inappropriate for a fair-trade stall to take place in the back of church on a Sunday morning, this is precisely where as a witness to resurrection life we should expect it to be! Indeed, it is possible to see the fair-trade table as an extension of the communion table: in a local church setting this might take the form of finding ways to incorporate the pictures of fair-trade producers into the service, and so emphasizing their participation in the communion of saints with whom the congregation shares food and drink. A step further might involve organizing reciprocal visits with producers, giving and receiving eucharistic hospitality.

To be sure, fair trade is still a tiny proportion of all international trade. However, from the point of view of eucharistic witness, the first criterion of discernment is not its effectiveness in reforming the world but its aptness as a symbol of the world renewed in Christ. This does not, of course, exclude the possibility that there might ripple out from it wider economic changes. (To give one example, as a result of the influence of fair-trade organizations, many UK supermarkets have begun to monitor labor standards in the supply chains of their own-label brands.) Nor, needless to say, is it the only form of witness against the inequities of the global economic order or the only way of addressing poverty. But it is one such way; while, of course, it may in the future yet become corrupted or turn out to have unexpected and undesirable long-term consequences, it is for now a sign of a world made new (on fair trade, see further Johnson and Sugden, 2001).

A second example is the Jubilee Debt Campaign's work for the relief of international debt. The roots of the international debt crisis lie in the 1970s, when a large number of developing countries took advantage of low interest rates and excess funds in the international banking system to take out major loans to finance economic growth. By the 1980s, however, interest rates had risen substantially, precipitating a sustained crisis for many developing countries that were no longer able to finance their debts. While much of the problem cannot be simply laid at the doors of the West (loans might be used to buy arms, finance dearer oil imports, line presidential slush funds, or build high-prestige development projects, for example), the manner in which Western banks and multilateral institutions have policed the loans has directly contributed to poverty in many developing countries. In particular, the International Monetary Fund's insistence on the adoption of economic policies that demand budgetary austerity have frequently resulted in severe cuts in food subsidies, health care, and education, with devastating consequences for the standard of living of the very poorest.

The Jubilee Debt Campaign (originally founded as Jubilee 2000), working in partnership with organizations in both North and South, was established with the aim of achieving the complete remission of all unpayable debts owed by poor countries and establishing instead an independent framework for resolving international debt crises. With strong backing from British churches, it has adopted many of the tactics of effective pressure groups: careful research, programs to raise awareness, large public petitions, meetings with politicians and civil servants, and, in Birmingham in 1998, a 70,000-strong chain of protesters around the place where the heads of the G8 leading industrialized nations were meeting – the first of many demonstrations that came to be associated with the anti-globalization movement.

In what sense might participation in the Jubilee Debt Campaign be eucharistic? The theological significance of the campaign lies not so much in the fact that it has managed to inject the biblical language of the Jubilee into public consciousness and so affirmed the continuing "relevance" of the Bible, as that it has witnessed to the nature of God who is about remitting debts, for whom forgiving debts is at the heart of human relationships. The Eucharist is the means of participation in the life of God and communion with one another, and the confession and sharing of peace enable that participation. Equally, at an international level, relief of unpayable debts enables poor countries to participate in the common life of global trade and cross-border communication.

The means adopted by Jubilee campaigners also point to the reality of a world renewed in Christ. The peaceable witness of the Birmingham protesters, for example, was appropriate not because peace is the best tactic, but because the Eucharist is a sacrament of reconciliation. (Indeed, it was not obviously true that peaceful means were the most effective: the violent protests that marked demonstrations at subsequent World Trade Organization and G8 meetings at Seattle, Genoa, and elsewhere gained more news coverage and were arguably more successful in concentrating global leaders' minds.)

These examples are, of course, not remotely complete. There are an indefinite number of practices, individual and corporate, which might express the Eucharist in the context of global poverty and hunger: these merely mark steps at the beginning of the journey. But each of them, whatever form they take, make clear that the Eucharist is not a private religious practice which might have "implications" for a separate and self-inclosed public sphere, but instead is seamlessly worked out in the world in ways that do not thereby cease to be eucharistic in fundamental identity. Of course, such forms may turn out to be flawed in practice. To inhabit a spatial location in the world is to be part of a network of cause and effect, which is a place of risk. It requires engaging with the complexity of the world, and this in turn implies the possibility of making mistakes, of being vulnerable to criticism. In attempting to establish the clarity of its witness, the Church may find that the consequences of its actions turn out to be in contradiction to the nature of the God it proclaims. But by being encompassed by the action of the Eucharist, it may find forgiveness for its sins, and so avoid the Pelagian anxiety of justification by effectiveness. In venturing its witness to Christ, the Church finds its identity not in being justified by its actions but in being held in love by the Christ who died for it.

The Case of Genetically Modified Foods

These latter considerations are especially important when thinking about another topic relevant to hunger, namely genetically modified (GM) crops and foods. The application of genetic engineering techniques to plants dates back to the development of recombinant DNA technologies in the 1970s. These enabled scientists to insert DNA sequences or whole genes into the chromosomes of organisms belonging to different species. Conventional selective breeding of variants over generations has produced many of the plants and crops that are the staples of modern agriculture. But, with the exception of some crossbreed hybrids, these have been limited to the breeding of variants within species, which is a cumbersome and inaccurate process. Genetic modification, by contrast, allows for the transfer of traits between species, dramatically increasing the possibilities open to plant breeders and eliminating many of the constraints of traditional methods.

Since the first transgenic plant (a herbicide-resistant tobacco) was produced in 1983, several GM products have been developed or proposed. Some are foods, such as slow-softening tomatoes modified for a longer shelf-life, or are food crops in which the genetically altered element is not the part of the plant that is eaten. Others are crops for non-food use, such as insect-resistant cotton which reduces pesticide spraying, or plant-based vaccines which could be grown locally in developing countries rather than imported.

Some of the anxiety surrounding transgenic food and crops is rooted in an instinctive perception that genetic modification is "playing God," a transgressive interference in the divine work of creation. But concern has also been expressed over possible health hazards: for example, allergic reactions to proteins derived from transferred genes, or the distant risk that antibiotic-resistant bacteria used in developing some GM foods might confer antibiotic resistance on human gut bacteria. Perhaps most significantly, critics have pointed to the environmental risks of GM crops, given the unpredictable effects of interference in the ecological balance of native habitats. Biodiversity loss as a result of negative impacts on the food chain, the evolution of insects that develop resistance to transgenic insecticidal crops, and herbicide-tolerant weeds arising from accidental gene transfer from GM crops into neighboring wild species, have all been cited as potentially irreversible environmental consequences of GM planting. (On GM foods and plants in general, see Pence, 2002; Deane-Drummond et al., 2003.)

In the context of global hunger, however, the most important question is whether GM foods will be needed in the coming decades to feed the world's growing population. This problem can be illustrated through the example of rice, on which half the world's population depends for the majority of its dietary needs. Between the 1960s and 1980s the rate of increase in rice production broadly matched the rate of human population growth. In the 1990s, however, it failed to do so, and the previously effective methods of increasing yields – more land, water, pesticides, and hybrid crops – appeared to have reached their limit. The publication of the complete sequence of the rice genome in 2002 opened up the possibility of the genetic modification of rice. Because this may in due course enable increased resistance of rice to diseases, insects and other pests, improved tolerance of high salinity levels, and so on, proponents argue that it may be the most effective way of ensuring the enormous increases in productivity necessary. Genetic modification might also provide other benefits, by enhancing the nutritional value of crops: for example, industry sources claim that genetically engineered "golden rice" could prevent blindness in many thousands of children each year and save millions of people from vitamin A deficiency.

How might Christians formed by a eucharistic vision respond to this? To start with, they will not wish to construe population growth *as such* as a problem, let alone a "crisis." Welcoming new life has been recognized from the earliest days of the Church as intrinsic to the vocation to hospitality, and this applies in this context as much as in the context of, say, the family. On the other hand, hospitality also requires working for all to have access to the means for living human life: eucharistic openness to the truth of the world must therefore mean not refusing in an attitude of denial the question of how an extra two billion people will be fed. That Christians live in the presence of the communion of saints past, present, and future, implies that future generations are also neighbors to whom hospitality is owed.

Yet Christians will also want to be suspicious of some elements of the narrative of biotechnology. Thus the idea that genetically engineered food is the *necessary* means to future food provision assumes that only technological solutions will solve the problems of the world. This reflects the Western cultural fixation with the promise of technology as the primary means of eliminating suffering and removing the burden of finitude, a mindset that has governed developments in every area of technology. Because of its hegemony, other ways of envisioning the world are hidden from view, in particular those ways which suggest that the issue is not so much how we may improve our technical ingenuity as how we may become better people.

For example, it is part of eucharistically formed identity that selves are shaped through sharing in communion, rather than through individual self-dependence (cf. 1 Corinthians 11: 21–2). This requires learning that the mutuality of giving and receiving is foundational to discipleship, however much or little one has: if one is unable to share what one has already, having more is scarcely likely to make one more generous – and, indeed, as the story of the widow's mite suggests, may even have the opposite effect (Mark 12: 41–4). The mentality that reaches toward GM as the solution assumes that such sharing is impossible, with the result that technological means must be found as compensation.

The dangers of this are much greater in an economic context of corporate capitalism. Innovations in agricultural biotechnology have on the whole been driven by the search for profit rather than a response to need, with inevitable implications for product development. This has reinforced the fears of some people in developing countries that GM technology might become another, neo-colonial means of extending Western corporate power over their access to food supplies. In India, for example, many small farmers have been afraid that the traditional practice of setting aside part of a crop for the next year's planting will be destroyed by the incorporation of "terminator" genes into genetically modified seeds; this renders them sterile and so ensures that farmers will be dependent on purchasing next year's supplies from the multinational seed company, making GM crops more expensive and pushing farmers potentially deeper into debt. While companies may work to meet the needs of people, it does not take too much skepticism about the motives of commercial interests to recognize the dangers.

The close interweaving of GM foods with technological capitalism, and Christian refusal of the logic of necessity of the latter, means that Christians should be open to alternative perspectives. For example, hunger is often the result of inequitable distribution, not of inadequate production: where people lack money to buy food or land to grow it on, the genetic improvement of food will make no difference. Sustainable, people-centered agriculture will pay attention to the economic structures and social practices of rural regions in poor countries, which with low-tech improvements can generate remarkable increases in productivity precisely in the localities where they are most needed. Other problems are beyond the control of developing countries: for example, massive agricultural subsidies in the United States and European Union lead to overproduction in the North, with consequent dumping of surplus food onto world markets at prices which may drive Southern farmers to destitution.

Addressing these issues does not finally rule out a possible role for biotechnology. Indeed, given projected world food needs, one would need to be very sure about the adequacy of alternatives before categorically rejecting GM – a stance that is especially problematic if it is the well fed rather than the poor or hungry who are making the decisions. But it does mean that those nourished by eucharistic vision will remain very suspicious of any logic of necessity, particularly when it is articulated by those who are powerful and will massively benefit as a result.

The Eucharist and the Judgment of God

"I hate, I despise your religious feasts; I cannot stand your assemblies . . . But let justice roll on like a river, righteousness like a never-failing stream!" (Amos 5: 21, 24, NIV). The possibility of "correctly" performing the liturgy of the Eucharist but failing to embody the righteousness of God remains a constant threat to the Church. Neglecting to practice the justice God requires is not just a matter of incidental disobedience to particular commands, but betrayal of the Church's very nature. For Paul, eating the bread or drinking the cup in an unworthy manner, failing to discern the body, will incur the Lord's judgment (1 Corinthians 11: 27–34). As William Cavanaugh notes, "Paul is not speaking metaphorically; *the Eucharist can kill you*" (1998: 236; emphasis in original). Christians may not assert that the Eucharist contains a greater story than the story of hunger, unless they also recognize the bread and wine as potentially toxic food.

And yet it is also always open to the Church to witness truthfully to the bread that gives life. As Christians pray every day to be given their daily bread, they learn to acknowledge their dependence on God and their need for God's mercy. As they participate in the death and resurrection of Christ in the Eucharist, they learn that communion with God is not possible without communion with one another. And as they begin to embody the divine life in acts of hospitality and care for the other, so they begin to witness to the God who is known in the breaking and the sharing of bread.

References

Attias, Monica (2001) "Reconciliation and the Eucharist: Heart and World," in *Living the Eucharist: Affirming Catholicism and the Liturgy*, ed. Stephen Conway, pp. 13–24 (London: Darton, Longman, and Todd).

Berkhof, Hendrik (1977) *Christ and the Powers*, trans. John H. Yoder (Scottdale, PA: Herald; orig. pub. 1953).

Blundy, David and Vallely, Paul (1985) *With Geldof in Africa* (London: Times Books/Band Aid).

Bonhoeffer, Dietrich (1996) *Discipleship*, ed. Geoffrey B. Kelly and John D. Godsey, trans. Barbara Green and Reinhard Kraus, *Dietrich Bonhoeffer Works*, vol. 4 (Minneapolis, MN: Fortress; orig. pub. 1937).

Cavanaugh, William T. (1998) *Torture and Eucharist: Theology, Politics and the Body of Christ* (Oxford: Blackwell).

Deane-Drummond, Celia, Szerzynski, Bronislaw E., and Grove-White, Robin (eds) (2003) *Reordering Nature: Theology, Society and the New Genetics* (Edinburgh: T. and T. Clark).

Johnson, Peter and Sugden, Chris (eds) (2001) *Markets, Fair Trade and the Kingdoms of God* (Oxford: Regnum).

Pence, Gregory E. (ed.) (2002) *The Ethics of Food: A Reader for the Twenty-first Century* (Lanham, MD: Rowman and Littlefield).

Wink, Walter (1984) *Naming the Powers: The Language of Power in the New Testament* (Philadelphia: Fortress).

—(1986) *Unmasking the Powers: The Invisible Forces that Determine Human Existence* (Philadelphia: Fortress).

—(1992) *Engaging the Powers: Discernment and Resistance in a World of Domination* (Minneapolis, MN: Fortress).

Yoder, John Howard (1992) *Body Politics: Five Practices of the Christian Community before the Watching World* (Nashville, TN: Discipleship Resources).

—(1994) *The Politics of Jesus*, 2nd edn (Grand Rapids, MI: Eerdmans).

CHAPTER 30

Eating Together: Friendship and Homosexuality

Joel James Shuman

> . . . I think that you
> forget the very issue which
> induced the Christ to take on flesh.
>
> . . . Yes,
> if you'll recall your Hebrew word
>
> just long enough to glimpse in its
> dense figure *power to produce*
> you'll see as well the damage Greek
>
> has wrought upon your tongue, stolen
> from your sense of what is holy,
> wholly good, fully animal –
>
> the *body* which he now prepares.
> Scott Cairns, "Loves: Magdalen's Epistle"

Christians who care to talk about "homosexuality" as a moral matter tend, with a few notable exceptions, to fall neatly into two groups, both of which are pretty sure they have the right answer to the question of whether Christians can "be homosexual." On the one hand, are those who read the Bible, note (in passages such as Leviticus 18, Romans 1, or 1 Corinthians 6) what they take to be those Scriptures' univocal condemnation of homosexual behavior as a voluntary and deliberate violation of the natural moral order, and pronounce without reservation that God and nature have spoken clearly and the matter is settled. Every instance of homosexual behavior is unequivocally wrong, and all those who engage in it are committing sin of the worst sort; they should stop what they are doing or risk eternal separation from God.

On the other hand, are those who for a variety of reasons see things quite differently, insisting that the kinds of same-sex relationship we call "homosexual" are fully compatible with Christian discipleship. Those on this side of the argument argue that certain things about the social location of the Biblical authors, which is very different from our own, requires that we read Scripture – a collection of historically contingent ancient texts, after all – not just carefully, but also through the lenses of scientific reason and contemporary experience. Such a reading will show, this party claims, that the views represented in the Bible reflect the limitations and prejudices of the authors and their times. Where sexual practices are concerned, the biblical authors were dealing with a fundamentally different set of questions from those facing Christians living in the twenty-first century. It simply would never have occurred to them to consider the possibility that homosexual (or bisexual, or transgendered) is "just the way some people are" (Countryman, 1988). Certainly, it is possible for gays and lesbians, as much as for straight people, to commit occasional sexual sins of various sorts, many of the advocates of this position concede, but that is something different from saying that all expressions of homosexual behavior are morally wrong. How could God create some people this way and then condemn them unequivocally simply for being who they are? Should such people not be permitted, after all, simply to exercise their capacity for sexual love in the way that best suits them as unique individuals created by a God who from the beginning declared the entire creation "good"?

The most significant thing about this debate is not the considerable strength of conviction with which those who join it defend their respective positions, nor is it the theologically attenuated and therefore finally problematic logic voiced by both sides. Rather, it is that most Christians do not participate actively in it at all. They do not argue a position because they do not know what to argue, or how; they recognize some of their own sentiments reflected in the reasoning of one, or more frequently, both, of the aforementioned positions, but they are unable fully to agree with the logic of either.

I frequently count myself among those in this position. Fundamentally suspicious of arguments based on "personal experience," I am unable (and unwilling) to disregard what the Church has taught about the authority of the Scripture and about marriage, understood as a "one flesh" union between one man and one woman, being the appropriate context for the expression of sexually explicit love. To this point, moreover, I am not persuaded by revisionist exegeses of relevant Scriptures or accounts of the tradition insisting that so-called *adelphopoiesis* rites from the medieval Church are essentially same-sex marriages (Rogers, 2002: 61–5). Yet, my life has been graced repeatedly by the presence of faithful gay and lesbian Christians, women and men with whom I have studied and conversed, played Church softball, prepared meals for the homeless, and passed the peace of Christ before gathering around the eucharistic table. I have been unable fully to reconcile my experience in the parish with all that I believe about what it means to be a Christian, and so, like so many of my sisters and brothers, I have often remained silent.

Bewildered

To the extent that such silence may be regarded as an implicit confession of bewilderment, it is not altogether a bad thing. Indeed, I believe that any faithful contemporary Christian response to the "homosexuality question" must begin with the confession that most of us who are Christians living in contemporary North Atlantic cultures do not fully know what to think or even where to begin thinking about the matter. This is not because those of us who are confused have no moral convictions, or because we do not trust the authority of Scripture or tradition, or even because we live as members of a community that includes faithful gay and lesbian Christians, but because we look around and see that we wander in what I have heard one of the editors of this volume refer to as a trackless, "sexual wilderness." Contemporary North Atlantic Christians cannot say anything interesting about homosexuality because they can no longer say anything interesting about sexuality at all. For reasons too numerous and complex to name here, many Christians have lost track of the meaning and significance of our bodies as God's good creatures. And because they do not understand that their bodies matter to God, or how they matter, their bodily existence – especially their existence as sexual bodies – is set adrift on the turbulent seas of the "wider" culture they inhabit.

This is not to say that contemporary North Atlantic culture is any more or less obsessed with or confused by sex than many of the cultures that precede it (consider, for example, Paul's first letter to the Christians in Corinth, a group that had plenty of problems where sexual morality was concerned). Rather, it is that the ways those of us who live in such cultures think about what it means to be sexual are formed to a significant extent by our having been shaped by the particular social and economic practices of the dominant political economy to see every aspect of our lives as self-interested, rational, "choices." The ways in which we express ourselves sexually, and with whom, we have learned to treat merely as lifestyle choices among others, appetites to be satisfied within and by a marketplace that exerts an increasingly expansive influence in our lives (Lowe, 1995: 2, 38–46, 121–37). Whether one "chooses" or not to be gay, lesbian, bisexual, or straight is not the point; it is that the market-shaped culture we inhabit treats such dispositions as if they are consumer choices among others, existing merely to offer personal fulfillment to the contemporary subject.

Those readers who doubt that this is the case should take a quick trip to the newsstand and peruse the wide assortment of "lifestyle" magazines to be found there. Nearly all of these are laden with articles and advertisements offering both male and female readers ways to enhance their attractiveness, locate and secure short- and long-term partners, and improve sexual performance and technique – and so to maximize each one's potential advantage in the sexual marketplace. Such publications are particularly overt expressions of a broader economy of consumption in which "lovestyles present themselves as an array of choices for our consumption and . . . our own proclivities for one style or another are determined ultimately by our personality traits and personal preferences" (McCarthy, 2001: 57; cf. 40, 50–6).

Certainly, even within the logic of the cultural marketplace, there are rules participants must follow, but these are primarily procedural, designed to preserve order by making sure the competition is fair and no one gets hurt. Seldom do we hear anyone suggest that our conversations about sex should be predicated upon, or at least include, some consideration of what our bodies properly are *for*. Blissfully ignorant of the ways in which culture shapes our perspective on such matters, we assume that we *know* what they are for; they are instruments of the autonomous, choosing self, apparatuses for the satisfaction of appetites and the actualization of choices. Within the parameters of this logic, it matters little whether these appetites are persistent or fleeting, or whether they are heterosexual, homosexual, or some variant thereof; the general assumption is that we at least need, and probably deserve, to have them fulfilled.

One need not plunge too deeply into the Christian tradition to see the significant gap that lies between the visions of human flourishing proffered by Christianity and those suggested by the post-industrial consumer capitalism dominating contemporary culture. Neither, however, is Christianity precisely coterminous with what some refer to as the "traditional family values" of earlier, pre-consumerist times, or with the self-evident goodness of "nature." We will not get faithful answers to our questions about homosexuality by beginning with a nostalgic look into a past era when people were not so consumptive and things were not so confused. Nor will we learn what is right by fleeing from the complexities of the post-industrial world back to the simple goodness of "nature," which may then be read by anyone like a book as a source of normative moral data. Every backward look, and every account of "nature," is always already part of a discourse with origins in particular social and political contexts, which suggests that any account of normal sexuality we take from "traditional family values" or from "nature" may be just as far from Christianity as an account shaped by the practices of consumer capitalism (Lowe, 1995: 121–7).

A Logic and Politics of the Christian Body

This means that the first step to thinking faithfully as Christians about sexual behavior of any kind is to re-establish a logic and politics of the body and its goods in close and careful conversation with the richly variegated texture of the Christian story and the liturgical practices of the Christian tradition. Although carefully reading the relevant scriptural texts is an integral part of such a re-establishment, it is important that Christians do not fall prey to the illusion that closer readings and more meticulous exegesis alone will answer our questions (Hays, 1996: 3). The texts in question hardly suffer from exegetical neglect, yet scholars seem farther than ever from unanimity as to their precise meaning. For example, in 1 Corinthians 6: 9, the words *malakoi* and *arsenokoitai* are offered as descriptions of particular sexual practices that are deemed inconsistent with Christian life; according to Liddell and Scott's *Greek-English Lexicon* (which undoubtedly carries its own biases), an *arsenokoitēs* is "one guilty of unnatural offences," while *malakos* simply means "soft." Among exegetes, disagreements about how to interpret the phrase in this particular passage center on whether the words in question are simple descriptions of the participants in a sexual act (i.e., consensual intercourse between two males) or are technical terms for persons engaging in same-sex prostitution, pederasty, or rape. And the term *para phusin*, a phrase found in Romans 1: 26 and describing the moral character of sexual activity between persons of the same sex, means either (according to one side of the debate) "contrary to nature," which is to say that it is morally wrong because it is by definition contrary to the divinely established natural moral order, or (according to the other side) "beyond nature," which is to say that it is morally wrong primarily because it is not in keeping with the particular, ostensibly heterosexual nature of the persons in question (Countryman, 1988; Hays, 1996: 379–406; Rogers, 1999: 17–36).

So, rather than trying to say what makes for faithful versus unfaithful expressions of sexuality by making presumptions based on the complementary shapes of genitalia or the phenomenology of desire, or by doing precise exegesis accounting for the *sitz im leben* of the biblical authors and the real meaning of words like *para phusin, malakoi,* or *arsenokoitai,* I propose to begin with the Eucharist. I will argue that we cannot learn properly to value the gift of sexual love and so learn to be good and faithful lovers, until we learn to be good and faithful friends; we cannot be good and faithful friends until we understand that our friendship with each other is fully established and perfected by our being made friends of God. And we can be friends of one another and of God only when we learn the significance of eating together. For it is only as we gather bodily around the common table of the Eucharist that we may learn properly to value the gifts that are our bodies.

Eating Together

The significance of faithful eating for faithful sex begins with the obvious: both activities are fundamental to our being bodied creatures. Both eating and sexual loving are responses to our most basic appetites and are potentially sources of tremendous joy; in this sense, they are both wonderful gifts. Yet both require, if we are to do them well, that we learn them as skills, over time and as members of a community of people mutually committed to one another's flourishing. For both are means which afford us the opportunity to participate in the life of God. In this sense, both eating and sex are moral (and so potentially immoral) acts.

No activity is more elementary to human existence than eating. "In the biblical story of creation," remarks Alexander Schmemann, "man is presented *first of all*, as a hungry being, and the whole world as his food" (Schmemann, 1973: 11; emphasis added). Yet eating is more than simply something women and men do in order to sustain their bodies while they are busy with, or so they can attend to, the more significant matters – that is, the "spiritual" matters – of life. Eating is life itself, first because women and men are never less than bodied members of God's good creation.

> Man must eat in order to live; he must take the world into his body and transform it into himself, into flesh and blood. He is indeed that which he eats, and the whole world is presented as one all-embracing banquet table for man. And this image of the banquet remains, throughout the whole Bible, the central image of life. It is the image of life at its creation, and also the image of life at its end and fulfillment: ". . . that you eat and drink at my table in the Kingdom." (Schmemann, 1973: 11)

Eating is life also because it is the most basic means by which women and men may participate in the life of God, and so also in the lives of one another. In this sense, eating is always an activity with great social significance. God gifts humanity with food, and that gifting, properly acknowledged, establishes between God and humanity, and so among humans, the bond we call *communion*. Schmemann explains: "all that exists is God's gift to man, and it all exists to make God known to man, to make man's life communion with God . . . the sign and means of His presence and wisdom" (1973: 14). Creation is for women and men intended by God as a blessing, and women and men are alone among the members of creation capable of responding by blessing God. "So the only *natural* (and not 'supernatural') reaction of man, to whom God gave and blessed and sanctified the world, is to bless God in return, to thank Him, to see the world as God sees it and – in this act of gratitude and adoration – to know, name and possess the world" (1973: 15; emphasis in original).

But gratitude scarcely describes the disposition of most women and men toward the creation and its author; it has forever been the human tendency, because of our self-chosen alienation from God, one another, and the non-human creation, to view and to treat God, people, and things instrumentally, as means *simpliciter* of satisfying whatever appetites we happen to have. Part of God's saving work to rescue us from this state of self-absorbed alienation is to teach us once again to be members of a people who receive all good things – including each other – as gifts. This teaching finds its clearest expression in the Eucharist, the Christian feast of thanksgiving. This holy meal is the center of the liturgy, the event toward which all of Christian worship points.

As the climax of the drama that is the liturgy, the Eucharist makes of those eating together a *reconciled people*. This, Schmemann reminds us, is the highest and most perfect expression of what *leitourgia* is, "an action by which a group of people become something corporately which they had not been as a mere collection of individuals – a whole greater than the sum of its parts . . . a function or 'ministry' of a man or of a group on behalf of and in the interest of the whole community" (1973: 25). The eating done in the Eucharist is thus fundamentally and inescapably social; one eats the bread and drinks the cup always and everywhere with and mindful of others; in that eating, moreover, one is united to those with whom one eats. In the Eucharist, those who eat together are "re-membered" by the triune God into and as the Body of Christ. By gathering around a common table, they agree to love each other as God loves each one of them. They become friends of God by their eating together the one loaf that is Christ's body and drinking together from the one cup that is Christ's blood; they are able to become friends of one another because of their mutual friendship with God. Those gathered to participate in the life of God offer to one another, as signs of their having been forgiven by and reconciled to God, bodily gestures of Christ's peaceable love, the hand of fellowship and the embrace of peace. These two kinds of friendship are thus inseparable; our disposition toward God and our disposition toward one another are part of the same grace-created, grace-sustained politics, a politics always and everywhere learned by and displayed in bodily gestures, both ritual and quotidian (Shuman, 1999: 92–7).

Just so, the language and gestures of the Eucharist also create a kind of classroom for the initiation of women and men into their roles as members of the political reality called the Body of Christ. It is as members of the Christian community that women and men learn of their true Good, and it is the community's practices, represented in the liturgy, that form the members to desire, pursue, and achieve that Good. The common life of the community, in other words, is both the medium for and the modality of the pursuit and achievement of friendship with God. As the "destination" of the ritual liturgical journey into the Kingdom of God (Schmemann, 1973: 26–46), the Eucharist is how God incorporates those eating together into the perfect love of the divine triune society, a society whose love is then to be displayed by the common life of the Body of

Christ. It is through this incorporation that sin-distorted "natural" bodily appetites are taken up, disciplined, and transformed, and ultimately oriented altogether toward the Good of friendship with God (Rogers, 1999: 219–36).

Living Together

Thus, the Eucharist reminds those who participate of the social significance of their more quotidian forms of eating. Eating together creates an intimacy that approaches and potentially even surpasses the intimacy of sexual love. In the New Testament, Jesus never takes a lover, but is often seen gathered around the table with those to whom he is ministering. It is his final common meal with his disciples that serves not simply as the model for the Eucharist, but also as the occasion for his telling them that they were no longer his servants, but his friends (John 15: 14–15). It is in this context of table-centered friendship, moreover, that Jesus establishes a new model for service; friends are those who serve one another, often in the basest of ways (John 13: 12–17; 15: 12–13). Such service flows from the school for friendship that is the common table, a place where social interactions are established and transformed.

Insofar as Christians are never *not* members of Christ's eucharistic social body, it is always within and through that body's common life that we discover how properly to make use of our (i.e., how to live as) individual bodies. "Although," as Eugene Rogers puts the matter, "this side of heaven Christians believe the redemption of their bodies will be incomplete, nevertheless they also believe that God's argument with the human being continues and retains its integrating, enhypostatic power, in the body of the Logos that is the Church" (Rogers, 1999: 28). The entirety of our lives as bodies, including our appetites for food and friendship and our capacity for sexual (erotic) love and whatever sexual appetites we might experience, are corrupted by our participation in the creation's brokenness; as such, they frequently further our alienation from God and each other. Yet, those very appetites are being restored, reoriented by God, through the disciplines of our ecclesial membership, toward our genuine flourishing as individual human bodies and the common good of Christ's human body.

The names Christians traditionally have given to the ecclesial practices within and through which this reorientation and disciplining takes place are marriage and celibacy. Marriage and celibacy, in other words, are the ways Christians name the particular friendships through which the gift of sexuality may properly be expressed, and the practices by which we learn to live well as sexual bodies within the Body of Christ. By *marriage*, Christians traditionally have meant a lifelong, monogamous union between one man and one woman, a relationship with three proximate ends, no one of which is fully separable from the others. Marriage is first the school and the proper context for those Christian friendships that include, on a continuing basis, the sharing of erotic love. The sexual act, Christians have believed, effects a "one flesh union" between woman and man. Second, marriage is the appropriate context for the procreation, welcoming, and raising of children. Finally, marriage is by its permanence a visible display to the watching world of the steadfast love with which God loves the creation.

Christian marriage is thus, like its complement, celibacy, a venue for discipleship. "Marriage in Christianity is best understood as an ascetic practice of and for the community by which God takes sexuality up into God's own triune life, graciously transforming it so as to allow the couple partially to model the love between Christ and the Church" (Rogers, 1999: 72–3; cf. 76–9). Marriage is not simply about the satisfaction of sexual desire; it is also about the rest of life – cooking and cleaning, paying bills and repairing houses, rearing children, and often about negotiating *not* having sex. In the simplest terms, marriage largely is a way of naming the difficulties of day-to-day life with another person with whom one also happens to have sex. As an aspect of discipleship, sex in marriage points to

> the essential meaning and natural ends of sexual intercourse. Sex is never "just sex," and desire is never just desire for its own sake. Within the thought and practices of the Church, sexual desire is shaped by our desire for unity with another person and by the duties and gifts that come with sharing our lives . . . Sexual relationships have less to do with fleeting moments and more to do with the passage of time. Marriage, in short, sets our desires in household time and place. (McCarthy, 2001: 42–3)

Both marriage and celibacy, then, are ways in which Christians live, as members of households, in their vocation to be a holy witness to the life and work of God. Through negotiating the bodily presence and the entire range of desires represented by the bodily presence of another (or perhaps, for celibates in particular, of multiple others) on a continual basis, Christians learn, in ways that may or may not include the periodic manipulation and/or union of each other's genitals, to be friends – of each other and so of God. Eugene Rogers is probably putting too great a burden on the Christian household when he claims that it is to be, whether based in marriage or celibacy, "a *micrabasilea*, a domestic Church . . . one of the purposes of which is to build up that larger polity under God, the community of the faithful" (Rogers, 1999: 29). Yet, undeniably, the Christian household is, as part of a constellation of likewise-oriented, open households, a place that forms as well as displays disciples.

It is against the background of the Christian household as part of a complex of open households that we may finally ask (in one of its many possible forms) the "right" question concerning Christianity and homosexuality. Given that *all* Christians are called to a sanctification of body to be accomplished (in part) *either* through marriage or celibacy, is it possible for the Christian community to understand (imagine?) *some* gay or lesbian relationships as sufficiently analogous to marriages to bless them as sanctifying relationships? That is, can such relationships be in some sense *sacramental?* Or is it the case, given the Church's traditional understanding of relationships between persons of the same sex, that all gay and lesbian Christians are de facto called to celibacy – that is, to membership in households within which the relationships between members do not include the manipulation or union of each other's genitals?

Another way of putting this is to ask whether some gay and lesbian relationships are capable of fulfilling the traditionally understood "goods" of Christian marriage. We can imagine that at least in principle such relationships could be permanent and monogamous, enduring the difficulties and unhappy contingencies befalling most households, and so bearing witness to the steadfastness of Christ's love for the Church and God's love for creation. The question becomes, then, whether (and how) gay and lesbian "marriages" can fulfill the so-called procreative and unitive goods of marriage.

Obviously gay and lesbian couples cannot conceive and give birth to children in the usual and customary way. Even by abstract analogy, sexual activity between two men or two women cannot be construed as procreative. As important as biology may be, however, we need to be careful not to *reduce* the procreative good of marriage to penis and vagina, sperm and ovum, conception and implantation, labor and birth. To some extent, every household that practices the virtue of hospitality by welcoming children participates as well in the procreative good. As members first of all of a community that is created and grows by the practice of baptism, Christians are freed from the absolute need to have "children of their own." This is the backdrop to Eugene Rogers' claim that "If marriage is not about procreation, although it promotes the virtue of hospitality to the stranger, then there too gay and lesbian Christians suffer no disadvantage, but can carry forward the great tradition of those other same-sex communities, the monasteries, in caring for the sick and the oblate" (Rogers, 1999: 84).

Yet, just as the procreative good is not reducible to fruitful copulation, neither is it fully reducible to hospitality. The "if" with which Rogers qualifies his claim about marriage and procreation is substantial, especially if he intends it as the basis for a normative practice. For it is one thing to deny that the procreative good of marriage is reducible to fruitful copulation, and another altogether to say that same- or opposite-sex couples can do whatever they like sexually so long as they are willing, in practice or in principle, for their household to be hospitable to children. This is not to say that contemporary, "natural law" neoconservatives, who imply that the "reproductive-like" character of heterosexual coitus makes it *by definition* morally superior to anything gay or lesbian couples do, are correct (George, 2001: 75–89). Such uncritically foundationalist accounts of nature and the natural law are useful only to the extent that they are disciplined by faithful close readings of Scripture and the liturgical practices of the Christian tradition. Yet, we cannot talk about the Christian body and its goods in the theological abstract, as if the biological given-ness of male and female do not matter. The crux of the conversation, therefore, must turn to *how* biology matters.

Eugene Rogers suggests that, within the context of lifelong monogamy, it is *possible* that any given sexual act, because it fulfills the desire of one person for another, can serve to unite lovers erotically – quite apart from the abstract or particular possibility that the act might also lead to a procreative end – and so to effect the "one flesh" union characteristic of properly Christian sexual love. Because the procreative good need not be linked biologically, even in the abstract, to the "one flesh" union, he says, gay and lesbian monogamous relationships are just as capable as heterosexual marriages of fulfilling the unitive good.

To say otherwise is to limit the freedom of God in an unbiblical manner. The first chapter of Matthew picks out several stories that lead up to Mary as the supreme example – she who represents the race as a whole – of departures from "normative" marriage and childbirth. Matthew picks out the stories by naming women – only four of them – in the entire genealogy of Jesus. Those women are Tamar, Ruth, Rahab, and "the wife of Uriah," a des-

ignation emphasizing that Bathsheba was married to Uriah when David had sex with her
... Tamar dresses as a prostitute and seduces her father-in-law by the side of the road,
bearing twins ... Rahab, a Gentile, is also a prostitute; she shows "hospitality" to the spies
of Israel against her home town of Jericho ... After the death of her husband, Ruth, a
Gentile, pledges herself to Naomi, her mother-in-law, and bears a son "to her"; she does
this by seducing Boaz, her husband's next of kin, on the threshing floor, following Naomi's
instructions to get him drunk and uncover his "feet," a Hebrew euphemism for "genitals."

In picking out those resourceful women with their irregular pregnancies, Matthew portrays God as capable – even delighting in – the use of irregular sexual unions for God's
own purposes. God not only chooses an unwed mother to bear Jesus, but, as one of my
students put it, "it runs in the family." (Rogers, 1999: 243–4)

Rogers' broad point here is that God's saving activity – activity in which women and
men called by God are to participate – is frequently unconventional, or, to use his
phrase, "in excess of nature." That God has in the past worked among the people of God
through unconventional sexual practices, Rogers suggests, is an indication that God is
disposed to do so again, and perhaps even to do so regularly. If this is the case, he asserts,
then it is reasonable to allow for the possibility that gay or lesbian relationships, which
are in their own way also "in excess of nature," can be avenues for God's saving work
analogous to Christian marriage traditionally understood.

There is *something* right about having tabs and slots, but the very language "reduces love
to an instrumental and utilitarian sexuality." Only because God gives slots more to be about
– namely God – than insert-tab-A-in-slot-B, it comes not amiss that God should give it to
some to admire others with tabs. Even Augustine was able to speculate about the placement of nipples on a man's chest: "they articulate the space of the chest, and they prove
that beauty is a value in itself, not tied inevitably to utility in the human body." Or better:
the utility is for bodies made aware of grace, the utility of joy. (Rogers, 1999: 246)

Rogers' first point is well taken; God works, as the old folks used to say, in strange
and mysterious ways, and some of those ways have involved atypical sexual behavior.
Yet, his conclusion about the goodness of same-sex relationships being kinds of marriages does not necessarily follow. It is one thing to observe that the saving work of God
in a broken world is from time to time surprisingly unconventional and "in excess of
nature," and another thing to use that observation as a warrant for normalizing the
human behaviors through which God has from time to time been known to work, even
if such behaviors have indisputably been occasions for human joy. The former is a
matter of discernment; the latter, especially in the absence of strong theological warrants, a matter of presumption. The second son of David and Bathsheba was indeed,
as Rogers notes, an ancestor of Jesus, but Solomon's place in the Messianic lineage did
not result in the overturning of the sixth commandment. To say that God's work is "in
excess of nature" is not to say that the *telos* of that work, the Kingdom of God, has
nothing to do with, or is contrary to, or altogether disregards, nature.

The distinction is significant. Insofar as the Kingdom of God is the restoration and
perfection of God's good creation (that is, of "nature"), those ritual practices constituting the Church's liturgical journey into the Kingdom of God are claims about what

it means to live in anticipation of harmonious membership in a restored and perfected nature. The world we see and experience day to day is "nature" only imperfectly; "real" nature is the nature we will know in the Kingdom of God, the world we are being trained to live in by our participation in the practices of the Church. Marriage is such a practice; it teaches us to live well with one another as sexual bodies in anticipation of being bodily present to one another in the Kingdom of God. Just so, to sanctify gay and lesbian relationships by naming them "marriages" is to say something about how we imagine relationships between bodies in the Kingdom of God, and so, it would seem, about the character of human life in a restored and perfected nature.

Our life in the restored and perfected nature of the Kingdom of God is to be a fully human life, in which, says Robert Jenson, "the redeemed . . . will be available to one another; they will be able to intend one another in love." The intention of another in love is necessarily embodied, for the "personal body is . . . personal availability" (Jenson, 1999: 355; cf. 88–9). Such availability is sexual at least in the sense that "we are humans only in that we are male or female . . . as Jesus interprets Scripture in Matthew, God 'made them at the beginning . . . male and female'" This is not to say that marriage as we know it will be part of our lives in the kingdom of God; neither, however, is it to say that life will be asexual. "Humanity's sexuality turns us to each other in *two* ways, of which only the turning to unborn generations must end with this age" (Jenson, 1999: 357). Sexuality, as we experience it in the Kingdom of God, whatever it may look like, will be the sexuality of a restored and perfected creation, a sexuality that is "perfectly natural."

Here we may turn for help to the creation stories, which, read through the lens of the consummated redemption, give us a sense of God's intention for us from the beginning. The human bodies in those stories are male and female bodies, bodies created to unite with each other as "one flesh." As Jenson explains, the "creation narratives contemplate no such thing as humanity that is not female humanity or male humanity, each in relation to the other" (Jenson, 1999: 90; see also Tribble, 1978). Marriage, in part, anticipates the restoration of that relation, and so requires for its one-flesh union male and female bodies. Gay and lesbian sexual unions, whatever else they may be, are not marriages. Yet this in itself does not mean that there is no place in the Christian community for those who identify themselves as gays and lesbians.

We have seen that the practice of good eating is central to the establishment of true friendships within and among networks of open, hospitable households. The kind of friendships that flow from a thick account of common eating clearly need not be limited to those based in marriage; indeed, the explicitly sexual character of marriage might even be an impediment to the formation of such friendships as are conducive to practices of hospitality. Surely then, households constituted by persons of the same sex are every bit as capable of bearing witness to the Kingdom of God and building up the Body of Christ as those founded on marriage. All those who gather around the table as Christians learn the skills of service, of regularly showing various kinds of hospitality not just to children or to other families, but also to the sick, the poor, and the lonely (Matthew 25: 31–46). Such households are able to put genital relations into their proper perspective; they are secondary to the prior vocation of welcoming others as if those others were representatives of Jesus himself.

This still leaves us with a significant pastoral problem; how do Christians account for the presence among us of faithful women and men who claim that they are called neither to celibacy nor to heterosexual marriage, but to a permanent, monogamous, same-sex relationship that does include genital exchange? Clearly, one answer is that we must proceed with a patient, generous conversation, for one of the most important characteristics of the Church is that it is a space within which God has given us the time to talk about matters that matter, and the body matters.

To begin this conversation, I suggest two questions. The first question is to be put to those who, like Eugene Rogers, admit that gay and lesbian relationships are extraordinary and in some sense "in excess of nature," yet argue that this is of little consequence to a God whose saving acts are frequently "in excess of nature," and that to deprive gays and lesbians of the Church's blessing of their relationships is to deprive them of the very means of grace by which they might be saved. To them the question must be: Why must sanctifying friendships be sexually explicit? Given the significance of other activities – eating together in particular – for the formation of friendships, can we not imagine *adelphopoiesis* without the stimulation of genitalia? If salvation is in part the restoration of nature, should the Christian community be in the business of liturgically sanctifying a way of life that has for most of Christian history been seen as in excess of nature?

The second question is one to be contemplated by those who, like myself, are not persuaded that the Church should sanctify sexually active gay or lesbian relationships because they fail to account for the continuity of life in the Church with life in the restored, perfected creation of the Kingdom of God. The question we eventually must ask is: Why must our anticipation of the Kingdom, expressed through the practices of the Church, focus so explicitly on sexuality? Clearly, we make accommodations in other areas of our lives for our being "not yet" fully redeemed. Many Christians continue, for example, to eat meat, even in the presence of compelling theological arguments that we were created to be herbivorous and will again be so in the Kingdom of God. If, as I have tried to show, there can for Christians be no such thing as "casual eating," why can the Church not see gay and lesbian unions analogously to the way we see our consumption of animal flesh in this time between the times? Does the perfection to which Christ calls us require us to forgo all forms of accommodation to those aspects of creation that are not as we anticipate they one day shall be, or can there be a space within our communities for those who believe they are called, as gay and lesbian Christians, to what Rogers calls "marriage-like" relationships, sanctified by the community?

I readily admit that these questions are not much, but they are a start. In the interim, we continue to long eagerly for the redemption of our bodies, looking forward to that day when such questions will trouble us no more.

References

Countryman, L. William (1988) *Dirt, Greed and Sex: Sexual Ethics in the New Testament and their Implications for Today* (Philadelphia: Fortress).

George, Robert (2001) *The Clash of Orthodoxies* (Wilmington: ISI).

Hays, Richard (1996) *The Moral Vision of the New Testament: A Contemporary Introduction to New Testament Ethics* (San Francisco: Harper Collins).

Jenson, Robert (1999) *Systematic Theology*, vol. 2: *The Works of God* (New York: Oxford University Press).

Lowe, Donald (1995) *The Body in Late-capitalist USA* (Durham, NC: Duke University Press).

McCarthy, David Matzko (2001) *Sex and Love in the Home* (London: SCM).

Rogers, Eugene F. (1999) *Sexuality and the Christian Body: Their Way to the Triune God* (Oxford: Blackwell).

— (ed.) (2002) *Theology and Sexuality: Classic and Contemporary Readings* (Oxford: Blackwell).

Schmemann, Alexander (1973) *For the Life of the World: Sacraments and Orthodoxy* (Crestwood, NY: St Vladimir's Seminary).

Shuman, Joel (1999) *The Body of Compassion* (Boulder, CO: Westview).

Tribble, Phyllis (1978) *God and the Rhetoric of Sexuality* (Philadelphia: Fortress).

CHAPTER 31

Being Silent: Time in the Spirit

Michael S. Northcott

Time in the modern world seems to be in short supply. In many households, the daily round of childcare, work and travel to work, meal preparation, and household management involves a constant struggle with time where there never seems to be enough of it. Time for worship and silent contemplation is squeezed out by the demanding cacophony of communication devices, transportation and cleaning machines which fill our neighbourhoods, homes, and workplaces. Anthropologists observe that "premodern" hunter-gatherers have considerably more time for friendship, feasting, the nurture of children, and religious celebration than do modern Europeans whose work to acquire the machines which are designed to "save" time absorbs far more of their lives than the minimalist material requirements of hunter-gatherers (Sahlins, 1972: 42). Promising liberation, the machine age eats up time, subjecting human life to its artifice of ceaseless governed movement of which the mechanical clock is the most powerful symbol.

The modern loss of time may be traced to a new account of the relation between God and created time amongst medieval theologians who, unlike the early fathers, began to envisage finite "being" in time apart from the infinite "being" of God. Existence in time was consequently problematized and finite, being seen as inherently sinful (Gunton, 1993). In this chapter I will suggest that time is redeemed because God has given time back to us in the Risen Lord who is "Alpha and Omega" and in whom created time finds its beginning and end. The recovery of time as gift requires us to re-imagine creation, nature, embodiment as proximate and continuously related to God as Trinity, and to enact such re-imaginings through practices of time-ful living, and especially eucharistic worship. Such practices, and the knowledge of time as gift, are made possible by the Spirit of God who illumines the minds of the people of God and empowers them to live in the renewed time of the Resurrection of Christ as creator and Lord, the time of the Church, the time between the Ascension and the *parousia*.

In many Churches in both the Western and non-Western worlds the time after communion is a time of collective as well as individual adoration and thanksgiving in which the prayers of the people of God are expressed in spiritual songs and meditative chants. In the Taizé community, located near Dijon in France, the monks and their often large numbers of youthful congregants and pilgrims have developed a practice of post-eucharistic meditative singing which has analogues in the post-communion chanting of folk melodies and rhythms in churches in Africa, Latin America, and Asia. The repetitive singing of simple harmonic chants creates a temple of sound, and allows the worshiper to receive the sacrament and to pray after communion, while being enfolded in musical praise.

I have arranged this chapter under three headings taken from the Taizé community's chant book which point to three key features of the Christian experience of the redeeming of created time: the eschatological feast of the Eucharist in which the reign of God is already breaking in to present reality; the focus of Christian eucharistic worship on the Lord's Day, the day of Resurrection, which sacramentally frames the weekly rhythm of life; and the gift of the Spirit who is the God who comes to dwell with us and renew our experience of created time as divine gift.

Maranatha: Veni Domine

Modernity arises from the idea that the future is empty, up for grabs, and that collectively humans make their own future and even the future of the planet (Schweiker, 2000: 129). This future is often conceived in terms of the idea of progress, so that human history is said to be evolving toward a higher moral or economic or technological plane, an end of human making which is superior to the present and the past. This approach is sometimes called historicism (O'Donovan, 1986: 58), and it finds characteristic expression among moral philosophers in the claim that contemporary concern with animal welfare, and in particular the advocacy of animal rights, represents an advanced stage in the development of human moral consciousness, whose earlier stages included the recognition of the rights of women and of slaves (Singer, 1975).

One-sided and distorted attitudes to time, especially to the future, are clearly exemplified in certain forms of consequentialist thinking. Consequentialism makes a system of the calculus by which moderns mostly seek to describe "ethics," that is the judgment of actions through the assessment of their likely consequences. Consequentialists are not so much concerned with the now of the ethical moment or the present character of a particular act as with the state of affairs that will pertain *after* the event or act in question. The consequentialist looks to the ends of actions, rather than to the intrinsic character of the actors or the meaning of their actions. The end in view, identified for example by Utilitarian consequentialists as the promotion of happiness, is the primary concern: the action and the agent are treated as instrumental to the desired end. As Philip Pettit puts it, under consequentialism, "agents are required to produce whatever actions have the property of promoting a designated value, even actions that fail intuitively to honour it" (Pettit, 1993: 231).

The consequentialist also refuses to judge actions according to criteria from inherited moral traditions. The archetypal attempt to eschew time past from present moral rationality is Kant's attempt to construe the moral agent as an amnesiac with no past or future, in his *Religion Within the Limits of Reason Alone*, an attempt which finds more recent analogy in John Rawls's idea of the "original position" by which Rawls hopes to produce a concept of justice untainted by personal interest or memory (Rawls, 1972). The attempt to construct a version of moral rationality with a distorted sense of time makes self-alienation a central feature of ethics for both consequentialists and certain kinds of deontologist, for on this view we can only make moral judgments when we view our moral projects as outside observers; that is, as if they were not valuable to *us* (Hauerwas and Burrell, 1989: 171–2).

Against the forgetful and unsituated consequentialist calculus of modern ethics, pre-modern and contemporary Christian ethics is intrinsically concerned with memory and tradition, for Christians believe that their future and the future of creation is already given and revealed as the "new creation" which God inaugurates in the events of the birth, life, death, resurrection, and ascension of Christ as narrated in the Christian Scriptures. For Christ is "before all things" (Colossians 1: 17), "he is the beginning" (Colossians 1: 18), "through him God was pleased to reconcile to himself all things, whether on earth or in heaven, by making peace through the blood of the cross" (Colossians 1: 20), and in him God promises to fulfill the creation at the end of time when Christ will come again and "gather up all things in him" (Ephesians 1: 10). Christians do not presume to know in advance the outcome of their actions except inasmuch as they remember that God has already determined their end, and the end of all things in the new creation which begins with the Resurrection of Christ from the dead and is being revealed between Christ's Ascension and his *parousia*. And this is the spring of hope and moral courage for Christians, who live in expectation that their lives, being caught up by grace in the life of the Spirit between the Ascension and the *parousia*, may manifest the goodness of God even in the midst of their sinfulness.

It is in the Eucharist that this view of history as memory and anticipation, what Christians call eschatology, takes bodied form as the sacramental feast brings into present reality the future that God has promised: "Those who eat my flesh and drink my blood have eternal life, and I will raise them up on the last day" (John 6: 4). From the beginning Christians practiced the Eucharist as an eschatological feast, in which the new creation which Jesus enacted in his parabolic acts of feasting with sinners and the outcast, and which God inaugurated at the Resurrection of Jesus, was brought into being in the life of the Church (Wainwright, 1971). In the earliest written account of the Eucharist in the New Testament, Paul describes the practice of Eucharist as a clear eschatological imperative: "For as often as you eat this bread and drink this cup, you proclaim the Lord's death until he comes" (1 Corinthians 11: 26). In the Synoptic Gospels a clear link is established between the Eucharist feast, as modeled on the Last Supper, and the coming eschatological kingdom of which the Eucharist is a sign and exemplar, for Jesus declares at the Last Supper "truly I tell you, I will never again drink of the fruit of the vine until that day when I drink it new in the kingdom of God" (Mark 14: 25). The Gospels describe three occasions on which Jesus ate and drank with the disciples after the Resurrection: at Emmaus (Luke 24: 28–35), later in the evening of the same day in Jerusalem (Luke 24: 36–43), and in the morning at the beach (John 21: 13) (Wainwright, 1971: 38). This recognition is powerfully expressed in the prayer *O Sacrum convivium* attributed to Aquinas: "O sacred banquet, in which Christ is received, the memory of His Passion is renewed, the mind is filled with grace, and a pledge of future glory is given to us." Eucharistic worship is then a realization, and not just an anticipation, of the heavenly feast of which Jesus often spoke in parables. The Eucharist, along with the gift of the Spirit, is one of the first fruits of the new era that dawned at the Incarnation and was revealed more fully in the Resurrection. When Christians celebrate the Eucharist they declare that the Kingdom is already coming in, that time has been remade, and that they are living in a new time, the time between the Ascension and the *parousia*.

The oblation of liturgical time, prayer and silence, music and celebration, set apart for God in the Eucharist, presents the worshiping community with a weekly experience of redeemed time in which the hidden end of human time is already displayed in the perfection of Christ present in the eucharistic elements and in whom death is overcome by life and all things are made new (Farrow, 1999: 72). Instead of human time being a meaningless progression from birth to death, or cosmic time being the birth and death of the sun, time is revealed as finding its origin and fulfillment in Christ who is the Alpha and the Omega, and in whose Resurrection and Ascension Christians discern the meaning of the future (Cullman, 1951). Because Christians already know their end, and the end of creation, this means that they are released from fear of the dead or of the past, and from anxiety about the future.

Surrexit Dominus Vere

The confident eschatological orientation toward an already revealed future helps explain the ambiguous civilizational power of Christianity in history. Hopeful orientation toward the future is a source of great energy and dynamism both for the individual and for society (Moltmann 1965: 15–36), but it is ambiguous because this future orientation has been secularized since the Renaissance and the rise of modernity. Modern humans believe that they are autonomous within time and hence the source of their own redemption and their own future. They also seek means to measure and control time, and to predict the future. According to Jacques Ellul, the mechanical clock turns time into an abstract quantity and renders time lifeless, momentary, and fleeting (Ellul, 1964: 329). This results in a loss of a sense of duration, a loss that has done much to shape the character of modern life, and its impact upon creation. Some locate this shift to time as non-relational quantity in the absolute conception of space–time developed by Isaac Newton (Funkenstein, 1986: 92). In the Newtonian schema the universe is a realm that subsists independently of the relations between Creator and creation, and obeys fixed laws that do not vary between one place or time and another. Time and space are fixed containers and this fixity displaces the traditional Christian account of creation as relationally dependent upon the Trinitarian God with whom the world, and human beings especially, are said to remain in constant interaction. Capitalism gives flesh to this shift in Western metaphysics. Industrial time, the reduction of time to the unrelenting cycle of factory machines and accounting measures, compresses our experience of time and space (Harvey, 1989). The industrial over-determination of time, and of life in the body, means that whereas the ancients measured time by the cycles of the heavenly bodies and the religious calendar, modern time is decontextualized both from the movements of the created earth and heavens, so that human eating, working, and sleeping are controlled by the clock instead of the divinely created time of sun and moon, and the rhythms of the seasons. Time-and-motion studies and strict scheduling involve the subjection of the mind–bodies of industrial and office workers to the rule of the machine and of monetary calculation. Accountants seek to maximize returns on monies invested in computers, manufacturing plants, or the stock market, through seven-day, night-and-day production systems, and, more recently, through non-stop global trading in stocks and commodities or twenty-four hour, seven-day telephone sales centers and banks. The invention of what Marx called "industrial time" has encroached on the traditional practice of Christian worship and rest on Sunday, or the Lord's Day, and this is one of the most significant anti-theological impacts of the ceaseless and restless culture of capitalism.

In a world dominated by the experience of mechanically ordered, non-relational time, the relations between the present and past and future are ruptured, as may be observed in the domination of modern life by the rituals of capitalism. Money's unceasing quest for the transformation of living creation into dead matter and wealth displays a practice of forgetfulness both of the past and the future, for capitalism has no memory (Hauerwas, 2000: 148). Modern economists discount the destruction of irreplaceable natural goods, such as ancient forest or biodiversity, as insignificant by-products of wealth creation. Their accounting mechanisms have no way of identifying the value of created diversity and conserving it for future generations. Neither do these mechanisms have a way of remembering the ascetic lives of our ancestors who bequeathed the earth's riches far more fulsomely to us than we may to our children's children. Modern corporations spend billions globally persuading us to participate in the rituals of consumerism to "keep the economy going." But the putative instant satiety promised by these increasingly seven-day-a-week rituals does not answer the hunger for a more enduring sense of meaning in a universe narrated by modern science as one of such duration and size as to render the sum of the history of human existence as no more than a minute blip in space–time (Schweiker, 2000: 124).

Modernity constructs the human experience of time as lack, as necessity, and as unreality. Lack arises from fear of death; necessity from the narration of the cosmos as a machine which is gradually unwinding, or a sun which is gradually dying, where finitude, limitation, being-without-end is problematized; unreality from the speed with which machines and communication devices bombard the individual with disconnected images and signs, stimulating and at the same time frustrating desire. The individual is consequently forced to "seize from within" the only enduring reality which is the memory of the self whose "continuity of progress, and unity of direction" seems more reliable than the sense perceptions of the real (Bergson, 1913). The mechanical over-determination of the real makes the modern subject skeptical of her encounters with the objects of nature and even her own body so that she is driven inside in a hubristic and individualistic quest for personal endurance.

Taking time for communion, time for silent prayer and worshipful adoration after communion, involves the claim that time is not rushing away from us, that time and death have been redeemed, and that Christians have all the time in the world to be God's people, and to worship in God's presence. In the meeting of time and eternity of the eucharistic present Christians recover the sense of time as gift rather than as necessity. In the transformation of matter into divine presence which is the miracle enacted in every Eucharist, Christians are enabled to see the reality of matter and bodies as created and completed in the Incarnate Lord of the cosmos rather than in human making and mechanical remaking.

But the practice of the Eucharist has not always, does not always, enable the recovery of time from the fear of finitude, the logic of necessity or skepticism of the real. Augustine in Book 11 of *The Confessions* expresses doubts about the reality of time, and fails fully to distinguish between the temporal and the fallen or sinful. He seems to forget that time is only given reality by its relation to God as both creator *and* redeemer (Gunton, 1993: 82). Similarly Barth's account of time and timelessness in the *Church Dogmatics* privileges the uncreated eternal over the created temporal, seeming to disallow the reality of grace-ful living, the realization of the eschaton in the present Spirit-indwelt reality of the Church and the lives of believers (Roberts, 1989). The underlying problem for both Augustine and Barth is what Gunton calls the "displacement of eschatology," a problem which results from a lack of a sense of the interweaving of times, of a way in which the divinely ordered destiny of life could, by the work of the Spirit, be anticipated in the present. According to such a view, the future destination of the world is, by grace, anticipated in the present. Indeed, in the teaching of Jesus the present is reconstituted – not *created* – by the breaking in from the future of the promised kingdom of God. It is to do justice to the biblical notion of the openness of the times to one another that "theologians of hope" have rightly attempted a shift in the temporal orientation of theology (Gunton, 1993: 92).

In the early Church, as I argue above, the simultaneity of the promised kingdom and the present life of the Church, the interweaving of time and eternity, was enacted in the practice of the Eucharist as eschatological feast on the Lord's Day, the day of Resurrection, and in the experience of the gift of the Spirit as the eschatological "first fruit" of eternal life to which I will turn in the final section of this chapter. It is possible that the earliest practice of the Lord's Supper was a continuation of the Sabbath observance of the Jewish Christians in Jerusalem, and that the Eucharist would have been celebrated late in the evening of the Sabbath as the Day of Resurrection approached. But, according to the Acts of the Apostles, the practice soon developed of the celebration of the Eucharist on Sunday morning, thus ultimately supplanting the Jewish Sabbath with the Christian Sunday (Wainwright, 1971: 75). Christians continue to practice the Sabbath for, as the writer to the Hebrews affirms, the "sabbath rest still remains for the people of God; for those who enter God's rest also cease from their labours as God did from his" (Hebrews 4: 9–10). But Christians observe the Sabbath on the eighth day, the day of Resurrection. In so doing they recognize that the Sabbath has been transformed by the Resurrection of Christ, and that God's call to worship and rest is no longer just for Israel but for all people and the whole creation (Hauerwas and Willimon 1999: 61). And Christians do not understand Sabbath *keeping* in the same way as their Jewish forebears for they recognize that the law is not the source of their reconciliation with God. Freedom from the tyranny of work is an essential part of a Christian understanding of the Lord's Day, but freedom to share hospitality or write a letter to a friend or climb a mountain (all activities proscribed by the original Sabbath tradition) is also important. For this reason I resist the attempt to frame the Christian understanding of time, and Christian ethics, around Sabbath keeping as proposed by Karl Barth (1961: 53 ff).

While establishing worship as a central and shaping activity of human life, eucharistic worship on the Lord's Day also recalls the fact that God rested after the work of creation. That Christians can rest from their labors is indicative of the fact that God originally ordered all things well, and that God has reordered them after the Ascension: "sabbath keeping is a sign of trust that God governs this world, therefore we don't have to work to make things come out right" (Hauerwas and Willimon, 1999: 57). The worship, and rest, of the Lord's Day remind us that the creation was perfected and abundant when it was originally blessed by the creator, and that the recovery of the divine benison is not therefore achieved through human actions but by waiting on God. The worship and rest of the Lord's Day recall the fact that, in Christ, God has already established a new redeemed physicality, a new time and a new space, within the boundaries of historical existence. Human work in the production of artifacts or of food and clothing is not then so central to the redemption of human life as moderns imagine, and certainly not so central that productive work cannot cease for worship and rest on the Sabbath.

The practices of eucharistic worship on the Lord's Day, and of waiting on the gift of the Spirit in prayer after communion, inculcate the timely virtues of patience and faithfulness and perseverance, for God saves time from futility by coming as Spirit to dwell with us in time, and so returns time to us as gift rather than as threat (Wells, 1998: 142). Waiting for God becomes then an opportunity for renewal and blessing in the *present*, rather than of frustration or despair at the long delay of the Second Coming (Vanstone, 1982). The practice of waiting on the Spirit, and the time-shaping virtues of patience and endurance are threatened, undermined, by the promise of technology to "save" time: waiting on God in the silence of prayer and meditation is then a sign of contradiction in relation to contemporary culture. Similarly, in a culture that idolizes speed and mobility and instant results, attention to such time-ful activities as feasting, hospitality, the nurture of children, care of the sick and the disabled is a sign and source of resistance and renewal. Technologies promise a whole range of short-cuts which are supposed to reduce the need to wait, and reduce the time involved in healing the sick, or growing and preparing food, or enjoying a piece of music. But time plays a key role in moral formation, for characterful living and the virtues are shaped over time, as well as giving meaning to the experience of time. What kinds of individuals are sustained by a culture of instant satisfaction of desire such as that offered by television watching, microwaveable food, or the video game? Some see a genealogical connection between the growth of incivility in public life, and increasing aggression and violence, and the repetition of these kinds of time-foreshortening experience, and between high suicide rates and high levels of technological mediation (Mander, 1991).

Albert Borgmann suggests that technological devices are potentially harmful to human flourishing because they displace what he calls "focal practices." Focal practices such as fly-fishing, cooking raw food, walking, and nurturing children provide experiences of moral agency which enable the discovery of true freedom and purposiveness, whereas technological devices that supplant such practices, while promising greater liberty, in fact fail to deliver it (Borgmann, 1984). Focal practices foster true agency by "centering" the individual, and by enabling disciplined engagement in relationships with particular people and places over time. Choice, comfort, pleasure, and security are the fruits promised by technological devices, but they do not make for rich and characterful living. Technological devices also promise us control over our lives and our destinies but, by subverting true self-mastery, this sense of control is illusory. The promise of technological control also subverts Christian eschatology, and the awareness that our times and the creation are not our own but in the hands of a good and generous creator who gives us time to become the kinds of people we are made to be, and to experience the richness of community in which the weak, the poor, the disabled, the unsuccessful, and our fellow beings in creation, are cared for and honored (Wells, 1998: 146).

Veni Sancte Spiritus

In the silence of prayer after communion Christians enter the presence of God without the aid of technology. They are reminded that before they are auto engineers or software designers or pharmacists they are children of God. In the silence they recall that their dependence on God goes deeper than their reliance on technological devices, and that God is the one who can supply all their needs. In the silence Christians reflect on the week that has gone by and the week that is beginning. They rest and rejoice in the rhythm of the weekly Eucharist in which what has been done is transformed through confession, forgiveness, and celebration and what will be done is laid before Christ who is the foundation of every good work. And Christians recall in the silence that Christ has not left them alone to do his work after he has met with them in the Eucharist, any more than he left his disciples alone after the Ascension. Instead, he promises to be with them in the presence of the Holy Spirit who is the source of all Christian action to transform the world toward the reign of God.

In churches influenced by the Pentecostal and charismatic traditions, the *nouveau liturgie* of the twentieth-century liturgical movement, or the French Taizé community, spiritual songs are often sung during the administration of communion, to aid worshipers in their reflections, to encompass their prayers in a musical temple of praise, and to invoke the empowering presence of the Holy Spirit. Many of these songs enjoin Christians to continually invite the Holy Spirit into their lives as the one who can heal them from sin, reframe their intentions, and transform their actions into a sharing of God's own life. Some of the most ancient songs of the Church are imprecations of the Spirit such as the plainsong chant *Veni Creator Spiritus*:

> Come Holy Ghost our souls inspire
> And lighten with celestial fire
> Thou the anointing Spirit art
> Who dost thy sevenfold gifts impart.

And a popular contemporary Holy Spirit incantation sung in St James's, Leith, where I worship, goes as follows:

Spirit of the living God, fall afresh on me
Spirit of the living God, fall afresh on me
Break me, melt me, mould me, fill me
Spirit of the living God, fall afresh on me.

Such invocations, sung in the time during the administration of the communion elements, amplify and bring to mind the eucharistic epiclesis in which the Spirit is invoked as the power of God to transform both the elements of bread and wine into the body and blood of Christ, and the lives of those who partake of the sacrament into sanctified lives which embody and display in the world the fullness of life lived in the presence and power of God.

In the New Testament, the Spirit is revealed as the presence of God in the new dispensation under which Christians live between the return of Christ to his heavenly home and his coming again. In Ephesians, the Spirit is described as "the earnest of our inheritance" as the newly adopted children of God waiting for redemption, which was the divine intention since "before the foundation of the world" (Ephesians 1: 3: 14), and in Romans the whole creation is said to wait in eager anticipation for the redemption of the children of God which the Spirit is bringing near (Romans 8: 21–3). The Spirit realizes the mystery hidden until the coming of Christ, which is the adoption of the children of God to become heirs of eternal life:

He saved us, not because of any works of righteousness that we had done, but according to his mercy, through the water of rebirth and renewal by the Holy Spirit. This Spirit he poured out on us richly through Jesus Christ our Saviour, so that, having been justified by his grace, we might become heirs according to the hope of eternal life. (Titus 3: 5–7)

As Yves Congar observes, it is through the Spirit that Christians experience the grace and gift of divine holiness in their lives in the present, for there is no objective presence of grace in worship or in Christian living apart from the Spirit for "only God is holy, and only he can make us holy" (Congar, 1983: 68). In other words, the sacraments are not objective channels of grace *apart from* the Spirit who dwells in the lives of the people of God who assemble to celebrate the Sacraments. This "indwelling" is not automatic or to be taken for granted by Christians for the gift of the Spirit is, and has often been, neglected by Christians (Congar, 1983: 69). Christians should emulate the advice that Paul gives to Timothy to "stir up the gift of God which is in you by the laying on of hands" (2 Timothy 1: 6).

This recognition is an important corrective to the overemphasis in Catholic theology, at least since Thomas Aquinas, on the outward performance of the sacrament, as if the performance of the sacrament alone can act as a guarantee of grace and as source of the moral life. There is plenty of evidence from the history of the Church that this is not the case; nor does anything in the New Testament justify this over-objectification of the graced action of the Holy Spirit in the sacraments. The Eucharist was celebrated in churches whose patrons burnt crofting communities out of their homes at the time of the Clearances in Scotland, and among the communities of settlers in North America who oversaw the genocide of Native American communities and the violent expropriation of their lands. The Eucharist was celebrated in German Lutheran churches that were literally next door to Nazi concentration camps where the Holocaust was taking place but to which the worshipers turned a "blind" eye (Forrester, 2000). The Eucharist was celebrated on the aircraft carriers that carried the planes that dropped the atomic bombs that devastated Hiroshima and Nagasaki.

The Catholic and sacramentalist understanding of the Eucharist as the *origin* of the new reality which characterizes ecclesial reality after the Ascension (Pickstock, 1998) neglects the eschatological provisionality of the institution of the Eucharist. But the New Testament witnesses all agree that it is the Spirit of God who is the one who transforms the prayers and the lives of Christians, including their engagement as citizens and neighbors with the "world," into a sweet incense whose fragrance is genuinely pleasing to God. And this transformation relativizes and exceeds reliance on outward ritual or satisfaction with inward piety.

Given that Christians live in this eschatological provisionality between the old and the new aeons, they have a twofold task of discernment in the present, for, as William Stringfellow puts it, they need to be able to

> interpret ordinary events in both apocalyptic and eschatological connotations, to see portents of death where others find progress or success but, simultaneously, to behold tokens of the reality of the Resurrection or hope where others are consigned to confusion or despair. Discerning signs does not seek spectacular proofs or await the miraculous, but, rather, it means sensitivity to the Word of God indwelling in all Creation and transfiguring common history, while remaining radically realistic about death's vitality in all that happens. (Stringfellow, 1973: 139)

The discernment of signs arises directly from the celebration of the Eucharist, and from the correspondence between worship in Word and Spirit and the truth of God as creator and redeemer of all that is. Just to the extent that God is truthfully worshiped, so Christians are invited and empowered to engage responsibly with God's world in such a way as to resist the principalities and powers and the worship of idols which bring death, and to promote the path of peace and of divine, rather than merely human, justice (Stringfellow, 1973: 139).

The authority for Christians to discern the signs of the times arises from the gift of the Spirit whom Jesus promised would enable the disciples to "testify on his behalf" (John 15: 26). But, for want of gratitude to the God who gives Godself graciously in the Spirit, Christians too often fail to "stir up the gift" that is in them (2 Timothy 1: 6) and so are disabled from testifying boldly and prophetically to the portents of death in modern consumer culture (Stringfellow, 1973: 140). For it is the work of the Spirit to alert us to the falsely structured nature of reality which continues to stand in contradiction to the Resurrection of Jesus and the gift of the Spirit which bring eternal life into the present sinful world, for the Spirit is the one who convicts the world, and us, of sin (John 16: 8; O'Donovan, 1986: 104).

Reliance on the Spirit as the one who makes present the reality of Christ's triumph over the powers is the true source of a genuinely eschatological ethic. The spiritual gift of discernment enables Christians critically to juxtapose the promised kingdom with the idolatrous claims of the fallen powers who continue to hold much of humanity in their thrall. And such an ethic does not just involve the claim that God has already done all that is needed for things to "come out right" (Hauerwas and Willimon, 1999: 57). It also means "utilizing the diverse and particular charismatic gifts as the ethics and tactics of resistance to the power of death in the assurance that these gifts are in their use profoundly radically triumphantly humanizing" (Stringfellow, 1973: 152).

We may discern the continuing cultural "power of death" in the willingness of the United States, Britain, and France to manufacture and sell technologies of mass destruction to governments in Africa, Asia, Latin America, and the Middle East; in the sacrifice of so many human lives in Africa to the tyranny of external debt repayments and the associated "deregulation" of the marketing of food, fiber, timber, and even water; in the sacrifice of indigenous communities for development projects like the Narmada dam in India which will submerge the lands and homes of 20 million Dalits; in the plunder of the environment, or the imprisonment of millions of animals in cages for the production of cheap protein; in the sacrifice of childrens' moral and spiritual formation on the altar of a fashion industry which would turn them into consumers almost as soon as they can talk.

Discerning and resisting the multiple manifestations of the death ethic does not mean announcing that humanity, or the Church, or Christians, are responsible for saving the world from itself. But it does mean that Christians who have learnt that ethics is sacramental, material, embodied in practices, and who are emboldened by the Spirit to seek the good and resist evil, are called to participate in "some forms of Christian direct action in the name of creating a responsible society" (Hauerwas, 1981: 220). Christians have no mandate to abandon the world as presently structured out of trust in the future that God has promised to bring in at the end of time, or out of a quietist enjoyment of the gift of the Spirit. On the contrary, the Spirit is the one who is the source of that moral agency and freedom that confirms Christians as moral subjects able to act confidently in the world God has declared God intends to redeem:

> in confirming us as subjects he teaches us how, within this age of eschatological judge-ment, we may act. To do this he does not take over our subjecthood: he enables us to realize it. In a sentence of critical importance for theological ethics Saint Paul wrote: "God is at work in you, both to will and to work for his good pleasure" (Phil 2: 13). (O'Donovan, 1986: 106)

The Spirit enables our moral agency by enlightening our minds to the reality of sin, and by removing the veil that sin placed over our minds so that when we hear the narratives of the Word in the liturgy we hear its message of freedom from sin and redemption for eternal life (2 Corinthians 3: 16). The Spirit frees us both to know and to participate in the redemption of the created order, which is inaugurated in the resurrection of Christ. And this freedom is the very basis of the possibility of moral enquiry: "that man is free implies that he can know and act; thus moral enquiry is a meaningful undertaking for him" (O'Donovan, 1986: 107). But this moral freedom is not freedom to live according to our own lights, for when our freedom is derived from the Spirit of God then it is immediately demonstrated in self-binding to the service of others:

"You, my friends, were called to be free; only beware of turning your freedom into licence for your unspiritual nature. Instead, serve one another in love" (Galatians 5: 13).

The spiritual gift of freedom drives the Church and Christians to express moral agency creatively in the present, not in excessive reliance on legal codes or religious rituals, nor in a deferral to the divine future. And this living in the present stands in direct opposition to the "pathological inability" of many of our contemporaries "to live in the present" (Gunton, 1993: 99). Only eucharistic eschatology united with pneumatology can overcome the modern state's endless deferral of the prospects of peace, both human and ecological, to some future state toward which present sacrifices on the twin altars of war and economics are said to bring us, and the rest of creation, closer.

After communion then, Christians recollect that they live between the Ascension and the *parousia* and are called, as Thomas Merton (1973) reminded us, to both contemplation *and* action. This liturgical moment between the sharing of communion and the sending out into the world ritualizes the need for Christians to hold together the Ascension and the *parousia*, the vision of the ascended one and the hope of the coming reign of peace, contemplation and action. Only when Christians embrace the creative tension between vision and hope can they truly discern the signs of the times and their eucharistic communities become loci of spiritual resistance to the ethic of death.

References

Barth, Karl (1961) *Church Dogmatics: The Doctrine of Creation*, trans. T. H. L. Parker et al., ed. G. W. Bromiley and T. F. Torrance, vol. III, part 4 (Edinburgh: T. and T. Clark).

Bellah, Robert N., et al. (1999) "Democracy Means Paying Attention," in *Scanning the Future: 20 Eminent Thinkers on the World of Tomorrow*, ed. Yorick Blumenfeld, pp. 217–34 (London: Thames and Hudson).

Bergson, Henri (1913) *An Introduction to Metaphysics*, trans. T. E. Hulme (London: Macmillan).

Borgmann, Albert (1984) *Technology and the Character of Contemporary Life: A Philosophical Inquiry* (Chicago: University of Chicago Press).

Congar, Yves (1983) *I Believe in the Holy Spirit*, trans. David Smith (London: Geoffrey Chapman).

Cullman, Oscar (1951) *Christ and Time: The Primitive Christian Conception of Time and History* (London: SCM).

Ellul, Jacques (1964) *The Technological Society* (New York: Vintage).

Farrow, Douglas (1999) *Ascension and Ecclesia: On the Significance of the Doctrine of the Ascension for Ecclesiology and Christian Cosmology* (Edinburgh: T. and T. Clark).

Forrester, Duncan B. (2000) "The Church and the Concentration Camp: Some Reflections on Moral Community," in *Faithfulness and Fortitude: In Conversation with the Theological Ethics of Stanley Hauerwas*, ed. Mark Thiessen Nation and Samuel Wells (Edinburgh: T. and T. Clark).

Funkenstein, Amos (1986) *Theology and the Scientific Imagination from the Middle Ages to the Seventeenth Century* (Princeton, NJ: Princeton University Press).

Gunton, Colin E. (1993) *The One, the Three, and the Many: God, Creation, and the Culture of Modernity* (Cambridge: Cambridge University Press).

—(1998) *The Triune Creator: A Historical and Systematic Study* (Edinburgh: Edinburgh University Press).

Harvey, David (1989) *The Condition of Postmodernity: An Enquiry into the Origins of Cultural Change* (Oxford: Blackwell).

Hauerwas, Stanley (1981) "The Nonresistant Church: The Theological Ethics of John Howard Yoder," in *Vision and Virtue: Essays in Christian Ethical Reflection* (Notre Dame, IN: Notre Dame University Press).

—(2000) *A Better Hope: Resources for a Church Confronting Capitalism, Democracy, and Postmodernity* (Grand Rapids, MI: Brazos).

—and Burrell, David (1989) "From System to Story: An Alternative Pattern for Rationality in Ethics," in *Why Narrative? Readings in Narrative Theology*, ed. Stanley Hauerwas and L. Gregory Jones (Grand Rapids, MI: Eerdmans), esp. pp. 158–90.

—and Willimon, William H. (1999) *The Truth about God: The Ten Commandments in Christian Life* (Nashville, TN: Abingdon).

Mander, Jerry (1991) *In the Absence of the Sacred: The Failure of Technology and the Survival of the Indian Nations* (San Francisco: Sierra Club).

Merton, Thomas (1973) *Contemplation in a World of Action* (San Francisco: Harper and Row).

Moltmann, Jürgen (1965) *Theology of Hope*, trans. J. Leitch (London: SCM).

O'Donovan, Oliver (1986) *Resurrection and Moral Order: An Outline for Evangelical Ethics* (Leicester: Inter-Varsity Press).

Pettit, Philip (1993) "Consequentialism," in *A Companion to Ethics*, ed. Peter Singer (Oxford: Blackwell), esp. pp. 230–40.

Pickstock, Catherine (1998) *After Writing: On the Liturgical Consummation of Philosophy* (Oxford: Blackwell).

Rawls, John (1972) *A Theory of Justice* (Oxford: Clarendon Press).

Roberts, Richard H. (1989) "Karl Barth's Doctrine of Time: Its Nature and Implications," in *Karl Barth: Studies in his Theological Methods*, ed. Stephen W. Sykes (Oxford: Clarendon Press).

Singer, Peter (1975) *Animal Liberation: A New Ethics for our Treatment of Animals* (New York: Random House).

Sahlins, Marshall (1972) *Stone Age Economics* (Chicago: Aldine).

Schweiker, William (2000) "Time as Moral Space: Moral Cosmologies, Creation and Last Judgement," in *The End of the World and the Ends of God*, ed. Michael Welker and John C. Polkinghorne (Harrisburg, PA: Trinity).

Stringfellow, William (1973) *An Ethic for Christians and Other Aliens in a Strange Land* (Waco, TX: Word).

Vanstone, William H. (1982) *The Stature of Waiting* (London: Darton, Longman and Todd).

Wainwright, Geoffrey (1971) *Eucharist and Eschatology* (London: Epworth).

Wells, Samuel (1998) *Transforming Fate into Destiny: The Theological Ethics of Stanley Hauerwas* (Carlisle: Paternoster).

CHAPTER 32

Being Thankful: Parenting the Mentally Disabled

Hans S. Reinders

I

Like most people in our present culture, many Christians have a problem with relating to those of their number often called "mentally disabled." Their presence in the congregational life is seldom a matter of course, nor is their participation in the liturgy always welcomed (Webb-Mitchell, 1994). Not unlike society in general, church life is influenced by social stigma that identifies them as not inhabiting the patterns of normal human behavior. Of course, the educated mind knows that the notion of normal behavior is contestable. Given the increasing variety of "lifestyles" in our times, we are used to widely diverging conceptions of what counts as "normal." Notwithstanding this growing range of cultural diversity, however, the fact is that people with mental disability are generally perceived to be different in a different way (Reinders, 2000). Particularly those often called "profoundly disabled," they are seen as being different in a way that affects contemporary culture's very notion of humanity. With its heavy emphasis on the self, this notion not only highlights the fact that disabled human beings have limited abilities, but that mentally disabled human beings in particular may not even have a clear conception of themselves. The lives of such people are not just seen as culturally diverse. They are perceived to be different in ways such that many people hardly recognize these lives as human lives at all.

As indicated, such perspectives do not remain undisputed. Critical social science suggests that they represent cultural patterns of domination. It is by means of "binary oppositions" – for example, the opposition between "rational" and "irrational," or between "normal" and "abnormal" – that contemporary culture provides the social order it represents with the necessary symbolic underpinnings. The opposition between "ability" and "disability" is just another example of this. Such oppositions function to identify people *vis-à-vis* the gravitational centers of cultural domination.

It is from these centers of power that people are divided between "us" and "them." But the concepts by means of which these identifications take place are "social constructs." This characterization is claimed to be true even for the most fundamental concepts such as the concept of the human. That is to say, there are no perceptions of what is "human" that are not culturally conditioned, any more than there are perceptions of what is "normal" or "rational" that are not so conditioned. Social constructivism, critical social scientists suggest, goes all the way down. However, social constructivism notwithstanding, when confronted with mentally disabled human beings, particularly when they are profoundly disabled, many people experience a sense of difference bordering on strangeness. Even though it is clear that the population of people with mental disability is as diverse as any other, this knowledge does not seem to have much influence on public perception.

Perhaps this perception of a difference beyond the scope of diversity explains why the response by Christians and the Christian churches to people with mental disability often resembles that of our culture at large. Christian responses may have been colored by sympathetic pity, but more often the response has been one of ignorance. Consequently, the presence of disabled people as members of Church communities continues to be the exception rather then the rule. It is against this background that I will consider the question of what it might mean for Christians to be grateful for the presence of mentally disabled human beings.

II

Before I start, a few preliminary remarks are appropriate. It is, indeed, through the influence of social constructivism that more people have come to understand that language and terminology are never innocent with regard to patterns of domination. Therefore, some points about composing a text on a sensitive topic such as the present one deserve to be made explicit. When in this text I speak of "we," "our," and "us" – as I frequently will – the reference of these pronouns will always be members of the Christian community. Among these members there will be many for whom a prayer of thanksgiving for the presence of a person with a mental disability requires an explanation. Mental disability appears to them a condition to be deplored, if anything, so what could it mean to be grateful for it? It is with this perspective that I identify myself in this text and try to explain what it is that we need to understand.

Furthermore, the exploration of my topic proceeds predominantly from the perspective of the parents of disabled children, which means that people with mental disability will appear in reflections about other people's experience with them. I hope that readers will not regard this as another example of "objectifying" a group of people who are not appropriately recognized as "subjects." As a careful reading of particularly the last sections will show, there they do appear as subjects in a very important sense. Nonetheless, the reason for taking the perspective of their parents seriously lies, again, in the expression of gratitude. Too often I have witnessed parents of disabled children getting very angry about the language of "gratitude" and "gift" with regard to these children, particularly when that language is spoken by other people. There is a sense in which the use of that language is cheap, namely when spoken by those who have not given themselves the trouble of sharing these children's lives. There may be much to be grateful for, but not everyone is in a position to say so. It is therefore appropriate, I think, to approach my topic holding in the back of one's mind the question of how their parents may respond to what is said.

Finally, in this text I will speak of people with mental disabilities as if they share one and the same identity, whereas in fact they are just as diverse as the members of any other group. I do not regard that as a problem, however. On the contrary. When diversity is claimed for these people as well, this is usually directed against those accounts of their lives that are focused on their disabilities, while ignoring whatever abilities they may have. The result of this conceptual move, I am afraid, is that what is claimed with regard to their lives is usually *not* true – or only marginally true – for people with profound mental disabilities. I support the view that whatever abilities any human being has, or might be capable of developing, need our full attention. But I also want claims about people with mental disabilities to be true of each and every one of them. So, what in their presence is claimed to be reason to be grateful for cannot be of a kind that excludes some of these people from the truth of such claims.

III

Let me relate this chapter to the general argument underpinning this volume. As that argument claims, Christian ethics is ethics from "within." It does not proceed on the basis of a fundamental philosophical account of what morality is, in order to identify subsequently what Christian morality is. Christian ethics properly understood is not adding its own "content" to a primary logic that is non-Christian. Instead, it is defined as reflection on the ecclesial practices that shape the moral lives of Christians participating in these practices. Among these practices the celebration of the Eucharist is central.

Following the liturgical order of this volume, it is now time to respond to God's gift of the Eucharist with the prayer of thanksgiving. Christians rejoice in the gift of the body of Christ that has been broken for us, and they express their gratitude for that gift in prayer. Is it appropriate to include the expression of gratitude for the presence of the mentally disabled in this prayer, and, if so, what is it that Christians have reasons to be grateful for? One way to approach this question is to say that God does not necessarily give us the gift that we think we should be given, and that the gift of the mentally disabled belongs in this category. As we will see later, there is a profound truth in this, but as it stands this answer has a ring of negativity to it that needs to be dispelled. God does not send disabled children into the world in order to teach us a lesson.

IV

In the Gospel of John the dialectic between seeing and blindness informs many of the stories it tells. The dramatic epitome of this dialectic is the story of the man born blind who receives eyesight from Jesus (John 9: 1–12, 13–34, 35–41).

As Jesus walks by a man who has been blind from birth, his disciples ask whether this man or his parents have sinned. The question suggests that the misfortune of being born blind is the result of somebody's fault. The logic that brings it about is the logic of retribution: who did the wrongdoing that was punished with blindness? As it stands, however, Jesus does not answer the question. In fact, he ignores the issue it raises ("Can guilt been passed on from one generation to another?"). Instead, he puts the question in an entirely new light. The man was born blind so that God's work may be revealed in him.

As it develops, the story nowhere reiterates the initial question but unfolds by telling how Jesus heals the man's blindness, which is again an occasion of hostile confrontation with the Pharisees. Having interrogated the man, they turn to his parents: "Is this your son, who you say has been born blind?" (John 9: 18–23). The parents confirm this, but refuse further comments because they are afraid of getting into trouble. Then they turn to the man again and ask him by whose authority Jesus can do such things. The man answers: "Here is an astonishing thing! You do not know where he comes from, and yet he opened my eyes. We know that God does not listen to sinners, but he does listen to one who worships him and obeys his will . . . If this man were not from God, he could do nothing" (John 9: 24–34). The Pharisees are offended and send him away. Jesus approaches him with the question of whether he believes in the Son of Man. When asked who that might be, Jesus answers "I am," whereupon the man confesses that he believes. Jesus states what is evidently the point of the story by saying that he came into the world so that those "who did not see may see and those who do see become blind."

V

What reasons do we have to be grateful for the presence of people with mental disability in our communities? How do they reveal the work of God? What does it mean to say that their presence is a gift?

From what the story in John 9 tells us, the notion to start with, in this connection, is the notion of "seeing as." There is in this story a hovering between metaphor and miracle. Surely the story of how Jesus heals the blind man is intended to be seen as a miracle, something unheard of. "Never since the world began has it been heard that anyone opened the eyes of a person born blind" (John 9: 32). But at the same time the ability to see has a spiritual meaning. The Pharisees, who claim to know God but reject the one he sent, are spiritually blinded. Because they do not see Jesus as the Son of Man, they must remain in the dark. ("If you were blind, you would not have sin. But now that you say, 'We see!,' your sin remains": John 9: 41.) The confrontation with Jesus reveals our blindness which needs to be healed. That is what the Pharisees fail to see. The question of how the blind man reveals the work of God, then, apparently depends on how that healing is to be understood.

The question now is what this story tells us about the presence of people with profound disabilities in our midst. Do they also partake in revealing the work of God, and, if so, how? What, if anything, do they teach us about our own need to be healed? Whatever we want to say about these questions will depend a great deal on how the presence of the disabled in our community is seen. In what light do we understand that presence? I suggest that we continue to explore the richness of the notion of "seeing as" in connection with these questions.

Outside the context of the Gospel, the lives of disabled people are seen in various lights depending on different practices. Those whose perception is shaped by medical practice usually see people with disabilities as people with a particular kind of pathology. Their bodies don't function well when compared with the "normal" functioning of other human bodies. Because of the fact that it has dominated the lives of disabled people for more than a hundred years, this way of "seeing as" has acquired a name. It is called "the medical model." The medical model is a defect model. It is now generally criticized for its tendency to regard people with disabilities as patients, not only in a medical, but also in a moral sense. Given their physical and/or mental "malfunctioning," they lack the ability to run their own life. To be labeled "mentally disabled" is to be seen as "defective" on both counts. Medical training creates a propensity to regard them as such.

The medical model has been replaced. In the past decade social services have adopted "the support model," which is based on seeing people with disabilities as human beings with their own potential. Their lives are to be given back into their own hands and they should receive adequate support to develop the skills enabling them to run their own lives. The support model is backed up by yet another model. The "civil rights model" perceives the disabled again in a different light, which is that of equal citizenship. This model prevails in political contexts where the issue of equality and justice is pursued. People with disabilities ought to have every possibility to live the lives that other citizens enjoy, which includes housing, paid labor, medical treatment, and recreation. Whether in a medical, a social, or a political context, each of these contexts is shaped by a particular understanding of the practices by which they are constituted. Each of these contexts has its own way of "seeing as."

In contrast, Christian ethics springs from the question of what it means to see in the light of the gospel. The story of the man born blind indicates an answer that is as simple as it is profound: it is our vocation to see a disabled person in the light of Jesus as sent by the Father. As his teaching tells us, that is the decisive point which decides between seeing or remaining in the dark. Depending on where our hearts are, we will see differently.

Seeing a disabled person in the light of the gospel is easier said than done, however. As documented by many stories told by parents of disabled children, their hearts are often torn apart by the experience of disappointment, of failure, and guilt. This is particularly true of the first stage of these children's lives. Accordingly, the question the disciples put before Jesus betrays a thought all too familiar to these parents. The devastation that most families experience in this initial stage causes a great crisis in their perception of the world. "Our world fell apart," is the expression that gives a voice to this experience. It evokes in many parents a sense of being victimized: "Why me? What did I do wrong to deserve this?" However, as we have learned from the story of John 9, this is not the question that Jesus wants us to think about. That question assumes a logic of retribution. If something bad happens to people, it must be somebody's fault. Jesus wants us to think about God in a different light, the light of the father who sends his Son. He therefore leaves the question and ignores the logic of retribution as if totally beside the point. The blindness of the man occurred, he says, so that God's work may be revealed in him. If this claim is not about punishment or retribution, then what is it about?

VI

Before we enter into this question let me bring in a few caveats. As already indicated in section II of this chapter, parents of disabled children are weary of those who believe that they can answer the question of "meaning." The first caveat therefore is a moral one. Obviously, things may go very wrong when the parents are told, for example, that their disabled child is a blessing, that she is a special gift of God, or that sharing their lives with her must be an enriching experience. Very often, when these things are said, they are said by the wrong people at the wrong time. The reason is that their saying does not match their doing. When Jesus tells his disciples that the man is born blind so that the work of God may be revealed, he immediately adds: "We must work the works of him who sent me while it is day." That is what distinguishes them from the Pharisees. They say "He is our God" though they do not know him, according to Jesus, to which he adds: "But I do know him and I keep his word" (John 8: 55).

In other words, true knowledge of God goes with keeping his word. Saying that a disabled life is a blessing can be utterly false and deceitful, therefore, when not underwritten by acts of compassion. This is particularly true with regard to suffering. Parents know when their children suffer. The sight of a child with, say, severe epileptic convulsions, is horrible. Parents cannot witness this sight without feeling the anxiety and panic in their own bodies. In that connection, words about a blessing or gift may become lies when people make such statements in order not to let the pain get under their skin. Without being embedded in acts of compassion, any statement about disabled lives revealing the works of God is a self-referential contradiction. *Pia fraus sed fraus* (It may be pious fraud to say so, but it is fraud anyway).

This does not mean that it is inappropriate to think about the life of a disabled child as a gift. Many wonderful stories about people sharing their lives with a disabled person use such words as "enrichment," "blessing," or "gift" (de Vinck, 1988; Meyer, 1995; Oe, 1996; Klein and Schive, 2001). When spoken in truth such words reflect experience. They are spoken truly by people who have acquired the skills to see the disabled person in such a light that her presence *does* appear a blessing. The statement cannot be intended as a moral claim about how disabled people ought to be viewed. Such statements are not properly made, that is to say, as statements to be used as a premise in an argument about how to think morally about the lives of disabled people. It is only for those who *do* partake in Jesus's task of "working the works" to speak of blessing. Consequently, anyone who believes the meaning of disabled lives to be that God's works may be revealed in them must be prepared to take up their part in making these works visible.

The second caveat is closely related. It is about repentance. Given who we are as Christians and what our lives are like, many of us are not very good in taking up our share of "working the works." I, for my part, have of late not been very faithful to my friends in the group home that I visit, beyond sending them postcards when I am traveling. This indicates another way in which a reference to Jesus's response to his disciples may turn into a lie. That happens whenever his words are spoken without connection to the confession of our sins. The Gospel of John epitomizes Jesus's confrontation with the Pharisees in a final judgment which says precisely this. The Pharisees will not be able to witness how God's work is revealed in the blind man because they are incapable of recognizing their blindness to God's truth. "If you were blind," Jesus tells them, "you would not have sin. But now that you say 'We see!,' your sin remains" (John 9: 41). If they were capable of confessing their sins their eyes would be opened.

Particularly the last of these caveats points in the right direction for answering our question. To be able to see disabled human beings in such a way that God's works may be revealed in them, it takes first of all to have appropriate self-knowledge. Unless our heart is with God we cannot see straight. We could not recognize his works even if they happen right under our noses. Appropriate self-knowledge in this connection begins with practicing humility to lay down our pride. It is clear that the Pharisees in the Gospel of John don't know how to do this. That is their sin. Because they don't see through their own hearts, they don't know God and vice versa. Self-knowledge and true knowledge of God are two sides of the same coin. Consequently, if we must learn to see the disabled such that God's work be revealed in them, we must learn to see ourselves in truth as we stand before them. Given the fact that our ways of seeing are shaped by the practices in which we are trained, the question comes down to where and how we acquire appropriate self-knowledge.

VII

With regard to this question I will turn to the witness of people who have shared their lives with mentally disabled persons in the communities of *l'Arche*, founded in 1964 by the Canadian Jean Vanier. Their stories tell us what it means to be part of a community that has chosen to live this kind of life. These stories witness how mentally disabled persons may bring people closer to God by bringing them closer to themselves. They account for the need to see the truth about ourselves in order to really understand what it means to be loved by God. Therefore I will look at some of the writings of Vanier and his friends about their experiences in *l'Arche* (l'Arche, 1982; Nouwen, 1997, 1998; Vanier, 1997).

The community houses of *l'Arche* are built on the conviction that it is important that there are people who chose *to be with* the disabled rather than *to do* something *for* them (Vanier, 1994: 18). "Being with" is the expression for wanting to share your life with somebody because you have chosen to be with that person.

> This is the challenge of l'Arche. It can be professionally interesting and profitable for someone to work with handicapped people as a teacher or a therapist. But who will live with them if they have no family or if they cannot get on with the family? And particularly, who will create a relationship with those who are severely handicapped and what

happens if the relationship is not immediately rewarding and gratifying? Who will be prepared to accept anger, violence or depression, hoping that under all the confusion and darkness lies the light of the person. Who will believe and trust in him more than they believe and trust in themselves? (Vanier, 1982: 260)

The difference between "doing for" and "being with" marks the crucial distinction between what professionals in social services for the disabled do and what the people of *l'Arche* communities intend to be doing. It is the distinction between professional intervention and personal presence. To do something for somebody is the intention of the professional worker whose job it is to provide services. To be qualified for the job one has acquired certain skills for certain specific tasks. But what kind of skills does one need, or what kind of qualifications are required, for healing a disabled person from not being loved? It is with regard to this practical question that the distinction between "intervention" and "presence" does its work.

> The handicapped person needs a warm, friendly, dynamic milieu where he or she can grow and develop. To create this type of atmosphere means essentially to create authentic relationships which are a source of security. If the handicapped person needs people who can do things for him, if he needs qualified educators, it is also vital for him to have people who are happy just to live and be with them, who are ready to commit themselves to a lasting relationship which becomes a deep friendship and a source of hope. (Ceyrac, 1982: 25–6)

The challenge of *l'Arche* is to be the kind of community where these things can happen. But for them to happen does not come easy. Community life is difficult, according to Vanier, because it takes more than a sufficient dose of energy, good will, and a noble ideal to commit yourself to a lasting friendship that can be a source of hope. The skills required for "being with" are of an unusual kind. There are many that come to *l'Arche* to get acquainted with its spirituality, to learn about its vision, or to make their relation with God more profound. All these, says Vanier, are objectives that constitute a school, but not a community (Vanier, 1994: 28). There are many, especially young people, who come because of their ideal to live in a community, or to be part of *l'Arche* to make the world a better place. But these are abstractions, which cannot but lead to disappointment (Vanier, 1994: 28). A community does not live from what its members think it should be, but from who they actually are. "Communities are only then communities," writes Vanier, "when they are open to others, when they are vulnerable and humble, when their members grow in love, compassion, and humility" (Vanier, 1994: 27). A community in Vanier's sense is constituted by a group of people "who have left the place where they lived before to be with others, to build mutual relations and live and work according to a new way of seeing human beings in their relationships to one another and to God" (Vanier, 1994: 17). This new way of seeing, what does it entail?

VIII

The most important, and most difficult, thing is to learn to see *oneself* in truth. Given the reality with which the mentally disabled confront us, this truth is about limitation, about fear, and about learning to see one's own brokenness. Consider the following quote by Odile Ceyrac, a French woman who joined the first l'Arche community in Trosly, and who was called to assist Vanier in his leadership. In that capacity she was responsible for overseeing the training of new assistants. Following the language of the beatitudes that people of l'Arche often use, Ceyrac speaks about the disabled as "the poor" (Phillippe, 1982). In describing the spiritual journey, she mentions a discovery that anyone who comes to l'Arche to live with disabled people has to make.

> The poor bring us to the discovery of our weakness, limitations, mental blocks, prejudices and handicaps. When we come to live in community with mentally handicapped people, we often feel we have to prove ourselves and show that we are someone. We need to be "successful." In fact, we are hiding our fragility behind the barriers of success. It is difficult to accept the challenge that our encounter with the handicapped person gives us. We have to pass through many trials before we are able to recognize that it is more often an attitude of domination behind our coming to be with the handicapped people, than a desire to listen. The discovery of this truth about ourselves implies a real stripping. The handicapped person has already lived through this stripping. If we cannot accept this, if we cannot accept our fragilities and handicaps as they are revealed to us, then we will probably not be able to live very long in community with our handicapped brothers and sisters. (Ceyrac, 1982: 34–5)

The most striking thing about this account – the example of which could multiplied with many others (Allier, 1982: 54; de Miribel, 1982: 72–3; Lenon and Lenon, 1982: 86–8) – is the lack of any self-congratulatory confidence about good deeds done. The dominant theme of the spiritual journey is not "giving to" but "receiving from." Yet this receiving comes from mentally disabled people who because of their need for assistance in the eyes of the world do not have much to give. This is what seeing the person in her relationship to oneself and to God entails. To learn how to receive from those who have nothing to give but what and who they are, this is the task that new assistants at l'Arche have to master. Without knowing how to receive, their days will be filled with frustrating experiences. The simplest acts – holding a spoon, drinking from a cup, opening one's mouth for a bite – are incredibly difficult and take all the patience you can muster, given the many other things that need to be done. Yet the only possible response is to accept all this without resentment. Responding in a rush, with impatience, with anger, with hidden agendas or pretexts, none of this will work. You will be stripped to the bone of whatever mood or motive there is behind your actions. There is no hiding yourself from people who know, better than anyone else, what it is to be exposed to someone else's will. The only thing that may work is to say: "OK, not my will, but your will be done." Trying to do it any other way will not bring you closer to the disabled person, nor will it lead to the friendship you seek as proof that you are doing all right.

It is important to note once again that this "new way of seeing" is not to be read as a prescription for moral virtue. Vanier and his friends are in no way concerned with "ethics" in the traditional sense of defending a normative account of what kind of people we ought to be as Christians. Instead, they are trying to describe the realities that govern their lives. Most striking is the description of how the spiritual journey of their being with the disabled actually works. It is in the mirror of their relationship with the disabled person that they renew their relationship with God. That is how the disabled reveal God's work in them.

IX

Of course, one can refuse to look into the mirror and blame the disabled person for not allowing a growing moral perfection through good deeds done – saying that she is "difficult," "demanding," "aggressive," or whatever predicate one may think of – but the most likely result, as Odile Ceyrac points out, is that one will leave the community. When we do look into the mirror, however, we will see our own fragility and limitation. The friendship given turns out to be conditional: it is given in the expectation of a return. What is received, therefore, is a truth about our own limits in the face of a human being who wants to be accepted unconditionally. That is the painful truth that has to be faced. The reason why it is painful is the discovery that the disabled person is still not seen as another human being in her own right, which is not very different from how the world sees her. As Odile Ceyrac indicates, however, this truth is likely to be exhibited in subtler ways than the world does, namely cloaked in the manner of sympathy.

Once this painful discovery is made, however, it may turn out to be for the good and become a salutary truth, according to the people of *l'Arche*. You begin to see that the initiative toward change does not come from acting but from responding. At this point, the accounts of the spiritual journey at *l'Arche* take this amazing turn that most people from outside find difficult to follow. These accounts speak in terms of a reversal of roles and talk about disabled people in their capacity as "teachers." Let me continue to quote from Odile Ceyrac.

> In the life we share together, we soon discover that they are our "teachers"; they give us more than we can ever give them, in terms of acceptance of our human condition, in the discovery of what is essential in our lives. This is a terribly demanding discovery. Frequently we want to flee from it. We need to be stimulated and encouraged, on a personal as well as on a communal level, in order to live it. The first moments of wonder in our encounter with the handicapped person have to be nourished and deepened. (Ceyrac, 1982: 27)

The "first moments of wonder" are those when the assistant begins to see that the disabled person may lead her or him toward greater openness to what is essential. What is essential in their lives is the discovery that those who are supposedly the ones who need healing become healers themselves. It is that the most important thing to know is not how to love and be good, but how to be loved despite our faults and failures. The most important thing is not to strive toward your own perfection but to learn to live with your imperfections.

To understand these things and how to live them is essential. Living with their imperfection is what mentally disabled people have been doing all their lives. That is how they become healers. "They can help and heal us; they can peel away our illusions and masks and thus they can liberate us. Little by little they can lead us to greater inner freedom. It is important for the handicapped person that we are free in our relationships with him" (Ceyrac, 1982: 35). The "moment of wonder" is the moment the possibility of love and friendship is discovered not in the fullness but in the brokenness of your life. The experience that the disabled person is leading in this discovery is the reason why their presence is seen in the light of the beatitudes, as the people of *l'Arche* do. Vanier makes a similar claim regarding this experience that sums up the point of their spiritual journey in a most profound way.

> Each of our Arche communities has experienced men and women, who are chaotic, broken and spiritually dead, evolving – after years in a big institution – into men and women of peace and light. These are not mere words. We have all seen the dead rise. It has happened before our eyes and in our homes. This has told us something about the depth, vulnerability and capacities of the human heart. (Vanier, 1982: 259)

X

Where have these reflections taken us with regard to the question with which I started? What does it take to see the mentally disabled in such a way that God's works may be revealed in them? Of course, the answer to this question largely depends on what one takes God's works to be. As we have seen, the disciples pose the issue of guilt, indicating that they think of retributive justice as God's work. Somebody must have sinned, otherwise there would be no blindness.

If people with disabilities are seen in this light, things tend to go wrong. First of all, when the disabled person is sent to balance the scales of retributive justice it is impossible not to see her existence as evil. Secondly, how do you manage to love what God has sent as punishment? As I indicated before, parents of disabled children often raise the question of personal guilt, but that question marks a catastrophe. Most parents, if not all, want to be grateful for the gift of life, but how to be grateful for a catastrophe?

These questions are suggestive, and many parents of newborn children with a disability have a hard time getting them out of their system. Their way of seeing their child needs to be transformed (Reinders, 2000: 175–92). But this is not only true of parents because the stories told by the people of *l'Arche* tell us exactly the same. Looking at the disabled from the perspective of frustrated expectations is the barrier that blocks the opening of our hearts to become their friends. We first have to learn to accept them as they are. Their lives are what we have received. The fact that we would rather have received something less frustrating and chaotic is largely beside the point. At least, this is what our Lord Jesus suggests when he responds to his disciples' question by ignoring it.

However, many Christians nowadays question the notion of God sending disabled people in the world so that we may become better people. The idea was once quite acceptable when a disabled person was seen as a *vehiculum caritatis*, a vehicle of charity. Some people in *l'Arche* have no problem with this traditional notion. Accordingly, Thomas Philippe wrote, referring to disabled people as the poor of the beatitudes: "The poor will become for him [the assistant at *l'Arche*] the *instruments of Providence* and will help him to discover the ultimate ends of his own being" (Phillippe, 1982: 40; emphasis added).

This notion does not go uncontested, however. To many contemporary Christians the very idea is appalling. They would rather argue that God would not be worthy of our praise if it were true. God cannot make innocent children suffer for his own purposes and still be God! Maybe. One has to be aware, however, that the interesting thing about this contemporary view of ethical Christianity is its hidden theological premise, which is that God the creator has to prove himself to be worthy of the praise of his creatures. One can, of course, stick to this theological premise, and blame God for not saving us from evil, but again the result is most likely to be that the disabled person is still perceived as the sign of an injustice.

As the story in the Gospel of John makes abundantly clear, Jesus does not see the blind man in that light. The disabled person is genuinely a gift. But in order to see that, we first have to learn to say words of thanksgiving to God for what we receive, which is not necessarily the same as what we would like to be given. As the stories from the houses of *l'Arche* suggest, we have to learn to receive the disabled person as God's child, which is quite different from receiving her in the light of our own dreams and expectations. To be capable of receiving another human being unconditionally takes appropriate self-knowledge. As said before, self-knowledge begins with practicing humility to lay down our pride. Once we know how to do that, we will find the way to receive the gift of the disabled person. We will open our hearts, the Spirit will enlighten us and send its love between us, and we will thank God for their presence among us.

The work of God that is revealed in the disabled person, then, is that she does not reject me for the limited person that I am. In that moment – the moment of wonder – it is revealed to me that the possibility of love persists against, and despite, my self-centeredness. It is in the mirror of this relationship that the disabled person reveals to me that God loves me in just that same manner. This is what the gospel of Jesus Christ is about. No doubt we can persist in our resentment and demand from God that he saves us from evil. As Jesus's judgment on the Pharisees indicates, however, this presumptuousness will leave us in the dark. Jesus wants us to see God differently.

XI

I want to conclude with a few lines by Sue Mosteller, who has spent many years in service of the Daybreak community of *l'Arche* in Toronto, Canada. Her account of her experience in sharing her life with disabled people says it about all.

> For me the quiet moments spent in God's presence at the beginning and at the end of each day are essential. These moments of silence in the presence of Jesus are necessary in order to try to integrate all the beauty and all the pain. And I feel so small. I am learning, however, that it is essentially in knowledge of my inability to look at the other, in my disappointment at my own reactions in a crisis, in my resentments and my harsh judgments that Jesus, the author of love, can touch me, can teach me, can heal me. In these precious

moments I learn to believe more deeply in the essential mystery underlying "blessed are the poor." I believe it, not because I live with handicapped people, the poor, but because I myself am so poor, so close to my limits, and at the same time so blessed in believing that I am a child of God, called to live with brothers and sisters, who journey together towards the Father. (Mosteller, 1982: 22)

The people of *l'Arche* are remarkable people. Not because of their moral achievement, but because of the way they have probed the gospel as it speaks to us in stories such as in John 9. Confronted with the brokenness of mentally disabled lives, they know there is no refuge in strength. Living with these people has taught them instead to accept the brokenness in their own lives. They have learned to accept this as a gift, the source of which is the gift of Christ. In the brokenness of his body, the Church proclaims the presence of God. That is what is celebrated in the Eucharist. The appropriate response to this celebration is a prayer to thank God for what we have received. In the eyes of the world what we have received does not count for much. For the world, the brokenness of God is as absurd as the brokenness of profoundly disabled human beings is scandalous. The world sees no cause whatsoever to be grateful for the presence of disabled people. Having enjoyed the communion of the Lord's Supper, Christians may begin to think and see differently.

References

Allier, Hubert (1982) "A Place for Human Growth," in l'Arche, *The Challenge of l'Arche*, pp. 51–68 (London: Darton, Longman and Todd).

l'Arche (1982) *The Challenge of l'Arche*, introduction and conclusion by Jean Vanier (London: Darton, Longman and Todd).

Ceyrac, Odile (1982) "The Poor at the Heart of our Communities," in l'Arche, *The Challenge of l'Arche*, pp. 24–36 (London: Darton, Longman and Todd).

Jonas, Robert A. (ed.) (1998) *Henri Nouwen: Writings Selected* (Maryknoll, NY: Orbis).

Klein, Stanley D. and Schive, Kim (eds) (2001) *You Will Dream New Dreams: Inspiring Personal Stories by Parents of Children with Disabilities* (New York: Kensington).

Lenon, Pat and Lenon, Jo (1982) "A Place for a Family," in l'Arche, *The Challenge of l'Arche*, pp. 84–96 (London: Darton, Longman and Todd).

Meyer, Donald J. (ed.) (1995) *Uncommon Fathers: Reflections on Raising a Child with a Disability* (Bethesda, MD: Woodbine House).

Miribel, Claire de (1982) "Growth Towards Covenant," in l'Arche, *The Challenge of l'Arche*, pp. 69–83 (London: Darton, Longman and Todd).

Mosteller, Sue (1982) "Living with," in l'Arche, *The Challenge of l'Arche*, pp. 11–23 (London: Darton, Longman and Todd).

Nouwen, Henry (1997) *Adam: God's Beloved* (Maryknoll, NY: Orbis).

—(1998) "The Road to Daybreak," in *Spiritual Journals*, pp. 292–448 (New York: Continuum).

Philippe, Thomas, OP (1982) "Communities of the Beatitudes," in l'Arche, *The Challenge of l'Arche*, pp. 37–50 (London: Darton, Longman and Todd).

Oe, Kenzaburo (1996) *A Healing Family* (Tokyo: Kodansha International).

Reinders, Hans S. (2000) *The Future of the Disabled in Liberal Society: An Ethical Analysis* (Notre Dame, IN: University of Notre Dame Press).

Vanier, Jean (1982) "Introduction and Conclusion," in l'Arche, *The Challenge of l'Arche*, pp. 5–13, pp. 256–73 (London: Darton, Longman and Todd).

——(1994) *La communauté: lieu de pardon et de fête* (Paris: Editions Fleurus).

——(1997) *Our Journey Home: Rediscovering a Common Humanity beyond our Differences* (Maryknoll, NY: Orbis).

Vinck, Christopher de (1988) *The Power of the Powerless* (Grand Rapids, MI: Zondervan).

Webb-Mitchell, Brett (1994) *Unexpected Guests at God's Banquet: Welcoming People with Disabilities into the Church* (New York: Crossroad).

CHAPTER 33

Washing Feet: Preparation for Service

Mark Thiessen Nation

"You know, we always have footwashing on Lord's Supper Sundays. And I'll tell you the truth, I wouldn't take the Supper if I couldn't wash feet" (Duke, 1995: 402). Perhaps many of us are not surprised to learn that this statement came from a mountain woman, a footwashing Baptist of Appalachia. We expect "this sort of person" to engage in the "primitive" practice of footwashing. But is footwashing a practice for all Christians?

Evidence from the New Testament and the writings of the early Church Fathers indicates that footwashing was both encouraged and practiced within the early Church (see Thomas, 1997: 174). Numerous Christian traditions since have also practiced it (see Knight, 1912). Many today continue to discover why footwashing can be a vital practice of the Church. But I suspect that a much larger number do not practice footwashing.

Why have many dismissed footwashing so easily? Has footwashing – and the New Testament text that authorizes the practice – too often been inadequately understood both by those who practice it and by those who don't practice it? Do those of us who call ourselves disciples of Jesus lack stories that demonstrate the significance of such a practice? Might footwashing have anything of significance to say to us about Christian ethics? This chapter attempts to move us toward responses to all of these questions.

Footwashing: The Text

An optional mandate?

In his careful and detailed study of John 13, John Christopher Thomas has shown that the practice of footwashing in this passage is mandated more clearly than the Lord's Supper (Thomas, 1991, 1997: 169–75). Not only does the lengthy narrative of the footwashing appear at a crucial juncture in the Gospel of John, but there is little ambiguity in the central admonition: "So if I, your Lord and Teacher, have washed your feet, you also *ought* to wash one another's feet" (John 13: 14, NRSV). So, why is it that many Christians do not feel that footwashing is mandated in the same way as the Lord's Supper?

Many of the churches that have practiced footwashing over the centuries have connected it to Maundy Thursday. The term is derived from the Latin, *Mandatum novum*, a new commandment. This new commandment appears in the same chapter, verse 34a: "I give you a new commandment: that you love one another." I sometimes wonder if it is not the starkness of the two mandates – whether to wash feet or to love – that has been less than alluring to many. Perhaps the Church needs to recapture the rich theological fabric of the text in order to hear the fullness of the gospel message that is communicated through this narrative.

The presence of Jesus as foundation for redefinition

John 13, like the gospel of Jesus Christ, like Christian ethics, does not begin with the utterance of a mandate, even one as important as "love one another." No, it begins with the presence of Jesus, the Christ. John begins this narrative by informing us that Jesus knows that his time is short. He will soon "depart from this world and go to the Father" (John 13: 1b). Of course, his departure will be protracted and painful. Painful not only to him but also to those who have attached their hopes for the future of Israel and of the redemption of the world to him, the one whom they have come to believe is the anointed one, the Messiah. That redemption – or the disciples' understanding of it – will need to be redefined on the far side of the crucifixion of their Savior. Jesus recognizes this need. In fact, that re-definition is already underway, especially around this supper table through the actions of the footwashing Lord and Master.

Jesus can face what lies ahead in Jerusalem because he is confident of his origin and destiny. He knows "that the Father had given all things into his hands" (John 13: 3). This confidence, this trust, is vital. Only with such trust do acts reflective of serious commitment make sense. Only with such knowledge can costly repercussions even be imagined as redemptive rather than merely painful. It is this "knowledge" that the disciples still desperately need.

And so, at this key juncture, a short time before he is to face execution, Jesus wants time alone with the inner circle of his disciples. John frames the scene in John 13 with the love of Jesus for his disciples. "Having loved his own who were in the world, he loved them to the end" (John 13: 1b). "Just as I have loved you . . ." (John 13: 34b). This is no stranger among them. This is Jesus, the Jesus they know, personally and intimately. It is not as if the enacted parable that is about to unfold will provide new information, but once again, on this redefining evening, Jesus visibly, powerfully, demonstrates his love for them. After Jesus shares a meal with them, perhaps his last meal with these close friends, Jesus rises from the table, takes off his outer garment, and ties a towel around himself. He then pours water in a basin and begins to wash the feet of his disciples.

Intimacy and cleansing

Paul Duke alerts us to an aspect of the context that we often miss. He writes of the disciples:

> We can feel them squirming. Their embarrassment is palpable, as enacted by Peter. But the dread is not so much centered in how menial an act Jesus has undertaken for them, as in how painfully intimate it is. It is often noted that Jewish slaves could not be required to wash feet, as if it were merely too servile a function. Overlooked is the fact that a man's feet were often washed by his wife or his children or by a welcoming host. An issue of intimate acquaintance seems to apply. The indignity for the disciples resides in their teacher's disarming initiative to touch them in this way, to bring himself so near and naked to their need, to apply himself to their private rankness, to cleanse for them what they would prefer almost anyone else to cleanse.

Duke continues: "No wonder Peter resists. He has signed up to follow Jesus, not to have the unpleasantness down at the foot of his life exposed and handled for him. He prefers the dignity of self-reliance, the fantasy of being heroic. The refusal of his feet to Jesus is precisely equivalent to his blithe belief that he is ready to follow and lay down his life for Jesus" (Duke, 1995: 399–400).

Like Peter, we, too, want our dirty feet kept to ourselves. We do not want them exposed, either to Jesus or to his followers. Along with Peter, we are more comfortable with the extraordinary deeds recorded earlier in John's Gospel. We delight in the extraordinary event in John, chapter two, where Jesus turns plain water into luxurious wine. But, together with Peter, we do not participate without hesitation in the miracle where Jesus turns clear water into dark murky water as he washes our feet. We squirm as he cleanses us of the dirt that accumulates on the soles of our feet and at the center of our lives. But if Jesus is to create a community of disciples who seriously follow him they will need to know that intimacy includes cleansing, vulnerability, and forgiveness.

We need this cleansing, this washing, not only once at our baptism but repeatedly. As Jesus is lovingly present with us, we need his cleansing, we need his washing of the filth that threatens to define our lives. Jesus knows that. Peter has been bathed, says Jesus. But still "unless I wash you, you have no share with me" (John 13: 8b).

Servanthood inspires faithfulness

Jesus could have expressed the cleansing of his disciples in any number of ways. However, he chose to express it through the intimate, yet humble act of washing feet, thereby demonstrating a lesson he had repeatedly taught. As we know from other texts, on earlier occasions Jesus had responded to the disciples' questions about greatness and leadership by contrasting the way he exercised authority with the ways of the Gentile rulers. He said, "I am among you as one who serves" (Luke 22: 27b; also Mark 10: 45).

But it is here, shortly before his departure, that Jesus chooses to leave the disciples with a visible image of who he has been, is, and will be among them. He recognizes that although this group of his friends knows who he is – "You call me Teacher and Lord" (John 13: 13a) – they need to know that central to his identity, his identity as Teacher and Lord, is his role as servant. And it is his love, his servanthood, and his sacrifice on their behalf that gives them life that already does and will continue to make their lives of faithfulness, their community of faithfulness, possible.

Karl Barth put it this way:

> It is surely worth noting that in the Fourth Gospel the story of the Last Supper is replaced by that of the foot-washing. The material message is the same, but how emphatically the latter emphasizes the fact that the service of Christ is His true power and majesty and therefore the grace by which man receives his life! – the revealed grace of God which was already the secret of the Old Testament, though operative then only in a vertical movement from above. In the New, however, it has really come down into the depths and manifested itself there, becoming itself service in accordance with this end of its way. The action of God which absolutely precedes all human action and therefore human service is that He has placed Himself wholly and unreservedly in the service of man as revealed and effectual in the sacrifice of Jesus. (Barth, 1961: 476–7)

Yes, indeed! Jesus "has placed Himself wholly and unreservedly" in the service of us mere mortals "as revealed and effectual in the sacrifice of Jesus."

Footwashing and the new commandment

After being reminded of their overall cleansing in baptism and of the loving and footwashing presence of Jesus, the disciples are ready to hear the New Mandate: "Just as I have loved you, you also should love one another" (verse 34). The meaning and shape of this love has just been demonstrated for them in the footwashing they have both witnessed and received. And they have just heard: "For I have set you an example, that you also should do as I have done to you . . ." (verse 15). Why then do we so readily separate the two mandates? Perhaps this is a good place to remember Barth's observation: "in the Fourth Gospel the story of the Last Supper is replaced by that of the footwashing." Most churches have seen the words "do this in remembrance of me" as a call regularly to repeat the action of eating together. Should the same churches not also hear the words "you also should do as I have done to you" as a call regularly to pick up the towel and basin? Is this not one way to fulfill the call to love one another as Christ has loved us?

And just as the Lord's Supper is not to be divorced from daily life, so here what Jesus is referring to is not simply a re-enactment of his washing of the disciples' feet (although that is not a bad place to begin). He has demonstrated what love is and what it means for them to love each other. It is interesting to note that John 13: 34 offers the first positive use of the verb *agapao* (love) for anyone other than Jesus or God in the Gospel of John. The verb has been used negatively three times in relation to humans (3: 19; 8: 42; 12: 43). Also, the only use of the noun, *agape*, in the Gospel has been negative (5: 42). It is as if only now – after the cleansing and after the perfect model – that human love can be spoken of positively as something that can bring life and redemption to the community of Jesus.

The Community of Footwashers

Here in John 13 Jesus is showing them how to have community, a redemptive and loving community. They are to be a community that confesses Jesus as teacher and Lord. They are to know that this Lord gave himself for them. They, too, are to give themselves to one another. Only so can they be true witnesses to the Great Footwasher. Only so can they know what it means to be in community in his name. Only so can they know what it means to serve and witness to him in the midst of the world.

Barth summarized it this way:

> To serve Jesus (Rom. 14.18, 16.18; Col. 3.24), and therefore to serve "the living and true God" (1 Thess. 1.9), to "serve him acceptably with reverence and godly fear" (Heb. 12.28), includes the reciprocal service that each should render the other (Gal. 5.13; 1 Pet. 4.10) in submission "one to another in the fear of God" (Eph. 5.21) . . . To belong to [Jesus], and to perform human action in this relationship, means *eo ipso* and *per se* to take His yoke upon oneself (Mt. 11.29), i.e., to serve and not to rule with Him, in His discipleship, according to His example and in correspondence with His action, and to do so, not in a self-chosen way which might well be a secret path of domination, but in participation in His commission and therefore among men and in the service of men. This is the criterion and test whether it is really the service of God, whether man is really obedient in His active life, whether in his own choice he is really responding to the divine choice and not going his own way and living for himself under the pretext of a self-chosen service. (Barth, 1961: 477)

Yes, we are called to a life of servanthood, as we follow the True Servant. However, it is not intended to be a life of drudgery. No, Jesus wants us to "know" what he knows, to know our destiny, our purpose in Christ. So, as Jesus assured his disciples he assures us: "If you know these things, you are blessed if you do them" (13: 17).

The narrative ends with a sober reminder. Yes, even in the midst of this holy room, at this sacred time, the disciples, and we, are reminded both of the reality that not everyone will embrace the love of Jesus and of the need for repeated cleansing. Peter, one of the inner circle, will soon deny Jesus (13: 36–8) – at least for a time. But, more ominously, Judas is present at this event. Judas is a reminder that "the light shines in the darkness" (1: 5a). However, it is also vital, at this time approaching the cross, that the disciples know that "the darkness did not overcome it" (1: 5b).

What might this text of Scripture mean within the life of the Church? What does the story of Jesus's intimate presence and cleansing, his servanthood and love, and his desire to prepare the disciples for the future teach us? How might individuals be formed by the practice of footwashing in the Church? Let me tell you a story.

Footwashing: A Story

It was the autumn of 1963. I was nine years old. I was with a small group of my friends. The school year was underway. We were happy to be alive. It wouldn't be long before the annual Fall Festival would be in town. There would be carnival rides, steam engines, games, a parade, and lots of friends gathered together in one place. (In my small home-town the Fall Festival was one of the highlights of the year.) As we talked, we strolled downtown, imagining out loud the transformation that would happen when the car-nival set up their equipment on the square. All of a sudden our excitement was eclipsed. We fell silent, each of us looking in the same direction. Then, as with one voice, we said: "If those niggers aren't out of this town by sundown they will be strung up."

I am not sure where we got these words. But our collective gut response to a black family walking around our downtown area probably echoed the sentiments of most of our parents, and the ethos of this proudly all-white community in southern Illinois.

This is a snapshot from my childhood. Of course, it is only a snapshot. There were many other realities that shaped who I was. Born in 1953, I was reared watching a considerable amount of television. Certainly my understandings of justice, righteous-ness, and violence were shaped by *Combat*, a drama about World War II; by *The Rifle-man*, an emotionally powerful drama about a single father in the "Wild West" of nineteenth-century America who protects his son and his community by killing many a bad man who is trying to do evil things; and by various other Westerns in which good and evil characters were fairly obvious and distinct. (One set of characters was worthy of doing the killing and the other deserving of the killing.)

Also, growing up in this small town, I had a strong sense of community, family, and the importance of friendships. Many different influences in my childhood, each in varying ways, defined my life and my understanding of reality. One shaping influence, however, that was almost completely absent within my childhood, was the Church. My father was fairly obviously not a Christian. And my mother was decidedly not connected to that entity that symbolized her own mother's overbearing religion.

But all of this was to change for me at the age of seventeen. New birth is quite an appropriate image for what happened to me in the autumn of 1970. It was the begin-ning of the acquisition of a new identity, a Christian identity. The inauguration of this identity was a dramatic conversion experience in a revival service at the First General Baptist Church of McLeansboro, Illinois. During most weeks over the next two years I attended church services at least three times per week. Various practices of the church served to re-shape me: Scripture reading (private and public), sermons, testimonies, music, the Lord's Supper, baptism, glimpses of Christians' lives – and one more which I vividly recall: footwashing.

I still remember Bob and Carlton Brockett on footwashing Sundays. Bob and Carlton were emotionally expressive brothers. Bob was a very big man with rough hands, a laborer on the railroad. He was also a humble and gentle man. When we washed feet, as during testimony services, Bob would almost always cry, confessing his unworthiness as well as his gratitude for the many good gifts God had given to him. He would express deep appreciation for the men standing there, kneeling there, washing one another's feet. These were his brothers in Christ and he was grateful for them.

Carlton could also hardly contain himself. He always wanted to communicate some-thing about the call upon our lives that was entailed by the reality that Christ had washed our feet and had enabled us to wash the feet of others. Carlton's words on footwashing days echoed his words uttered repeatedly during times of testimony, testimonies in which he would call upon all of us to link our lives of praise and worship within a Sunday church service to the lives we lived during the week.

I also remember the image of my pastor, Bill Duncan, getting down on his hands and knees and washing feet. Bill powerfully preached and embodied the Good News of Jesus Christ. Now, in this act, he was physically underscoring that message: Christ had given himself for us that we might give ourselves for others.

These intermittent footwashing services underscored, deepened, and broadened what I was coming to learn of the gospel within this church. Repeatedly, I heard sermons assuring me that God loved the world, loved it so much that Jesus died for everyone in the world. God desired that everyone be redeemed. Everyone! God was no respecter of persons. Furthermore, I was learning – through testimony services and songs – that our lives given to worship on Sunday mornings were to be congruous with the way we lived our lives throughout the week. This sense was reinforced through my own reading of the Scriptures and my glimpses of the lives of some of those I knew within this church. Our lives should echo the gift of salvation we had received, the repeated graciousness of God within our lives, and the call to live lives of faithfulness in whatever we were called to do.

For me this meant, among other things, that when I had to register for military service in October of 1971, I registered as a conscientious objector. At that point in my life I didn't even know the word pacifism. What I knew was that the One who washed my feet called me not only to wash the feet of my brothers and sisters in Christ. He also called me to love my enemies as well as my neighbors.

Some twenty years later, in 1992, I was not only living more than two thousand miles from my hometown, I had also metaphorically traveled a great distance from the person I was in 1971. Pacifism, as I learned to name my set of Christian convictions, was rooted in my Christian faith. My life-long journey of reflections on this peculiar "position" grew out of the realization that love and servanthood were inherent in the gospel.

Part of my journey during the twenty years since I first became a conscientious objector included learning from and with African Americans. The writings and testimonies of Martin Luther King Jr and John Perkins deepened my understanding of pacifism, reconciliation, forgiveness, and servanthood. That these extraordinary Christian leaders could simultaneously confront and forgive white people for their profound sin of racism was a testimony to the astonishing power of the gospel, and of the willingness to live out its implications in daily life.

This was no minor challenge, as my African American friends were to teach me. Glen Perkins, a young black man who shared a home with me for one and a half years, was the son of a man who had for many years been a consistent voice for justice for African Americans. Glen knew about injustice. He was a committed servant of God. Alton Trimble, a Pentecostal pastor, became a significant friend and conversation partner in Los Angeles. He shared with me what it meant to be a black man in Los Angeles. Alton told of how he, a black pastor, dressed in a three-piece suit, driving to a Bible study, was forced by the cops to get down on all fours on the pavement – simply because he is a black man. He told of being under constant surveillance when shopping, again simply because suspicions are attached to him because he is black. Alton's willingness to engage in honest and vigorous exchanges with me during the trial of O. J. Simpson was agonizingly instructive. I live with these stories from my African American friends and have been repeatedly taught what love, even love of enemies looks like, and what it might cost in real life. Again and again, I have marveled at the astonishing power of the gospel, in their lives and in mine. What a gift they were and are to me!

I tell of these relationships to set the context for an experience I had in the small church I pastored in Los Angeles. Every Maundy Thursday this church would practice footwashing. Several black Christians, including Ralph Ferguson, were members of the congregation. Having come from Alabama, Ralph knew what racism was up close and personal. He would not have been surprised to learn that my childhood included stereo-typing and ugly epithets intended to demean people of his color. And yet it never occurred to him – a profoundly Christian man – not to pick up a towel, place my feet, the feet of a white man, in the basin and wash my feet and allow me to wash his. More-over, it was our practice to embrace after the footwashing. The footwashing and the embrace reminded me that there is cleansing, there is redemption for those of us who have drunk the sin of racism with our mother's milk. Ralph taught me both physically and symbolically that reconciliation is possible, even in our painfully sinful world. The footwashing and the embrace, of course, are only symbols, but they are potentially potent. This is who Christ has been to us and who we are to be as his followers. So Ralph, a former military veteran-turned pacifist, believed; so Ralph lived.

Toward the end of 1997 I preached for the first time in over twenty-five years at the same church in which I became a Christian. In my sermon I mentioned how I had acquired a passion for serious discipleship, peace, and justice – particularly mentioning my convictions against war and racism – from this church, partly through the practice of footwashing. The congregation expressed appreciation for my words. I am delighted that my mother became a Christian and a member of this church several years ago. I have noted that on several occasions when my mother has been ill, the members of this church have visited her and taken food to her home. She has also learned to serve in ways she never did before.

I have been fortunate to have many people to help me see the "primitive" Christian practice of footwashing as something luminous, instructive, and vital for the life of the Church. So why is it that this potentially transforming practice has been quite uncom-mon in much of the Church?

Footwashing: An Uncommon Practice

Why is it that we so readily participate in communion, but shy away from footwash-ing? Unlike eating bread and drinking wine (or juice), which are common everyday practices in our lives, having our feet washed by others is decidedly not common. As such, it presents a far greater challenge to our sensibilities. We immediately sense that this practice includes a touch of intimacy, it exposes our need for cleansing, it reminds us of the call to humility and servanthood, and it moves our love for our sisters and brothers in Christ from a nice idea to a tangible expression. In short, many character qualities, which we praise with our words, are here graphically expressed, reminding us that Christ desires an embodied life in the Spirit.

Yes, footwashing is simply not the kind of ritual that we choose to do because it is pleasant. Unlike the candles, gold-plated chalices, white napkins, and gilded Bibles, and the carefully guided procedures for partaking of the bread and wine, footwashing cannot easily be made beautiful. It is simply earthy, no matter how clean the bowl or crisp the towel. Bending down to wash another person's feet challenges us on many levels – our dignity, our poise, our position.

Some have argued that because washing each other's feet, even within intimate relationships, is no longer a common practice, we ought to find an analogous practice within our culture, rather than practicing something so foreign and no longer necessary. They suggest that serving each other in practical, even costly ways, is more useful. Although such acts of service may indeed express that Christ is present among us, there are few ritual acts which combine the dynamic composite of experiences present during footwashing: service, intimacy, humility, and the need for cleansing.

So what kind of church practices footwashing? And when, or how often, should this ritual be practiced? Churches that practice footwashing are likely to be those that are committed to the components of footwashing in their daily lives and practices. By this I mean, the structures and procedures within the church will reflect servanthood rather than abusive power; the community will practice care for one another throughout the week; there will probably be opportunity for telling and hearing each other's stories of faith as experienced in daily life; members will know and enjoy the cleansing grace as well as the pain of forgiveness, not only during footwashing but as a necessary part of life; and they will know each other well enough to risk the intimacy of touching each other's feet. If these qualities are not part of the continuing life of the church, few people will choose to participate in a footwashing service.

As for the question of when or how often footwashing should be practiced, I am convicted by the story in John 13 to respond: often enough to remind us of who Christ is among us and who we are to be to each other. Although in many traditions, Maundy Thursday has been a natural and, in many ways, an appropriate time for this practice, perhaps serious reflection ought to be given to whether once a year is sufficient to remind us of these integral components of following the example of our Lord and Teacher.

If we are tempted to ignore or avoid this uncommon, possibly unpleasant, and in many ways convicting practice, we may need to hear again the accompanying words of Jesus: "If you know these things, you are blessed if you do them" (John 13: 17). It is indeed an uncommon, extraordinary blessing to belong to a community of footwashers who are led by a Footwasher.

Footwashing: An Adequate Preparation for the Christian Life

According to John Christopher Thomas, within the cultural context of John 13, the washing of feet was considered an act of preparation. In fact, it was such a basic act of preparation – for religious duties, the sharing of a meal, or intimate relationships – that "unwashed feet" had become an idiomatic expression meaning "without adequate preparation" (Thomas, 1991: 59).

Footwashing, properly understood, is indeed adequate preparation – repeated preparation – for Christian living, for Christian ethics. We, all of us, need the gentle repeated cleansing that only Jesus can provide. We need a cleansing that will soothe our aching feet, a cleansing that will remove the filth that attaches itself at the very base of our existence. We serve a compassionate Lord, a teacher whose patience and tenderness beckon us to faithfulness in the midst of a world that he loves and yet a world that sometimes betrays him and even crucifies him.

The resurrected Lord not only continues to wash but also calls his followers to wash the feet of one another, as they learn from him to love, to serve, and to live within this world. We need to know that we are not on this journey alone. As willing disciples, we join ourselves to others who, like us, are in need of cleansing and, like us, are extending their hands to wash our feet as we wash theirs. We embrace, knowing we need love, knowing we need forgiveness and care, knowing that if we have "unwashed feet" we are inadequately prepared for the journey of Christian discipleship. Furthermore, we need reminders, embodied acts of faithfulness to beckon us forward in faithfulness. As we rise from the washing of feet we know that we are to "wash feet" in the world through living lives of love and servanthood, testifying to our Lord. We also know we will be enriched and challenged through the lives of other brothers and sisters whose lives are, in their various and complex ways, embodiments of the wondrous love of our footwashing Lord.

Perhaps if we can see footwashing within this broader theological context more of us can grow in our appreciation of its importance. In fact, it might even be that as preparation for faithfulness, many of us will come to say with the Appalachian Baptist: "I wouldn't take the Supper if I couldn't wash feet."

Acknowledgments

I want to express gratitude to two people. First, my wife, Mary, gave very generously of her time in editing this chapter. She even wrote the section "Footwashing: An Uncommon Practice," beautifully reflecting what I had tried to say, as well as her many years of service in South Central Los Angeles and the practice of footwashing she experienced in the Pasadena Mennonite Church. It is much improved because of her work. Second, Paul Duke's wonderful essay is much more important than one might guess from its length. I went back to it many times as I wrote this.

Bibliography

Allison, Richard E. (2001) "Foot Washing," in *The Encyclopedia of Christianity*, vol. 2, ed. E-I. Erwin Fahlbusch, et al. (Grand Rapids, MI: Eerdmans), esp. pp. 322–3.
Barth, Karl (1961) *Church Dogmatics*, vol. III, part 4, ed. G. W. Bromiley and T. F. Torrance (Edinburgh: T. and T. Clark).

Brodie, Thomas L. (1993) *The Gospel According to John: A Literary and Theological Commentary* (Oxford: Oxford University Press).

Duke, Paul D. (1995) "John 13: 1–17, 31b–35," *Interpretation*, 49 (4) (October): 398–400, 402.

Enniss, P. C., Jr (1987) "Lenten Discipline," *Journal for Preachers*, 10 (2) (Lent): 3–9.

Foster, Richard J. (1983) "The Ministry of the Towel: Practicing Love through Service," *Christianity Today*, 27 (1) (January 7): 19–21.

Graber-Miller, Keith (1992) "Mennonite Footwashing: Identity Reflections and Altered Meanings," *Worship*, 66 (2) (March): 148–70.

Hernhold, Robert M. (1983) "Foot Washing and Last Things," *Christian Century*, 100 (7) (March 9): 205.

Howard-Brook, Wes (1994) *Becoming Children of God: John's Gospel and Radical Discipleship* (Maryknoll, NY: Orbis).

—(1997) *John's Gospel and the Renewal of the Church* (Maryknoll, NY: Orbis).

Kennedy, D. Robert (1995) *The Politics of the Basin: A Perspective on the Church as Community* (Lanham, MD: University Press of America).

Knight, G. A. Frank (1912) "Feet-Washing," in *Encyclopedia of Religion and Ethics*, ed. James Hastings (Edinburgh: T. and T. Clark), esp. pp. 814–23.

Macchia, Frank D. (1997) "Is Footwashing the Neglected Sacrament? A Theological Response to John Christopher Thomas," a Review Essay in *The Journal of the Society for Pentecostal Studies*, 19 (2) (Fall): 239–49.

Moloney, Francis J. (1998) "The Gospel of John," in *Sacra Pagina Series*, vol. 4, ed. Daniel J. Harrington (Collegeville, MN: The Liturgical Press).

O'Day, Gail R. (1995) "The Gospel of John: Introduction, Commentary and Reflections," in *The New Interpreter's Bible*, vol. IX (Nashville, TN: Abingdon).

Schneiders, Sandra M. (1981) "The Foot Washing (John 13: 1–20): An Experiment in Hermeneutics," *The Catholic Biblical Quarterly*, 43 (1) (January): 76–92.

Thomas, John Christopher (1991) "Footwashing in John 13 and the Johannine Community," *Journal for the Study of the New Testament Supplement Series*, no. 61 (Sheffield: Sheffield Academic Press).

—(1997) "Footwashing within the Context of the Lord's Supper," in *The Lord's Supper: Believers Church Perspectives*, ed. Dale R. Stoffer (Scottdale, PA: Herald).

Tschackert, Paul (1952) "Foot-washing," in *The New Schaff-Herzog Encyclopedia of Religious Knowledge*, ed. Samuel Macauley Jackson (Grand Rapids, MI: Baker Book House), esp. pp. 339–40.

Vanier, Jean (1998) *The Scandal of Service: Jesus Washes our Feet* (New York: Continuum).

PART VI
Being Commissioned

CHAPTER 34

Being Blessed: Wealth, Property, and Theft

Stephen Fowl

The Ambiguous Relationship between Blessing and Possessions

After being fed at the Lord's Table, Christians typically pray for several things. They thank God for feeding them with the body and blood of the Lord Jesus Christ, thus assuring them that they are indeed living members of Jesus's body. In the light of such nourishment, Christians then look toward being sent out into the world. They pray for strength and courage to live and work to God's praise and glory. Typically, then, the one presiding at the Eucharist will pronounce a blessing on the community. This blessing is to abide and remain on each member of the community as they go out into the world in a way that recalls the resurrected Christ's promise at the end of Matthew's Gospel to abide with his followers (28: 20).

What should Christians expect in the light of being blessed at the close of the Eucharist in this way? One initial temptation is to think that blessing is a reward that believers receive for worshiping God. First, Christians worship, then, at the end, we receive a blessing. If God needed our worship, then we might be correct in seeing God's blessing as a sort of payment for services rendered. While it is true that God loves us as if we were God, and desires our worship, this is not because of any lack in God that is completed by our worship. Thus, the first thing Christians should think about being blessed at the end of the Eucharist is that it is something that overflows from God's boundless love for us.

Once Christians think of God's blessing as a gracious gift, we need to reflect on what sort of gift this is. Of course, one way to think of God's blessing is in terms of getting more – usually more things – from God. Even if it didn't involve an increase in possessions, God's blessing would allow us to keep what we already have with greater assurance that God really wants us to have it. It is not difficult to find various characters, usually television preachers, who proclaim a gospel of health, wealth, and ever-increasing prosperity. In response to this, believers may well be tempted to downplay or eliminate any connection between blessing and material goods. This would be a mistake. Although Christians might enumerate any number of "spiritual blessings," Scripture clearly links (but does not confine) God's blessing to material goods. As created by God, the garden is a place of material abundance where humans are free from having to toil for their food, struggle with predatory animals, or seek protection from the elements. When God leads the Israelites out of slavery into the land of promise, it is to be a land flowing with milk and honey (see Exodus 3: 8). When the prophets speak of the restoration of Israel, it is common to note that at least one aspect of that restoration is material abundance (for example, Isaiah 65: 17–25; Jeremiah 33: 6–7; Amos 9: 11–15).

There is really no option but to think that God's blessing is tied (but not limited) to material goods. This recognition raises new problems and prospects for believers. First, we may be tempted to think that the amount and quality of our possessions is directly proportional to the amount and quality of God's pleasure with us. While Scripture clearly links God's blessing to possessions, there is an even more persistent theme within Scripture warning us against making any sort of systematic inferences that move from the amount and quality of our possessions to judgments about the degree to which God is pleased with us. Two, among many, scriptural examples make this plain. Think of Amos and his prophetic mission to Israel. In the midst of their material prosperity, the Israelites find it impossible to imagine that God is not pleased with their common life and their worship. God, however, finds Israelite life and worship corrupt, unjust, and oppressive to the most vulnerable in society. This message, delivered by Amos, is inconceivable to the Israelites. As Amaziah, the priest at Bethel, tells the king, "The land cannot bear all his [Amos's] words" (7: 10). In short, the Israelites assume that their material prosperity can only be the result of God's deep pleasure with them and their society.

The friends of Job provide an even more striking example of those who operate with this sort of economy of blessing. Interestingly, when God rebukes Job's friends it is not for their false accusations against Job, or for their failure accurately to judge Job's situation and character. Rather, it is because the friends have spoken falsely about God (Job 40: 7). Because of a failure to understand God properly, they assume a false ratio between material possessions and God's pleasure.

It would seem, then, that believers have little hope of understanding what to think about and expect from God's blessing apart from a prior proper understanding of the God who does the blessing. Only in the light of this understanding could we then hope to understand the ways in which the blessing with which we are sent out from the Eucharist will help us order all of our lives – including our possessions – so that we live and work to God's praise and glory.

Considering the ways in which Jesus conveys blessings in the beginning of the Sermon on the Mount (Matthew 5: 1–11) lends further support to this way of thinking. Here Jesus pronounces God's blessing on a host of unlikely characters, the poor in spirit, the meek, the merciful, the peacemakers, the persecuted, and so forth. In these verses Jesus is not directly commanding his followers to become these sorts of people. Rather, he is declaring that just these sorts of people are blessed because they are those whom God values highly, they are the premier citizens of God's in-breaking kingdom. By indicating those whom God values highly, Jesus is primarily telling us something about God and God's deepest desires for the way in which the Kingdom of God will be ordered. Christians come to understand these characters as blessed, we come to value them as God does, and we may seek to become like them, only to the extent that we come to understand these blessings as reflecting some of the deepest desires of God's heart. Apart from understanding God as decisively displayed by the Son, by Immanuel (Matthew 1: 23), it will be impossible to understand the blessings pronounced in the Sermon on the Mount.

This is hardly a comprehensive examination of biblical texts on blessing. I hope it is enough to show that as believers begin to think about being blessed, two things need to be recognized. On the one hand, then, there are some pretty good scriptural reasons for thinking that the blessing we receive at the end of the Eucharist is related to the ways in which we get and hold our possessions. On the other hand, it appears that we will not properly understand the relationships between blessing and possessions unless we have a proper understanding of the God who blesses us. For Christians, one of the primary ways we may come to a proper understanding of the God who blesses us is through regular attentive participation in the Eucharist. This indicates that we should direct our attention back from this final eucharistic blessing to other parts of the Eucharist.

Blessing, Possessions, and the Knowledge of God

Recall that our blessing in the Eucharist is taken to be the proper response to the prayer thanking God for feeding us with the body and blood of Christ. This recollection points back to that moment in the Eucharist when the consecrated elements are offered to us as "The gifts of God for the people of God." These gifts are the transformed gifts we have earlier in the service offered to God as bread and wine. It would appear that the giving and receiving of gifts is one of God's primary eucharistic actions.

From this, believers might infer that we should think of God's blessing in terms of God receiving our gifts and then, after transforming them, giving them back to us. That is, in the Eucharist, God's character is primarily displayed in receiving and giving gifts. Thus, if understanding the relationship between blessing and possessions is dependent on a proper understanding of God, we should understand our possessions as gifts, giving them as God has given to us.

This certainly fits with the earlier recognition that God's blessing is neither reward nor payment for services rendered. The notion of gift rightly conveys the gratuity of God's blessing. If we leave things at this point, however, we have not yet said enough. This is because no gift is given in a vacuum. Giving and receiving gifts invokes a range of cultural and interpersonal conventions, expectations, and practices. These conventions, expectations, and practices arise out of particular relationships and continue to form those relationships over time. Giving and receiving gifts invokes and presumes webs of social and interpersonal obligation, power, and status. Gifts can thereby be used to situate people in terms of their status and power. Of course, this all depends on who does the giving, how much is given, and what is expected in return. Giving and receiving gifts can just as easily work to cement unholy, manipulative, and, ultimately, oppressive relationships as they can reflect the character of God as displayed in the Eucharist.

Moreover, this is not simply a modern phenomenon of gift-giving. Paul, in particular, understands how receiving gifts from his congregations shapes and is shaped by the sorts of relationships he has with them. In the case of the Corinthians, Paul refuses to accept their offer of financial gifts to him. This creates tensions, but he considers addressing those tensions better than the distortion in his ministry that would have occurred had he accepted the Corinthians' gifts while he was ministering among them (see Marshall, 1987: 233–51).

In the case of the Philippians, Paul receives gifts from them at various points in his travels (Philippians 4: 15). In his epistle to the Philippians Paul recognizes their most recent gift, sent with Epaphroditus to an imprisoned Paul. Because giving and receiving gifts is so bound up with issues of power, status, need, and obligation, Paul goes to great lengths to put the Philippians' gift in a properly theological context so that it does not shape his friendships with them in deleterious ways (4: 10–20). In this passage Paul views both his needs and the Philippians' gift in the light of their common friendship in God. Paul receives the Philippians' gift with joy (4: 10). At the same time, he notes that God (rather than the Philippians or any other congregation) has met his needs (4: 11). Because he lacks nothing in Christ, the Philippians' gift does not put Paul in a position of supplicant or debtor. Rather, he and the Philippians are partners in the gospel (1: 5, 7) and fellow slaves of Christ (1: 1). Their giving and receiving must be understood in the light of the three-way friendship they share with each other in Christ. As it turns out, Paul's joy stems from the fact that the Philippians' gift is really an offering to God (4: 17–18). Throughout this passage, Paul never directly thanks the Philippians for their gift. This would invoke conventions of indebtedness. Instead, Paul seeks to present the Philippians' gift in the light of his understandings of what God has done in Christ, befriending both Paul and the Philippians, and calling them to a common life worthy of the gospel of Christ (1: 27). In this case, Paul views financial gifts as simply part of a circulation of goods between Christian friends that takes place as they make common offerings to God (see Fowl, 2002).

As Paul understood, giving and receiving gifts, even between Christians, can work to undermine friendships in Christ, unless those gifts are set within a properly theological context. The example of Philippians 4 should make one pause in considering God's blessing simply in terms of the giving and receiving of gifts. Gift-giving, and, thus, eucharistic blessing, may turn out to be more complex than it at first appeared.

In this light, believers might well return to examine the gift-giving character of God as displayed in the Eucharist. Within the Eucharist there is an extraordinary exchange of gifts. At the offering, the community offers its gifts at the altar. These gifts are financial as well as offerings of bread and wine. At the same time, the words and prayers said over these offerings make it clear that these are not gifts in the normal sense of the term. For example, our giving does not fill up any lack in God. Moreover, because all things come from God, believers are only offering what is already God's.

Nowhere is this more clearly stated than in David's prayer over the materials that the Israelites offered for the building of the Temple (1 Chronicles 29: 10–19). This prayer seems to undergird prayers and statements made during our eucharistic offerings. In fact, some Christians recite one or other verses from this prayer at the offering such as: "All things come from you, O Lord, and of your own do we give you" (1 Chronicles 29: 14). Lest we are tempted to think otherwise, David's prayer makes it clear that the entire question of desert is eliminated when it comes to our offerings (29: 14–15). We are not giving to God from our own well-deserved abundance. Rather, we are simply returning God's bounty to God. In this light, our offerings are not gifts that believers beneficently bestow on God. Rather, in the light of the recognition that "Yours, O Lord, is the greatness, and the power, and the glory and the victory, and the majesty; for everything that is in heaven and on earth is yours" (29: 11), they represent no more than the appropriate return of God's bounty (Episcopal Church, 1979: 376–7).

Moreover, when our offerings of bread and wine have been transformed into the body and blood of Christ, they are offered to us as "the gifts of God for the people of God." In taking them, however, Christians do not become recipients who must then reciprocate. There are two reasons for this. First, if everything is already God's it becomes difficult to imagine what might be given to God. The second reason has to do with what our eucharistic practice actually does to us, to our relationship to God. In the words of William Cavanaugh, "Although it is true that we can never make a return to God, 'since there is nothing extra to God which *could* return to him,' in the economy of the divine gift we participate in the divine life such that the poles of giver and recipient are folded into God" (Cavanaugh, 1999: 195). Eucharistic practice, then, draws believers into the divine life. We are "folded into God" in such a way that we are neither giver nor really receiver. As we are drawn into the life of the triune God, we find that the world is transformed in ways that tend to collapse any straightforward notions of gift, giver, and recipient.

Once believers recognize this, then conceiving God's eucharistic gift-giving as the foundation for our understanding of being blessed by God will have a very different set of implications for the way we come to hold and reflect on our possessions. For example, the notion of "our" in the phrase "our possessions" becomes very problematic. Exploring this may further help illumine the relationships between God's blessing and possessions. If Christians take seriously the ways in which David's prayer clearly underwrites the offertory prayer, then we are pushed to say that we "own" either nothing or everything in God. Further, once we conceive of our eucharistic practice as part of our participation in the divine life in which giver and recipient are "folded into God," we may then begin to think differently about how the blessing we receive at the end of the Eucharist might form the ways in which we come to think of and hold our possessions in relationship to others. In addition, I hope to show that believers need to think of the relationship between blessing and possessions in the light of the shape of Christian communities.

Blessing, Possessions, and the Shape of Christian Communities: Acts and Ephesians

Our eucharistic practice identifies the triune God as the creator and source of all things. Further our eucharistic practice enhances and deepens our communion with the triune

God, as we anticipate ultimately being completely gathered into the life of God. Thus, being blessed at the end of the Eucharist by this God presents Christians with a distinct set of challenges as we struggle to hold our possessions in ways that appropriately witness to God's identity and desires for us.

In the light of these challenges, we must admit that the New Testament does not present us with a single normative pattern. Nevertheless, a few patterns do seem commended. Moreover, there are two important things to note here. First, while we learn about distinct characters such as the "rich ruler", or Zacchaeus, and how they hold their possessions in the light of their encounters with Jesus, the New Testament has a persistent interest in Christian communities. When the New Testament addresses how followers of Jesus hold their possessions, which are blessings from the triune God, the concern is with how these followers hold their possessions as part of a set of larger issues related to their common life in Christ. Second, and following from this first point, it becomes clear that the ways in which Christians hold their possessions shape and are shaped by other aspects of their common life. Thus, one cannot simply make a recommendation about how Christians ought to hold possessions without other practices already being in place and in good working order.

Consider two examples of this. The first is the well-known passage in Acts 4–5 about the earliest community of believers in Jerusalem. We are told "no one called anything their own, but everything they owned was held in common" (4: 32). The upshot of this is that there was no need among them (4: 33). In many respects, this practice bears powerful testimony to the notion that "all things come from you, O Lord, and of your own have we given you." There is, however, much more to say here. First, before we learn anything about the ways in which these disciples held their possessions, we are told that these believers were all "of one heart and of one mind" (4: 32). Their unity was not simply a unity of possessions. Rather, the way they held their possessions was just a part of a more comprehensive unity enabled by the Spirit and enacted in their common life. If they had "one heart and one mind," it is only natural that they would hold their possessions in common.

Further, we learn that those with possessions sold them and handed the proceeds over to the apostles (4: 35, 37). Although they were of one mind and one heart, holding all things in common, they granted authority to particular members of the community to distribute the common purse to address the needs of members of the community. Indeed, Acts 6 makes it clear that they revised and corrected this pattern in the light of specific problems. This presumes an enormous amount of trust in each other. The apostles were trusted to use these blessings faithfully. Those in need were trusted to speak truthfully about their needs. Without this mutual trust and mutual truthfulness, holding all things in common cannot properly work. This is why when Ananias and Sapphira fail to speak truthfully about the possessions they bring to the disciples, the response from God is so terrifying. Failures of truthfulness strike at the very heart of the unity and trust which underlies a common life in which believers hold all things in common.

I suspect that the openness and trust in matters of possessions, which lies at the heart of the practice of the earliest believers in Jerusalem, seems largely inconceivable to most churchgoers today. To the extent that we are willing to part with our possessions at all, we are not willing simply to leave them at the feet of the apostles and walk away. We want full disclosure about how the money is spent. We often want some say in how it is spent, and we hold out the prospect of withholding our possessions in the future as a way of exerting some control on this process.

We may feel particularly justified in these attitudes as Churches come to grips with the financial repercussions of recent clergy sex-abuse cases in the US and Canada. Large numbers of lay people feel that they should have been more suspicious of the apostles and threaten to withhold future gifts. There are calls for bishops to resign as if they were failed CEOs. Without question, in these cases serious, devastating, and repeated sin has been committed at almost all levels of Church leadership. Alternatively, if Christians continue to treat these matters as another form of corporate scandal such as that of Enron, they will primarily demonstrate that they are more deeply shaped by individualism and patterns of accountability more at home in corporate America than the Church.

If we cannot conceive of holding our blessings in common, laying them at the feet of the apostles, then it may well be because we operate in the almost total absence of the unity of heart and mind which Acts so closely links to holding of possessions in common. Acts makes it clear that this unity and trust is a fragile achievement, which depends on truthfulness. It does not, however, depend on moral perfection. That is, the oneness of mind and heart characteristic of Acts is not the result of sinlessness, but of being reconciled, reconciling people. Truthfulness can really only flourish in the ways that it must for us to hold all things in common, if a community's practices of forgiveness and reconciliation are in good working order. We can only learn to speak truthfully in the ways envisioned in Acts 4–6 when we know that we can speak truthfully about our sin and realize that our sin need not ultimately destroy our relationship with God and others.

Acts 4–6 demonstrate that Christians and Christian communities cannot think about and act upon the getting and holding of possessions apart from thinking and acting upon issues of unity, trust, truthfulness, forgiveness, and reconciliation. We can see further how these issues are connected and how failure in one area can result in failure in other areas by looking at the epistle to the Ephesians. Clearly, the Ephesians do not hold all things in common in the manner of Acts. Neither does Paul assume they should. Nevertheless, consider the following passage:

So then, putting away falsehood, let each of us speak the truth with our neighbor, for we are all members of one another. Be angry yet do not sin; do not let the sun go down on your anger and do not make room for the devil. Those who steal must stop stealing. Rather, let them do honest work with their own hands, so as to have something to share with those in need. Let no evil talk come out of your mouths, but only what is good for building up as fits the occasion, that it may impart grace to those who hear. Do not grieve the Holy Spirit of God in whom you were sealed for the day of redemption. Put away from you all bitterness and wrath and anger and wrangling and slander together with all malice, and be kind to one another, tenderhearted, forgiving one another, as God in Christ forgave you. Therefore, be imitators of God, as beloved children and walk in love as Christ loved us and gave himself for us a fragrant offering and sacrifice to God. (Ephesians 4: 25 – 5: 2)

This passage offers a series of sharp injunctions about the way in which Christians ought to use words. Paul (or whoever wrote the letter) admonishes the Ephesians to put away falsehood and to speak truthfully with one another. He warns of the dangers of letting one's anger fester, thus giving the devil opportunity to lead the Ephesians into sin. These injunctions about word use lead to a further series of injunctions proscribing a whole range of attitudes. Each of these attitudes is generally, but not exclusively, manifested in certain types of speech. All of these injunctions lead to the final demand of this passage, that the Ephesians "walk in love as Christ loved us . . ." Paul's instructions in this paragraph seem concerned precisely with how and what Christians ought to speak, which attitudes and emotions they ought to cultivate, and which they should avoid in order to build up one another.

It comes as a surprise, then, to read in Ephesians 4: 28 that Paul says that those who steal must stop and take up honest work so that they may have something to share with those in need. Why, in the midst of a discussion about "word care," does Paul raise the issue of stealing? Indeed, this verse seems so out of place that if it were removed from chapter 4 I don't think anyone would notice. Why was such an earthy, material, physical action as stealing brought into this discussion about words and attitudes? Was there a particularly large number of practicing cat burglars in the Ephesian Church? Was there some sort of deviant teaching running through the congregation advocating that Christians ought to steal from the rich to give to the poor? If this were the case, such a teaching would seem to merit more than the almost off-hand attention it receives here.

Alternatively, the text is phrased in such a way that, false teaching or not, it seems clear that there were those in the congregation who were stealing. Without mitigating this disturbing fact, it is probably important to recognize that Paul does not use the Greek word for "thief" here (contra the NRSV). Rather he uses a participle, which is better rendered into English as "those who steal" as opposed to those who have made stealing their vocation. In this light, the types of things that might be considered stealing in this passage include the numerous small-scale ways in which slaves might pilfer their master's goods (see Philemon 18). Those in the marketplace who use unfair scales or engage in price fixing and petty con artists might also fit the bill. Calvin seems to have grasped this point quite well. In his thirty-first sermon on Ephesians (preached sometime between 1558 and 1559) he says:

> Now when St Paul speaks here of thefts, he does not refer to such thieves as men punish with whipping or with hanging, but to all kinds of sly and crafty dealing that are used to get other men's goods by evil practices such as extortion, deeds of violence and all other similar things . . . Although a merchant may be accounted a man of good skill, yet he will still have a store of tricks and wiles, and they will be like nets laid for the simple and such as are without experience, who do not perceive them. The case is the same with those who follow the mechanical arts, for they have the skill to counterfeit their works in such a way that men shall be deceived by them. Again, with regard to prices, there is no trusting the sellers . . . In short, there is no class of men in which there are not infinite faults and extortions to be seen for every man wishes to get the upper hand and make himself stronger than the rest. (Calvin, 1979: 451–2)

In addition to Calvin's account, there is a further tradition regarding stealing within Christianity. This tradition is typified by Basil of Caesarea (see Homily on Psalm 14 and Homily on Luke 12: 18; Basil of Caesarea, 1963) and Thomas Aquinas (see *Summa theologiae* 2a2ae q.66; Aquinas, 1963), who argue that those with the means to give to the needy, yet do not do so, deserve the name "thief" as much as those who take what belongs to another. It would seem, however, that Paul's demand that those who steal both stop stealing and work in order to have something to share with the needy does not have this type of thief in mind (see also Ryan, 1942).

We may get a further picture of the type of situation Paul is addressing when we recognize that this whole passage, with its repeated use of phrases like "one another" (vv. 25, 32) and its emphases on building up the body of Christ, is directed at the common life of the Ephesian Church. It may well be the case that those who were stealing were stealing from other members of the congregation. This, of course, is not a foreign notion to the New Testament. The story of the "neglect" of the widows of the "Hellenists" in Acts 6 might serve as an appropriate example of the type of stealing Paul proscribes in 4: 28. Alternatively, Paul might be talking about a scenario in which some members of the congregation, who either through idleness or misplaced views about the *parousia*, were living as parasites off the charity of the Church like those addressed in 2 Thessalonians 3. It would not be unreasonable to characterize similar activities in the Ephesian Church as stealing. While all these examples show that disputes over possessions are not unknown to the New Testament, we must admit that we do not know exactly what types of behavior Paul was addressing when he told certain Ephesians to stop stealing. Presumably, those who first read the epistle had a pretty good idea of what Paul was talking about.

I have already noted that this entire passage is directed toward maintaining the common life of the Church. These are not demands addressed to isolated individuals to make of what they will. Rather, they are admonitions to a community about how they must talk and live with each other in order to maintain their unity and faithfulness under Christ. In this light, it is not hard to see that lying (v. 25), allowing one's anger to lead one into temptation (vv. 26–7), stealing (v. 28), destructive speech (v. 29), grieving the Spirit (v. 30), along with bitterness, rage, wrath, quarreling, blaspheming, and the like (v. 31), and the inability to forgive one another (v. 32) are all potentially mortal wounds to the common life of the Church. Such practices stand in sharp opposition to the life of *agape* commended by Paul and exemplified by Christ (5: 1–2). Given that Paul's aim in this passage is maintaining the common life of the Church as a faithful testimony to the work of God, it is no more odd for him to address the issue of Christians stealing (particularly from each other) than it is for him to emphasize truth-telling.

Further, it is not difficult to imagine that the fact that certain Ephesians were stealing would be quite destructive of the trust and honesty needed to speak truthfully, and to engage in all the other verbal activities that contribute to the building up of the Church. The combination of all of these injunctions in 4: 25 – 5: 2 makes clear that some Ephesians were engaged in stealing (probably from other members of the congregation) and that such activity was a distinct threat to the common life of the Church. In particular, stealing posed a distinct threat to the Ephesians' abilities to speak the truth, to be angry without sinning, to put away bitterness, rage, and so forth. This much seems relatively straightforward.

There are two further points I wish to develop from this. The first concerns the specific issue of stealing and its deleterious effects on a community's abilities to manifest the unity, trust, and truthfulness Paul enjoins in this passage. The second point examines the presumptions about the common life of the Ephesian Church lying behind this passage and the relevance of this sort of common life to contemporary Christian communities.

First, if stealing frustrates unity, truthfulness, and trust in the ways Paul implies, it may be fruitful to explore the relationships between unity, truthfulness, and trust and the alternative to stealing. Once one recognizes that this passage is not directed to isolated individuals but to a community of believers, it also becomes evident that this passage presumes a certain level of intensity in the common life of the Ephesians, an intensity largely absent from most churches in the US. The verbal activities of this passage, both those encouraged, and those discouraged, are all public sorts of activities. That is, to be performed at all they have to be performed in the presence of others. As I already noted, Paul addresses the issue of stealing in 4: 28 as if his audience would understand what he meant without saying much more. This means that the Ephesians had enough knowledge about each other's lives to know that some among them were stealing. For the reality of stealing to be as great a danger to the fabric of the common life of the Ephesians as lying or slandering one another, the lives and, indeed, the possessions of the members of the community had to be relatively accessible to other members of the community. This text presupposes that the common life of the Ephesian Church was such that they had some access to each other's possessions.

While the Ephesian Christians did not hold all things in common after the manner of Acts 4–6, it is also the case that they had not taken excessive precautions to secure their possessions from the intrusions of one another. They could not have made the issue of possessions an entirely private matter separate from the continuing life of the community. The line constructed between public and private seems to have located possessions squarely in the public realm. It is a profound testimony to the poverty of the common life of most contemporary churches that Christians have so secured their possessions from each other that they can barely imagine what it might be to acknowledge openly, in the manner of Ephesians 4, that Christians might steal (even from each other).

This, of course, is not because of the excessive virtue of contemporary Christians. It would not be surprising that on any given Sunday, in almost any church, embezzlers sit next to those who cheat on their taxes or steal from their employers or customers. Any astonishment one registers would result from finding out about such stealing. Nevertheless, the manner in which Paul addresses this issue in Ephesians 4 makes it painfully clear that the fact that such stealing was going on in the Ephesian Church was no secret. Alternatively, should I or anyone else in the church I attend be caught stealing, particularly stealing from others in the congregation or the congregation as a whole, the general response would be that such news should be buried under a thousand layers of silence. To the extent that such stealing became known it would only be through gossip and innuendo. Whether it remains covered up or exposed only in limited ways, we would treat this stealing as if it were irrelevant for a contemporary community's abilities to speak truthfully with each other.

Such fragmentation of issues related to possessions, truth-telling, trust, and unity would have deeply troubled Paul (and even the Ephesians). This is because the community's ability to speak truthfully has already been shown to be deficient by the way in which it has addressed the matter of stealing.

One can, in a small way, understand the importance and interconnectedness of these issues of stealing and the verbal practices of the Ephesians if one has ever lived or worked in a situation where several people share a refrigerator. This small manifestation of common life can quickly threaten the harmony of a social group when one goes to get a can of soda only to find that the Coke put there yesterday to get cold for today is no longer there. Further, it does not take much imagination to see that in this situation the boundary between stealing and borrowing becomes very fluid. Our assumptions about what is appropriate to share will bang up against the assumptions of others. Under such conditions disputes and arguments are bound to arise. If disputes about the use of goods in the refrigerator are not to tear the house or office apart, the relevant parties will have to enter into the sorts of communal practices where issues of truth-telling, forgiveness, and the other practices mentioned in Ephesians 4 will play major roles.

In the course of writing an earlier version of this chapter I was told about a church where the staff shared a refrigerator. Stealing became such a divisive issue that the church secretary spent the best part of a week dividing up the refrigerator into individual bins assigned to each staff member. Each individual's bin is sacrosanct. One is not to interfere in any way with the bin of one's neighbor.

It appears that Christians can either have the sort of community in which possessions are made accessible to one another and stealing and/or knowledge of stealing is a real possibility, or they can privatize their possessions as best they can, thus securing their goods at the expense of their common life. It is ostensibly the case that stealing led to the division of the refrigerator into individual cubicles. This, however, is only a surface problem. When the stealing began, these Christians also suffered from an inability to put away falsehood and to speak the truth with each other. Their anger got the better of them; they failed to engage in the practices of confession and forgiveness and repentance. For any particular group of Christians, privatization of property, that is, making possessions merely a personal matter, is both the easiest and least threatening way to deal with the impoverishment of their common life. To do anything else not only raises the specter of stealing, it will demand that they be truthful, able to deal with conflict without lapsing into sin and capable of asking for and receiving forgiveness from each other. Yet it is precisely these practices that must be cultivated if Christians are to treat their possessions as blessings from the God from whom all things come.

The practices and presumptions behind the treatment of possessions in Acts 4–6 and Ephesians 4 stand as profound challenges to the common life of any contemporary Christian community. The challenge is to counter the tendencies in modern life to individualize and privatize large sections of our lives, including our wealth. There are some rare exceptions to this. For example, all United Methodist clergy are required to publish their salaries in the journal of their annual conference and I gather that this often pro-

vides a basis for some stimulating conversation. Any attempt to make this a requirement for all baptized Methodists, however, would provoke widespread rebellion.
Without a common life, in which the ways in which Christians get and hold possessions
are much more accessible to each other, Christians will also find it much more difficult
to engage in the other practices presumed and/or prescribed in these passages: truthfulness rather than triviality, anger that leads to forgiveness rather than bitterness, gracious words which build up as opposed to vacuous compliments which support one
another's self-deceptions (see also Fowl, 1998: ch. 6).

Conclusion

This chapter was initiated and directed by the bestowing of God's blessing on Christians
at the conclusion of the Eucharist. I began by noting Scripture's unambiguous assertion that one of the primary ways of thinking about God's blessing is in terms of possessions. There are, however, numerous ambiguities and asymmetrical patterns in
God's blessing that make it impossible and dangerous to think that one can assume that
many possessions is a direct sign of God's favor. If believers are to understand the relationships between blessing and possessions properly we need to deepen our understanding of the God who blesses us. One of the most important ways of deepening our
understanding of God is by attentive participation in the Eucharist.

The many ways in which gifts seem to be exchanged in the Eucharist can initially
tempt us into thinking of God's blessing in terms of a straightforward exchange of gifts,
aiming at some sort of reciprocity. To do this would so misjudge what is going on in the
Eucharist that we would be in danger of eating and drinking to our own condemnation (1 Corinthians 11: 23). Instead, proper attention to the God who blesses us in the
Eucharist reminds us that "all things come from God" and our gifts are merely an
appropriate return of God's bounty. Moreover, as we come to see that the Eucharist is
fundamentally about how we are enfolded into the life of God, we also come to see that
distinctions between giver and recipient are transformed. Because we are being drawn
into the life of the triune God from whom all things come, the blessing at the end of the
Eucharist is implicitly a challenge to hold our possessions in a way that bears witness
to God's character.

The New Testament indicates that there is no single way by which Christians might
faithfully offer such testimony. Nevertheless, we find in the New Testament several
points that both direct and challenge contemporary Christians. First, for the most part,
the issues of blessing and possessions are primarily issues for Christian communities
and not individual believers. If eucharistic practice is communal, it is reasonable to
think that the blessing at the end of the Eucharist should shape the ways in which
Christian communities get and hold their possessions.

Secondly, texts such as Acts 4–6 and Ephesians 5 show Christians making their possessions a matter of public concern. It also becomes clear that one cannot treat matters
of possessions apart from matters of Church unity, trust, truth-telling, forgiveness, and
reconciliation. Indeed, failure in any of these areas tends to bring about and/or result
from failure in the others. Thus, the blessing, which we so often unthinkingly receive

at the conclusion of the Eucharist, calls us to think about our possessions in the light of some of the deepest theological truths about God and God's desires for us. It also challenges us to order our communal lives in ways that ardently desire the unity, truthfulness, and grace that are essential gifts of the Spirit.

References

Aquinas, Thomas (1963) *Summa theologiae*, Blackfriars translation (New York: McGraw-Hill).

Basil of Caesarea (1963) "Homily on Psalm 14," in *Exegetic Homilies*, Fathers of the Church, trans. Agnes C. Way (Washington, DC: CUA); "Homily on Luke 12: 18," in *Patrologiae Grecae*, vol. 31, esp. cols 275–6.

Calvin, John (1979) *Sermons on Ephesians*, revision of 1577 translation of A. Golding (London: Banner of Truth Trust).

Cavanaugh, W. (1999) "The City: Beyond Secular Parodies," in *Radical Orthodoxy*, ed. John Milbank, Catherine Pickstock, and Graham Ward, pp. 182–200 (London: Routledge).

Episcopal Church (1979) *The Book of Common Prayer* (New York: The Church Hymnal).

Fowl, S. (1998) *Engaging Scripture* (Oxford: Blackwell).

—(2002) "Know your Context: Giving and Receiving Money in Philippians," *Interpretation* (January): 45–58.

Marshall, P. (1987) *Enmity in Corinth: Social Conventions in Paul's Relationship with the Corinthians* (Tübingen: Möhr).

Ryan, John (1942) *Distributive Justice* (New York: Macmillan).

CHAPTER 35

Bearing Fruit: Conception, Children, and the Family

Joseph L. Mangina

Since it may not be obvious why issues surrounding conception, children, and the family should be considered under the rubric of "the blessing," let us begin with some thoughts on blessing in Scripture and the Church's liturgy.

The God of the Bible is the God who blesses, being indeed blessed in himself. Jews acknowledge this when they conclude references to "the Holy One" by exclaiming "Blessed be He!" For Christians, the divine blessedness is closely tied to God's being as Trinity. As the triune life shared by Father, Son, and Holy Spirit, God eternally gives and eternally receives – and just so is blessed. It is no accident that liturgical blessings are so often trinitarian in form: "The blessing of God almighty, the Father, the Son, and the Holy Spirit, be upon you and remain with you forever."

God blesses by creating a people. Pouring out blessings upon his people Israel, God extends these riches even to the Gentiles in the creation of the *ekklesia*. The community of Jesus's followers bears witness to the astonishing gift enacted through his cross and resurrection. The bishop's or pastor's spoken benediction reminds us that we do not have to go out in search of God's blessing. In Jesus Christ, that blessing has come to us (cf. Ephesians 1: 3).

Finally, God's blessing is concrete and historical, bound up with the complexities of embodied existence. For Israel, blessing – along with its opposite, the curse – was a matter of lands and fields, children and wealth, fertility and birthright. Thus, the puzzle Abraham confronts on receiving God's promise of a blessing is the very practical question, "How will Sarah conceive?" Likewise, in the New Testament, the way to God's blessing passes through the womb of Mary, "blessed" among women (Luke 1: 42, 48). Though rarely thought of in this way, the blessing at the end of the liturgy encapsulates these themes, pointing the Church to a life deeply involved in the reciprocities of sex, procreation, and the family. To claim God's blessing means neither to escape these created reciprocities, nor to idolize them, but to discern how they fit in the way of life known as discipleship.

How one hears the blessing may depend literally on where one stands. I once worshiped in a congregation that celebrated the Lord's Supper in the round, each person receiving the bread and wine from his or her neighbor. This circle remained unbroken through the final hymn and the blessing. The congregation thus received the blessing as they had received the Eucharist itself: not as individual agents, but as the odd collection of parents, children, elders, teenagers, and students (this was in a university town) making up one particular community of Christ's body. Significantly, this congregation was one in which children played a highly visible role. In this way, the reciprocal character of divine blessing becomes manifest: rather than simply being received "vertically," the blessing is mediated through the gift of a life shared in common. This insight will shape everything we have to say about conception, children, and the family as being likewise forms of participation in the one blessing.

In the remainder of this chapter, I will take up the themes of the title in reverse order: the next section offers a biblical and historical perspective on the role of families in the Church; the following section explores the ways in which Christians consider children to be a blessing; and the final part turns to particular questions concerning conception, especially in the light of the revolution in "reproductive technologies." As we engage all three areas, it will be important not to lose sight of the conviction cited earlier: that in Jesus Christ God's blessing has come among us, and that all our work of moral reflection takes place in the light of this gift.

Saying the Blessing: The Family

Of all the labels one might apply to a contemporary Christian congregation, perhaps the most damning would be to say that it is not "family-friendly." Churches pursue couples with children the way TV networks seek the market of 18 to 35-year-old males. Conversely, a church composed mainly of older members is often perceived as a failure. Implied here is a strong correlation between the Church and the family, both of which seem to embody similar values of trust, caring, and life in community. Surely discipleship to Jesus goes hand in hand with a strong sense of family.

This would have been news to the young man who approached Jesus with a simple request: " 'Lord, first let me go and bury my father.' But Jesus said to him, 'Follow me, and let the dead bury their own dead' " (Matthew 8: 21–2). This rude answer is paralleled by other passages in the Gospels:

> Do not think that I have come to bring peace to the earth; I have not come to bring peace, but a sword. For I have come to set a man against his father, and a daughter against her mother, and a daughter-in-law against her mother-in-law; and one's foes will be members of one's own household. Whoever loves father or mother more than me is not worthy of me; and whoever loves son or daughter more than me is not worthy of me. (Matthew 10: 34–8; cf. Mark 3: 31–5)

Though brimming with good intentions, the celebration of family reflects the sentimentalist captivity of the modern Church. Contemporary Christians tend to forget that the nuclear, intimate family is a relatively recent development. In pre-modern societies, families were almost always economic units. This was true of the first-century Jewish families disrupted by Jesus: significantly, the sons of Zebedee leave their father "in the boat with the hired men" (Mark 1: 19–20). The same holds true of the Roman households that nurtured the early Church. As Wayne Meeks notes, the household (*oikos*) would have included not only relatives but slaves, freedmen, and hired workers, dependent on their patron for support; such were probably "Chloe's people" (1 Corinthians 1: 11; cf. Meeks, 1983: 75). The patronage family of this sort has probably been more the rule than the exception throughout the Church's history. Local economies of necessity breed "home economics."

With the development of industrial capitalism in the nineteenth century, all this begins to change. The father as breadwinner now works for the family's livelihood outside the home, while domestic industries like spinning and sewing fade in importance. With this relativizing of the household comes a decline in the economic status of women. No longer a producer, the middle-class woman becomes the shopper/consumer *par excellence*. But the same might be said for the family as a whole: it becomes largely a consumer of goods and services provided by others.

But in one of those delicious ironies of history, the decline of the family ushered in a whole new era of the family. As social historian Christopher Lasch (1977) has argued, the nineteenth- and twentieth-century family creatively reinvented itself, precisely as a refuge from the ravages of modern life. The Victorian household became the domain of affection, morality, and religion, private values in a world of harsh public facts. The home is, above all, a feminine space, with Woman assigned the role of nurturer and culture-bearer. One need only think of *Huckleberry Finn*, where the Widow Douglas sets about "sivilizing" Huck by teaching him Bible stories and improving his table manners.

Families in contemporary Western societies differ in many ways from those of our Victorian ancestors. Women have moved into the workplace in large numbers; fathers have assumed – at least in theory – a more direct role in raising their children; no longer a stigma, divorce has become an accepted fact of social life. (A nineteenth-century time-traveler would no doubt find this last development most shocking of all.) Despite these changes, perhaps in large part because of them, the family continues to be prized as a unique zone of safety and contentment – Lasch's "haven in a heartless world." Indeed, one could argue that the cult of family amounts to virtually a religious practice in secular middle-class society. Christians have found the pull of this religion almost irresistible, depicting the Church as a warm, caring community, modeled on the so-called "natural" family.

To such claims we must utter a clear and emphatic "No." The Church is the elect people of God. It is a community formed not by kinship, or even by shared affections, but by baptism and confession of faith. Attempts to treat the Church as "one big, happy family" are thus doomed to failure. Even if the New Testament picture of the *ekklesia* does have certain family-like aspects, as Gerhard Lohfink makes clear in his *Jesus and Community*, this is far from saying that Christianity valorizes family life in the abstract (Lohfink, 1984: esp. ch. 2). Indeed, the very opposite is the case: precisely in that disciples are made brothers and sisters to each other, their ties to their families of origin are weakened.

None of this is to deny a legitimately natural element in those structures we name as "family." The Old Testament strongly affirms the biological ties that bind one generation to the next: "Sons are indeed a heritage from the Lord, the fruit of the womb a reward" (Psalm 127: 3). Even in the eschatologically charged atmosphere of the

Gospels, we find acknowledgment of the divine ordering of human life through such structures; thus Jesus endorses – and even radicalizes – the Torah's teaching about the marriage bond, and criticizes those who would weaken the mandate to honor father and mother (Mark 7: 9–13, 10: 2–9). To ignore such texts would be to situate Christianity in a gnostic space above creation, rather than in the earthy and profoundly material witness of the Old Testament.

The question, therefore, is not whether the family is to be affirmed as part of creation, but how much we can deduce from this fact for purposes of Christian ethics. The short answer is "not very much." As Karl Barth points out, the Bible is simply not interested in the family for its own sake (Barth, 1961: 241–3). We are certainly not entitled to speak of the family as an "order of creation," as did some older forms of Protestant ethics. Rather than giving us a neat picture of the normative family, Scripture shows us families caught up in the larger drama of God's purposes. In the Old Testament, this drama is that of God's covenant with Israel: "in you [that is, Abraham and his descendants] all the families of the earth shall bless themselves." In the New Testament we see the family only as it is engaged by God's grace, drawn into the new creation through the cross and resurrection of Jesus.

A traditional term for this divine drama is *oikonomia*, the economy of redemption. We might put the theological question of the family this way: how does the *oikos* (household) serve God's *oikonomia* (literally, "household rule" or "governance")? And how are both related to the "household of God," the Church? There are advantages to this approach beyond mere word-play. Asking about the family's usefulness lowers the stakes in a healthy way. We are not talking about perfect families here, but about ordinary, messy, conflicted families – families that in their very ordinariness may serve the divine purpose. This is not the only area of ethics where the doctrine of justification by faith should be kept firmly in view! At the same time, to speak of the family's usefulness helps us to reclaim its unique dignity. One reason why the modern celebration of family rings so hollow is that it gives families so little to do. Once we acknowledge that the family is not an end in itself, we may begin to discover something of its role in the life of the Church.

What kind of work, then, does the family perform? Even in our economy of consumption, the family still performs the basic task of nurturing the body. Rent must be paid, food put on the table, diapers changed, and babies washed. These unglamorous aspects of life are rooted in the material character of creation itself. For the believing family, they also offer a particular occasion for gratitude. Nowhere is such gratitude more clearly expressed than in the practice of "saying the blessing" – surely one of the most basic rituals of the Christian household; it is no accident that works like *The Book of Common Prayer* and Luther's *Large Catechism* contain forms for grace at table. Indeed, this simple practice can help to focus some of the challenges that confront the Christian household. Consider the following traditional Anglican grace: "Give us grateful hearts, our Father, for all thy mercies, and make us mindful of the needs of others; through Jesus Christ our Lord." The prayer opens with a request that we may be grateful for all God's gifts, especially the gift of food. Yet this petition is immediately followed by a second: "make us mindful of the needs of others." That Christians should be mindful of others' needs may seem fairly self-evident; is not a concern for the poor and helpless an integral part of Christian faith? Yet the force of the prayer becomes more clear when we view the family precisely in economic terms – as part of what Wendell Berry calls the "little economy" of the local community, which itself exists only within the "great economy" of the Kingdom (Berry, 1987).

Viewing the family as an economy inevitably raises basic questions about the deployment of resources. For example, nothing is more literally "economic" about a family than its monthly and yearly budget. What does mindfulness of others' needs mean in terms of, say, a family's contributions of time and money to the Church? In terms of service to the local food bank? How is this particular household related to the society's larger patterns of production and consumption? For example, buying a box of cereal at the supermarket is such an obvious act that I hardly think about it. Yet those oats, wheat, or corn came from somewhere. Who grew them? On how large a farm, and with what use of genetic engineering? What mechanisms of exchange brought them to my table? This may seem a lot to ask of a box of cornflakes; yet such questions are, I think, implied by the act of giving thanks to God and remembering the needs of all who belong to the "great economy." It does not seem too much to ask that a Christian household raise questions about its relation to the pagan marketplace – as, indeed, did Paul himself (1 Corinthians 10: 23 – 11: 1).

Another key role the family plays is that of socialization. In any society, families are a prime means by which individuals acquire language, cultural skills, and a sense of personal identity. What sets the Christian family apart is not these functions themselves, but the fact that the culture learned is that of discipleship to Jesus Christ. The reading of Scripture, the singing of hymns, the saying of prayers at meals and other times all contribute to such formation. Thus children learn about God by the fact that, in this household, God is spoken to. As with more strictly economic questions, those who seek to embody the Christian way in the home will inevitably find themselves drawn into a process of discernment with respect to other cultures that claim their loyalty: the cultures implied by the secular educational system, for example, or of the entertainment industry. Culture is not a static thing, and the goal should not be that of turning the home into a pure zone of Christian influence (the "haven in a heartless world" idea again). Nonetheless, there will be times when Christian families are called to say a definite and perhaps painful "No" to the cultural principalities and powers. A strong congregation will not leave families to fend for themselves, but will engage such questions precisely as a community.

It is good to remind ourselves once more of the family's limitations. The family does not save us. The family is not the Church. The family is at best a particular local manifestation of the Church, gathered for bed and board and good fellowship along the way. That we may taste the Kingdom in this odd company is one of the many blessings of the Christian life.

On Not Hindering the Blessing: Children

We commonly speak of children as a "blessing" without giving too much thought to just what we mean by this. Is it just another way of saying that babies are nice? Or is a more substantive claim being made here?

Two key passages from Mark's Gospel can help to focus our reflections. The first occurs in Mark 9, where the context is the disciples' argument over who is "greatest." Jesus rebukes them, insisting that real greatness consists in service to others (9: 35). He then offers a kind of living parable: "Then he took a little child and put it among them; and taking it in his arms, he said to them, 'Whoever welcomes one such child in my name welcomes me, and whoever welcomes me welcomes not me but the One who sent me'" (9: 36–7). It is a brief episode, yet it speaks volumes about the sort of community the Church is called to be. In the ancient world, children were "nobodies," creatures without much status or claim to protection (Gundry-Volf, 2001). Yet it is precisely such nobodies whom disciples are called to welcome in Jesus's name. No wonder he utters such dire warnings against anyone who would harm his "little ones" – a term that embraces more than children, yet which surely includes them (Mark 9: 42).

The second Marcan passage is one of the most familiar stories in the entire New Testament:

> People were bringing little children to him in order that he might touch them; and the disciples spoke sternly to them. But when Jesus saw this, he was indignant and said to them, "Let the little children come to me, do not stop them; for it is to such as these that the kingdom of God belongs. Truly I tell you, whoever does not receive the kingdom of God as a little child will never enter it." And he took them up in his arms, laid his hands upon them, and blessed them. (Mark 10: 13–16)

Even more strongly than in Mark 9, this story emphasizes Jesus's special concern for children: they belong to him, and therefore the disciples are not to "stop" their coming – intriguingly, the same word used in Acts 8: 36, where the Ethiopian asks Philip "what's to stop me from being baptized?" Defenders of infant baptism have long cited this passage as a key scriptural warrant (cf. Calvin, *Institutes*, 4.16.7). At the very least, the passage suggests that the welcoming of children must be a basic practice of the Christian Church. I will return to this point below.

The other accent sounded here, however, is that children offer a paradigm for receiving the Kingdom. Surely it is significant that this story immediately precedes that of the rich man who turned away when Jesus commanded him to sell his possessions (Mark 10: 22). Children typically do not come burdened with hindrances of this sort. The point is not so much that they are innocent, but that their frankness and spontaneity – their simple willingness to be embraced by Jesus – offers a kind of parable of life with God. The rich man, after all, kept the commandments (Mark 10: 20); what he lacked was simple freedom to follow.

From these stories we can draw two conclusions; first, that children's place is in Church – which means in the worshiping assembly; second, that their presence may help the whole community discover aspects of God to which it might otherwise be blind. It is important to distinguish the latter claim from any sentimental valorization of the child as such. Children are not necessarily purer, or better, or closer to God, though they may be possessed of astonishing spiritual insight; witness the children who populate the fiction of Flannery O'Connor and Fyodor Dostoevsky. The point is not really about children at all, but about how God chooses to bless his Church. The claim is that God does so in part by giving adults children, and children adults, within a larger economy of blessing.

How best to involve children in the worshiping assembly is, of course, no simple matter. Perhaps the best place to begin is by not excommunicating them. I mean this first of all in a literal sense. If a Church baptizes infants – and, of course, not all do – it makes little sense to defer their participation in the Eucharist. If children are genuinely members of the people of God, how can one exclude them from the event that stands at the center of the Church's life? Happily, many Western churches are beginning to embrace historic Orthodox practice in this area (see Holeton, 1991). One can but hope that this movement will be informed by a vigorous theology of baptism itself.

Excommunication, however, can happen in far more subtle ways than exclusion from the Lord's table. For example, congregations sometimes treat children as though they were mainly candidates for condescending instruction by adults. The so-called "children's sermon" is a chief symptom of this disease. However creatively it is conceived, the children's sermon nearly always – yes, there are exceptions – reflects the view that children's main access to faith is cognitive and didactic, and that they are best served by having the gospel "brought down to their level." Now there is, indeed, a time and place for explicit catechesis (and even, I would claim, for rote memorization), yet the larger context in which catechesis makes sense is the liturgy. Worship is the central activity that rehearses believers in the life of faith. Thus the best way of deepening children's grasp of faith turns out to be the means that works best for adults: immersion within the overall sacramental economy of the Church. The child who serves as acolyte, reader, or choir member is honored not simply as a child but as a member of the congregation, with a particular and important gift to share. The same goes for the child who is involved in worship in less formal ways – perhaps simply by being present, a keen observer who occasionally adds her own exhuberant voice to the proceedings.

Two larger considerations for a Christian ethics of the child flow from the points just made. First, children's presence in worship reminds us that they are not simply their parents' responsibility, but that of the entire community of the baptized. If the Church, and not the family, is the primary social loyalty of believers, then Christian parents will acknowledge that their claim on their children is, while real, also limited: parents do not "own" their children. Membership in the Church gives one "houses, brothers and sisters, mothers and children" beyond the biological family (Mark 10: 30). A congregation must therefore hold parents accountable for the care they provide their children; yet the congregation is itself committed to offering spiritual and material resources to underwrite that care. No Christian parents should feel that they have to go it alone, or that the state is the only place to which they can turn for help.

Second, the presence of children in worship can help us address a basic, yet surprisingly difficult, question, namely, why have children at all? There are, of course, many answers one can give to this question: because it is what people do, because we want to experience parenthood, because we want to make the world a better place. None of these answers is necessarily "wrong." Yet they miss what is, for Christians, the central point: that having children is an affirmation that the ordinary time of dirty diapers, trips to the doctor, and football practice *is* the grace-filled time of life "in Christ." As Stanley Hauerwas has argued, children "bind existence temporally, as through them we are given beginnings, middles, and ends" (Hauerwas, 1998: 258). We are bound by our children to the time and tasks of this world. One of the things liturgy teaches us, however, is that "this world" is precisely not an autonomous sphere following its own laws, but God's good creation – a creation undergoing the birth pangs of eschatological renewal. Having children seems such an ordinary, even trivial thing to do. Yet for Christians it is not so. The willingness to have children in a world like ours serves as nothing less than a sign of hope. Though not all Christians are called to have children, those who are help to mediate God's blessing in a very particular way.

Conceiving the Blessing: Procreation

Any theological account of family and children will eventually have to address questions about conception. At one level this is simply a matter of biology: the way to children lies through the sexual act. Yet to say even this much is to invite misunderstanding. On the one hand, Christians clearly believe that more than biology is involved; humans are not simply organisms but embodied persons, destined for communion with God and with one another. On the other hand, we must guard against the modern tendency to construe the "more than biology" in terms of sheer intimacy. As David McCarthy argues elsewhere in this volume, the Christian understanding of marriage is badly served when we place intimacy at the center of the picture. Intimacy there may well be, but marriage Christian-style is a companionship grounded in the larger practices of the Church's life, for example, the couple's baptismal vows; the modern priority given to personal fulfillment just will not do.

A better place to begin thinking about conception is with a New Testament passage I alluded to earlier: Jesus's affirmation of the marriage bond. " 'For this reason [God's creating humans as male and female] a man shall leave his father and mother and be joined to his wife, and the two shall become one flesh'. So they are no longer two, but one flesh. Therefore what God has joined together, let no one separate" (Matthew 19: 5–6, quoting Genesis 2: 24). Two things should be apparent here. First, the reference is to the biological "fact" of sexual union; second, this "fact" has been sovereignly inscribed within *God's* purpose for the man and woman, as institutionalized in the marriage bond. If reducing this bond to sheer biology is impossible, spiritualizing it in terms of affection or intimacy is equally absurd.

This is not to say that, Christianly viewed, the relation of husband and wife is impersonal or uncaring. On the contrary! Christians have always understood marriage to be a sacrament or icon of Christ's own self-giving to the Church (cf. Ephesians 5: 32). The point, rather, is that the "unitive" end of marriage – to use the traditional shorthand for marriage as friendship, companionship, the making of a common life – has more to do with constancy over the long haul than with affection in the short term. The one-flesh union of husband and wife does not so much express their ethereal "love," as it enacts (along with many other things) the larger economy of their life together. Thus the economy of a marriage also involves the sharing of time, money, work, and play. Not least does it involve the sharing of food – the kitchen being the second most important room in any house.

In addition to this "unitive end," traditional ethics has also spoken of marriage as having a "procreative end" – the making of babies. Sometimes the tradition has seemed to imply that this is the *only* legitimate good to be realized in marriage; in this sense, more recent personalist approaches have served as a healthy corrective. Nonetheless, Christian tradition has maintained that openness to having children is essential to the overall integrity of the marriage bond. Marriage is precisely not a dyadic, closed circle for the mutual benefit of the parties involved (as modern contractual views would have it). It is not just "self" and "other," the "I" and the "Thou," but these two in the presence of an Other (God); and because in God's presence, then also in the presence of the child who is God's gift.

Christian Churches have been virtually unanimous in teaching that these complex ends of marriage belong together. Any purposeful severing of unitive from procreative goes against the grain of Christian marriage (infertility is quite a different matter). Yet does this mean that the unity must be maintained in each individual act of sexual intercourse? Here the Churches have parted ways. Traditional Roman Catholic moral theology has said "yes": a couple must always be open to having children, and therefore all forms of contraception are off-limits for Catholics – a view officially confirmed by Pope Paul VI in the encyclical *Humanae vitae* (1968). This teaching does, to be sure, allow Catholics to engage in "natural family planning" (NFP) by avoiding sex during the times of highest fertility in a woman's cycle. Defenders of this view claim there is no inconsistency here, since the couple that employs NFP is still "open" to children in principle – i.e., NFP doesn't really count as "contraception" at all. Most Protestant ethicists (and not a few Catholics) have been dubious about this claim. If contraception consists in the use of rational means to control human fertility, they argue, then NFP certainly looks like a form of contraception. And if the Church finds this method acceptable, why not others?

An alternative view is that advanced by many Protestant theologians. They argue that it is indeed important that marital companionship and procreation be kept together; but the level at which these cohere is the relationship as a whole, rather than the individual sexual act. On this view, the use of contraception need by no means signal a self-absorbed, contractual understanding of marriage. Rather, artificial means of contraception are simply that – means, subordinated to the greater end of covenant fidelity. As the tone of these remarks no doubt indicates, I find this second line of argument to be the more persuasive. Nonetheless, the traditionalist position at least has the virtue of reminding us that that sanctification is worked out in the body, and that marriage has more to do with sharing a bed and changing diapers than it does with mere "love"; or rather, that Christian love consists precisely in such mundane acts as sharing a bed and changing diapers.

As Gilbert Meilaender points out, if contraception raises concerns over sex without babies, assisted reproduction raises just the opposite worry: the possibility of babies without sex (Meilaender, 1996: 17). The past few decades have seen extraordinary developments in the technology of human fertility. It was only in 1978 that a child was conceived by means of *in vitro* fertilization (IVF). Since then a dizzying array of possibilities has opened up. While this chapter cannot hope to address all the technical issues involved, it may be helpful to review briefly some of the more important options couples are likely to face:

- *Artificial insemination* This is not a new technology, the first successful effort having occurred in 1884. In this procedure, sperm provided by the woman's husband or other donor is inserted into her body via a syringe.
- *In vitro fertilization (IVF)* This is a procedure (in fact, a number of related procedures) in which eggs are removed from a woman's ovary and fertilized with sperm in the laboratory. The embryo is then returned to the uterus for gestation and birth. Usually the gametes (sperm and ovum) come from the husband and wife involved, although this need not be the case. It is an expensive procedure, and the success rate is low; perhaps one in five couples who attempt IVF succeeds in having a child by this method. It is not uncommon for multiple eggs to be fertilized and (sometimes) implanted all at once, in hopes of boosting the chances for success.
- *Surrogate motherhood* In this most complex form of assisted reproduction, a woman bears another woman's child for her. She may be inseminated using sperm from the husband of the genetic mother, or she may carry a child conceived *in vitro* from the gametes of both parents.

All forms of assisted reproduction raise ethical questions. Surrogate motherhood has commanded more public attention, largely because of the dramatic possibilities involved in conflicts between the genetic parents and the surrogate. For the purposes of this chapter, however, I will focus simply on *in vitro* fertilization, since it is the most widespread and accepted form of assisted reproduction.

A theological approach to IVF may wish to begin with the desire expressed by couples who turn to this and similar technologies: namely, the having of biological offspring. It is very tempting simply to take this wish at face value. If the end is self-evidently good, the presumption runs strongly in favor of methods such as IVF. Yet, as Karl Barth reminds us, the wish to have children is by no means a simple matter for the Christian. While it may have been the case under the old covenant that one "had" to have children – for perpetuation of the covenant was by biology and inheritance – this is no longer the case after the Messiah's coming:

> *Post Christum natum* [after the birth of Christ] there can be no question of a divine law in virtue of which all these things must necessarily take place. On the contrary, it is one of the consolations of the coming kingdom and expiring time that this anxiety about posterity, that the burden of the postulate that we should and must bear children, heirs of our blood and name and honour and wealth, that the pressure and bitterness and tension of this question, if not the question itself, is removed from us all by the fact that the Son on whose birth alone everything seriously and ultimately depended has now been born and has now become our Brother. No one now has to be conceived and born. We need not expect any other than the One of whose coming we are certain because He is already come. Parenthood is now only to be understood as a free and in some sense optional gift of the goodness of God. It certainly cannot be a fault to be without children. (Barth, 1961: 266; translation altered)

Stated in other terms, having children is a matter of gospel rather than law; conversely, it must be made clear that, while infertility is often a source of great sadness, the childless couple is nonetheless welcome in the Church, and may indeed have a crucial role to play there. I will return to this point below.

Still, no one would dispute that the infertile couple with a call to be parents may seek some forms of assistance. Blocked Fallopian tubes can be treated with surgery, while conditions like endometriosis may respond to drugs. Such treatments are no more problematic than other forms of medical care, in that they seek to remedy a disorder in the body. The problem, of course, is whether one takes the next step, employing alternative means for the actual process of conception.

Some Christian ethicists, such as Oliver O'Donovan (1984) and Gilbert Meilaender (1996), worry that IVF inevitably crosses the line from receiving life as a gift to fashioning it as a product. They argue that, while the naturally conceived child is "begotten, not made," the child conceived outside the womb reflects modern humanity's aspiration to be its own maker. At one level this argument seems hard to refute: there is little doubt but that IVF will eventually be employed to create "designer babies," selected for gender, intelligence, or even body type. In the years ahead Christians will be called on to confront and resist the overall politics represented by such technocracy. There are practices to which the Church must and will say "No."

But is every instance of IVF itself a step toward this sort of politics? I am less certain than O'Donovan and Meilaender that this is the case. One can at least imagine the possibility of a couple whose life is shaped by the faith and practice of the Church, who turn to IVF – not in denial of their one-flesh union, but in an extraordinary (that is, exceptional) confirmation of it. In a marriage between believers, might not having children by IVF be precisely the faithful thing to do? To be sure, the couple choosing this path will find themselves bound in certain respects. Christian resort to IVF must presume, for instance, fertilization employing the couple's own sperm and ova; donor gametes are not an option. Only so, can one maintain that IVF serves as an extension of the couple's union realized in these particular bodies – the bodies they pledged to each other in marriage. By contrast, the use of donor gametes suggests the desire to "make a baby" in circumvention of the life they share.

Yet if this exception really is an exception, it serves to underscore the rule: that Christians should approach IVF and related procedures with a healthy dose of suspicion. They do so not because they are anti-technology, much less because they lack sympathy for the childless, but because IVF in our society is bound up with practices that tend to undermine the biblical witness concerning human life. A key example is the fertilization and storage of embryos as a by-product of the IVF process. One need not view the embryo as a "person" to find this practice problematic; the larger issue is that of treating the body as a source of raw material, whether for reproductive or for research purposes – most notably the harvesting of stem cells. Stem-cell therapy may one day bring huge benefits for the treatment of illness; but, for the Christian, this gain should not be at the cost of treating the embryo as so much impersonal stuff, to be manipulated as the "medical community" sees fit.

All this may very well sound more like law than like gospel, yet I do not wish to end on a critical note. Recall once again Barth's assertion that there is no *necessity* in Christians' producing heirs, given that in Christ the end of the ages has come. Having said that, we may consider two forms in which the infertile couple can nonetheless fulfill a vocation to be parents.

The first and most obvious form is adoption. The couple who welcome someone else's child into their home acts to "receive one of these little ones" no less than do biological parents. There is even a peculiar appropriateness about adoption for Christians, in that all confess themselves to be adopted children, strangers welcomed into the household of God (Romans 8: 15). This is not, of course, to romanticize adoption, which often brings peculiar challenges of its own. Yet how better to fulfill the mandate of welcoming children in Christ's name?

Second, there is the kind of informal parenting that goes on within the Church itself. This takes us back to a point made earlier: that when a child is baptized, the entire congregation assumes responsibility for his or her upbringing. It is easy enough to say this, though hard to overcome the liberal habit of treating the family as a sacrosanct, self-enclosed unit. Nonetheless, there is a space of hospitality here waiting to be filled. The childless couple may offer their services as Sunday school teachers or catechists; they might be willing to work with teenagers, a modern group (there were, of course, no teenagers in biblical times) notoriously difficult to integrate into the Church's life; the couple might play a crucial role as baptismal sponsors or godparents. While their freedom for these roles may be unintended, this freedom is nonetheless real and an opportunity to be exploited. Whether this happens depends not only on the couple themselves, but on the willingness of the congregation to receive their gifts.

I began this chapter by recalling a circle of blessing – of men and women, parents and children, young and old, gathered in prayer and praise around the Lord's table. The Church does not *make* the blessing. But the Church does celebrate it, acknowledging that "the Son on whose birth alone everything seriously and ultimately depended has now been born and has now become our Brother." To conceive children and live in families is to affirm the goodness of created life, whose end is the *oikonomia* of the new creation. It is to this great economy that the Church bears its own small witness.

References

Barth, Karl (1961) *Church Dogmatics*, ed. G. W. Bromiley and T. F. Torrance, vol. 3, part 4 (Edinburgh: T. and T. Clark).

Berkow, Robert (ed.) (1992) "Assisted Reproductive Technologies," in *The Merck Manual*, 16th edn (Rahway, NJ: Merck and Co.), esp. pp. 1772–3.

Berry, Wendell (1987) "The Two Economies," in *Home Economics* (New York: North Point Press).

Catholic Church, Congregatio pro Doctrina Fidei (1987) *Instruction on Respect for Human Life in its Origin and on the Dignity of Human Procreation: Replies to Certain Questions of the Day* (Washington, DC: US Catholic Conferences).

Clapp, Rodney (1993) *Families at the Crossroads: Beyond Traditional and Modern Options* (Downers Grove, IL: InterVarsity).

Gundry-Volf, Judith (2001) "The Least and the Greatest: Children in the New Testament," in *The Child in Christian Thought*, ed. Marcia Bunge (Grand Rapids, MI: Eerdmans).

Hauerwas, Stanley (1998) "Taking Time for Peace: The Ethical Signficance of the Trivial," in *Christian Existence Today* (Durham, NC: The Labyrinth).

Holeton, David (1991) "Communion, Children, and Community," in *The Identity of Anglican Worship*, ed. Kenneth Stevenson and Bryan Spinks (London: Mowbray).

Lasch, Christopher (1977) *Haven in a Heartless World: The Family Besieged* (New York: Basic).

Lohfink, Gerhard (1984) *Jesus and Community* (Philadelphia: Fortress).

Meeks, Wayne (1983) *The First Urban Christians: The Social World of the Apostle Paul* (New Haven, CT: Yale University Press).

Meilaender, Gilbert (1996) *Bioethics: A Primer for Christians* (Grand Rapids, MI: Eerdmans).

Noonan, John P. (1985) *Contraception: A History of its Treatment by the Catholic Theologians and Canonists* (Cambridge, MA: Belknap).

O'Donovan, Oliver (1984) *Begotten or Made?* (Oxford: Clarendon Press).

Pope Paul VI (1968) *Encyclical of Pope Paul VI: Humanae vitae, on the Regulation of Birth* (Glen Rock, NJ: Paulist).

Soulen, Kendall (1996) *The God of Creation and Christian Theology* (Philadelphia: Fortress), esp. the treatment of "blessing" in chs 5–6.

CHAPTER 36

Being Sent: Witness

Michael G. Cartwright

While Christians throughout the world face challenges specific to the diverse communities in which they live and work, they share a common mandate to go into the world (Matthew 28: 19–20) as heralds of the peaceable Kingdom of God. They are to be "resident aliens in a country belonging to others" (Acts 7: 6). Christians are *not* to be conformed to the social order around them, but rather to embody the renewal that God has already begun in the world by being a different kind of *polis* (Gwyn et al., 1991). In Paul's words, Christians are to be "ambassadors for Christ," participating in the reconciling work of God in the world (2 Corinthians 5: 17–20). *How* Christians go into the world matters, then. And the "good news" to which they bear witness as they are sent out has much to do with the character of their gatherings for worship.

Consider the following narrative about a Christian congregation that is about to conclude its Sunday liturgy. Shortly, the people are to be dismissed to return to their homes in the Galilean village of Ibillin where Christians are a minority of the population. The time is Palm Sunday 1966. Fr Elias Chacour stands before this Melkite Catholic congregation, a church not far from Capernaum where the public ministry of Jesus of Nazareth began circa AD 27–30. This Israeli Arab priest is visibly disturbed by what he sees before him: an unreconciled congregation made up of Israeli Arab policemen, divided families, and sworn enemies. He recalls the pathos of that moment at the conclusion of the liturgy: "every time I turned around to bless the congregation, to give them Christ's peace, I was reminded all over again that there was no reality [of reconciliation] among these people. Such peace had always been refused (Chacour, 1992: 30). Although week after week, the congregation had the opportunity to share the "kiss of peace" – as a sign of their participation in God's reconciling work in the world – their public witness to God's peace was deficient.

As the liturgy ended and the people prepared to be dismissed, the priest suddenly acted in a very uncharacteristic way. Before anyone could leave, he hurried down the center aisle. The worshipers were startled at this unusual sight of a priest wearing his vestments outside the iconostasis screen. They were even more startled to see that their beloved *Abuna* was locking the two doors on either side of the church! The congregation sat frozen in silent disbelief, as Fr Chacour took the big, old key out of the door and marched up the aisle to the front of the sanctuary where he turned to face the people. Loudly and firmly, he said,

> I want you to know . . . how saddened I am to find you hating and decrying each other. I have tried so often in the six months I have been here to help you reconcile with each other, but I have been unable to do so. I have wondered if all the villages have the problems you have here, and I tell you the truth when I say that I have looked about in Galilee and have found that you are alone in such bitterness and hatred. You are very, very complicated people here in Ibillin. (Chacour, 1992: 30)

As the congregation looked at him in stunned silence, the priest continued:

> This morning while I celebrated this liturgy, I found someone who is able to help you. In fact, he is the only one who can work the miracle of reconciliation in this village. This person who can reconcile you is Jesus Christ, and he is here with us. We are gathered in his name, this man who rode in triumph into Jerusalem with hosannas from the people ringing in his ears.
>
> So on Christ's behalf, I say this to you: The doors of the church are locked. Either you kill each other right here in your hatred and then I will celebrate your funeral gratis, or you use this opportunity to be reconciled together before I open the doors of the church. If that reconciliation happens, Christ will truly become your Lord, and I will know I am becoming your pastor and your priest. That decision is now yours. (Chacour, 1992: 31)

Having heard this startling challenge, members of the congregation started looking around at one another. A few people looked as if they were about to leave. At that point, *Abuna* Chacour put up his hand and stopped them. "And, don't try to get out. The doors are locked. And the key is in my hand. You can take this key only if you kill me. The only other way you will get out of here is to make peace among yourselves by being reconciled to those who you have hurt and who have hurt you" (Chacour, 1992: 31). Fr Chacour stood in the archway with his hands folded in front of him, looking out over his captive flock with firm but benevolent intensity. "No one said a word," he recalls. "They looked at me, they looked at each other, they looked at the peeling paint on the dome and arches, they looked at the floor. The silence continued" (Chacour, 1992: 31).

After ten minutes passed, someone moved. To the pastor's amazement, he saw Abu Muhib slowly get to his feet. This man, who was dressed in an Israeli police uniform, stretched out his arms to the congregation, looked around and then looked toward his pastor. "Abuna, I ask forgiveness of everybody here and I forgive everybody. And I ask God to forgive me my sins." Fr Chacour recalls that he stepped down to the church floor and reached out to his parishioner, crying. "Come here, come here, Abu Muhib! Let me hug you!" As he embraced this man who many viewed with suspicion because of his role as an agent of the state of Israel, Chacour turned to the congregation, and called out: "Why don't we all hug each other now? I will hug everybody, and everybody will hug each other, all right?" (Chacour, 1992: 31–2).

The entire congregation proceeded to share the kiss of peace with one another. They had already exchanged the peace earlier in the liturgy, but *this time* their performance embodied tears of joy, sorrow, and repentance. After this time of reconciliation had concluded, the priest dismissed his congregation with the following words of blessing:

> Don't listen to the gossipers and to people who are only interested in seeing you dispersed, divided from each other again. Now you are one community. Brothers and sisters, this is not Palm Sunday any longer. This is our resurrection! We are a community that has risen from the dead; we have new life. I propose that we don't wait until next Sunday, until Easter, to celebrate the resurrection. I will unlock the doors and then let us go from home to home all over the village and sing the resurrection hymn to everyone! (Chacour, 1992: 32)

As the congregation exited through the open church doors – sent into a world populated by Muslims, Jews, Druze, and other Christians – they sang the ancient hymn: "Christ is risen from the dead! / By his death he has trampled upon death / And has given life to those / Who are in the tomb!" (Chacour, 1992: 32).

Fr Chacour recalled: "All afternoon I could hear singing, ululations, happy voices, and laughter. I knew this was a whole new life for Ibillin . . . I . . . saw this vision of my parish reconciling together" (Chacour, 1992: 33). Where fear had once reigned, now reconciling love ruled. In the midst of a land torn by wars and rumors of wars, the community of faith at Ibillin celebrated the peace of the "crucified and risen" King. They had realized the witness of reconciliation that the kiss of peace is supposed to signify to the peoples of the world.

What Does it Mean for Christians to be Witnesses in and for the World?

This story about a particular congregation in a particular setting calls attention to the importance of the embodiment of Christian witness in a world of conflict. As Stanley Hauerwas has argued, the primary problem confronting the Christian Church in a postmodern world is not whether Christian claims about God can be debated in credible ways with alternative accounts (*logos*) of abstract reasoning. Rather, the challenge is about *ethos* of Christian witness. Can particular Christian communities produce and sustain the kind of witness to God in which their practices of discipleship can serve as credible signs of God's reconciling work in the world? According to Hauerwas, "there can be no argument to the truth of God in Jesus Christ without witnesses" (2001: 697–8).

As theologians as diverse as John Howard Yoder and Gerhard Lohfink agree, the work of God as described in the Bible is best described as *the calling of a people*. This is true no less for the Church than it was for the people of Israel. How we understand the significance of Christian "peoplehood" makes a difference to how we think about the message of the gospel itself.

> The church is then not simply the bearer of the message of reconciliation, in the way a newspaper or a telephone company can bear any message with which it is entrusted. Nor

is the church simply the result of a message, as an alumni association is the product of the school or the crowd in the theater is the product of the reputation of the film. That men and women are called together to a new social wholeness is itself the work of God, which gives meaning to history, from which both personal conversion (whereby individuals are called into this meaning), and missionary instrumentalities are derived. (Yoder, 1994: 74)

This commentary on Ephesians 3: 9–10 takes seriously the apostolic vision of the Church as the means God has chosen to convey the good news of Jesus Christ to the "principalities and powers" of the cosmos. This is why the practices of the Church should always be done in the awareness that the integrity of performance of such practices has a direct bearing on the credibility of the Church's witness before the eyes of "the watching world" (Yoder, 1992).

The content of the Church's witness is inseparable from the apostolic confession that Jesus of Nazareth is the Messiah of God. The conversation between Peter and Jesus recorded in Matthew 16: 13–19 is prototypical for all Christians. Jesus posed a question for his disciples: "Who do you say that I am?" Peter declares that Jesus is "the Messiah, the Son of God" (Matthew 16: 15–16). Through Jesus Christ, the Christians see what it means to participate in God's reconciling work in the world (2 Corinthians 5: 16–20). Empowered by the Holy Spirit of God, the Church is sent forth to embody this good news, however imperfectly and provisionally, as a reconciled community engaged in sacrificial service (Shenk, 1997: 192–206).

The preceding narrative of "The Palm Sunday Prisoners" in Ibillin reveals seven features of the ethos of witness of those who are called to live "in but not of" the world.

(1) *Mission*   To begin with, the priest had been sent out by the bishop of the Melkite Catholic Church to lead the congregation. Although Elias Chacour had a strong sense that God had called him to be a peacemaker (Chacour, 1984: 146), he also understood that, as an ordained priest, his vocation must be enacted in the context of the Church's mission of making disciples of Jesus Christ. As the one charged with responsibility to preside at the congregation's celebration of the Eucharist, the priest is responsible for leading the congregation on behalf of the wider community of Christians. Chacour was initially sent by the Bishop in Haifa to the Galilean village to serve for a short time: three to six months (Chacour, 1984: 147–50). As it turned out, however, he would stay in Ibillin for the greater part of the next *thirty-six years* – until he was appointed to be Bishop of Haifa. This unlikely location turned out to be the place where his peacemaking vocation was enacted.

(2) *Praising God*   The Christians of Ibillin gathered to praise the triune God in worship. When they left the church, marching through the village singing hymns about the resurrection of Jesus, they were announcing the good news of the gospel to the world with a sense of wonder that God was doing something in their midst that was beyond measurement. In fact, Christians proclaim that their very capacity to offer themselves in worship is made possible by the *superabundance* of God's grace (Ford, 1998).

(3) *Keeping Time*   The Christians of this Galilean village offered their witness from a temporal perspective shaped by the *eschaton*. The end of history has come in the life, ministry, death, and resurrection of Jesus Christ. Christians gather to celebrate the res-

urrection each Sunday. Living in this "new creation" (2 Corinthians 5: 16) requires that they embrace the "politics of Jesus" even as they renounce the politics of a world ordered by more utilitarian ways of keeping time. Fr Chacour's directive to his congregation to celebrate the resurrection of Jesus Christ – even though they found themselves gathered on "Palm Sunday" in the cycle of the Christian year – is instructive in another sense. Christians dare not forget that those who shouted hosanna in the highest at the beginning of the passion narrative were the ones who later turned against him. The possibility of betrayal and falsification of our witness to Jesus as Messiah is ever present. "Were you there when they crucified my Lord?" remains a penetrating question that reminds Christians that the way to Easter is by way of the cross, not by a different route.

(4)   *Remembering God's Story*   By linking the narrative of what they had and had not done to the narrative of what God has done and is doing in the world, the Christians of Ibillin displayed their capacity to remember the "storied" character of the Christian gospel. While their witness to the gospel was certainly informed by the particularities of individual journeys, the proper focus of that witness is to the story of God's interaction with Israel and the Church. There is a deep tension between the story of the dreams and aspirations of Western nation-states and the story of Israel's deliverance from Egypt (McClendon, 2000: 359–60). In contrast to the individualist narrative of freedom *from* social constraints, Jews and Christians bear witness to a freedom that coincides with service (Goldberg, 1995: 15). The image of the people of God as a "royal priesthood" or "kingdom of priests" is found in Exodus 19: 5–6 as well as in the New Testament (1 Peter 2: 9–10). For Christians, this imagery is understood in the context of the narrative of the life, ministry, death, and resurrection of Jesus. Christian freedom, then, is properly understood as freedom *for obedience*. While Christians and Jews tell different stories about how God has acted in human history, both of these "holy peoples" have been called to serve, and the Christian narrative of God in the New Testament cannot be separated from the narratives of the Hebrew Bible.

(5)   *Serving God*   By stopping the service, Chacour reminded his congregation about the Church's proper vocation. James William McClendon, Jr concurs with the Jewish theologian Michael Goldberg in locating the "missionary character" of Jewish peoplehood in Israel's vocation to serve God. From this perspective, the shared priesthood of the Israelite people exists in the context of "serving God by bringing others into his service also" (McClendon, 2000: 360). When stated this way, it is possible to see the ways that Christians and Jews have both been "sent out" by God. This aspect of the story of God's purposes has been obscured by two assumptions: (a) the identification of the Church as the people of God with the authority of the civil "powers that be" (locally, regionally, or at the level of the nation-state); and (b) the substitution of the Church for Israel, a "supersession" of peoplehoods, which has resulted in the erasure of Jewish vocational identity as "children of Abraham" within the economy of salvation history. Such "Constantinian" assumptions have in turn led to overstated views of the Jewish–Christian schism, which has contributed to an inadequate awareness of the Church's own provisionality for God's purposes in human history (Yoder, 2003: 43–66). It follows, then, that historic communions (Baptist, Methodist, Anglican, and so on) are justified "only if they serve as the provisional means toward that one great peoplehood that embraces all, the Israel of God" (McClendon, 2000: 374). Jews and

Christians share a common covenant, although they have very different understandings of their vocations as peoples of God.

(6)   *Performing Liturgy*   As the narrative of the "Palm Sunday Prisoners" illustrates, witness derives it meaning from the work of the people (*leitourgia*) as displayed
in their public gatherings for worship. Early Christian communities gathered in those
places in Jerusalem that were associated with the life, ministry, death, and resurrection
of Jesus. In fact, the earliest "stational" liturgies of the early Church took shape as
Christians gathered for processionals and prayers at sites in Galilee and Jerusalem associated with the life, ministry, death, and resurrection of Jesus to bear witness to the
good news. Properly understood, when Christians gather for worship, what they are
doing is nothing less than bearing witness to what God has done and is doing in human
history.

(7)   *Exercising Authority*   When Fr Chacour locked the doors of the church, he was
exercising authority in a highly visible way. The power associated with the "keys to the
kingdom" – "binding and loosing" (Yoder, 1994: 323–58) – is closely associated with
Peter's confession that Jesus is Messiah (Matthew 16: 13–16). Jesus confers the authority to forgive sins upon Peter as representative of the Church. The wisdom to know
when it is appropriate to forgive transgressions and when forgiveness must be withheld
for the sake of the integrity of the Church's witness is a key index for understanding
how each Christian community is constituted. Congregations that cannot "bind and
loose" are unable to exercise their apostolic mandate precisely because they have lost
the capacity to embody the skills of discernment and forgiveness (Yoder, 1994: 350).
Christian communions display "the power of the keys" in different ways, but in all cases
the community's own witness to the Kingdom of God is authorized by its public structures and traditions of accountability. By refusing to let the congregation leave until
they had reconciled with each other, Fr Chacour bound them to confront their responsibility for living in ways that nullify their witness to the gospel. When he invited them
to go forth into the world rejoicing in their newly reconciled relationship with one
another, he set them free to live lives of obedience.

These seven aspects of the Church's ethos make visible the decisive distinction
between Church and world. As John Howard Yoder rightly observed, the oft-used distinction between "Christ and Culture" fails to engage "the Christian community as a
sociological entity in its own right" (Yoder, 1996: 75). "It is this specificity of the church
as a new phenomenon within history, sharing the uniqueness of the Incarnation as
humanly possible obedience, which seals the impossibility of reasoning as if 'culture'
were a 'monolithic' unity. The call to 'transformation' can only have substance if there
has already been some modeling of that to which the hearers are called" (Yoder, 1996:
75).

Evangelization: What Does it Mean for Christians to Evangelize their Neighbors?

The gospel calls for conversion. That cannot be denied without ignoring "the hospitality of God in Jesus Christ" (Shenk, 1997: 204). Unfortunately, some Christians attempt

to evangelize as if the Church's role is to distribute information or sell a product and in doing so they forsake their vocation to live in the world as "ambassadors for Christ." Those Christians who understand that the medium for the message matters will pay attention to those who have embodied their role as envoys to the Kingdom God in ways that display wisdom.

St Francis of Assisi once advised his "little brothers and sisters" to go forth into the world proclaiming the good news of the gospel wherever they went. He added: "if necessary, use words." The point of Francis's directive, of course, is that *the way* his friends embodied their witness for Christ as mendicants who have renounced all in order to follow Christ was the most powerful articulation of their vocation as "royal ambassadors" of the Kingdom of God. The same kind of evangelical imagination informed Francis's conviction that the bloody Crusade of the twelfth century was not an appropriate witness of the gospel to the Muslims.

Indeed, one of the most striking stories told about Francis concerns his "bloodless Crusade" to Arab peoples at a time when other Christians were killing Muslims in the name of Christ. Francis dissented from Cardinal Pelagius's vision of a Church powerful enough to conquer evil. In doing so, Francis reminded the Church hierarchy that it only existed as a means to another end – the Kingdom of God. Declaring that God uses the weak, not the powerful, to accomplish God's purposes in the world, Francis offered his witness about the peaceable Kingdom of God to Church leaders (Lehn, 1980: 34). They chose to ignore his witness. Having been dismissed by the leadership of the Church, Francis deliberately crossed the lines of battle to go directly to the Sultan al-Kamil, the leader of the Arab armies. Francis addressed the Sultan as a "brother" created by God and spoke to him about the good news of the Kingdom of God (Lehn, 1980: 34–5).

There is no historical evidence to suggest that Francis's witness resulted in the immediate conversion of the Arab general any more than it resulted in the immediate transformation of the Christian cardinal. That does not mean that Francis's witness was offered in vain. Years later the Sultan encountered a group of Christian Crusaders in the Holy Land led by Cardinal Pelagius. Upon discovering that these Christians were from Francis's homeland, he remembered the non-violent witness of Francis and decided to let them go free (Lehn, 1980: 35–6). Christians also remember the ways in which Francis's wisdom called the Church as a whole to renewed focus on embodying the kinds of Christ-like habits that are consistent with the renunciation of evil.

Some Christians have taken such stories about St Francis as confirmation of their sense that only "saints" – extraordinary Christians – can embody the gospel fully, while "ordinary" Christians will need to stick to more manageable techniques of evangelizing the world like "revival crusades" and "church marketing." In effect, this way of thinking about evangelism creates a "two-level ethic" (Lohfink, 1984: 39) in the way Christians go about bearing witness to the gospel. Such conceptions of evangelism offer truncated images of what it means to make disciples of Jesus Christ. By reducing the gospel to a product that can be mass-produced, they actually "sell out" the Church (Kenneson and Street, 1997). This results in the elimination of the prospect of martyrdom, as if one could "admire" Jesus without having to "follow" Jesus in the way of the cross (Hauerwas, 2001: 257–8).

Such images of evangelism and conversion are perpetuated by misreadings of the New Testament that ignore the context of Jewish practices in which would-be disciples heard the good news of Jesus Christ. As Gerhard Lohfink explains, it is a mistake to read the narratives of the Acts of the Apostles without recalling that those Gentiles who responded to the gospel were *already* "God-fearers," persons who worshiped the God of Israel. In fact, the very possibility of "immediate baptism" such as is described in the encounter between Philip and the Ethiopian eunuch (Acts 8: 26–40) presumes that such persons "were already members of the people of God, or at least were strongly shaped by God's people" (Lohfink, 1999: 266). While these "God-fearers" had not been circumcised (in the case of men), they were already attending Sabbath services, worshiping the one God of Israel, keeping the Sabbath and the food prescriptions. In very important ways, then, "Judaism was the catechumenate of the primitive Church." Only when the danger emerged that the Church would lose its roots in Judaism did it become "necessary to introduce the catechumenate as a separate institution" (Lohfink, 1999: 268–9).

As this example illustrates, the role of Church teaching in evangelism is very important. As Michael Budde has observed, Christian catechesis is best imaged not as a mass-production assembly line for making disciples, but rather as a "workshop of witnesses" in which Christians are formed "one person at a time, with different groups of people requiring differing modes of training and teaching – with the further wrinkle that the craftspersons themselves are unfinished, are themselves 'on the way' of Christian discipleship and practices" (Budde, 1997: 130). When the New Testament writings are read with greater attention to context, it becomes clear that discipleship was learned in the context of apprentice relationships. The disciples did not immediately grasp the gospel. Over time, and with the assistance of one another, they came to understand the ways in which the gospel called them into new relationships, through which they learned the disconcerting truth of the gospel. Without Cornelius, Peter would not have been able to grasp the radical inclusivity of the Kingdom of God; without Peter, Cornelius would not have been able to grasp the holiness of the Christian way (Shenk, 1997: 205).

Re-envisioning evangelism as requiring an apprenticeship in which one learns to practice the "crafts" of discipleship shifts our attention in two important ways. First, it illumines the necessity of "rites of initiation" in the socialization process of making Christian disciples. Second, it refocuses attention on the timeful nature of making disciples; "conversion" takes place over the course of a lifetime. Third, it helps to clarify the ways in which God may use groups like the Franciscan friars to reform the Church while also bearing witness to the world. Sometimes, Christian witness can be enacted by small communities of Christians, who confess Jesus as Lord by taking a stand against corrupt Church structures. By displaying what it can mean for the Church to live as a "contrast society" (Lohfink, 1984: 50) in the world, such groups call the Church to fulfill its mission of living as an "alternative society" (1984: 55) in the world.

The process of learning what is truly necessary for Christians to bear witness in the world begins with understanding what is involved in the rites of Christian baptism and Eucharist. Consider the following story. Bishop George Bashore was standing before a group of people who were about to be baptized in a United Methodist congregation in the USA where the pastor *had not taken the time* to teach those who were "joining the church" the significance of baptism. He asked the first question: *"Do you renounce the spiritual forces of wickedness, reject the evil powers of this world, and repent of your sin?"* One young man was visibly surprised by this question, and he was not immediately sure how to respond. The bishop repeated the question. Again the man stood there looking at his pastor and the bishop in stunned silence. Finally, after the bishop addressed the question to him a third time, the would-be disciple of Jesus stammered his response: "Well, I will if you will!"

The words of this uneasy would-be Christian disciple are worth pondering. Bishop Bashore told this story to a group of men and women who were about to be ordained as ministers to proclaim the word and celebrate the sacraments of the Church. He drew two lessons from this anecdote. First, pastors and congregations must take responsibility for teaching people that baptism does in fact involve renouncing particular forms and practices of evil and injustice. Second, would-be disciples can only dare to undertake the journey of discipleship in the company of others who are also committed to learning what it means to embrace the daunting freedom for obedience.

This story also reminds us that the social significance of baptism has everything to do with the wisdom and skills members of a congregation bring to the practices of public worship. One of these skills is a memory shaped by the life, ministry, death, and resurrection of Jesus. Christian anamnesis is a way that Christians learn to "remember" their past, present, and future in the context of narratives shaped by baptism and Eucharist. Over time, Christian disciples are formed to recognize that some convictions and patterns of behavior are simply inconsistent with our renunciation of evil and injustice, while other beliefs and practices embody the kind of freedom for obedience that is enacted in the Eucharist of the Church.

To imagine a *life-long catechumenate* as the proper form of the evangelistic task is to take seriously the responsibility that would-be disciples have to and for one another. Of course, the exercise of such oversight and nurture must take various forms. Some congregations have formalized sequences of discipleship formation that are linked to continuing covenant discipleship groups in which an experienced Christian works with a group of new disciples to help them foster the habits of accountability that sustain discipleship. Other congregations seek the same end through more informal ad hoc means. The congregation of the Church of the Servant King (a house-church of less than thirty-five people) assigns one member of the congregation to be a "pastoral assistant" to work with an adult who is preparing for baptism and entry into this community of people committed to living as Christian disciples. The amount of time that this intensive process of Christian formation may take varies, but it typically takes a period of years. Even after someone has become an "affirmed member" of the congregation, he or she continues to learn the craft of discipleship alongside those brothers and sisters who have been his or her mentors.

To imagine evangelism as taking place in the rather modestly described "workshop for witnesses" also serves as a caution to Christians about not locating "success" in numerical tallies or other quantitative measures. Christians should not seek a world in which non-Christians have been vanquished nor should they imagine themselves on a "crusade" in which non-Christian peoples will ultimately disappear. Rather, they should bear witness in ways that are consistent with the non-violence of the gospel. This requires mastering the disciplines of hospitality and gentleness in their relationships as well as the discernment to know how and when to "give and receive counsel" to one another. Further, it involves learning to recognize the ways in which particular human beings have excelled as Christian disciples. Not surprisingly, the skills needed to grasp the significance of the life-witness of a "saint" such as Francis of Assisi can only be acquired in the context of practices of accountability that sustain apprentice-disciples who learn from other would-be saints what it means to excel in the way of the Cross.

Witnesses in a Pluralistic World?

Christians are sent to a world in which the "others" around them may or may not be able to comprehend their witness. It is instructive to be reminded of the social signifi-cance of the site where Peter is believed to have responded to Jesus's question "Who do you say that I am? (Matthew 16: 13–20). Caesarea Phillipi or "Banias" was the site of several well-known temples to pagan deities. In other words, Peter's confession of faith took place in a scene in which the first Christian witness was already contested by a wider polytheism. Although not every Christian community faces the same situation, it is nevertheless true that many other social and political convictions compete for their allegiance and that of their non-Christian neighbors.

How Christians make sense of the pluralistic environment in which they find them-selves is itself a challenge that many Christians find confusing, particularly given that more and more Christians live in environments in which their neighbors may practice other religions. Christian thinking about how to regard the status of Christian truth claims in relation to other religious beliefs that make contrary claims ranges from exclu-sivity to inclusivity and pluralism (Shenk, 1997: 21–73). "Exclusivists" believe that the Christian tradition has sole possession of religious truth and offers the only path to sal-vation. "Inclusivists" affirm that salvation is available through other traditions because the God most decisively acting and most fully revealed in Christ is also present within or through those traditions. "Pluralists" maintain that various religious traditions are independently valid paths to salvation (Heim, 1995: 4).

These views have different implications for the witness that a Christian community offers in its specific context. For example, if the pluralist view is taken as accurate, then the Christians of Ibillin do not need to be concerned about the truth claims of their Muslim neighbors because the validity of their neighbor's understanding of salvation is subject to that tradition's own internal standards of validity.

With this typology of "theologies of religions" in mind, some Christians have been tempted to think that all religious communities have the same ultimate end (i.e., redemption). However, this is not the case: *not all religious traditions are focused on the question of salvation* (Heim, 1995: 124–5). If Christians take seriously the possibility that non-Christian neighbors are asking a different set of questions about matters reli-gious than they are, then they will discover that they need a more adequate perspective than the "pluralistic hypothesis." Mark Heim suggests that, in addition to thinking carefully about those circumstances in which particular religious claims of different religious traditions may or may not be warranted, Christians also need to focus on "the actual practice of witness on the part of believers commending their visions to others" (1995: 143). This kind of "orientational" pluralism preserves the possibility of offering (internal and external) critique of the witness(es) of particular religious traditions without prematurely concluding that the visions of religious fulfillment that inform such witnesses are necessarily invalid. Indeed, the credibility of such visions is properly linked to the character of the witness that is offered by such communities of conviction.

When Christians reassert the importance of *ethos* in their witness to the world, new possibilities for inter-religious dialogue and cooperation also emerge. For example, Fr Chacour has drawn on local traditions and the New Testament to encourage his Melkite congregation (as well as other Christians around the world) to think seriously about what it means for Christians and Muslims and Jews to claim to be "children of Abraham." He reminds them of the biblical image of the olive tree used by Paul (Romans 11: 13–24) to describe the relationship of Christians as a branch that has been grafted onto the original tree of Judaism (Chacour, 1984: 137–42). Further, recalling the biblical stories in Genesis about Isaac and Ishmael, Jacob and Esau – the ancestors claimed in different ways by Jews, Christians, and Muslims – Chacour encourages contemporary Jews, Christians, and Muslims to think of one another as "blood brothers." By reminding his congregation of their biblical identity, Chacour urges his fellow Christians to think of Jews and Muslims as created in the image and likeness of God. Indeed, as Chacour continually reminds the Christians of Galilee, this message of reconciliation is *at the heart of the witness that they offer* locally as well as in the wider world.

How Should Christians Go About Making Common Cause with Non-Christians?

Christians and non-Christians face common challenges even if they have different reasons for engaging those challenges. In a world that often is engulfed in war, a Christian witness for peace may be appreciated for practical reasons, particularly if that witness makes it possible for hope to be sustained for the next generation of Muslims and Jews. Here again, the Christians of Ibillin are a reminder of the potential power for Christian witness in a world in which Christians are a minority. Today, nearly four decades after their congregational reconciliation on Palm Sunday 1966, the Christians of Ibillin are working with local Muslims and Jews to provide educational opportunities for the under-educated Muslim population of Israel. In doing so, their actions are consistent with Jesus's directive that the disciples not view their neighbors as opponents of the gospel but rather as potential participants in God's transformation of the world.

The kindergarten and elementary school that Fr Chacour began in the Melkite Church in 1982 have provided a much-needed opportunity not only for the Christians of Ibillin but also for their Muslim and Jewish neighbors throughout the region of Galilee. This shared concern is imaged in a variety of ways on campus. The word peace is painted on a rock wall in Hebrew, Arabic, and English, the three languages used by the students. The name of the school – "Mar Elias" – is Arabic for Elijah, a prophet recognized in Judaism, Christianity, and Islam. Finally, the teaching staff of Mar Elias Educational Institutions displays an intentionally inter-faith mix that is magnified in the population of the students.

In an environment that is continually tested by the prospect of violence, the very fact that the Melkite Church in Ibillin has initiated this inter-faith collaboration is note-worthy. Perhaps even more significant, however, is the fact that the Mar Elias commu-nity has been able to sustain such relationships even when violence has threatened the lives of students and faculty. For example, in the fall of 2000 at the beginning of the *Al Aqsa intifidah*, one of the high-school students was killed by mistake by Israeli sol-diers near his home in Nazareth. Whether this was a case of mistaken identity, or a tragic instance of simply being in the wrong place at the wrong time, this young man's death shocked the communities in Lower Galilee. This young man was the acknowl-edged leader of "Seeds of Peace," an inter-faith group of high-school students who were committed to offering a peaceable witness in the midst of the continuing conflict between the state of Israel and the Palestinian people.

The way this young man is now remembered by the Muslim and Jewish communi-ties of the Galilee displays the influence of the Christian community associated with Mar Elias School. Fr Chacour was invited by the student's family to offer the eulogy for him at a nearby mosque. Several weeks later, the school held its own service of com-memoration, to which the public was invited. At the memorial ceremony, the Israeli education minister and an Arab political leader had been designated to lay wreaths at the place the school has set aside to remember all those people who have died in the conflict that has racked the region for decades. The memorial is comprised of two curved walls of stone that face one another. On one wall, the Hebrew words for *"To the martyrs of the Palestinian people"* are engraved on the wall. On the facing wall, the Arabic words for *"To the martyrs of the Jewish people"* are engraved.

When it came time for the officials to lay the wreaths at the memorial in remem-brance of this young man's life, the Israeli official stepped forward. Just as the Israeli minister was about to lay the wreath at the wall that commemorated the Jewish martyrs, Fr Chacour intervened. As the host of the event, Chacour reminded the Israeli leader of the purpose of the occasion and of the memorial, and bid him to lay his wreath at the site of the Palestinian's martyred children. Shortly thereafter, the local Arab offi-cial laid his wreath at the memorial marking those Israelis who had died for their people. What could have been a cause for taking offense was turned into an occasion for sowing seeds of reconciliation.

This display of authority by Fr Chacour is instructive. While Chacour's intervention on this occasion is different in several ways from the action that he took almost four decades before when he locked the doors of the church, his action is no less significant. In this latter instance, he invokes the authority of the host – as president of Mar Elias College – to thwart inhospitable behavior by guests at a public event hosted by an inter-faith community of learning. At the same time, Chacour's action embodies the Church's commitment to fostering the kind of hospitality that sustains the Christian vocation to be "ambassadors for Christ" in the world.

The story of the many ways that Fr Chacour and the Christian community in Ibillin have been able to bear witness in this Galilean village off the beaten path can remind Christians in Church-related institutions of higher education through the world that they, too, have opportunities to bear witness in the places to which they have been sent. Whatever may have appeared to be the case once upon a time, Church-related universities are no longer in a position to choose whether they will be inter-faith or not. Rather, it is a question of how they choose to deal with the inter-faith character of their campus populations. In this respect, there may be more parallels between the situation faced by Fr Chacour at Mar Elias School and the situation faced by Church-related universities in Europe and the USA than would appear on first glance.

Christians in higher education must lead the way in offering the kind of radical hospitality that invites conversation between people of different religious traditions about religious convictions and practices. While university leaders should never forget that the Church is the proper locus for lifelong apprenticeship to the gospel, Church-related universities can still play a role in the lives of young adults by helping them to acquire the skills necessary for engaging non-Christians peaceably, including learning to talk with persons from other religious traditions. In educational contexts, therefore, Christians will prize the freedom of religious practice not only for themselves but also for those non-Christians. Some advocates for the gospel may object that such hospitality to non-Christian religious practices in Church-related universities appears to cede too much control to non-Christians and threatens to become its own form of idolatry, but this concern is misplaced. One of the false hopes that Christian communities in Europe and the USA must learn to renounce is the illusion that they possess the power and authority to direct their own course. Just as Fr Chacour could not know that he would spend the greater part of his ministry serving in Ibillin, neither could the Christians of that village know the outcomes of the initiatives that they took with non-Christian neighbors in the early 1980s.

What Christians throughout the world can do – with confidence and humility – is to bear witness to the good news by fostering the kinds of habits and practices that enable would-be disciples of Jesus Christ to remember the saints and the martyrs, including those whose lives may even constitute a judgment against past failures of the Church's witness. To forget those who have died as witnesses to the Kingdom of God is to risk forgetting the apostolic mandate. To forget those who have died as a result of Christian "crusades" – medieval or modern – is to pretend that it is possible to make disciples of Jesus Christ without going through the kind of lifelong apprenticeship in which we learn that cruciform living involves continuing renunciation of evil and injustice. For those who have been sent into the world as heralds of the gospel of Jesus Christ, this begins with renouncing the assumption that Christians control the direction of history while embracing the freedom of *being sent* into the world as "ambassadors" for Christ. Wherever the ethos of the Church displays such renunciation and freedom, the Church's witness to the world starts to become visible.

References

Budde, Michael (1997) *Magic Kingdom of God: Christianity Amid the Global Culture Industries* (Denver, CO: Westview).

Chacour, Elias, with Hazard, David (1984) *Blood Brothers* (Grand Rapids, MI: Chosen).

—, with Jensen, Mary E. (1992) *We Belong to the Land: The Story of a Palestinian Israeli who Lives for Peace and Reconciliation* (San Francisco: Harper).

Ford, David F. (1998) *Self and Salvation: Being Transformed* (Cambridge: Cambridge University Press).

Goldberg, Michael (1995) *Why Should Jews Survive? Looking Past the Holocaust to a Jewish Future* (New York: Oxford University Press).

Gwyn, Douglas, Hunsinger, George, Roop, Eugene F., and Yoder, John Howard (1991) *A Declaration of Peace: In God's People the World's Renewal has Begun* (Scottdale, PA: Herald).

Hauerwas, Stanley (2001) *The Hauerwas Reader*, ed. John Berkman and Michael G. Cartwright (Durham, NC: Duke University Press).

Heim, S. Mark (1995) *Salvations: Truth and Difference in Religion* (Maryknoll, NY: Orbis).

Kenneson, Philip and Street, James L. (1997) *Selling Out the Church: The Dangers of Church Marketing* (Nashville, TN: Abingdon)

Lehn, Cornelia (1980) *Peace Be With You* (Newton, KS: Faith and Life).

Lohfink, Gerhard (1984) *Jesus and Community: The Social Dimension of Christian Faith* (Philadelphia: Fortress).

—(1999) *Does God Need the Church?* (Collegeville, MN: The Liturgical Press).

McClendon, James Wm (2000) *Witness*, vol. 3 of *Systematic Theology* (Nashville, TN: Abingdon).

Shenk, Calvin (1997) *Who Do You Say That I Am? Christians Encounter Other Religions* (Scottdale, PA: Herald).

Yoder, John Howard (1992) *Body Politics: Five Practices of Christians before the Watching World* (Nashville, TN: Discipleship Resources).

—(1994) *The Royal Priesthood: Essays Ecumenical and Ecclesiological*, ed. Michael G. Cartwright (Grand Rapids, MI: Eerdmans).

—(1996) "How H. Richard Niebuhr Reasoned: A Critique of *Christ and Culture*," in *Authentic Transformation: A New Vision of Christ and Culture*, ed. Glen H. Stassen, D. M. Yeager, and John Howard Yoder (Nashville, TN: Abingdon Press).

—(2003) *The Jewish–Christian Schism Revisited*, ed. Michael G. Cartwright and Peter Ochs (London: SCM).

Afterword

Rowan Williams

"Contemplative experience wants to speak of 'God's will' as 'God's wishing-to-be-in-us'" (Moore, 1977: 209). This pregnant observation by Sebastian Moore instantly puts into proper perspective the unfruitfulness of certain classical puzzles in theological thinking about ethics. Is good good because God commands it or does God will the good because it is good? It depends how you are thinking about the very notion of the good: if it is substantively related to actual relationship with God, if human beings are made so that their final and complete flourishing as humans is in relation with God, then the terms of the argument change somewhat. The good life is not a condition of winning God's pleasure but the very form of "God's pleasure" in us; that is, it is a life in which reconciliation with God shapes what is thought and done in such a way that, in some sense, the "form" of God's life becomes perceptible. What God wants is to be manifestly there in what God has created; thus what God wants in the shape of human lives is the fading away of what prevents divine life being visible in us. The good is grounded neither in a divine *decision*, a setting of rules solely by an abstract divine freedom, nor in a divine acknowledgment of some eternal and independent ideal; it is grounded in the character of God as "wishing to be in the other," as acting so as to diffuse divine life.

As the chapters in this volume amply show, this would have been pretty obvious to Christian theologians for some three-quarters of Christian history; it is – by a rather roundabout route, I agree – the theological impulse that molded some of the Reformers' language about justification, no less than it molded the earlier refusals of Augustine and St Thomas to separate God's will from God's nature, or Pseudo-Dionysius and his followers and commentators, including Thomas, to define the divine goodness as "self-diffusion." God's nature is to be active, and the act that is God-being-God is essentially one of self-imparting, self-sharing. That is the God discerned and responded to as a result of the events of the life and death and rising of Jesus. Any moral discourse that suggests a passive or reactive God misses the central point; so, to consider forms of behavior simply in terms of whether they are pleasing to God, in any way that implies a God who reacts to and judges them from a distance, presents problems for a fully theological ethic. For a human act to be pleasing to God is for a human act to be the "carrier" of some quality of divine action, to participate in divine action; for a human act to be unpleasing to God, to be sinful, is for it to be opaque to divine action (and it is not prevented from being opaque by the good will or good faith of the human agent; theological ethics needs to challenge a certain religious sentimentality about good intentions, and to take the consideration of sin beyond the level of individual achievement or failure).

Christians exist, so they claim, because God's action has become visible and tangible in an unsurpassable way in the events of Jesus's earthly life. In reflection on what it was that brought into being a distinctive human group with these practices and these priorities in worship and action, Christians drew conclusions about the character of God which became the normative grammar for talking of God: divine life is threefold, and it is so because of a "generativity" in that life, an irreducible movement into what is other – the Father and the Word, the Father and the Spirit, the Spirit's entire absorption in witness to the Word, the Word's self-emptying in witness to the Father. If divine life were not like that, we couldn't make sense of there being anything other than divine life; but if God is by nature generative of "the other," it makes perfect sense that the "will," the specific direction of intelligence and purpose, that is exercised by that divine nature should generate what is by nature other than God – the contingent universe. But just as in the divine life itself otherness is reconciled in what we could call a mutual transparency (the Father's life flowering "in" the Son, the Spirit existing as the bearer of the Son's radiance, and so on), so in the relation of God to creation: the non-divinity of creation achieves its full purpose when it bears and manifests the glory of God. Hence the Wisdom traditions which see the world, including the world of human habit and behavior, as tracing and transmitting the divine life.

And hence the vision of ethical reflection that animates this book: to learn what the good life is, we have to enquire about where the "pressure" of God, to use another phrase from Sebastian Moore, is encountered, recalled, reinforced. Vigen Guroian, in an essay on "Tradition and Ethics" (Guroian, 1994: 42), draws attention (following Wayne Meeks) to the way in which Paul, discussing matters of behavior, regularly appeals to the fact of baptism and what is learned in preparation for baptism: the fundamental truth about the Christian is that he or she has died to the slavery of fallenness and been raised to the life of Christ. Behavioral priorities follow from this, not from any general argument about the good life. Baptism is the point of transition between lives, even identities, the place where transparency to God's otherness begins in earnest as both a fact and a project that is shared, talked about, explored, and consciously worked at. And, a few pages later (1994: 50), Guroian writes of what the icon represents in Orthodox practice: "It is a material representation of the human and divine dialogue that constitutes the church and in which the church invites others to participate . . . Orthodox ethics is, in a fundamental sense, iconic ethics."

"Iconic ethics" is not a bad summary of what the present volume has attempted to present as the primary character of a theological ethic. If we wanted to put it very radically, we could say that behavior is not, for the Christian, "good" or "bad"; it is transparent or opaque, truthful or illusory, grounded in life or leading to death, in the sense that it is assessed in relation to its response to God's "wishing-to-be-in-us." To borrow the language of another eastern Christian writer, Christos Yannaras (1984), theological ethics has to be "ontological" in character. The good life is the life in which reality (God's reality) is dominant – a view which has nothing to do with the modern rhetoric of authenticity or truth to the "real self," since the self's reality is wholly dependent on its relation with God. And to the degree that this relation is known as freely and unreservedly bestowed on the human agent, the good life is one in which anxiety is characteristically absent: "every good work is in itself nothing but faith or confidence," as John Milbank puts it (1997: 230), accurately summarizing Luther's account of Christian virtue.

Baptism is the moment of critical transition; the Eucharist is where the transition is newly presented and activated by the community. Here God's wishing-to-be-in-us is made immediate in two inseparable ways: by the recital of the story of incarnation and kenosis, in the proclamation of the Word and the recitation of the Institution narrative; and in the offer of divine life as physical food, given at the hand of a Christ who is present, actively inviting the congregation and at the same time actively giving himself on their behalf to the Father. To accept the invitation is not to receive a gift that is simply assimilated into the receiver; the receiver is transformed into one who enacts Christ's action, first and foremost in sharing Christ's prayerful movement into the life of the Father, derivatively in assuming again the baptismal role in the world at large, which is to proclaim and make visible what Christ is and does. And crucial to this process, of course, is that it happens as the *whole* Church gathers, offering no definition of itself other than that of the assembly convened by Christ as his praying Body on earth. Thus, a eucharistic ethic, as the preceding pages again make plain, is far more than an affirmation that "community" and material sharing are good and God-worthy things, or that human fellowship around a religious focus is highly significant for our flourishing. It is rather a statement about how God comes to be in us, because of God's nature and action in eternity, God's nature and action in the history of divine dealings with human agents, and because of the specific covenantal promise of Jesus to renew his invitation and welcome to us when we break bread in his name and presence and power.

One corollary of much of the argument of the chapters in this volume is that the stumblings and tangles of a good deal of contemporary moral argument on ethical questions arise from an impoverished doctrine of the Church and of the will of God. We have obscured the centrality of understanding the Church as *creatura Verbi*, the community brought into being by God's communication, which is a communication not only of words or information but of new life; we have misconstrued the will of God as a wanting of specific outcomes, apparently rather arbitrary in character, rather than a way of speaking about the "pressure" of God's self-diffusion (see Moore, 1977: 204–5 and 208 for the notion of divine will as pressure). To step back a little from the heat of some such contemporary debates enables us not only to look freshly at what have become stale arguments, but also to see something of what has been lost in our theology more generally. Contrary to what is often said, there is no ultimate contradiction between a narratively shaped theology and a robust theological metaphysic (see Williams, 2000: 239–64 for an attempt to counter the perception of such a contradiction). Understand the energy of the narrative as deriving from the unconstrained energy of the self-diffusing God, and you can see the connections. The *real* contradiction is between a narrative theology that never quite allows itself to claim that the story of God's dealings with us "inscribes" in time the character of the eternal God, and a metaphysic that divorces behavior from the manifestation of God on the grounds that the divine nature is not truly bestowed or participated in the world. Modern relativism (ethical or religious) regularly includes both of these flawed approaches; a theological ethics of the sort here sketched may have the welcome effect of bringing to light their inadequacy.

There are important tactical and rhetorical differences in Christian usage between talking about "goodness" and talking about "holiness." But they depend largely on our prevailing conventions: "holiness" can be opposed to "goodness" to the extent that it is culturally assumed that goodness is a matter of either temperament or achievement, whereas holiness can be presented as gift and epiphany. But, of course, this will not do in the long run. All that has been said here assumes that the only kind of goodness worth nurturing is gift and epiphany; there is really no gap between this and holiness. We may from time to time get into the habit of speaking of certain sorts of harmlessness or benevolence, self-disciplined or cooperative behavior as "good," but our theology ought to make us uncomfortable with such usage. Even (or especially) when we speak of the "goodness" of the unbeliever, we ought to be doing more than ascribing to them an inoffensive tractability; instead, we should be aware of the theological challenge that is posed by the experience of *seeing* in a life that is not conventionally a life of faith more than the liver of that life sees, seeing something of epiphany, response to the wanting-to-be-in-us of God. The good we are interested in is simply God's presence among us.

And that takes us back to where we started. Recognizing and responding to God's presence among us means recognizing something about the very nature of God: a God the "pressure" of whose being is toward the other, so intensely that the eternal divine life itself is a pattern of interweaving difference that then animates a world of time, change, differentiation, in which the unifying calling for all things and persons is to show forth God in the way each one is uniquely capable of doing. Or, more succinctly, Christian ethics is about giving glory to the giver of glory.

References

Guroian, Vigen (1994) "Tradition and Ethics: Prospects in a Liberal Society," in *Ethics After Christendom: Toward an Ecclesial Christian Ethic*, pp. 29–52 (Grand Rapids, MI: Eerdmans).

Milbank, John (1997) *The Word Made Strange: Theology, Language, Culture* (Oxford: Blackwell).

Moore, Sebastian, OSB (1977) "Some Principles for an Adequate Theism," *The Downside Review* (July), 320: 201–13.

Williams, Rowan (2000) "Interiority and Epiphany: A Reading in New Testament Ethics," in *On Christian Theology* (Oxford: Blackwell), esp. pp. 239–64.

Yannaras, Christos (1984) *The Freedom of Morality* (Crestwood, NY: St Vladimir's Seminary).

Index

Key Reference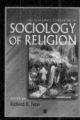

Volumes in
Religion &
Theology

Offering original, state-of-the-art essays by internationally recognized scholars, the Blackwell Companions to Religion provide outstanding reference sources.

THE BLACKWELL COMPANION TO JUDAISM
Edited by Jacob Neusner & Alan J. Avery-Peck
756 PAGES / 2000 / 1-577-18058-5 HB / 2003 / 1-577-18059-3 PB

THE BLACKWELL COMPANION TO SOCIOLOGY OF RELIGION
Edited by Richard K. Fenn
512 PAGES / 2000 / 0-631-21240-X HB / 2003 / 0-631-21241-8 PB

THE BLACKWELL COMPANION TO THE HEBREW BIBLE
Edited by Leo G. Perdue
504 PAGES / 2001 / 0-631-21071-7 HB

THE BLACKWELL COMPANION TO POSTMODERN THEOLOGY
Edited by Graham Ward
560 PAGES / 2001 / 0-631-21217-5 HB

THE BLACKWELL COMPANION TO HINDUISM
Edited by Gavin Flood
616 PAGES / 2003 / 0-631-21535-2 HB

THE BLACKWELL COMPANION TO POLITICAL THEOLOGY
Edited by Peter Scott & William T. Cavanaugh
560 PAGES / 2003 / 0-631-22342-8 HB

THE BLACKWELL COMPANION TO PROTESTANTISM
Edited by Alister E. McGrath & Darren C. Marks
496 PAGES / 2003 / 0-631-23278-8 HB

THE BLACKWELL COMPANION TO MODERN THEOLOGY
Edited by Gareth Jones
608 PAGES / 2003 / 0-631-20685-X HB

THE BLACKWELL COMPANION TO CHRISTIAN ETHICS
Edited by Stanley Hauerwas & Samuel Wells
544 PAGES / 2004 / 0-631-23506-X HB

THE BLACKWELL COMPANION TO RELIGIOUS ETHICS
Edited by William Schweiker
544 PAGES / 2004 / 0-631-21634-0 HB

Forthcoming:

THE BLACKWELL COMPANION TO THE STUDY OF RELIGION
Edited by Robert A. Segal

THE BLACKWELL COMPANION TO EASTERN CHRISTIANITY
Edited by Ken Parry

THE BLACKWELL COMPANION TO CHRISTIAN SPIRITUALITY
Edited by Arthur Holder

THE BLACKWELL COMPANION TO THE BIBLE AND CULTURE
Edited by John Sawyer & Paul Fletcher

THE BLACKWELL COMPANION TO THE NEW TESTAMENT
Edited by David Aune

For more information on our Companions to Religion & Theology series, visit www.blackwellpublishing.com/reference

Blackwell
· Publishing